TWENTIETH CENTURY VIEWS

The aim of this series is to present the best in contemporary critical opinion on major authors, providing a twentieth century perspective on their changing status in an era of profound revaluation.

Maynard Mack, *Series Editor*
Yale University

Joyce writing a sentence

Drawn by Guy Davenport

JOYCE

A COLLECTION OF CRITICAL ESSAYS

Edited by

William M. Chace

Prentice-Hall, Inc. *Englewood Cliffs, N.J.*

A SPECTRUM BOOK

Library of Congress Cataloging in Publication Data

CHACE, WILLIAM M. COMP.
 Joyce: a collection of critical essays.

 (Twentieth century views) (A Spectrum Book)
 CONTENTS: Dubliners: Cixous, H. Political ignominy;
"Ivy day." Ellmann, R. The backgrounds of "The dead."—
A portrait of the artist as a young man: Kenner, H.
The portrait in perspective.—Ulysses: Wilson, E.
James Joyce. Goldberg, S. L. Homer and the nightmare
of history. Cronin, A. The advent of Bloom. Ellmann, R.
Why Molly Bloom menstruates. [etc.]

 1. Joyce, James, 1882–1941. I. Title.
PR6019.09Z52638   823'.9'12   73–18496
ISBN 0–13–511303–2
ISBN 0–13–511295–8 (pbk.)

10 9 8 7 6 5 4 3 2

PRENTICE-HALL INTERNATIONAL, INC. (*London*)
PRENTICE-HALL OF AUSTRALIA PTY. LTD. (*Sydney*)
PRENTICE-HALL OF CANADA LTD. (*Toronto*)
PRENTICE-HALL OF INDIA PRIVATE LIMITED (*New Delhi*)
PRENTICE-HALL OF JAPAN, INC. (*Tokyo*)

Acknowledgments

Quotations from the following works of James Joyce are used by kind permission of The Viking Press, Inc., Jonathan Cape Ltd, and The Society of Authors, literary representative of the Estate of James Joyce:

A Portrait of the Artist as a Young Man. Copyright © 1964 by the Estate of James Joyce. All rights reserved.

Dubliners. Copyright © 1967 by the Estate of James Joyce. All rights reserved.

Quotations from *Finnegans Wake* by James Joyce are used by kind permission of The Viking Press, Inc. and The Society of Authors, literary representative of the Estate of James Joyce. Copyright © 1939 by James Joyce; © 1967 by George Joyce and Lucia Joyce.

Quotations from *Ulysses* are used by kind permission of Random House, Inc. and The Bodley Head. Copyright 1914, 1918 by Margaret Caroline Anderson and renewed 1942, 1946 by Nora Joseph Joyce.

Quotations from *Stephen Hero* are used by kind permission of Jonathan Cape Ltd and The Society of Authors, literary representative of the Estate of James Joyce.

The frontispiece is used by the kind permission of Guy Davenport. It originally appeared in *Flaubert, Joyce and Beckett: The Stoic Comedians,* by Hugh Kenner (Boston: Beacon Press, 1963).

Contents

Finnegans Wake

Retrospection

Introduction

In "The Dead," we learn of a horse named Johnny, inured to the steady circular labor of driving a mill in a glue factory. He was brought out one day by his master to review a military parade, and "everything went on beautifully until Johnny came in sight of King Billy's statue: and whether he fell in love with the horse King Billy sits on or whether he thought he was back again in the mill, anyhow he began to walk round the statue." James Joyce, who sometimes pleasured himself by thinking of events in his fictional works as prophetic, might have drawn some enjoyment from today's continuing spectacle of the horse, the mill, and the statue. In the world of Joycean scholarship, the horse forever circles the statue, habituated to its labor; the mill operates ceaselessly.

And Joyce, whose entire writing life was a protracted struggle against time, poverty, emotional crises, semiblindness, and public misunderstanding, might have found something to admire in the steadiness with which the mill grinds on. One of those now harnessed to the labor, his attention loyally fixed to one part of Joycean statuary, has declared of the story "The Boarding House": "If it was written by Joyce, there should be things to explicate." Having in his later years discovered the advantages of collecting about himself a small team of workers to whom questions, errands, and learning projects could be given, Joyce would have found interesting the ways in which his own amateur helpers have by now been supplanted by professional exegetes and commentators (mostly American, a nationality that had never gained his affections) whose efforts are a model of relentlessly systematic investigation. They do, in every aspect of Joyce's achievement, find things to explicate.

Just as their unremitting labors are now a part of the Joycean spectacle, so also are comments akin to mine above. One customarily explores the landscape of Joycean scholarship by first noting how densely crowded it is; one then looks about for a place to deposit one more interpretation. Here, however, the custom will not be observed. No new interpretation can be offered. Instead, a few observations on the statue, the horse, and the mill.

The statue itself, Joyce's achievement, seems to have proved awesome enough over the years to dissuade most critics from doing much more than walking round it with respect, remarking on parts and pieces. Having invited little serious criticism of its ultimate value (save from those, such as publishers and printers, anxious about its alleged obscenity),

Joyce's work has become known to many readers for its prefect integrity in part and whole, the production of an encyclopedic and infallibly disciplined mind. This Joyce serves the explicators well; they may begin with the assumption of absolute control on the part of the author, and then proceed to show how the wizardry manifests itself. Against this kind of reverence few writers have spoken out. The most important of the early iconoclasts was Wyndham Lewis, whose boisterous and overwritten attack on what he thought was the formlessness of Joyce's work is not now much read. Lewis saw Joyce's mind as one more victim of the Bergsonian time-cult, caught in a flux of objects without means of judgment or escape. Joyce was the logical end result of Naturalism, of a fascination with *matter,* of absorption in detail without recourse to the ventilating power of abstraction.

Lewis's pugnacious refusal to be awed by the statue has had two important results for readers today. The first was Stuart Gilbert's pioneering analysis, chapter by chapter, of *Ulysses* (1930). The second has been Hugh Kenner's view of Joyce. Gilbert's book, composed with Joyce's own help and in reaction to Lewis's attack, is a patient elaboration of the minutely organized structural details of the novel. It offers a picture of Joyce as one wholly consumed in organization and pattern: organ, art, color, symbol, and technic are the terms out of which the novel is shown to have grown. Not flux, but mastery and control. Gilbert's book and its famous schema of correspondences have since been central to any classroom reading of Joyce; so central, in fact, that a few readers have transported its vision of Joyce to other of his works than *Ulysses*. Thus, in 1944 two scholars, Richard Levin and Charles Shattuck, brought forth the finding that *Dubliners* is no mere collection of stories somehow connected with the social paralysis of Dublin life, but a work whose organization also issues from a parallel, finely conceived, with Homer. Just as *Ulysses,* with its Telemachiad and Nostos, mirrors the *Odyssey,* so do the fifteen stories, held in tight structural union, from "The Sisters" through to "The Dead."

Although such exegetical performances today seem embarrassing ways to honor the statue, they permit us to see the awe the statue can evoke. So strong is that power that even with one of the first of the sustained critical achievements, unaided by Joyce himself and written with more than exegesis in mind—that by Hugh Kenner (*Dublin's Joyce,* 1956)— the reverence remains almost wholly pure. Kenner, all of whose brilliant encounters with certain great modernists (Pound, Eliot, Lewis, Beckett) are a function of his mimetic adoption of their vocabulary and stance, was able to imagine Joyce from the inside out. As temporary owner of the Joycean mask, Kenner could pontificate that Joyce's books were the work of a master ironist, and although he agreed with Lewis that Joyce was preoccupied with the matter of the universe, that this was no weakness derived from Bergson, but a strength. Joyce's willing absorption in detail, his fact-ridden Naturalism, his exploitation of the emotional and linguistic clichés of Dublin—all are means to high parody. Dublin is a city of the paralyzed and dead, Joyce's characters speak lifeless language, spirituality is inert. Behind and above this meaninglessness, the artist reigns supreme. Having given his absurd characters a world evacuated of sense in which to bang about, he suffuses them with irony. Thus Bloom, a mere "sentimental Jew," is amorphous and pathetic; his wife Molly is smugly given over to the body, and her famous "Yes" is one that "kills the soul" and "has darkened the intellect and blunted the moral sense of all Dublin." Stephen, in both *Ulysses* and *A Portrait of the Artist as a Young Man,* is an "indigestibly Byronic hero," and he shows what happens when idealistic Romanticism runs free. When we read the later book, we are asked by Kenner to see what an insufferable prig Stephen is in *A Portrait.* The earlier novel is to be read, in fact, as the tale of one who becomes no artist, but only an esthete, and whose final vision of freedom is "murderously lambasted" in *Ulysses.* Only when Kenner admits that his reading of *A Portrait* renders the last forty pages of that novel very heavy going—"an intolerable strain on the reader"—and when he warns that *A Portrait* cannot truly be appreciated without *Ulysses* on the reading table beside it, does his gaze at the statue seem to flicker.

The care, however, with which he disentangles the many elements of *A Portrait* and *Ulysses,* and the intellectual sophistication that he brings to the novels, make his approach a turning point in the critical history. His animadversions about the unsatisfactory end of *A Portrait* have called forth many answers and "solutions"—none wholly satisfactory.[1] His assumption that Joyce must be taken primarily as an ironist is a provocation to which every reader will find himself again and again returning.

Much of the criticism before Kenner's book, some of it gathered in Seon Given's *James Joyce: Two Decades of Criticism* (1948), reflects the need felt by earlier writers to legitimize Joyce, to transcend the legal controversy surrounding him, to separate him from Dadaism, Surrealism, and Expressionism, to insist on the order manifest in his achievements. T. S. Eliot saw him in 1923 as a "classicist" who, in pursuing an ancient myth within modern circumstances, was helping to give shape to "the immense panorama of futility and anarchy which is contemporary history."[2] He was also, by peculiar coincidence, combining past and present in ways similar to Eliot's own. Ezra Pound, who had done much to get Joyce into print, saw *Ulysses* in the year of its publication, 1922, as a con-

---

[1] But for two particularly admirable efforts, see Wayne Booth, "The Problem of Distance in *A Portrait of the Artist as a Young Man,*" in his *The Rhetoric of Fiction* (Chicago: The University of Chicago Press, 1961), pp. 323–36; and F. Parvin Sharpless, "Irony in Joyce's *Portrait:* The Stasis of Pity," *James Joyce Quarterly* (Summer 1967), pp. 320–30.
[2] "Ulysses, Order and Myth," *Dial* LXXV, 5 (November 1923), 480–83.

tinuation of the art of writing "where Flaubert left it." [3] Eliot rather thought the novel as a possible art form to have passed into obsolescence before Joyce got to it; Pound thought Joyce had moved it a quantum jump ahead. But both, as early watchers of the statue, were willing to let the term "novel" stand for what Joyce had done.

With Gilbert's Homeric reading available as a semiofficial pronouncement, however, other terms were set by which many readers could approach *Ulysses*: not as a novel, but as a compendium of symbols, esoteric knowledge, labyrinthine connections. The work as mosaic, the reader as initiate, the artist as lord of his creation; such things early became staples of Joycean study. Cutting against the mystique was the analysis presented by Edmund Wilson (in *Axel's Castle*, 1931). Determined to read *A Portrait, Ulysses,* and even *Finnegans Wake* as novels, even while praising their symbolic richness, Wilson offered an approach to Joyce still eminently solid today: an approach emphasizing the accessibility of the works once certain rules are understood, but not succumbed to. Wilson sets forth many of the most compelling Homeric parallels, but urges us to see that Joyce was not enclosed by them. Seeing Joyce's world, particularly that of *Ulysses,* as informed by both the omnivorous grasp of Naturalism and the special interior density of Symbolism, he treats Joyce's mind as that of a poet, "playing a rôle absolutely impersonal and always imposing upon itself all the Naturalistic reactions in regard to the story it is telling at the same time that it allows itself to exercise all the Symbolistic privileges in regard to the way it tells it." While thus preserving for Joyce his standing as a poet (something Joyce's own poems fall short of doing), Wilson also gives us a way to appreciate his much-acclaimed technical virtuosity—not as an end in itself but as a new means to enlarge our apprehension of the psychological life all around us. As Wilson moved beyond mere praise of Joyce's ability with words ("I have discovered I can do anything I want with language," Joyce once grandiosely said), he pointed out a step that every serious reader of the novelist one day takes.

Wilson's essay not only represents a departure in the steady movement round the statue; it is unusual for quite another kind of reason. That is, Wilson criticizes Joyce. Negative criticism had hitherto largely been the preserve of weekly reviewers (". . . inartistic, incoherent, unquotably nasty—a book that one would think could only emanate from a criminal lunatic asylum," wrote one of *Ulysses*) and certain other notable writers of the period—like Virginia Woolf, E. M. Forster, and G. B. Shaw—all of whom, while politely respecting Joyce's abilities, were disgusted by the irregular uses to which he put them. Wilson's criticism, by contrast, is concerned not with irregularity of any sort but with prodigality. He sees Joyce's work as suffering from the "excess of design" brought

[3] "Paris Letter," *Dial,* LXXII, 6 (June 1922), 623–29.

to bear on it. Joyce, possessing no solicitude for his reader, simply gave him too much to absorb. Therefore, while Gilbert's authorized *vade mecum* shows us how much is there to be dug out, it also reveals how much we are inevitably missing. Joyce has overwhelmed us, and he has done so because, as a novelist, he lacks the ability to move things ahead dramatically, as a novelist should. He responds to dramatic opportunity with verbal resourcefulness. His fiction suffers from being static.

Wilson's criticism has been echoed in various ways by, among others, Harry Levin and, more lately, S. L. Goldberg. Levin's compact study (1941), which is still the very best of all the introductory books, also points to the essential stasis of Joyce's picture of that one extraordinary and unexceptional Dublin day, June 16, 1904. Levin locates, moreover, the appropriate aesthetic principle governing not only the stasis of *Ulysses* but, by implication, the paralysis of *Dubliners,* the circularity of *Finnegans Wake.* "Characterization in Joyce," says Levin, "is finally reducible to a few stylized gestures and simplified attitudes." He argues that Joyce's works are limited in their psychological insight to the degree that they are rich in technical brilliance because Joyce remained true to the rules of art enunciated first in *A Portrait:* "Aristotle has not defined pity and terror. I have. . . . Pity is the feeling which arrests the mind in the presence of whatsoever is grave and constant in human sufferings and unites it with the human sufferer. Terror is the feeling which arrests the mind in the presence of whatsoever is grave and constant in human sufferings and unites it with the secret cause. . . . You see, I use the word *arrest* . . . the esthetic emotion . . . is therefore static." These words, evoked by virtually all Joyce's commentators and evaluated with greatest care and thoroughness in 1946 by Irene H. Chayes[4]—who also provides a detailed analysis of the importance of the Joycean epiphany—are crucial to Levin because they explain why so little happens in Joyce, and why such negligibility is stuffed with such tumultuous linguistic energy.

The vexing question of Joyce's success or failure as a dramatic novelist is given its most complex and satisfying treatment in S. L. Goldberg's extraordinarily good book on *Ulysses* (*The Classical Temper,* 1961). Its excellence stems in part from Goldberg's recognition that Joyce calls for criticism as much as explication, and that Wilson was wise indeed in refusing to treat *Ulysses* or any of Joyce's works as sacred books of the arts. Goldberg sustains for the length of his book one central thesis: the meaning of the novel lies in the ways its human experience is realized and ordered. Joyce is not primarily a parodist, a philosopher, a linguist, or a maker of myths. He is a novelist, faced with the same obligation as any novelist—to give imaginative illumination to the moral experience of certain human beings. Goldberg, who owes much of his own critical sensi-

---

[4] See her essay "Joyce's Epiphanies" in Seon Givens, ed., *James Joyce: Two Decades of Criticism* (New York: Vanguard Press, 1948), pp. 27–46. The essay appeared originally in *The Sewanee Review,* LIV, 3 (July–September 1946), 449–67.

bility to F. R. Leavis, responds to the criticism offered by Wilson and by Levin by simply treating the acclaimed technical virtuosity of Joyce's method as trivial compared to the dramatic situation posed by the existences, within *Ulysses,* of Molly and Leopold Bloom and of Stephen Dedalus. Joyce, in coming to terms with the opportunities they presented, achieved the temper by which dogma, explicit belief, metaphysics, and abstractions are repulsed. That temper is open instead to what is centrally human; Goldberg opens himself to the lives of the three central characters as the meanings of those lives are enacted.

In bringing the criticism of *Ulysses,* and thereby of Joyce in his other works, to a new level of intelligence and sophistication, Goldberg's book does not terminate the critical discussion. Rather, in true Joycean terms, such ends mean only new beginnings, new revolutions in the progress round the statue. Thus, two of the most interesting readings of Joyce since Goldberg, those by Anthony Cronin and Richard Ellmann, return to the employment of critical techniques acclaimed in early years, then later discarded as obsolete. Cronin will have nothing to do with the idea that *Ulysses* is to be read for its plot, for its dramatic sequences. Joyce has liberated the novel from such artificialities and, in directing the reader to the "profane joy" of living, dispenses with the many corrupt falsehoods of traditional novels while infusing his work with ephiphanies, with the power of words themselves, with poetry. The result is a novel of comic joy, of tolerance and liberation. Moreover, in lifting from the world of Dublin the heavy hand of societal judgment, Joyce resolved for himself the painfully deep tensions of love and hate he had held for many years toward his fatherland. And in settling upon Leopold Bloom as his chief character, Joyce accepted the sordid, fallible, comic, and absurd father he had once, as the proud esthete Stephen, held at arm's length. Incorporating and redeeming what is most embarrassing and most noble in humanity, Joyce showed at last what a Stephen grown into artistic maturity could do, and what such a man as Leopold Bloom could be.

Ellmann's book, *Ulysses on the Liffey* (1972), returns, by "commodious vicus of recirculation," to the world of Joyce as it had been charted out some forty years before by Gilbert. The return, however, is illuminated by a brilliance and a sympathy unachieved by Gilbert. In joining the circle back to Gilbert, Ellmann also advances beyond the kind of purely biographical criticism within whose limits he had so brilliantly written his essay on "The Dead." He is in his way also fascinated by Homeric parallels, and he too makes available a schema of correspondences. His schema, that originally sent by Joyce to his friend Carlo Linati in 1920, antedates Gilbert's by one year. The differences between Gilbert and Ellmann consist, however, of rather more than this. Where Gilbert's authorized version of *Ulysses* can quickly prove mechanical—can prove, in fact, a burden, for all its knowledge—Ellmann's version is elegant, witty, and profoundly responsive to the Joyce who would see the oceanic forces of nature overcoming the denying forces of man-made power, the Joyce who would marry the real to the ideal in order that each might have its splendor, the Joyce who would praise the affirmative power of art. As Leopold and Stephen close the distance between them, bringing forth a harmony from such apparent discord in character, and as Stephen learns to unite the sordid and the rarefied in his own life, so the novel is everywhere founded on syntheses between unlikely partners. Many years ago, Frank O'Connor drew attention to the way Joyce could evoke the beautiful while keeping his eyes glued to a Dublin city directory. Later students have suffered to learn that Joyce, at ease as well with Blake as with Defoe, constructed his most sublime story, "The Dead," partly out of literary materials left behind by Bret Harte.[5] One recent writer, Hélène Cixous, has found it quite difficult to exhaust Joyce's sense of polarity, contradiction, and irony. Her tangled and fascinating book, *The Exile of James Joyce,* as long as *Ulysses* itself but not as nicely ordered, is given over to rich meditations on tensions within Joyce's life and work. Her essay on "Ivy Day in the Committee Room" indicates how well Joyce had learned to explore and refine those tensions.

Ellmann shows us that as that day in 1904 comes to an end, we are left with a strange trinity, balanced so precariously and beautifully, assembled at 7 Eccles Street: a cuckolded advertising canvasser who, having masturbated that day, now represents love; a semi-inebriated and homeless intellectual of sorts who has come into possession of a vision of love "as the basic act of art"; and a somnolent bleeding woman, no better than she should be, representing love as "the final penetration by the wisdom of the body of the wisdom of the mind." None of the three is complete in himself; together they "sum up what is affirmable." By fusions and reconciliations intricately brought into being by Joyce and subtly exposed by Ellmann, *Ulysses* is formed by a geometry that balances each thing against itself, each balance then posed against a synthesis elsewhere in force. Behind the complex structure, moreover, grows a figure manlike in form. Each episode of *Ulysses,* keyed to a part of the body, contributes to his creation. He is more than Bloom, more than Molly and Stephen: "The androgynous man who stands within and behind and beyond might be called Hibernion. One day he will be Finnegan."

Of *Finnegans Wake,* where Joyce at last lodged that figure, almost anything might be, and has been, said by the critics. The extremes have by now been struck. S. L. Goldberg: "I do not believe *Finnegans Wake* is worth detailed exegesis." To such a critic, so responsive to *Ulysses,* *Finnegans Wake* is no novel, and no drama, but only a disastrous experiment. But to Robert Martin Adams, ". . . in the near future it is *Finne-*

---

[5] See Gerhard Friedrich, "Bret Harte as a Source for James Joyce's 'The Dead,'" *Philological Quarterly,* XXXIII (October 1954), 442–44.

gans Wake on which the major reputation of Joyce will depend. . . .
It carries to their logical conclusion the modalities of visionary insight
and multiple imitation which we have learned to admire in *Ulysses* and
The Portait; it is an immense mine of verbal invention, from which artists will be quarrying for years to come."

Between such contrariety, so appropriate to Joyce's sense of opposi-
tions, lies *Wake* scholarship. Its history is not unlike that of the circular
path of Joycean criticism in general. At first, awe before the mystery,
and admiration conditioned by the belief that Joyce could do no wrong.
Thus the early volume, evangelical in spirit, published while the *Wake*
was still being written: *Our Exagmination Round his Factification for
Incamination of "Work in Progress."* Then, Edmund Wilson with another sober propaedeutic approach.[6] Both had received some help from
Joyce himself, who once again was faced with a largely uncomprehending,
and even hostile, world of readers. Then, in the year of Joyce's death,
Harry Levin's book, containing as useful and as encouraging a reading of
the *Wake* as has been written. Afterwards, virtual silence from those who
would offer a general analysis of the book; rather, the steady movement
of explication, positivistic and sensible in the face of all that must be
known for the book to be understood, but Swiftian in the way certain
questions of value are tabled while the work proceeds. Thus Joseph
Campbell and Henry Morton Robinson's *A Skeleton Key to Finnegans
Wake*, Adaline Glasheen's *A Census of Finnegans Wake: An Index of
the Characters and Their Roles* (particularly the first edition), and,
among many other noteworthy efforts, the *Wake Newslitter*. As Gilbert's
book has proved of greatest classroom serviceability for *Ulysses,* so the
Skeleton Key and William York Tindall's *Reader's Guide to Finnegans
Wake* are most often consulted for the later work. They introduce the
well-known mythological patterns, the Viconian cycles, the emphasis on
mankind's Fall and Resurrection, the rituals and repetitions by which
man knows and makes himself known. Glasheen indexes and cross-references the specific elements and characters so that a base for general analysis will be at the ready. That such analysis, at once critical in the freest
sense, and well informed in the widest sense, is not yet forthcoming is
evident from the pages of the *Wake Newslitter*. There, as in the *James
Joyce Quarterly,* the struggle for first principles is constantly bogged
down by preoccupation with textual detail, linguistic reference, and
previous error on the part of other professionals. It is probably correct to
argue, as a number of Joyce scholars do, that *Finnegans Wake* will not
be known until a great deal of spadework has been done. That argument, most happily formulated after setting aside the consideration that
life is short, is in fact now in the ascendant among Joyce scholars. One

[6] Contained in two essays, one in *Axel's Castle* (New York: Charles Scribner's Sons,
1931), pp. 225–36; the other in *The Wound and the Bow* (New York: Oxford University
Press, 1947), pp. 243–71.

of them, Clive Hart, has written well of Joyce, and brilliantly of the structure of the *Wake,* even after confessing that "whether the riches are sufficient to repay the considerable labour which must be expended" is a question sure to bother him, and us, for as long as we turn our attention to Joyce's last work.

But, as Mr. Hart surmounts his own doubts, so also do scholars such as James S. Atherton, in his *The Books at the Wake,* and David Hayman, in his *A First Draft Version of Finnegans Wake.* The result is a tough, hard-edged scholarship, long on fact and short on subjective treatment. Hart shows that the text of the *Wake,* so difficult even after renewed attacks upon it, its themes apparently so inaccessible, is in fact given order and some accessibility by Joyce's use of certain motifs. These motifs had to be substantial in length because they had to serve as conspicuous fixed points in a work saturated by verbal flux. One such motif was lifted by Joyce from Edgar Quinet's *Introduction à la philosophie de l'histoire de l'humanité.* The spirit of Quinet's paragraph, so congenial to Joyce's own temper, serves to remind us of permanence amid change, of the circularity of history, of the vanity of man. Joyce, fleeing from the nightmare of Irish politics and history, sought to organize his own emotional and intellectual life so that contemporary folly or tyranny could be seen as merely local—and therefore ephemeral—instances of perennial human weaknesses. The same device that allowed him to put distance between himself and his own troubled historical circumstances was used to provide structural order to his last, and most troubled, artistic achievement.

Joyce's preoccupation with the folly of man, with the ways in which his loudly proclaimed journeys arrive at only their starting point, with the repetitions of life that provide the illusion of meaning, was nonetheless a loving preoccupation. Joyce was absorbed by the vanities and the repetitions; he was also compelled to see through them. He did not seek a hasty reduction of life, or an art that would cruelly puncture its noble silliness. His, as Lionel Trilling implies, was a skepticism that fully embraced. It moved, as Trilling says, "through the fullest realization of the human, the all-too-human, to that which transcends and denies the human." Its ultimate station is something other than the *stasis* the young writer had sought; it is the full acceptance of *nullity.* That acceptance is governed by gigantic curiosity and industry; it slights nothing on its way to denying everything. Trilling also implies, I think, that to challenge Joyce's denial is possible only for those who have made a preliminary acceptance as large as Joyce's. To quarrel with Joyce, we must embrace that bewildering profusion of life mirrored in *Ulysses* and *Finnegans Wake.* No smart, easy negativism is possible. In this way, Joyce's arrogant claim that he expected his readers to spend as much time in understanding *Finnegans Wake* as he spent in writing it loses some of its arrogance. Joyce, we come again and again to see, is a writer great enough to be an imposition. That is a distinction not easily gained. As

Adams points out, it is an imposition to which we as readers have responded now in one way, now in another. To see him as lord supreme over his perfectly integrated and ordered work is one way to respond to the imposition. To see him as a cosmic ironist is another. To see him, as Adams decides to do, as the great modern humorist is yet another. That we feel constrained to make such responses is a measure of the gravity, or the greatness, of the imposition. To that imposition we will continue to respond imperfectly in our progress round the statue.

Political Ignominy—"Ivy Day"

by Hélène Cixous

This was Joyce's favourite of his own novellas; if "Cyclops" satirises the disproportionately vast ambition of Irish nationalism, then inversely "Ivy Day," written in 1905, satirises the Irish political situation, which derived its meaning and relative proportion from the presence of an invisible giant, present and alive in people's minds. This, it could be said, is the Lilliputian method of satire at work, reducing everything by reference to a superior, larger being. On this 6 October, a group of Dubliners from various social strata assemble in Wicklow Street to make their preparations for a municipal election, and the day is the anniversary of Parnell's death. Some of the agents, assembling at the end of a rainy day, have remembered this and wear an ivy leaf behind their lapel. The ivy is perennially green, but memory is less lasting; this 6 October soon appears as a day of forgetfulness, of shame, or of inconvenient recollections. The agents discuss local politics, and their conversation bears witness to the disintegration of political and moral values that has come about since the Leader's death. The rain matches both the mourning of the past and the sadness of the present, while the imagery that lights up the darker corners of this evening and its events only accentuates the shadows.

In the small bare room, the ancient caretaker fans a fire which is in danger of being choked by ashes; and the commemoration begins under the auspices of a dying fire, guarded by a weeping old man. The Phoenix would find it difficult to arise from these ashes, and despite the direct allusion to resurrection in the poem recited at the end ("They had their way: they laid him low./ But Erin, list, his spirit may/ Rise, like the Phoenix from the flames,/ When breaks the dawning of the day"), it is clear that there is no faith now, and that no one really wishes to revive the spirit of Parnell, for he would be too intransigent and too honest to suit anyone in this new generation, except perhaps (this is the Triestine, socialist Joyce speaking) the workers. But the workers would have very little chance in competition with the two parties capable of financing election campaigns, the Nationalist party in whose favour the Conservative candidate has stood down, and the unnamed party of Mr. Tierney, for which

"Political Ignominy—'Ivy Day.'" From Hélène Cixous, *The Exile of James Joyce*, pp. 266–72. Copyright © 1972 by Hélène Cixous. Reprinted by permission of David Lewis, Inc.

the O'Conners, Croftons, Henchys, and Lyons are working. It is Joe Hynes who speaks up for the working classes, in Marxist terms which suggest that all the virtues have taken refuge among the proletariat:

> —The working-man, said Mr. Hynes, gets all kicks and no halfpence. But it's labour produces everything. The working-man is not looking for fat jobs for his sons and nephews and cousins. The working-man is not going to drag the honour of Dublin in the mud to please a German monarch.
> —How's that? said the old man.
> —Don't you know they want to present an address of welcome to Edward Rex if he comes here next year? What do we want kowtowing to a foreign king?

We shall see that Joe Hynes, "a tall, slender young man with a light brown moustache," who looks like Joyce, is a "loyalist"; as his friend O'Connor says, "poor Joe is a decent skin." He clearly has a sense of humour, a certain firmness, and real loyalty to Parnell and to the Socialist creed. If Parnell were alive, say Hynes, O'Connor, and old Jack, things would be different now; and old Jack says, "Musha, God be with them times! There was some life in it then." And this is true; then, Parnell was God. But the door opens and a little man bustles in, hurries to the fire, "rubbing his hands as if he intended to produce a spark from them," and Mr. Henchy has arrived. It can be seen that he does not like Hynes, or the working class, or the "hillsiders and fenians" whom he confuses together and insults in a most conventional fashion: "Some of these hillsiders and fenians are a bit too clever if you ask me, said Mr. Henchy. Do you know what my private and candid opinion is about some of those little jokers? I believe half of them are in the pay of the Castle" (that is, of the English government).

In the half-light there come and go various representatives of the alienation from which Dublin suffers, the most typical being the indefinable person, "resembling a poor clergyman or a poor actor," whose face has "the appearance of damp yellow cheese," and whose voice is "discreet, indulgent, velvety." It eventually turns out that he is a poor, unbeneficed priest, "travelling on his own account." Everything rings false in this devalued world, except the elementary desires: Everyone is thirsty and impatiently awaits the arrival of the promised bottles of stout. Here can be observed the beginnings of that downgrading technique Joyce was to use so freely in *Ulysses*; just as the princess Nausicaa is replaced by a lame schoolgirl, the times of Parnell and his glory are cheapened by the succeeding age. The ambitions of Ireland are limited to the consumption of alcohol, and Mr. Henchy, the most active and unscrupulous of the Dubliners present, burlesques the rise of a citizen to the highest bourgeois honours thus: "You must owe the City Fathers money nowadays if you want to be made Lord Mayor. . . . Would I do for the job? . . . Driving out of the Mansion House, in all my vermin, with Jack here standing up behind me in a powdered wig, eh? . . . And I'll make Father Keon my private chaplain. We'll have a family party."

Henchy has a sense of humour that springs from his awareness of the country's degradation. This is not a source of grief to him, however; on the contrary, he exploits it. He knows how to make use of circumstances as best he can, for purely selfish ends. He is the anti-idealist, who sees politics as nothing more than a business proposition. The well-told joke may make his audience forget the date of this day which for Henchy has been profitably employed; but pettiness is apparent in all his jokes and actions. Everything that is done or said is appallingly trivial, even when it is not a matter of vulgar sentiments or cowardice; the assembled agents carry out their campaign, not for a beloved or trusted leader, but for "Tricky Dicky," who is known for his untrustworthiness, and who "only wants to get some job or other." The agents are not deceived by him, because there is no question of politics in the business for them; they have simply taken temporary jobs as agents, in order to pay some urgent debt, and all that counts is that they should be paid. As they wait, because the trickster "with those little pig's eyes" for whom they work is in no hurry to honour his debts, they fall back upon the drink, which they have also been awaiting with growing impatience.

The scene is indeed far from the majesty of Ireland's "uncrowned King." The imaginary presence of Parnell embarrasses them, and the behaviour of these men who live with the times expresses their embarrassment or their excessive joviality. This meeting is quite a close parody of an "heroic" political gathering; but these Dubliners have assembled at a time when politics is the exact opposite of heroism; Mr. Henchy pretends to act energetically, bustling about, talking loudly, calling for more light and warmth. There can be little honesty and less dignity when the deified leader is replaced by a mean little man whose father was a money-lender and pawnbroker. Worst of all, this downfall is accompanied by a renewal of treachery; there is no longer such a thing as individual honour, and soon there will be no national honour left either. The only subject which evokes any reaction from the agents' guilty consciences is the possibility of King Edward's projected visit to Ireland.

The tone changes abruptly from the sordid to the slanderous. The comedy acts as a disguise for unscrupulousness; for Henchy, for example, the king is not a symbolic figure and his visit ought not to be treated sentimentally, but accepted for what it is, an opportunity to revive the Irish economy. "The King's coming here will mean an influx of money into this country. The citizens of Dublin will benefit by it." We are no longer concerned with freedom, but with profit; "It's capital we want." Mr. Henchy takes no account of any sense of honour, for, after all, "Parnell is dead." This is of course true, but here it sounds like a repetition of the treachery, a denial of all he stood for. "Look at all the money there is in the country if we only worked the old industries, the mills, the shipbuilding yards and factories." Mr. Henchy knows where his interests lie, and Ireland needs money. The citizens, the ratepayers, everyone concerned would benefit, if this "jolly fine, decent fellow," Edward VII, came to Dublin.

Some of those present feel that they must, rather inconveniently, raise objections; Mr. Lyons points out that "King Edward's life, you know, is not the very . . ." But Henchy will not have any moralising in political matters, and judiciously recommends that they "let bygones be bygones"; he reminds them that Edward is a human being, which is true, and that he likes his amusements like the rest of them—"he's just an ordinary knockabout like you and me." Basically, what can they find in him to complain about? He is a "man of the world," [1] and if he were not English, he would have all the qualities of a good Irishman: "He's fond of his glass of grog and he's a bit of a rake, perhaps, and he's a good sportsman. Damn it, can't we Irish play fair?" This is a good example of the impeccable logic of treachery. Mr. Lyons is not fully convinced by the argument, though: "That's all very fine. . . . But look at the case of Parnell now," he says.

But Mr. Henchy replies, "Where's the analogy between the two cases?" In the name of what does Mr. Lyons claim that one can compare Edward with Parnell? But there is no answer; Henchy pretends not to understand "the connection," and with the skill of all those who practise the political trade, he changes the subject, ignoring the contradictions of the doubtful morality involved and acting the part of the generous, forgiving man who reconciles opposing views. Everything falls back into the chaos of degeneracy and lies again. "Don't let us stir up any bad blood," says Mr. O'Connor with subtle hypocrisy, quietening his own conscience by this act of reconciliation. "We all respect him now that he's dead and gone," he adds, meaning that Parnell no longer frightens us, though while he was alive his frankness and honesty hindered and embarrassed us because we were cowards. This is what Bloom thought also, in the cabmen's shelter. Even the conservatives forgive the adulterer, now that he is dead, and respect him "because he was a gentleman." Parnell, of course, as gentleman is not of the same species as Edward, "a man of the world" and "a jolly, fine, decent fellow, and no damn nonsense about him."

"Parnell is dead," and nothing need hinder Ireland from welcoming the English king. And so, who *is* worthy to revive the flame, and who is not unworthy to wear the ivy leaf? Not the younger generation, to judge by old Jack's son, who is at the worst stages of degeneracy; if he is forced to get himself a job, "he drinks it all." Another proof is offered by the boy who brings the bottles of stout; Mr. Henchy offers him a drink, much against old Jack's will, and as Jack gives the boy a bottle, he asks him how old he is, as though trying to recall him to sense and health before it is too

[1] Like the Jesuits in "Grace," who are "men of the world like ourselves."

late. But the lad already knows whom to heed and whom to respect, not the distressed old father but the tempter Henchy; "That's the way it begins," says the old man, but in fact that is how it ends. They suddenly remember that today is the anniversary of Parnell's death, and feel slightly embarrassed by this. Parnell exists so little that when the need to communicate is felt, they do not know quite what to do, not having thought of preparing any ceremony. Hynes, who had vanished during the discussion, as though Joyce had obscurely wished to keep him from being a witness to this deadly wake, now returns, and the vague Parnell wake that takes place has this in common with the wake for Finnegan the mason: that if the shade of Parnell has made even a timid appearance in people's minds, they have hastened to reduce it again to its customary impotence, and similarly the guests at the wake persuade Tim Finnegan, whom the scent of whiskey has recalled to life, to lie down again. Parnell, however, resembles Hamlet's father much more than he resembles Finnegan; and whatever they do to exorcise him, he remains firmly ensconced in the individual conscience.

At the end, Joyce's intention is to evoke more concretely the death of the Leader, because the presence of their eternally absent king is so strongly felt by all the characters, *as it was felt by Joyce himself,* as a perpetual reproach and remorse for their decadent state. Through a paradox which represents the highest achievement of his deceptively realistic art in *Dubliners,* Joyce is, in the writing of "Ivy Day," doubly present; he is every Irishman, and thereby guilty of the murder of Parnell, and he also *is* Parnell, invisible but present behind every line and every word, to such an extent that one can sense his irony informing everything that is said. It is all written down in the characters' uneasy consciences. Mr. Henchy shamelessly invites Joe Hynes to recite "that thing you wrote," as though to demonstrate that the break between living present and dead past is complete, and that Parnell henceforth belongs to literature rather than to history.

The poem is ambiguous; what the metaphor actually alludes to and what it makes manifest can be interpreted on many levels, some of them liable to become mutually contradictory, and we must examine all of these levels and not just the apparently literary one which is the first to be perceived. The thematic tension thus established acts upon the reader's mind, making him sensitive to the smallest variations in tone; and "The Death of Parnell" is seen to be a poem of several different degrees of irony. To begin with, there is the literal irony of reciting a poem of grief and indignation to an audience that remains completely cold and unmoved. Then, by its relationship with this audience, the poem acquires an aggressive tone, because Parnell died betrayed by people whose description ("modern hypocrites," "coward hounds") identifies them with the audience, who are complacently listening to the poem; they behave as though they were not the people being criticised in the poem, as though they had nothing to do with it, and applaud their own condemnation. Next, the irony becomes historical too; the contrast is established between the message of hope which the poet cries prayerfully towards the future and the reality of this future, made concrete as the moment in which the poem is being read—and the hope is seen to be both vain and ridiculous.

> "His spirit may/ Rise, like the Phoenix from the flames,/ When breaks the dawning of the day," cries the poet, and on this echo of the Psalms, the fire in the grate goes out. Erin is compared to an Eastern queen who sees all the hopes of her life perish on the pyre where her dead king is burned:—"He lies slain by the coward hounds/ He raised to glory from the mire;/ And Erin's hopes and Erin's dreams/ Perish upon her monarch's pyre.// In palace, cabin, or in cot/ The Irish heart where'er it be/ Is bowed with woe—for he is gone/ Who would have wrought her destiny./ He would have had his Erin famed,/ The green flag gloriously unfurled,/ Her statesmen, bards, and warriors raised/ Before the nations of the world./ He dreamed (alas, 'twas but a dream!)/ Of Liberty: but as he strove/ To clutch that idol, treachery/ Sundered him from the thing he loved."

Yet in reality Erin had taken great delight in raising that pyre and in burning her "hopes and dreams," for fear that they might come true.

Insensibly the distance grows, between Parnell's death, theatrically deplored as a great loss, and the real indifference of his so-called followers; between the tragedy of the hero's death and the meanness of the chorus who bewail it; between the swollen rhetoric of the lamentations that are recited and the actual paucity of the Dubliners' vocabulary; between the dead dream and the living nightmare; and as it grows, the irony is further modified. Read before an innocent audience it would simply be an expression of some puerile optimism; but, to a guilty audience, it denounces their crimes clearly and candidly. Hynes reciting "The Death of Parnell" is like the actors in *Hamlet* acting out the murder of a king before the king's murderer; the whole tragedy is in Claudius' silence. Similarly, when Hynes finishes his poem, there is a silence, lasting for a moment while everyone hastens to adjust his mind to the consciousness of guilt and to decide on the appropriate behaviour to adopt; this moment of mutual admission of guilt is broken by their applause, for the guilty have found their line of defence, and their reply to the indirect accusation. They choose the role of spectators, excusing themselves thus from any responsibility, and they congratulate the poet on his mastery of the art.

Yet there was that moment in which Parnell almost began to exist again, that silence which he occupied so fully that he almost returned to them; and in that silence, that moment, was produced their awareness of the discord between the last verse and its echo in time present, in actuality as they knew it. It was not the silence of shamefaced reluctance to speak, but the silence in which the dishonourable Dubliner was faced with the image of the honourable man who was to exist when Parnell returned, when freedom ruled, in the psalmist's ideal future.

"And on that day may Erin well/ Pledge in the cup she lifts to Joy/ One grief—the memory of Parnell." Each knows that the memory of Parnell is only a form of remorse, and each lifts the bitter drink of guilty conscience to his lips, but no toast is drunk to freedom, because they are soon to drink to King Edward. All the themes which could have led to tragedy have been turned aside into farce.

The Backgrounds of "The Dead"

by Richard Ellmann

The silent cock shall crow at last. The west shall shake the east awake.
Walk while ye have the night for morn, lightbreakfastbringer. . . .

—*Finnegans Wake* (473)

The stay in Rome had seemed purposeless, but during it Joyce became aware of the change in his attitude toward Ireland and so toward the world. He embodied his new perceptions in "The Dead." The story, which was the culmination of a long waiting history, began to take shape in Rome, but was not set down until he left the city. The pressure of hints, sudden insights, and old memories rose in his mind until, like King Midas's barber, he was compelled to speech.

Although the story dealt mainly with three generations of his family in Dublin, it drew also upon an incident in Galway in 1903. There Michael ("Sonny") Bodkin courted Nora Barnacle; but he contracted tuberculosis and had to be confined to bed. Shortly afterwards Nora resolved to go to Dublin, and Bodkin stole out of his sickroom, in spite of the rainy weather, to sing to her under an apple tree and bid her goodbye. In Dublin Nora soon learned that Bodkin was dead, and when she met Joyce she was first attracted to him, as she told a sister, because he resembled Sonny Bodkin.[1]

Joyce's habit of ferreting out details had made him conduct minute interrogations of Nora even before their departure from Dublin. He was disconcerted by the fact that young men before him had interested her. He did not much like to know that her heart was still moved, even in pity, by the recollection of the boy who had loved her. The notion of being in some sense in rivalry with a dead man buried in the little cemetery at Oughterard was one that came easily, and gallingly, to a man of Joyce's jealous disposition. It was one source of his complaint to his Aunt Josephine Murray that Nora persisted in regarding him as quite similar to other men she had known.[2]

"The Backgrounds of 'The Dead.'" From Richard Ellmann, *James Joyce* (New York: Oxford University Press, 1959), pp. 252–63. Copyright © 1959 by Richard Ellmann. Reprinted by permission of Oxford University Press, Inc.

[1] Letter to me from Mrs. Kathleen Barnacle Griffin.

[2] See p. 222 [of *James Joyce* by Ellmann].

A few months after expressing this annoyance, while Joyce and Nora Barnacle were living in Trieste in 1905, Joyce received another impulsion toward "The Dead." In a letter Stanislaus happened to mention attending a concert of Plunket Greene, the Irish baritone, which included one of Thomas Moore's *Irish Melodies* called 'O, Ye Dead!' [3] The song, a dialogue of living and dead, was eerie enough, but what impressed Stanislaus was that Greene rendered the second stanza, in which the dead answer the living, as if they were whimpering for the bodied existence they could no longer enjoy:

> It is true, it is true, we are shadows cold and wan;
> And the fair and the brave whom we loved on earth are gone;
>> But still thus ev'n in death,
>> So sweet the living breath
> Of the fields and the flow'rs in our youth we wandered o'er,
>> That ere, condemn'd, we go
>> To freeze, 'mid Hecla's snow,
> We would taste it awhile, and think we live once more!

James was interested and asked Stanislaus to send the words, which he learned to sing himself. His feelings about his wife's dead lover found a dramatic counterpart in the jealousy of the dead for the living in Moore's song: It would seem that the living and the dead are jealous of each other. Another aspect of the rivalry is suggested in *Ulysses*, where Stephen cries out to his mother's ghost, whose "glazing eyes, staring out of death, to shake and bend my soul, . . . to strike me down," he cannot put out of mind: "No, mother. Let me be and let me live." [4] That the dead do not stay buried is, in fact, a theme of Joyce from the beginning to the end of his work; Finnegan is not the only corpse to be resurrected.

In Rome the obtrusiveness of the dead affected what he thought of Dublin, the equally Catholic city he had abandoned, a city as prehensile of its ruins, visible and invisible. His head was filled with a sense of the too-successful encroachment of the dead upon the living city; there was a disrupting parallel in the way that Dublin, buried behind him, was haunting his thoughts. In *Ulysses* the theme was to be reconstituted, in more horrid form, in the mind of Stephen, who sees corpses rising from their graves like vampires to deprive the living of joy. The bridebed, the childbed, and the bed of death are bound together, and death "comes, pale vampire, through storm his eyes, his bat sails bloodying the sea, mouth to her mouth's kiss." [5] We can be at the same time in death as well as in life.[6]

[3] S. Joyce, "The Background to 'Dubliners,'" *Listener*, LI (March 25, 1954), 526–7.
[4] *Ulysses* (New York: Vintage Books, 1961), p. 10.
[5] *Ibid.*, p. 48.
[6] The converse of this theme appears in *Ulysses* (113 [107]), when Bloom, walking in

By February 11, 1907, after six months in Rome, Joyce knew in general what story he must write. Some of his difficulty in beginning it was due, as he said himself,[7] to the riot in Dublin over *The Playboy of the Western World*. Synge had followed the advice of Yeats that Joyce had rejected, to find his inspiration in the Irish folk, and had gone to the Aran Islands. This old issue finds small echoes in the story. The nationalistic Miss Ivors tries to persuade Gabriel to go to Aran (where Synge's *Riders to the Sea* is set), and when he refuses, twits him for his lack of patriotic feeling. Though Gabriel thinks of defending the autonomy of art and its indifference to politics, he knows such a defense would be pretentious, and only musters up the remark that he is sick of his own country. But the issue is far from settled for him.

"The Dead" begins with a party and ends with a corpse, so entwining "funferal" and "funeral" as in the wake of Finnegan. That he began with a party was due, at least in part, to Joyce's feeling that the rest of the stories in *Dubliners* had not completed his picture of the city. In a letter of September 25, 1906,[8] he had written his brother from Rome to say that some elements of Dublin had been left out of his stories: "I have not reproduced its ingenuous insularity and its hospitality, the latter 'virtue' so far as I can see does not exist elsewhere in Europe." He allowed a little of this warmth to enter "The Dead." In his speech at the Christmas party, Gabriel Conroy explicitly commends Ireland for this very virtue of hospitality, though his expression of the idea is distinctly after-dinner: "I feel more strongly with every recurring year that our country has no tradition which does it so much honour and which it should guard so jealously as that of its hospitality. It is a tradition that is unique as far as my experience goes (and I have visited not a few places abroad) among the modern nations." This was Joyce's oblique way, in language that mocked his own, of beginning the task of making amends.

The selection of details for "The Dead" shows Joyce making those choices which, while masterly, suggest the preoccupations that mastered him. Once he had determined to represent an Irish party, the choice of the Misses Morkans' as its location was easy enough. He had already reserved for *Stephen Hero* a Christmas party at his own house, a party which was also to be clouded by a discussion of a dead man. The other festive occasions of his childhood were associated with his hospitable great-aunts Mrs. Callanan and Mrs. Lyons, and Mrs. Callanan's daughter Mary Ellen, at their house at 15 Usher's Island, which was also known as the "Misses Flynn school." [9] There, every year the Joyces who were old enough would go, and John Joyce carved the goose and made the speech.

Glasnevin, thinks, "They are not going to get me this innings. Warm beds: warm fullblooded life."

[7] See p. 248 [of *James Joyce* by Richard Ellmann].
[8] See p. 239 [of *James Joyce* by Richard Ellmann].
[9] Interview with Mrs. May Joyce Monaghan, 1953.

Stanislaus Joyce says that the speech of Gabriel Conroy in "The Dead" is a good imitation of his father's oratorical style.[10]

In Joyce's story, Mrs. Callanan and Mrs. Lyons, the Misses Flynn, become the spinster ladies, the Misses Morkan; and Mary Ellen Callanan becomes Mary Jane. Most of the other party guests were also reconstituted from Joyce's recollections. Mrs. Lyons had a son Freddy, who kept a Christmas card shop in Grafton Street.[11] Joyce introduces him as Freddy Malins, and situates his shop in the less fashionable Henry Street, perhaps to make him need that sovereign Gabriel lent him. Another relative of Joyce's mother, a first cousin, married a Protestant named Mervyn Archdale Browne, who combined the profession of music teacher with that of agent for a burglary insurance company. Joyce keeps him in "The Dead" under his own name. Bartell d'Arcy, the hoarse singer in the story, was based upon Barton M'Guckin, the leading tenor in the Carl Rosa Opera Company. There were other tenors, such as John McCormack, whom Joyce might have used, but he needed one who was unsuccessful and uneasy about himself; and his father's often-told anecdote about M'Guckin's lack of confidence furnished him with just such a singer as he intended Bartell d'Arcy to be.

The making of his hero, Gabriel Conroy, was more complicated. The root situation, of jealousy for his wife's dead lover, was of course Joyce's. The man who is murdered, D. H. Lawrence has one of his characters say, desires to be murdered,[12] some temperaments demand the feeling that their friends and sweethearts will deceive them. Joyce's conversation often returned to the word "betrayal," [13] and the entangled innocents whom he uses for his heroes are all aspects of his conception of himself. Though Gabriel is less impressive than Joyce's other heroes, Stephen, Bloom, Richard Rowan, or Earwicker, he belongs to their distinguished, put-upon company.

There are several specific points at which Joyce attributes his own experiences to Gabriel. The letter which Gabriel remembers having written to Gretta Conroy early in their courtship is one of these; from it Gabriel quotes to himself the sentiment, "Why is it that words like these seem to me so dull and cold? Is it because there is no word tender enough to be your name?" These sentences are taken almost directly from a letter Joyce wrote to Nora in 1904.[14] It was also Joyce, of course, who wrote book reviews, just as Gabriel Conroy does, for the *Daily Express*. Since the *Daily Express* was pro-English, he had probably been teased for writing for it during his frequent visits to the house of David Sheehy, M. P. One of the Sheehy daughters, Kathleen, may well have been the model for Miss Ivors,

[10] He excepts the quotation from Browning, but even this was quite within the scope of the man who could quote Vergil when lending money to his son.

[11] Interview with Mrs. Monaghan.

[12] Birkin, in *Women in Love*.

[13] Information from Professor Joseph Prescott.

[14] At Cornell [the Joyce Collection of the Cornell University Library].

for she wore that austere bodice and sported the same patriotic pin.[15] In Gretta's old sweetheart, in Gabriel's letter, in the book reviews and the discussion of them, as well as in the physical image of Gabriel with hair parted in the middle and . . . glasses, Joyce drew directly upon his own life.

His father was also deeply involved in the story. Stanislaus Joyce recalls that when the Joyce children were too young to bring along to the Misses Flynn's party, their father and mother sometimes left them with a governess and stayed at a Dublin hotel overnight instead of returning to their house in Bray.[16] Gabriel and Gretta do this too. Gabriel's quarrels with his mother also suggest John Joyce's quarrels with his mother, who never accepted her son's marriage to a woman of lower station.[17] But John Joyce's personality was not like Gabriel's; he had no doubts of himself, in the midst of many failures he was full of self-esteem. He had the same unshakable confidence as his son James. For Gabriel's personality, there is among Joyce's friends another model.[18] This was Constantine Curran, sometimes nicknamed "Cautious Con." He is a more distinguished man than Joyce allows, but Joyce was building upon, and no doubt distorting, his memories of Curran as a very young man. That he has Curran partly in mind is suggested by the fact that he calls Gabriel's brother by Curran's first name, Constantine, and makes Gabriel's brother, like Curran's, a priest.[19] Curran has the same high color and nervous, disquieted manner as Gabriel, and like Gabriel he has traveled to the continent and has cultivated cosmopolitan interests. Curran, like Conroy, married a woman who was not a Dubliner, though she came from only as far west as Limerick. In other respects he is quite different. Gabriel was made mostly out of Curran, Joyce's father, and Joyce himself. Probably Joyce knew there was a publican on Howth named Gabriel Conroy; or, as Gerhard Friedrich has proposed,[20] he may have borrowed the name from the title of a Bret Harte novel. But the character, if not the name, was of his own compounding.[21]

Joyce now had his people, his party, and something of its development. In the festive setting, upon which the snow keeps offering a different perspective until, as W. Y. Tindall suggests,[22] the snow itself changes, he

[15] Interview with Mrs. Mary Sheehy Kettle, 1953.

[16] *My Brother's Keeper* (New York: The Viking Press, 1958), p. 38.

[17] See p. 17 [of *James Joyce* by Richard Ellmann].

[18] Interview with S. Joyce, 1953.

[19] Suggested to me by Professor Vivian Mercier.

[20] Gerhard Friedrich, "Bret Harte as a Source for James Joyce's 'The Dead,'" *Philological Quarterly*, XXXIII (October 1954), 442–44.

[21] The name of Conroy's wife Gretta was borrowed from another friend, Gretta (actually Margaret) Cousins, the wife of James H. Cousins. Since Joyce mentioned in a letter, at the same time that he was meditating "The Dead," the danger of becoming "a patient Cousins," this family was evidently on his mind.

[22] W. Y. Tindall, *The Literary Symbol* (New York: Columbia University Press, 1955), p. 227.

develops Gabriel's private tremors, his sense of inadequacy, his uncomfortable insistence on his small pretensions. From the beginning he is vulnerable; his well-meant and even generous overtures are regularly checked. The servant girl punctures his blithe assumption that everyone is happily in love and on the way to the altar. He is not sure enough of himself to put out of his head the slurs he has received long ago; so in spite of his uxorious attitude towards Gretta, he is a little ashamed of her having come from the west of Ireland. He cannot bear to think of his dead mother's remark that Gretta was "country cute," and when Miss Ivors says of Gretta, "She's from Connacht, isn't she?" Gabriel answers shortly, "Her people are." He has rescued her from that bog. Miss Ivors's suggestion, a true Gaelic Leaguer's, that he spend his holiday in the Irish-speaking Aran Islands (in the west) upsets him; it is the element in his wife's past that he wishes to forget. During most of the story, the west of Ireland is connected in Gabriel's mind with a dark and rather painful primitivism, an aspect of his country which he has steadily abjured by going off to the continent. The west is savagery; to the east and south, lie people who drink wine and wear galoshes.

Gabriel has been made uneasy about this attitude, but he clings to it defiantly until the ending. Unknown to him, it is being challenged by the song, "The Lass of Aughrim." Aughrim is a little village in the west, not far from Galway. The song has a special relevance; in it a woman who has been seduced and abandoned by Lord Gregory comes with her baby in the rain to beg for admission to his house. It brings together the peasant mother and the civilized seducer, but Gabriel does not listen to the words; he only watches his wife listening. Joyce had heard this ballad from Nora; perhaps he considered also using Tom Moore's "O, Ye Dead" in the story, but if so he must have seen that "The Lass of Aughrim" would connect more subtly with the west and with Michael Furey's visit in the rain to Gretta. But the notion of using a song at all may well have come to him as the result of the excitement generated in him by Moore's song.

And now Gabriel and Gretta go to the Hotel Gresham, Gabriel fired by his living wife and Gretta drained by the memory of her dead lover. He learns for the first time of the young man in Galway, whose name Joyce has deftly altered from Sonny or Michael Bodkin to Michael Furey. The new name implies, like the contrast of the militant Michael and the amiable Gabriel, that violent passion is in her Galway past, not in her Dublin present. Gabriel tries to cut Michael Furey down. "What was he?" he asks, confident that his own profession of language teacher (which of course he shared with Joyce) is superior; but she replies, "He was in the gasworks," as if this profession was as good as any other. Then Gabriel tries again, "And what did he die of so young, Gretta? Consumption, was it?" He hopes to register the usual expressions of pity, but Gretta silences

and terrifies him by her answer, "I think he died for me." [23] Since Joyce
has already made clear that Michael Furey was tubercular, this answer of
Gretta has a fine ambiguity. It asserts the egoism of passion, and unconsciously defies Gabriel's reasonable question.

Now Gabriel begins to succumb to his wife's dead lover, and becomes
a pilgrim to emotional intensities outside of his own experience. From
a biographical point of view, these final pages compose one of Joyce's
several tributes to his wife's artless integrity. Nora Barnacle, in spite of
her defects of education, was independent, unselfconscious, instinctively
right. Gabriel acknowledges the same coherence in his own wife, and he
recognizes in the west of Ireland, in Michael Furey, a passion he has himself always lacked. "Better pass boldly into that other world, in the full
glory of some passion, than fade and wither dismally with age," Joyce
makes Gabriel think. Then comes that strange sentence in the final paragraph: "The time had come for him to set out on his journey westward."
The cliché runs that journeys westward are towards death, but the west
has taken on a special meaning in the story. Gretta Conroy's west is the
place where life had been lived simply and passionately. The context and
phrasing of the sentence suggest that Gabriel is on the edge of sleep, and
half-consciously accepts what he has hitherto scorned, the possibility of
an actual trip to Connaught. What the sentence affirms, at last, on the
level of feeling, is the west, the primitive, untutored, impulsive country
from which Gabriel had felt himself alienated before; in the story, the
west is paradoxically linked also with the past and the dead. It is like
Aunt Julia Morkan who, though ignorant, old, grey-skinned, and stupe-
fied, seizes in her song at the party "the excitement of swift and secure
flight."

The tone of the sentence, "The time had come for him to set out on
his journey westward," is somewhat resigned. It suggests a concession, a
relinquishment, and Gabriel is conceding and relinquishing a good deal
—his sense of the importance of civilized thinking, of continental tastes,
of all those tepid but nice distinctions on which he has prided himself.
The bubble of his self-possession is pricked; he no longer possesses himself, and not to possess oneself is in a way a kind of death. It is a self-
abandonment not unlike Furey's, and through Gabriel's mind runs the
imagery of Calvary. He imagines the snow on the cemetery at Oughterard,
lying "thickly drifted on the crooked crosses and headstones, on the spears
of the little gate, on the barren thorns." He thinks of Michael Furey who,
Gretta has said, died for her, and envies him his sacrifice for another kind
of love than Christ's. To some extent, Gabriel too is dying for her, in giving up what he has most valued in himself, all that holds him apart from

[23] Adaline Glasheen has discovered here an echo of Yeats's nationalistic play, *Cathleen
ni Houlihan* (1902), where the old woman who symbolizes Ireland sings a song of
"yellow-haired Donough that was hanged in Galway." When she is asked, "What was
it brought him to his death?" she replies, "He died for love of me; many a man has
died for love of me." I am indebted to Mrs. Glasheen for pointing this out to me.

the simpler people at the party. He feels close to Gretta through sympathy if not through love; now they are both past youth, beauty, and passion; he feels close also to her dead lover, another lamb burnt on her altar, though she too is burnt now; he feels no resentment, only pity. In his own sacrifice of himself, he is conscious of a melancholy unity between the living and the dead.

Gabriel, who has been sick of his own country, finds himself drawn inevitably into a silent tribute to it of much more consequence than his spoken tribute to the party. He has had illusions of the rightness of a way of life that should be outside of Ireland; but through this experience with his wife he grants a kind of bondage, of acceptance, even of admiration to a part of the country and a way of life that are most Irish. Ireland is shown to be stronger, more intense than he. At the end of *A Portrait of the Artist,* too, Stephen Dedalus, who has been so resolutely opposed to nationalism, makes a similar concession when he interprets his departure from Ireland as an attempt to forge a conscience for his race.

Joyce did not invent the incidents that conclude his story, the second honeymoon of Gabriel and Gretta which ends so badly. His method of composition was very like T. S. Eliot's, the imaginative absorption of stray material. The method did not please Joyce very much because he considered it not imaginative enough, but it was the only way he could work. He borrowed the ending for "The Dead" from another book. In that book a bridal couple receive, on their wedding night, a message that a young woman whom the husband jilted has just committed suicide. The news holds them apart, she asks him not to kiss her, and both are tormented by remorse. The wife, her marriage unconsummated, falls off at last to sleep, and her husband goes to the window and looks out at "the melancholy greyness of the dawn." For the first time he recognizes, with the force of a revelation, that his life is a failure, and that his wife lacks the passion of the girl who has killed herself. He resolves that, since he is not worthy of any more momentous career, he will try at least to make her happy. Here surely is the situation that Joyce so adroitly recomposed. The dead lover who comes between the lovers, the sense of the husband's failure, the acceptance of mediocrity, the resolve to be at all events sympathetic, all come from the other book. But Joyce transforms them. For example, he allows Gretta to kiss her husband, but without desire, and rarefies the situation by having it arise not from a suicide but from a memory of young love. The book Joyce was borrowing from was one that nobody reads any more, George Moore's *Vain Fortune*; but Joyce read it,[24] and in his youthful essay, "The Day of the Rabblement," overpraised it as "fine, original work." [25]

[24] He evidently refreshed his memory of it when writing "The Dead," for his copy of *Vain Fortune,* now at Yale, bears the date "March 1907."
[25] *The Critical Writings of James Joyce,* ed. Ellsworth Mason and Richard Ellmann (New York: Viking, 1959), p. 71.

Moore said nothing about snow, however. No one can know how Joyce conceived the joining of Gabriel's final experience with the snow. But his fondness for a background of this kind is also illustrated by his use of the fireplace in "Ivy Day," of the streetlamps in "Two Gallants," and of the river in *Finnegans Wake*. It does not seem that the snow can be death, as so many have said, for it falls on living and dead alike, and for death to fall on the dead is a simple redundancy of which Joyce would not have been guilty. For snow to be "general all over Ireland" is of course unusual in that country. The fine description, "It was falling on every part of the dark central plain, on the treeless hills, falling softly upon the Bog of Allen and, farther westward, softly falling into the dark mutinous Shannon waves," is probably borrowed by Joyce from a famous simile in the twelfth book of the Iliad, which Thoreau translates:[26] "The snowflakes fall thick and fast on a winter's day. The winds are lulled, and the snow falls incessant, covering the tops of the mountains, and the hills, and the plains where the lotus-tree grows, and the cultivated fields, and they are falling by the inlets and shores of the foaming sea, but are silently dissolved by the waves." But Homer was simply describing the thickness of the arrows in the battle of the Greeks and Trojans; and while Joyce seems to copy his topographical details, he uses the image here chiefly for a similar sense of crowding and quiet pressure. Where Homer speaks of the waves silently dissolving the snow, Joyce adds the final detail of "the mutinous Shannon waves" which suggests the "Furey" quality of the west. The snow that falls upon Gabriel, Gretta, and Michael Furey, upon the Misses Morkan, upon the dead singers and the living, is mutuality, a sense of their connection with each other, a sense that none has his being alone. The partygoers prefer dead singers to living ones, the wife prefers a dead lover to a live lover.

The snow does not stand alone in the story. It is part of the complex imagery that includes heat and cold air, fire, and rain, as well as snow. The relations of these are not simple. During the party, the living people, their festivities, and all human society seem contrasted with the cold outside, as in the warmth of Gabriel's hand on the cold pane. But this warmth is felt by Gabriel as stuffy and confining, and the cold outside is repeatedly connected with what is fragrant and fresh. The cold, in this sense of piercing intensity, culminates in the picture of Michael Furey in the rain and darkness of the Galway night.

Another warmth is involved in "The Dead." In Gabriel's memory of his own love for Gretta, he recalls incidents in his love's history as stars, burning with pure and distant intensity, and recalls moments of his passion for her as having the fire of stars. The irony of this image is that the sharp and beautiful experience was, though he has not known it until

---

[26] Professor Walter B. Rideout kindly called my attention to the similarity of these passages.

this night, incomplete. There is a telling metaphor: He remembers a moment of happiness, standing with Gretta in the cold, looking in through a window at a man making bottles in a roaring furnace, and suddenly calling out to the man, "Is the fire hot?" The question sums up his naïve deprivation; if the man at the furnace had heard the question, his answer, thinks Gabriel, might have been rude; so the revelation on this night is rude to Gabriel's whole being. On this night he acknowledges that love must be a feeling which he has never fully had.

Gabriel is not utterly deprived. Throughout the story there is affection for this man who, without the sharpest, most passionate perceptions, is yet generous and considerate. The intense and the moderate can meet; intensity bursts out and declines, and the moderated can admire and pity it, and share the fate that moves both types of mankind towards age and death. The furthest point of love of which Gabriel is capable is past. Furey's passion is past because of his sudden death. Gretta is perhaps the most pitiful, in that knowing Furey's passion, and being of his kind, she does not die but lives to wane in Gabriel's way; on this night she too is fatigued, not beautiful, her clothes lie crumpled beside her. The snow seems to share in this decline; viewed from inside at the party, it is desirable, unattainable, just as at his first knowledge of Michael Furey, Gabriel envies him. At the end as the partygoers walk to the cab, the snow is slushy and in patches, and then, seen from the window of the hotel room, it belongs to all men, it is general, mutual. Under its canopy, all human beings, whatever their degrees of intensity, fall into union. The mutuality is that all men feel and lose feeling, all interact, all warrant the sympathy that Gabriel now extends to Furey, to Gretta, to himself, even to old Aunt Julia.

In its lyrical, melancholy acceptance of all that life and death offer, "The Dead" is a linchpin in Joyce's work. There is that basic situation of cuckoldry, real or putative, which is to be found throughout. There is the special Joycean collation of specific detail raised to rhythmical intensity. The final purport of the story, the mutual dependency of living and dead, is something that he meditated a good deal from his early youth. He had expressed it first in his essay on Mangan in 1902, when he spoke already of the union in the great memory of death along with life;[27] even then he had begun to learn like Gabriel that we are all Romes, our new edifices reared beside, and even joined with, ancient monuments. In *Dubliners* he developed this idea. The interrelationship of dead and living is the theme of the first story in *Dubliners* as well as of the last; it is also the theme of "A Painful Case," but an even closer parallel to "The Dead" is the story, "Ivy Day in the Committee Room." This was in one sense an answer to his university friends who mocked his remark that death is the most beautiful form of life by saying that absence is the

[27] *The Critical Writings*, p. 83.

highest form of presence. Joyce did not think either idea absurd. What binds "Ivy Day" to "The Dead" is that in both stories the central agitation derives from a character who never appears, who is dead, absent. Joyce wrote Stanislaus that Anatole France had given him the idea for both stories.[28] There may be other sources in France's works, but a possible one is "The Procurator of Judaea." In it Pontius Pilate reminisces with a friend about the days when he was procurator in Judaea, and describes the events of his time with Roman reason, calm, and elegance. Never once does he, or his friend, mention the person we expect him to discuss, the founder of Christianity, until at the end the friend asks if Pontius Pilate happens to remember someone of the name of Jesus, from Nazareth, and the veteran administrator replies, "Jesus? Jesus of Nazareth? I cannot call him to mind." The story is overshadowed by the person whom Pilate does not recall; without him the story would not exist. Joyce uses a similar method in "Ivy Day" with Parnell and in "The Dead" with Michael Furey.

In *Ulysses* the climactic episode, *Circe*, whirls to a sepulchral close in the same juxtaposition of living and dead, the ghost of his mother confronting Stephen, and the ghost of his son confronting Bloom. But Joyce's greatest triumph in asserting the intimacy of living and dead was to be the close of *Finnegans Wake*. Here Anna Livia Plurabelle, the river of life, flows toward the sea, which is death; the fresh water passes into the salt, a bitter ending. Yet it is also a return to her father, the sea, that produces the cloud which makes the river, and her father is also her husband, to whom she gives herself as a bride to her groom. Anna Livia is going back to her father, as Gabriel journeys westward in feeling to the roots of his fatherland; like him, she is sad and weary. To him the Shannon waves are dark and mutinous, and to her the sea is cold and mad. In *Finnegans Wake* Anna Livia's union is not only with love but with death; like Gabriel she seems to swoon away.

That Joyce at the age of twenty-five and -six should have written this story ought not to seem odd. Young writers reach their greatest eloquence in dwelling upon the horrors of middle age and what follows it. But beyond this proclivity which he shared with others, Joyce had a special reason for writing the story of "The Dead" in 1906 and 1907. In his own mind he had thoroughly justified his flight from Ireland, but he had not decided the question of where he would fly *to*. In Trieste and Rome he had learned what he had unlearned in Dublin, to be a Dubliner. As he had written his brother from Rome with some astonishment, he felt humiliated when anyone attacked his "impoverished country." [29] "The Dead" is his first song of exile.

[28] Letter to S. Joyce, February 11, 1907.
[29] Letter to S. Joyce, September 25, 1906.

The *Portrait* in Perspective

by Hugh Kenner

From wrong to wrong the exasperated spirit
Proceeds, unless restored by that refining fire
Where you must move in measure, like a dancer.

T. S. Eliot

Faites votre destin, âmes désordonnées,
Et fuyez l'infini que vous portez en vous!

Baudelaire

And yet he felt that, however he might revile and mock her
image, his anger was also a form of homage.

Portrait (P259/251)

A Portrait of the Artist as a Young Man, which in its definitive form
initiates the second cycle, was some ten years in the writing. A 1,000-page
first draft was written around 1904–1906, about the same time as the
bulk of *Dubliners.* This was scrapped and a more compressed version undertaken in 1908; the third and final text was being composed in 1911,
and was finished early in 1914.[1] About one-third of the first draft (the
Stephen Hero fragment) survives to show us what was going on during the
gestation of this book, the only one which it cost Joyce far more
trouble to focus than to execute.

Joyce first conceived the story of Stephen Dedalus in a picaresque mode.
The original title was meant to incorporate the ballad of Turpin Hero,
a reference to which still survives in the final text. Turpin spends most

"The *Portrait* in Perspective." From Hugh Kenner, *Dublin's Joyce* (Bloomington,
Ind.: Indiana University Press, 1956), pp. 109–33. Reprinted by permission of Indiana
University Press and A D Peters and Company.

[1] [Herbert Gorman, *James Joyce* (New York: Rinehart & Co., 1939; rev. ed., 1948), pp.
142–45, 190–97, 202–9, 220–23.] See also Theodore Spencer's introduction to *Stephen
Hero* [(New York: New Directions Publishing Corporation, 1963), pp. 7–18.]

of the ballad achieving gestes at the expense of a gallery of middle-class
dummies, beginning with a lawyer:

> . . . As they rode down by the powder mill,
> Turpin commands him to stand still;
> Said he, your cape I must cut off,
> For my mare she wants her saddle cloth.
> > O rare Turpin Hero,
> > O rare Turpin O.
> This caus'd the lawyer much to fret,
> To think he was so fairly bit;
> And Turpin robb'd him of his store,
> Because he knew he'd lie for more.
> > O rare Turpin Hero,
> > O rare Turpin O.

The lawyer's mistake was to admit the plausible stranger to his intimacy.
Stephen in the same way achieves a series of dialectical triumphs over
priests, parents, and schoolfellows. The typical dialogue commences amid
courtesies:

> Stephen raised his cap and said "Good evening, sir." The President an-
> swered with the smile which a pretty girl gives when she receives some
> compliment which puzzles her—a "winning" smile:
> —What can I do for you? he asked in a rich deep calculated voice. . . .

But cut-and-thrust soon follows:

> —May I ask you if you have read much of [Ibsen's] writing? asked
> Stephen.
> —Well, no . . . I must say . . .
> —May I ask you if you have read even a single line?
> —Well, no . . . I must admit . . .

Stephen always relieves the interlocutor of his complacence:

> —I should not care for anyone to identify the ideas in your essay with
> the teaching in our college. We receive this college in trust. . . .
> —If I were to publish tomorrow a very revolutionary pamphlet on the
> means of avoiding potato-blight would you consider yourself responsible
> for my theory?
> —No, no, of course not . . . but then this is not a school of agriculture.
> —Neither is it a school of dramaturgy, answered Stephen.

The ballad ends with Turpin in jail condemned to the gallows; *Stephen
Hero* was presumably to end, as the *Portrait* does, with Stephen Proto-
martyr on the brink of continental exile, acknowledged enemy of the
Dublin people. This Stephen is an engaging fellow with an explosive
laugh, an image of the young Joyce whom Yeats compared to William

Morris "for the joyous vitality one felt in him," or of the student Joyce who emerges from his brother's *Memoir*:

> Uncompromising in all that concerned his artistic integrity, Joyce was, for the rest, of a sociable and amiable disposition. Around his tall, agile figure there hovered a certain air of youthful grace and, despite the squalors of his home, a sense of happiness, as of one who feels within himself a joyous courage, a resolute confidence in life and in his own powers. . . . Joyce's laugh was characteristic . . . of that pure hilarity which does not contort the mouth.[2]

When Stephen's uncompromising side occasionally becomes absurd, Joyce the recorder is always at hand to supply a distancing phrase: "the fiery-hearted revolutionary"; "this heaven-ascending essayist"; "he was foolish enough to regret having yielded to the impulse for sympathy from a friend." Toward the end of the existing fragment we find more and more of these excusing clauses: "No young man can contemplate the fact of death with extreme satisfaction and no young man, specialised by fate or her stepsister chance for an organ of sensitiveness and intellectiveness, can contemplate the network of falsities and trivialities which make up the funeral of a dead burgher without extreme disgust." This clumsy sentence, its tone slithering between detachment, irony, and anger, is typical of the bad writing which recurs in the *Stephen Hero* fragment to signal Joyce's periodic uncertainty of Stephen's convincingness.

The book ran down unfinished in 1906, stalled partly by its own inner contradictions, partly by the far maturer achievement of *Dubliners*. It had never, Joyce saw, had a theme; it was neither a novel, nor an autobiography, nor a spiritual or social meditation. It contained three sorts of materials that would not fuse: documentation from the past, transcribed from the Dublin notebooks; Joyce's memories of his earlier self, transmuted by a mythopoeic process only partly controlled; and his present complex attitude to what he thought that self to have been.

Fortunately, the catalytic theme was not long in coming. In the late fall of 1906, he wrote from Rome to his brother about a new story for *Dubliners*, "Ulysses." On February 6, 1907, he admitted that it "never got any forrarder than the title." It coalesced, instead, with the autobiographical theme, and both subjects were returned to the smithy. A novel, *Ulysses*, as Joyce told a Zurich student ten years later, began to be planned as sequel to a rewritten *Portrait*. In 1908 *Stephen Hero* was discarded for good, and the job of lining up the two works began. And once the final balance of motifs for the *Portrait* had been at last struck and the writing of the definitive text completed, the last exorcism, *Exiles*, took only three spring months. *Ulysses* and *Finnegans Wake* took seven and seventeen years, but their recalcitrance was technical merely. The *Portrait* includes

[2] Stanislaus Joyce, "James Joyce: A Memoir," *Hudson Review*, II. 4, [(Winter 1950)] 496.

their scenario: first "the earth that had borne him" and "the vast indifferent dome" (Penelope, Ithaca), then sleep and a plunge into "some new world, fantastic, dim, uncertain as under sea, traversed by cloudy shapes and beings." These are lyric anticipations of the dense epic and dramatic works to come; the actual writing of those works went forward during the next quarter-century with scarcely a false step.

Linking Themes

In the reconceived *Portrait,* Joyce abandoned the original intention of writing the account of his own escape from Dublin. One cannot escape one's Dublin. He recast Stephen Dedalus as a figure who could not even detach himself from Dublin because he had formed himself on a denial of Dublin's values. He is the egocentric rebel become an ultimate. There is no question whatever of his regeneration. "Stephen no longer interests me to the same extent [as Bloom]," said Joyce to Frank Budgen one day. "He has a shape that can't be changed." [3] His shape is that of aesthete. The Stephen of the first chapter of *Ulysses* who "walks wearily," constantly "leans" on everything in sight, invariably sits down before he has gone three paces, speaks "gloomily," "quietly," "with bitterness," and "coldly," and "suffers" his handkerchief to be pulled from his pocket by the exuberant Mulligan, is precisely the priggish, humourless Stephen of the last chapter of the *Portrait* who cannot remember what day of the week it is, sentimentalizes like Charles Lamb over the "human pages" of a second-hand Latin book, conducts the inhumanly pedantic dialogue with Cranly on mother-love, writes Frenchified verses in bed in an erotic swoon, and is epiphanized at full length, like Shem the Penman beneath the bedclothes, shrinking from the "common noises" of daylight:

> Shrinking from that life he turned towards the wall, making a cowl [!] of the blanket and staring at the great overblown scarlet flowers of the tattered wall-paper. He tried to warm his perishing joy in their scarlet glow, imaging a roseway from where he lay upwards to heaven all strewn with scarlet flowers. Weary! Weary! He too was weary of ardent ways. [*Portrait,* 221–222.]

This new primrose path is a private Jacob's ladder let down to his bed now that he is too weary to do anything but go to heaven.

To make epic and drama emerge naturally from the intrinsic stresses and distortions of the lyric material meant completely new lyric techniques for a constatation exact beyond irony. The *Portrait* concentrates on stating themes, arranging apparently transparent words into configurations of the utmost symbolic density. Here is the director proposing that Stephen enter the priesthood:

[3] Budgen, 107. [Frank Budgen, *James Joyce and the Making of "Ulysses" and Other Writings* (London: Oxford University Press, 1972), p. 107.—Ed.]

> The director stood in the embrasure of the window, his back to the
> light, leaning an elbow on the brown crossblind, and, as he spoke and
> smiled, slowly dangling and looping the cord of the other blind, Stephen
> stood before him, following for a moment with his eyes the waning of
> the long summer daylight above the roofs or the slow deft movements of
> the priestly fingers. The priest's face was in total shadow, but the waning
> daylight from behind him touched the deeply grooved temples and the
> curves of the skull.   [*Portrait,* 153–154.]

The looped cord, the shadow, the skull, none of these is accidental. The
"waning daylight," twice emphasized, conveys that denial of nature which
the priest's office represented for Stephen; "his back to the light" co-
operates toward a similar effect. So "crossblind": "blind to the cross";
"blinded by the cross." "The curves of the skull" introduces another
death-image; the "deathbone" from Lévy-Bruhl's Australia, pointed by
Shaun in *Finnegans Wake,* is the dramatic version of an identical symbol.
But the central image, the epiphany of the interview, is contained in the
movement of the priest's fingers: "slowly dangling and looping the cord
of the other blind." That is to say, coolly proffering a noose. This is the
lyric mode of *Ulysses'* epical hangman, "The lord of things as they are
whom the most Roman of Catholics call *dio boia,* hangman god."

The Contrapuntal Opening

According to the practice inaugurated by Joyce when he rewrote "The
Sisters" in 1906, the *Portrait,* like the two books to follow, opens amid
elaborate counterpoint. The first two pages, terminating in a row of
asterisks, enact the entire action in microcosm. An Aristotelian catalogue
of senses, faculties, and mental activities is played against the unfolding
of the infant conscience.

> Once upon a time and a very good time it was there was a moocow
> coming down along the road and this moocow that was down along the
> road met a nicens little boy named baby tuckoo. . . .
>
> His father told him that story: his father looked at him through a glass:
> he had a hairy face.
>
> He was baby tuckoo. The moocow came down along the road where
> Betty Byrne lived: she sold lemon platt.
>> *O, the wild rose blossoms*
>> *On the little green place.*
>
> He sang that song. That was his song.
>> *O, the green wothe botheth.*
>
> When you wet the bed, first it is warm then it gets cold. His mother put
> on the oilsheet. That had the queer smell.

This evocation of holes in oblivion is conducted in the mode of each of
the five senses in turn; hearing (the story of the moocow), sight (his father's face), taste (lemon platt), touch (warm and cold), smell (the oil-

sheet). The audible soothes: the visible disturbs. Throughout Joyce's work, the senses are symbolically disposed. Smell is the means of discriminating empirical realities ("His mother had a nicer smell than his father" is the next sentence), sight corresponds to the phantasms of oppression, hearing to the imaginative life. Touch and taste together are the modes of sex. Hearing, here, comes first, via a piece of imaginative literature. But as we can see from the vantage-point of *Finnegans Wake*, the whole book is about the encounter of baby tuckoo with the moocow: the Gripes with the Mookse.[4] The father with the hairy face is the first Mookse-avatar, the Freudian infantile analogue of God the Father.

In the *Wake*,

> Derzherr, live wire, fired Benjermine Funkling outa th'Empyre, sin right hand son.

Der Erzherr (arch-lord), here a Teutonic Junker, is the God who visited his wrath on Lucifer; the hairy attribute comes through via the music-hall refrain, "There's hair, like wire, coming out of the Empire."

Dawning consciousness of his own identity ("He was baby tuckoo") leads to artistic performance ("He sang that song. That was his song.") This is hugely expanded in chapter IV:

> Now, as never before, his strange name seemed to him a prophecy . . . of the end he had been born to serve and had been following through the mists of childhood and boyhood, a symbol of the artist forging anew in his workshop out of the sluggish matter of the earth a new soaring impalpable imperishable being.   [*Portrait*, 168–169.]

By changing the red rose to a green and dislocating the spelling, he makes the song his own ("But you could not have a green rose. But perhaps somewhere in the world you could.")

> His mother had a nicer smell than his father. She played on the piano the sailor's hornpipe for him to dance. He danced:
>
> > *Tralala lala,*
> > *Tralala tralaladdy,*
> > *Tralala lala,*
> > *Tralala lala.*   [*Portrait*, 7.]

Between this innocence and its Rimbaudian recapture through the purgation of the *Wake* there is to intervene the hallucination in Circe's sty:

> *The Mother. (With the subtle smile of death's madness.)* I was once the beautiful May Goulding. I am dead. . . .

---

[4] Compare the . . . sentence: "Eins within a space and a wearywide space it wast ere wohned a Mookse." . . . Mookse is moocow plus fox plus mock turtle. The German "Eins" evokes Einstein, who presides over the interchanging of space and time; space is the Mookse's "spatialty."

Stephen. (Eagerly.) Tell me the word, mother, if you know it now. The word
  known to all men. . . .
The Mother. (With smouldering eyes.) Repent! O, the fire of hell!

[*Ulysses,* 580–581.]

This is foreshadowed as the overture to the *Portrait* closes:

He hid under the table. His mother said:
—O, Stephen will apologise.
Dante said:
—O, if not, the eagles will come and pull out his eyes.—

> Pull out his eyes,
> Apologise,
> Apologise,
> Pull out his eyes.
>
> Apologise,
> Pull out his eyes,
> Pull out his eyes,
> Apologise.   [*Portrait,* 8.]

The eagles, eagles of Rome, are emissaries of the God with the hairy face:
the punisher. They evoke Prometheus and gnawing guilt: again-bite. So
the overture ends with Stephen hiding under the table awaiting the
eagles. He is hiding under something most of the time: bedclothes, "the
enigma of a manner," an indurated rhetoric, or some other carapace of
his private world.

Theme Words

It is through their names that things have power over Stephen.

> —The language in which we are speaking is his before it is mine. How
> different are the words *home, Christ, ale, master,* on his lips and on mine!
> I cannot speak or write these words without unrest of spirit. His language,
> so familiar and so foreign, will always be for me an acquired speech. I
> have not made or accepted its words. My voice holds them at bay. My
> soul frets in the shadow of his language.   [*Portrait,* 189.]

Not only is the Dean's English a conqueror's tongue; since the loss of
Adam's words which perfectly mirrored things, all language has con-
quered the mind and imposed its own order, askew from the order of
creation. Words, like the physical world, are imposed on Stephen from
without, and it is in their canted mirrors that he glimpses a physical and
moral world already dyed the colour of his own mind since absorbed,
with language, into his personality.

> Words which he did not understand he said over and over to himself
> till he had learnt them by heart; and through them he had glimpses of
> the real world about him.   [*Portrait*, 62.]

Language is a Trojan horse by which the universe gets into the mind.
The first sentence in the book isn't something Stephen sees but a story he
is told, and the overture climaxes in an insistent brainless rhyme, its jingle
corrosively fascinating to the will. It has power to terrify a child who
knows nothing of eagles, or of Prometheus, or of how his own grownup
failure to apologise will blend with gathering blindness.

It typifies the peculiar achievement of the *Portrait* that Joyce can cause
patterns of words to make up the very moral texture of Stephen's mind:

> Suck was a queer word. The fellow called Simon Moonan that name be-
> cause Simon Moonan used to tie the prefect's false sleeves behind his
> back and the prefect used to let on to be angry. But the sound was ugly.
> Once he had washed his hands in the lavatory of the Wicklow hotel and
> his father pulled the stopper up by the chain after and the dirty water
> went down through the hole in the basin. And when it had all gone down
> slowly the hole in the basin had made a sound like that: suck. Only louder.
> To remember that and the white look of the lavatory made him feel
> cold and then hot. There were two cocks that you turned and the water
> came out: cold and hot. He felt cold and then a little hot: and he could
> see the names printed on the cocks. That was a very queer thing.
>   [*Portrait*, 11.]

"Suck" joins two contexts in Stephen's mind: a playful sinner toying with
his indulgent superior, and the disappearance of dirty water. The force
of the conjunction is felt only after Stephen has lost his sense of the reality of the forgiveness of sins in the confessional. The habitually orthodox
penitent tangles with a God who pretends to be angry; after a reconciliation the process is repeated. And the mark of that kind of play is disgrace-
ful servility. Each time the sin disappears, the sinner is mocked by an impersonal voice out of nature: "Suck!"

This attitude to unreal good and evil furnishes a context for the next
conjunction: whiteness and coldness. Stephen finds himself, like Simon
Moonan,[5] engaged in the rhythm of obedience to irrational authority,
bending his mind to a meaningless act, the arithmetic contest. He is being
obediently "good." And the appropriate colour is adduced: "He thought
his face must be white because it felt so cool."

The pallor of lunar obedient goodness is next associated with damp re-
pulsiveness: the limpness of a wet blanket and of a servant's apron:

> He sat looking at the two prints of butter on his plate but could not
> eat the damp bread. The table-cloth was damp and limp. But he drank

---

[5] Joyce's names should always be scrutinized. Simon Moonan: moon: the heatless
(white) satellite reflecting virtue borrowed from Simon Peter. Simony, too, is an activity naturally derived from this casually businesslike attitude to priestly authority.

> off the hot weak tea which the clumsy scullion, girt with a white apron,
> poured into his cup. He wondered whether the scullion's apron was damp
> too or whether all white things were cold and damp.   [*Portrait,* 12–13.]

Throughout the first chapter an intrinsic linkage, white-cold-damp-obedient, insinuates itself repeatedly. Stephen after saying his prayers, "his shoulders shaking," "so that he might not go to hell when he died," "curled himself together under the cold white sheets, shaking and trembling. But he would not go to hell when he died, and the shaking would stop." The sea, mysterious as the terrible power of God, "was cold day and night, but it was colder at night"; we are reminded of Anna Livia's gesture of submission: "my cold father, my cold mad father, my cold mad feary father." "There was a cold night smell in the chapel. But it was a holy smell." Stephen is puzzled by the phrase in the Litany of the Blessed Virgin: Tower of Ivory. "How could a woman be a tower of ivory or a house of gold?" He ponders until the revelation comes:

> Eileen had long white hands. One evening when playing tig she had
> put her hands over his eyes: long and white and thin and cold and soft.
> That was ivory: a cold white thing. That was the meaning of *Tower of
> Ivory.*   [*Portrait,* 36.]

This instant of insight depends on a sudden reshuffling of associations, a sudden conviction that the Mother of God, and the symbols appropriate to her, belong with the cold, the white, and the unpleasant in a blindfold morality of obedience. Contemplation focussed on language is repaid:

> *Tower of Ivory. House of Gold.* By thinking of things you could under-
> stand them.   [*Portrait,* 43.]

The white-damp-obedient association reappears when Stephen is about to make his confession after the celebrated retreat; its patterns provide the language in which he thinks. Sin has been associated with fire, while the prayers of the penitents are epiphanized as "soft whispering cloudlets, soft whispering vapour, whispering and vanishing." And having been absolved:

> White pudding and eggs and sausages and cups of tea. How simple and
> beautiful was life after all! And life lay all before him. . . .
> The boys were all there, kneeling in their places. He knelt among
> them, happy and shy. The altar was heaped with fragrant masses of white
> flowers: and in the morning light the pale flames of the candles among
> the white flowers were clear and silent as his own soul.   [*Portrait,* 146.]

We cannot read *Finnegans Wake* until we have realized the significance of the way the mind of Stephen Dedalus is bound in by language. He is not only an artist: He is a Dubliner.

The Portrait As Lyric

The "instant of emotion," of which this 300-page lyric is the "simplest verbal vesture," is the exalted instant, emerging at the end of the book, of freedom, of vocation, of Stephen's destiny, winging his way above the waters at the side of the hawklike man: the instant of promise on which the crushing ironies of *Ulysses* are to fall. The epic of the sea of matter is preceded by the lyric image of a growing dream: a dream that like Richard Rowan's in *Exiles* disregards the fall of man; a dream nourished by a sensitive youth of flying above the sea into an uncreated heaven:

> The spell of arms and voices: the white arms of roads, their promise of close embraces and the black arms of tall ships that stand against the moon, their tale of distant nations. They are held out to say: We are alone—come. And the voices say with them: We are your kinsmen. And the air is thick with their company as they call to me, their kinsman, making ready to go, shaking the wings of their exultant and terrible youth.   [*Portrait*, 252.]

The emotional quality of this is continuous with that of the *Count of Monte Cristo,* that fantasy of the exile returned for vengeance (the plot of the *Odyssey*) which kindled so many of Stephen's boyhood dreams:

> The figure of that dark avenger stood forth in his mind for whatever he had heard or divined in childhood of the strange and terrible. At night he built up on the parlour table an image of the wonderful island cave out of transfers and paper flowers and strips of the silver and golden paper in which chocolate is wrapped. When he had broken up this scenery, weary of its tinsel, there would come to his mind the bright picture of Marseilles, of sunny trellises and of Mercedes.   [*Portrait*, 62.]

The prose surrounding Stephen's flight is empurpled with transfers and paper flowers too. It is not immature prose, as we might suppose by comparison with *Ulysses*. The prose of "The Dead" is mature prose, and "The Dead" was written in 1908. Rather, it is a meticulous pastiche of immaturity. Joyce has his eye constantly on the epic sequel.

> He wanted to meet in the real world the unsubstantial image which his soul so constantly beheld. He did not know where to seek it or how, but a premonition which led him on told him that this image would, without any overt act of his, encounter him. They would meet quietly as if they had known each other and had made their tryst, perhaps at one of the gates or in some more secret place. They would be alone, surrounded by darkness and silence: and in that moment of supreme tenderness he would be transfigured.   [*Portrait*, 65.]

As the vaginal imagery of gates, secret places, and darkness implies, this is the dream that reaches temporary fulfilment in the plunge into profane love. But the ultimate "secret place" is to be Mabbot Street, outside Bella

Cohen's brothel; the unsubstantial image of his quest, that of Leopold Bloom, advertisement canvasser—Monte Cristo, returned avenger, Ulysses; and the transfiguration, into the phantasmal dead son of a sentimental Jew:

> *Against the dark wall a figure appears slowly, a fairy boy of eleven, a changeling, kidnapped, dressed in an Eton suit with glass shoes and a little bronze helmet, holding a book in his hand. He reads from right to left inaudibly, smiling, kissing the page.*   [*Ulysses*, 609.]

That Dedalus the artificer did violence to nature is the point of the epigraph from Ovid, *Et ignotas animum dimittit in artes;* the Icarian fall is inevitable.

> In tedious exile now too long detain'd
> Dedalus languish'd for his native land.
> The sea foreclos'd his flight; yet thus he said,
> Though earth and water in subjection laid,
> O cruel Minos, thy dominion be,
> We'll go through air; for sure the air is free.
> *Then to new arts his cunning thought applies,*
> *And to improve the work of nature tries.*

Stephen does not, as the careless reader may suppose, become an artist by rejecting church and country. Stephen does not become an artist at all. Country, church, and mission are an inextricable unity, and in rejecting the two that seem to hamper him, he rejects also the one on which he has set his heart. Improving the work of nature is his obvious ambition ("But you could not have a green rose. But perhaps somewhere in the world you could"), and it logically follows from the aesthetic he expounds to Lynch. It is a Neoplatonic aesthetic; the crucial principle of epiphanization has been withdrawn. He imagines that "the loveliness that has not yet come into the world" is to be found in his own soul. The earth is gross, and what it brings forth is cowdung; sound and shape and colour are "the prison gates of our soul"; and beauty is something mysteriously gestated within. The genuine artist reads signatures, the fake artist forges them, a process adumbrated in the obsession of Shem the Penman (from *Jim the Penman,* a forgotten drama about a forger) with "Macfearsome's Ossean," the most famous of literary forgeries, studying "how cutely to copy all their various styles of signature so as one day to utter an epical forged cheque on the public for his own private profit."

One can sense all this in the first four chapters of the *Portrait,* and *Ulysses* is unequivocal:

> Fabulous artificer, the hawklike man. You flew. Whereto? Newhaven-Dieppe, steerage passenger. Paris and back.   [*Ulysses*, 210.]

The Stephen of the end of the fourth chapter, however, is still unstable; he had to be brought into a final balance, and shown at some length as a being whose development was virtually ended. Unfortunately, the last chapter makes the book a peculiarly difficult one for the reader to focus, because Joyce had to close it on a suspended chord. As a lyric, it is finished in its own terms; but the themes of the last forty pages, though they give the illusion of focussing, don't really focus until we have read well into *Ulysses*. The final chapter, which in respect to the juggernaut of *Ulysses* must be a vulnerable flank, in respect to what has gone before must be a conclusion. This problem Joyce didn't wholly solve; there remains a moral ambiguity (how seriously are we to take Stephen?) which makes the last forty pages painful reading.

Not that Stephen would stand indefinitely if *Ulysses* didn't topple him over; his equilibrium in Chapter V, though good enough to give him a sense of unusual integrity in University College, is precarious unless he can manage, in the manner of so many permanent undergraduates, to prolong the college context for the rest of his life. Each of the preceding chapters, in fact, works toward an equilibrium which is dashed when in the next chapter Stephen's world becomes larger and the frame of reference more complex. The terms of equilibrium are always stated with disquieting accuracy; at the end of Chapter I we find:

> He was alone. He was happy and free: but he would not be anyway proud with Father Dolan. He would be very quiet and obedient: and he wished that he could do something kind for him to show him that he was not proud.   [*Portrait*, 59.]

And at the end of Chapter III:

> He sat by the fire in the kitchen, not daring to speak for happiness. Till that moment he had not known how beautiful and peaceful life could be. The green square of paper pinned round the lamp cast down a tender shade. On the dresser was a plate of sausages and white pudding and on the shelf there were eggs. They would be for the breakfast in the morning after the communion in the college chapel. White pudding and eggs and sausages and cups of tea. How simple and beautiful was life after all! And life lay all before him.   [*Portrait*, 146.]

Not "irony" but simply the truth: the good life conceived in terms of white pudding and sausages is unstable enough to need no underlining.

The even-numbered chapters make a sequence of a different sort. The ending of IV, Stephen's panting submission to an artistic vocation:

> Evening had fallen when he woke and the sand and arid grasses of his bed glowed no longer. He rose slowly and, recalling the rapture of his sleep, sighed at its joy. . . .   [*Portrait*, 173.]

—hasn't quite the finality often read into it when the explicit parallel with the ending of II is perceived:

> . . . He closed his eyes, surrendering himself to her, body and mind, conscious of nothing in the world but the dark pressure of her softly

parting lips. They pressed upon his brain as upon his lips as though they were the vehicle of a vague speech; and between them he felt an unknown and timid pressure, darker than the swoon of sin, softer than sound or odour. [*Portrait*, 101.]

When we link these passages with the fact that the one piece of literary composition Stephen actually achieves in the book comes out of a wet dream ("Towards dawn he awoke. O what sweet music! His soul was all dewy wet"), we are in a position to see that the concluding "Welcome, O life!" has an air of finality and balance only because the diary form of the last seven pages disarms us with an illusion of auctorial impartiality.

Controlling Images: Clongowes and Belvedere

Ego *vs.* authority is the theme of the three odd-numbered chapters, Dublin *vs.* the dream that of the two even-numbered ones. The generic Joyce plot, the encounter with the alter ego, is consummated when Stephen at the end of the book identifies himself with the sanctified Stephen who was stoned by the Jews after reporting a vision (Acts VII, 56) and claims sonship with the classical Daedalus who evaded the ruler of land and sea by turning his soul to obscure arts. The episodes are built about adumbrations of this encounter: with Father Conmee, with Monte Cristo, with the whores, with the broad-shouldered moustached student who cut the word "Foetus" in a desk, with the weary mild confessor, with the birdgirl. Through this repeated plot intertwine controlling emotions and controlling images that mount in complexity as the book proceeds.

In Chapter I the controlling emotion is fear, and the dominant image Father Dolan and his pandybat; this, associated with the hangman-god and the priestly denial of the senses, was to become one of Joyce's standard images for Irish clericalism—hence the jack-in-the-box appearance of Father Dolan in Circe's nightmare imbroglio, his pandybat cracking twice like thunder. Stephen's comment, in the mode of Blake's repudiation of the God who slaughtered Jesus, emphasizes the inclusiveness of the image: "I never could read His handwriting except His criminal thumbprint on the haddock."

Chapter II opens with a triple image of Dublin's prepossessions: music, sport, religion. The first is exhibited via Uncle Charles singing sentimental ballads in the outhouse; the second via Stephen's ritual run around the park under the eye of a superannuated trainer, which his uncle enjoins on him as the whole duty of a Dubliner; the third via the clumsy piety of Uncle Charles, kneeling on a red handkerchief and reading above his breath "from a thumb-blackened prayerbook wherein catchwords were printed at the foot of every page." This trinity of themes is unwound and entwined throughout the chapter, like a net woven round Stephen; it underlies the central incident, the Whitsuntide play in the Belvedere chapel (religion), which opens with a display by the dumb-bell team (sport) preluded by sentimental waltzes from the soldier's band (music).

While he is waiting to play his part, Stephen is taunted by fellow students, who rally him on a fancied love affair and smiting his calf with a cane bid him recite the *Confiteor*. His mind goes back to an analogous incident, when a similar punishment had been visited on his refusal to "admit that Byron was no good." The further analogy with Father Dolan is obvious; love, art, and personal independence are thus united in an ideogram of the prepossessions Stephen is determined to cultivate in the teeth of persecution.

The dream-world Stephen nourishes within himself is played against manifestations of music, sport, and religion throughout the chapter. The constant ironic clash of Dublin *vs.* the Dream animates Chapter II, as the clash of the ego *vs.* authority did Chapter I. All these themes come to focus during Stephen's visit with his father to Cork. The dream of rebellion he has silently cultivated is externalized by the discovery of the word *Foetus* carved in a desk by a forgotten medical student:

> It shocked him to find in the outer world a trace of what he had deemed till then a brutish and individual malady of his own mind. His monstrous reveries came thronging into his memory. They too had sprung up before him, suddenly and furiously, out of mere words. . . .   [*Portrait*, 90.]

The possibility of shame gaining the upper hand is dashed, however, by the sudden banal intrusion of his father's conversation ("When you kick out for yourself, Stephen, as I daresay you will one of these days, remember, whatever you do, to mix with gentlemen. . . ."). Against the standards of Dublin his monstrous reveries acquire a Satanic glamour, and the trauma is slowly diverted into a resolution to rebel. After his father has expressed a resolve to "leave him to his Maker" (religion), and offered to "sing a tenor song against him" (music) or "vault a fivebarred gate against him" (sport), Stephen muses, watching his father and two cronies drinking to the memory of their past:

> An abyss of fortune or of temperament sundered him from them. His mind seemed older than theirs: it shone coldly on their strifes and happiness and regrets like a moon upon a younger earth. No life or youth stirred in him as it had stirred in them. He had known neither the pleasure of companionship with others nor the vigour of rude male health nor filial piety. Nothing stirred within his soul but a cold and cruel and loveless lust.   [*Portrait*, 95–96.]

After one final effort to compromise with Dublin on Dublin's terms has collapsed into futility ("The pot of pink enamel paint gave out and the wainscot of his bedroom remained with its unfinished and illplastered coat"), he fiercely cultivates his rebellious thoughts, and moving by day and night "among distorted images of the outer world," plunges at last into the arms of whores. "The holy encounter he had then imagined at

which weakness and timidity and inexperience were to fall from him"
finally arrives in inversion of Father Dolan's and Uncle Charles' religion:
his descent into night-town is accompanied by lurid evocations of a Black
Mass:

> The yellow gasflames arose before his troubled vision against the vapoury
> sky, burning as if before an altar. Before the doors and in the lighted
> halls groups were gathered arrayed as for some rite. He was in another
> world: he had awakened from a slumber of centuries.   [*Portrait,* 100.]

Controlling Images: Sin and Repentance

Each chapter in the *Portrait* gathers up the thematic material of the preceding ones and entwines them with a dominant theme of its own. In
Chapter III the fear-pandybat motif is present in Father Arnall's crudely
materialistic hell, of which even the thickness of the walls is specified;
and the Dublin-*vs.*-dream motif has ironic inflections in Stephen's terror-
stricken broodings, when the dream has been twisted into a dream of
holiness, and even Dublin appears transfigured:

> How beautiful must be a soul in the state of grace when God looked
> upon it with love!
> Frowsy girls sat along the curbstones before their baskets. Their dank
> hair trailed over their brows. They were not beautiful to see as they
> crouched in the mire. But their souls were seen by God; and if their
> souls were in a state of grace they were radiant to see; and God loved
> them, seeing them.   [*Portrait,* 140.]

A *rapprochement* in these terms between the outer world and Stephen's
desires is too inadequate to need commentary; and it makes vivid as nothing else could the hopeless inversion of his attempted self-sufficiency. It
underlines, in yet another way, his persistent sin: and the dominant
theme of Chapter III is Sin. A fugue-like opening plays upon the Seven
Deadly Sins in turn; gluttony is in the first paragraph ("Stuff it into you,
his belly counselled him"), followed by lust, then sloth ("A cold lucid indifference reigned in his soul"), pride ("His pride in his own sin, his love-
less awe of God, told him that his offence was too grievous to be atoned
for"), anger ("The blundering answer stirred the embers of his contempt
for his fellows"); finally, a recapitulation fixes each term of the mortal
catalogue in a phrase, enumerating how "from the evil seed of lust all the
other deadly sins had sprung forth."

Priest and punisher inhabit Stephen himself as well as Dublin: When
he is deepest in sin he is most thoroughly a theologian. A paragraph of
gloomy introspection is juxtaposed with a list of theological questions
that puzzle Stephen's mind as he awaits the preacher:

> . . . Is baptism with mineral water valid? How comes it that while the
> first beatitude promises the kingdom of heaven to the poor of heart, the

second beatitude promises also to the meek that they shall possess the
land? . . . If the wine change into vinegar and the host crumble into
corruption after they have been consecrated, is Jesus Christ still present
under their species as God and as man?
       —Here he is! Here he is!
       A boy from his post at the window had seen the rector come from the
house. All the catechisms were opened and all heads bent upon them
silently.   [*Portrait*, 106–107.]

Wine changed into vinegar and the host crumbled into corruption fits
exactly the Irish clergy of "a church which was the scullery-maid of
Christendom." The excited "Here he is! Here he is!" following hard on
the mention of Jesus Christ and signalling nothing more portentous
than the rector makes the point as dramatically as anything in the book,
and the clinching sentence, with the students suddenly bending over
their catechisms, places the rector as the vehicle of pandybat morality.
       The last of the theological questions is the telling question. Stephen
never expresses doubt of the existence of God nor of the essential validity
of the priestly office—his *Non serviam* is not a *non credo,* and he talks of
a "malevolent reality" behind these appearances—but the wine and bread
that were offered for his veneration were changed into vinegar and
crumbled into corruption. And it was the knowledge of that underlying
validity clashing with his refusal to do homage to vinegar and rot that
evoked his ambivalent poise of egocentric despair. The hell of Father
Arnall's sermon, so emotionally overwhelming, so picayune beside the
horrors that Stephen's imagination can generate, had no more ontological
content for Stephen than had "an eternity of bliss in the company of the
dean of studies."
       The conflict of this central chapter is again between the phantasmal
and the real. What is real—psychologically real, because realized—is
Stephen's anguish and remorse, and its context in the life of the flesh.
What is phantasmal is the "heaven" of the Church and the "good life"
of the priest. It is only fear that makes him clutch after the latter at all;
his reaching out after orthodox salvation is, as we have come to expect,
presented in terms that judge it:

       The wind blew over him and passed on to the myriads and myriads of
       other souls, on whom God's favour shone now more and now less, stars
       now brighter and now dimmer, sustained and failing. And the glimmer-
       ing souls passed away, sustained and failing, merged in a moving breath.
       One soul was lost; a tiny soul; his. It flickered once and went out, for-
       gotten, lost. The end: black cold void waste.
              Consciousness of place came ebbing back to him slowly over a vast tract
       of time unlit, unfelt, unlived. The squalid scene composed itself around
       him; the common accents, the burning gasjets in the shops, odours of
       fish and spirits and wet sawdust, moving men and women. An old woman
       was about to cross the street, an oilcan in her hand. He bent down and
       asked her was there a chapel near.   [*Portrait*, 140–141.]

That wan waste world of flickering stars is the best Stephen has been able
to do towards an imaginative grasp of the communion of Saints sustained
by God; "unlit, unfelt, unlived" explains succinctly why it had so little
hold on him, once fear had relaxed. Equally pertinent is the vision of
human temporal occupations the sermon evokes:

> What did it profit a man to gain the whole world if he lost his soul?
> At last he had understood: and human life lay around him, a plain of
> peace whereon antlike men laboured in brotherhood, their dead sleeping
> under quiet mounds.   [*Portrait,* 126.]

To maintain the life of grace in the midst of nature, sustained by so
cramped a vision of the life of nature, would mean maintaining an intolerable tension. Stephen's unrelenting philosophic bias, his determination
to understand what he is about, precludes his adopting the double standard of the Dubliners; to live both the life of nature and the life of grace,
he must enjoy an imaginative grasp of their relationship which stunts
neither. "No one doth well against his will," writes Saint Augustine, "even
though what he doth, be well"; and Stephen's will is firmly harnessed to
his understanding. And there is no one in Dublin to help him achieve
understanding. Father Arnall's sermon precludes rather than secures a
desirable outcome, for it follows the modes of pandybat morality and
Dublin materiality. Its only possible effect on Stephen is to lash his dor-
mant conscience into a frenzy. The description of Hell as "a strait and
dark and foul smelling prison, an abode of demons and lost souls, filled
with fire and smoke," with walls four thousand miles thick, its damned
packed in so tightly that "they are not even able to remove from the eye
the worm that gnaws it," is childishly grotesque beneath its sweeping
eloquence; and the hair-splitting catalogues of pains—pain of loss, pain
of conscience (divided into three heads), pain of extension, pain of intensity, pain of eternity—is cast in a brainlessly analytic mode that effectively prevents any corresponding Heaven from possessing any reality at
all.

Stephen's unstable pact with the Church, and its dissolution, follows
the pattern of composition and dissipation established by his other
dreams: the dream for example of the tryst with "Mercedes," which found
ironic reality among harlots. It parallels exactly his earlier attempt to
"build a breakwater of order and elegance against the sordid tide of life
without him," whose failure, with the exhaustion of his money, was
epiphanized in the running-dry of a pot of pink enamel paint. His regimen at that time:

> He bought presents for everyone, overhauled his rooms, wrote out reso-
> lutions, marshalled his books up and down their shelves, pored over all
> kinds of price lists . . .   [*Portrait,* 97–98.]

is mirrored by his searching after spiritual improvement:

> His daily life was laid out in devotional areas. By means of ejaculations
> and prayers he stored up ungrudgingly for the souls in purgatory centuries
> of days and quarantines and years. . . . He offered up each of his three
> daily chaplets that his soul might grow strong in each of the three theo-
> logical virtues. . . . On each of the seven days of the week he further
> prayed that one of the seven gifts of the Holy Ghost might descend upon
> his soul.   [*Portrait,* 147–148.]

The "loan bank" he had opened for the family, out of which he had
pressed loans on willing borrowers "that he might have the pleasure of
making out receipts and reckoning the interests on sums lent" finds its
counterpart in the benefits he stored up for souls in purgatory that he
might enjoy the spiritual triumph of "achieving with ease so many fabulous ages of canonical penances." Both projects are parodies on the doctrine of economy of grace; both are attempts, corrupted by motivating
self-interest, to make peace with Dublin on Dublin's own terms; and both
are short-lived.

As this precise analogical structure suggests, the action of each of the
five chapters is really the same action. Each chapter closes with a synthesis of triumph which the next destroys. The triumph of the appeal to
Father Conmee from lower authority, of the appeal to the harlots from
Dublin, of the appeal to the Church from sin, of the appeal to art from
the priesthood (the bird-girl instead of the Virgin) is always the same
triumph raised to a more comprehensive level. It is an attempt to find
new parents; new fathers in the odd chapters, new objects of love in the
even. The last version of Father Conmee is the "priest of the eternal imagination"; the last version of Mercedes is the "lure of the fallen sera-
phim." But the last version of the mother who said, "O, Stephen will
apologise" is the mother who prays on the last page "that I may learn
in my own life and away from home and friends what the heart is and
what it feels." The mother remains.

The Double Female

As in *Dubliners* and *Exiles,* the female role in the *Portrait* is less to arouse
than to elucidate masculine desires. Hence the complex function in the
book of physical love: The physical is the analogue of the spiritual, as
St. Augustine insisted in his *Confessions* (which, with Ibsen's *Brand,* is
the chief archetype of Joyce's book). The poles between which this affection moves are those of St. Augustine and St. John: the Whore of Babylon
and the Bride of Christ. The relation between the two is far from simple,
and Stephen moves in a constant tension between them.

His desire, figured in the visions of Monte Cristo's Mercedes, "to meet
in the real world the unsubstantial image which his soul so constantly
beheld" draws him toward the prostitute ("In her arms he felt that he had
suddenly become strong and fearless and sure of himself") and simultane-

ously toward the vaguely spiritual satisfaction represented with equal vagueness by the wraithlike E— C—, to whom he twice writes verses. The Emma Clery of *Stephen Hero,* with her loud forced manners and her body compact of pleasure, was refined into a wraith with a pair of initials to parallel an intangible Church. She is continually assimilated to the image of the Blessed Virgin and of the heavenly Bride. The torture she costs him is the torture his apostasy costs him. His flirtation with her is his flirtation with Christ. His profane villanelle draws its imagery from religion—the incense, the eucharistic hymn, the chalice—and her heart, following Dante's image, is a rose, and in her praise "the earth was like a swinging swaying censer, a ball of incense."

The woman is the Church. His vision of greeting Mercedes with "a sadly proud gesture of refusal":

> —Madam, I never eat muscatel grapes.   [*Portrait, 63.*]

is fulfilled when he refuses his Easter communion. Emma's eyes, in their one explicit encounter, speak to him from beneath a cowl. "The glories of Mary held his soul captive," and a temporary reconciliation of his lust and his spiritual thirst is achieved as he reads the Lesson out of the Song of Solomon. In the midst of his repentance she functions as imagined mediator: "The image of Emma appeared before him," and, repenting, "he imagined that he stood near Emma in a wide land, and, humbly and in tears, bent and kissed the elbow of her sleeve." Like Dante's Beatrice, she manifests in his earthly experience the Church Triumphant of his spiritual dream. And when he rejects her because she seems to be flirting with Father Moran, his anger is couched in the anti-clerical terms of his apostasy: "He had done well to leave her to flirt with her priest, to toy with a church which was the scullery-maid of Christendom."

That Kathleen ni Houlihan can flirt with priests is the unforgivable sin underlying Stephen's rejection of Ireland. But he makes a clear distinction between the stupid clericalism which makes intellectual and communal life impossible, and his long-nourished vision of an artist's Church Triumphant upon earth. He rejects the actual for daring to fall short of his vision.

The Final Balance

The climax of the book is of course Stephen's ecstatic discovery of his vocation at the end of Chapter IV. The prose rises in nervous excitement to beat again and again the tambours of a fin-de-siècle ecstasy:

> His heart trembled; his breath came faster and a wild spirit passed over his limbs as though he were soaring sunward. His heart trembled in an ecstasy of fear and his soul was in flight. His soul was soaring in an air beyond the world and the body he knew was purified in a breath and delivered of incertitude and made radiant and commingled with the

element of the spirit. An ecstasy of flight made radiant his eyes and wild
his breath and tremulous and wild and radiant his wind-swept limbs.

—One! Two! . . . Look out!—
—O, Cripes, I'm drownded!—   [*Portrait*, 169.]

The interjecting voices of course are those of bathers, but their ironic appropriateness to Stephen's Icarian "soaring sunward" is not meant to
escape us: divers have their own "ecstasy of flight," and Icarus was
"drowned." The imagery of Stephen's ecstasy is fetched from many
sources; we recognize Shelley's skylark, Icarus, the glorified body of the
Resurrection (cf. "His soul had arisen from the grave of boyhood, spurn-
ing her graveclothes") and a tremulousness from which it is difficult to
dissociate adolescent sexual dreams (which the Freudians tell us are frequently dreams of flying). The entire eight-page passage is cunningly organized with great variety of rhetoric and incident; but we cannot help
noticing the limits set on vocabulary and figures of thought. The empurpled triteness of such a cadence as "radiant his eyes and wild his breath
and tremulous and wild and radiant his wind-swept face" is enforced by
recurrence: "But her long fair hair was girlish: and girlish, and touched
with the wonder of mortal beauty, her face." "Ecstasy" is the keyword,
indeed. This riot of feelings corresponds to no vocation definable in mature terms; the paragraphs come to rest on images of irresponsible motion:

> He turned away from her suddenly and set off across the strand. His
> cheeks were aflame; his body was aglow; his limbs were trembling. On
> and on and on and on he strode, far out over the sands, singing wildly
> to the sea, crying to greet the advent of the life that had cried to him.
>   [*Portrait*, 172.]

What "life" connotes it skills not to ask; the word recurs and recurs. So
does the motion onward and onward and onward:

> A wild angel had appeared to him, the angel of mortal youth and beauty,
> an envoy from the fair courts of life, to throw open before him in an in-
> stant of ecstasy the gates of all the ways of error and glory. On and on
> and on and on!   [*Portrait*, 172.]

It may be well to recall Joyce's account of the romantic temper:

> . . . an insecure, unsatisfied, impatient temper which sees no fit abode
> here for its ideals and chooses therefore to behold them under insensible
> figures. As a result of this choice it comes to disregard certain limitations.
> Its figures are blown to wild adventures, lacking the gravity of solid
> bodies. . . .   [*Stephen Hero*.]

Joyce also called *Prometheus Unbound* "the Schwärmerei of a young
jew."

And it is quite plain from the final chapter of the *Portrait* that we are not to accept the mode of Stephen's "freedom" as the "message" of the book. The "priest of the eternal imagination" turns out to be indigestibly Byronic. Nothing is more obvious than his total lack of humour. The dark intensity of the first four chapters is moving enough, but our impulse on being confronted with the final edition of Stephen Dedalus is to laugh; and laugh at this moment we dare not; he is after all a victim being prepared for a sacrifice. His shape, as Joyce said, can no longer change. The art he has elected is not "the slow elaborative patience of the art of satisfaction." "On and on and on and on" will be its inescapable mode. He does not *see* the girl who symbolizes the full revelation; "she seemed like one whom magic had changed into the likeness of a strange and beautiful seabird," and he confusedly apprehends a sequence of downy and feathery incantations. What, in the last chapter, he does see, he sees only to reject, in favour of an incantatory "loveliness which has not yet come into the world."

The only creative attitude to language exemplified in the book is that of Stephen's father:

> —Is it Christy? he said. There's more cunning in one of those warts on his bald head than in a pack of jack foxes.   [*Portrait,* 28.]

His vitality is established before the book is thirty pages under way. Stephen, however, isn't enchanted at any time by the proximity of such talk. He isn't, as a matter of fact, even interested in it. Without a backward glance, he exchanges this father for a myth.

James Joyce

by Edmund Wilson

Ulysses was published in Paris in 1922. It had originally been conceived as a short story for *Dubliners,* and was to have been called "Mr. Bloom's Day in Dublin" or something of the sort. But this idea was afterwards combined with the further history of Stephen Dedalus, the hero of the autobiographical *Portrait of the Artist as a Young Man. Ulysses,* however, in its final form as a volume of seven-hundred-odd large pages, took shape as something entirely different from either of Joyce's earlier books, and it must be approached from a different point of view than as if it were merely, like the others, a straight work of Naturalistic fiction.

The key to *Ulysses* is in the title—and this key is indispensable if we are to appreciate the book's real depth and scope. Ulysses, as he figures in the *Odyssey,* is a sort of type of the average intelligent Greek: among the heroes, he is distinguished for cunning rather than for exalted wisdom, and for common sense, quickness and nerve rather than for, say, the passionate bravery of an Achilles or the steadfastness and stoutness of a Hector. The *Odyssey* exhibits such a man in practically every situation and relation of an ordinary human life—Ulysses, in the course of his wanderings, runs the whole gauntlet of temptations and ordeals and through his wits he survives them all to return at last to his home and family and to reassert himself there as master. The *Odyssey* thus provides a classical model for a writer attempting a modern epic of the ordinary man—and a model particularly attractive to a modern writer by reason of the apparently calculated effectiveness, the apparent sophistication, of its form. By a device suggestive of some of the novels of Conrad, Homer has framed the wanderings of Ulysses between an introductory group of books in which our interest is aroused in the hero before we meet him by Telemachus's search for his lost father, and a culminating group of books which present dramatically and on a larger scale the wanderer's return home.

Now the *Ulysses* of Joyce is a modern *Odyssey,* which follows closely the classical *Odyssey* in both subject and form; and the significance of the characters and incidents of its ostensibly Naturalistic narrative cannot properly be understood without reference to the Homeric original. Joyce's Telemachus of the opening books is Stephen Dedalus—that is, Joyce himself. The Dedaluses, as we have already learned from *A Portrait of the Artist as a Young Man,* are a shabby-genteel family of Dubliners. Stephen's father, Simon Dedalus, has run through a great variety of employments to end up as nothing in particular, a drinker, a decayed sport, an amateur tenor, a well-known character of the bars. But Stephen has been given a good education at a Jesuit college, and we have seen him, at the end of the earlier novel, on the point of leaving for France to study and write. At the beginning of *Ulysses,* he has been back in Dublin a year: he had been summoned home from Paris by a telegram that his mother was dying. And now, a year after her death, the Dedalus family, already reduced to poverty, has become completely demoralized and disintegrated. While Stephen's young sisters and brothers have hardly enough to eat, Simon Dedalus makes the rounds of the pubs. Stephen, who has always resented his father, feels now that in effect he has none. He is more isolated in Dublin than ever. He is Telemachus in search of a Ulysses. His friend, the medical student, Buck Mulligan, with whom he is living in an old tower on the coast and who believes himself to share Stephen's artistic tastes and intellectual interests, really humiliates him by patronizing him and turns to ridicule his abilities and ambitions. He is Antinous, that boldest of Penelope's suitors, who, while Ulysses is away, tries to make himself master of his house and mocks at Telemachus. Stephen has announced at the end of the earlier book that he is going forth "to forge in the smithy of my soul the uncreated conscience of my race"; and now he has returned to Dublin baffled and disinherited— his life with Mulligan is dissolute and unproductive. Yet as Telemachus finds friends and helpers, so Stephen is reminded by the old woman who brings the milk for breakfast in the tower of that Ireland whose uncreated conscience it is still his destiny to forge: "Old and secret . . . maybe a messenger." She is Athene in the guise of Mentor who provides Telemachus with his ship; and the memory of Kevin Egan, an Irish exile in Paris, is the Menelaus who speeds him on his way.

The scene now shifts, as it does in the *Odyssey,* to the lost Ulysses himself. Joyce's Ulysses is a Dublin Jew, an advertisement canvasser named Bloom. Like Stephen, he dwells among aliens: a Jew and the son of a Hungarian father, he is still more or less of a foreigner among the Irish; and a man of something less than mediocre abilities, but of real sensibility and intelligence, he has little in common with the other inhabitants of the lower-middle-class world in which he lives. He has been married for sixteen years to the buxom daughter of an Irish army officer, a professional singer, of prodigious sexual appetite, who has been continually and indiscriminately unfaithful to him. They have had one daughter, who is already growing up and apparently going the way of her mother; and one son, of whom Bloom had hoped that he might resemble, that he might refine upon, himself, but who died eleven days after he was born. Things have never been the same between the Blooms since the death of this son; it is now more than ten years since Bloom has attempted complete intercourse with his wife—it is as if the birth of the sickly Rudy had discouraged him and made him doubt his virility. He is aware that his wife has lovers; but he does not complain or try to interfere—he is even resigned to her accepting money from them. He is a Ulysses with no Telemachus and cut off from his Penelope.

We now follow Bloom's adventures on the day of June 16, 1904 (the whole of *Ulysses* takes place within less than twenty-four hours). Lotoseaters allure him; he is affrighted by Laestrygonians. He assists at the burial of an Elpenor and descends with him in imagination to the underworld; he suffers from the varying favor of an Æolus. He escapes by ruse from the ferocity of a Cyclops and he disengages himself through prudence from the maiden charms of a Nausicaa. And he emerges finally a man again from the brothel of a Circe who had transformed him into a swine.

The comings and goings of Stephen during the day are woven in and out among the wanderings of Bloom: the two encounter each other twice but do not recognize each other. Both men, we become aware, are constantly accompanied and oppressed by ideas which they have tried to dismiss from their minds: the family situation of each really lies back of and explains all that he does that day. In Stephen's case, it is only a few days from the anniversary of his mother's death, and he is haunted by the memory of it: she had begged him on her deathbed to kneel down and pray for her soul and, in rebellion against the Catholic education which had disciplined and maimed his spirit, jealous of the independence he had won and in fear of the past to which he had returned, he had cruelly refused and had allowed her to die without the comfort of believing that he had repented of his apostasy. But now that she is dead, this incident tortures him. He has in the early morning reproached Mulligan—accusing really himself—for something the latter had said about Stephen's mother at the time of her death which Stephen had overheard and resented; and, as he has looked out upon the bright morning sea, the pathos and horror of her life have become suddenly vivid to him—he has been dragged back to relive all that she had suffered. Then, "No, mother!" he has cried out within himself as he thrust her memory down out of his mind, "let me be and let me live!" But through his whole bitter and baffled day, it is his helpless feeling of guilt toward his mother, his hopeless discouragement and disgust with his father, which govern all his thoughts and movements. When he teaches school, he brings the class to a close by a hysterical joke about "the fox burying his grandmother under a hollybush," and in a stupid boy who cannot do his sums he can see now only his own graceless youth which his mother had shielded from the world. After school, he has gone to walk on the beach and has contemplated paying a visit to the family of a maternal uncle whom he despises, as if he could do penance in this fashion for his hardness to his mother and somehow make it up to her now by kindness to her wretched relatives; but again the counter-impulse which had proved too strong on the former occasion comes into play to block his intention: his mind drifts off to other things and he walks beyond where he should have turned. The artist still conflicts with the son—the two are irreconcilable: he sets out to compose a poem, but the poem itself breaks down and he is left gazing at a silent homing ship.—Visiting the library later in the day, he improvises a long, pretentious lecture on the relation of Shakespeare to his father—a lecture which has little to do with Shakespeare, but a good deal to do with Stephen himself.

And as Stephen is ridden by thoughts of his parents, so Bloom is ridden by thoughts of his wife. He has seen Molly at breakfast get a letter which he suspects—and suspects rightly—to be from Blazes Boylan, a flashy buck about town who is managing a concert tour for her and with whom she is having a love affair. All day he has to change the subject when Boylan's name is mentioned—all day he avoids meeting him in the street. In the afternoon, while Bloom is eating at the Ormond Hotel, Boylan comes into the bar, gets a drink and sets off to call on Mrs. Bloom, and when he has gone, Bloom hears the men in the bar talking and laughing about Molly's easy favors. And the conversation, later on in the pub, about Boylan's having won money in a boxing match—in spite of Bloom's gently insistent efforts to induce the company to talk about tennis—is one of the incidents which give rise to an antagonism between Bloom and the rest of the company and eventually to the quarrel between the Cyclops-Citizen and Bloom. At the end of the Nausicaa episode, the voice of the cuckoo-clock from the priest's house tells Bloom that he is now a cuckold.

In the evening, Bloom goes to a maternity hospital to inquire after the wife of a friend, who has been having a hard delivery: there he meets and recognizes Stephen, who is drinking with the medical students. In the *Odyssey*, the final shipwreck of Ulysses and his subsequent misfortunes are the result of the impiety of his companions, who in defiance of all his warnings have killed and eaten the Oxen of the Sun. So Bloom is pained by the impiety of the medical students as they joke obscenely about childbirth and maternity. On the part of Stephen, whose mother died only a year ago, this levity seems especially shocking, but Stephen's very feeling of guilt about her makes him particularly blasphemous and brutal. Yet Bloom has himself in his own way offended against the principle of fertility by his recent prolonged neglect of Molly: the Calypso who has detained him since his shipwreck is the nymph who hangs in his bedroom and whom he makes the object of amorous fantasies. It is this sin against fertility which—at the hour when Mrs. Bloom is entertaining Boylan—has landed Bloom on the Phæacian strand indulging in further erotic daydreams in connection with little Gerty MacDowell, the Nausicaa of the Dublin beach.

When Mrs. Purefoy's child has finally been born, the party rushes out to a public house; and, later on—after a drunken altercation between Dedalus and Buck Mulligan at the tram station, in which Antinous and Telemachus apparently dispute over the key to the tower and Telemachus goes away homeless—Stephen, with one of his companions and with Bloom following some distance behind, proceed to a brothel. Both, by this time, are pretty drunk—though Bloom, with his invincible prudence, is not so drunk as Stephen. And in their drunkenness, in the sordid gaslight and to the tune of the mechanical piano of the brothel, their respective preoccupations emerge fully for the first time since the morning into their conscious minds: Bloom beholds himself, in a hideous vision, looking on at Blazes Boylan and Molly, an abject cuckold, the laughing-stock of the world; and there rises suddenly in Stephen's imagination the figure of his dead mother come back from the grave to remind him of her bleak disheartened love and to implore him to pray for her soul. But again he will not, cannot, acquiesce; in a desperate drunken gesture, intolerably torn by his conflict of impulses, by his emotions which deadlock each other, he lifts his stick and smashes the chandelier—then rushes out into the street, where he gets embroiled with two English Tommies and knocked down. Bloom has followed and, as he bends over Stephen, beholds an apparition of his own dead son, little Rudy, as Bloom would have had him live to be—learned, cultivated, sensitive, refined: such a youth, in short, as Stephen Dedalus. Ulysses and Telemachus are united.

Bloom picks Stephen up and takes him first to a coffee-stand, then home to his own house. He tries to talk to him of the arts and sciences, of the general ideas which interest him; but Stephen is morose and exhausted and makes little response. Bloom begs him to spend the night—to come and live with them, but Stephen declines and presently takes his leave. Bloom goes up, goes to bed with Molly, describes to her his adventures of the day, and soon drops off to sleep.

But Bloom's encounter with Stephen is to affect both Stephen's life and the relations between the Blooms. To have rescued and talked with Stephen has somehow restored Bloom's self-confidence. He has gotten into the habit in the past of cooking breakfast for Molly in the morning and bringing it to her in bed—it is the first thing we have seen him doing at the beginning of the day; but tonight, before he goes to sleep, he gives her to understand that he expects her to get breakfast next morning herself and to bring it up to him. This amazes and disconcerts Mrs. Bloom, and the rest of the book is the record of her meditations as she lies awake thinking over Bloom's homecoming. She has been mystified by his recent behavior, and her attitude toward him now is at first a mixture of jealousy and resentment. She congratulates herself upon the fact that, if Bloom neglects her nowadays, her needs are ably supplied by Blazes Boylan. But as she begins to ruminate on the possibility of Stephen Dedalus's coming to live with them, the idea of Blazes Boylan's coarseness becomes intolerable to her: the thought of Stephen has made her fastidious, and, rapidly becoming very tender about him, she prefigures a relation between them of an ambiguous but intimate character, half-amorous, half-maternal. Yet it is Bloom himself who has primarily been the cause of this revolution in Molly's mind: in telling her about Stephen, he has imposed upon her again his own values; in staying away from the house all day and coming back very late at night, and in asking for his breakfast in bed, he has reasserted his own will. And she goes back in her mind over her experience of Bloom—their courtship, their married life. She remembers how, when she had promised to marry him, it had been his intelligence and his sympathetic nature, that touch of imagination which distinguished him from other men, which had influenced her in his favor—"because he understood or felt what a woman is and I knew I could always get around him"; and on the day when he had first kissed her, he had called her "a flower of the mountain." It is in the mind of his Penelope that this Ulysses has slain the suitors who have been disputing his place.

As for Stephen, unresponsive as he has seemed to Bloom's interest and cordiality, he has at last, none the less, found in Dublin someone sufficiently sympathetic to himself to give him the clew, to supply him with the subject, which will enable him to enter imaginatively—as an artist—into the common life of his race. It is possible that Molly and Bloom, as a result of Bloom's meeting with Stephen, will resume normal marital relations; but it is certain that Stephen, as a result of this meeting, will go away and write *Ulysses*. Buck Mulligan has told us that the young poet says he is going "to write something in ten years": that was in 1904—*Ulysses* is dated at the end as having been begun in 1914.

II

This is the story of *Ulysses* in the light of its Homeric parallel; but to describe the book in such a way gives no idea of what it is really like—of its psychological and technical discoveries or of its magnificent poetry.

Ulysses is, I suppose, the most completely "written" novel since Flaubert. The example of the great prose poet of Naturalism has profoundly influenced Joyce—in his attitude toward the modern bourgeois world and in the contrast implied by the Homeric parallel of *Ulysses* between our own and the ancient world, as well as in an ideal of rigorous objectivity and of adaptation of style to subject—as the influence of that other great Naturalistic poet, Ibsen, is obvious in Joyce's single play, *Exiles*. But Flaubert had, in general, confined himself to fitting the cadence and the phrase precisely to the mood or object described; and even then it was the phrase rather than the cadence, and the object rather than the mood, with which he was occupied—for mood and cadence in Flaubert do not really vary much: he never embodies himself in his characters nor identifies his voice with theirs, and as a result, Flaubert's own characteristic tone of the sombre-pompous-ironic becomes, in the long run, a little monotonous. But Joyce has undertaken in *Ulysses* not merely to render, with the last accuracy and beauty, the actual sights and sounds among which his people move, but, showing us the world as his characters perceive it, to find the unique vocabulary and rhythm which will represent the thoughts of each. If Flaubert taught Maupassant to look for the definitive adjectives which would distinguish a given cab-driver from every other cab-driver at the Rouen station, so Joyce has set himself the task of finding the precise dialect which will distinguish the thoughts of a given Dubliner from those of every other Dubliner. Thus the mind of Stephen Dedalus is represented by a weaving of bright poetic images and fragmentary abstractions, of things remembered from books, on a rhythm sober, melancholy and proud; that of Bloom by a rapid staccato notation, prosaic but vivid and alert, jetting out in all directions in little ideas growing out of ideas; the thoughts of Father Conmee, the Rector of the Jesuit college, by a precise prose, perfectly colorless and orderly; those of Gerty-Nausicaa by a combination of schoolgirl colloquialisms with the jargon of cheap romance; and the ruminations of Mrs. Bloom by a long, unbroken rhythm of brogue, like the swell of some profound sea.

Joyce takes us thus directly into the consciousness of his characters, and in order to do so, he has availed himself of methods of which Flaubert never dreamed—of the methods of Symbolism. He has, in *Ulysses,* exploited together, as no writer had thought to do before, the resources both of Symbolism and of Naturalism. Proust's novel, masterly as it is, does perhaps represent a falling over into decadence of psychological fiction: the subjective element is finally allowed to invade and to deteriorate even those aspects of the story which really ought to be kept strictly objective if one is to believe that it is actually happening. But Joyce's grasp on his objective world never slips: his work is unshakably established on Naturalistic foundations. Where *A la Recherche du Temps Perdu* leaves many things vague—the ages of the characters and sometimes the actual circumstances of their lives, and—what is worse—whether they may not be merely bad dreams that the hero has had, *Ulysses* has been logically thought out and accurately documented to the last detail: everything that happens is perfectly consistent, and we know precisely what the characters wore, how much they paid for things, where they were at different times of the day, what popular songs they sang and what events they read of in the papers, on June 16, 1904. Yet when we are admitted to the mind of any one of them, we are in a world as complex and special, a world sometimes as fantastic or obscure, as that of a Symbolist poet—and a world rendered by similar devices of language. We are more at home in the minds of Joyce's characters than we are likely to be, except after some study, in the mind of a Mallarmé or an Eliot, because we know more about the circumstances in which they find themselves; but we are confronted with the same sort of confusion between emotions, perceptions, and reasonings, and we are likely to be disconcerted by the same sort of hiatuses of thought, when certain links in the association of ideas are dropped down into the unconscious mind so that we are obliged to divine them for ourselves.

But Joyce has carried the methods of Symbolism further than merely to set a Naturalistic scene and then, in that frame, to represent directly the minds of his different characters in Symbolistic monologues like "Mr. Prufrock" or "L'Après-midi d'un Faune." And it is the fact that he has not always stopped here which makes parts of *Ulysses* so puzzling when we read them for the first time. So long as we are dealing with internal monologues in realistic settings, we are dealing with familiar elements merely combined in a novel way—that is, instead of reading, "Bloom said to himself, 'I might manage to write a story to illustrate some proverb or other. I could sign it, Mr. and Mrs. L. M. Bloom,'" we read, "Might manage a sketch. By Mr. and Mrs. L. M. Bloom. Invent a story for some proverb which?" But as we get further along in *Ulysses*, we find the realistic setting oddly distorting itself and deliquescing, and we are astonished at the introduction of voices which seem to belong neither to the characters nor to the author.

The point is that of each of his episodes Joyce has tried to make an independent unit which shall blend the different sets of elements of each —the minds of the characters, the place where they are, the atmosphere about them, the feeling of the time of day. Joyce had already, in *A Portrait of the Artist,* experimented, as Proust had done, in varying the form and style of the different sections to fit the different ages and phases of his hero—from the infantile fragments of childhood impressions, through the ecstatic revelations and the terrifying nightmares of adolescence, to the self-possessed notations of young manhood. But in *A Portrait of the Artist,* Joyce was presenting everything from the point of view of a single particular character, Dedalus; whereas in *Ulysses* he is occupied with a number of different personalities, of whom Dedalus is no longer the centre, and his method, furthermore, of enabling us to live in their world is not always merely a matter of making us shift from the point of view of one to the point of view of another. In order to understand what Joyce is doing here, one must conceive a set of Symbolistic poems, themselves involving characters whose minds are represented Symbolistically, depending not from the sensibility of the poet speaking in his own person, but from the poet's imagination playing a rôle absolutely impersonal and always imposing upon itself all the Naturalistic restrictions in regard to the story it is telling at the same time that it allows itself to exercise all the Symbolistic privileges in regard to the way it tells it. We are not likely to be prepared for this by the early episodes of *Ulysses*: they are as sober and as clear as the morning light of the Irish coast in which they take

place: the characters' perceptions of the external world are usually distinct from their thoughts and feelings about them. But in the newspaper
office, for the first time, a general atmosphere begins to be created, beyond
the specific minds of the characters, by a punctuation of the text with
newspaper heads which announce the incidents in the narrative. And in
the library scene, which takes place in the early afternoon, the setting and
people external to Stephen begin to dissolve in his apprehension of them,
heightened and blurred by some drinks at lunchtime and by the intellectual excitement of the conversation amid the dimness and tameness of
the library—"Eglintoneyes, quick with pleasure, looked up shybrightly.
Gladly glancing, a merry puritan, through the twisted eglantine." Here,
however, we still see all through Stephen's eyes—through the eyes of a
single character; but in the scene in the Ormond Hotel, which takes place
a couple of hours later—our reveries absorb the world about us progres-
sively as daylight fades and as the impressions of the day accumulate—
the sights and sounds and the emotional vibrations and the appetites for
food and drink of the late afternoon, the laughter, the gold-and-bronze
hair of the barmaids, the jingling of Blazes Boylan's car on his way to
visit Molly Bloom, the ringing of the hoofs of the horses of the viceregal
cavalcade clanging in through the open window, the ballad sung by Simon
Dedalus, the sound of the piano accompaniment and the comfortable
supper of Bloom—though they are not all, from beginning to end, perceived by Bloom himself—all mingle quite un-Naturalistically in a harmony of bright sound, ringing color, poignant indistinct feeling and de-
clining light. The scene in the brothel, where it is night and where Dedalus and Bloom are drunk, is like a slowed-up moving picture, in which the
intensified vision of reality is continually lapsing into phantasmagoric
visions; and the let-down after the excitement of this, the lassitude and
staleness of the cabmen's shelter where Bloom takes Stephen to get him
some coffee, is rendered by a prose as flavorless, as weary, and as banal as
the incidents which it reports. Joyce has achieved here, by different methods, a relativism like that of Proust: he is reproducing in literature the
different aspects, the different proportions and textures, which things and
people take on at different times and under different circumstances.

III

I do not think that Joyce has been equally successful with all these
technical devices in *Ulysses*; but before it will be possible to discuss them
further, we must approach the book from another point of view.

It has always been characteristic of Joyce to neglect action, narrative,
drama, of the usual kind, even the direct impact on one another of the
characters as we get it in the ordinary novel, for a sort of psychological
portraiture. There is tremendous vitality in Joyce, but very little movement. Like Proust, he is symphonic rather than narrative. His fiction has

its progressions, its developments, but they are musical rather than dramatic. The most elaborate and interesting piece in *Dubliners*—the story called "The Dead"—is simply a record of the modification brought about during a single evening in the relations of a husband and wife by the man's becoming aware, from the effect produced on the woman by a song which she has heard at a family party, that she has once been loved by another man; *A Portrait of the Artist as a Young Man* is simply a series of pictures of the author at successive stages of his development; the theme of *Exiles* is, like that of "The Dead," the modification in the relations of a husband and wife which follows the reappearance of a man who has been the wife's lover. And *Ulysses*, again, for all its vast scale, is simply the story of another small but significant change in the relations of yet another married couple as a result of the impingement on their household of the personality of an only slightly known young man. Most of these stories cover a period of only a few hours, and they are never carried any further. When Joyce has explored one of these situations, when he has established the small gradual readjustment, he has done all that interests him.

All, that is, from the point of view of ordinary incident. But though Joyce almost entirely lacks appetite for violent conflict or vigorous action, his work is prodigiously rich and alive. His force, instead of following a line, expands itself in every dimension (including that of time) about a single point. The world of *Ulysses* is animated by a complex inexhaustible life: We revisit it as we do a city, where we come more and more to recognize faces, to understand personalities, to grasp relations, currents, and interests. Joyce has exercised considerable technical ingenuity in introducing us to the elements of his story in an order which will enable us to find our bearings: yet I doubt whether any human memory is capable, on a first reading, of meeting the demands of *Ulysses*. And when we reread it, we start in at any point, as if it were indeed something solid like a city which actually existed in space and which could be entered from any direction—as Joyce is said, in composing his books, to work on the different parts simultaneously. More than any other work of fiction, unless perhaps the *Comédie Humaine*, *Ulysses* creates the illusion of a living social organism. We see it only for twenty hours, yet we know its past as well as its present. We possess Dublin, seen, heard, smelt and felt, brooded over, imagined, remembered.

Joyce's handling of this immense material, his method of giving his book a shape, resembles nothing else in modern fiction. The first critics of *Ulysses* mistook the novel for a "slice of life" and objected that it was too fluid or too chaotic. They did not recognize a plot because they could not recognize a progression; and the title told them nothing. They could not even discover a pattern. It is now apparent, however, that *Ulysses* suffers from an excess of design rather than from a lack of it. Joyce has drawn up an outline of his novel, of which he has allowed certain of his

commentators to avail themselves, but which he has not allowed them
to publish in its entirety (though it is to be presumed that the book on
Ulysses which Mr. Stuart Gilbert has announced will include all the information contained in it); and from this outline it appears that Joyce has
set himself the task of fulfilling the requirements of a most complicated
scheme—a scheme which we could scarcely have divined except in its
more obvious features. For even if we had known about the Homeric
parallel and had identified certain of the correspondences—if we had
had no difficulty in recognizing the Cyclops in the ferocious professional
Fenian, or Circe in the brothel-keeper, or Hades in the cemetery—we
should never have suspected how closely and how subtly the parallel had
been followed—we should never have guessed, for example, that when
Bloom passes through the National Library while Stephen is having his
discussion with the literary men, he is escaping, on the one hand, a Scylla
—that is, Aristotle, the rock of Dogma; and, on the other, a Charybdis—
Plato, the whirlpool of Mysticism; nor that, when Stephen walks on the
seashore, he is reënacting the combat with Proteus—in this case, primal
matter, of whose continual transformations Stephen is reminded by the
objects absorbed or washed up by the sea, but whose forms he is able to
hold and fix, as the Homeric Proteus was held and vanquished, by power
of the words which give him images for them. Nor should we have known
that the series of phrases and onomatopoetic syllables placed at the beginning of the Sirens episode—the singing in the Ormond Hotel—and selected from the narrative which follows, are supposed to be musical
themes and that the episode itself is a fugue; and though we may have
felt the ironic effect of the specimens of inflated Irish journalism introduced at regular intervals in the conversation with the patriot in the pub
—we should hardly have understood that these had been produced by a
deliberate technique of "gigantism"—for, since the Citizen represents the
Cyclops, and since the Cyclops was a giant, he must be rendered formida-
ble by a parade of all the banalities of his patriotic claptrap swollen to
gigantic proportions. We should probably never have guessed all this,
and we should certainly never have guessed at the ingenuity which Joyce
has expended in other ways. Not only, we learn from the outline, is there
an elaborate Homeric parallel in *Ulysses,* but there is also an organ of the
human body and a human science or art featured in every episode. We
look these up, a little incredulously, but there, we find, they all actually
are—buried and disguised beneath the realistic surface, but carefully
planted, unmistakably dwelt upon. And if we are tipped off, we are able
further to discover all sorts of concealed ornaments and emblems: in the
chapter of the Lotos-Eaters, for example, countless references to flowers;
in the Laestrygonians, to eating; in the Sirens, puns on musical terms;
and in Æolus, the newspaper office, not merely many references to wind
but, according to Mr. Gilbert—the art featured in this episode being
Rhetoric—some hundred different figures of speech.

Now the Homeric parallel in *Ulysses* is in general pointedly and charmingly carried out and justifies itself: It does help to give the story a universal significance and it enables Joyce to show us in the actions and the relations of his characters meanings which he perhaps could not easily have indicated in any other way—since the characters themselves must be largely unaware of these meanings and since Joyce has adopted the strict objective method, in which the author must not comment on the action. And we may even accept the arts and sciences and the organs of the human body as making the book complete and comprehensive, if a little laboriously systematic—the whole of man's experience in a day. But when we get all these things together and further complicated by the virtuosity of the technical devices, the result is sometimes baffling or confusing. We become aware, as we examine the outline, that when we went through *Ulysses* for the first time, it was these organs and arts and sciences and Homeric correspondences which sometimes so discouraged our interest. We had been climbing over these obstacles without knowing it, in our attempts to follow Dedalus and Bloom. The trouble was that, beyond the ostensible subject and, as it were, beneath the surface of the narrative, too many other subjects and too many different orders of subjects were being proposed to our attention.

It seems to me difficult, then, not to conclude that Joyce elaborated *Ulysses* too much—that he tried to put too many things into it. What is the value of all the references to flowers in the Lotos-Eaters chapter, for example? They do not create in the Dublin streets an atmosphere of lotus-eating—we are merely puzzled, if we have not been told to look for them, as to why Joyce has chosen to have Bloom think and see certain things, of which the final explanation is that they are pretexts for mentioning flowers. And do not the gigantic interpolations of the Cyclops episode defeat their object by making it impossible for us to follow the narrative? The interpolations are funny in themselves, the incident related is a masterpiece of language and humor, the idea of combining them seems happy, yet the effect is mechanical and annoying: in the end we have to read the whole thing through, skipping the interpolations, in order to find out what has happened. The worst example of the capacities for failure of this too synthetic, too systematic, method seems to me the scene in the maternity hospital. I have described above what actually takes place there as I have worked it out, after several readings and in the light of Joyce's outline. The Oxen of the Sun are "Fertility"—the crime committed against them is "Fraud." But, not content with this, Joyce has been at pains to fill the episode with references to real cattle and to include a long conversation about bulls. As for the special technique, it seems to me in this case not to have any real appropriateness to the situation, but to have been dictated by sheer fantastic pedantry: Joyce describes his method here as "embryonic," in conformity to the subject, maternity, and the chapter is written as a series of parodies of English literary styles from the bad Latin of the early chronicles up through Huxley and Carlyle, the development of the language corresponding to the growth of the child in the womb. Now something important takes place in this episode —the meeting between Dedalus and Bloom—and an important point is being made about it. But we miss the point because it is all we can do to follow what is happening at the drinking party, itself rather a confused affair, through the medium of the language of the Morte d'Arthur, the seventeenth-century diaries, the eighteenth-century novels, and a great many other kinds of literature in which we are not prepared at the moment to be interested. If we pay attention to the parodies, we miss the story; and if we try to follow the story, we are unable to appreciate the parodies. The parodies have spoiled the story; and the necessity of telling the story through them has taken most of the life out of the parodies.

Joyce has as little respect as Proust for the capacities of the reader's attention; and one feels, in Joyce's case as in Proust's, that the *longueurs* which break our backs, the mechanical combinations of elements which fail to coalesce, are partly a result of the effort of a supernormally energetic mind to compensate by piling things up for an inability to make them move.

We have now arrived, in the maternity hospital, at the climactic scenes of the story, and Joyce has bogged us as he has never bogged us before. We shall forget the Oxen of the Sun in the wonderful night-town scene which follows it—but we shall be bogged afterwards worse than ever in the interminable let-down of the cabman's shelter and in the scientific question-and-answer chapter which undertakes to communicate to us through the most opaque and uninviting medium possible Dedalus's conversation with Bloom. The night-town episode itself and Mrs. Bloom's soliloquy, which closes the book, are, of course, among the best things in it—but the relative proportions of the other three latter chapters and the jarring effect of the pastiche style sandwiched in with the straight Naturalistic seem to me artistically absolutely indefensible. One can understand that Joyce may have intended the colorless and tiresome episodes to set off the rich and vivid ones, and also that it is of the essence of his point of view to represent the profoundest changes of our lives as beginning naturally between night and morning without the parties' appreciating their importance at the time; but a hundred and sixty-one more or less deliberately tedious pages are too heavy a dead weight for even the brilliant flights of the other hundred and ninety-nine pages to carry. Furthermore, Joyce has here half-buried his story under the virtuosity of his technical devices. It is almost as if he had elaborated it so much and worked over it so long that he had forgotten, in the amusement of writing parodies, the drama which he had originally intended to stage; or as if he were trying to divert and overwhelm us by irrelevant entertainments and feats in order that we might not be dissatisfied with the flatness—except for the drunken scene—of Dedalus's final meeting with Bloom; or even perhaps as if he did not, after all, quite want us to understand his story, as if he had, not quite conscious of what he was doing, ended by throwing up between us and it a fortification of solemn burlesque prose —as if he were shy and solicitous about it, and wanted to protect it from us.

IV

Yet even these episodes to which I have objected contribute something valuable to *Ulysses*. In the chapter of parodies, for example, Joyce seems to be saying to us: "Here are specimens of the sort of thing that man has written about himself in the past—how naïve or pretentious they seem! I have broken through these assumptions and pretences and shown you how he must recognize himself today." And in the question-and-answer chapter, which is written entirely from the conventional point of view of science and where we are supplied with every possible physical, statistical, biographical, and astronomical fact about Stephen's visit to Bloom: "This is all that the twentieth-century man thinks he knows about himself and his universe. Yet how mechanical and rigid this reasoning seems when we apply it to Molly and Bloom—how inadequate to explain them!"

For one of the most remarkable features of *Ulysses* is its interest as an investigation into the nature of human consciousness and behavior. Its importance from the point of view of psychology has never, it seems to me, been properly appreciated—though its influence on other books and, in consequence, upon our ideas about ourselves, has already been profound. Joyce has attempted in *Ulysses* to render as exhaustively, as precisely, and as directly as it is possible in words to do, what our participation in life is like—or rather, what it seems to us like as from moment to moment we live. In order to make this record complete, he has been obliged to disregard a number of conventions of taste which, especially in English-speaking countries, have in modern times been pretty strictly observed, even by the writers who have aimed to be most scrupulously truthful. Joyce has studied what we are accustomed to consider the dirty, the trivial and the base elements in our lives with the relentlessness of a modern psychologist; and he has also—what the contemporary Naturalist has seldom been poet enough for—done justice to all those elements in our lives which we have been in the habit of describing by such names as love, nobility, truth and beauty. It is curious to reflect that a number of critics—including, curiously enough, Arnold Bennett—should have found Joyce misanthropic. Flaubert is misanthropic, if you like—and in reproducing his technique, Joyce sometimes suggests his acrid tone. But Stephen, Bloom and Mrs. Bloom are certainly not either unamiable or unattractive—and for all their misfortunes and shortcomings, they inspire us with considerable respect. Stephen and Bloom are played off a little against the duller and meaner people about them; but even these people can scarcely be said to be treated with bitterness, even when, as in the case of Buck Mulligan or the elder Dedalus, Stephen's feeling about them is bitter. Joyce is remarkable, rather, for equanimity: in spite of the nervous intensity of *Ulysses,* there is a real serenity and detachment behind it— we are in the presence of a mind which has much in common with that of a certain type of philosopher, who in his effort to understand the causes of things, to interrelate the different elements of the universe, has reached a point where the ordinary values of good and bad, beautiful and ugly, have been lost in the excellence and beauty of transcendent understanding itself.

I believe that the first readers of *Ulysses* were shocked, not merely by Joyce's use of certain words ordinarily excluded today from English literature, but by his way of representing those aspects of human nature which we tend to consider incongruous as intimately, inextricably mingled. Yet the more we read *Ulysses,* the more we are convinced of its psychological truth, and the more we are amazed at Joyce's genius in mastering and in presenting, not through analysis or generalization, but by the complete recreation of life in the process of being lived, the relations of human beings to their environment and to each other; the nature of their perception of what goes on about them and of what goes on within themselves; and the interdependence of their intellectual, their physical, their professional and their emotional lives. To have traced all these interdependencies, to have given each of these elements its value, yet never to have lost sight of the moral through preoccupation with the physical, nor to have forgotten the general in the particular; to have exhibited ordinary humanity without either satirizing it or sentimentalizing it—this would already have been sufficiently remarkable; but to have subdued all this material to the uses of a supremely finished and disciplined work of art is a feat which has hardly been equalled in the literature of our time.

In Stephen's diary in *A Portrait of the Artist,* we find this significant entry apropos of a poem by Yeats: "Michael Robartes remembers forgotten beauty and, when his arms wrap her round, he presses in his arms the loveliness which has long faded from the world. Not this. Not at all. I desire to press in my arms the loveliness which has not yet come into the world."

And with *Ulysses,* Joyce has brought into literature a new and unknown beauty. Some readers have regretted the extinction in the later Joyce of the charming lyric poet of his two little books of poems and the *fin de siècle* prose writer of the *fin de siècle* phases of *A Portrait of the Artist as a Young Man* (both the prose and verse of the early Joyce showed the influence of Yeats). This poet is still present in *Ulysses:* "Kind air defined the coigns of houses in Kildare Street. No birds. Frail from the housetops two plumes of smoke ascended, pluming, and in a flaw of softness softly were blown." But the conventions of the romantic lyric, of "æsthetic" *fin de siècle* prose, even of the æsthetic Naturalism of Flaubert, can no longer, for Joyce, be made to accommodate the reality of experience. The diverse elements of experience are perceived in different relations and they must be differently represented. Joyce has found for this new vision a new language, but a language which, instead of diluting or doing violence to his poetic genius, enables it to assimilate more materials, to readjust itself more completely and successfully than that of perhaps any other poet of our age to the new self-consciousness of the modern world. But in achieving this, Joyce has ceased to write verse. I have suggested, in connection with Valéry and Eliot, that verse itself as a literary medium is coming to be used for fewer and fewer and for more and more special purposes, and that it may be destined to fall into disuse. And it seems to me that Joyce's literary development is a striking corroboration of this view. His prose works have an artistic intensity, a definitive beauty of surface and of form, which make him comparable to the great poets rather than to most of the great novelists.

Joyce is indeed really the great poet of a new phase of the human consciousness. Like Proust's or Whitehead's or Einstein's world, Joyce's world is always changing as it is perceived by different observers and by them at different times. It is an organism made up of "events," which may be taken as infinitely inclusive or infinitely small and each of which involves all the others; and each of these events is unique. Such a world cannot be presented in terms of such artificial abstractions as have been conventional in the past: solid institutions, groups, individuals, which play the parts of distinct durable entities—or even of solid psychological factors: dualisms of good and evil, mind and matter, flesh and spirit, instinct and reason; clear conflicts between passion and duty, between conscience and interest. Not that these conceptions are left out of Joyce's world: they are all there in the minds of the characters; and the realities they represent are there, too. But everything is reduced to terms of "events" like those of modern physics and philosophy—events which make up a "continuum," but which may be taken as infinitely small. Joyce has built out of these events a picture, amazingly lifelike and living, of the everyday world we know—and a picture which seems to allow us to see into it, to follow its variations and intricacies, as we have never been able to do before.

Nor are Joyce's characters merely the sum of the particles into which their experience has been dissociated: we come to imagine them as solidly, to feel their personalities as unmistakably, as we do with any characters in fiction; and we realize finally that they are also symbols. Bloom himself is in one of his aspects the typical modern man: Joyce has made him a Jew, one supposes, partly in order that he may be conceived equally well as an inhabitant of any provincial city of the European or Europeanized world. He makes a living by petty business, he leads the ordinary middle-class life—and he holds the conventional enlightened opinions of the time: he believes in science, social reform and internationalism.

But Bloom is surpassed and illuminated from above by Stephen, who represents the intellect, the creative imagination; and he is upheld by Mrs. Bloom, who represents the body, the earth. Bloom leaves with us in the long run the impression that he is something both better and worse than either of them; for Stephen sins through pride, the sin of the intellect; and Molly is at the mercy of the flesh; but Bloom, though a less powerful personality than either, has the strength of humility. It is difficult to describe the character of Bloom as Joyce finally makes us feel it: it takes precisely the whole of *Ulysses* to put him before us. It is not merely that Bloom is mediocre, that he is clever, that he is commonplace—that he is comic, that he is pathetic—that he is, as Rebecca West says, a figure of abject "squatting" vulgarity, that he is at moments, as Foster Damon says, the Christ—he is all of these, he is all the possibilities of that ordinary humanity which is somehow not so ordinary after all; and it is the proof of Joyce's greatness that, though we recognize Bloom's perfect truth and typical character, we cannot pigeonhole him in any familiar category, racial, social, moral, literary or even—because he does really have, after all, a good deal in common with the Greek Ulysses—historical.

Both Stephen and Molly are more easily describable because they represent extremes. Both are capable of rising to heights which Bloom can never reach. In Stephen's rhapsody on the seashore, when he first realizes his artist's vocation, in *A Portrait of the Artist as a Young Man,* we have had the ecstasy of the creative mind. In the soliloquy of Mrs. Bloom, Joyce has given us another ecstasy of creation, the rhapsody of the flesh. Stephen's dream was conceived in loneliness, by a drawing apart from his fellows. But Mrs. Bloom is like the earth, which gives the same life to all: she feels a maternal kinship with all living creatures. She pities the "poor donkeys slipping half asleep" in the steep street of Gibraltar, as she does "the sentry in front of the governor's house . . . half roasted" in the sun; and she gives herself to the bootblack at the General Post Office as readily as to Professor Goodwin. But, none the less, she will tend to breed from the highest type of life she knows: she turns to Bloom, and, beyond him, toward Stephen. This gross body, the body of humanity, upon which the whole structure of *Ulysses* rests—still throbbing with so strong a rhythm amid obscenity, commonness and squalor—is laboring to throw up some knowledge and beauty by which it may transcend itself.

These two great flights of the mind carry off all the ignominies and trivialities through which Joyce has made us pass: they seem to me—the soaring silver prose of the one, the deep embedded pulse of the other— among the supreme expressions in literature of the creative powers of humanity: they are, respectively, the justifications of the woman and the man.

Homer and the Nightmare of History

by S. L. Goldberg

At the beginning, Stephen's crisis is portrayed in terms of his rejection of Mulligan, or rather of the image of him that Mulligan wishes to impose. Against Mulligan's easy compromises with the material values he affects to despise, and his possessiveness and aesthetic provinciality—both of which are neatly exemplified in *his* naming of the tower in which they live the *omphalos*—Stephen opposes his scorn in return, a scrupulous evasion of commitment, and a contemptuous compliance with Mulligan's desire for the key to the Martello tower. When Mulligan (and the peasant milk-woman whose respect for him identifies the nature of his power) usurp what Stephen regards as his place, he is ready to go. The key is, of course, a symbol of his attachment to a centre; he is willing enough to give it up when he feels the centre (home and country) usurped, but he goes with the burden of bitterness. And as Wyndham Lewis and Mr. Kenner have pointed out, his emotional attitudes do seem rather theatrical. In this first chapter, he gives the impression of posturing—an impression only the more heightened by the contrast with his more private attitudes as they are revealed in the third chapter ("Proteus"): the rigid and somewhat operatic posture largely dissolves once we see him from the inside. Here, in "Telemachus," he is presenting an image of himself to the world; but he is presenting it in deliberate opposition to those Mulligan and others wish him to adopt. His own image may be false and immature; theirs, he feels, would involve a fundamental lie to his true nature and vocation. "To discover the mode of life or of art whereby [his] spirit could express itself in unfettered freedom" (*Portrait,* p. 280): his own youthful image, inadequate as it is already beginning to appear to him, at least offers a negative ideal, and he uses it as a shield. If he cannot be much more positive, he does know what he does not want.[1]

"Homer and the Nightmare of History." Abridged from S. L. Goldberg, *The Classical Temper: A Study of James Joyce's "Ulysses,"* pp. 154–63; 170–80. Copyright © 1961 by S. L. Goldberg. Reprinted by permission of Barnes & Noble Books, Division of Harper & Row, Publishers, Inc. and Chatto and Windus Ltd. Two footnotes have been deleted.

[1] Cf. [Stuart] Gilbert [*James Joyce's "Ulysses"* (New York: Alfred A. Knopf, Inc., 1952),] p. 107, though Mr. Gilbert seems to imply that Stephen is presenting his true personality to Mulligan and Haines.

The waves of his personal crisis spread wider than the immediate struggle with Mulligan, however. For one thing, he is entangled with a kinetic remorse, a sense of guilt arising from his rejection of Roman Catholicism and the fear that his rejection may have contributed to his mother's death. This, it must be said, is an aspect of his character that does seem wholly theatrical, an unpleasant combination of self-accusation, self-pity and pride. He can evidently see through the current "romantic" and pretentious twaddle about Ireland, as his speculations about the milk-woman suggest. But although he savours that sentimentality with a dry irony, it is in fact very like many of his own thoughts about his mother:

> In a dream, silently, she had come to him, her wasted body within its loose graveclothes giving off an odour of wax and rosewood, her breath bent over him with mute secret words, a faint odour of wetted ashes.
>
> Her glazing eyes, staring out of death, to shake and bend my soul. On me alone. The ghostcandle to light her agony. Ghostly light on the tortured face. Her hoarse loud breath rattling in horror, while all prayed on their knees. Her eyes on me to strike me down. *Liliata rutilantium te confessorum turma circumdet: iubilantium te virginum chorus excipiat.*
>
> [*Ulysses*, 10.]

Yet it is worth noticing that, even despite the self-pity, the unfortunately Gothic horrors, and the overelaborate cadences (which it is hard to be quite sure whether to ascribe to Stephen or to Joyce), the passage does conclude with an instinctive, and significantly direct, cry for freedom and life:

> Ghoul! Chewer of corpses!
> No, mother. Let me be and let me live.

It is hardly a conscious critical response, an appeal to ideals positively held; Stephen is too divided for that. It is still a kinetic reaction, but it is very much in the right direction.

Similarly with the other false images of himself: he regards them, as he had regarded them in the *Portrait,* as nets to be avoided. The Englishman, Haines, comments,

> —After all, I should think you are able to free yourself. You are your own master, it seems to me.
> —I am the servant of two masters, Stephen said, an English and an Italian. . . .
> —And a third, Stephen said, there is who wants me for odd jobs.
> [20.]

As Haines replies, "It seems history is to blame." To Stephen the past does seem almost overwhelmingly determinant. He sees tradition not as a liberating force but (with a more intimate knowledge of some traditions than has every *laudator temporis acti*) as constricting and deadening. Yet again, although his freedom seems little more than the minimum of mere escape, he is shown groping towards something more. Carefully placed beside this conversation with Haines is a passage about a man drowned in the bay, which reinforces the point already implicit in Stephen's rejection of possible masters. Throughout *Ulysses* the sea appears as a symbol of the chaotic flux of experience, the element;[2] drowning is defeat, submergence, the death of the spirit in the overwhelming flood of kinetic appetencies. Stephen fears death by water. The drowned man objectifies his fear of suffocation, his need to rise above the waves, to swim in the element—in other words, to achieve a free *stasis* of spirit by understanding and accepting himself, his predicament, and his necessities. He must, as he clearly realizes, launch out. When the chapter ends, he is literally homeless. We do not know where he is going, nor does he.

The second chapter explores the historical aspects of his situation further. It begins by crystallizing our feeling, and Stephen's too, about his "victory" over Mulligan and his other potential masters: it is not enough, not decisive, indeed Pyrrhic. And the main theme of the chapter is Stephen's hostility to, and fear of, the past. Time seems to him only to repeat itself in "the same room and hour, the same wisdom. . . . Three nooses round me here," or in the repeated experience of the Jews:

> Time surely would scatter all. A hoard heaped by the roadside: plundered and passing on. Their eyes knew the years of wandering and, patient, knew the dishonours of their flesh.
> —Who has not? Stephen said.   [34.]

In short, "history was a tale like any other too often heard." The individual seems helplessly bound to the pattern; the "dear might of Him that walked the waves" does not exist for Stephen. He can see as little in the present as he can see in Elizabethan England—"an age of exhausted whoredom groping for its god." The ages, as John Eglinton puts it, seem only to "succeed one another" without change or hope. So conceived, history must seem a nightmare.

> —History, Stephen said, is a nightmare from which I am trying to awake.
> From the playfield the boys raised a shout. A whirring whistle: goal.
> What if that nightmare gave you a back kick?

[2] Cf. [William York] Tindall, *James Joyce* [(New York: Charles Scribner's Sons, 1950)], p. 30: "water means reality." Professor Curtius and Mr. Gilbert take the sea as the "primordial element, giver and taker of life" (Gilbert, p. 128). Mr. Kenner [in *Dublin's Joyce* (Bloomington: Indiana University Press, 1956)], on the other hand, takes it as "matter" (p. 211), with the implication, which I think unjustified, of *mere* matter. Of course the sea is a traditional Neo-Platonic symbol for matter or the amorphous substance in which natural forms are embodied, but, as with all such symbols, its meaning in *Ulysses* is what the work *makes* of it. The most thorough discussion of Joyce's related symbols of woman, moon, water and life, together with Stephen's fear of drowning, is Maurice Beebe, "James Joyce: Barnacle Goose and Lapwing," *Publications of the Modern Language Association of America*, LXXI, 1956, pp. 302–20.

—The ways of the Creator are not our ways, Mr Deasy said. All history
moves towards one great goal, the manifestation of God.
    Stephen jerked his thumb towards the window, saying:
    —That is God.
    Hooray! Ay! Whrrwhee!
    —What? Mr Deasy asked.
    —A shout in the street, Stephen answered, shrugging his shoulders.
                                                                    [34.]

Stephen cannot accept that history moves to any supernatural end outside itself. If God exists, He manifests Himself here and now, in all life
however pointless or trivial it may seem. History is not like a detective
story; there are no comforting revelations to follow. When Stephen uses
teleological arguments himself later on, he does so only analogously for
another and very different conclusion.

His obsessive fear of the past is partly balanced, however, by a different strain of thought about history. If past events limit the present and
the future, they also, as acts of will, liberate possibilities into the world
of fact. Stephen ponders this dual aspect of history in Aristotelian terms:

> Had Pyrrhus not fallen by a beldam's hand in Argos or Julius Caesar
> not been knifed to death. They are not to be thought away. Time has
> branded them and fettered they are lodged in the room of the infinite
> possibilities they have ousted. But can those have been possible seeing
> that they never were? Or was that only possible which came to pass?
> Weave, weaver of the wind.   [25.]

And during the schoolboys' reading of *Lycidas,* the grounds of hope occur to him: time is not only a burden, it is also a means to the fruition
and fulfilment of the soul in action. As he tells himself a little later, he
could, if he willed it, break free of his present nooses—and in fact he
does. History involves more than the ossification of life; it is also dy-
namic:

> It must be a movement then, an actuality of the possible as possible.
> Aristotle's phrase formed itself within the gabbled verses and floated out
> into the studious silence of the library of Sainte Geneviève where he had
> read, sheltered from the sin of Paris, night by night. By his elbow a delicate
> Siamese conned a handbook of strategy. Fed and feeding brains about me:
> under glowlamps, impaled, with faintly beating feelers: and in my mind's
> darkness a sloth of the underworld, reluctant, shy of brightness, shifting
> her dragon scaly folds. Thought is the thought of thought. Tranquil bright-
> ness. The soul is in a manner all that is: the soul is the form of forms.
> Tranquillity sudden, vast, candescent: form of forms.   [25–26.]

The relevance of this (even the Siamese student) to his moral problems
as an artist, his desire to mature and freely and creatively to act, requires
no emphasis. Mr. Deasy's ambiguous wisdom confirms the implications

of Stephen's drift: "to learn one must be humble. But life is the great teacher." For Stephen's situation, that cliché is the wisdom of Nestor.

"Proteus" develops these implications still further, both in Stephen's reflections about them and in the dramatic presentation of the way his reflections themselves progress. Joyce's writing here has often been praised for its sensitive delicacy, but it is not always realized how much more it is than that, how finely and firmly the chapter is organized as a poetic, dramatic unit. Generally speaking, the chapter explores the Protean transformations of matter in time—matter, as we should expect from Stephen's aesthetic theory, both as object, the "ineluctable modality of the visible and audible," apprehensible only in the condition of flux,[3] and as subject, Stephen himself. In the one aspect, Stephen is seeking the principles of change and the underlying substance of sensory experience; in the other, he is seeking his self among its temporal manifestations. Consequently, he seems narcissistic, self-conscious, *lisant au livre de lui-même* like Hamlet. Yet, although he is still egocentric and still in uneasy kinetic relationship to his environment and himself, he exhibits in this chapter more of the incipient irony he had displayed at the end of the *Portrait,* a dawning capacity to stand off from himself and criticize what he sees, and concomitantly, to observe external reality with a certain detachment. His potentiality of growth is perhaps here most clearly visible. The humourless and priggish aesthete appears much less certain about his poses; he has after all, we discover, some sense of the ridiculous and some glimmerings of maturer values. "Proteus," in fact, is the crucial chapter for our conception of him. Without it, his other appearances in the book would hardly convince us of his solidity or interest as a protagonist; as it is, they are all enriched and qualified by his presentation here.

The setting on the seashore has an obvious metaphorical significance. Stephen speculates at the edge of life about the meanings in, and beyond, the immediate sensible world—his material as an artist. Bloom, who finds himself on the same shore in the evening, can make nothing of it:

> All these rocks with lines and scars and letters. O, those transparent!
> Besides they don't know. What is the meaning of that other world. I
> called you naughty boy because I do not like.
> [He draws with a stick: I. AM. A.]
> No room. Let it go.
> Mr Bloom effaced the letters with his slow boot. Hopeless thing sand.
> Nothing grows in it. All fades. . . .   [381.]

But Stephen has the intellectual and imaginative capacity to read the "signatures of all things," to penetrate the diaphanous sensible world

---

[3] See Joseph E. Duncan, "The Modality of the Audible in Joyce's *Ulysses*," *Publications of the Modern Language Association of America,* LXXII, 1957, pp. 286–95, for an exposition of the Aristotelian terminology Stephen uses here.

and the ineluctable *nacheinander* and *nebeneinander* placed before the individual consciousness, the world that is "there all the time without you: and ever shall be, world without end."[37.]

His thoughts turn to the permanent patterns of change—in particular, to the pattern of the life-cycle within which the individual's destiny is played out. He scorns theosophical hocus-pocus about the navelcord, but he acknowledges the common bond of continuity it represents. For him —and for Bloom, too—womankind represents the permanent force and pattern of biological history: birth, copulation, family and death. Indeed, when we recall the figure of Molly Bloom, it is true to say that this is one of the constant symbolic values of the book as a whole. Women do not figure in it as people but as biological symbols. And the polarity some of Joyce's critics have observed between Stephen ("intellectual life") and Molly ("biological life") already exists in Stephen's own point of view—especially in the rather abstractly "deep" speculations about Woman in which both he and Bloom sometimes indulge.

The first transformation of "matter" lies in the changing substance of Stephen's thoughts from the life-cycle in general towards his family and its particular life, and equally in his rejection of their "paralysis": "Houses of decay, mine, his and all. . . . Come out of them, Stephen. Beauty is not there." His father, as he says to Bloom later, is "all too Irish," and his criticism here includes the whole "hundred-headed rabble of the cathedral close," the general state of Ireland.

Swift provides the link to the second transformation—Stephen's "temptation" to enter the priesthood, or, more generally, to achieve and exercise magical powers; and, correspondingly, in "subjective" terms, his rejection of the possibility in both its religious and aesthetic aspects:

> Cousin Stephen, you will never be a saint. . . . You were awfully holy, weren't you? . . . On the top of the Howth tram alone crying to the rain: *naked women!* What about that, eh?
>
> What about what? What else were they invented for?
>
> . . . You bowed to yourself in the mirror, stepping forward to applaud earnestly, striking face. . . . No-one saw: tell no-one. Books you were going to write with letters for titles. . . . Remember your epiphanies on green oval leaves, deeply deep. . . . Someone was to read them there after a few thousand years, a mahamanvantara. Pico della Mirandola like. Ay, very like a whale. When one reads these strange pages of one long gone one feels that one is at one with one who once . . .   [40.]

The sharp juxtaposition of this mystico-Symbolist nonsense with the "grainy sand" in the following line adds Joyce's endorsement to Stephen's self-criticism; clearly, we are not invited to take the aesthetic attitude Stephen parodies very seriously. Nor, for that matter, are we Stephen's third transformation, which begins with the sight of a "maze of dark cunning nets." He himself punctures the attitude of the *esprit libre* he

had adopted on his flight to Paris: "My latin quarter hat. God, we simply must dress the character."

With his latest transformation—failed missionary to Europe, bedrag-
gled Icarus—he is naturally less detached and less critical. He recognizes
his failure, but the recognition is qualified by his sense of undefeated
pride:

> His feet marched in sudden proud rhythm over the sand furrows, along
> by the boulders of the south wall. He stared at them proudly, piled stone
> mammoth skulls. Gold light on sea, on sand, on boulders. The sun is there,
> the slender trees, the lemon houses.   [42.]

Despite the earlier *débâcle,* Paris still represents something of value to
him, though he also recognizes the meaning for himself in Kevin Egan,
exiled revolutionary in Paris, forgotten, remembering Sion. But all his
retrospection leads him finally to a crucial decision which involves a crucial perception:

> He has the key. I will not sleep there when this night comes. . . . Take
> all, keep all. My soul walks with me, form of forms.   [44.]

The decision to leave again is more than a recognition that he has been
forced out; it is based on a firmer knowledge of what his nature positively
seeks—the discovery of itself in a deeper experience of ordinary life.

His self-identification with the introspectively heroic Hamlet is the last
transformation of matter portrayed. The significance of the parallel is
mainly suggested and dramatically qualified by Stephen's theory in
"Scylla and Charybdis," but it is also partly qualified (and naturally it
can only be partly) by his own self-critical reflections here. The significant point emerges from his fear of attack by a dog on the beach: "Respect his liberty. You will not be master of others or their slave." He
rejects all violence. The nightmare of history is within him—

> Famine, plague and slaughters. Their blood is in me, their lusts my waves.
> I moved among them on the frozen Liffey, that I, a changeling, among
> the spluttering resin fires. I spoke to no-one: none to me.   [45.]

As he says at the end of "Circe," it is *within* that he must kill the king
and the priest, symbols of spiritual tyranny and slavery. His means to
freedom are still silence, exile, and cunning—the evasion of action and
violence—but they also seem like cowardice. He wonders if he too is not
another "pretender": he fears drowning, he is not a strong swimmer; he
hates water; life may well overwhelm him. In short, ironic self-scrutiny
has begun to temper his will.

His reflections now turn reflectively upon themselves. He identifies
himself with the sniffing dog, "tatters," "poor dogsbody," fox who has
buried his mother under a hollybush; he sees himself "vulturing the
dead," "looking for something lost in a past life"—

Dogskull, dogsniff, eyes on the ground, moves to one great goal.   [46.]

His search for the self beneath the protean flux of life concludes with
such partial knowledge as he is capable of discovering and with a recognition of the nature of his search. The future can be only prefigured:
in a symbolic dream ("That man led me, spoke. I was not afraid"); in his
adolescent longing for contact with the female tides of life; in his continual effort to find his self in reality yet avoid the sterility of solipsism,
to grasp the significance of the sensible world, where subject and object
unite by "parallax":

> Hold hard. Coloured on a flat: yes, that's right. Flat I see, then think
> distance, near, far, flat I see, east, back. Ah, see now. Falls back suddenly,
> frozen in stereoscope. Click does the trick.   [48.]

The scribbled note for his poem is part of the action of the chapter, a
transformation that transcends all those that precede it, an emblem of
the "great goal" of his process of self-scrutiny, a symbol in little of *Ulysses*
itself. History, understood, moves towards the goal of art, but art is itself
a symbol of the wider spiritual life it ideally embodies. The phrase from
Yeats that Stephen quotes—"and no more turn aside and brood" [4]—sig-
nalizes his progress to a precarious *stasis,* or at least to a less kinetic frame
of mind, in which he tries to express the sound and unending movement
of water, his sense of the life into which he must plunge. That his present
stasis is precariously unstable is implicit in the way he tries to accept his
fear and the necessary rôle of death in life; the language reflects an intention, an effort, more than achieved assurance:

> God becomes man becomes fish becomes barnacle goose becomes feather-
> bed mountain. Dead breaths I living breathe, tread dead dust, devour a
> urinous offal from all dead. Hauled stark over the gunwale he breathes
> upward the stench of his green grave, his leprous nosehole snoring to
> the sun.
>   A seachange this, brown eyes saltblue. . . . Just you give it a fair
> trial. . . .
>   . . . Evening will find itself.
>   . . . Yes, evening will find itself in me, without me. All days make their
> end. . . .   [50.]

This is a passage less important for the symbolic relationships it suggests
(father—sea—life, urine—death, etc.) than for the dramatic significance
of its tone. Stephen's trust in the future is no mere involuntary drifting
with the stream. As the rest of the chapter has established, he has some
appreciation of the direction he must take and of the importance of

---

[4] From "Who will drive with Fergus now," which Joyce himself set and used to sing,
and which was one of his mother's favourites: see Stanislaus Joyce, *My Brother's Keeper*
[(New York: The Viking Press, Inc., 1958)], p. 143, and Patricia Hutchins, *James Joyce's
World* (London: [Methuen,] 1957), pp. 186–7.

growing towards it as well as simply willing it. His attitude still remains tentative, largely a passive, but watchful, waiting. In order to crystallize its positive value, Joyce must direct us outside Stephen's consciousness, and this he does with the "objectively" rendered episode of the ship at the very end of the chapter. Revealed to Stephen's significantly "rere regardant" gaze, her sails "brailed up on the crosstrees, homing, upstream, silently moving, a silent ship." With the final hint that he too is silently moving homeward, Stephen is dismissed, and the stage is set for Bloom. . . .

. . . Unlike Stephen, Bloom is not much aware of his own individual character, nor is he concerned with establishing any special relationship between himself and "life." He *is* alive. Of course, as we have seen, we cannot take him as fully alive, an unqualified hero, but his common humanity does represent that "life" against which Stephen is placed.

Bloom engages with everyday life at many points—that is the primary and obvious significance of the Odyssean parallel: he is an "allround-man." More important, however, is the way in which he engages—the sense in which his completeness is a sign of moral vitality and his consciousness the expression of a man truly, if not ideally, alive. For all his comparative unselfconsciousness he is not unreflective; for all his absorption in everyday matters, he is far from completely absorbed by them. His active consciousness is the clearest basis of his moral stature and his dramatic significance; he is a modern Odysseus, expressing himself less in outward action than in inward awareness. Much of his pathos, much of the dramatic irony, derives from this limitation of his capacity for physical action, but neither this, nor the limitations of his intelligence and sensibility, destroy his fundamental dignity. This dignity, however, lies ultimately in his unselfconscious being, in what he *is* unknown to himself, which it is one of Joyce's prime intentions to reveal to us in "Circe" and "Ithaca." The most important difference between Bloom and Stephen is that while Stephen aspires to a special dignity of his own as an artist, he has not achieved it, where Bloom does possess his dignity, and all the more securely because he is never for one moment aware that he does—or that he possesses heroic dimensions.

His first appearance places him in careful *contrast* to Stephen. The first fact we learn about him is his liking for the inner organs of beasts and fowls: "most of all he liked grilled mutton kidneys which gave to his palate a fine tang of faintly scented urine." We recall Stephen's reflection on the previous page, at the end of "Proteus": "dead breaths I living breathe, tread dead dust, devour a urinous offal from all dead." Where Stephen can slip free of the dead hand of the past and accept the necessity of death only fitfully and with difficulty, Bloom accepts death easily and transforms it into life.[5] One need not solemnly trace the symbolism of offal and urine through the whole book—though it is important to remember that Stephen and Bloom urinate together before they part—in order to perceive this major difference between the attitude of the two men to the dead past.[6] But so far this is not a realized difference, only the symbol of one dramatically established in the acts and consciousness of Bloom as the action proceeds.

In "Calypso," where Bloom's racial and familial relationships are first outlined, his awareness of them is inevitably his awareness of time. He considers a prospectus for recultivating Palestine; his mind turns to a sudden vision of the Holy Land as barren, exhausted, dead: "Grey horror seared his flesh. . . . Cold oils slid along his veins, chilling his blood: age crusting him with a salt cloak. Well, I am here now." From the horror of the past he turns to the living flesh of the present: "to smell the gentle smoke of tea, fume of the pan, sizzling butter. Be near her ample bedwarmed flesh. Yes, yes." This does not represent the whole of his attitude to the past, of course, but already it is clear that he does not agonize in the manner of Stephen. Even when he is immediately reminded that the ample bedwarmed flesh is waiting for Blazes Boylan, and the thought of the future chills him like the thought of the dead Promised Land, he does not remain fixed in his pain. His mind constantly shifts between past, present and future. The little discussion about "metempsychosis" establishes one of the verbal symbols of this movement: they say we have forgotten the lives we are supposed to have lived in the past, Bloom tells Molly; "some say they remember their past lives." Bloom himself forgets and remembers as a human being active in the present. If he recalls his ghosts, he salutes them and passes on. Where Stephen fights and struggles and has suicidal impulses, Bloom wears the past, and hence the present, more easily. At the end of "Hades," after he has faced the shadow of death, his thoughts "turn aside and no more brood": "Back to the world again. Enough of this place. . . . Plenty to see and hear and feel yet. Feel live warm beings near you. Let them sleep in their maggoty beds. They are not going to get me this innings. Warm beds: warm fullblooded life." He recognizes the savagery of life, the necessity even of killing ("Eat or be eaten. Kill! Kill!"), but, unlike Stephen, he can accept this without the knowledge corrupting the springs of action. He moves on always, rejecting the false *stasis* of imprisoning frustration: "Life those chaps out there must have, stuck in the same

---

[5] But contrast Kenner's comment on this passage, p. 213.

[6] In his article on "Dante and Mrs. Bloom," *loc. cit.*, p. 89, Mr. Tindall briefly discusses the symbolism of urine, which he takes as water: "to Joyce water meant life and making water was not only creating life but, by extention, creating art." This seems questionable, both physiologically and poetically. Making water in this sense is to eliminate waste-matter; urine is not the same as water; and Stephen creates neither life nor art.

spot. Irish Lights board. Penance for their sins." To Bloom, life presents itself as an inescapable activity, the moral exigencies of which control the influence of the past as much as the influence of the past controls them.

Like Stephen, he recognizes the general patterns that circumscribe the life of the individual, though his awareness has a very different tone: "It's the blood sinking in the earth gives new life. Same idea those jews they said killed the christian boy. Every man his price." He preserves the same tone in his reflections about himself too:

> June that was too I wooed. The year returns. History repeats itself. . . .
> Life, love, voyage round your own little world. And now? . . .
>   All quiet on Howth now. The distant hills seem. Where we. The rho-dodendrons. I am a fool perhaps. He gets the plums and I the plumstones. Where I come in. All that old hill has seen. Names change: that's all. Lovers: yum yum.
>   . . . She kissed me. My youth. Never again. Only once it comes. Or hers. Take the train there tomorrow. No. Returning not the same. . . . The new I want. Nothing new under the sun. . . . Think you're escaping and run into yourself. Longest way round is the shortest way home. . . . All changed. Forgotten. The young are old. . . .   [376–377.]

Bloom's pathos here arises from his helpless recognition of ineluctability; it is the helplessness of humanity itself. As the contrasting echoes of Stephen's parable of the plums and of his speculations about the actualization of the self in experience suggest, Bloom's recognition is an experiential one, not a merely theoretical acceptance like Stephen's. For him, the life-cycle, the biological limits of the individual's experience, are a felt part of his actual life. He accepts the universe not because he has found any intellectual formula into which he can fit it, but for the more compelling reason that he simply has to. Inasmuch as he does so, moreover, he represents one of the values Joyce expresses in the work. Bloom's simple awareness of these natural patterns is not offered as stupidity or moral surrender, but as a kind of unthinking wisdom. Thus, when Bloom hears of Mrs. Purefoy's difficult lying-in, "his heavy pitying gaze absorbed her news. His tongue clacked in compassion. Dth! Dth!"—the suggestion of the life-cycle is Joyce's as much as, if not more than, Bloom's. Or again, when Bloom actually visits the hospital and hears of the death of a friend, he stands silent "in wanhope," whereupon the narrative comments in general terms on the inevitability of death. Even though Joyce makes no unqualified endorsement of Bloom, he does in this endorse his characteristic attitude. So that when Bloom's attitude to time and Stephen's are finally juxtaposed in "Ithaca," we should recognize the sense in which the former's is a criticism of the latter's. Standing beneath the stars and ready to part, they hear, as Bloom had heard among his thoughts of Dignam's death in the morning, the bells of St. George's church striking the passage of time:

What echoes of that sound were by both and each heard?

By Stephen, an echo of his unpurged remorse:

> *Liliata rutilantium. Turma circumdet.*
> *Iubilantium te virginum. Chorus excipiat.*

By Bloom, an echo of death, and yet also an incipient turn from it:

> *Heigho, heigho,*
> *Heigho, heigho.*   [704.]

His attitude can be easily mistaken for a completely passive resignation. In fact, it is something rather different, an *active* resignation, so to speak. Certainly, Bloom does not do obvious battle with his world, though we should remember that he has lost one job "for giving lip" and stands up to the Citizen where no one else does.[7] He does occasionally surrender to a sentimental and uselessly nostalgic acceptance of things as they are —his daughter, Milly, usually provokes this reaction: "A soft qualm, regret, flowed down his backbone, increasing. Will happen, yes. Prevent. Useless: can't move . . ." He submits without overt protest or resistance to the petty indignities that mark his social exclusion. On the other hand, his important acceptances are made with an awareness of the complexities; they are not easy resignations by any means. His proposals to Stephen for future meetings—meetings that William Empson has argued are to be regarded as having really taken place and to be the real point of the book[8]—are the product of his deep and pathetic desire for friendship. The proposals are, in fact, accepted by Stephen. Bloom, however, knows more than to take the arrangement at face-value:

> What rendered problematic for Bloom the realisation of these mutually selfexcluding propositions?
> The irreparability of the past: once at a performance of Albert Hengler's circus . . . an intuitive particoloured clown . . . had publicly declared that he (Bloom) was his (the clown's) papa. The imprevidibility of the future: once in the summer of 1898 he (Bloom) had marked a florin . . . for possible, circuitous or direct, return.
>
> Was the clown Bloom's son?
> No.
>
> Had Bloom's coin returned?
> Never.   [696.]

---

[7] J. Mitchell Morse also warns against over-estimating Bloom's passivity; see "The Disobedient Artist: Joyce and Loyola," *Publications of the Modern Language Association of America*, LXXII, 1957, pp. 1018–35, now chapter 6 of *The Sympathetic Alien* [(New York: New York University Press, 1959)]. As Mr. Morse points out, it is Bloom's moral *activity* that is the most striking thing about him, and he is in some ways set off, as predominantly a moralist, against the ambivalent and relativistic imagination of Stephen.

[8] William Empson, "The Theme of *Ulysses*," *Kenyon Review*, XVIII, 1956, pp. 26–52.

In short, if Bloom accepts the past as it has been and life as it is, it is not because he does not also desire them otherwise.

Probably the most important illustration of his whole general attitude is provided by his feelings about Molly's adultery. These change, or rather crystallize, during the course of the book, and in fact this crystallization is one of the central threads of the action. Bloom's first reactions are distress and emotional flight; when he sees Boylan in the street, for example, he meets the insupportable by escaping into the Museum, turning to the refuge of "cold statues" and "the Greek architecture." When he does allow his mind to dwell on the situation, it is with a certain self-pity and nostalgia: "Me. And me now." Later on, the art of song in the "Sirens" chapter induces another mood, more reflective, more detached, in which he is able to generalize his situation:

> Thou lost one. All songs on that theme. Yet more Bloom stretched his string. Cruel it seems. Let people get fond of each other: lure them on. Then tear asunder. . . . Human life. . . .
> Yet too much happy bores. He stretched more, more. Are you not happy in your? Twang. It snapped.   [277.]

His personal isolation is heavily emphasized in this chapter, of course, but it is an isolation which is partly an active movement of his mind towards a fuller understanding of his past and present situation (that the chapter is focused upon an *art,* and that Bloom's capacity to comprehend his situation is as limited as the elasticity of his string, are equally significant). But understanding of a sort he does achieve:

> I too, last my race. Milly young student. Well, my fault perhaps. No son. Rudy. Too late now. Or if not? If not? If still?
> He bore no hate.
> Hate. Love. Those are names. Rudy. Soon I am old.   [285.]

By evening ("Nausicaa"), he has begun to see Molly's behaviour in an even wider context as only one more illustration of the laws of attraction, of a universal natural process. And his reconciliation to her proposed tour with Boylan is significantly juxtaposed with his charitable thoughts about the Citizen who had abused and assaulted him. His mood is not quite a surrender to mere amoral natural processes; it includes a positive charity, a compassionate realization of the common human lot. The mocking sound of the cuckoo that concludes the chapter seems cheap, almost irrelevant, by comparison; its irony leaves his substance untouched. Still further, in "Circe" and "Eumaeus," he comes to recognize that his own sexual failure has a good deal to do with Molly's infidelity. Gradually he moves from *kinesis* to "a silent contemplation," which is summed up in "Ithaca":

> With what antagonistic sentiments were his subsequent reflections affected?
> Envy, jealousy, abnegation, equanimity.   [732.]

Envy of Boylan, jealousy of Molly, abnegation for complicated motives, and equanimity because, finally, Molly's act is "more than inevitable, irreparable."

> Why more abnegation than jealousy, less envy than equanimity?
> From outrage (matrimony) to outrage (adultery) there arose nought but outrage (copulation) yet the matrimonial violator of the matrimonially violated had not been outraged by the adulterous violator of the adulterously violated. . . .   [733.]

> By what reflections did he, a conscious reactor against the void of incertitude, justify to himself his sentiments?
> [The naturalness of the attraction and the act]: the futility of triumph or protest of vindication: the inanity of extolled virtue: the lethargy of nescient matter: the apathy of the stars.   [744.]

The equanimity results in a final satisfaction in the warmth and beauty of Molly's female "mute immutable mature animality"—the eternally given, but never to be possessed, richness of the flesh.

> The visible signs of antesatisfaction?
> An approximate erection: a solicitous adversion: a gradual elevation: a tentative revelation: a silent contemplation.

> Then?
> He kissed the plump mellow yellow smellow melons of her rump, on each plump melonous hemisphere, in their mellow yellow furrow, with obscure prolonged provocative melonsmellonous osculation.

> The visible signs of postsatisfaction?
> A silent contemplation: a tentative velation: a gradual abasement: a solicitous aversion: a proximate erection.   [734–735.]

That Bloom's silent contemplative *stasis* is followed by a kind of *kinesis* (characteristically weak and ambiguous, we might notice) marks the difference between the continuing process of life and the fixity of art. If Bloom's slaying of the suitors by a victory over himself seems paltry or despicable by contrast with Ulysses' more conclusive methods, we must not therefore suppose that Joyce is being simply ironical at Bloom's expense.[9] He rarely supports his characters in postures of moral violence; his notion of true moral activity is less overtly militant. Bloom kills his enemies, as Stephen hopes to do, within, and they are not Molly's suitors so much as his own inner frustrating imbalance of envy, jealousy and excessive abnegation. He wins a temporary equanimity, but clearly no final victory. Life, Joyce implies, is not art; there is nothing concluded, no absolute command possible.

---

[9] This *is* the view taken by [Douglas] Knight, "The Reading of *Ulysses,*" [*ELH,* XIX (March 1952)], pp. 72–3, 65–6. But [W. B.] Stanford [*The Ulysses Theme* (Oxford: Basil Blackwell, 1954)], pp. 218–19, seems to me to be closer to the truth in his description and evaluation of this part of the story.

Bloom's comparative freedom from guilt, remorse, nostalgia, jealousy, egotistic assertion and other nightmares of history is to be contrasted with Stephen's bondage. Similarly, his curiosity and openness to experience, unlike Stephen's search for "life," express a desire to place the past at the disposal of the future. Where Stephen is a novice, incapable as yet of using the past and so in search of a spiritual father, Bloom is oppressed by the complementary frustration that, as the last of his race, he has no one to whom he can hand on his spiritual gift.

The problem haunts him all through the book, emerging perhaps most explicitly as he sits with the young men in the hospital ("Oxen of the Sun") where he has been drawn by his compassion for Mrs. Purefoy and kept by his half-conscious attraction to Stephen. After a passage in which Mulligan mocks Stephen's divine analogies ("the black panther was himself the ghost of his own father"),[10] Bloom, contemplating the label on a bottle of Bass, passes to the "incorruptible eon of the gods." "What is the age of the soul of man?" Bloom relives his own youth—"he is young Leopold, as in a retrospective arrangement, a mirror within a mirror (hey, presto!), he beholdeth himself." But the mirror clouds; "now he is himself paternal and these about him might be his sons. Who can say? The wise father knows his own child." His intense regret that he has not fathered a living man-child, his unwilled frustration, reflects mirror-wise the deliberate contraception that forms the abstract theme of the chapter:

> No, Leopold! Name and memory solace thee not. That youthful illusion of thy strength was taken from thee and in vain. No son of thy loins is by thee. There is none now to be for Leopold, what Leopold was for Rudolph. [413–414.]

For Bloom, as his "soul is wafted over regions of cycles of cycles of generations that have lived," the past is barren, "Agendath is a waste land," horrible and damned. But womankind, "link between nations and generations . . . sacred life-giver," still remains, with her potentialities for the future—"And, lo, wonder of metempsychosis, it is she, the everlasting bride, harbinger of the daystar, the bride, ever virgin. It is she, Martha, thou lost one, Millicent, the young, the dear, the radiant."

Bloom cannot understand, any more than Stephen, what he can offer the younger man. It is certainly not his good advice, nor anything he could formulate consciously; the essence of his gift is that he is unconscious of it—it is what he represents and is. Partly, of course, he is Stephen's possible "material" as an artist, the City against which Stephen reacts and which is therefore the necessary subject of his self-reflective art. More, however, he represents a relationship to the history of his own people that is analogous to Stephen's and yet unlike it. It is part of Bloom's relevance that, like Stephen, he also embodies a racial tradition

---

[10] For the identification of the black panther with Christ, see [A. M.] Klein ["The Black Panther: A Study in Technique," *Accent*, X, 1950].

(which is also a spiritual tradition), even though it is consciously present to him only in fragments.[11] His "defective mnemotechnic" links him with attitudes and patterns of life that he unwittingly re-experiences in his own circumstances. They are not Jewish in the narrowest sense; they have a wider reference, which emerges in "Circe," and to Bloom himself Christ is a symbol both of his values and the mixed tradition whence they derive: "Well, his uncle was a jew, says he. Your God was a jew. Christ was a jew like me." The racial parallel with Stephen is explicitly drawn in "Ithaca": both inherit a long and rich tradition, both are conscious only of fragments of it. Yet the contrast between the two men is equally explicit and equally important. Where Stephen consciously (and uneasily) rejects, Bloom accepts. Once, earlier, Bloom had impatiently criticized his father's beliefs and practices; now, they appear to him "not more rational than they had then appeared, not less rational than other beliefs and practices now appeared." As we shall see, this detachment is by no means the whole of Bloom's attitude, for much else in it is, as it should be, quite unconscious; his significance, nevertheless, is as an example, parallel to but contrasting with Stephen's case, of an involuntary involvement, an involuntary exile, but a real if unemphatic freedom.

Such contrasts between Bloom and Stephen would have little point without the relationship that lies at the centre of the whole book: they are here, as always, complementary counterparts, "fundamental and dominant," actuality and potentiality. The father-son theme is one metaphor for this; the theory about Shakespeare another; the figure of Christ, in whom are expressed the dichotomies of crucified citizen (Man) and crucified artist (God), of action and passion, of involvement and freedom, is yet a third. By its different aspects, the symbol of Christ links the diverse facts of the situation Joyce explores, but the meaning of Joyce's *symbol* lies in the facts it orders. Unless the values it relates and expresses are themselves realized, imaginatively established as denotations, the symbol remains empty and inert. Stephen cannot be portrayed as the suffering and crucified Artist redeeming the world; in the very terms of the book, he lacks the freedom, the love, and the capacity, and has only the desire to become an artist and the uneasy realization of what is involved. For the most part, he rejects. He is Christ as the "black panther," and the very incompleteness of his state provokes the metaphor of Lucifer. Stephen as Christ often passes over into Stephen as Satan: it is a sign of his immaturity that he is ready to adopt either rôle at any time. He is not quite *der Geist, der stets verneint*, of course; it is rather that his affirmations seem only velleities, or at best unachieved intentions. Bloom, therefore, must carry the heavier burden of significance—be not merely passive but active, not merely involved but free, not merely representa-

---

[11] J. Prescott has collected and annotated many of these fragments in his articles in the *Modern Language Quarterly*, XIII, 1952, pp. 149–62; and *Modern Language Notes*, LXVII, 1952, pp. 334–6.

tive of, but crucified by, his world, the scapegoat and redeemer, and tied all the while by close analogy and parallel with Stephen, so that the reader may perceive what Stephen must learn to perceive: the values Bloom represents and the deep similarity between the two of them. Bloom's ambiguous position, his example, his love, his freedom, if only he could understand them, are what Stephen must come to. For the parallels between the two men are fundamental: Bloom's exclusion from society reflects Stephen's spiritual exile from it (a situation neatly portrayed early in the book when they are both at the newspaper office). Each is an alien in the life of Dublin. They are both isolated by "parallax," each in his personal world, and only a full spiritual outgoing— or its symbol, art—can alleviate their condition. They both reject violence and the senseless agitations of the mob as incompatible with the freedom and order they seek. They are both keyless, citizen and artist, yet both "born adventurers" and committed to the essential isolation of their individuality. They both have personal courage, one in his pride, the other in his humility. Both strive to awake from the nightmare of history, though Stephen cannot yet realize what values he seeks, and Bloom cannot express what he means. But his attempts are the justification for the Christ metaphor—his positive courage in "Cyclops" for example, but more especially his unalienated integrity in "Circe." The most important structural parallel between the two protagonists, in fact, is that between Stephen's self-examination of the past, which is conducted consciously, and Bloom's, which is necessarily much less conscious; between "Proteus" and "Circe." The connections between these two chapters, with all that is implied by those connections, is what really establishes the metaphor of paternity.

The Advent of Bloom

by Anthony Cronin

Those who are intent on turning *Ulysses* into mere anagram and allegory are perhaps so because they are incapable of appreciating the "profane joy" with which ordinary mundanities are invested in it. Perhaps too they are unsympathetic towards the kind of life which in large part it portrays; incapable of savouring, for example, the citizen's language as Joyce himself savours it, to some extent even uninterested in the primary satisfactions we derive from language and the representation of life. Whatever Joyce's secondary purposes may have been, whatever elaborations of technique and allusion he indulges in, that is not where the true greatness of the book lies. Mr. Bloom may be Shakespeare; what is important to us is that he is Bloom. The fact that he is not only Odysseus but Shakespeare and Sinbad the sailor as well, does not account for his fascination: as if Joyce's talents lay simply in the ability to invent more and more "meaningful" parallels. Nor is the worth of the book to be suggested by explaining what it is really "about," as if Joyce was a nostrum vendor, a mystic or a philosopher. What the book is "about" may be important in the sense that every writer may have to be judged by the *quality* of his vision as well as by his ability to express it, though this is a debatable point which would require a lot of definition. It is irrelevant, if we mean by what it is "about" a mere attitude hidden in the hermeneutics which, if discovered, would only have the force of an attitude and not the force of art. To speak of the quality of a man's vision is not to speak of the worth of his mere, paraphrasable opinions about history or religion or our place in the cosmos: an ideology which could be discovered and exclaimed over like that of any other fashionable sage. Every recorded statement we have exhibits Joyce's total contempt for abstract ideas, his cheerful and not at all hag-ridden scepticism about religion, his indifference to the profundities of the new psychology. A good deal of confusion exists about the nature of his vision; he has been accused of everything from sentimentality, to indifference, to rage; but before asking what his book is about, it is equally, if not more important, to enquire into the almost totally neglected question of what in fact it is.

What it is can perhaps be seen more clearly by a preliminary examination of what it is not. It is to begin with unlike almost any other novel ever written. Almost all other novels are patterned dramatically. They are concerned not only with a situation, but with a situation that unfolds itself, a plot, which progresses through a chain of causation, often involving coincidence, frequently violence or at least death. Life in such books is to a greater or lesser degree subordinated to event. We get little or no static living, but only those events which contribute more or less to the main stream. Irrelevancies may be included but they are usually said to have had some influence on the behaviour of the characters in the crises of event. Life has to be contained within the pattern of event; it is therefore neater and smaller than real living. The events, being patterned, are also neater than the events in life, which have usually no pattern. Plot events are dialectic, being explainable in terms of each other, whereas events in life are frequently isolated and inexplicable, or, if explicable, they are so only in terms of an infinite conglomeration of factors which would stretch outside the book. The events out of which the pattern of event is made are both more clear-cut and more probable than the events in life, though the pattern as a whole is usually highly improbable.

The justification for this patterning in most serious works is presumably more than the amusement of the reader with a good story, the satisfaction of his aroused curiosity, or the gratification of his delight in violence or intrigue. The justification, if there is one, must rest both on the negative claim that much is allowable in letters that does not obtain in life, like speaking in iambic pentameters; and on the positive claim that the dramatic arrangement of life in a book is a means of producing pity, terror, catharsis or any other emotion that it is proper to feel in the presence of a work of art. The latter claim rests on the assumption that an artificial arrangement of life in a pattern of event and a curtailment of life in the interests of a pattern of event can be a source of aesthetic satisfaction.

Still the falsification of life remains. We may say that this falsification is tacitly admitted between the writer and the reader, just as a composer of opera tacitly agrees with the audience that people do not communicate by singing at each other; it exists all the same. There is no such falsification of life in *Ulysses*. Of course *Ulysses* is not just a "slice of life," as it was once assumed to be, though even as a slice of life, if that were conceivable, it would still be very great. (Samuel Beckett has said that Joyce thought it was perhaps "over-constructed": some of the commentators seem to suggest that it is constructed to the exclusion of everything but the construction and is the "greater" for that.) But the necessary limitations of Joyce's form do not result in a falsification of life as do those of the ordinary novel of self-sustaining event. In *Ulysses,* for the first time in fiction, life could be almost completely itself. Where in the novel of event each picture, each person, each happening, each thought has to be subordinated to the overall pattern, in *Ulysses* they are allowed their own importance. Nothing is a mere turning point in the narrative, a mere link in a chain of causation, a puppet called upon to give the story a twist or a push. Though there is event—there is a good deal of real drama in the episode of the funeral carriage: the stony silence with which, as Irish Catholics believing in the last sacraments, his companions greet Bloom's assertion that sudden death is the best, and the unfortunate reference to suicide—it has its own right to exist independently. Conversation, anecdote, thought, desultory impression, image and happening are freed at last from their long subordination to plot. They do not have to play a part; or to suffer drastic curtailment because they are counted as irrelevant. Of course they have to have some significance: *Ulysses* would be a terrifying monstrosity if they had not. Each is, in fact, an epiphany, to use Joyce's own term, of greater or lesser importance; but their importance is not that of mere contributing factors to a story. This is the texture of life, not the artificiality of contrived event; and, as a result, *Ulysses* is a prose work much of which one can read as one does a poem, for the epiphanies and the words themselves, not for the sake of a story to which they contribute, though they do, of course, contribute to the total impression the book makes.

Succeeding in this, Joyce has succeeded in eliminating the underlying falsehood of the novel. Though there may be a tacit agreement between the reader and the writer that things do not happen as the novel suggests, that they are not so isolated, nor clear-cut, nor interlocked, nor dramatic; and that most of life is composed of experiences which do not serve the novelist's purposes, there nevertheless remains a residual feeling on the reader's part that things ought to be like this, that fiction is in some way better than fact, a feeling that is bad for fact, for living, and, one might add, bad for fiction too. The various confusions about "naturalism" and "realism" do not help matters. Zola, the great prophet of naturalism, is full of the most preposterous melodrama. Nor, for all that we hear about the influence or non-influence of *Ulysses,* has the novel, even the so-called serious novel, altered very much, if at all, in this respect: event is still preponderant at the expense of texture.

But along with this liberation of ordinary living from the shackles of plot, goes an enormous extension of the range of life included. If one of the simplest but most important functions of the writer is to extend the recorded area of human experience, Joyce has flung the frontiers further out than any writer of this century—and it is to the particular honour of this century that whole new tracts of human experience, never before explored, have been brought under the amending and meliorating rule of the artist's compassion. Whatever his secondary purposes may have been, whatever intertwining strands of meaning and experience *Ulysses* contains, whatever the point of the story, if there is a point, all his statements go to show that Joyce considered it a major, indeed *the* major part of his vocation as a writer to speak the truths that had never before been spoken. As his brother points out, he was a realist and an extremist who had had the advantage over most writers of having to conduct his after-dinner discussions about life in a country in which the dinner itself was often lacking. From the time when he told Stanislaus that "he had no doubt that most artists, even the greatest, belied the life they knew," so that "literature . . . was a parody of life" and came to believe, according to Stanislaus, that "the poetry of noble sentiments, the romantic music, and the dramatic passions, with a dominant love theme, which culture offered him as a true poetic insight into the universal problems of human life, did not fit in with life as he knew it"—his primary purpose as an artist was clear. He ended his first adolescent manifesto with a quotation from Ibsen: " 'What will you do in our society, Miss Hessel?' asked Rorlund—'I will let in fresh air, pastor,' answered Lona." And in *Ulysses* itself he writes of the "secrets, silent, stony" which "sit in the dark palaces of both our hearts: secrets weary of their tyranny: tyrants willing to be dethroned."

Part of this process was technical: ordinary living had to be freed from the distortions of plot, from the skimping and twisting essential in the novel of event, of men and women in dramatic conflict, so that it could achieve its own entelechy. But along with this liberation from the tyranny of narrative went a tremendous extension of the amount of life included. Joyce includes so much that had never been included in art before, of man not only in his basic sexuality but in his basic sordidity as well, that he must stand as one of the great liberators of the human spirit from the tyranny of its own secrets. And not only did he bring such things within the scope of expression; he brought them, which is more important, within the scope of art.

A man's message is his way of seeing. Instead of asking whether Bloom will or will not get his breakfast in bed in the morning, and what, if anything, is the significance of the meeting between Bloom and Stephen, it is perhaps better to ask what spirit pervades and informs *Ulysses*. The mood of a book should operate on the reader more surely and a great deal more subtly than anything that could be described as its message.

"The theme of *Ulysses* is simple," says Mr. Richard Ellmann in his book, *James Joyce,* "casual kindness overcomes unconscionable power." Mr. Harry Levin in *James Joyce,* however, will have nothing to do with such calendar mottoes. He thinks that the book offers no hope and no comfort, that there is only the author's creative intensity, beating down "like an aroused volcano upon an ancient city, overtaking its doomed inhabitants in forum or temple, at home or at brothel, and petrifying them in the insensate agonies of paralysis." (Incidentally, it is difficult to make out from Mr. Levin's celebrated study whether he enjoyed reading the book or not.) Mr. Hugh Kenner thinks the book is a gargantuan, ironic machine, and he favours the dilemma of Modern Industrial Man, the dead remains of classical and Christian civilisation being incapsulated in the speech of the characters, whose language is the language of eighteenth-century Dublin, in order to show how the mighty are fallen. That the language of the nameless narrator of the Cyclops episode is the language of eighteenth-century Dublin one is inclined to doubt. It is sufficiently obvious that neither he nor the citizen are Industrial Men, or industrious men either, for the matter of that. Many people have found the book terrible. George Orwell believed that it was "the product of a special vision of life, the vision of a Catholic who has lost his faith. What Joyce is saying is, 'Here is life without God. Just look at it!' " (Apart altogether from whether we really feel that Joyce is saying anything like this when we read the book, it is perhaps worth remarking here that though all the evidence goes to show that he was a cheerful sort of unbeliever, it is rather to be doubted whether, as Mr. Eliot has pointed out to the present author, anybody brought up as an Irish Catholic could ever, deep in his being, envisage the world as "godless.") Mr. William Empson thinks that Bloom's isolation and Stephen's megalomania are so monstrous that, if the book is to be bearable, it must have a happy ending. He thinks Joyce meant to indicate that Stephen went to bed with Molly, the first woman not a whore he had ever been to bed with, and that this not only produced an enormous improvement in his character, but was the means of restoring conjugal relations between the Blooms.

All this disagreement would seem to suggest that there is a deep inherent difficulty in deciding what are the values of the book, even, let us say, to put it perfectly simply, in deciding whether it is a cheerful book or a very gloomy one.

The values with which we are surrounded in life are, so to speak, concentric: near at hand are those of the parental, or, later, the human circle in which we move, outside them the values of society and beyond that again what are alleged to be the values of God or of the grave. Before discussing his larger vision it would be as well to see whether Joyce accepts, rejects, endorses or modifies the ordinary close-at-hand values of society and it is perhaps instructive to compare him with a famous, and in many ways remarkable, novelist who is said to have attacked them. . . .

Thackeray quite obviously expects the reader to share his beliefs, his prejudices and his values: his book [*Vanity Fair*] is written in the assurance that there is a common ground and that it is quite easily reached by people of good will. Joyce does not seem to have any prejudices whatever about values or beliefs. As far as can be seen, initially at least, what he expects from the reader is only a level of literacy and a freedom from atavistic reaction to sexual abnormality, dirt, drink, dishonesty, failure (how failure sets Thackeray off, one way or the other!) and all societal obstacles to admiration or compassion, or at least a cool regard. The people of *Ulysses* are a pretty battered lot. Debt, drink, idleness afflict practically all of them, Stephen included. Bloom is not idle, but he is not very industrious either, and his record of false starts and lost jobs in Cuffe's, Wisdom Hely's, Thom's and elsewhere certainly amounts to failure, a failure from which only the nine hundred pounds and the insurance policy inherited from his father protect him. Parts of his past, the making up to Mrs. Riordan, for example, or the suggestion to Molly that she should pose in the nude for the rich dilettantes in Merrion Square, are not very creditable in terms of the sort of values we imbibe from Thackeray or indeed any of the writing of the past. Nor would the rest of the people in the book appear, by these standards, very prepossessing. The three old men who foregather in the Ormonde would not have much to say for themselves in most courts of judgment of life. Ben Dollard of the bass baritone has squandered his substance and reduced himself to penury; Bob Cowley is in the hands of the bailiffs, Simon Dedalus's daughters are near starving while he drinks. Yet there seems to be nothing much on their consciences that a ball of malt and a bar of a song will not amend. Is Joyce's attitude towards them condemnatory, compassionate or indifferent? Are we supposed to admire them as they evidently to some extent admire themselves?

The first thing one is forced to conclude is that if *Ulysses* is an examination of hell, or futility, or an unredeemed decay, or anything else of that nature—which it is frequently alleged to be—it presents some very curious characteristics. Here is a passage from *Stephen Hero* which is an illuminating contrast to the tone of *Ulysses*. Stephen has gone to the Adelphi Hotel to look for Cranly. He finds him in the billiard-room and sits down beside him to watch the game:

> It was a three-handed game. An elderly clerk, evidently in a patronising mood, was playing two of his junior colleagues. The elderly clerk was a tall stout man who wore gilt spectacles on a face like a red shrivelled apple. He was in his shirt-sleeves and he played and spoke so briskly as to suggest that he was drilling rather than playing. The young clerks were both clean-shaven. One of them was a thickset young man who played doggedly without speaking, the other was an effervescent young man with white eyebrows and a nervous manner. Cranly and Stephen watched the game progress, creep from point to point. The heavy young man put his ball on the floor three times in succession and the scoring was so slow that the marker came and stood by the table as a reminder that the twenty minutes had passed. The players chalked their cues oftener than before and, seeing that they were in earnest about finishing the game, the marker did not say

anything about the time. But his presence acted upon them. The elderly clerk jerked his cue at his ball, making a bad stroke, and stood back from the table blinking his eyes and saying "Missed that time." The effervescent young clerk hurried to his ball, made a bad stroke and, looking along his cue, said "Ah!". The dogged young man shot his ball straight into the top pocket, a fact which the marker registered at once on the broken marking-board. The elderly clerk peered for a few critical seconds over the rim of his glasses, made another bad stroke and, at once proceeding to chalk his cue, said briefly and sharply to the effervescent young man "Come on now, White. Hurry up now."

The hopeless pretence of those three lives before him, their unredeemable servility, made the back of Stephen's eyes feel burning hot. He laid his hand on Cranly's shoulder and said impetuously:

"We must go at once. I can't stand it any longer."

If this is hell, and it is, we are out of it in *Ulysses*. There is no one in *Ulysses* whose life is a hopeless pretence or who presents an aspect of unredeemable servility. Indeed there is scarcely anyone who does not bear himself with panache, with gaiety, with scurrility or with pride. Bloom, though insulted, certainly feels no inferiority. And it is instructive to compare the mood of the portraiture in *Ulysses* with Joyce's treatment of the same people in *Dubliners*. It comes as something of a shock to realise that the Ignatius Gallagher whose scoop we hear about in the *Freeman's Journal* office is the vulgarian who appeared from London in "A Little Cloud." The Lenehan of *Ulysses* is a great deal less insufferable (and more cheerful) than the Lenehan who hangs about while Corley extracts money from the slavey in "Two Gallants.") Martin Cunningham, Jack Power, McCoy, Tom Kernan are all treated harshly and satirically in the earlier book but with what almost amounts to gentleness in the later. But the strangest blossoming concerns someone who had appeared only in the *Portrait* and *Stephen Hero*. Simon Dedalus now at last attains those legendary dimensions that the *Portrait* had grudgingly hinted at. He is given size, humour, style and pathos; it is made quite clear that he retains his daughter's amused affection even though he refuses her the money he proceeds to spend in the Ormonde; and his song in that place is given its full worth of beauty. We see him well away now on his downward path, in the glory of his scandalous autumn, and we leave him in full voice.

Joyce openly enjoys his material in *Ulysses* and grants it a worth which, for any but satirical purposes, is denied to it in *Dubliners*. I have no wish to suggest that the book is Pickwickian or that Simon Dedalus is a first cousin of the Cheeryble brothers; nor that the book presents a happier view of experience simply because it is funnier than *Dubliners* or the *Portrait*. But the humour of *Ulysses* can scarcely be other than sympathetic, for the simple reason that most of it is made by the characters themselves. It is their tongues and imaginations, the vitality of their language, the grotesquery of their wit which, as much as anything else, draw us back to the book and make it, whatever else it may be, one of the funniest in the language.

And there can hardly be any question but that Joyce enjoys them just as they enjoy themselves. The Citizen is well aware that he is giving a performance, albeit straightfaced, and he is certainly enjoying himself. In *Dubliners* the comedy is of a kind that gives Joyce and the reader bitter and mordant amusement—the asinine conversation about the doctrine of infallibility in the story, "Grace," for example—but which the characters themselves can hardly be said to share. *Dubliners* may be comic; it is anything but humorous. If the man who wrote *Dubliners* has looked upon the Gorgon's head, the man who wrote *Ulysses* has certainly not been turned to stone.

And it is often forgotten how much of *Ulysses* explores the lives of people other than simply Bloom and Stephen: when Joyce's narrowness of scope as a novelist is complained of, it should be remembered how skilfully and often how movingly he touched in the whole background of a minor character's life: Martin Cunningham's wife, J. J. O'Molloy's attempts to borrow money, the Dignam household, Mrs. Breen's marriage, Father Conmee's complacency, Zoe's patter. Hundreds of such details, flitting across Bloom's mind or emerging from some conversation, evoke, seldom without compassion, the lives of a dozen others.

The people of *Ulysses* are not a cross-section of the bourgeois world: they are Joyce's father's world, that narrow world of drink and song, of debt and redemption, of vulgarity, wit and seedy gentility that his father inhabited. It is through singing that they are, for the most part, acquainted; and Joyce himself loved song. "The humour of *Ulysses* is his; its people are his friends. The book is his spittin' image," he said to Louis Gillet after his father's death. And, apart from their feeling for song, the people of *Ulysses* are by no means without their virtues: their ready understanding of misfortune, their willingness to help each other beat the rap, their refusal to judge each other by the standards of mere respectability are apparent. *Ulysses*, says Mr. Harry Levin in his book, *James Joyce: A Critical Introduction*, is an epic "entirely lacking in the epic virtues of love, friendship and magnanimity," but he seems to be forgetting or ignoring something deeply important in the characters' attitude to each other:

> For a few days tell him, Father Cowley said anxiously.
> Ben Dollard halted and stared, his loud orifice open, a dangling button of his coat wagging brightbacked from its thread as he wiped away the heavy shraums that clogged his eyes to hear aright.
> What few days? he boomed. Hasn't your landlord distrained for rent?
> He has, Father Cowley said.
> Then our friend's writ is not worth the paper it's printed on, Ben Dol-

lard said. The landlord has the prior claim. I gave him all the particulars. 29 Windsor Avenue. Love is the name?

That's right, Father Cowley said . . . But are you sure of that?

You can tell Barabbas from me, Ben Dollard said, that he can put that writ where Jacko put the nuts.

He led Father Cowley boldly forward linked to his bulk.

Filberts I believe they were, Mr. Dedalus said, as he dropped his glasses on his coatfront, following them.

And along with their readiness to help, however desultory, idle or unreliable it may be, they have a gaiety and courage in face of their own usually well-deserved misfortunes, which is part of an attitude to life that may at bottom be weak and self-deceiving, but which also augurs a certain generosity and recklessness of spirit not markedly characteristic of the bourgeois world. Apart from Stephen's student friends and the librarians these people are all, or nearly all, failures of one kind or another. Even the editor of the *Freeman* is, according to Ned Lambert, a "sad case" of "incipient jigs." That Joyce should have thought an exposure of their limitations and weaknesses worth the full weight of so much of the book is inconceivable. Many judgments on the people of *Ulysses* seem to proceed from a sort of upset liberalism or shocked Protestantism which finds them and their humour an outrage, but these judgments are certainly not shared by Joyce himself. Yeats was nearer the mark when he agreed that *Ulysses* was "cruel" but added that it was "our Irish cruelty, and also our kind of strength." A great deal of the humour of these people is admittedly cruel, but then it is *Galgenhumor,* the product of misfortune, and those who find it too cruel would probably find most Irish humour so, from Lever's to Samuel Beckett's, and might profitably even take a closer look at some of the humour of Somerville and Ross.

The confusion of morality with mere respectability which is almost endemic in the English mind is entirely absent in Joyce, and the vulgarity of judgment by mere status is entirely absent from his book. The people of *Ulysses,* though they belong, very roughly speaking, to a certain social class, form an almost completely classless community. Though the realities of money and survival are known to them, the irrelevancies of the social structure are not important to Joyce. Nor does *Ulysses* contain any lingering traces of a morality—sexual, social, monetary or hygienic— unconsciously adopted from respectable society and silently assumed to be held in common with the respectable reader. Joyce has shifted the process of judgment of human behaviour altogether away from that governed merely by social reflex. And this is one of the ways in which he is a specifically modern writer, reflecting the real consciousness of our time; for whatever else may be said about it, and with all its vulgarities, its violences, its half-baked caricatures of serious creative purposes on its head, ours is a time of liberation from merely societal values. That his book is in large part governed by this spirit of tolerance and liberation is all the more remarkable in that it is populated not by artists or anarchists or beats or professional rebels of one kind or another, but by some of the outwardly ordinary people of Dublin in 1904. It is as if the lid had been pulled off ordinary society to reveal the falsity of the lie that people are divided into the respectable and the criminal: to reveal in all its outrageousness the unbiddable eccentricity, weakness, humour and unreliability of man. . . .

It is striking how clearly Joyce, in his own career, sums up the *fin de siècle* and its immediate aftermath, the advent of modern literature. There is an aesthetic revolt. A brave, proud, Satanic but "languid" young man scorns the world as it is and rejects its paths in favour of his own right to follow and create an ideal beauty. The *fin de siècle* artist turns his back on the meanness, squalor and ignobility of the world. Then suddenly in the aftermath we find modern art as never before concerned with that world and attempting to bring all that very squalor within its compass: within, that is to say, in some way or other, the compass of "beauty."

Stephen is right to revolt against and abandon the Dublin he knew, and the parental environment into which he had been born. While remaining personally within it he was unlikely to accomplish much. "When the soul of man is born in this country there are nets flung at it to hold it back from flight. You talk to me of nationality, language, religion. I shall try to fly by those nets." Physically and spiritually of course he did. *Ulysses* is in no sense a double apostasy. Its author is not finding sustenance or illumination in the spiritual values of its characters. But he is in their human value, and in their human reality. In the Proteus episode, while Stephen is communing with himself on the strand, contemplating a visit to his uncle, he reflects on his family. We hear, in this reflection, his real, "consubstantial father's voice" for the first time, commenting on his in-laws:

> O weeping God, the things I married into. The drunken little costdrawer and his brother, the cornet player. Highly respectable gondoliers. And skeweyed Walter sirring his father, no less. Sir. Yes, sir. No, sir. Jesus wept: and no wonder by Christ.

And Stephen imagines also his uncle's greeting:

> Sit down or by the law Harry I'll knock you down.
> Walter squints vainly for a chair.
> He has nothing to sit down on, sir.
> He has nowhere to put it, you mug. Bring in our Chippendale chair. Would you like a bite of something? . . . the rich of a rasher fried with a herring? Sure? So much the better. We have nothing in the house but backache pills.

And he reflects:

> Houses of decay, mine his and all. You told the Clongowes gentry you had
> an uncle a judge and an uncle a general in the army. Come out of them,
> Stephen. Beauty is not there.

Yet, if the purpose of Stephen's revolt, and, in whatever sense, the purpose of the artist, was the creation or extraction of some form of beauty,
and if *Ulysses* was the justification of that revolt and the fulfilment of
that purpose, then beauty must lie there, even in those "houses of decay"
which are its subject. If, to put it simply, the book was his father's "spit-
ting image," it is in the contemplation of that image that beauty must lie.

Ulysses executes a complex movement of reconciliation and acceptance:
towards the world of its author's father, towards the "sordid and deceptive" world of ordinary living; and, because the self, having abandoned
the heroic lie, is now seen to be part of that world, towards the self as
well. For Stephen and, ultimately, because art achieves the general
through the particular instance, for us, they are one and the same. He
had been tempted to reject the world of mundane, sordid and deceptive
detail, as well as his father's houses of decay, in favour of an ideal beauty.
That to reject the mundanities and sordidities of this world is also to
reject a great deal of the self, every human being knows, in whom "the
monster" who favours the ideal has not grown to dominatingly "heroic
proportions." It was through the concept and the creation of Leopold
Bloom that Joyce, with many characteristic ironies and subtleties, but
also with an immense simplicity, achieved the multiple apotheosis he
desired.

"There is," says Lenehan, "a touch of the artist about old Bloom. He's
a cultured allroundman, Bloom is. . . . He's not one of your common
or garden . . . you know . . . There's a touch of the artist about old
Bloom."

There is indeed, for "As we . . . weave and unweave our bodies, Stephen said, from day to day, their molecules shuttled to and fro, so does
the artist weave and unweave his image." And a few pages later we are
reminded of another Jewish character in the same young man's assertion
that Shakespeare "drew Shylock out of his own long pocket."

There are many parallels between Bloom and Stephen, just as there
are many resemblances between Bloom and the mature Joyce. Boylan
stands in relation to Bloom as Mulligan does to Stephen: accenting his
isolation, making a mockery of his attitudinisings, representing a worldly
glitter and a sexual flamboyance which neither Bloom nor Stephen possesses.

> Wit. You would give your five wits for youth's proud livery he pranks in.
> Lineaments of gratified desire.

To a large extent, though not nearly to the same extent as Stephen,
Bloom rejects the values of the society within which he moves. Both are
humiliated; both are excluded, partly by choice and partly by force. Both

are infidels, though both are concerned with and coloured by the ancient faiths within which they were nurtured. Both of them have deep and complex feelings about the histories of their races and their ancestral religions; but, nevertheless, to both of them history is a nightmare from which one must struggle to awake. Both have reason to feel remorse about the dead.

But their contrasts in resemblance are no less interesting than the resemblances themselves. Whereas Stephen is almost overwhelmed by his remorse, Bloom recovers his balance comparatively easily. In the brothel Bloom finds the thought of his ancestral background a source of strength; Stephen finds the thought of his merely another source of remorse. Parallel to Stephen's dramatic defiance of convention and society runs Bloom's comic, often shaken, often degraded, seldom dignified, never wholly triumphant, but still stubborn, courageous and, in the main, successful attempt to achieve the same end: to be oneself. But Bloom has merely to remain himself, whereas Stephen has to become. Confronted like Stephen by mockery, assault, the temptations of the flesh, Messianic ambition and remorse, Bloom, unlike Stephen, has attained to a certain magnanimity.

In general, where we find a resemblance, in circumstance or personality, between the two, and when we see its end, we can say that the difference is that Bloom is more mature than Stephen and seems to body forth— with some irony of course and some caricature, but nonetheless fairly faithfully—the differences between Stephen and the mature Joyce.[1]

But Bloom had to be made inclusive not only of the circumstantial Joyce, but of the human nature that Joyce and all men shared. If the pretences to heroism were to be stripped away and *Ulysses* was to be the first great masterpiece of unheroic literature; if Bloom was to survive as the first great anti-hero, standing in for all unheroic men, including the self, if the "silent secrets" sitting in the dark palaces of all men's hearts which were "weary of their tyranny" were to be dethroned, the avatar had to be subjected to and his power of survival tested against the most open and the most cruel tests.[2]

---

[1] Bloom is of course important also, as an instrument of Joyce's return to his father's world, though it is also true that he emphasises his differences from it. He, who "knows your old fellow" is also "middler the Holy Ghost," the third person of the blessed Trinity, mediator between the son and his consubstantial father's world. This theme is made so plain and is so constantly returned to that to suggest it as a central motif in the book is not to indulge in any arcane exegesis. It is not necessary for any of the three characters to become other than they are, in order that we may grasp Bloom's middle position between Dublin and Trieste, between the father and his associates in Ireland and the artist in the Austro-Hungarian empire—where, incidentally, old Virag, Bloom's father, was born. Joyce came to delight in the existence and the creative possibilities of his father's world, but he did not desire to be part of it. Hence his hero is Bloom, the common man who is also the outsider, and Dubliner who is also a stranger.

[2] There is a sense in which Bloom stands in for all humanity: like Kafka's K, Chaplin's

This frequently ridiculous, often humiliated man is seen in every possible intimacy and exposed to every possible nuance of contempt. He is
put to flight by physical threats; he is cuckolded; he masturbates before
our eyes; most of the atavisms born of fear and shame by which we are
accustomed to react to others and judge ourselves are flouted. Nor does
Joyce spare him his humour. From the episode of John Henry Menton's
hat to the silly questions about Gibraltar in the coffee stall, he is exposed
to it. Even such ambiguous qualities as his wariness at fence sometimes
desert him in favour of a boyish and ridiculous vanity for the truth. And
the cruellest cut of all is reserved till last. Molly may or may not be Gea
Tellus or the Great Earth Mother; she is certainly Bloom's wife. She
knows him through and through and she spares him nothing. If she remembers his romantic insistence on Howth Head, she also remembers his
peculiar request in Harold's Cross Road. Joyce's purpose in ending the
book with Molly's monologue has been much debated; yet it seems fairly
obvious that if his purpose was the total exposure of Bloom, and the
exposure of him in the most candid light, no tribunal could equal in
intimate knowledge and ultimate frankness the thoughts of his woman.

Yet the remarkable thing is that in some way Bloom survives all this,
even Molly's inquisition, though shakily as usual. "Let them go and get
a husband first that's fit to be looked at," Molly says of the Miss Kearneys;
and she recognises that he is in some sense or other superior to his
mockers:

> . . . theyre a nice lot all of them well theyre not going to get my husband
> again into their clutches if I can help it making fun of him then behind
> his back I know well when he goes on with his idiotics because he has
> sense enough not to squander every penny piece he earns down their
> gullets and looks after his wife and family goodfornothings . . .

Her final "yes" may or may not have the allegorical implications her
admirers have read into it; it may or may not be a "yes" to life; it is
certainly a repetition of her original acceptance of Bloom.

Nor does the reader withhold his assent, as the long book draws to a
close and we get to know Bloom through intimacies of body and soul

---

tramp or Beckett's old man. Endlessly interesting, unmistakably real though he is in
the personal detail which is piled up, he is yet sufficiently outside his immediate environment to take on a certain universality. His position is ambiguous in several respects. Though no anarchist, he is at least a failure. He stands far enough outside
the society to present a contrast and suggest, however comical it may be, a conflict:
in this he again resembles K, anxious to cooperate but denied the opportunity, or
Chaplin's tramp, gazing wistfully at the lighted ballroom, or Beckett's old men who
are anonymously fed and maintained in their solitude. That Bloom should be Odysseus,
Sinbad the sailor, the wandering Jew and whatnot, may help to confer this universality
upon him. It is done in more important ways by a series of carefully arranged ironies
and ambiguities in his personal position: orphaned son and bereaved father, worldly-
wise and yet a failure, Irish and non-Irish, husband yet cuckold, faithful and faithless.

to which no other character in literature had ever previously been subjected. Joyce set out to show man in a light he had never been seen in before; to expose him to a gaze more omnipresent and more exacting than any to which he had ever previously been exposed. He weighted the circumstances against his man; he put him in situations which normally arouse only our contempt; he exposed him to the jibes of the cruellest wits in Europe; he brought the elaborations of his own irony gleefully to bear upon him. Yet it is the measure of his success in his ultimate purpose that the man not only survives but survives triumphantly, as the first great hero of unheroic literature; that he arouses not only our compassion and sympathy, our affection and humorous understanding, but, before his long chapter of humiliations is over, our profoundest respect.

That Bloom's own qualities, often overlooked by criticism, and always derided by the other characters, had something to do with this miracle we must admit; though they are certainly not the whole story. He is at least averagely kind. He performs, for example, most of what are known in Catholic theology as "the corporal works of mercy" during the day: he visits the sick, comforts the afflicted, buries the dead, shelters the homeless, etc. Though no combatant, he can bring himself to assert vital truths in the teeth of the opposition.

> But it's no use, says he. Force, hatred, history, all that. That's not life for men and women, insult and hatred. And everybody knows that it's the very opposite of that that is really life.
> What? says Alf.
> Love, says Bloom. I mean the opposite of hatred.

And he pays for this, and for similar pronouncements, in more ways than one. It is typical of Joyce's method that it is the enunciation of this simple and terrible truth that brings down upon him Hynes's cruel and brilliant sneer about his own abilities as a lover—"I wonder did he ever put it out of sight"—just as it is his display of learning in Lenehan's story of coming home beside Molly in the sidecar which exposes him to the jibe, so amusing to the teller that he momentarily collapses with laughter, about "that's only a pinprick."

His own humour, his irony, his subtlety and his intelligence are, in general, easy to underestimate. His mind only works in clichés in the coffee stall scene when he is tired, and it does not seem to have been noticed that he is here making a mistaken attempt to impress Stephen as a sort of literary man and thinker. What he utters are the clichés of editorial journalism, particularly provincial journalism of a sort that is written in Ireland to this day, though it was probably more widespread everywhere in 1904. It is just the sort of language we might expect Bloom to use in order to impress Stephen intellectually at the beginning of their acquaintance. (The general unpopularity of this extremely funny and engaging section of the book with critics who are not particularly well

acquainted with Ireland, may stem from their lack of recognition of the
precise kind of language he is talking.) Before that, as Dr. S. L. Goldberg
has pointed out (he is very good on Bloom's process of thought, suggesting that his stream of consciousness, far from being "jellyfish," is actually
composed of illuminating and rewarding epiphanies), Bloom's quiet ability to think for himself, his equanimity without insensitivity, above all,
perhaps, his combination of moral seriousness with a generally humorous,
caustic, but tolerant cast of mind are remarkable enough. Joyce's purpose
would not have been well served either if Bloom had been merely the
sort of stupid, acquiescent, bumbling mediocrity which earlier criticism
often made him out to be. It was necessary that he should be deprived
of certain dignities and exposed in certain lights, that he should be the
opposite of Napoleonic and often the apotheosis of the foolish, but it
would not have done, either, to make him out merely a dull cretin. In
his kindness and his gropings after better things he is surely as human
as in his *niaiseries*. Joyce had to be fair twice over.

Nor is he dull in any other sense. The fact that he is not a scurrilous
wit like most of the others, that he is grave and quiet in demeanour and
talks seriously when he believes the issues are serious, should not disguise
the fact that his mind has a constant and perhaps predominantly humorous cast:

> All kinds of places are good for ads. That quack doctor for the clap used to
> be stuck up in all the greenhouses. Never see it now. Strictly confidential.
> Dr Hy Franks. Didn't cost him a red like Maginni the dancing master self
> advertisement. Got fellows to stick them up or stick them up himself for
> that matter on the q.t. running in to loosen a button. Fly by night. Just
> the place too. POST NO BILLS. POST NO PILLS. Some chap with a
> dose burning him.

But it must be repeated that it is in no way primarily because of his
intellectual or moral qualities that Bloom so arouses our interest and
so commands our affection. (It should not, really, except to critics, be
necessary to prove that he does the latter: no character in contemporary
fiction has such a widely variegated personal following.) I mean my
Ulysses to be a good man, said Joyce to Frank Budgen right enough; and
we can see that he is, however strange the definition of goodness might
seem by orthodox standards, but it is not this in the end. When we ask
what it is, we are forced ultimately, I think, to recognise that here is the
familiar: the worn, familiar, comical, shabby, eroded but not collapsed
face of humanity. In his vulnerability, his weakness, his secrecies, his
continuous but uncertain ability to remain upright, his clinging to a
few props, his constantly threatened dignity, Bloom commands that affection in the midst of comedy which we give to our own image, stained and
worn as it is. Joyce has given him an almost infinite complexity as well;
because the book is technically, for all its faults, a *tour de force,* we learn

about Bloom as we learn about nobody else in fiction while we go along. And his creator has also breathed life into him and surrounded him, on this one day, with a world masterfully rich in the comic and in living detail. But his ultimate triumph was to extract this ordinary poetry of humanity from him; and it is a strange one, for his creator was Stephen Dedalus, that well-known aesthete.

Joyce's movement, as he was subsequently to demonstrate at length, was circular. By "the commodious vicus of recirculation" one came back to where one started, to the father and the race. He had, in particular (as, it is alleged, has all humanity in general), a fallen father, "foosterfather." The fall began in the dark wet winter of Parnell's downfall and death, when John Joyce began that long downward progress in which the instincts of a dandy and a gentleman, a Corkman and a boaster, a whiskey-drinking "praiser of his own past" were to consort oddly with, and to succeed only in accelerating, that decline into "squalor and insincerity" of which Stephen Hero speaks. The two falls, Parnell's and his Parnellite father's, were forever after symbolically one in Joyce's mind. He was to harmonise them humorously and to entwine them with all other falls and fathers in *Finnegans Wake*. In *Ulysses* he has achieved out of the resentments and limitations of adolescence, even out of the justified attitudes of revolt and the judgments he was entitled to make about his spiritual and carnal inheritance, an attitude of compassion, tolerance and delight, which returns to that inheritance what it gave him: pride, humour, a love of song, a sense of style and a knowledge of the obverse of these coins, the degradations, the inescapable Irishnesses of life. The contrast between Stanislaus's attitude to his father, as expressed in *My Brother's Keeper*, and Joyce's is almost a parable of the difference between the viewpoint of the good man and the artist. The one is a judgment, harsh, clear and unforgiving. The other is an acceptance.

Yet, important though this movement was for Joyce—this achievement, like Shakespeare (according to Stephen), of the spiritual paternity of his own father—it is not the whole story. Like "the greyedauburn Shakespeare," walking in Fetter Lane Joyce was "weaving and unweaving his own image" and seeing himself as he then was "by reflection from that which then I shall be"; and he was also attempting to incorporate and to redeem aspects of our common humanity which had never been incorporated victoriously into literature before. It is here that Leopold Bloom enters, contrasted in his humility yet his continuing, if comic, integrity, with Stephen Dedalus; the self-image transmuted into an Irish Jew with ancestry somewhere in central Europe, with "a touch of the artist" and yet without the artist's redemption from the conditions of ordinary living. For Bloom does represent ordinary living, though isolated and set apart. He is pragmatic, yet a visionary; mean and careful, yet often in trouble out of generosity or fineness of spirit; betrayed and betraying, yet loyal after his fashion in the primary instances of love; ridiculous, yet dignified; spat upon, yet victorious; sensitive yet complacent, with the complacency which turns out in the end to be one of humanity's great defences, a clinging to the moment and the necessities of the moment, a form of continuing courage. All this adds up to the inescapable Jewishness of life. Bloom is not heroic, in the old sense. Nor is he abysmal, in the old sense, as any character in literature with certain of his characteristics would have had to be before him. In him, for the first time, our unpromising, unpoetic, unheroic image is found to have surprising possibilities for pride and for poetry.

The greatness of *Ulysses* is partly technical.[3] A new prose form has been achieved, free from the distortions of dramatic narrative, and not dependent for its intensity on dramatic confrontations and resolutions. Yet it has intensity: a matter of language, of density of life, of immediacy of texture; in a word, of poetry. That the texture is yet "ordinary" proves that intensity, poetry, resides here too, its extraction being a matter of language and of the pitch of interest with which the ordinary is contemplated and then evoked.

In this sense it can hardly be otherwise than "on the side of life," ordinary, continuing life, as against dogmatisms of one kind or another. Such poetry cannot avoid possessing, in Coleridge's word, geniality; and if this were all that were to be said it would still be enough. Poetry is enough. The book does not have to be "about" anything, except, of course, Leopold Bloom.

Yet over such a large area, an uncoloured contemplation and evocation of life is tantamount to impossible. There remains the question of the author's vision. One cannot prove syllogistically that the temper of the book is what Joyce called "the classic temper," that it is an act of acceptance and an act of *pietas*. One can only appeal to the reader's response to its abounding humour, its creative zest, its ability to anneal the spirit (all of which are inseparably bound up with its poetry and its "geniality"); and one can only try, as I have tried, to show that Joyce meant it to be received in this way and that, in part, he wrote a saga about a young man who achieved this classic temper. It is not necessary to seek profundities of meaning in *Ulysses*. Criticism has performed no service for Joyce by the suggestion that we must unravel the book before we can understand it; and that patience, skill and drudgery in unravelment are the primary qualities required of its ideal reader. They are not the sort of qualities commonly found in those most remarkable for receptivity and generosity of response to art or anything else. The suggestion that they are essential is part of the academic claim to indispensability—let alone

---

[3] *Ulysses* and *The Waste Land*, published so near together in time, began in English that attempt to find new forms to accommodate more images in a new relationship, which remains characteristic of much of the most interesting work of this century, though not always of the most praised.

usefulness—which has followed in our time as a result of the vesting of academic interests in literature. Yet it is also the duty of the critic to seek to interpret a book in the spirit in which it is written. Whether the facts that *Ulysses* is partly a strange act of *pietas* on Joyce's part; that Bloom, as well as being plain Leopold Bloom of Eccles Street, is a mediator between the artist and mankind; or that the book is a work of abounding comedy, full of "profane joy," make it greater than if it were a work of hatred and disgust, is a question difficult to answer. We can only fruitfully say that all great works of art are full of intensity, and that there is not therefore so much difference between opposing visions as criticism may be tempted to suggest.

It is certain, however, that if we can describe *Ulysses* in this way, we claim it to be more important than it would be if the whole enormous structure had been raised in support of some theory about metempsychosis, some illumination of comparative myth, or some conviction about the decline of Western man. It is in the redemption of our common and ordinary humanity from its own "deceits and sordities," and the totality as well as the poetic intensity of its statement of the conditions of ordinary living, that its originality and its importance for us lies. More than any other book, *Ulysses* marks the end of heroic literature, and with the advent of Bloom, man takes on a new poetic interest for his complex mundanity rather than as an actor of greater or lesser strength and tragic resonance. The resonance is there, and the tragedy as well as the triumph, but they are otherwise revealed. In no previous work, to take but one of his characteristics, had a "good" man been shown who was not altogether "normal" sexually.

We are rightly suspicious of the notion of progress, but there is a sense in which there is progress in the arts. We cover more ground, we say what has not been said; partial and limited like the visions of other artists of other eras though ours may be, we extend both the ordinary recorded area of human experience and the reclaimed area of poetic compassion; and we in our time have been honest. *Ulysses* has faults, of eccentricity, of mere display, of mechanical thoroughness. Yet in the way it encompasses ordinary living and the way it gives to much that had been denied it the intensity and texture of poetry, *Ulysses* is a landmark, perhaps the most important single event in the great breakthrough that has been achieved in this century.

Why Molly Bloom Menstruates

by Richard Ellmann

The denouement of Ulysses has been much disputed. What seems to end the book is that Bloom, who nodded off at the end of the "Ithaca" episode, and his more wakeful wife Molly, both snore away in the arms of Morpheus, or as Joyce puts it, in the arms of Murphy. But is this really the end? Did Joyce have no future in mind for his characters? The question is particularly likely to be asked because *A Portrait* is often said to find its sequel in *Ulysses* where Stephen appears after an interval of about two years. But *A Portrait* seems self-contained, it celebrates the birth first of Stephen's body and then of his soul, it brings him from inchoate to real selfhood, from possibility to decision. If he reappears in *Ulysses,* and I won't deny that he does, he is there for a different purpose, not to present his further adventures.

What then does happen to Bloom and Stephen? One critic declares that Stephen goes out into the night and writes—*Ulysses.* But *Ulysses* is not the work of Stephen, any more than *Hamlet* is the work of Hamlet; it issues from that mind of which Stephen, Bloom, Molly, and even Mulligan and Boylan are only aspects. Two other critics regard the ending as proleptic, but the events they foresee are not the same. William Empson remembers that Stephen, after refusing to stay the night, agrees to exchange with Mrs. Bloom Italian for singing lessons, and proposes that Stephen returns on 17 June or anyway in the next few days, with his grammar book. The mutual instruction then takes a predictable turn. Bloom tolerates the affair, Empson feels, because he wants desperately to have a son, even if through the agency of another man.

On a practical level, this theory offers a number of difficulties. Apart from Molly's impending concert tour, which will make other alliances than with Boylan complicated for her, Empson leans heavily upon what appears to be a mere gesture of politeness on Stephen's part. Having been rescued from a jam, and having turned down an invitation to stay the night, he avoids twice refusing his host pointblank by appearing to accept a vague and unscheduled exchange of lessons. But Bloom recognizes—

"Why Molly Bloom Menstruates." From *Ulysses on the Liffey,* by Richard Ellmann (London: Faber and Faber Ltd., 1972), pp. 159–76. Copyright © 1972 by Richard Ellmann. Reprinted by permission of Oxford University Press, Inc. and Faber and Faber Ltd. One of Mr. Ellmann's footnotes has been shortened.

and Joyce at once underlines the recognition—that Stephen's return is problematic. That Molly dandles the idea as an erotic fancy does not make it more likely. The notion of a Stephen–Molly affair outside the book is so skimpily supported that it becomes a nineteenth-century parlour game like "Describe Desdemona's girlhood" or "Fortinbras's reign in Denmark."

The other theory for 17 June is exactly opposite. According to it, Bloom, instead of relaxing further his marriage tie, tightens it and becomes a proper husband. Edmund Wilson proposed this idea some years ago in an uncharacteristic burst of optimism; he contended that Bloom's request for breakfast in bed proved that Bloom was once more becoming master in his own house. A difficulty with this oatmeal theory is that it rests heavily upon the notion that not to make breakfast himself is Bloom's assertion of male authority. This in turn would be more convincing if Bloom had seemed put upon when he made breakfast on the morning of June 16, but actually he likes cooking and doesn't feel degraded by it. Moreover he has apparently done it, except when ill, during the whole of their married life, including the period when they enjoyed complete conjugal relations. Need he feel degraded? After all, if cooks are always women, chefs are always men.[1] His request for breakfast may be just what it appears to be, an expression of fatigue after a late night which is most unusual for him. Molly indicates that she expects to return to the usual pattern after one morning's exertions. At any rate, it seems an unwarranted assumption that breakfast in bed will restore anyone's sexual relations to normalcy. It is harder to reject Wilson's theory than Empson's, but both suffer from a desire, vestigial even among modern readers of novels, to detain the characters a little longer in their fictional lives. Yet a warning must be taken from Eugammon of Cyrene, who tacked his unfortunate sequel onto the *Odyssey*.

Joyce declared in his aesthetic notebook that the excellence of a comedy depended upon its joy, which in turn depended upon its fulfilment of desire. To the extent that a work was not sufficient to itself, it was deficient in joy. He could scarcely then have intended to encourage speculation about the future of his characters. He meant what he said in a letter, that in the "Ithaca" episode Bloom and Stephen become like the stars at which they gaze, and that in "Penelope" Bloom and Molly with him are off to eternity. The conjugal future at 7 Eccles street no longer interests him, any more than future doings of Odysseus and Penelope interest Homer or of Dante and Beatrice interest the author of *The Divine Comedy*. Joyce leaves possibilities at the end like dangling threads, just as Homer leaves an unfulfilled prophecy of Tiresias, but he has his mind set on other things. At the end of his Linati schema Joyce shows Bloom going off to *"Alta Notte"* ("Deep Night") and Stephen to *"Alba"*

---

[1] Mary Ellmann, in *Thinking About Women* (New York and London, 1968).

("Dawn"), but since these opposites coincide, the point is that there is
no more to say. If Joyce had wanted to, he could certainly have given the
book either Empson's or Wilson's conclusion: to please Empson he might
have let Stephen stay the night, to please Wilson he could have had husband and wife resume complete sexual relations for the first time in
eleven years. He does neither of these, though in Homer Telemachus presumably sleeps in the palace and Odysseus and Penelope share a bed. Instead of sexual intercourse in the present, Joyce has Molly think of a
sexual scene in the past. He did so not because Flaubert had prescribed
to the writer of fiction, *ne pas conclure,* but because he had another conclusion in mind.

He said himself that "The last word (human, all too human) is left to
Penelope. This is the indispensable countersign to Bloom's passport to
eternity." Beyond eternity his characters could scarcely be expected to go.
The episode was, he said, the book's *clou,* the star turn of the show. In a
jocular mood he said also that "Ithaca" was the true ending of the book
because "Penelope" had neither beginning, middle, nor end. But it is not
so formless as that, since it begins with a capital letter and ends with a
full stop. Moreover, the first word in the book is *Stately* and the last
Yes, the first and last letters of each being reversed so that the serpent
has his tail in his mouth at last.[2] It would be more accurate to say that the
form of "Penelope" is ungirdled than that it is nonexistent. Molly's
countersign may be deciphered, and an explanation given for her thoughts
of Mrs. Riordan, an elderly widow now dead, for her menstruation, and
for her memories of adolescence on Gibraltar. These prove necessary
rather than improvisatory.

Coming after the dry, impersonal, and pseudoscientific order of most of
the "Ithaca" episode, the final monologue offers a personal, lyrical efflores-
cence. It is the only episode to which Joyce assigns no specific hour—the
time is no o'clock, or as he said in one schema, it is the time indicated
mathematically by the slightly disproportioned figure ∞ or lemniscate
lying on its side—the number of eternity and infinity. It might be more
exact to say that the ruins of time and space and the mansions of eternity
here coexist, at least until the very end. Molly presents herself without
portentousness as spokesman for nature. Like the Wife of Bath, she
contends that God has not endowed us with sensual proclivities if these
are not to be indulged. "Nature it is," she insists, falling into the fallacy

---

[2] Joyce probably regarded *S* as a male letter (Gerty MacDowell relates Bloom to a
snake staring at its prey), and *Y* as a female one. (He said in a letter that "yes" was
a female word.) For this literary symbolism he had precedents in Mallarmé and
Rimbaud, not to mention Dante. It may be noted here that he draws another circle
by making the *Telemachiad* begin with *S* and end with *P,* and the *Nostos* begin with
P and end with *S.*

Compare *Stephen Hero,* p. 32: ". . . he put his lines together not word by word
but letter by letter. He read Blake and Rimbaud on the values of letters and even
permuted and combined the five vowels to construct cries for primitive emotions.

of identifying virtue with what is natural that Hume had criticized. (Joyce too knew it was a fallacy; Richard Rowan in *Exiles,* when Robert poses a "law of nature," retorts, "Did I vote it?") Yet Molly's nature is not indiscriminate; as she sees and represents it, nature is choosy—Darwin thought it choosy too. Still she is acceptant enough to plant the almost desert globe of the "Ithaca" episode with vegetables and people and animals and curious objects. Most of all, she covers it with flowers. In the Linati plan, the part of the body allotted to "Penelope" is fat ("Eumaeus" having offered nerves, and "Ithaca" bones). Philosophy is fleshed. Stephen had recalled earlier the medieval legend that Aristotle was enticed by a "light o' love" to let her bit, bridle, and ride him, and Molly's nature, so much more earthy, trivial, sexualized, and lyrical than Aristotle's or Hume's, appears as a final penetration by the wisdom of the body of the wisdom of the mind. (Molly's only acquaintance with Aristotle is the apocryphal and semipornographic *Aristotle's Masterpiece*; she malaprops his name into "some old Aristocrat or whatever his name is.") *"Ich bin das Fleisch das stets bejaht,"* Joyce says of her, confirming her as the opposite pole to Mulligan's denying spirit. But her yeasaying is mixed with much naysaying—until the very end of her monologue, "Yes" and "No" (with a great many "knows" for good measure) are rivals for pre-eminence. Her final affirmation is a victory over strong resistance.

Molly Bloom's birthday is 8 September, and in tribute to this anniversary, and to the symbol of eternity-infinity, Joyce writes her monologue in eight sentences. "It begins and ends," Joyce wrote Budgen,

> with the female word *yes*. It turns like the huge earth ball slowly surely and evenly round and round spinning, its four cardinal points being the female breasts, arse, womb and cunt expressed by the words *because, bottom* (in all senses bottom button, bottom of the class, bottom of the sea, bottom of his heart), *woman, yes.* Though probably more obscene than any preceding episode it seems to me to be perfectly sane full amoral fertilisable untrustworthy engaging shrewd limited prudent indifferent *Weib*.

He delights in mythologizing Molly as Gea-Tellus, then, by bringing her down with a thump onto the orangekeyed chamberpot at 7 Eccles street, in demythologizing her into an old shoe.

Molly's animadversions begin with thoughts of Mrs. Riordan, a widow whom Bloom befriended:

> Yes because he never did a thing like that before as ask to get his breakfast in bed with a couple of eggs since the *City Arms* hotel when he used to be pretending to be laid up with a sick voice doing his highness to make himself interesting to that old faggot Mrs Riordan that he thought he had a great leg of and she never left us a farthing all for masses for herself and her soul greatest miser ever was actually afraid to lay out 4d for her methylated spirit telling me all her ailments she had too much old chat in her about politics and earthquakes and the end of the world let

us have a bit of fun first God help the world if all the women were her
sort down on bathingsuits and lownecks of course nobody wanted her to
wear I suppose she was pious because no man would look at her twice I
hope Ill never be like her a wonder she didnt want us to cover our
faces . . .

Joyce's purpose is served by having Molly establish her own point of view
against its counterpart, Mrs. Riordan's prudery, the latter associated with
miserliness and piety here, as earlier in the book with occultism and aes-
theticism. Molly might seem to run more danger from the opposite faction, of Mistress Moll Flanders. She says herself, however, that she is not
a whore or a slut, and she is right. Only the most rigorous interpretation
of adultery—Christ's in the Sermon on the Mount, "Whosoever looketh
on a woman to lust after her hath committed adultery with her already in
his heart"—could consider Molly's friendships, except that with Boylan,
and perhaps that with D'Arcy, as adulterous. The book makes clear that
this first relationship is something new. June 16 may in fact be the first
day that Boylan and Molly have had "carnal," as Bloom puts it. It may
also be, though this is never established, the day in June that Bloom and
Molly climaxed their courtship by proposal and consent among the rhododendrons on Howth sixteen years before. Joyce plays on the coincidence without bearing down too hard. Fidelity and infidelity coexist.

Essentially Molly is right about herself—she is not the wholly sexual
being that to Boylan she must appear to be. She hopes that he is pleased
with her, but she is not really pleased with him. She complains about his
too familiar manners in slapping her on the behind—"I'm not a horse
or an ass am I"—but she remembers that Boylan's father was a horse-
trader and hopes this fact may explain his conduct. Boylan writes bad
loveletters ending, "Yours ever Hugh Boylan." Molly detects that he is
basically a "strange brute" with an unconscionableness that Stephen had
earlier described as the *sentimental* desire to "enjoy without incurring the
immense debtorship for a thing done." So while Molly is not planning to
break with Boylan, she is not expecting the relationship to last, and
thinks of other men as more perceptive and congenial. For the same reason she rejects sado-masochism, in books about flagellants, "Sure theres
nothing for a woman in that." She steers between Mrs. Riordan's maso-
chistic prudery and Boylan's loutishness.

Bloom has as much trouble as Ulysses had in winning recognition as
Penelope's husband. Joyce complained once of his wife that she did not
appear to see much difference between him and other men, though in
fact Nora Joyce remarked to a friend that her husband was like nobody
else. The seeming (though not real) inability to differentiate finely is
characteristic of Molly, who falls into calling the various men she has
known by the pronoun "he," without much further identification. (Stephen Dedalus did the same in "Proteus": "She she she. What she?" But
he had no particular woman to think about.) Against Stephen's effort

to make women mythical, "handmaidens of the moon," "wombs of sin," and the like, Molly regards men as either natural or unnatural. Basically she is earth to Bloom's sun, modifying his light by her own movements. She is thoroughly aware of his many failings, but notes also a few virtues. He is kind to old women like Mrs. Riordan, he has a few brains, he was handsome when young, he wipes his feet on the mat. On the other hand, his atheism, his socialism, his talk of persecution, put her off. She gradually acknowledges his pre-eminence by the frequency with which she returns to thinking about him. As compared with Boylan, her husband is the more complete man, with the supreme virtue that he wishes her well. She cannot say as much for Boylan. Molly, as the earth, prefers in Bloom the more complete to the less complete example of a biological species.

In the book's characterology, Molly is needed to contribute a quality not often present in either Bloom or Stephen, her naturalness and spontaneity. The two men are thoughtful, detached, Bloom because he sees all round, Stephen because he looks deep in. Molly's monologue is therefore less an addition than a correction. The "Ithaca" episode had offered a heliocentric view of Bloom, Molly offers a geocentric one, the two together forming the angle of parallax (a word which had baffled Bloom earlier in the day). Bloomsday becomes everymansday, and everywomansday, in that all necessary elements of desirable life have been gathered together. None of the principal figures is complete in himself, but together they sum up what is affirmable. At the end we are brought back to the earth, to spring, to vegetation, and to sexual love.

Molly has a capacity for intense yet fastidious feeling which makes Joyce's altitudinous ending possible. The peroration of her monologue is morose delectation, theologically speaking, but moroseness plays no part in it. She is thinking of that day among the rhododendrons on Howth when she and Bloom came to an understanding, but she marvellously collocates such elements as land and sea to have them all "swimming in roses."

> I love flowers Id love to have the whole place swimming in roses God of heaven theres nothing like nature the wild mountains then the sea and the waves rushing then the beautiful country with fields of oats and wheat and all kinds of things and all the fine cattle going about that would do your heart good to see rivers and lakes and flowers all sorts of shapes and smells and colours springing up even out of the ditches primroses and violets nature it is

She quickly resolves the questions of belief and incertitude which have dogged Stephen and western philosophy, and with which Bloom has bothered her, by finding them not worth asking:

> as for them saying theres no God I wouldnt give a snap of my two fingers for all their learning why dont they go and create something I often asked him atheists or whatever they call themselves go and wash the cobbles

off themselves first then they go howling for the priest and they dying and
why why because theyre afraid of hell on account of their bad conscience
ah yes I know them well who was the first person in the universe before
there was anybody that made it all who ah that they dont know neither
do I so there you are they might as well try to stop the sun from rising
tomorrow the sun shines for you he said the day we were lying among
the rhododendrons on Howth head in the grey tweed suit and his straw
hat the day I got him to propose to me yes first I gave him the bit of
seedcake out of my mouth and it was leapyear like now yes 16 years ago

This recollection of the seedcake, which Bloom also experienced in the
"Lestrygonians" episode, is vaguely reminiscent of something else, and if
we remember that *Finnegans Wake* speaks of the apple in the Garden of
Eden as the seedfruit, there is a momentary connection with the apple
which Eve passed to Adam as Molly to Bloom. This is what St. Augustine
called the happy fault, *felix culpa*, but Bloom calls it *copula felix*, happy
not because it brought about redemption by Christ, but in itself. As in
Dante's Earthly Paradise, Adam and Eve have been absolved of original
sin. Moist with spittle, the seedcake offers its parallel also to the host, and
the lovers' rite is contrasted with the black mass of "Circe."

> my God after that long kiss I near lost my breath yes he said I was a
> flower of the mountain yes so we are flowers all a womans body yes that
> was one true thing he said in his life and the sun shines for you today
> yes that was why I liked him because I saw he understood or felt what a
> woman is and I knew I could always get round him and I gave him all
> the pleasure I could leading him on till he asked me to say yes and I
> wouldnt answer first only looked out over the sea and the sky I was think-
> ing of so many things he didnt know of Mulvey and Mr Stanhope and
> Hester and father and old captain Groves and the sailors playing all birds
> fly and I say stoop and washing up dishes they called it on the pier and
> the sentry in front of the governors house with the thing round his white
> helmet poor devil half roasted and the Spanish girls laughing in their
> shawls and their tall combs and the auctions in the morning the Greeks
> and the jews and the Arabs and the devil knows who else from all the
> ends of Europe and Duke street

Duke street is in Dublin. East and West join here, as in "Circe" greekjew
and jewgreek meet, with the Arabs added here to the pot:

> and the fowl market all clucking outside Larby Sharons and the poor
> donkeys slipping half asleep and the vague fellows in the cloaks asleep
> in the shade on the steps and the big wheels of the carts of the bulls and
> the old castle thousands of years old yes and those handsome Moors all in
> white and turbans like kings asking you to sit down in their little bit of
> a shop and Ronda with the old windows of the posadas glancing eyes a
> lattice hid for her lover to kiss the iron and the wineshops half open at
> night and the castanets and the night we missed the boat at Algeciras the
> watchman going about serene with his lamp and O that awful deep-
> down torrent O and the sea the sea crimson sometimes like fire

Water and fire combine, and so does the crimson sea of the straits of Gibraltar with Molly's menstruation, about which she has complained earlier, as if the natural forces of earth and woman were synonymous. This synthesis was prepared long before in the book; in the "Proteus" episode Stephen brooded on the oddity of God's transubstantiation into flesh occurring in so many communions in so many times and places:

> And at the same instant perhaps a priest round the corner is elevating it. Dringdring! And two streets off another locking it into a pyx. Dringadring! And in a ladychapel another taking housel all to his own cheek. Dringdring! Down, up, forward, back.

Then in "Nausicaa," Bloom meditated on the same identity-variety in the process of menstruation:

> How many women in Dublin have it today? Martha, she [Gerty]. Something in the air. That's the moon. But then why don't all women menstruate at the same time with same moon, I mean? Depends on the time they were born, I suppose. Or all start scratch then get out of step.

These two passages seem at first to be idle. But Joyce is establishing a secret parallel and opposition: the body of God and the body of woman share blood in common. In allowing Molly to menstruate at the end Joyce consecrates the blood in the chamberpot rather than the blood in the chalice, mentioned by Mulligan at the beginning of the book. For this blood is substance, not more or less than substance. The great human potentiality is substantiation, not transubstantiation, or subsubstantiation. It is this quality which the artist has too, in that he produces living human characters, not ethereal or less than human ones. It is human blood,[3] not divine. Menstruation is Promethean.

> and the glorious sunsets and the figtrees in the Alameda gardens yes and all the queer little streets and pink and blue and yellow houses and the rosegardens and the jessamine and geraniums and cactuses and Gibraltar as a girl where I was a Flower of the mountain yes when I put the rose in my hair like the Andalusian girls used or shall I wear a red yes and how he kissed me under the Moorish wall

Molly confuses, or rather conflates, an incident when in her early youth she lay on the rock of Gibraltar beside Lieutenant Mulvey, with the moment of her courtship by Bloom on another eminence, the hill of Howth.

And now her reference to all the men she has known as "he" has a sudden relevance: Mulvey glides into Bloom in the next line: "and I thought well as well him as another." In Homer, Tiresias had prophesied that Ulysses would, after some years with Penelope, set sail once again but return at last to Ithaca. Dante, however, as Keats said, brought "news" of Ulysses, for in the *Inferno* Ulysses tells Dante of a last, presumptuous

---

[3] Molly's menstruation also establishes that she is not with child by Boylan.

voyage beyond the pillars of Hercules and out into the unknown and for him fatal sea. In Molly's mind, Mulvey, who was her Ulysses on Calpe's mount at Gibraltar, blends into Bloom, her Ulysses on Howth. She stamps an Irish visa on Ulysses' Greek passport. There is also an Italian visa, for Dante and Beatrice in Canto XXVII of the *Paradiso* look down on the straits of Gibraltar just as Bloom-Mulvey and Molly do. It is now clear why Molly Bloom had to be born so far from Ireland, at the pillars of Hercules.

In the last non-sentences of her monologue, Molly, having as she said got Bloom to propose to her, joins activity to passivity, aggression to surrender:

> and I thought well as well him as another and then I asked him with my eyes to ask again yes and then he asked me would I yes to say yes my mountain flower and first I put my arms around him yes and drew him down to me so he could feel my breasts all perfume yes and his heart was going like mad and yes I said yes I will Yes.

But why then does Molly end with an act of sixteen years before? She seems to burst the confines of her present situation, and fly from her jingly bed to a time which is beyond present time and a place beyond present place. In fact, she bursts through them to "that other world" mentioned by Martha Clifford, which is not death but an imaginative recreation, like *le temps retrouvé* of Proust. Like Adam and Eve's, it is a paradise lost, for as Proust says, the only true paradise is the one we have lost. According to Dante, Adam and Eve's paradise lasted only six hours, Bloom and Molly's is about the same. At the beginning of Molly's monologue she had thought of Mrs. Riordan predicting the end of the world, and here, in memory and imagination, the world does end and is created afresh. Joyce said that this episode had no art, but his book is consummated by the principle that art is nature's self. Molly, like Gerty MacDowell, like Bloom, like Stephen, has a touch of the artist about her, but that is because art is a natural process, which begins and ends with impure substance, and bids the dead to rise. There is sadness too, since Molly's present is so bleak in comparison with that lost paradise where, as Yeats said, all was "blossoming and dancing." The sadness is muted, however. Time and space are, at least for an instant, mere ghosts beside eternity and infinity.

Not Stephen then—though he defined the eucharistic element of art— but Molly, re-bears paradise, and Bloom, who earlier evoked the same scene, is her husband in art as in law. But Joyce has other nuptials in mind as well. "Penelope" ends the second half of the book as "Scylla and Charybdis" ended the first. The idea that Stephen brought to birth in "Scylla" is that Shakespeare's life provided him with the matter of his plays and poems, or in grander terms, that art is nature. Molly, by demonstrating that nature is art, may be seen as reaching across nine chapters of the book to offer Shakespeare her hand. As Shakespeare says in *A Winter's Tale,* "o'er that art/Which you say adds to nature is an art/That nature makes." [4] Deliberate and spontaneous creation are joined.

As if to render this contract more licit, Joyce in the "Circe" episode had Bloom and Stephen look together into a mirror, and see there not their own faces but the beardless face of Shakespeare. The cuckolded Shakespeare and Bloom, the betrayed Shakespeare and Stephen, are more closely akin than anyone would have suspected. All three out of victimization, as Molly out of present deprivation, create their artistic moments. There is a famous late-nineteenth-century edition of Shakespeare edited by F. J. Furnivall, which is known as the *Leopold Shakespere,* and Joyce makes this strange amalgam credible, with Stephen, now fused with Bloom, also a part of it. He announces the nuptials of Mrs. Marion Bloom and Mr. Leopold Shakespeare.

But another ingredient is necessary for art as for nature. Bloom's statement that the very opposite of hatred is truly life is borne out by Molly's last words, for it is love which empowers the imagination to overcome time, just as it is love which, in Wallace Stevens's words, "tips the tree of life." The first nine episodes of the book ended with a vision of the act of love as the basic act of art. The last nine episodes end with a vision of love as the basic act of nature. Joyce affirms this union of the two halves of his book by uniting the ship, which appears so heraldically and mysteriously at the end of the "Telemachiad," with the straits which appear at the end of the "Return." The ship sails through the straits, even navigation constituting an amorous movement. The ship is the *Rosevean,* and its name is taken up in Molly's epithalamion where she thinks about wearing a white rose or a red. Thus is fulfilled Stephen's prophecy in the "Oxen of the Sun," "Desire's wind blasts the thorntree but after it becomes from a bramblebush to be a rose upon the rood of time." Yeats, Dante, and Joyce all agree, though Joyce corrects Dante (and Plato) by placing sexual love above all other kinds of love. Red-rosed Molly and Bloom, himself a flower, fertilize the terrestrial paradise. Their youth and age, their innocence and experience, blend. In their dark bed at dead of night the summer sunlight shines.

The narrative level of the book has by this time become less important, and Joyce will not pursue his characters literally because he has negotiated their symbolic reconciliation. On the ethical level Bloom and Stephen have succeeded in taking the city of Dublin by exposing enthusiasm and superstition there, and by disclosing a truer way of goodwill and freedom. Molly's hardwon approbation confirms their enterprise. On the historical level, the characters have awakened from the Circean nightmare of history by drawing the past into the present (a timeless present)

[4] The whole passage in *The Winter's Tale,* IV, iv, 86–97, is relevant. . . . In the same vein, Dante has Virgil explain in the *Inferno,* XI, that "Vostr'arte a Dio quasi è nipote," that is, that God's child is nature whose child is art.

and making it an expression of love instead of hatred, of fondness rather than remorse. Art has been shown to be a part of nature, and in all its processes an imitation of natural ones. These processes have their summit in love, of which the highest form is sexual love.

Joyce outflanks the individual lives of his characters by these ultimate implications. But he outflanks them also by making each episode a part of the body. It seems at first that this slow accretion of a human form was gratuitous, but it must now be seen to be essential. Stephen says that literature is the eternal affirmation of the spirit of man, but pure spirit is something never endorsed in this book. For the body of man must be affirmed with his spirit. So the pervasive physicality of *Ulysses* goes with its spirituality. The identity of the archetypal man whose body the whole book limns is never given; it can scarcely be Bloom, since the book is larger than he; it must include Molly and Stephen, a trinity and a unity. On the analogy of Blake's giant Albion, the androgynous man who stands within and behind and beyond might be called Hibernion. One day he will be Finnegan.

In the final stages of his book, Joyce, with all his boldness, shows a certain embarrassment and reticence. He speaks of love without naming it; he celebrates art as an essential part of nature, but offers his proofs without ceremony or explanation; his moral criticism of his time is sharp yet couched entirely in images; without warning he raises his narrative from a literal to an anagogic plane. He is determined that his book, unlike some of the works of his master Tolstoy, should not be didactic. What claims he has to make for various possibilities in experience he puts forward with the utmost delicacy. That we are all members of the one body, and of the one spirit, remains implicit rather than explicit. This message he will give us only obliquely and in Greek, in Dublin Greek.

The Language of the Outlaw

by Harry Levin

Thinking of Swift, said Thackeray, is like thinking of an empire fall-ing. To think about Joyce is to allow our thoughts to dwell upon a buried city. As they have traversed the stages of his career, we have seen the soaring aspirations of young Icarus lead to the underground labyrinth of the aging Dædalus. We see how his subject broadens as his style dark-ens; the hero of the *Portrait of the Artist* is the author, the hero of *Ulysses* the common man, of *Finnegans Wake* mankind. The past which Joyce tries to recapture, in the throes of his "traumaturgid" [496] night-mare, is not personal reminiscence but collective experience. The burial mound of his sleeping giant contains an enormous and heterogeneous time capsule. H. C. Earwicker's subconscious mind is the historical con-sciousness of the human race. Thus modern culture, rounding out Vico's cycle, cowers before the thunder and returns to the cave—to Plato's cave via Saint Patrick's purgatory. [80] With contemporary ruins accumulating above ground, we seek refuge in the underworld of Homeric shades, in the eternal places of Dante's hell, in Shakespeare's dark backward and abysm of time, in the subterranean passages of Sir Thomas Browne, in the hollow caverns under Wagner's foreboding earth, in Lewis Carroll's rabbit-hole of fantasy, Henry James' deep well of memory, T. S. Eliot's contrived corridors of history, or Thomas Mann's *coulisses* and abysses of the past.

Happily, an Irish wake is apt to rise above its melancholy occasion. Here is Joyce talking to himself: [189-190]

> Sniffer of carrion, premature gravedigger, seeker of the nest of evil in the bosom of a good word, you, who sleep at our vigil and fast for our feast, you with your dislocated reason, have cutely foretold, a jophet in your own absence, by blind poring upon your many scalds and burns and blisters, impetiginous sore and pustules, by the auspices of that raven cloud, your shade, and by the auguries of rooks in parlament, death, with

"The Language of the Outlaw." From Harry Levin, *James Joyce: A Critical Intro-duction.* Copyright 1941 by New Directions, Norfolk, Conn., © 1960 by New Directions Publishing Corporation. Reprinted by permission of the author, New Directions Pub-lishing Corporation, Faber and Faber Ltd., and Lawrence P. Pollinger Ltd.

Superscripts refer directly to pages in the Viking Press edition of *Finnegans Wake,* or, in the case of *Ulysses,* to the 1961 Random House edition.

every disaster, the dynamatisation of colleagues, the reducing of records to ashes, the levelling of all customs by blazes, the return of a lot of sweetempered gunpowdered didst unto dudst but it never stphruck your mudhead's obtundity (O hell, here comes our funeral! O pest, I'll miss the post!) that the more carrots you chop, the more turnips you slit, the more murphies you peel, the more onions you cry over, the more bullbeef you butch, the more mutton you crackerhack, the more potherbs you pound, the fiercer the fire and the longer your spoon and the harder you gruel with more grease to your elbow the merrier fumes your new Irish stew.

The parenthesis is the outcry of the great writer who has come too late. In the times of the Tuatha De Danaan, the legendary tribe that left Greece to colonize Ireland and to be driven into the hills by the later conquests of the Celts, he might have been the Dagda, their poet, priest, and king, whose harp enchanted all his listeners and whose appetite was equal to untold messes of pottage. In a time when universities are bombed and books are burned, the confiscation of the banned English edition of *Ulysses* by the New York post office authorities is an omen of "the levelling of all customs by blazes." The last of the bards, half blinded and long exiled, Shem stirs a magic cauldron at the funeral feast of civilization. His international potpourri is brewed from an Irish recipe, with a dash of everything else he has ever read or heard. *Ulysses* is seasoned with the same ingredients, but *Finnegans Wake* is the richer concoction. The old themes of the artist and the city are combined in the person of the mythical hod-carrier, the builder of cities. Dublin is now merely the local habitation for history itself. Artifice, by a supreme effort, is bent upon creating a language of its own.

The thwarted filial impulse, still prompting Joyce to look up to some intellectual godfather, goes beyond Homer to the scholar who refined Homer out of existence, beyond the authority of Aquinas to the skepticism of Bruno, and beyond Shakespeare's immediacy to Swift's detachment. If a poet is a maker, a prose writer is *altus prosator*—in the Latin of a venerable Irish hymn attributed to Saint Columba—the sublime begetter.[185] As the son becomes a father, he ceases to be a disciple and becomes a rival. Like "Great Shapesphere," [295] he emulates God and rivals nature. The note of banishment, which Stephen Dedalus overheard in Shakespeare, is sounded defiantly. The reception of *Ulysses* has lengthened the distance between Joyce and Ireland, or any other English-speaking country. Ruefully, in *Finnegans Wake,* he glances back at "his usylessly unreadable Blue Book of Eccles." [178] There are moments of startling candor, when he doubts his mission and questions himself: "Was liffe worth leaving?" [230] Or conversely, *à la Henri Quatre,* "was Parish worth thette mess." [199] When he addressed his friend, John Sullivan, whose remarkably pure tenor range was better appreciated abroad than at home, it was "a Banned Writer to a Banned Singer." So much public apathy and

so little critical discernment, together with such excruciating treatment
at the hand of the publishers and censors, tangibly reinforced his sense
of persecution. "A hundred cares, a tithe of troubles," moans the river,
"and is there one who understands me?" [627]

Since Joyce lived to write, though he never wrote for a living, he went
on writing to please himself, with an almost paranoid disregard of any
other reader. The authors of the so-called *Exagmination,* it must be acknowledged, were more of a claque than an audience, like Victor Hugo's
friends on the first night of *Hernani.* Yet Joyce's disregard was touch-
ingly sensitive to the slightest sign of outside interest. His friends report
that his last year was clouded by the indifferent response to *Finnegans
Wake*—as if it could have been otherwise. The indifference was quite
natural, and so was his disappointment. What was unnatural is that he
should have cultivated both for seventeen years "with a meticulosity bor-
dering on the insane." [173] His work in progress he came to regard as "that
letter selfpenned to one's other, that neverperfect everplanned." [489] To
be a writer under such circumstances, for Shakespeare, would have meant
"speechless death"; for Joyce's garrulous fellow Parisian, Gertrude Stein,
it meant a chance to be "alone with English." For Joyce, exile meant a
renewal of silence and, under the tutelage of the Defense of the Realm
Act, a new and diabolical cunning: "Mum's for's maxim, ban's for's book
and Dodgesome Dora for hedgehung sheolmastress." [228]

The silence behind *Finnegans Wake,* like the silence that Carlyle
preached in forty volumes, is the oracular sort that requires comment.
Having abandoned his hopes of direct communication, Joyce turned his
efforts to symbolic expression. "In a Symbol there is concealment and yet
revelation," opined Carlyle's oracle, Dr. Teufelsdroeckh, "hence, therefore, by Silence and by Speech acting together, comes a double significance." But this augmented meaning will be hardly audible to those
whose patience is not intrigued by the metaphorical diction of Vico's
heroic age. To say that Joyce's writing smells of the lamp is to make a
pallid understatement. It reeks of the thurible. No writer, not Flaubert
himself, has set a more conspicuous example of the cult of style. Joyce's
holy grail, *la dive bouteille,* is Shem's inkbottle. For its sake he has given
up his church along with his city, and by its virtue he would recover
them. In the discipline and tradition of literature, perhaps, he finds com-
pensations for the rootlessness of his life. "Suffoclose! Shikespower! Seu-
dodanto! Anonymoses!" he exclaims, transported by his own ingenuity.[47]
He has identified himself with the greatest writers; he has recapitulated
the development of English prose; now he must synthesize his language.

English was only an acquired speech to the artist as a young man. Latin
was an educational and ecclesiastical idiom. Gaelic was one of those nets
that Stephen flew by. The hard years of Trieste and Zurich were weath-
ered by teaching English and other foreign languages in the cosmopolitan
babel of the Berlitz schools. Joyce's synthetic language had to distort, if

not disown, the tongue of Shakespeare and Swift; it had to preserve the hieratic intonations of the liturgy, excite the enthusiasms of a literary movement, and reverberate with the polyglot humors of the professional linguist. To fulfil these conditions, it had to assume what I. A. Richards calls a severance of poetry and belief: it had to be "sanscreed." [215] A ripe specimen of patriotic eloquence, quoted in the newspaper episode of *Ulysses*,[142-143] compares the plight of the Jews under the Pharaohs to that of Ireland in the British Empire. *Why will you jews not accept our culture, our religion and our language?*" the high priest asks Moses. The answer, when Joyce himself declaims it, even through the imperfections of an acoustical recording, is his *apologia* for the nomadic life of the banished writer. His expatriation is an exodus, a deliverance from slavery. The bearer of the curse is destined to be the bringer of the word:

> —*But, ladies and gentlemen, had the youthful Moses listened to and accepted that view of life, had he bowed his head and bowed his will and bowed his spirit before that arrogant admonition he would never have brought the chosen people out of their house of bondage nor followed the pillar of the cloud by day. He would never have spoken with the Eternal amid lightnings on Sinai's mountaintop nor ever have come down with the light of inspiration shining in his countenance and bearing in his arms the tables of the law, graven in the language of the outlaw.*

Saint Patrick, who spent forty days on a mountain in his turn, fasting and praying for the conversion of Ireland, stands by the side of Moses in the hierarchy of *Finnegans Wake*.[307] Here the implied relation of the Irish to the Israelites is that of Stephen to Bloom, of artist to prophet. Inspiration, in the most transcendental sense of the word, holds both terms of the comparison together. A work of art, according to those tenets of esthetic mysticism which Joyce so devoutly professed, is among the varieties of religious experience. His earliest sketches were epiphanies and his choice of a career was a kind of ordination. His maturest work still conforms to the Catholic pattern: as Valery Larbaud observed, it is closer to the Jesuit casuists than to the French naturalists. And, if Joyce's naturalism seems to stem from the confessional, we may also observe that his symbolism is deeply rooted in the sacrament of the mass. The black mass of *Ulysses* follows the *confiteor* of the *Portrait of the Artist*. The hero of *Finnegans Wake,* in the character of a cricketeer named "Hosty," is again united with the body of Christ. "How culious an epiphany!" [508] The church is broad enough to touch the extremes of confession and mystery, both the appalling frankness and the labored obscurity with which Joyce alternately expresses himself. As the artist's stature enlarges, he is no longer a visionary but a demiurge, no longer waiting for revelations but arranging them. With godlike equivocation he can reveal or conceal, mystify or make manifest, fashion myths and forge words.

Words are the stuff that Earwicker's dream is made on. The darker shadings of consciousness, the gropings of the somnolent mind, the states between sleeping and waking—unless it be by Proust—have never been so acutely rendered. But Joyce's technique always tends to get ahead of his psychology. *Finnegans Wake* respects, though it garbles and parodies, the literary conventions. It brims over with ad libs and misplaced confidences and self-conscious stage-whispers. Now and then it pauses to defend itself,[112] to bait the censorship,[179] or to pull the legs of would-be commentators.[453] It mentions the working title,[497] throws in such items as "The Holy Office"[190] and "Gas from a Burner,"[93] and freely discusses the suppression of *Dubliners.*[185] It includes a brief outline of *Ulysses*[229] and even a letter to the author from a dissatisfied reader.[113] In reply, frequent telegraphic appeals from the author to his "abcedminded" readers[18] (". . . stop, please stop, do please stop, and O do please stop respectively . . ."[124]) punctuate[232] the torrent[379] of his soliloquy[560] periodically.[609] These *obiter dicta* cannot be traced, with any show of plausibility, to the sodden brain of a snoring publican. No psychoanalyst could account for the encyclopedic sweep of Earwicker's fantasies or the acoustical properties of his dreamwork.

The strangest feature of this dream vision is that it lacks visual imagery. Joyce's imagination, as his light is spent, concentrates on the "mind's ear."[477] Though he offers us a *"verbivocovisual presentment,"*[341] it is no easier to visualize a Mookse or a Gripes than to gather a clear-cut impression of slithy tove or a mome rath. "Ope Eustace tube!" is his sound advice.[535] When he promises us a view of Dublin, he enjoins us to listen: "Hush! Caution! Echoland!"[13] The isle is full of noises. Gradually, after we have become accustomed to the darkness, we recognize familiar voices. From the pedantic jargon[121] and childish lisping,[396] the young men's blarney[407] and old women's chatter,[101] we distinguish Earwicker by his intermittent stutter[45] and catastrophic hiccup.[454] He is usually submerged in a welter of dialects and documents—pidgin English,[485] American slang,[455] vulgar Latin,[185] liturgical responses,[470] legal forms,[545] advertisements,[181] riddles.[170] To this confusion of tongues the radio lends a spasmodic continuity, comparable to the influence of the film on *Ulysses*. The loudspeaker, with its summons to sales and revolutions, its medley of raucous chamber music and prefabricated repartee, its collaboration between Dædalean engineering and blind static, is the medium of *Finnegans Wake*. With a "tolvtubular high fidelity daildialler,"[309] we tune in on the "sponsor programme" from Howth Castle, "Haveth Childers Everywhere."[531]

Everyone who has played Joyce's captivating phonograph record from "Anna Livia Plurabelle" will agree that the best introduction to his book is to hear him read it aloud. Yet even the author's expressive brogue cannot convey all the inflections, unless it is supplemented by the text. If he ever appeals to the eye, it is to the eye of a reader. A full reading must be simultaneously oral and literary, "synopticked on the word,"[367] dividing our attention between vocal and verbal images. Joyce is interested in both the sound of a word and the figure it cuts on the page. In a disquisition on the alphabet, when he tells us "how hard a thing it is to mpe mporn a gentlerman," he would remind us that, since *beta* has the value of V in modern Greek, B must be indicated by a *mu* and a *pi*.[120] When he speaks of school days, his book takes on the temporary appearance of a schoolbook. One set of marginalia, in pompous capitals, exhibits Vico's terminology. The other set, in shrewd italics, betrays Joyce's own accents. The footnotes are infantile *scholia*. "Traduced into jingish janglage for the nusances of dolphins born" recalls the *in usum Delphini* of an edition of the classics notorious for its expurgations.[275] A geometrical diagram demonstrates the equivalence of one delta-shaped triangle lettered *ALP* to another, or of mother to daughter.[293] An uncivil nose and a pair of crossbones, childishly scrawled at the end of the chapter, are the least abstruse of Joyce's symbols.

The impatient reader, perpetually admonished to look out for typographical ambushes and to keep listening for surreptitious rhythms, may come to feel that *Finnegans Wake* is a grim business. Actually it is a wonderful game—by no means a private affair, but one in which many may join, each with his own contribution, and the more the merrier. This realization may prove equally disturbing to the reader whose conception of art is rather grim. He should realize that all art is a game, the object of which is to make the problems of life and death—with as much insight, skill, and originality as possible—a source of enjoyment. For enjoying *Finnegans Wake*, we need scarcely insist, the prerequisite is not omniscience. It is no more than a curiosity about Joyce's unique methods and some awareness of his particular preoccupations. His work is enriched by such large resources of invention and allusion that its total effect is infinite variety. But, when we are able to scan the variety, we notice that it is controlled by a few well-defined themes and a number of characteristic devices. Myriads of minute details boil down to a handful of generalizations.

The very reverse, of course, is true of the process of composition: it takes the bare elements and exposes them to unceasing elaboration. Writing is primarily a basis for rewriting, and revision is a form of self-caricature. Every word of the first draft is subject to a series of gross exaggerations. Each successive version, even after publication, is a palimpsest for further accretions. We can well believe that the final version of one chapter, previously published as "Anna Livia Plurabelle," cost Joyce more than 1600 intensive working hours. His "warping proccess"[497] enables him to expand and condense at a single stroke; the alteration of a letter will widen the orbit of a phrase. By including all the alternatives, rather than choosing and discarding, he eliminates the writer's chief torture, hesitation between phrases. Incidentally, he throws economy to the winds. Since the essence of his method is not to select but to accumulate, his readers seldom have that feeling of inevitability which is the touchstone of a more reserved style. They feel a continual surprise. Sooner or later, they feel the reservation voiced by Dr. Johnson, when he said of James Macpherson's earlier attempt to revive the spirit of Finn MacCool: "Sir, a man might write such stuff for ever, if he would *abandon* his mind to it."

The differences in mood between *Ulysses* and *Finnegans Wake* are underlined by the contrast between the Homeric poems and that prodigious literary hoax, "Makefearsome's Ocean." [294] Joyce's recourse to the Ossianic poems, like his use of the counterfeit word, "hesitancy," evinces a growing addiction to the idea of forgery. Jim the Penman is forging, with a vengeance, the uncreated conscience of his race. His creative ideals have found their unforeseen fulfilment in "an epical forged cheque on the public for his own private profit." [181] The artist, god of his own world, is no better than a criminal in this one, Joyce obliquely admits; the finest literary imitations of life are fakes. It should be unnecessary to add that the only person who has the right to accuse Joyce of being "a low sham" [170] is himself, and that his accusation is a self-searching testimonial of sincerity. However unintelligible he may seem, he is never incoherent. His idiom is based on a firm command of the usages of popular speech. His habit of sudden generalization is backed by his facility with proverbs. Look at Shem's "bodily getup": "all ears, . . . not a foot to stand on, a handful of thumbs, . . . a deaf heart, a loose liver, . . . a manroot of all evil . . ." [169]

Consciously, by extending his range of reference, Joyce limits our appreciation of his work. Because *po-russki* means "in Russian" in Russian, "Paud the russky" is at once an apology for, and an explanation of, a macaronic Anglo-Russian interlude about the Crimean War. [335] "Pratschkats at their platschpails," for old women by the Liffey, is wasted on us, if we do not know that *prachka* and *plach* are Russian for "laundress" and "crying." [101] But the words we know should teach us not to conclude, from the words we miss, that Joyce can be vague or loose. Whenever we happen to catch the overtones, we are impressed by his philological accuracy and logical rigor. With *Finnegans Wake* the circular exposition of *Ulysses* is carried to its logical conclusion, which is no conclusion at all. The peculiarity of Joyce's later writing is that any passage presupposes a reading knowledge of the rest of the book. On the other hand, to master a page is to understand the book. The trick is to pick out a passage where a breakthrough can be conveniently effected. For this sort of exercise, such set-pieces as the "Tales Told of Shem and Shaun" are both revealing and entertaining. "When a part so ptee does duty for the holos we soon grow to use of an allforabit." [18]

A book must have a beginning, a middle and an end; but a dream may be a jumble of excluded middles. The first page of *Finnegans Wake* is an orderly thematic statement, and the following pages bring their own tautologies and encores. But the reader must be prepared for continuous digression, instead of consecutive narration. Instead of a table of contents, he may take his bearings from a rough summary of the miscellaneous chapters. The first episode of the first section is an epical invocation;[3] the second episode sets Earwicker's peccadillo to the ribald strains of "The Ballad of Persse O'Reilly";[30] the third prolongs the hearsay after closing hours;[48] and the fourth proceeds, with due solemnity, to the trial.[75] All four are unified by the theme of Earwicker's fall; the fifth episode takes up the question of Anna's letter.[104] The sixth consists of twelve leading questions and evasive answers, passing in review the hero (HCE), the heroine (ALP), their tavern (the Bristol), their city (Dublin), their man of all work (Joe), their maid of all work (Kate), their twelve patrons (variously denominated Murphys, Doyles, or Sullivans), their daughter (Isabel), the theory of history (Vico), the theory of love (Swift), the theory of time and space (illustrated by Shem's fable of the Mookse and the Gripes), and the signature of the author (*"Semus sumus!"*) respectively. Shem is the villain of the next episode, unmasked by his twin in an allegorical debate between Justius and Mercius.[169] The rhythm of the river, emerging toward the end of the seventh, is fully orchestrated in the eighth episode, the haunting "Anna Livia Plurabelle" colloquy.[196]

There are four lengthening episodes to the second section, and again to the third. If a dream may be assigned to a definite location, the first section was located in and around the Phoenix Park; the second is at Chapelizod, and the third will be on the hill of Howth. The second section starts to be the program of a play, "The Mime of Mick, Nick, and the Maggies," with cast, credits, and a lively synopsis.[219] When the diversion ends in a thunderstorm, the party retreats into the book of childhood.[260] The third episode takes us on a voyage of discovery, with the patrons of Earwicker's pub as Viking sea-farers.[309] The fourth eavesdrops upon the romance of Tristan and Isolde, through the censorious ears of the quartet of old men ("Mamalujo").[383] After the watchman has told the hour, the third section gives Shaun a chance to tell his fable of the Ondt and the Gracehoper.[403] He is back again, in a second episode, with his sermon.[429] Shaun, by now "Yawn," is his father's boy, and his "dream monologue" leads naturally to Earwicker, as Shem's has led to his mother. The third episode marks the climax with a keen over the barrow of the hero.[474] The fourth, a half-waking evocation of the slumbering household, should be carefully scrutinized for its clues to the literal situation.[555] The fourth section is a brief coda, which heralds the dawn and completes the Viconian revolution.[593]

This enumeration, if it clarifies anything, confronts us with something more like vaudeville than narrative. The deafmute dialogue of a prehistoric comedy team, Mutt and Jute,[16] is revived on the day of judgment by Muta and Juva,[609] and provides a *divertissement* by Butt and Taff in the midst of the battle of Sebastopol.[338] The tabloid scandal of "Peaches" and "Daddy" Browning is warmed over to suit Earwicker's fancy.[65] One red herring after another, pursued by the dreamer, turns out to be an *idée-fixe*. While the main themes are never absent from the background, the foreground is always crowded with topical matters. In the middle distance, ordinarily the center of interest, the action is shadowy and capricious. Avid for a story, the reader will find little in Joyce's "meandertale" [18] to reward his pains. He will track down Saint Michael and Satan to their picture-frame on the wall of Earwicker's bedroom, and rationalize the Garden of Eden into a mantelpiece in the Adelphian style of the brothers Adam.[559] The penultimate episode, he will find, is as detailed a survey of domestic arrangements as the corresponding inventory of *Ulysses*. He will find a more substantial residue of human sympathy in the most tenuous sketch of *Dubliners* than in the whole of *Finnegans Wake*.

And tastes will differ, when he complains of being given an intolerable deal of sack to wash down his half-pennyworth of bread. The richness of Joyce's symbolism helps us to tolerate the realities of the situation. Considered for its vestiges of naturalistic fiction, a night with the Earwickers is weary, flat, and stale. Its most dramatic event, signalized by the vulgar name of a quaint fountain in Brussels,[267] occurs when a child wets his bed.[427] Its *dénouement* is the interruption of Earwicker's connubial performance by a rooster,[595] whose chiliastic "cocorico" is anticipated by numerous alliterations in K.[193] Joyce's perverse passion for the inert and the undistinguished could not have directed him to a less eventful subject. Nor could he, having sacked history and despoiled language, have endowed this unpromising material with more liveliness and distinction. From his own Olympian imaginative level, he causes the all but unmentionable trivialities of daily and nightly routine to produce earth-shaking consequences. Earwicker's flatulence produces Vico's thunder.[258] Pedestrian readers will not forgive a novelist or a dramatist for such conceits, though they accept them from a humorist or even a poet. When we come to sum up Joyce's work, however, we must admit that it was never strong in scenic description, sympathetic characterization, or the other virtues of the novel. His peculiar strength lay in speculation, introspection, and an almost hyperesthetic capacity for rendering sensations. These are poetic attributes, and his successes are the achievements of a poet—in arranging verbal harmonies and touching off emotional responses.

Joyce demands the same degree of absorption that Yeats and Donne receive. We are bound to be disappointed, if we approach him with the notion of extracting a quintessential content from the encumbrances of form. The two, in *Ulysses*, were intended to coalesce. Where they fail to do so, it is because he has imposed a formal requirement that is too rigid to be satisfied without hindering the advance of the plot. The Siren episode is too cluttered up with verbiage to be an effective scene, and too broken up with comment to be an authentic fugue. The drastic solution of this dilemma, in *Finnegans Wake,* is to subordinate content to form: to forego the normal suspenses and sympathies that bind the reader to the book, reduce the plot to a few platitudes that can be readily stylized, and confer complete autonomy upon words. They are now matter, not manner. Nothing could be farther from the fallacy of imitative form than Joyce's latter tendency toward abstract content. We are borne from one page to the next, not by the expository current of the prose, but by the harmonic relations of the language—phonetic, syntactic, or referential, as the case may be. The mythological themes, recurring, varying, modulating into a new context, have a consistency of their own. When we have an index to them, we shall comprehend the book.

The relation between chapters is abrupt and arbitrary, as with the movements of a symphony. As with music, as with any composition in time, the structure seems to dissolve into the texture, when we examine it closely. At close range, *Finnegans Wake* seems to realize the aspiration of the other arts toward the condition of music. The obvious musical analogies are misleading, for they imply a limitation, rather than an enlargement, of our means of expression. They encourage a doctrine of pure poetry, or prose that exists solely for the sake of euphony. Joyce is a consummate master of the music of words, but he is also a master of "the music of ideas," the complex orchestration of associated images which symbolist poets have taught us to appreciate. His innovation is to harmonize the two modes. Now, when you bring discordant sounds and associations together, you have created a pun. If the associations remain irrelevant, it is a bad pun; if they show an unlooked-for relevance, it is better; if the relevant associations are rich enough, it is poetry. The Elizabethans regarded this as a legitimate rhetorical resource. The Victorians degraded it into a parlor trick. Joyce has rehabilitated the pun for literary purposes. Again, as he was fond of pointing out, he has a theological precedent: the church itself was founded on a pun ("thuartpeatrick" [3]).

Having laid down such vast reserves of potential association, Joyce can easily and adroitly pun his way through 628 pages. From Saint Peter and his rock, on one excursion, he can move on to a Greek wine, by a devious route that stops at Petrarch, Laura, laurel, Daphne, and Mavrodaphne.[203] Often these roundabout progressions, like the motions of the mind, disclose unexpected shortcuts. Who would have expected the initial letter of "victory," translated into Morse code and timed to the opening bar of Beethoven's *Fifth Symphony,* to become a symbol by which millions live and die? The dream convention is Joyce's license for a free association of ideas and a systematic distortion of language. Psychoanalysis insinuates its special significances into his calculated slips of the tongue. Under cover of a drowsy indistinctness and a series of subconscious lapses, he has developed a diction that is actually alert and pointed, that bristles with virtuosity and will stoop to any kind of slapstick. His neologism is the joint product of the three types of verbal wit that Freud has discriminated—condensation, displacement, allusion.

Joyce perceived that all attempts to make the subconscious intelligible break down into nonsense. This, of course, did not deter him. He perfected a species of "double-talk," like the convincing gibberish of certain comedians, superficially adjusted to the various norms of discourse, and fundamentally nonsensical. The twofold ambiguity is that, by playfully harping on his obsessions, Joyce makes a modicum of sense. He can contradict himself with a clear conscience and a straight face. Consider his most sustained *double-entendre:* Shaun preaching a sermon on chastity to twenty-nine adolescent girls is really Earwicker professing a more than fatherly love for his daughter. The psychological censor has dictated a sanctimonious tone, and the chapter is scrupulously modelled on the soundest lenten homiletics; but prurience will out. "Oop, I never open momouth but I pack mefood in it," Shaun leers genially.[437] Recommending safe books for the *jeune fille*—to quote one of his few safe examples —he debauches the household words of Dickens into "Doveyed Covetfilles" and "the old cupiosity shape." [434] After the sermon in the *Portrait of the Artist,* and the youthful tragedy of Stephen's first recoil from carnal sin, Jaunty Jaun's homily comes as a monstrous satyr-play.

How did Joyce manage to concoct these "messes of mottage?" [183] By accentuating the purely formal values of words, and by linking them together with as many devices as he could manipulate. Some of these devices are auditory—rhyme,[371] alliteration,[250] assonance,[216] onomatopoeia.[258] Others are morphological—back-formations,[266] infixes,[191] etymologies,[120] spoonerisms.[189] Others are alphabetical—acrostics,[88] anagrams,[140] palindromes,[496] inversions.[311] Still others, more sportive, run through a sequence of words by changing a letter at a time,[142] or weave groups of related names into narratives—one still runs across specimens of this *genre* in school magazines. The material ranges the Joycean gamut from Irish counties ("cold airs")[595] to Ibsen's plays ("peers and gints")[540] and musicians ("peer Golazy" and "mere Bare").[360] Insects and philosophers collaborate in the cosmic irony of the Ondt and the Gracehoper, by this procedure, and hundreds of rivers accommodate themselves to the main stream of the Liffey. Other devices are peculiar to Joyce—like the four polysyllables terminating in the pretentious suffix *-ation,* which he employs now and then to call the discussion to order.[372]

The official guide to his vocabulary is Lewis Carroll's student of semantics, Humpty Dumpty, who could explain all the poems that were ever invented and a good many that hadn't been just yet. Through "portmanteau-words" Joyce is able to instil a Freudian undertone in his small talk. The extra compartment permits the transient word to assimilate local color: a Siberian atmosphere turns the Bristol into an "isbar" and the *spécialité de la maison* into "irsk irskusky." [70] "Potapheu's wife" lends a touch of domestic warmth to an otherwise chilling story.[193] The adjective, "lidylac," applied to curtains, has an appropriate aroma of lavender and old lace.[461] And what better word than "umbroglia" could have been coined to fit the foreign policy of the late Neville Chamberlain? [284] "Umprumptu" [93] colors Humpty Dumpty's fall with a tinge of onomatopoetic spontaneity; "wenchyoumaycuddler" is more specific than it sets out to be.[608] A typical phrase, which telescopes Joyce's prepossessions, is "viceking's graab": Ireland is both the grave of Norse heroes and the spoil of the British viceroy.[18] When, "by the waters of babalong," we sit down and laugh, we are exiled to that border region which is disputed by wit and poetry.[103] "The flushpots of Euston and the hanging garments of Marylebone" have a retrospective poignance that is not unworthy of T. S. Eliot.[192] And, in a fresher vein, the paragraph about the sleeping infant Isobel, "like some losthappy leaf," is a delicate lyric that suggests Hopkins' "Spring and Fall." [556]

On the whole, there were not many obstacles to keep Swift from living up to his definition of style: "proper words in proper places." The wear and tear on language since his time, the corruptions of usage, the vulgarizations of journalism, the affectations of scholarship, have so relaxed the standard that we are no longer surprised to find proper words in improper places. Joyce, with Swift's feeling for linguistic elegance and sense of outraged propriety, has a very different language to handle; the style of *Finnegans Wake,* which shocks us into an awareness of the difference, may be defined as "improper words in proper places." Joyce utilizes the malapropism as the literary expression of social maladjustment, the language of the outlaw. The boyish inscription in a closet of Clongowes Wood College, *Julius Caesar wrote The Calico Belly,* was more than a reduction to absurdity; it was a protest against things as they are. But the genius of Mrs. Malaprop offers a means of escape, as well as a mode of criticism, and sometimes casts a temporary glamor over familiar things. Joyce revised the nursery rhyme, "Ride a cock horse," to advertise "Anna Livia Plurabelle." The one quality she had in common with the fine lady was music, so that is the one word of the last line that does not undergo a sea-change: *Sheashell ebb music wayriver she flows.*

Portmanteau-words and malapropisms can be isolated and analyzed; heavier luggage and longer passages are more securely embedded in the text. When every word of a simple declarative sentence is subjected to the same sort of alteration, the result is not too complex. "Nobirdy aviar soar anywing to eagle it" is simply an ornithological fashion of stating that nobody ever saw anything to equal it.[505] Most of Joyce's sentences are acted upon by more complicating forces. The result is a polyphonic phrasing which takes its key from its most consistent combination of sounds and meanings, but may be modified by substitution or addition at any point. One of the simplest questions of the book is, "How hominous his house, haunt it?" [560] Here the subdominant would be "How ominous his house, ain't it?" The tonic, through the allusive and alliterative influence of the key-word, "house," has introduced "home" and "haunt." The dominant augments the chord by bringing out the latinate adjective for humanity and shifting the question to an injunction. There is a further consonance between "ominous" and "haunt," and between the whole sentence and the main theme. In comparison with the contrapuntal possibilities of this way of writing, the Siren scene from *Ulysses* is plain-song.

Another instance, more strictly measured, is a line from Shaun's account of the Gracehoper's despair: "Was he come to hevre with his engiles or gone to hull with the poop?" [416] Here the honors seem fairly divided between crossing the North Sea and finding out someone's destination in the next world. Not quite fairly. "Hevre" is equally Havre and heaven, as "engiles" refers impartially to the ship's engines and God's angels; but hell hides behind the redoubled opacity of Hull, and "poop" is literal because of the blasphemous suggestion about the Pope. Since the answer to the equation is already hinted by the symmetrical relationship of both parts of the two clauses, no meaning is lost by the displacement, and a certain emphasis is gained. Every sentence is a wilful divagation from the expectations raised by the last. While the rhythmic undercurrent is pulling us in one direction, the drift of associations carries us the other way. By listening carefully, we can make out a number of recurrent lilts and metrical patterns, pulsating through the fluctuations of verbalism. Bear in mind this concise formulation of Vico's doctrine: [215]

Teems of times and happy returns. The seim anew.

The children's hour is responsible for a variation: [277]

We drames our dreams tell Bappy returns. And Sein annews.

The *Götterdämmerung* has a terrifying effect on the words, and leaves the tune unchanged: [510]

—Booms of bombs and heavy rethudders?
—This aim to you!

By the time the Phoenix arises, it is an old story, and we are ready—as in the song about Old Man Finnegan—to begin again: [614]

Themes have thimes and habit reburns. To flame in you.

The system of *leitmotif* borrows more heavily from literary echoes than *Ulysses,* although the cadences of nature are a crucial exception. Rain has its own distinctive rhythm, which adapts itself to an impression of Earwicker's drunken discomfort, as he tosses about at the end of an episode: [74]

Liverpoor? Sot a bit of it! His braynes coolt parritch, his pelt nassy, his heart's adrone, his bluidstreams acrawl, his puff but a piff, his extremities extremely so.

Later on, when deeper slumber has made him deaf to the rain, he is personified as a bridge crossing Dublin Bay:[266]

> Rivapool? Hod a brieck on it! But its piers eerie, its span spooky, its toll but a till, its parapets all peripateting.

The "hitherandthithering waters of" the Liffey are presented with endless versatility;[265] Earwicker is represented by the incremental repetition of "The House That Jack Built." [511] "John Peel," as a drinking song, owes its authority to a hunting print on display at the Bristol.[31] There are doubtless a number of signs advertising Guinness' stout. The ubiquitous slogan is broadcast on the final day: hustled from your graves, when the conquering hero appears in triumph, you are informed that "genghis is ghoon for you." [593] The noble motto of the Order of the Garter is quoted,[113] only to be flouted,[495] and the Lord's prayer is taken in vain by Kate, the cross-grained housemaid, with searing Joycean blasphemy.[530] Joyce, in his echolalia, is revisited by fragments and reminiscences so profusely scattered and so deeply charged, that his maltreatment of them is a culminating gesture of dissent from a lifelong disciple of the fallen archangel. His work is a gargantuan burlesque, not of any other given work, but of the entire cultural heritage.

Often his allusions to other writers justify themselves by enlivening a trite refrain: "Walhalloo, Walhalloo, Walhalloo, mourn in plein!" is a manifest improvement upon Victor Hugo's *"Waterloo, Waterloo, Waterloo, morne plaine!"* [541] On the Belgian battlefield, which it lets you keep in sight, it heaps Valhalla, a war cry, full mourning, and full morning. Joyce is not afraid to hinge the critical point of an episode on an elusive reference. He sketches out the setting for Earwicker's downfall, without mentioning the arsenal, by parodying an epigram that Swift wrote when it was built:

> Behold a proof of Irish sense,
>   Here Irish wit is seen!
> Where nothing's left that's worth defence,
>   They build a magazine!

Joyce falls short of the biting Anglophobia of his model, though he touches, somewhat self-consciously, on Swift's visit to England in the matter of tithes: "Behove this sound of Irish sense. Really? Here English might be seen. Royally? One sovereign punned to petery pence. Regally? The silence speaks the scene. Fake!" [12] The nearer Joyce comes to a scene or an emotion, the more prone he is to indulge in literary byplay. When Earwicker's *cri du cœur* is muffled in a travesty of *Macbeth*, we may assume a studied evasion on the author's part, a determination to detach himself from his characters at all costs: "For a burning would is come to dance inane. Glamours hath moidered's lieb and herefore Coldours must leap no more. Lack breath must leap no more." [250]

These distractions are quite deliberate. If Earwicker's plight really held our attention and solicitude, we should consider them heartless, far-fetched, and even cheap. Joyce shows no more concern for his hero than a geneticist for a fruit-fly; he happens to be interested in the peculiarities of the *genus* earwig. Indifferent, he pares his fingernails, having reached the stage of artistic development that passes over the individual in favor of the general. The divine, far-off event toward which Joyce's doomsday book moves is a "general election." [253] By associating ideas and multiplying parallels he is attempting to universalize his limited subject-matter. Universality, insofar as he can be said to have attained it, is a mosaic of particulars. When he reverts to basic situations, primary emotions, and final values, he is willing to take them for granted. His serious interest is focussed on the manifold permutations of shape, color—in the last analysis—language. Of the romance between his hero and heroine he has a good deal to say, but no more to express than the schoolboy who carves "HCE loves ALP" on a tree-trunk. Instead of selecting the *mot juste,* Joyce accumulates a Rabelaisian catalogue of epithets: ". . . neoliffic smith and magdalenian jinnyjones . . . martial sin with peccadilly . . . solomn one and shebby . . . Regies Producer with screendoll Vedette." [576]

Here the characters, grotesquely magnified and romantically draped, are lay figures. The real romance is between Joyce and the language. Even when his subject is moribund, his writing is alive. The result of his experiments fits in surprisingly well with the conclusions toward which critical theories and poetic practice, propaganda studies and pedagogical tests, semantics and logical positivism, have lately been pushing us. We used to lament that words were such a shadowy approximation of objective reality. We have learned to look upon them as objects of immediate apprehension, more real in themselves than their penumbras of meaning. They were always symbols, to be sure, but we had fallen into the careless habit of confounding the symbol with its referents. Joyce, conceding the priority of the word to the thing, renews our perception of language as an artistic medium. When he sought words, in the hospital chapter of *Ulysses,* to reproduce the origins of life, he was foiled by the intervention of literary history, embryology, and other excrescences. Turning from representation to presentation, he allows nothing to intervene between the prose of *Finnegans Wake* and the flow of the Liffey.

Joyce's book, with more reason than Jules Romains' interminable pot-boiler, is describable as a *roman-fleuve.* Its most authentic voice is the prosopopoeia of the river, rippling upwards to the surface of consciousness in all her feminine moods and changes. When Anna Livia is introduced, she is a vivacious young girl in a shower of spring rain: "Arrah, sure, we all love little Anny Ruiny, or, we mean to say, lovelittle Anna Rayiny, when unda her brella, mid piddle med puddle she ninnygoes nannygoes nancing by." [7] Later she makes a mature appearance, convey-

ing words of maternal comfort to the feckless Shem, "babbling, bubbling,
chattering to herself, deloothering the fields on their elbows leaning
with the sloothering slide of her, giddgaddy, grannyma, gossipaceous
Anna Livia." [195] By the end, her remembrance of girlhood ("just a young
thin pale soft shy slim slip of a thing" [202]) has been transferred to her
daughter *con variazioni* ("just a whisk brisk sly spry spink spank sprint of
a thing" [627]). A shower, a stream, a freshet, the river rises until it drowns
out the other sounds. Meanwhile, on the banks of the Liffey, two old
washerwomen gossip about Earwicker and his family, proceeding "to make
his private linen public" until nightfall has transformed them into a tree
and a stone:[215]

> Can't hear with the waters of. The chittering waters of. Flittering bats,
> fieldmice bawk talk. Ho! Are you not gone ahome? What Thom Malone?
> Can't hear with bawk of bats, all thim liffeying waters of. Ho, talk save
> us! My foos won't moos. I feel as old as yonder elm. A tale told of Shaun or
> Shem? All Livia's daughtersons. Dark hawks hear us. Night! Night! My
> ho head halls. I feel as heavy as yonder stone. Tell me of John or Shaun?
> Who were Shem and Shaun the living sons or daughters of? Night now!
> Tell me, tell me, tell me, elm! Night night! Telmetale of stem or stone.
> Beside the rivering waters of, hitherandthithering waters of. Night!

This paragraph, the last of the first section, is among the few that yielded
to a committee of seven French translators, collaborating with Joyce.
Their task, like Urquhart's with Rabelais, was to translate a style—
double entendre for pun, "*le parc de l'Inphernix*" for "the Fiendish
Park"—where a literal translation would have been meaningless. They
proved, at all events, that the application of Joyce's technique is not restricted to English. Assonance is easier in French, and orthography is
harder:

> *N'entends pas cause les ondes de. Le bébé babil des ondes de. Souris
> chauve, trottinette cause pause. Hein! Tu n'es pas rentré? Quel père
> André? N'entends pas cause les fuisouris, les liffeyantes ondes de. Eh!
> Bruit nous aide! Mon pied à pied se lie lierré. Je me sens vieille comme
> mon orme même. Un conte conté de Shaun ou Shem? De Livie tous les
> fillefils. Sombre faucons écoutent l'ombre. Nuit. Nuit. Ma taute tête
> tombe. Je me sens lourde comme ma pierre-stone. Conte moi de John ou
> Shaun. Qui furent Shem et Shaun en vie les fils ou filles de. Là-dessus nuit.
> Dis-mor, dis-mor, dis-mor, orme. Nuit, nuit! Contemoiconte soit tronc ou
> pierre. Tan rivierantes ondes de, couretcouranies ondes de. Nuit.*

Difficulties of the opposite kind were met by C. K. Ogden, when he
turned the same passage into Basic English, as an accompaniment to
Joyce's recording. His problem was not to imitate the suggestiveness of
the original, but to reduce it to direct statement. Hence he is forced to
ignore harmonies and conceits, and to rule out ambiguities, sometimes
rather arbitrarily. There is not much left:

No sound but the waters of. The dancing waters of. Winged things in flight, field-rats louder than talk. Ho! Are you not gone, ho! What Tom Malone? No sound but the noise of these things, the Liffey and all its waters of. Ho, talk safe keep us! There's no moving this my foot. I seem as old as that tree over there. A story of Shaun or Shem but where? All Livia's daughters and sons. Dark birds are hearing. Night! Night! My old head's bent. My weight is like that stone you see. What may the John Shaun story be? Or who were Shem and Shaun the living sons and daughters of? Night now! Say it, say it, tree! Night night! The story say of stem or stone. By the side of the river waters of, this way and that way waters of. Night!

This self-denying paraphrase juxtaposes the simplest and the most complex English, Mr. Ogden's language of strict denotation and Joyce's language of extreme connotation. Both are reactions against our modern Babel, and Mr. Ogden has hailed Joyce as "the bellwether of debabelization." While his enemies have attacked him for conducting a campaign to disintegrate literature, his friends have rallied to "the revolution of the word." In sober fact, Joyce is neither an obscurantist nor a logodedalist, neither a destroyer nor a creator of language. He could scarcely achieve his microscopic precision and polysemantic subtlety unless he were a neutral. His restless play of allusion depends, to the vast extent of his knowledge, on the acceptance of a linguistic *status quo*. Within his top-heavy frame of reference, everything must be in its place. Whatever is capable of being sounded or enunciated will find its echo in *Finnegans Wake*: Joyce alludes glibly and impartially to such concerns as left-wing literature,[116] Whitman and democracy,[263] Lenin and Marxism,[271] the Gestapo,[332] the Nazis,[375] the Soviets,[414] and the "braintrust." [529] The sounds are heard, the names called, the phrases invoked, as it were by a well-informed parrot. The rest is "SILENCE." [501]

Quinet

by Clive Hart

The more repetition a book contains, the less easy it must obviously be for the writer to create motifs whose recurrence will arrest the attention of the reader. In writing a book so consistently repetitive as *Finnegans Wake*, Joyce set himself the considerable technical problem of creating, for major architectonic or thematic purposes, a few outstanding motifs which would not be entirely swamped by the general flow of mutating material. His simplest solution to this difficulty was to turn aside from his normal custom of building up motifs from insignificant little phrases and to construct, or borrow, a number of very long motifs which, by virtue of their unusual proportions might readily be picked out even on a casual reading—if anyone ever reads *Finnegans Wake* casually. The misquotation from Quinet* is in some ways the most remarkable of these long motifs.

Stuart Gilbert quite correctly defined the technique of *Finnegans Wake* as "*pointilliste* throughout." [1] The development of a style which involved the manipulation of ever smaller and more autonomous units eventually led Joyce to the point where, as I have suggested above, he could insert short, detached phrases in any one of a number of places in the text. Yet in spite of the unusually fragmentary nature of Joyce's own mature literary methods, he seems never to have abandoned his youthful admiration for "supple periodic prose" in the work of other writers. Even as late as 1935 he stuck to his unpopular assertion that Newman was the greatest of English prose-stylists.[2] This love of simplicity in others may well have been a psychological reaction against the complexity of his own writing very similar to that which induced him momentarily to lower his defences and publish *Pomes Penyeach*. In a somewhat lyrical mood he incorporated the

---

"Quinet." From *Structure and Motif in Finnegans Wake*, by Clive Hart (London: Faber and Faber Ltd., 1962), pp. 182–200. Reprinted by permission of Northwestern University Press and Faber and Faber Ltd. A few of Mr. Hart's footnotes have been deleted.

* [Edgar Quinet (1803–1875) French historian and romantic nationalist. A violent anticleric, he was dismissed from his teaching post at the Collège de France for advocating the annihilation of Roman Catholic influence in France.—Ed.]

[1] S. Gilbert, *James Joyce's Ulysses*, London, 1952, p. 96.
[2] *Letters*, p. 366.

Quinet sentence into the text of *Finnegans Wake* in the original French
(281). While this is the only quotation of any length to be included in the
book, it is interesting to note that Joyce has misquoted no less than six
times, almost certainly due to faulty memory:[3]

> *Aujourd'hui, comme aux jours de Pline et de Columelle, la jacinthe se*
> *plaît dans les Gaules, la pervenche en Illyrie, la marguerite sur les ruines*
> *de Numance; et pendant qu'autour d'elles les villes ont changé de maîtres*
> *et de nom, que plusieurs sont rentrées dans le néant, que les civilisations*
> *se sont choquées et brisées, leurs paisibles générations ont traversé les âges*
> *et se sont succédé l'une à l'autre jusqu'à nous, fraîches et riantes comme*
> *aux jours des batailles.*

The sentence is taken from the *Introduction à la philosophie de l'histoire
de l'humanité* [1827], a general and attractively written essay which Joyce
probably found congenial, but which he does not seem to have used in
Finnegans Wake in any other way.[4] The version in *Finnegans Wake* reads
as follows:

> *Aujourd'hui comme aux temps de Pline et de Columelle la jacinthe se*
> *plaît dans les Gaules, la pervenche en Illyrie, la marguerite sur les ruines*
> *de Numance et pendant qu'autour d'elles les villes ont changé de maîtres*
> *et de noms, que plusieurs sont entrées dans le néant, que les civilisations*
> *se sont choquées et brisées, leurs paisibles générations ont traversé les*
> *âges et sont arrivées jusqu'à nous, fraîches et riantes comme aux jours des*
> *batailles.*

Joyce's change of *jours* to *temps* renders the echoes at the beginning and
end of the sentence less exact; the changes of punctuation and the substitution of *noms* for *nom* are not serious (though *nom* is the more usual
French), but by reading *entrées* for *rentrées*, Joyce has surely thrown away
much of the sentence's power to suggest the cyclic nature of history. The
final change—*sont arrivées* for *se sont succédé l'une à l'autre*—may perhaps be intentional, since it considerably improves the rhythmic balance,
but this is in any case just the kind of stylistic improvement we should
expect Joyce to make unconsciously when quoting from memory.

There is rather more to the sentence than its simple content might suggest, for it may be interpreted as a type-example of imitative form on a
small scale—an idea which may never have occurred to Quinet, but of
which Joyce makes full use. A brief analysis will show how well suited it
is to Joyce's purposes. Perhaps the most immediately obvious thing about
the sentence is that, like *Finnegans Wake*, it is a closed circle. After the
word *Aujourd'hui* with which it begins, we step immediately back into
the past: *comme aux temps de Pline et de Columelle.* For Vico, whom

---

[3] *See* the plate between pp. 128 and 129 in Mrs. Maria Jolas' *A James Joyce Yearbook*,
Paris, 1949, which reproduces an even more corrupted version in Joyce's hand; this
shows clear signs of having been written out from memory.
[4] *Œuvres Complètes*, Paris, 1857, vol. II, pp. 367–8. . . .

Quinet studied and translated, the days of Pliny and Columella, when western Rome was on the way toward its destruction, represented the *ricorso* period of transition between two great historical cycles and formed the prelude to a new Theological Age. The historians presiding over the sentence are a symbolic brother-pair who, apart from the role they play in the five variations of the motif, appear twice more in *Finnegans Wake* (255, 319). They are particularly relevant to II.2, where the brother-battle is beginning to be openly expressed during the geometry and history lessons. The symbolic flowers, clearly identified throughout the book with the tempting young girls, follow hard on the heels of these illustrious "twins." Having rapidly established the primary male and female principles, Quinet now lets the sentence move forward again in time from late Roman days, so that it passes over what are in fact three Viconian Ages (post-Roman times, feudal Europe, Vico's own times) until it "rearrives" (*sont arrivées*) at the next Age of dissolution and changeover which Joyce obviously equates with the twentieth century (*jusqu'à nous*). A return to the past is implied in the concluding phrase, *comme aux jours des batailles,* echoing the words *comme aux temps* [or *jours*] *de Pline et de Columelle* with which the sentence began; the cyclic pattern, the BELLUM-PAX-BELLUM (281) is thus clearly established. This verbal echo further justifies Joyce's identification of the twin historians—who might otherwise seem to be no more than passive onlookers—with the eternal combatants. The continuity of the female element, the flowers, is expressed through a neat counterpoint of form and content: even in the central phrases of the sentence, where the transitory nature of the rough male City is under discussion, the rhythm is fluent and gentle.

Joyce was essentially an indoor man, a city dweller. All his books before *Finnegans Wake* are urban. Nature in the Wordsworthian sense seems to have meant little to him, and although in *Finnegans Wake* river and mountain, flower and tree are for the first time used as major recurrent symbols, they are little more than stylised icons which rarely develop into sensuous, living images. In *A Portrait,* the rural setting of Clongowes Wood College is barely mentioned and fulfills no important function as it might have done in, say, a Lawrence, while the more recently published pages from *Stephen Hero,*[5] dealing with rural Mullingar, show how out of touch Joyce felt when he attempted to write naturalistically about events in settings outside his native city. The biographies have little to say about holidays spent away from city life, and the *Letters* contain very little mention of the natural world (except, of course, for the frequent allusions to the Liffey, which formed an essential part of Joyce's urban Dublin). Mr. Frank Budgen insists that Joyce detested flowers, and indeed even the graceful periwinkle, hyacinth and daisy of Quinet's sentence are prized

[5] M. Magalaner (ed.), *A James Joyce Miscellany, second series,* Carbondale, Ill., 1959, pp. 3–8.

more for the abstractions they embody than for their sensuous qualities. Soon after Joyce begins to rework the sentence, he transforms the flowers into a giggling group of lewd schoolgirls, and then into a variety of other rapidly mutating symbols. This is not to say that the book would be better otherwise. In too many places it is already dangerously near to a sentimentality which any softening of Joyce's hard, stylised approach to natural objects could only tend to exaggerate.

The Quinet motif is intimately bound up with the "change-of-sex" theme, the "MUTUOMORPHOMUTATION" (281), as I shall presently demonstrate. First, however, a few comments about Joyce's numerology are needed. All the numbers up to seven, and a few beyond that, are associated with major characters, or groups of characters. The following are the most important identifications:

0 Anna, "Mother Zero"; a female symbol

1 Earwicker, the ithyphallic father

2 Isolde and her "looking-glass" girl; the pair of tempting girls in the Park; the washerwomen (All of these pairs are of course equivalent.)

3 the English soldiers who apprehend Earwicker in the Phoenix Park

4 the Old Androgynes

5 the Four, with their Ass

6 the twelve customers often seem to be made up of six men, each playing two parts (e.g., "a choir of the O'Daley O'Doyles doublesixing the chorus," 48)

7 the "Rainbow-girls," allied to the "2"

10 the Father and Mother in union (see 308, and SK 162–3)

12 the Customers

28 the "February-girls"—an expanded form of the "7" (The algebraical sum of 7 = 28.)

29 Isolde, the leap-year-girl

40 always associated with Anna; possibly her age at the naturalistic level

111 Anna's three children multiplied by a trick of notation; also the kabbalistic total of "A–L–P" (A = 1, L = 30, P = 80)[6]

These are the primary identifications, but Joyce likes the idea of cosmic reciprocity and hence whenever possible he balances a numerical group of one sex with an identical group of the opposite sex, so creating an analogy with the concept of "anti-particles" in modern physics.[7] Thus the female duo is reflected in the Shem-Shaun partnership, while the three soldiers —who seem to be Shem, Shaun, and a form of their father, HCE—are balanced by a female trinity made up of Isolde, her mirror-image, and "their" mother, Anna Livia. In the Quinet sentence, the female duo and

---

[6] See S. L. MacGregor Mathers, *The Kabbalah Unveiled,* London, 1887, p. 3.

[7] It will be noticed that "4" and "10" are the only numbers which Joyce makes intrinsically androgynous; 4 is the "perfect number," . . . and the algebraical sum of 4 = 10.

the male trio are made to appear in their inverted forms, but each of
these groups plays a part which is a combination of the activities of the
"primary" "2" and the "primary" "3"—the tempting of the sinner and
his subsequent apprehension. Thus the belligerent Pliny and Columella,
whose rather feminine-sounding names seem to have suggested to Joyce
that they were inverts,[8] solicit homosexually, while the three nympho-
maniac flowers peep through the shrubbery as do the spying soldiers.
Joyce makes this point in a marginal gloss: the two historians are *"Dons
Johns"*—two gallants—while the three flowers are *"Totty Askins,"* that is,
they are both juvenile ("totty") seducers who ask for the attention of the
males whom they always rebuff, and also three enemy (English) soldiers.
This succinct identification of the girls and the soldiers is further emphasised in the right-hand note, "BELLETRISTICS," which seems to be
Joyce's coinage for Amazons with a literary bias.

Isobel writes two footnotes to Quinet, in the second of which she suggests that the flatus of his very spiritual style be transmuted into the rather
more solid matter to be found on Anna Livia's cloacal scrap of tissue:[9]

> Translout that gaswind into turfish, Teague, that's a good bog and you,
> Thady, poliss it off, there's a nateswipe, on your blottom pulper.

Joyce takes Isobel's advice and parodies the sentence in five places in
Finnegans Wake, thus "translouting" it into his Irish "turfish" and thoroughly assimilating it into the book. (I have used the word "parody" here
for want of a better. Joyce is not really parodying Quinet at any point, but
refashioning his sentence word by word to suit new contexts—an altogether different art for which no adequate term seems to exist. The five
"parodies" are more like free translations into various dialects of
"Djoytsch.") Stylistically, Quinet's sentence is direct, lyrical, and simple
—in short, all that *Finnegans Wake* is not. By the time Joyce was composing his last book, he was long past the stage when he could comfortably
write such simple stuff at this, however much he may have admired it.
The result is that all his reworkings inevitably annihilate Quinet's rather
too self-conscious grace and delicacy. As I shall show below, Joyce has in
every case considerably elaborated and extended the original material,
but it is interesting to see how the necessity to compose within a more or
less predetermined form has very largely curbed his habit of expansion
and interpolation. The first three parodies (those on pages 14–15, 117,
and 236) were incorporated relatively early in their respective chapters,
and although in successive manuscript versions the surrounding passages
have in each case been greatly developed and expanded, the parodies have
remained almost untouched. In their earliest forms they read as follows:

---

[8] E.g., "medams culonelle" (351).
[9] Cf. the Russian General's cleaning himself with a sod of Irish turf (353).

Since the high old times of Hebear and Hairyman the cornflowers have
been staying at Ballymun, the duskrose has choosed out Goatstown's crossroads, twolips have pressed togatherthem by sweet Rush, townland of
twinlights the whitethorn and redthorn have fairygayed the mayvalleys
of Knockmaroon and though for rings round them during a hundred
thousand yeargangs, the Formoreans have brittled the Tooath of the Danes
and the Oxman has been pestered by the Firebugs & the Joynts have
thrown up wallmutting & Little on the Green is childsfather of the city,
these paxsealing buttonholes have quadrilled across the centuries and here
now whiff to us, fresh & made-of-all-smiles as on the day of Killallwhoo.
[British Museum Add. MS 47482 A, ff. 101–2. This was the first of the
parodies to be written, and dates from 1926. See *Letters,* p. 246.]

Since nozzy Nanette tripped palmyways with Highho Harry there's a
spurtfire turf a'kind o'kindling whenoft as the souffsouff blows her peaties
up and a claypot wet for thee, my Sitys, and talkatalka till Tibbs have
eve: and whathough billiousness has been billiousness during milliums of
millenions and our mixed racings have been giving two hoots or three
jeers for the grape, vine, and brew and Pieter's in Nieuw Amsteldam and
Paoli's where the poules go and rum smelt his end for him and he dined
off sooth american this oldworld epistola of their weatherings and their
marryings and their buryings and their natural selections has combled
tumbled down to us fersch and made-at-all-hours like an auld cup on tay.
[Add. MS 47473, f. 102. This version dates from the second half of 1927,
when Joyce was revising the *Criterion III* text of I.5 for *transition* 5,
August 1927. See J. J. Slocum and H. Cahoon, *A Bibliography of James
Joyce 1882–1941,* London, 1953, pp. 99, 101, sections C.64, and C.70.]

Since the days of Roamaloose and Rehmoose the pavanos have been
stridend through the struts of Chapelldiseut, the vaulsies have meed and
youdled through the purly ooze of Ballybough, many a mismy cloudy has
tripped tauntily along that hercourt strayed reelway and the rigadoons
have held ragtimed revels on the plateauplain of Grangegorman; and
though since then sterlings and guineas have been replaced by brooks and
lions and some progress has been made on stilths and the races have come
and gone and Thyme, that chef of seasoners, has made his usual astewte
use of endadjustables and what not willbe isnor was, those danceadeils
and cancanzanies have come stummering down for our begayment through
the bedeafdom of po's greats, the obcecity of pa's teapuc's, as lithe and
limb free limber as when momie played at ma. [Add. MS 47477, f. 21.
This was the third of the parodies to be written, and dates from 1930.
See *Letters,* p. 295. It is interesting to note that in all later versions the
word "stilths" has been corrupted to "stilts."]

The fourth parody (354) is a special case, since the passage in question
went through two stages of composition before it occurred to Joyce to turn
it into a fresh treatment of Quinet:

Forfife and formicular allonall and in particular till budly shoots the
rising germinal badly. [Add. MS 47480, f. 68.]

When old the wormd was a gadden opter and apter were Twummily
twims and if fieforlife fells farforficular allonalls not too particular so till
budly shoots the rising germinal let bodley chew the fat of his auger and
budley bite the dustice of the piece. [Add. MS 47480, f. 67; it is possible
that "auger" should read "anger."]

Joyce worked this up into a parody of Quinet for the *transition* text; once
again the earliest version of the parody is almost identical to the final
printed text:

When old the wormd was a gadden and Anthea first unfoiled her limbs
Wanderloot was the way the wold wagged and opter and apter were
samuraised twimbs. They had their mutthering ivies and their murdhering
idies and their mouldhering iries in that muskat grove but there'll be
bright Plinnyflowers in Calomella's cool bowers when the magpyre's babble
towers scorching and screeching from the ravenindove. If thees liked the
sex of his head and mees ates the seeps of his traublers he's dancing
figgies to the spittle side and shoving outs the soord. And he'll be buying
buys and gulling gells with his carme, silk and honey while myandthys
playing lancifer lucifug and what's duff as a bettle for usses makes cosyn
corallines' moues weeter to wee. So till butagain budly budly [*sic*] shoots
thon rising germinal let bodley chew the fatt of his anger and badley bide
the toil of his tubb. [Add. MS 47480, f. 105; J. J. Slocum and H. Cahoon,
A Bibliography of James Joyce 1882–1941, London, 1953, p. 101, section
C.70.]

The final parody (615) was apparently one of the last passages of *Finnegans Wake* to be composed, since it was not added to Book IV until after
the proofs had been set up. The printed text is almost exactly the same as
the MS insertion.[10] (The decision to include the quotation in French in
II.2 also seems to have been made quite late.)

The original quotation and all the finished parodies are closely associated in the text with commentaries on them which rehearse the basic situation, or much of it, in fresh terms, and in some cases can almost be said
to represent further minor variations on the motif. The paragraph following the quotation in II.2 discusses Quinet's ideas with vivacity and dis-
respectful wit:

Margaritomancy! Hyacinthinous pervinciveness! Flowers. A cloud. But
Bruto and Cassio are ware only of trifid tongues the whispered wilfulness,
('tis demonal!) and shadows shadows multiplicating (il folsoletto nel falso-
letto col fazzolotto dal fuzzolezzo), totients quotients, they tackle their
quarrel. Sickamoor's so woful sally. Ancient's aerger. And eachway both-
wise glory signs. What if she love Sieger less though she leave Ruhm
moan? That's how our oxyggent has gotten ahold of half their world.
Moving about in the free of the air and mixing with the ruck. Enten eller,
either or.

[10] British Museum Add. MS 47488, ff. 195–6.

One can sense in the outburst of exclamation points the relief with which Joyce, for all his praise of Quinet, turned again to the freedom of his own manner. That the sentence in its original and parodied forms is an important touchstone for the whole of *Finnegans Wake* is suggested by the marginal gloss to this commentary: "SORTES VIRGINIANAE"—for those with eyes to see, all our fates are to be found written in the Book of the Virgins, whose mystic invincibility (deriving perhaps from invincible ignorance) seems to be implicit in Joyce's translation of their names. These names once again allude to the masculine, soldierly aspect of the flowers, for Hyacinthus was a homosexual Spartan boy, "Margaritomancy!" may be read "Margaret, a man, see!" and Joyce seems to derive *pervinca* from *pervinco*.

In a charming prelude to the first parody (14), the basic materials of the sentence are presented in a pastoral setting. The polar principles underlying the scene of battles, death and regrowth, are to be found "neath the stone pine" where the "pastor lies with his crook." [11] The androgynous twins are a pair of grazing sheep—"pricket" and "pricket's sister"—while the "herb trinity" seem once again to be female, as on page 281: "amaid" (14). The eternal scene having been set—"Thus, too, for donkey's years"— the parody of Quinet may follow: "Since the bouts of Hebear and Hairyman . . ."

Joyce's inevitable elaborations have allowed the flowers to increase their number to six: "cornflowers . . . duskrose . . . twolips . . . whitethorn . . . redthorn . . . may-," while the garden in which they grow is now located in Ireland. The parody is pregnant with cross-references to other themes and motifs, as we should expect. The word *"riantes"* of the original is rendered by "made-of-all-smiles," which recurs in the next parody as "made-of-all-hours" (117), thus suggesting both the girls' timeless qualities and their constant sensual willingness; the important figure 1000 appears here as "chiliad"; the round of twenty-nine words for "Peace" (470–71)—which forms a complete cycle in itself, and recurs in III.3 as twenty-nine words for "Dead" (499.04)—is heralded in both forms by the phrase "paxsealing buttonholes," implying that the flowers both bring peace and seal up with wax the Letter of life that they help to write. (There is, as I shall show, a constant and close association of the Letter with Quinet's sentence.) The most important of the cross-references, however, is the inclusion of the old dance to the rhythm of which the flowers are made to arrive *jusqu'à nous*: "quadrilled across the centuries." The dance is continually used in *Finnegans Wake* as a symbol of communication and of cyclic progress. When they chant "Peace," the leap-year girls dance widdershins around Shaun-Osiris, as if around a phallic may-pole

[11] The crook is Eve, made from Adam's bent rib; cf. *"Hic cubat edilis. Apud libertinam parvulam"* (7).

and, even more significantly perhaps, they execute a sacred "trepas" [12] when they change this chant to "Dead," on the occasion of his *sparagmos* (499). I have already mentioned Joyce's repeated assertion that the cyclic scheme of *Finnegans Wake* "is like a rumba round my garden." Quinet's flowers grow in the garden of the world as civilisations clash and break, so that in the "rumba" of historical progress we may now perhaps hear a suggestion of the rumble of "toppling masonry."

Into the commentary which follows the first parody, Joyce pours all the superfluity of material that could not be squeezed into the parody itself; useful ideas apparently flowed all too fast. This is one case where the very richness of Joyce's thinking became something of an embarrassment to him. He had already blown the sentence up to more than one and a half times its original length (119 words against Quinet's 75) and had left only the vaguest rhythmic similarity. The decoration of the classical model with a mass of baroque ornamentation had to stop before poor Quinet disappeared altogether. But, as usual, Joyce manages to turn difficulty to his own advantage, for repetition "in outher wards" is, after all, what he is looking for most of the time in *Finnegans Wake*; if he has too much material for any given thematic statement, he simply repeats himself until the material is exhausted. This new flow of rich and evocative symbols gives further valuable insights into the primary situation. The rhythmic superiority of Joyce's free style is at once apparent:

> The babblers with their thangas vain have been (confusium hold them!) they were and went; thigging thugs were and houhnhymn songtoms were and comely norgels were and pollyfool fiansees. Menn have thawed, clerks have surssurhummed the blond has sought of the brune: Elsekiss thou may, mean Kerry piggy?: and the duncledames have countered with the hellish fellows: Who ails tongue coddeau, aspace of dumbillsilly? And they fell upong one another: and themselves they have fallen. And still nowanights and by nights of yore do all bold floras of the field to their shyfaun lovers say only: Cull me ere I wilt to thee!: and, but a little later: Pluck me whilst I blush! Well may they wilt, marry, and profusedly blush, be troth! For that saying is as old as the howitts. Lave a whale while in a whillbarrow (isn't it the truath I'm tallin ye?) to have fins and flippers that shimmy and shake. Tim Timmycan timped hir, tampting Tam. Fleppety! Flippety! Fleapow!
> Hop!

In the second parody, on page 117, the brother-pair, who had been incarnated on page 14 as cavemen equivalents of Heber and Heremon, take on the form of a music-hall song-and-dance team: "Since nozzy Nanette tripped palmyways with Highho Harry . . ." The three flowers, on the other hand, no longer figure as individuals, but as a collective symbol, the Letter: "this oldworld epistola." In identifying the flower-girls with their Letter, Joyce is even more literally putting into practice Isolde's sugges-

---

[12] *Trépas* (Fr.) = death.

tion in her second footnote on page 281. It is significant that while this is the version in which the Quinet-Letter identification is made most explicit, it is also the parody which departs most from the rhythms and general organisation of the original (except for the special case on page 354); Joyce is opting for more "turfish" and less French. It is particularly rich in allusions to other motifs and their associated symbols, the most salient of these being the cup-of-tea-and-pot still-life which is usually in evidence somewhere in the middle-ground whenever the Letter is under discussion. The water for the wetting of the tea and the consequent creation of a new world is heated over the fire of "Pat's Purge" (117)—an amusing conceit by means of which Joyce closely associates the tea symbol with the ubiquitous Phoenix-Magic-Fire theme. Bridget and Patrick enter with their constant litany of "tauftauf"–"mishe mishe," modified here to "souffsouff" and "talkatalka," and since Bridget and Patrick are a constantly recurring brother-and-sister pair, their solemn ritual is evidently to be identified with the theatrical frivolities of "Nanette" and "Harry."

The survival of the Letter-posy over the "billiousness" of infirm "mixed racings" is developed in a very direct statement of the Viconian cyclic principle:

> this oldworld epistola of their weatherings and their marryings and their buryings and their natural selections has combled tumbled down to us fersch and made-at-all-hours like an ould cup on tay.

The scene of the rise and fall of masculine glory has meanwhile been shifted from Ireland (15) back to Europe—"Pieter's in Nieuw Amsteldam and Paoli's where the poules go"—or perhaps even farther afield—"he dined off sooth american"—but wherever the comedy may be played out, the slow progress of history is seen to be like nothing so much as the gigantic drinking party of *Finnegans Wake*: "two hoots or three jeers for the grape vine and brew." The whole of this parody is in fact a further stage in Joyce's reduction of the nightmare of history to a "shout in the street."

The *jours des batailles*, which in the first parody were metamorphosed into an Irish bloodbath on the "eve of Killallwho," are now no more than a storm in "an ould cup on tay." [13] Joyce is identifying the fighting in the field with the sexual battle which assures the continued existence of the race of flowers, and in so doing he is postulating the ultimate interdependence of Quinet's opposed principles of war and peace, mortality and continuity. This is yet another example of the far-reaching ways in which *leitmotivs* work for Joyce, for without the structural correspondence "*jours des batailles*–ould cup on tay," which the motif establishes, Joyce's point would be lost.

In the brilliantly concise version of the sentence on page 236, the two

---

[13] See F. M. Boldereff, *Reading Finnegans Wake*, New York, 1959, pp. 182ff. for some interesting comments on the function of tea-symbolism in *Finnegans Wake*.

Roman historians have been transformed into the traditional founders of their city—"Roamaloose and Rehmoose"—a rather less pacific couple. After having quadrilled across the centuries which separate I.1 and II.1, the flowers have been refined away until nothing remains of them but the essence of their dances—the pavans, waltzes, reels, and rigadoons—while the scene of their seductive frolics has once more been shifted back to Ireland. The alternations of Irish and overseas backgrounds to the parodies (14–15, Ireland; 117, Europe and South America; 236, Ireland; 354, Eden; 615, "our mutter nation") parallel the many other oscillations of locality in *Finnegans Wake*—Tristan's loves in Brittany and Ireland, Shem's trips to Australia, Shaun's to the United States. Later on in the sentence, after it has moved forward in time, the older dances mentioned above are seen to have developed into the crazy modern gaiety of the Parisian cancan ("cancanzanies"), which stimulates the frustrated Earwicker to the point of *bégayement* ("begayment").

The destruction of the expendable male aspects of the world is equated with the preparation of food—"Thyme, that chef of seasoners, has made his usual astewte use of endajustables" (236)—which is one of the favourite pastimes of fat-bellied Shaun to whom the "dimb dumbelles" (236) pander at every turn. (The dumb-bell—the mathematical sign for infinity, ∞—is, of course, an especially suitable symbol for Joyce's immortal but empty-headed and vulgar flower-girls.) The seasoning of history's stew is just one more aspect of the "Eating the God" theme which Joyce took over from Frazer, and, after all, says Joyce, no matter how often the Host may go a progress through the guts of a communicant, the true God remains whole, inviolate. However destructive and degenerate Shaun's gourmandising may seem, nothing is really destroyed in the process; the laws of conservation always hold, so that "whatnot willbe isnor." History, like the kaleidoscope of *Finnegans Wake*, simply rearranges a number of "endadjustables," and the sharing out of the God among the congregation, though it symbolises the continuity of life, is no more than a juggling with the distribution of the same particles of Being. Through past eons and past epochs (236) the flower-dancers have continued to survive the *jours des batailles* which are no longer equated, as on page 117, with the lively and "fizzin" (308) cup of tea, but with the struggles of the ageing Anna to remain fertile. Book II is the Book of the Children; Anna has been replaced, and we watch the pitiful spectacle of the already mummified woman playing at the motherhood of which she is no longer capable (236). The cup of tea that was once her most important fertility symbol reappears in this parody, but only in association with the deaf, purblind, and obsessed old man of a past age, who has been supplanted just as his wife has: "the bedeafdom of po's taeorns, the obcecity of pa's teapucs." Furthermore, as Joyce uses back-slang for the cup ("teapucs"), we may fairly assume that it is upside down and hence, like Omar's glass, empty. The word "teapucs" may also contain the "specs" necessary to combat pa's approaching blindness; there seems to be at least one physical defect that Earwicker shares with his myopic second-best son, Shem.

In the preceding paragraph, Anna Livia's *billet doux* ("billy . . . coo") is identified with the Missal used at the communion, but when an office from it is sung—"and sing a missal too"—this is discovered, rather surprisingly, to be no more than the latest version of Quinet. Joyce could hardly have made greater claims for his motif.

The fourth parody is by far the most difficult of the set, and at the same time one of the most significant. The supreme importance of Quinet's sentence in *Finnegans Wake* is emphasised by the use to which Joyce puts this version—namely, to conclude the central "Butt and Taff" conversation as the two speak in unison for the first and only time. The passage is so dense with meaning that it will be as well to quote the final polished text in full:

> When old the wormd was a gadden and Anthea first unfoiled her limbs wanderloot was the way the wood wagged where opter and apter were samuraised twimbs. They had their muttering ivies and their murdhering idies and their mouldhering iries in that muskat grove but there'll be bright plinnyflowers in Calomella's cool bowers when the magpyre's babble towers scorching and screeching from the ravenindove. If thees lobed the sex of his head and mees ates the seep of his traublers he's dancing figgies to the spittle side and shoving outs the soord. And he'll be buying buys and go gulling gells with his flossim and jessim of carm, silk and honey while myandthys playing lancifer lucifug and what's duff as a bettle for usses makes coy cosyn corollanes' moues weeter to wee. So till but-again budly shoots thon rising germinal let bodley chow the fatt of his anger and badley bide the toil of his tubb.

This is the only occasion on which Quinet's single sentence has been broken down by Joyce into more than one—a fact which must be accounted for by the peculiar circumstances of the parody's genesis. The flowers have been transported away from time and space and made to blossom in the Garden of Eden, the site at which so many of Joyce's motifs are allowed to play themselves out. It will be seen that Pliny and Columella are once again present in person and that Anna Livia herself makes a third with her girls, in the guise of Aphrodite Antheia. In this passage, however, Joyce has gone far beyond Quinet, on to whose little sentence he has piled allusion after allusion to virtually every major theme in *Finnegans Wake,* including the Fall, ritual murder, blindness, Wagnerian Magic-Fire, the dance, Irish nationalism, homosexuality, simony, and micturition.

On page 615, where the last of the parodies immediately precedes the fullest and most important version of the Letter, the association of the two motifs is given its final and simplest expression. Since Book IV is the Age of Vico's *ricorso,* in which dawn begins to disperse many mists, Joyce reverts to a rather closer adherence to the rhythms and content of the original sentence. Pliny and Columella reappear almost undisguised, and the three flowers flourish again in the forms which Quinet gave them. Even here, however, there are numerous complexities. Columella doubles with Columkille, thus making another link in the long chain of correspondences that Joyce is always at pains to establish between Ireland and Rome.[14] The three flowers, from Gaul, Illyria, and Numancia, now show by their names that they in fact owe allegiance to more than one nation: the hyacinth from Gaul ("all-too-ghoulish") is also Italian ("Giacinta"); the Illyrian periwinkle has French ancestry ("Pervenche"); the Spanish daisy among the ruins of Numancia is half English ("Margaret"). In the last analysis they all belong to Ireland: "our mutter nation."

The most interesting change in this final parody is the inclusion for the first time of a clear symbol of male immortality. "Finnius the old One" also endures through the "hophazzards" of history. Though the manifestations of the masculine principle seem more transient than those of the feminine, the underlying essence of Finn the Giant is no less real or indestructible than that of Anna Livia with her twenty-nine tributaries. Finn will wake again at "Cockalooralooraloomenos." (This is one of the last appearances in *Finnegans Wake* of the cockcrow motif which throughout the book forms a trinity with the thundervoice (Father) and the Word "whiskey" (holy spirit), and shares with them the privilege of awakening the fallen hero to new life.)

The tea-table with cup, saucer, and teapot is now reset as the morning breakfast-table at which eggs are to be eaten: "there'll be iggs for brekkers come to mournhim" (12). At least one version of the Letter is written on the shells of these eggs—"there's scribings scrawled on eggs" (615)—and as they are broken open to be eaten, we at last understand how it is that the "punctuation" of the Letter is supplied by the fork of the Professor at the Breakfast Table (124), although the attempt to eat boiled eggs with a fork seems to brand the Professor as one of the absent-minded variety. As always, Joyce aims for a duality of function in his symbolism, so that the "piping hot" morning teapot is made to serve also as Molly-Josephine's orange-keyed night-utensil, the "Sophy-Key-Po" of 9. Having so firmly established the association of the Letter with the eggs on which it is written, with the generative power of tea, and with the cycle of ingoing and outgoing water, Joyce then hatches the complete text (615–19).

[14] Cf., for example, "The seanad and the pobbel queue's remainder" (434).

James Joyce in His Letters

by Lionel Trilling

In 1935, near the end of a long affectionate letter to his son George in America, James Joyce wrote: "Here I conclude. My eyes are tired. For over half a century they have gazed into nullity, where they have found a lovely nothing."

It is not a characteristic utterance. Joyce was little given to making large statements about the nature of existence. As Dr. Johnson said of Dryden, he knew how to complain, but his articulate grievances were not usually of a metaphysical kind. They referred to particular circumstances of practical life, chiefly the lets and hindrances to his work; at least in his later years, such resentment as he expressed was less in response to what he suffered as a person than to the impediments that were put in his way as an artist.

And actually we cannot be certain that Joyce did indeed mean to complain when he wrote to George of his long gaze into *"nulla"*—his letters to his children were always in Italian—or that he was yielding to a metaphysical self-pity when he said he had found in it *"un bellissimo niente."* The adjective may well have been intended not ironically but literally, and Joyce can be understood to say that human existence is nullity right enough, yet if it is looked into with a vision such as his, the nothing that can be perceived really *is* lovely, though the maintenance of the vision is fatiguing work.

To read the passage in this way is in accord with our readiness nowadays to see Joyce as preeminently a "positive" writer, to be aware of the resistance he offered to nullity through his great acts of creation. From the famous climactic epiphany of *A Portrait of the Artist as a Young Man*, in which life "calls" in all imaginable erotic beauty and is answered in ecstasy, he went on to celebrate human existence even in the pain, defeat, and humiliation that make up so large a part of its substance. He consciously intended Molly Bloom's ultimate "Yes" as a doctrinal statement, a judgment in life's favor made after all the adverse evidence was in. He contrived a rich poetry out of the humble and sordid, the sad repeated round of the commonplace, laying a significant emphasis on the little, nameless, unremembered acts of kindness and of love—it is much to the point that Joyce as a young man could speak of Wordsworth in superlative praise, with particular reference to *The Excursion,* for much of the power of his own work derives from the Wordsworthian purpose of discovering a transcendence by which life, in confrontation with nullity, is affirmed.

But this does not tell the whole story of the relation in which Joyce stood to nullity. He was not only resistant to it but also partisan with it. He loved it and sought to make it prevail. The transcendent affirmation of hypostasized life went along with a profound indifference, even a hostility, to a great many of the particularities in which the energies of life embody themselves. He could speak in thrilling archaic phrase of "the fair courts of life," yet the elaborations of developed society were for the most part of no account to him, and to much of the redundancy of culture as it proliferates in objects and practices that are meant to be pleasing he was chiefly apathetic. His alienation from so many of the modes and conditions of human existence is sometimes chilling.

Among life's processes, that of entropy makes an especial appeal to Joyce. The "paralysis" which is represented in *Dubliners* as the pathology of a nation at a particular moment of its history was also known to him as a general condition of life itself, and if he found it frightening, he also found it tempting. *Dubliners* does indeed have the import of social criticism that its author often said it was meant to have. This "chapter in the moral history" of his nation levels an accusation to which the conscience of his race, when at last it will have been forged in the smithy of his soul, must be sensitive. But if the devolution of energy to the point of "paralysis" is, in a moral and social view, a condition to be deplored and reversed, it is also for Joyce a sacred and powerful state of existence. The attraction it had for him is nearly overt in the first story of *Dubliners,* "The Sisters," and in the last, "The Dead." "The special odor of corruption which, I hope, floats over my stories" is the true scent by which life is to be tracked to its last authenticity. It is not without reason that Samuel Beckett is often said to have represented Joyce in the Hamm of *Endgame,* the terrible blind storyteller who presides over the quietus of Nature, himself on the verge of extinction but grimly cherishing and ordering what little life remains, setting against the ever-encroaching void, which he himself has helped bring about, an indomitable egoism that is itself an emptiness.

The power of Joyce's work derives, we must see, not only from the impulse to resist nullity but also, and equally, from the impulse to make nullity prevail. Something of the destructive force was remarked by T. S. Eliot when, taking tea with Virginia Woolf and trying to convince his hostess that *Ulysses* was not to be dismissed as the work of one or an-

other kind of "underbred" person, he characterized the author's achievement and the magnitude of his power by saying that he had "killed the
19th century." Eliot meant that Joyce by his radical innovations of style
had made obsolete the styles of the earlier time, and also that, as a result
of or in concomitance with the obsolescence that Joyce had effected, the
concerns and sentiments to which the old styles were appropriate had
lost their interest and authority. In 1922, the 19th cenutry was not in
high repute and one might suppose that the report of its having been
killed would make an occasion for hope: with the old concerns and
sentiments out of the way, those of the new day might be expected to
flourish. But Eliot expressed no such expectation. Although he took it
to be part of the great achievement of *Ulysses* that it had shown up "the
futility of all the English styles," he went on to say that Joyce had destroyed his own future, for now there was nothing left for him to write
about. Nor for anyone else: Eliot later said that with *Ulysses* Joyce had
brought to an end the genre of the novel.

If there is truth in Eliot's observation, a phrase of Walter Pater's helps
us understand what concerns and sentiments of the 19th century Joyce
may be said to have killed. In a famous paragraph of the Conclusion to
The Renaissance, Pater spoke of "success in life." It doesn't matter that
he was saying that success in life was the ability to burn with a hard
gemlike flame, to make all experience into an object of aesthetic contemplation. The point is that, at the high moment of his exposition of
a doctrine directed against crass practicality, Pater could use a phrase that
to us now can seem only vulgar, a form of words which scarcely even
stockbrokers, headmasters, and philistine parents would venture to use.
In the 19th century a mind as exquisite and detached as Pater's could
take it for granted that upon the life of an individual person a judgment
of success or failure might be passed. And the 19th-century novel was in
nothing so much a product of its time as in its assiduity in passing this
judgment.

It was of course moral or spiritual success that the novel was concerned
with, and this "true" success often—though not always—implied failure
as the world knows it. But a characteristic assumption of the novel was
that the true success brought as much gratification as conventional opinion attributed to worldly success, that it was just as real and nearly as
tangible. The conception of moral or spiritual achievement was, we may
say, sustained and controlled by the society from whose conventions the
triumph was wrested. The houses, servants, carriages, plate, china, linen,
cash, credit, position, honor, power that were the goods of the conventional world served to validate the goods of the moral or spiritual life.
At the heart of the novel is the idea that the world, the worldly world,
Henry James's "great round world itself," might have to be given up
in the interests of integrity or even simple decency. What made this idea

momentous was the assumption that the surrender is of something entirely real, and in some way, in the forcible way of common sense, much to be desired. Upon the valuation of what is given up depends much of the valuation of what is gotten in exchange. Poor Julien Sorel! Poor Pip! Poor Phineas Finn! It was a dull-spirited reader indeed who did not feel what a pity it was that the young man could not make a go of Things As They Are and at the same time possess his soul in honor and peace. But since the soul was one of the possible possessions, it was of course to be preferred to all others, the more because the price paid for it was thought real and high. In the degree that the novel gave credence to the world while withholding its assent, it established the reality of the moral or spiritual success that is defined by the rejection of the world's values.

Credence given, assent withheld; for a time this position of the novel *vis-à-vis* the world was of extraordinary interest. At a certain point in the novel's relatively short history, in the first quarter of this century, there burst upon our consciousness a realization of how great had been its accomplishment, how important its function. It was on all sides seen to be what Henry James in effect said it was, what D. H. Lawrence explicitly called it, "the book of life."

Yet no sooner had the novel come to this glory than it was said, not by Eliot alone, to have died. In all likelihood the report is true. The question of the viability of the novel today is probably to be answered in the spirit of the man who, when asked if he believed in baptism, replied that of course he did, he had seen it performed many times. Novels are still ceaselessly written, published, reviewed, and on occasion hailed, but the old sense of their spiritual efficacy is ever harder to come by. One thing is certain: to whatever purposes the novel now addresses itself, it has outgrown the activity which, in the 19th century and in the early days of the 20th, was characteristic of the genre, virtually definitive of it, the setting of the values of the moral and spiritual life over against the values of the world. This is a confrontation that no longer engages our interest. Which is by no means to say that getting and spending are not of great moment, or that moral and spiritual sensibility have declined. As to the latter, indeed, it flourishes in a way that is perhaps unprecedented—it may well be that never before have so many people undertaken to live enlightened lives, to see through the illusions that society imposes, doing this quite easily, without strain or struggle, having been led to the perception of righteousness by what literature has told them of the social life. Whatever we may *do* as persons in the world, however we behave as getters and spenders, in our other capacity, as readers, as persons of moral sensibility, we *know* that the values of the world do not deserve our interest. We know it: we do not discover it, as readers once did, with the pleasing excitement that the novel generated as it led toward understanding. It is a thing taken for granted. That the world is a cheat, its social arrangements a sham, its rewards a sell, was patent to us from our moral infancy, whose first spoken words were, "Take away that bauble."

So entirely, and, as it were, so naturally do we withhold our assent from the world that we give it scarcely any credence. As getters and spenders we take it to be actual and there; as readers our imagination repels it, or at most accepts it as an absurdity. What in the first instance is a moral judgment on the world intensifies and establishes itself as a habit of thought to the point where it transcends its moral origin and becomes a metaphysical judgment.

More and more the contemporary reader requires of literature that it have a metaphysical rather than a moral aspect. Having come to take nullity for granted, he wants to be enlightened and entertained by statements about the nature of nothing, what its size is, how it is furnished, what services the management provides, what sort of conversation and amusements can go on in it. The novel in some of its experimental and theoretical developments can gratify the new taste, but this is more easily accomplished by the theater, which on frequent occasions in its long tradition has shown its natural affinity for ultimate and metaphysical considerations. By means of the irony which it generates merely through turning a conscious eye on its traditional devices of illusion, the theater easily escapes from its servitude to morality into free and radical play with the nature of existence as morality assumes it to be. That life is a dream, that all the world's a stage, that right you are if you think you are—such propositions can be forcibly demonstrated by the theater, which, defined by its function of inducing us to accept appearance as reality, delights in discovering in itself the power of showing that reality is but appearance, in effect nothing.

At least at one point in his life, Joyce rated drama above all literary forms and made what he called the "dramatic emotion" the type of the "aesthetic emotion" in general. With the metaphysical potentialities of drama he was not concerned in an immediate way, but his famous account of the "dramatic emotion" has an obvious bearing upon the theater's ability to control, even to extirpate, the credence given to the worldly reality. Dedalus explains to Lynch that this emotion is "static," that it is brought into being by the "arrest" of the mind. "The feelings excited by improper art are kinetic, desire and loathing. Desire urges us to possess, to go to something; loathing urges us to abandon, to go from something. The arts which excite them, pornographical or didactic, are therefore improper arts. The aesthetic emotion (I use the general term) is therefore static. The mind is arrested and raised above desire and loathing."

Nothing, of course, could be further from the aesthetic of the novel in its classic phase. The novel was exactly, in Joyce's sense of the words, both pornographical and didactic, having the intention to generate desire and loathing, to urge the possession of the good, the abandonment of the bad. Assuming the prepotency of the will, the novel sought to educate and direct it by discriminating among the objects to which it might address itself. But Joyce characteristically represents the will in entropy, in its movement through ambiguity and paralysis to extinction. In *Ulysses,* for example, the objects of desire or intention of virtually all the characters are either of no great moment as the world judges, or they exist in unrealizable fantasy, or in the past.

There is one exception. The will of one person is represented as being, although momentarily in abeyance, on the point of becoming prepotent, and its object is represented as both capable of attainment and worth attaining: Stephen Dedalus means to become a great writer and we know, of course, that he does. The will of the artist is accepted in all its legendary power and authority, fully licensed. And the worldly traits of the particular artist Stephen Dedalus are entirely acknowledged—his bitter intention of fame, his pride, his vanity, his claim to unique personal superiority, touched with class feeling, his need to be ascendant in every situation. Yet the world to which these traits refer, that world to which Yeats—the admirer of Balzac!—gave so lively a recognition, in which the artist wins his prizes, has no existence in *Ulysses.* On the evidence that the book provides, there is nothing that can signalize the artist's achievement of success in life. There is no person, let alone a social agency, competent and empowered to judge his work and tell him that he has triumphed with it, that he has imposed his will upon the world and is now to be feared and loved. The honor he deserves cannot be accorded him, since the traditional signs of honor are wanting—there is no fine house to inhabit, no comfort or elegance that can gratify his heroic spirit after strenuous days, no acclaim or deference appropriate to his genius. His prepotent will lifts him above the primitive life, the everlasting round of birth, copulation, and death, making him peerless: his only possible peers are a certain few of the preeminent dead, among whom God is one, on the whole the most congenial of the small company. It is chiefly in emulation of the work of this particular colleague that Joyce undertakes his own creation, intending that his book shall be read as men formerly "read" the "book of the universe." In his eyes a thousand years are as but a day, or the other way around, and the fall of the sparrow does not go unnoticed. The round of birth, copulation, and death receives his sanction under the aspect of eternity and in the awful silence of the infinite spaces, and his inscrutable but on the whole affectionate irony is directed upon all that men contrive in their cities for their survival, with a somewhat wryer glance toward what they contrive for their delight. Who that responds to the subtle power of his work can ever again, as a reader, give serious thought to the appointments of the house, the ribbon in the buttonhole, the cash in the bank and the stocks in the portfolio, the seemliness of the ordered life, the claims of disinterested action (except as they refer to certain small dealings between one person and another, especially between father and child), the fate of the nation, the hope of the future? And however else we read *Finnegans Wake,* we cannot fail to understand that it is a *contra-Philosophie der Geschichte,* that its transcendent genial silliness is a spoof on those segments of the solemn 19th-century imagination— History, and World Historical Figures, and that wonderful Will of theirs which, Hegel tells us, keeps the world in its right course toward the developing epiphany of *Geist.*

But if Joyce did indeed kill the 19th century, he was the better able to do so because the concerns and sentiments he destroyed made so considerable a part of the fabric of his being. To read his letters as we now have them is to be confirmed in our sense of his denial of the world, but it is also to become aware that what is denied was once affirmed with an extraordinary intensity. It is to understand how entirely Joyce was a man of the century in which he was born, how thoroughgoing was his commitment to its concerns and sentiments, how deeply rooted he was in its ethos and its mythos, its beliefs and its fantasies, its greedy desires, its dream of entering into the fair courts of life.

In 1957 Stuart Gilbert brought out a volume called *Letters of James Joyce,*[1] which gave us most, though not all, of the letters that were available at the time. Taken as a whole, the collection proved disappointing. It included relatively few letters of the early years, always likely to be the most interesting period of a writer's correspondence; by far the greater number date from the years of maturity, beginning at a time when, although not yet famous, Joyce was already a figure, and of these a great many are devoted to business in the unremitting and often trifling detail in which Joyce carried it on. Nothing that bears upon Joyce's life can fail to command attention, but there is not much in Mr. Gilbert's collection that goes beyond the well-known public aspects of the career to make the appeal of intimacy.

It is true that some reviewers remarked on a quality of warmth and gaiety that they found in the letters and on how much more "human" this showed Joyce to be than had hitherto been supposed. By his middle years Joyce had developed a talent, if not for friendship, then at least for friendliness; whatever else his friends may have been to him, they were his aides, adjutants, and ambassadors, and in the letters in which he did business with them and through them, there sounds a note of geniality, often of a whimsical kind, which, as the reviewers noted, is at variance with what is often reported of his forbidding reserve. But it is possible to feel that the genial air is rather *voulu,* even contrived,[2] and at least

---

[1] [New York: The Viking Press.—Ed.]
[2] The letters to Frank Budgen are exceptional in suggesting Joyce's actual enjoyment of a relationship with another person.

one reviewer put the matter of the "humanness" in a qualified way—Philip Toynbee said no more than that the letters "reveal a far less inhuman man than the myth had led us to believe." They may be thought to reveal a man who, out of his sense of what is seemly, or perhaps for reasons of policy, wished to conceal the full extent of his "inhumanness," of his detachment from the affections. On the evidence of the first published letters, only one event of his middle age seems ever actually to have reached Joyce, his daughter's extreme mental illness. Even here the *apatheia* is to some degree in force, in part through the self-deception as to the true state of affairs that Joyce practiced, although we are in no doubt about the bitterness of his grief.[3] For the rest, the personal life seems to have been burned out, calcined. The difficulties of the once obsessing marriage appear to have been settled one way or another and no new erotic interests are to be discerned. The dialectic of temperament has come to an end—there are scarcely any indications of an interplay between the self and the life around it, the existence of which is recognized only as the world rejects or accepts Joyce's art.

Immediately after the appearance of Mr. Gilbert's collection there came to light a great trove of Joyce's letters, preserved through many vicissitudes. They were available to Richard Ellmann in the research for his definitive life of Joyce, and Professor Ellmann has edited them with the erudition and intelligence that make his biography the superlative work it is. The two collections have been conjoined to make a new *Letters of James Joyce* in three volumes,[4] of which Mr. Gilbert's is now Volume I, Professor Ellmann's Volumes II and III. The arrangement is anomalous and of course awkward, since the collections cover the same span of time although in different degrees of completeness. But the practical nuisance should not be exaggerated. The Joyce scholars are inured to worse difficulties than those to which the arrangement subjects them. And the general reader will inevitably conclude that Volumes II and III make the corpus of the *Letters* to which Volume I serves as a supplement. His conclusion will be based not merely on the greater scope of the later volumes but on the extent of their interest, which is beyond comparison with that of their predecessor.

The letters of the mature years that are given in Professor Ellmann's collection do not change in any decisive way the impression made by those of Volume I, although they do modify it in some respects. It turns out not to be true, for example, that there are no moments of crisis in the marriage after the removal to Paris. In 1922 Nora Joyce went off to

---

[3] Joyce's long refusal to recognize the seriousness of Lucia's condition was abetted by the doctors, who, whether out of ignorance or compunction, seem never to have offered a firm diagnosis.

[4] [New York: The Viking Press.—Ed.]

Ireland with the children, threatening that she would not return. Joyce writes in desperate appeal to "my darling, my love, my queen," telling her that the check for her fur is on the way, that he will live anywhere with her so long as he can be "alone with her dear self without family and without friends. Either this must occur or we must part for ever, though it will break my heart." He goes on to report in detail his "fainting fit in Miss Beach's shop," and concludes: "O my dearest, if you would only turn to me even now and read that terrible book which has now broken the heart in my breast[5] and take me to yourself alone to do with me what you will!"

The substance of the marital correspondence at forty is not different from that of the twenties: the same belief in the importance of gifts, especially of fur; the extravagant demand for devotion made through the avowal of infantile weakness; the plea to be dealt with ruthlessly in his total and pathetic dependence. But as compared with the earlier letters of similar import that we now have, the energy of this one seems but dutiful, almost perfunctory. It appears early in Volume III and is the last expression not only of erotic feeling but of strong personal emotion of any kind.

From here on, the new letters of the later years are at one with those of the 1957 collection in suggesting that, however powerful Joyce's creative will continued to be, his affective will had been outlived. *"Only disconnect!"* had long been an avowed principle of his life, but not until now had it been put fully in force. It is true that the paternal tenderness and solicitude do not abate, that the form of courteous geniality is maintained, that an enterprise of helpfulness is not precluded, such as involved Joyce with the career of the tenor Sullivan, and we must suppose that some other magnetism in addition to that of his genius drew many people to his service. But nothing in the ordinary way of "humanness" contradicts our sense that the letters of the years of fame were written by a being who had departed this life as it is generally known and had become such a ghost as Henry James and Yeats imagined, a sentient soul that has passed from temporal existence into nullity yet still has a burden of energy to discharge, a destiny still to be worked out.

We are tempted to deal with the uncanny condition by bringing it into the comfortable circle of morality. Joyce's disconnection from the world, we may want to say, is the ground of his indomitable courage, before which we stand in awed admiration. The man who had ventured and won so much with *Ulysses* now pushes on with *Finnegans Wake* under the encroaching shadow of blindness and to the disapproval of his patron and virtually all his supporters: how else save by a disconnection amounting to "inhumanness" can he pursue the enterprise? Or our mor-

---

[5] Even two years later, Nora had not yet consented to read *Ulysses*.

alizing takes the adversary tack and notes the occasions when the disconnection issues in an ugly coarseness of behavior in regard to others.
Joyce, who concerned himself with every detail of the promotion of his
own books and enlisted everyone he could in the enterprise, when asked
to support one of the posthumous novels of Italo Svevo, whose work
he admired, not only refuses the request but sneers at the very idea of
literary publicity. When his daughter-in-law, Giorgio's first wife, suffers
an extreme mental collapse, he writes of the disaster in anger and describes the deranged conduct with contemptuous bitterness.

Eventually, however, we come to feel that no moral judgment can
really be to the point of Joyce's state of being in his latter years. And
psychology seems as limited in its pertinence as morality. It is inevitable
that psychological speculation will be attracted to the often strange and
extreme emotional phenomena that the new letters record, especially to
what the early ones tell us of the extravagant energy of affective will that
was to devolve into the disconnection from the world, the existence in
nullity. Neither Joyce's representation of himself as Dedalus, nor Professor Ellmann's detailed account of his youthful temperament, nor yet the
two taken together quite prepare us for the intimacy and violence of
Joyce's early relation to the world, the urgency with which he sought
to requisition the world's goods. And certainly the devolution (if that is
the word) from this early egotism of the world to the later egotism of
nullity is a biographical event that asks for explanation. But however
brilliant and even true may be the insights into the disposition of the
internal forces that brought it about, they will fail to do justice to its
significance, which is finally not personal but cultural. The process recorded by the letters proposes itself as a paradigm of the 19th-century
will *in extremis*. It leads us to reflect less on what transpired in the life
of James Joyce than on what could formerly happen and cannot happen
again—never in our time will a young man focus this much power of
love and hate into so sustained a rage of effectual intention as Joyce was
capable of, so ferocious an ambition, so nearly absolute a commitment
of himself to himself.

Joyce was of course not exceptional in being a continuator of the ti-
tanism of the 19th-century artistic personality. The literary culture of
the first quarter of the 20th century is differentiated from that of our own
time by nothing so much as the grandiosity, both in purpose and in
achievement, of its preeminent figures. In this respect their sense of life
is alien from ours and is not uncommonly felt to alienate them from us.
In one point of temperament, in the unremitting energy of their inner-
direction, they have a closer affinity with their 19th-century predecessors
than with their successors. But as compared with Joyce, none of the great
modern chieftains of art put himself so directly and, as one might say,
so *naively*, in the line of the powerful personalities of the age before

his own. None so cherished the purpose of imposing himself upon the world, of being a king and riding in triumph through Persepolis.

If Joyce did indeed derive the impetus to his achievement from his acceptance of the ethos and mythos of the 19th century, a first salient example is his response to an idea that we take to be characteristic of the ideology of the period, the idea of the nation. One of the best-known things about Joyce is his ambivalence toward Ireland, of which the hatred was as relentless as the love was unfailing. With this passionate relationship his lust for preeminence and fame is bound up, and the more so because his erotic life is intricately involved with it. He is twenty-seven and on his first visit to Dublin after his exile and he is writing to Nora, telling her of the part she plays in his inspiration. "My darling," he says, "tonight I was in the Gresham Hotel and was introduced to about twenty people and to all of them the same story was told: that I was going to be the great writer of the future in my country. All the noise and flattery around me hardly moved me. I thought I heard my country calling to me or her eyes were turned toward me expectantly." He goes on to tell Nora that she is more important to him than the world and that everything comes from her. But in his thought of fame he cannot separate her from the nation, the "race": "O take me into your soul of souls and then I will indeed become the poet of my race." And among the things he has loved in her—"the image of the beauty of the world, the mystery and beauty of life itself . . . the images of spiritual purity and pity which I believed in as a boy"—there are "the beauty and doom of the race of whom I am a child." He calls her "my love, my life, my star, my little strange-eyed Ireland!"

And yet, of course, "I loathe Ireland and the Irish. They themselves stare at me in the street though I was born among them. Perhaps they read my hatred in my eyes." The hatred was of the essence of his ambition quite as much as the love. Three years later he is again in Dublin and he writes: "The Abbey Theater will be open and they will give plays of Yeats and Synge. You have a right to be there because you are my bride and I am one of the writers of this generation who are perhaps creating at last a conscience in the soul of this wretched race."

Some considerable part of Joyce's ambition consisted of what the 19th century called aspiration and conceived to be a mode of feeling peculiarly appropriate to generous minds, artists perhaps especially but also soldiers, statesmen, engineers, industrialists. Aspiration was the desire for fame through notable and arduous achievement. The end in view which defined it was the realization of one's own powers. That in order to reach this end one might be involved in competition with others, seeking to surpass and overcome them, was a frequent but accidental circumstance of aspiration which was not thought to qualify its noble disinterestedness.

That this is a reasonable way of looking at the matter is suggested by the astonishing letter the nineteen-year-old Joyce addressed to Ibsen. He makes a full and grandiose communication of his admiration and then goes on to say to the sick old man, "Your work on earth draws to a close and you are near the silence. It is growing dark for you." But there is a comfort that he can offer, the assurance that One—an unnamed but unmistakable One—comes after to carry on the great work. It is in all conscience a crueller letter than the young writer chose to know, yet the competition with the Father, the Old King, is sanctioned not only by tradition but by the very nature of life, and Joyce invests it with an absurd but genuine nobility by which the Master Builder, after a wince or two, might well have been grimly pleased.

But Joyce's competitiveness, which was extreme, was not always, not characteristically, in the grand style; as it showed itself in his relations with his age-mates it was often vindictive and coarse. Through all the early years in Trieste and Rome, Joyce lived in bitter jealous hatred of his former friends and companions in Dublin. He cannot mention them and their little successes without an expression of disgust: "Their writings and their lives nauseate [me] to the point of vomiting." The new letters make clear to how great an extent Joyce in his youth conceived of his art as a weapon to be used in personal antagonism, especially in vengeance. "Give me for Christ' sake a pen and an ink-bottle and some peace of mind and then, by the crucified Jaysus, if I don't sharpen that little pen and dip it into fermented ink and write tiny little sentences about the people who betrayed me send me to hell." The chief object of his bitterness, of course, was Gogarty, from whom, after the quarrel, he would accept no tender of reconciliation. It was his belief that the man who had so terribly offended him sought to make peace out of fear of how he would be delineated—the belief finds expression in the first chapter of *Ulysses:* "He fears the lancet of my art as I fear that of his. Cold steelpen."—and as early as 1905 it was assumed by Joyce's Dublin friends that a great revenge was in train; the form it would take was already known. "[Elwood] says," writes Stanislaus Joyce, "he would not like to be Gogarty when you come to the Tower episode. Thanks be to God he never kicked your arse or anything." Gogarty himself had every expectation that revenge would be duly taken, and Joyce coolly confirmed him in this; he reports that in refusing Gogarty's attempt to renew the friendship, he had said: "I bear you no ill will. I believe you have some points of good nature. You and I of 6 years ago are both dead. But I must write as I have felt!" To which Gogarty replied, "I don't care a damn what you say of me so long as it is literature." [6]

───────

[6] In the event this proved not to be true—Gogarty cared many a damn when *Ulysses* appeared. As well he might, if only because Joyce led all the world to believe forever that he and not Gogarty-Mulligan was the rightful tenant of the tower and that the famous key was his: any statement of the fact of the matter, that the opposite

The unremitting bitterness with which Joyce remembered and com-memorated his relation with Gogarty serves to remind us of the great authority that the ideal of male friendship formerly had. In this, as in so many other respects, the 19th century maintained its connection with the courtly cultures of earlier epochs. Out of the dream of the true friend arose the possibility of the false friend, and it is an element of the *Heldenleben,* as the 19th century understood the genre, that the hero is beset by treacherous comrades envious of his powers and eager to sub-vert them. Had these dwarfish natures been lacking in the actuality of his life, Joyce would have been quick to supply the want. His genius throve upon his paranoia, which was capable of anything—it is quite in his style to say in an early letter to Lady Gregory that the college authorities were determined that he should not study medicine, "wishing I dare say to prevent me from securing any position of ease from which I might speak out my heart." A belief in a hostile environment, in perse-cution and personal betrayal, was necessary to his mission. But in point of fact the false friends and the malice of their envy were real enough; they were fostered by Dublin life before they were cherished by Joyce as a condition of his art and the testimony of his being a dedicated spirit, singled out. Long before Joyce had anything like a career, his promise of genius was taken for granted by those who knew him, and Stanislaus's diary records the envy with which he was regarded by his contemporaries. In his early days of exile, when his thoughts turned homeward, it was to inquire what these lesser impotent beings said of his courage, his free-dom, his unconventional marriage, and, as time passed, his approach to success. Their mischievous impulses in relation to him came fully to light in the strange episode of his friend Cosgrove telling him, falsely and seemingly out of the gratuitous impulse to play Iago to this Othello, that before the elopement Nora had been unfaithful to him, a commu-nication that for a time had all its intended effect of making chaos come again.

The social life of late 19th-century Dublin as Joyce's class situation permitted him to know it was obviously in most respects quite elementary, but it was certainly not wanting in concern with social status, in judging who was "better" and stood higher than whom, and to such questions the young Joyce gave the most solemn attention. It was surely an important circumstance of the last interview with Gogarty that it took place in Gogarty's elaborate house and that the former friend, now set up in

---

was the case, will always be received with surprise and incredulity and soon for-gotten. Such is the power of the literary imagination in the service of self-justification. Partisans of simple justice—alas, there are virtually none of Gogarty—may find some encouragement in the display of the actual lease in the tower; that a signboard calls the tower James Joyce's should not dismay them: the rights of the ultimate possession are now absolute.

medical practice, well-to-do and well married, should have invited Joyce
to come with him in his motorcar to have lunch in his country home.
The social advantages that Gogarty had previously enjoyed, perhaps especially his having gone to Oxford, were of the greatest moment to
Joyce, who was at constant pains to enforce the idea that, when it came
to social establishment, Stephen Dedalus, if the truth were seen, was the
superior of anyone.[7] Joyce was in nothing so much a man of the 19th
century as in the sensitivity of his class feelings. No less than Dickens
he was concerned to be a *gentleman* and he was as little shy as Dickens
about using the word, the Victorian force of which maintained itself for
at least two of the Joyces in the face of the family's rapid downward
mobility. In the midst of an expression of disgust with his situation at
Rome, James remarks to Stanislaus, "I feel somehow that I am what
Pappie said I wasn't [,] a gentleman." [8] He was at the time working in a
bank as a correspondence clerk; he lived with his wife and infant son
in a single small room; often his wages did not meet his weekly expenses
and the letters of the period are chiefly to Stanislaus in Trieste, their
whole burden being that money must be sent at once. The conversation
of his fellow clerks, as he describes it, is simian; he has no ordinarily
decent social intercourse with anyone, yet he finds it in his heart to describe his circumstances not as unfit for a human being but as unfit for
a gentleman.

His feeling for the social forms could be strict, often in a genteel,
lower-middle-class way. Although in 1910 black-edged writing paper was
still used by proper people in a period of mourning, the faintly barbaric
custom was not universally observed, but Joyce, at the death of his uncle
John Murray, thought it necessary to his sense of how things should be
done.[9] When he was virtually starving during his first sojourn in Paris,
he regretted that he could not attend the Irish Ball because he had no
dress suit. He is still working as a Berlitz teacher in Trieste and the

[7] In the tower scene Mulligan tells Stephen. "You know, Dedalus, you have the real
Oxford manner." And he speculates that this is why Haines, the Englishman who is
staying with them, can't make Stephen out. Haines is rich and himself an Oxford
man and Mulligan twice remarks that he thinks Stephen isn't a gentleman.

[8] The occasion of the judgment was John Joyce's reading *Gas from a Burner*.
Stanislaus seems not to have shared the social feelings of his father and elder brother.
Perhaps it was his puritanical rationalism that led him to adopt a rather plebeian
stance. The youngest surviving Joyce brother, Charles, apparently laid no continuing
claim to being a gentleman; when last we hear of him he is a postal clerk in London.
The idea of social status was part of the fabric of the Joyce family life—it is well
known how preoccupied John Joyce was with the superiority of his own family to
his wife's, which of course had some bearing on James's choice of a wife whose pretensions to breeding were notably less than his own.

[9] Joyce took account in *Ulysses* of his response to the claims of funeral pomps. "He
can't wear them," Mulligan says when his offer of a pair of gray trousers has been
refused by Dedalus because he is in mourning for his mother. "Etiquette is etiquette.
He kills his mother but he can't wear gray trousers."

family in Dublin is on the verge of destitution, but he directs his father to arrange to sit for his portrait. The family crest was his treasured possession.

At the present time, feelings about class in their old form are in at least literary abeyance and it is hard to remember the force they once had and the extent to which they defined the character and aspirations of the artist.[10] In an age when the middle classes seemed to be imposing their stamp upon the world, a young writer was led to set store by what he imagined to be the aristocratic qualities of grace, freedom, and indifference to public opinion, and the aristocratic mode of life seemed the model for what all men's lives should be. It was the rare writer who did not think himself to be "well born" in some sense of the phrase, and if he had any reason to think that he was actually of distinguished blood, he was pretty sure to find the circumstance of value. George Moore said no more than the simple truth when he remarked that "Yeats's belief in his lineal descent from the great Duke of Ormonde was part of his poetic equipment." Writing in admiration of Tolstoy, Joyce associates his genius with his class position and his ability to remember "the Christian name of his great-great-grandfather." And the young man who felt himself excluded from the patrician literary circle of Dublin and expressed his resentment in rude mockery of its members shared Yeats's dream of the culture—the word is Joyce's own—of the great houses and the ancient families. Writing to Nora, who had been a chambermaid in a Dublin hotel when he had first met her and whose lack of grammar he was not above mocking to his brother, he explains to her the inspiration of *Chamber Music:* "You were not in a sense the girl for whom I had dreamed and written the verses you now find so enchanting. She was perhaps (as I saw her in my imagination) a girl fashioned into a curious grave beauty by the culture of generations before her, the woman for whom I wrote poems like 'Gentle Lady' or 'Thou leanest to the shell of night.' " He goes on, surely in entire sincerity: "But then I saw that the beauty of your soul outshone that of my verses. There was something in you higher than anything I had put into them. And so for this reason the book of verses is for you. It holds the desire of my youth, and you, darling, were the fulfillment of that desire." Yet the discrepancy between the robust, barely literate chambermaid who had to be told not to copy her love-letters out of a letter-book and the girl fashioned into a curious grave beauty by her lineage was often a pain to Joyce, and much as he needed Nora's earthy strength, he flinched at the rudeness—so he called it—that

---

[10] A few years ago I had occasion to remark in an essay that my students, no matter what their social origins, were not prevented by Yeats's snobbery from responding to his poetry. One reviewer took me sternly to task for obscuring the transcendent achievement of the great poet by speaking of him as a snob. What made especially interesting the view of life and letters implied by the rebuke was that the reviewer was Leon Edel, the biographer of Henry James.

went with it. It was certain that he was a gentleman, but whatever else Nora was, she was, alas, no lady.

That Joyce's preoccupation with his social status should go along with an avowed interest in subverting the society in which he held his valued rank does not make a contradiction. It was quite common in the 19th century for gifted men to find sanction for their subversive intentions toward society in such aristocracy or gentility as they could claim.[11] But that Joyce should ever have been political at all will for most of his readers make an occasion for surprise. For a few years of his young manhood, between the ages of twenty-two and twenty-five, Joyce called himself a socialist. Again and again in his letters to Stanislaus he insists on the importance to the artist of a radical political position: "I believe that Ibsen and Hauptmann separate from the herd of writers because of their political aptitude—eh?" "It is a mistake for you to imagine that my political opinions are those of a universal lover: but they are those of a socialistic artist." He scolds Stanislaus for not sharing his "detestation of the stupid, dishonest, tyrannical and cowardly burgher class." He explains the opposition of the Church to "the quite unheretical theory of socialism" as being an expression of the belief that a socialist government would expropriate ecclesiastical "landed estates . . . and invested moneys." His cogent objection to the Irish nationalist movement is that it takes no account of economic realities and is not aware that "if the Irish question exists, it exists for the Irish proletariat chiefly." And it is a further black mark against Gogarty that his political views exclude economic considerations. "Gogarty would jump into the Liffey to save a man's life but he seems to have little hesitation in condemning generations to servitude." [12]

Joyce never committed himself to political action or association, and although he had a knowledgeable interest in the Italian radical parties, he seems never to have put himself to the study of socialist theory; the only reference to Karl Marx occurs in the course of an excited and rather confused account of the apocalyptic Jewish imagination derived from Ferrero's *Young Europe*. By 1907 his socialism had evaporated, leaving as its only trace the sweet disposition of Leopold Bloom's mind to imagine the possibility of rational and benevolent social behavior and the brotherhood of man. This, however, is a residue of some importance in the history of literature: it makes *Ulysses* unique among modern classics for its sympathy with progressive social ideas.

In one of his early poems Yeats speaks of the places where men meet "to talk of love and politics." To us at our remove in time, the conjunction of the two topics of conversation seems quaint, for of course by love

---

[11] This was especially true of the anarchists in Russia, France, and Italy.

[12] Joyce's disgust with Gogarty on political grounds was made the more intense by Gogarty's anti-Semitism.

Yeats did not mean the rather touching interfusion of *eros* and *agape* that young people have lately come to use as a ground of social and political dissidence: he meant a love much more personal and egotistic, that ultimate relation between a man and a woman the conception of which had descended from courtly love, the "gay science" of the late Middle Ages, to become one of the powerful myths of the 19th century. Its old force has greatly diminished, perhaps to the point of extinction. No matter how gravely and idealistically we may use our contemporary names for the relation between a man and a woman, "sex" and "marriage," and even the phrase that is a vestige of the old name, "in love with," do not suggest, as "love" did for an age in whose sensibility *Tristan and Isolde* occupied a central position, the idea of life realized and transfigured by the erotic connection, fulfilled by its beauty, sustained by the energy and fidelity that constituted its ethos.[13] In the 19th century, politics was a new activity of free spirits and it naturally found affinity with a conception of love that made large promises of perceptivity, liberty, and happiness. Love was understood to be art's true source and best subject, and those who lived for love and art did harm to no one, lived the right life of humanity: so Tosca in a passion that reaches B-flat informs the tyrant Scarpia. The operatic example is much in point, for opera was the genre in which love and political virtue joined hands to make a lyric affirmation of life. The contemptuous indifference in which opera is held by our intellectual culture is not qualified by recognition of its political tendency. For Joyce, as everyone knows, opera was a passion. With a most engaging simplicity he gave the genre the response it asked for; he found it, as people used to say, ravishing. He would have been astonished and dismayed by the contemporary snootiness to Puccini; he held *Madame Butterfly* to be a work of transcendent beauty and power, most especially the aria *"Un bel di"* which at one period seems to have woven itself into the very fabric of his emotional life; when Butterfly sang the "romance of her hope" of what would come to her over the sea, his soul (as he wrote bitterly to Nora, who was not similarly moved) "sway[ed] with languor and longing": in the face of the harshness of circumstance, life is affirmed in erotic ecstasy, as when, in *A Portrait of the Artist*, Stephen has sight of the girl on the strand, gazing out to sea. For Joyce, as still for many men of the time in which he was young, human existence was justified by the rapture—lost archaic word!—of love.

Perhaps nothing in Joyce's life is more poignant and more indicative of the extent to which his imagination was shaped by the mythos of his time than the episode, on the threshold of his middle age, in which the famous vision of the lovely girl standing with high-kilted skirts at the water's edge, the most grandiose of the epiphanies, seemed to have pre-

---

[13] For an account of what *Tristan and Isolde* meant to the epoch, see Elliot Zuckerman's admirable *The First Hundred Years of Wagner's Tristan*, Columbia University Press, 1964.

sented itself as an attainable actuality. Martha Fleischmann was a young woman, seemingly Jewish, though not so in fact, beautiful, provocative but apparently not disposed to go beyond elaborate flirtation, whom Joyce came to know in Zurich in the autumn of 1918. As Martha recalled their meeting nearly a quarter of a century later, the scene stands all ready for the librettist. She was coming home "one evening at dusk" when a passerby stopped and looked at her "with an expression of such wonder on his face that she hesitated for just a moment before entering the house." The stranger spoke, explaining his astonishment by saying that she reminded him of a girl he had once seen "standing on the beach of his home country."[14] Martha's erotic temperament was ambiguous to a degree. She had a devoted "guardian," as she called him, and he expressed jealousy of her relation with Joyce, but there is some question as to whether her connection with this man was sexual in any ordinary sense of the word. On one occasion Joyce addressed her as "Nausikaa," signing himself "Odysseus,"[15] and it would seem that the Gerty Mac-Dowell of the "Nausikaa" episode of *Ulysses* commemorates her genteel narcissism and sentimentality. Joyce's own erotic disposition at this time was scarcely of a more direct kind. His lust, like Mr. Bloom's, was chiefly of the eye and the mind. What seems to have been the climactic assignation of these two fantasts of love took place in Frank Budgen's studio on February 2, which was Joyce's birthday and the feast of Candlemas, and Joyce borrowed from a Jewish friend a *menorah* so that he might gaze on Martha's beauty by candlelight, perhaps the sole intention of the meeting.[16] With the passage of years the exquisite virgin, *La Princesse lointaine*, came to be represented in the great "Nausikaa" episode as nothing more than the sad, silly figment of ladies' magazines, and the dream of love-and-beauty as an occasion of masturbation. But at the

[14] The quoted passages are from Professor Straumann's account of his interview with Martha when, in Zurich in 1941, she called to inquire about selling the four letters and the postcard that Joyce had written to her. Professor Straumann did not make the purchase on that occasion, but he did so at a later time, in 1943, when, Martha being ill, her affairs were in the charge of her sister—at least he bought the letters; the postcard had vanished. Professor Straumann's account of the relationship of Martha and Joyce appears as a preface to the letters as given in Volume II, pp. 426–436; it is less full and circumstantial than Professor Ellmann's earlier account in his biography.

[15] The salutation and the subscription were, Professor Straumann says, the whole message of the lost postcard.

[16] Candlemas commemorates the purification of the Virgin Mary and the presentation of Christ in the Temple. "The blessing of candles is now the distinctive rite of this day. . . . Beeswax candles, which are blessed, distributed, and lit whilst the Nunc Dimittis is sung, are carried in a procession commemorating the entrance of Christ, the 'True Light (cf. Jn. 1.9) into the Temple."—*The Oxford Dictionary of the Christian Church*. In his second letter to Martha, remarking on his impression that she was a Jewess, Joyce says, "If I am wrong, you must not be offended. Jesus Christ put on his human body: in the womb of a Jewish woman."

time his feelings for Martha seemed to Joyce to challenge comparison with Dante's for Beatrice and Shakespeare's for the Dark Lady; at least he meant them to. "And through the night of the bitterness of my soul," he wrote in the last of his letters to Martha, "the kisses of your lips fell on my heart, soft as rosepetals gentle as dew," and concludes, "O rosa mistica [*sic*], ora pro me."

One of the four letters is mutilated—we are told that Martha "tore off the lower right-hand edge of the second sheet . . . because it contained what she considered an indelicate expression." The judgment on the offending word or phrase cannot be set aside out of hand as one of Martha's neurotic gentilities. The chances are that Joyce did actually write an indelicacy, even an obscenity, for his concern that the erotic object and situation be of an extreme refinement and beauty went together with a no less exigent desire for all that is commonly thought to sully, besmirch, and degrade the erotic activity, and he derived a special pleasure from expressing this desire in writing.

The dialectic between the essential innocence and the essential shamefulness of the sexual act has in our time lost much of its old force, at least overtly. If nowadays we obey the command of Blake's Los to "Consider Sexual Organization," it does not seem naturally to follow, as the demiurge thought it would, that we "hide . . . in the dust" for shame. Crazy Jane's observation that love has pitched his mansion in the place of excrement is received as an interesting reminder of the actual state of affairs rather than as the expression of a distressing (or exciting) thought in the forefront of consciousness. The words of Yeats's poem echo those of another divine utterance in *Jerusalem:* "For I will make their places of love and joy excrementitious," but the circumstance as Yeats refers to it is not conceived to be a curse: we understand Yeats to be remarking on an anomaly that makes human existence more complex and difficult than his long celebration of the *Rosa Mystica* would suggest, or more "ironic," or more "tragic," but for that reason more substantive and the more interesting. His sense of the shameful arrangements of the erotic life stands midway between the neutralizing view of them that our contemporary educated consciousness seems determined to take and the eager response to them made by Joyce, for whom shame was a chief condition of sexual fulfilment.

In the course of the two visits he made to Ireland in 1909, Joyce in his letters to Nora ran through the whole gamut of his erotic emotions and in full voice. Within a week of his first arrival in Dublin, Cosgrove imparted the news of Nora's double dealing in the betrothal time, and although the false friend spoke only of kisses, Joyce of course imagined more and questioned whether Nora had actually come to him a virgin —"I remember that there was very little blood that night. . . ."—and whether Giorgio is in truth his son. He is shattered by the dreadful revelation—"I shall cry for days"—but a fortnight has not passed before he can report blandly that everything has been cleared up by Byrne's having said that Cosgrove's tale is "all a 'blasted lie' "; and after having called himself a "worthless fellow," he vows to be "Worthy of your love, dearest," and goes on to speak of a shipment of cocoa he has sent, that same cocoa that he later urges Nora to drink a good deal of so that she will increase the size of "certain parts" of her body, pleasing him by becoming more truly womanly. His marital resentments are bitter and explicit: Nora, whose great fault is her rudeness, had called him an imbecile, had disagreed with his expressed opinion that priests are disgusting, had been indifferent to *"Un bel di"*; his apologies, when his recriminations have proved offensive, are abject. He is much given to expressions of tender and poetic regard and is engagingly proud of the courtly ingenuity of a gift of jewelry he has designed and had executed, a necklace of gold links, five cubes of old ivory and an ivory plaque bearing in ancient lettering words from one of his poems, which is to symbolize the lovers' years together and their sadness and suffering when they are divided; his Christmas present is *Chamber Music* copied out in his own hand on parchment, bound with his family crest, on the cover the lovers' interlaced initials. But his lively imagination of the elegances of love goes along with fantasies and solicitations that, as he says, make him the object of his own disgust and, he insists on supposing, of Nora's.

Professor Ellmann has not found it possible to carry out his intention of publishing in its entirety the group of obscene love-letters from Dublin preserved in the Cornell Library. What he is able to publish does indeed, as he says, suggest the tenor of these extraordinary documents (the adjective is Joyce's) but not the force and the strange dignity that they seemed to me to have when I read them at Cornell some years ago. It may be, of course, that my memory plays me false, but I recall the letters read in the completeness of the holograph as making the effect of having been written under a more driving compulsion, a more exigent possession, than appears in the curtailed printed version. Perhaps it was the holograph itself that contributed to the impressiveness, enforcing the situation in something like the awesomeness that Joyce himself felt it to have: the man who may well be the greatest literary genius of his age submits to the necessity of taking in hand his sacred cold steel pen and with it to sully sheet after virgin sheet of paper with the filthy words that express all that he feels in the way of delight at the dirtiness of his exalted nature. The words themselves have for him a terrifying potency. One of his letters has induced Nora in her reply to use what he can refer to in no other way than as "a certain word." The sight of it, he says, excites him terribly—"There is something obscene and lecherous in the very look of the letters. The sound of it too is like the act itself, brief, brutal, irresistible and devilish."

His longed-for perversities and depravities—we had best call them that without permissive apologies, since he thought of them so and we ought not deny the ground of his pleasure—were not of an especially esoteric kind. He expresses the wish to be flogged and not merely in show but fiercely, to the end of his feeling real pain; he blames himself for writing "filth" and instructs Nora, if she is insulted by it, to bring him to his senses "with the lash, as you have done before." Nora is an "angel" and a "saint" who guides him to his great destiny, and he longs to "nestle" in her womb, and he seeks to "degrade" and "deprave" her, he wants her to be insolent and cruel and obscene. Perhaps the controlling and to him most puzzling and most significant component of his polymorphous perversity is his delight in the excrementitiousness of the places of love and joy, what he called his "wild beast-like craving . . . for every secret and shameful part" of his wife's body, "for every odor and act of it." "Are you offended because I said I loved to look at the brown stain that comes behind on your girlish white drawers? I suppose you think me a filthy wretch."

No one, I think, will be so armored in objectivity as not to be taken aback by the letters. But their shocking interest fades as we become habituated to them, or to the idea of them. In the way of all drastic personal facts, especially in our time, they cease to be dismaying or amazing soon after they are brought into the light of common day and permitted to assume their institutional status—one might say their prestige—as biographical data. What does not fade, however, is the interest of the literary use to which Joyce put the erotic tendencies that the letters disclose and indulge.

To a reader of *Ulysses* nothing in the substance of the letters comes as a surprise. All the fantasies are familiar to us through our having made acquaintance with them in the mind of Leopold Bloom. But what exists in the mind of Mr. Bloom is of a quite different import from the apparently identical thing as it exists in the mind of James Joyce or might exist in the mind of his surrogate Stephen Dedalus. The reader of the letters will not fail to conclude that it required a considerable courage for Joyce to write them. His doing so went against the grain of a decisive and cherished part of his nature, his austere, almost priestly propriety. "As you know, dearest," he writes in one of the letters, "I never use obscene phrases in speaking. You have never heard me, have you, utter an unfit word before others. When men tell in my presence here filthy or lecherous stories I hardly smile." Yet he put on paper and sent through the mail what was not to be countenanced and, although he urged Nora to be watchful in guarding the secrecy of the letters, since he did not destroy them when he might have done so, he must be thought to have wished that they be preserved. One thing, however, he would not—could not—do: attribute the fantasies of the letters to the mind of Stephen Dedalus.

By assigning them to Mr. Bloom, he of course quite changes their character. As elements of Mr. Bloom's psyche, they become comic, which is to say morally neutral. Our laughter, which is gentle, cognizant, forgiving, affectionate, has the effect of firmly distancing them and at the same time of bringing them within the circle of innocence and acceptability. We understand that nothing very terrible is here, nothing awesome, or devilish, or wild-beast-like—only what we call, with a relishing, domesticating chuckle, *human*. And the chuckle comes the more easily because we recognize in Mr. Bloom, as we are intended to, the essential innocence of the child; his polymorphous perversity is appropriate to his infantile state. This innocence, it would appear, is part of Joyce's conception of Jews in general, who, he seems to have felt, through some natural grace were exempt from the complexities of the moral life as it was sustained by Christians. Writing to Stanislaus of his son having been born early, with nothing prepared, he says, "However, our landlady is a Jewess and gave us everything we wanted." The implication is that a Christian might or might not have provided the necessary things; Christian kindness would result from the making of a choice between doing the good deed and not doing it, and would therefore, by the Aristotelian definition, be moral; but a Jewish good deed was a matter of instinct, natural rather than moral. It is in natural goodness rather than in morality that Mr. Bloom has his being, and in the ambience of his mind the perverse fantasies have nothing of the fearsome significance they had for Joyce when he entertained them.

It is possible to say that the translation of the fantasies as they existed in the mind of James Joyce, and might have existed in the mind of Stephen Dedalus, into what they become in the mind of Leopold Bloom is a derogation of Joyce's courage as an artist. A Stephen Dedalus whose rigorous moral being is assailed and torn by sinful desires is readily received as a heroic figure so long as the desires can be supposed sinful in a received way. But a polymorphous-perverse hero would make a difficulty, would be thought a contradiction in terms. For Joyce the Aristotelian categories of tragedy and comedy, the one showing men as "better," i.e., more dignified, than they really are, the other showing men as "worse," i.e., more ignoble, than they really are, had an authority that, at the time of *Ulysses*, was not to be controverted.

It is also possible to say that Joyce's refusal to assign the perverse fantasies to Stephen is a derogation of personal courage. A polymorphous-perverse Leopold Bloom stands as testimony to his author's astonishing powers of imagination, of sympathetic insight into the secret places of nature at the furthest remove from his own. But a polymorphous-perverse Stephen Dedalus must advertise the polymorphous perversity of the author whose fictive surrogate he is inevitably understood to be. To this personal disclosure Joyce could not consent.

His fictional disposition of the polymorphous perversity must make a salient question in any attempt to understand the mind of James Joyce. What I have called—with, I should make plain, no pejorative force— a derogation of courage is an answer that has a kind of provisional cogency. But a comment on the obscene letters made by Professor Ellmann in his Introduction seems to me to initiate an explanation that goes deeper. Professor Ellmann says of the letters that they have an "ulterior purpose," that Joyce, in writing them, had an intention beyond immediate sexual gratification. One thing he intended was "to anatomize and reconstitute and crystallize the emotion of love." And, Professor Ellmann says, "he goes further still; like Richard Rowan in *Exiles,* he wishes to possess his wife's soul, and have her possess his, in nakedness. To know someone else in love and hate, beyond vanity and remorse, *beyond human possibility almost* [my italics], is his extravagant desire."

If this is so, as I think it is, it brings the obscene letters into accord with what I have proposed as the controlling tendency of Joyce's genius —to move through the fullest realization of the human, the all-too-human, to that which transcends and denies the human. It was a progress he was committed to make, yet he made it with some degree of reluctance. Had the obscene fantasies been assigned to Stephen Dedalus, they would have implied the import that Professor Ellmann supposes they had for Joyce himself. But Joyce, we may believe, did not want, not yet, so Hyperborean a hero as he then would have had. The ethos and mythos of the 19th century could still command from him some degree of assent. The merely human still engaged him, he was not wholly ready to go beyond it. The fair courts of life still beckoned invitation and seemed to await his entrance. He was to conclude that their walls and gates enclosed nothing. His genius is defined by his having concluded this rather than taking it for granted, as many of the generation that came after him have found it possible to do.

The Bent Knife Blade:
Joyce in the 1960's

by Robert Martin Adams

The critic who undertakes to reexamine and revaluate James Joyce in the light of the modern tradition obviously implies that he has a pretty precise sense of that tradition, of what the *Zeitgeist* is and where it's headed; my first step will have to be a vigorous disclaimer on that score. Professors of literature don't direct the *Zeitgeist* and have no special claim to an insider's understanding of it—or if some do, I'm not one of them. Yet it is scarcely possible for even a backward academic to avoid recognizing that Joyce in the sixties is not by any means the same force he was in the twenties. His books have changed, for one thing, by standing still in the stream of time; they have changed in the mere process of becoming classics, and so a part of the recognized cultural atmosphere; they have changed as a result of changes in our cultural and intellectual weather. All this quite apart from the more or less conscious changes brought about by exegetes and commentators. Defining a few of these gradual changes, which have crept over Joyce and us, may accentuate new aspects of his relevance, and irrelevance.

At least in America, we are no longer obliged to defend Joyce's morals. There is something of a relief in this development, for moral controversy about a work of art usually resolves itself into repetition and denial of the axiom that the artist can treat any subject he wants; and Joyce's subject is not exactly the most edifying thing about him. Bloom on his jakes, Stephen in the whorehouse, and Molly Bloom in bed—these are elements which we find it a good deal easier to digest than the genteel tradition possibly could. We have digested them, without ill effects of any obvious sort; and so, rather gratified by our exercise of broadmindedness, we may well have carried the hygienic view of Joyce further than the facts will sustain it. A few recent apologists have gone far toward maintaining that Joyce was a kind of Irish Homer Lane—morally and socially therapeutic, intellectually farsighted as well as consistent, a kind of moral surgeon plying his steely art upon the conscience of the western world. The facts as we are coming to see them appear rather more complex and less dramatic. Like Swift, Joyce was a prurient author, as a result of both his temperament and his background. Dirty words and fecal images had a powerful inflammatory influence on his mind; he didn't generally use them (any more than Swift did) for therapeutic or cathartic effect. (Whether they can possibly have such an effect, I leave to the sexologists.) With his vigorous sense of obscenity and filth he combined a characteristically late-nineteenth-century worship of woman as the great redemptive force of modern life. Joyce found in sex a fearful and rapturous experience, the more dramatic because of all the taboos and cosmic rewards he grafted onto it. This combination of extreme attitudes on the subject of sex seems to me rather remote from any attitudes I recognize as widespread in the educated sixties. It is remote from healthy-minded "realism," from romantic promiscuity, or from the impersonal, empty mechanism which is the characteristic form of most modern literary sex. Joyce found in woman a doorway to heaven and/or hell; I think historical distance is making it easier to understand this view and less necessary to react for or against it.

Joyce's view of sex—no longer a revelation from Erebus or Olympus—is starting to be recognizable as a set of dramatic properties supplied by his social circumstances and personal temperament; much the same thing can be said of his politics, his "philosophy," his esthetics. I don't mean to sound condescending or triumphant here—as if at last, after all these years, we were starting to see around old Joyce. I mean only that, having been distracted all too long by questions about whether Joyce is bad or good for the young, or for Ireland, for the recognition of the truth, or the freedom of the psyche, we are finally coming to judge him as an artist, whose work is a structure of impressions. In building that structure, he came about as close to producing a durable scheme of philosophically impregnable positions as artists usually do. As a matter of fact, he had scruples all his life (honorable but probably quite unnecessary scruples) about his own power to create impressions, and thought himself a forger and a fraud precisely by virtue of his art. That he was a verbal prestidigitator is not the final truth about Joyce, nor is it even true of him in the same degree as of Eliot—whose flats and contrivances I take to be, by now, almost scandalously visible. But it is a real and inevitable part of the Joyce of the sixties, that the things he was able to hang people up on in the twenties—like the theory of epiphany, the bit about Dedalus the maze-maker, and the great Earth-mother image—are starting to look a little threadbare. This fact, which inevitably involves loss as well as gain, still frees us to recognize some interesting things about his art.

Though it is an important element in the working of Joyce's books and necessarily absorbs a good deal of the exegete's energy, the sort of intellectual and mythical scaffolding that he erected has remained largely idiosyncratic. During the twenties the use of classical myth as a principle of structure and order seemed an outstanding innovation of *Ulysses*; so no doubt it was, but this is not the feature which subsequent novelists have seen fit to use, any more than they have been inspired by the Viconian cycles of *Finnegans Wake*. The fact is that for a work of anything less than epic proportions, the mythical parallel is better used as adornment, as allusion, as passing commentary, than as structural principle. Joyce found it particularly handy as a groundwork for verbal and thematic embroidery; but Joyce's habit of mind was peculiar, indeed unique, in its passion for involuted decoration. He may well have inherited this trait, as he liked to think, from progenitors who had produced the Book of Kells; one may also feel that his intricate arabesques serve as a gigantic, complicated trap in which to involve and defeat the reader's conscious mind, in preparation for an appeal to deeper and darker levels of response. But neither rationale is capable of very general application. Whatever its function, whatever its origins, the crustacean, exoskeletal quality of Joyce's patterning has not been accepted as viable by other novelists, and seems likely to remain a personal oddity.

Much more interesting to people who are not professional Joyceans is Joyce's use of language. Here one has a considerable span of performance to deal with, from the stripped and polished subtleties of *Dubliners* to the dark oddities of *Finnegans Wake*. The first thing to say is that Joyce helped clean English fiction of its thick crust of nineteenth-century gingerbread, and made it impossible to write as badly as was commonplace before him. Of course many others took part with him in this cleaning of the stables, and it is impossible to sort out his specific contribution. But anyone who has prowled the jungle of late-nineteenth-century fiction, fiction written not by abysmal incompetents but by intelligent and often perceptive men, will testify to the stifling quality of the conventions which Joyce and his contemporaries inherited. Puffy and overstuffed language, a flat style, and a general disdain of literary effects—from Gissing to Galsworthy, and not excluding Hardy, these qualities were the rule. Now that the conventions are safely surmounted, it is easy to underestimate the considerable energy which was necessary to overcome them. But this is still only a historical reason for remembering Joyce, and he has better claims on our attention.

When one says that Joyce enriched the speech of English fiction, there is a natural tendency to think of the various taboos he violated, the various censorships he knocked down. The matter is more considerable than this. One has only to look at the first chapter of *Ulysses*, less than twenty pages of prose, to sense the dramatic richness, flexibility, and complexity of the language. The scene moves with elegance and under its own power; the hand of the novelist does not have to tug it along. Symbols are pervasive, vivid yet undemanding. The tonality of the chapter is sunlit, yet under the surface one senses the sulky, resentful power of Stephen's mind, cuddling its enmity. A complex of energies is effortlessly set moving in these pages; the economy of means and richness of achievement mark a genuine imaginative achievement. In the diction of a passage like this, Joyce worked to standards of subtlety, economy, and exactness by which English novels will be measured for years to come; his ability to do so was quite independent of technical innovations—stream of consciousness, mythic parallels, multilingual puns, and so forth.

As it was not Joyce's invention, the "stream-of-consciousness" device which he did so much to popularize can not be laid at his personal doorstep. Historically viewed, it actually does not seem to have been any one individual's contribution, and literary historians of the future will no doubt see it as simply one episode in a process by which the action of the modern novel was interiorized, its definition of reality changed from social to psychological. Seen simply as a shift in representational conventions, it is less than startling. Experience is caught at an earlier and less complete stage of digestion, but the artifice of expressing it is just as apparent as in the fully formed, grammatically articulated sentences of Jane Austen and Walter Scott. If the novelist had to go into the pre-articulate stages of his characters' existence, and stay there permanently, it is not clear that the device would be justified; used intermittently, it adds extraordinary mobility to the novelist's repertoire of effects, enabling him to move from inner fantasy to outward reality and back again, with a minimum of explanation. What he finds under the surface, too, can be expressed poetically without the implication that his character is a frightfully arty chap. A character like John Updike's Rabbit Angstrom displays, alongside an appallingly nebulous blank of mind and almost no verbal subtlety, an intricate gift of feeling conveyed in complex poetic metaphors. His brains are buried some where in his nerves, deeper than words, deeper even than neuroses, in his perceptions themselves; and I think it was Joyce, as much as anyone, who encouraged Updike to see them there. Flaubert said with a sneer that the debris of a poet is to be found in the corner of every notary's heart; Joyce makes good the observation without the sneer.

Of the prose of *Finnegans Wake* it is less easy to speak. If it was an experiment, it was given the most splendid and exhaustive tryout of any on record, and has left a whole generation of writers with no experiments to make which don't look puny by comparison. But the word "experiment" represents a weak evasion here; *Finnegans Wake* is a rigorously rational adaptation of language to the expression of the irrational. There is nothing tentative about it, and one has no sense that Joyce is trying to see what can be done with a technique. Joyce saw the history of a culture and a personality under the image of an immense litter-pile, its clutter arranged in vague layers and suggesting dim but complicated patterns. The manner of *Finnegans Wake* is a direct outcome of a mode of vision. Considered as a complete style of writing (not just a ragbag of occasional tricks), this manner is of relatively slight value independent of the insight it implies. The chief writers who seem inclined to share Joyce's point of view, nowadays, are the absurd-theatre fellows, who are barred from using *Finnegans Wake* prose by their medium. One wouldn't anticipate that a technique so exacting could supplant the conventional English of prose fiction (which is rather more a business these days than an art form), and so it hasn't. But the exploration of *Finnegans Wake* by a gallant band of enthusiasts continues with unslackened vigor, even though the book's broader influence remains mostly peripheral. If Joyce's last novel is to make its way, there seems no doubt now that it will have to do so as a unit—linguistic oddities, world view, structural principles, and all. As I shall argue presently, there are some signs that it may do just that; but at the moment, society is moving up on the book, not vice versa.

The Joyce we have had up to now was Daedalian—that is, he exercised over many minds the authority of a puzzle, which has to be solved on its own given terms and which promises, tacitly but nonetheless distinctly, that it has a final solution. It is truly amazing how many solutions, of remarkably different sorts, have been found for Joyce's remarkably various problems; it is also amazing how widely they are distributed across the surface of Joyce's work. Henry James' criticism centers perceptibly around the old *Turn of the Screw* problem, with secondary clusters around *The Ambassadors* and *The Portrait of a Lady;* Conrad's critics show a notable affinity for *Heart of Darkness* and *Lord Jim.* But of Joyce's major (and even minor) work, only *Exiles* has failed to attract a vigorous swatch of detailed exegesis. Whatever reservations one has about its solidity, almost all of this work has been resourceful, inventive, flexible, learned, and practically indefatigable. Outside the great epic poets, I don't suppose any author (much less any novelist) has accumulated so much exegesis; not even the epic poets accumulated their masses of commentary in less than half a century. Joyce, in short, has had an unprecedented amount of critical and biographical attention. Now, of course, nobody can tell with complete assurance that these researches will not someday yield the complete coherent pattern of symbolic relationships which their creators tacitly or explicitly envisage. (A few of the more visionary have announced it as a fact—every element in Joyce's entire canon is part of a single controlled composition; but most seem to hold it out as a hope or an ideal for criticism to work toward.) But by this time, I think we are in a position to say that the pattern very probably won't work out. Joyce is not, like Dante, a rigorous and utterly consistent systematizer. The more rigorously you read him, the more loose ends you uncover. The more intricately you explain one set of details, the less chance there is that this explanation can be made to dovetail with anything else in the book or the career. The more ingenious your explanations, the more explanation they seem to need themselves. At the moment, we are under no immediate compulsion to give up on the big-pervasive-pattern presumption—but it seems like a terribly apt time to start looking for alternatives. The reason is not simply that evidence on hand fails to establish the existence of such a pattern; it is that almost all the new evidence which keeps turning up works directly against it. There comes a time in the history of certain projects when someone has to say "We're never going to get a concert violin out of this thing, no matter *how many* toothpicks we use in it."

What, then, is the shape of the new Joyce? I think we must look for him in the figure of a visionary vulgarist, a man whose extraordinary view of life grew out of a defeat for, and disillusion with, the conscious, rational mind. The narrow young man whom Joyce calls Stephen Dedalus exemplifies one terminus of the conscious mind, when he tells prudent, flabbergasted Bloom that "Ireland must be important because it belongs to me." The sort of impressionism he has learned from Walter Pater (see the famous conclusion to *The Renaissance*) culminates in this near-solipsism. On another level, and within the same book, the long dry catechism of "Ithaca" contracts itself into that famous round black dot (which the Random House edition shamefully omits), and disappears into permanent darkness. Having tied itself in tighter and tighter knots throughout the book, rationality blacks out altogether, and the book culminates, not with the achievement of a symbolic pattern, but with the absorption of all thought in the endless spinning motion of the blindly appetitive life-force. Common as dirt, majestic, luminous, and all-embracing, the sensual life of Molly Bloom is, imaginatively, the beginning and end of us all. From the dark of "Penelope," Joyce passed to the deeper darkness of *Finnegans Wake*, and found there such rewards as, after rationality is defeated, remain to a great artist—a religion of man which he could scarcely formulate without deriding it; occult and pantheist notions which he took only half-seriously; a kind of know-nothing indifference to all ideas and causes, an indifference which he associated with Mr. Dooley; an immense and intricate structure of history which he borrowed from Vico as a frame to hang his artistic patterns on; language-games, macaronic puns, and lists. These materials are contemptible neither in themselves nor as the elements of great art (artists are traditionally, and properly, indifferent to the inherent nobility, if any, of their materials); but their very nature is evidence of the fact that Joyce in the last years of his life surrendered structural control over his materials to certain sorts of accident. There are stories from the biography which illustrate this trend. For instance, Samuel Beckett reports that one day when Joyce was dictating *Finnegans Wake* to him, they were interrupted by a knock at the door. Joyce said "Come in," Beckett incorporated the phrase in the manuscript, and there Joyce, despite the protests of his amanuensis, insisted on keeping it. Even more telling evidence of accident in the composition of *Finnegans Wake* is found in the collection of manuscripts at the University of Buffalo. Among them are various worksheets made by Joyce and his helpers in preparation for the version of *Finnegans Wake*

which was published as "Work in Progress." A few of these papers have
been edited under the title of *Scribbledehobble*. But this edition was
savaged because the unhappy editor, caught between Joyce's deliberate,
significant distortions and those due to his bad handwriting, was altogether without a clear rule for his text. No doubt he copied blindly at
best, inaccurately at worst. Yet there is every reason to believe that he was
better equipped for deciphering the scrawls in front of him than Joyce,
whose eyes were very bad, or many of Joyce's amanuenses, for whom English was not a native language. And the *Scribbledehobble* manuscripts
are at least all by Joyce. There are other worksheets in the collection, by
the amanuenses, which are disfigured by errors of primitive simplicity
and staggering grossness. The problem isn't that the manuscript is illegi-
ble; more often than not, one knows what the writer it trying to say, but
is appalled by inaccuracies which have not the slightest claim to significance. They are the obvious result of someone listening with a French ear
to an Irish mumble on an incomprehensibly private topic and trying to
write down the result. There is no evidence that anyone, at any stage of
the proceedings, tried to straighten out any of this confusion; or if Joyce
himself tried to do so, it seems inevitable that thousands of adventitious
errors got past him. There are plenty of them in *Ulysses* (errors of tran-
scription, errors of usage, errors of inconsistency and unintentional in-
accuracy), where for the most part Joyce had the conventions of English
speech and spelling to help him; whether one thinks they matter or not
—whether, in fact, they are all discoverable or not—there are unquestion-
ably even more in *Finnegans Wake*. And it is part of the argument for a
"bent" Joyce that in the last part of his life he was writing in such a way
that one cannot distinguish significant and purposeful from insignificant
and accidental elements of his writing.

His nickname in youth, bestowed by Gogarty, was "Kinch the knife-
blade"; and he pursued the metaphor with relish, describing his brother
Stanislaus and various other acolytes on whom he used to sharpen his
mind as his "whetstones." That the mind so assiduously sharpened
buckled in mid-career, and surrendered to accident, to whim, or to circumstance a great part of its control over its own materials may imply a
sort of defeat on Joyce's part. This isn't a point to be lightly conceded,
and there's not much doubt that Joyce would deserve well of any critic
who showed us a feasible way around it. At the moment, one would have
to describe informed opinion as regretfully sceptical that such a way will
ever appear.

Yet how much occasion for regret do we (as readers of the 1960's) really
have? Joyce was not a consistent, inclusive, or coherent philosopher, any
more than he possessed the power of transmuting metals; but he would
not be a man of our times if he had these powers, or believed that he did.
The medieval synthesis, out of which Dante wrote so firm and controlled
a world-poem, has long since been shattered; there is even doubt now

that it was ever as firm as it has since seemed to the eye of nostalgia. Neither Joyce nor any modern writer can count upon that framework of arching, intricate logic which entitles Dante to inscribe, without irony, over Hell-gate:

FECEMI LA DIVINA POTESTATE
LA SOMMA SAPIENZA E IL PRIMO AMORE.

Power, wisdom, and love, here invoked as coordinate forces without the slightest hesitation that they can be shown to work together, simply did not work together for Joyce—as they don't for our world, generally. There is nothing idiosyncratic about Joyce's "bending"; he took it, perhaps, harder than most because the early sense of unusual power and discipline engendered in him the conviction of a special intellectual destiny. No man who sets before him, as Joyce did in youth, the austere and rigorous example of Dante, can fail to be disappointed when he discovers that it is just not possible to write like Dante any more. An early review speaks with lofty contempt of "a young generation which has cast away belief and thrown precision after it, for which Balzac is a great intellect and every sampler who chooses to wander amid his own shapeless hells and heavens a Dante without the unfortunate prejudices of Dante." Except for admiring Balzac, the elder Joyce might be thought to exemplify precisely these terms of disdain formulated by his younger self.

In a famous essay of the twenties much hacked over lately, T. S. Eliot spoke of the "dissociation of sensibility" characteristic of our times as distinguished from the seventeenth century. Whether our sensibility is more dissociated now than it was then may be debated; what causes led to this dissociation (whenever we suppose it to have begun) may provide further subject of speculation. But the fact, simply as a fact, is scarcely open to question. The division between scientific knowledge and human feeling is not, however, the only "dissociation" we have to contend with; rifts and schisms in the world of the mind are so many and so deep that the modern sensibility can't be called simply "dissociated"—it is fractured, splintered, Balkanized. For good or evil, the characteristic arts of our age are unstructured; the invertebrate, episodic novel, music improvised or only loosely patterned, maze-like painting, these are our characteristic products. Not only this, but our social life seems to me more and more unstructured. We are in the age of the independent voter, responsive not to the principles but to moods, in the age of the wildcat strike, directed against union bureaucracy as much as against management. Distinctions between cultures, classes, even levels of mental organization are breaking down; witness, for instance, the peculiar ambivalence taken on by a word like "primitive." I even hear rumors of places where the distinction between the sexes is getting ambiguous.

To such a world, the very ideal of a monolithic structure of compelling belief is irrelevant. Setting aside the nostalgia of my conservative prejudices as unprofitable, I take Joyce as a type of the artist who is willing to live in and write for the future. The world he chose or was forced to choose, seemingly against the very nature of his gift, is the one we now inhabit. Having passed through the latter stages of *Ulysses,* we are entering upon the first pages of *Finnegans Wake,* a murky passage of confused time enlivened only by the incidental jokes of the indifferent. Joyce found not only the available structures of ideas and beliefs, but the very texture of language corrupted; and so undertook, not to build anew, but to write in a way that needed neither conventional ideas nor conventional language. His problem was one which it may not seem too pretentious to describe as a general problem of our time—how to wash clean in dirty water, how to do worthwhile work with bent, second-hand tools. *Finnegans Wake* may be perceived very handsomely as a game of billiards played

> *On a cloth untrue*
> *With a twisted cue*
> *And elliptical billiard balls.*

In its pages, Joyce has successfully performed the reduction of the arts to philology, and so far as is possible reenacted the creation of the cosmos (a new and private cosmos) within the proscenium of his peculiar gift. That he was able to do this using only the junk and litter of the original cosmos is a splendid achievement; but its splendor need not blind us to its perversity, and its perversity cannot be judged independently of the age to which it is a response. Thus we circle back to the *Zeitgeist,* about which it seems we must have opinions.

What Joyce saw (and it is an inevitable part of my argument that he saw truly) was an age of bind and smudge; of consciousness and above all of self-consciousness almost infinite in extent but foggy and unformulated in its topography. A peculiarity of modern feeling, as evident in Franz Kafka and Jackson Pollock as in *Finnegans Wake,* is loss of horizon, obliteration of perspective. Experience flickers through the darkroom of our consciousness like a film projected immensely too fast—out of control, altogether. With straining eyes and anxious small gestures we try to follow the flicker or even react to it; but our best postures are hollow and irrelevant. The language itself is *vermoulu;* the wells of thought and feeling have been fouled. The art of the later Joyce lies in extracting a kind of bubbling gaiety, a verbal vaudeville, from the desolation of this landscape. The old controversy roused by *Ulysses* over Joyce's alleged pessimism or optimism thus fades, for the 1960's, into a mere matter of emphasis. In particular, the view of Joyce as an intricate, unwearying cosmic ironist (a view which leads Hugh Kenner, for example, to see the *Portrait* as primarily an extended assault on Stephen and *Ulysses* as primarily an extended assault on Bloom) seems bound to fade. Joyce did not seek or make a desolation, he found it as in the air we breathe, and extracted from it the juice of a small and flickering joy. He is not the greatest modern ironist, he is the only great modern humorist.

One last speculation. The less we see Joyce's work as an intricate, logically arranged machinery of glittering, sterile edges, and the more we emphasize the commonness of his materials, the more we are likely to think his art itself a work of magic—one which touches, through intuitive insight, the chords of secret, irrational sympathies. These are not fashionable concepts in modern criticism, any more than in modern psychology; but modern criticism and psychology may well be obsolete before *Ulysses* is. In any event, Joyce (following Baudelaire and Mallarmé) himself accepted and made use of substantially this view of his art. An age more impressed than our own by its inability to understand its own reactions may well revert to a view of Joyce as verbal necromancer, if only because the fact of his impact is there, and the available ways of accounting for it are patently inadequate. The middle ages, Bloomishly fond of adapting antique temples into habitable hovels, reworked Apuleius and Virgil into the semblance of warlocks; very probably, in a century or so, the same process will be under way with Joyce. The new age will find, though, that Joyce has been beforehand with them—having not only constructed his own inimitable architectures, but himself pulled some of them down to make shanties and outhouses.

Chronology of Important Dates

1882   James Joyce born February 2 in Rathgar, Dublin. Eldest son in the large family of John Stanislaus Joyce, improvident rate collector and "praiser of his own past," and of Mary Jane ("Mae") Joyce.

1888   Joyce sent to Clongowes Wood College, a Jesuit school, remaining there until 1891.

1891   Death of Charles Stewart Parnell, "the uncrowned King of Ireland," on October 6. Joyce composed his first printed work, *Et Tu, Healy,* which praised the dead leader and attacked his chief political enemy.

1893–1898   Joyce's family in financial decline. Joyce sent to Belvedere College, another Jesuit school.

1899–1902   Joyce at University College, Dublin.

1900   Joyce read his paper "Drama and Life" before the Literary and Historical Society; his essay "Ibsen's New Drama" was published in the *Fortnightly Review.*

1901   His pamphlet attacking the Irish Literary Theatre, "The Day of the Rabblement," was composed.

1902–1903   Joyce left for Paris. Intending to be a medical student, he instead read, studied, wrote reviews, and lived on little food. In April he received a telegram: "MOTHER DYING COME HOME FATHER." He returned and watched her slow death.

1904   First draft of *Stephen Hero.* In June, Joyce met Nora Barnacle and fell in love with her. Together they left Dublin for Zurich, where Joyce expected to teach at the Berlitz School. The Zurich position was not open; they left for Pola, where one was. This year saw the publication, for the first time, of some of his poems and stories.

1905   Joyce was transferred to the Berlitz school in Trieste. His son Giorgio was born. Publishing difficulties with respect to *Dubliners,* not resolved until 1914, began.

1907   *Chamber Music* published. "The Dead" written. His daughter Lucia Anna was born.

1912   Joyce's last trip to Dublin.

1913   Joyce met Ezra Pound, who was able to interest *the Egoist* in the manuscript of *A Portrait of the Artist as a Young Man.*

1914   *Annus mirabilis. Dubliners* published by Grant Richards. Serial publication of *A Portrait* begun in *the Egoist. Ulysses* begun, but put aside for work on *Exiles.*

1915   Joyce departed Trieste for Zurich. After letters from Pound and Yeats, the Royal Literary Fund awarded him a small amount of money.

1916–1917   Publication of *A Portrait* in New York and London, successively. Joyce's eye troubles, not to end in his lifetime, began.

1918   *The Little Review* (New York) began to serialize *Ulysses. Exiles* published in London and New York.

1919   The subsidy of one of his benefactors withdrawn, Joyce took up teaching English at a commercial school in Trieste. His work on *Ulysses* continued.

1920   Pound persuaded Joyce to move to Paris. In New York, publication of *Ulysses* in the *Little Review* was discontinued after a complaint from the Society for the Suppression of Vice.

1922   *Ulysses* published on Joyce's birthday. His eye troubles worsened.

1923   The first pages of *Finnegans Wake* (known until 1939 only as *Work in Progress*) were composed.

1924   The first fragment of *Wake* published in the *Transatlantic Review* (Paris). Most of the book was thereafter to be published in fragments, later to be reworked.

1931   Joyce and Nora Barnacle were married, in London, "for testamentary reasons." Joyce's father died at age 82.

1932   A grandson, Stephen, was born. Lucia Joyce suffered a mental breakdown from which she was never to recover.

1933   In New York, Judge John M. Woolsey decided that *Ulysses* was not pornographic and that its American publication could be permitted.

1934   Lucia's mental health continued to deteriorate, as did Joyce's eyes.

1936   *Collected Poems* published.

1937   The last separate fragment of the *Wake* was published.

1939   Joyce was able to show the first bound copy of the *Wake* on his birthday. Official publication came later in the year.

1940   Joyce and Nora entered Switzerland after a hurried flight from France.

1941   James Joyce died January 13 of a perforated ulcer, in the Schwesterhaus vom Roten Kreuz in Zurich.

Notes on the Editor and Contributors

WILLIAM M. CHACE, the editor of this volume, is Assistant Professor of English at Stanford University. He is the author of *The Political Identities of Ezra Pound and T. S. Eliot* and articles on those two figures.

HÉLÈNE CIXOUS is Professor of English Literature, Université de Paris, Vincennes, and editor of *Poétique*. Her novel *Dedans* was awarded the Prix Medicis in 1969.

RICHARD ELLMANN is Goldsmiths' Professor of English Literature in the University of Oxford. He has also taught at Yale, Northwestern, and Harvard. Among his many publications are *Yeats: The Man and the Masks; The Identity of Yeats; James Joyce;* and *Eminent Domain: Yeats Among Wilde, Joyce, Pound, Eliot and Auden,* and *Ulysses on the Liffey. Golden Codgers: Biographical Speculations* is his most recent book.

HUGH KENNER is Professor of English at Johns Hopkins University; he has also taught at the University of California at Santa Barbara and the University of Virginia. The author of books on Wyndham Lewis, Eliot, Pound, Joyce, and Samuel Beckett, Professor Kenner has most recently published *The Pound Era* and *Bucky: A Guided Tour of Buckminster Fuller.*

EDMUND WILSON, the most widely accomplished and authoritative American man of letters in the last several decades, was, among other things, an early and brilliant student of the Joycean world..

S. L. GOLDBERG is Robert Wallace Professor of English Literature at the University of Melbourne and has also taught at the University of Sydney. He is editor of *The Critical Review: Melbourne-Sydney.* He has published two books on Joyce.

ANTHONY CRONIN, poet, novelist, playwright, critic, and editor, has recently published his *Collected Poems 1950–1973.* His play *The Shame of It* was presented in 1973 by the Abbey Company at the Peacock Theatre, Dublin. A prose narrative, *Dead As Doornails: A Chronicle of Life,* is forthcoming.

HARRY LEVIN is the Irving Babbitt Professor of Comparative Literature at Harvard University. He is the author of myriad books and articles, among them studies of Christopher Marlowe; of Hawthorne, Poe, and Melville; of *Hamlet;* and he has written extensively on general problems of literary criticism.

CLIVE HART is Professor of Literature at the University of Essex. He has written or edited several books on Joyce, including *A Concordance to "Finnegans Wake"* and *James Joyce's "Ulysses";* one on aeronautics and one on kites; and he is co-editor of the *Wake Newslitter.*

LIONEL TRILLING, until his retirement the George Edward Woodberry Professor of Literature and Criticism at Columbia University, and now University Professor there, is the author of *Matthew Arnold, The Liberal Imagination, The Opposing Self, Beyond Culture,* and lately, *Sincerity and Authenticity.*

ROBERT MARTIN ADAMS is Professor of English at the University of California at Los Angeles. Among his extensive and wide-ranging publications are books on Milton and the critics, on Stendhal, and on Joyce. His most recent books are *Nil: Episodes in the Literary Conquest of Void During the Nineteenth Century; Proteus: His Lies, His Truths;* and *The Roman Stamp.*

Selected Bibliography

The Texts

Collected Poems. New York: The Viking Press, Inc., 1937. Compass Books, 1957.

Critical Writings of James Joyce. Edited by Richard Ellmann and Ellsworth Mason. New York: The Viking Press, Inc., 1959.

Dubliners: Text, Criticism, and Notes. Edited by Robert Scholes and A. Walton Litz. Viking Critical Library. New York: The Viking Press, Inc., 1969.

Exiles: A Play in Three Acts, Including Hitherto Unpublished Notes by the Author, Discovered after His Death, and an Introduction by Padraic Colum. New York: The Viking Press, Inc., 1951. Compass Books, 1961.

Finnegans Wake. New York: The Viking Press, Inc., 1939.

A First-Draft Version of Finnegans Wake. Edited and annotated by David Hayman. Austin: University of Texas Press, 1963.

Giacomo Joyce. Edited by Richard Ellmann. New York: The Viking Press, Inc., 1968.

The Letters of James Joyce. Vol. 1. Edited by Stuart Gilbert. New York: The Viking Press, Inc.., 1957. New ed. with corrections, 1966. Vols. 2 and 3. Edited by Richard Ellmann. New York: The Viking Press, Inc., 1966.

A Portrait of the Artist as a Young Man: Text, Criticism, and Notes. Edited by Chester G. Anderson. Viking Critical Library. New York: The Viking Press, Inc., 1968.

Stephen Hero. Edited by Theodore Spencer. New ed. with additional material, edited by John J. Slocum and Herbert Cahoon. New York: New Directions Publishing Corporation, 1963.

Ulysses. New York: Random House, Inc., 1934. Rev. ed., 1961.

Bibliographies

Beebe, Maurice, Phillip F. Herring, and Walton Litz. "Criticism of James Joyce: A Selected Checklist." *Modern Fiction Studies,* 15 (Spring 1969), pp. 105–82.

Deming, Robert H. *A Bibliography of James Joyce Studies.* Lawrence: University of Kansas Libraries, 1964.

Slocum, John J., and Herbert Cahoon. *A Bibliography of James Joyce, 1882–1941.* New Haven: Yale University Press, 1953.

Journals

James Joyce Quarterly. Thomas F. Staley, editor. Vol. 1, no. 1 (Fall 1963) to the present.

James Joyce Review. Edmund J. Epstein, editor. Vol. 1, no. 1 (February 2, 1957); ended publication with Vol. 3, no. 1/2 (1959).

Wake Newslitter. Clive Hart and Fritz Senn, editors. No. 1 (March 1962) to no. 18 (December 1963); New Series, Vol. 1, no. 1 (February 1964) to the present.

Biography

Ellmann, Richard. *James Joyce.* New York: Oxford University Press, 1959.

General Criticism and Scholarship

Adams, Robert Martin. *James Joyce: Common Sense and Beyond.* New York: Random House, Inc., 1967.

Burgess, Anthony. *Re Joyce.* New York: W. W. Norton & Company, Inc., 1965. Ballantine Books, Inc., 1966.

Cixous, Hélène. *The Exile of James Joyce.* New York: David Lewis, Inc., 1972.

Givens, Seon, ed. *James Joyce: Two Decades of Criticism.* New York: Vanguard Press, Inc., 1948. Augmented ed., 1963.

Goldberg, S. L. *James Joyce.* New York: Grove Press, Inc., 1962. Capricorn Books, 1972.

Goldman, Arnold. *The Joyce Paradox: Form and Freedom in his Fiction.* Evanston: Northwestern University Press, 1966.

Gross, John. *James Joyce.* New York: The Viking Press, Inc., 1970.

Kenner, Hugh. *Dublin's Joyce.* Bloomington: Indiana University Press, 1956. Beacon Paperbacks, 1962.

Levin, Harry. *James Joyce: A Critical Introduction.* New York: New Directions Publishing Corporation, 1941. Rev. ed., 1960.

Lewis, Wyndham. "An Analysis of the Mind of James Joyce." In *Time and Western Man,* pp. 75–113. New York: Harcourt Brace Jovanovich, Inc., 1928.

Litz, Walton. *The Art of James Joyce: Method and Design in "Ulysses" and "Finnegans Wake."* New York: Oxford University Press, 1961. Galaxy Books, 1964.

Magalaner, Marvin, and Richard M. Kain. *Joyce, the Man, the Work, the Reputation.* New York: New York University Press, 1956.

Noon, William T., S.J. *Joyce and Aquinas.* New Haven: Yale University Press, 1957.

Pound, Ezra. *Pound/Joyce: The Letters of Ezra Pound to James Joyce, with Pound's Essays on Joyce.* Edited by Forrest Read. New York: New Directions Publishing Corporation, 1967.

Tindall, William York. *James Joyce: His Way of Interpreting the Modern World.* New York: Charles Scribner's Sons, 1950.

——. *A Reader's Guide to James Joyce.* New York: Farrar, Straus & Giroux, Inc., The Noonday Press, 1959.

Wilson, Edmund. "James Joyce." In *Axel's Castle: A Study in the Imaginative Literature of 1870–1930,* pp. 191–239. New York: Charles Scribner's Sons, 1931.

Dubliners

Garrett, Peter K. *Twentieth Century Interpretations of "Dubliners": A Collection of Critical Essays.* Englewood Cliffs, N.J.: Prentice-Hall, Inc., 1968.

Gifford, Don. *Notes for Joyce.* New York: E. P. Dutton & Co., Inc., 1967.

Hart, Clive, ed. *James Joyce's "Dubliners": Critical Essays.* London: Faber & Faber, 1969.

Magalaner, Marvin. *Time of Apprenticeship: The Fiction of Young James Joyce.* New York: Abelard-Schuman Limited, 1959.

A Portrait of the Artist as a Young Man

Connolly, Thomas E., ed. *Joyce's "Portrait": Criticisms and Critiques.* New York: Appleton-Century-Crofts, 1962.

Gifford, Don. (See entry under *Dubliners.*)

Morris, William E., and Clifford A. Nault, Jr., eds. *Portraits of an Artist: A Casebook on James Joyce's "A Portrait of the Artist as a Young Man."* New York: Odyssey Press, 1962.

Scholes, Robert E., and Richard M. Kain. *The Workshop of Daedalus: James Joyce and the Raw Materials for "A Portrait of the Artist as a Young Man."* Evanston: Northwestern University Press, 1965.

Schutte, William M., ed. *Twentieth Century Interpretations of "A Portrait of the Artist as a Young Man": A Collection of Critical Essays.* Englewood Cliffs, N.J.: Prentice-Hall, Inc., 1968.

Ulysses

Adams, Robert M. *Surface and Symbol: The Consistency of James Joyce's "Ulysses."* New York: Oxford University Press, 1962.

Blamires, Harry. *The Bloomsday Book: A Guide Through Joyce's "Ulysses."* New York: Barnes & Noble Books, 1966.

Cronin, Anthony. "The Advent of Bloom." In *A Question of Modernity,* pp. 58–96. London: Secker and Warburg, 1966.

Eliot, T. S. "*Ulysses,* Order and Myth." *The Dial,* 75 (November 1923), 480–83.

Ellmann, Richard. *Ulysses on the Liffey.* New York: Oxford University Press, 1972.

Empson, William. "The Theme of *Ulysses.*" *Kenyon Review,* 18 (Winter 1956), 26–52.

Gilbert, Stuart. *James Joyce's "Ulysses."* 2d rev. ed. New York: Alfred A. Knopf, Inc., 1952.

Goldberg, S. L. *The Classical Temper: A Study of James Joyce's "Ulysses."* London: Chatto and Windus, 1961.

Hart, Clive. *James Joyce's "Ulysses."* Sydney, Australia: Sydney University Press, 1968.

Jung, C. C. *"Ulysses:* A Monologue." Translated by W. Stanley Dell. *Nimbus,* 2 (June–August 1953), pp. 7–20.

Kain, Richard M. *Fabulous Voyager: James Joyce's "Ulysses."* Chicago: University of Chicago Press, 1947.

Schutte, William M. *Joyce and Shakespeare: A Study in the Meaning of "Ulysses."* New Haven: Yale University Press, 1957.

Shechner, Mark. *Joyce in Nighttown: A Psychoanalytic Inquiry into "Ulysses."* Berkeley: University of California Press, 1974.

Sultan, Stanley. *The Argument of "Ulysses."* Columbus: Ohio State University Press, 1964.

Thornton, Weldon. *Allusions in "Ulysses": An Annotated List.* Chapel Hill: University of North Carolina Press, 1968.

West, Alick. "James Joyce: *Ulysses.*" In *Crisis and Criticism and Selected Literary Essays,* pp. 104–27. London: Lawrence and Wishart, 1975.

Finnegans Wake

Atherton, James S. *The Books at the Wake: A Study of Literary Allusions in James Joyce's "Finnegans Wake."* New York: The Viking Press, Inc., 1960.

Beckett, Samuel, et al. *James Joyce—"Finnegans Wake": A Symposium.* Original title: *Our Exagmination Round his Factification for Incamination of "Work in Progress."* New York: New Directions Publishing Corporation, 1942.

Benstock, Bernard. *Joyce-Again's Wake.* Seattle: University of Washington Press, 1965.

Campbell, Joseph, and Henry Morton Robinson. *A Skeleton Key to "Finnegans Wake."* New York: Harcourt Brace Jovanovich, Inc., 1944. Compass Books, 1961.

Dalton, Jack P., and Clive Hart, eds. *Twelve and a Tilly: Essays on the Occasion of the 25th Anniversary of "Finnegans Wake."* Evanston: Northwestern University Press, 1965.

Glasheen, Adaline. *A Census of "Finnegans Wake."* Evanston: Northwestern University Press, 1956.

———. *A Second Census of "Finnegans Wake."* Evanston: Northwestern University Press, 1963.

Hart, Clive. *Structure and Motif in "Finnegans Wake."* Evanston: Northwestern University Press, 1962.

———, and Fritz Senn, eds.. *A "Wake" Digest.* Sydney, Australia: Sydney University Press, 1968.

Tindall, William York. *A Reader's Guide to "Finnegans Wake."* New York: Farrar, Straus & Giroux, Inc., 1969.

Wilson, Edmund. "The Dream of H. C. Earwicker." In *The Wound and the Bow*, pp. 243–71. New York: Oxford University Press, 1947.

Hunting Whitey

ALSO BY THE AUTHORS

Casey Sherman

The Finest Hours (coauthored by Michael J. Tougias)

Above & Beyond (coauthored by Michael J. Tougias)

12: The Inside Story of Tom Brady's Fight for Redemption
(coauthored by Dave Wedge)

The Ice Bucket Challenge (coauthored by Dave Wedge)

Boston Strong (coauthored by Dave Wedge)

*Animal: The Bloody Rise and Fall of
the Mob's Most Feared Assassin*

Bad Blood: Freedom and Death in the White Mountains

Black Dragon

Black Irish

A Rose for Mary: The Hunt for the Real Boston Strangler

Dave Wedge

12: The Inside Story of Tom Brady's Fight for Redemption
(coauthored by Casey Sherman)

The Ice Bucket Challenge (coauthored by Casey Sherman)

Boston Strong (coauthored by Casey Sherman)

Hunting Whitey

The Inside Story
of the Capture & Killing of
America's Most Wanted
Crime Boss

Casey Sherman
and Dave Wedge

HARPER LARGE PRINT

An Imprint of HarperCollins*Publishers*

HarperCollins books may be purchased for educational, business, or sales promotional use. For information, please e-mail the Special Markets Department at SPsales@harpercollins.com.

FIRST HARPER LARGE PRINT EDITION

ISBN: 978-0-06-299992-4

Library of Congress Cataloging-in-Publication Data is available upon request.

20 21 22 23 24 LSC 10 9 8 7 6 5 4 3 2 1

For my darling Kristin, thank you for embarking on life's journey with me, for Bella and Mia, and in memory of my beloved stepfather, Kenneth Dodd, a trusted editor of my work and a kind and gentle soul.

—CASEY SHERMAN

For Jessica, thank you for the love, support, and daily conversations about writing, news, and life that inspire me to do what I do. And to my amazing children, Danielle and Jackson, you guys are everything to me and I love you both.

—DAVE WEDGE

Perseverance, secret of all triumphs.

—VICTOR HUGO

James J. "Whitey" Bulger's Hit List

March & April 1973—Michael Milano, Al Plummer, William O'Brien, James Leary, and Joseph Notorangeli

December 1973—James O'Toole

February 1974—Al Notorangeli

October 1974—James Sousa

November 1974—Paul McGonagle

June 1975—Edward Connors

November 1975—Tommy King, Francis "Buddy" Leonard

December 1976—Roger Wheeler

December 1976—Richard Castucci

Late 1981—Debra Davis

May 1982—Brian Halloran, Michael Donahue

August 1982—John B. Callahan

July 1983—Arthur "Bucky" Barrett

November 1984—John McIntyre

Early 1985—Deborah Hussey

Prologue

Santa Monica, California, 2010

It's dusk in Santa Monica and a gentle breeze blows off the Pacific Ocean near the famed Santa Monica Pier. One hundred and thirty feet above the platform, a giant Ferris wheel turns slowly while nearby a steel roller coaster rumbles along at thirty-five miles per hour to the delight of screaming passengers.

On the beach nearby, Whitey Bulger is strolling hand in hand with his longtime girlfriend Catherine Greig just beyond Pacific Park. Both are dressed in white and are illuminated against the pinkish hue of the setting sun. They look like any other retired couple enjoying a warm evening outside. They also look vulnerable.

Whitey savors these nightly walks, as they give him a sense of freedom that he lacks while being cooped up most days inside their two-bedroom apartment at the Princess Eugenia less than a mile away. But Bulger senses that something is wrong—that they are being followed. He notices a vagrant walking a few paces behind them, studying their every move.

Is it an FBI agent working undercover? Bulger thinks to himself. *Is it finally the end of the line?* The living on edge, always prepared for someone to recognize him, these were realities that Bulger had grown comfortable living with ever since he fled Boston just before Christmas in 1994. His vigilance was constant—it was how he'd survived on the run for so long—it didn't matter whether he was sleeping in his Santa Monica apartment or strolling on the beach.

After a few more steps, a homeless man senses an opportunity and rushes the couple.

But instead of pulling out a badge, he shows them a knife.

"Give me your fucking money, old man," the robber shouts while holding up the long, steel blade.

Bulger smiles, rubs the white whiskers of his neatly trimmed beard, and lifts his arm slowly. He's holding a gun close to his body.

"Kid, never bring a knife to a gunfight," Whitey snarls.

Bulger, the avid movie buff, has no doubt lifted the line from the Brian De Palma film *The Untouchables* about the most legendary mobster of all—Al Capone.

The threat works.

The vagrant puts his blade away and disappears into the night.

And Whitey continues on his way.

PART I

The Hunt

1

Noreen Gleason carried a cardboard box bulging with personal and professional mementos up the elevator and into the Boston office of the FBI. It was February 3, 2008, her first day on the job as assistant special agent in charge of the criminal division (ASAC), and as she stepped off the lift, she walked past a bull-pen of agents who were glued to their computer screens or reviewing stacks of files dedicated to the one case that had haunted the office and the city for decades. The agents kept their heads down, going about their work without passion or energy. The New England Patriots had just lost the Super Bowl the night before to the New York Giants, ending their bid for a perfect season. There was reason to be glum. But the feeling here was different.

Gleason studied their mannerisms and recognized the problem immediately.

These agents look haggard and beat down, she said to herself.

Gleason placed the box on her desk, sat down, and took a deep breath. Gazing around her office, she realized how far she'd come from her strict, military-style upbringing in her sleepy hometown of Hawthorne, New Jersey, and the seven long years she'd toiled as a trooper in the state police there.

Her desk phone rang.

"Mr. Bamford will see you now," the secretary informed her.

Mr. Bamford was Gleason's new boss, Warren T. Bamford, the special agent in charge (SAC) of the Boston field office. Gleason walked confidently into Bamford's office, where he stood by the window with arms folded, staring out at Government Center and City Hall. He didn't waste time.

"I have one job for you, Agent Gleason," he said. "My top priority is capturing James Bulger and bringing him to justice."

Gleason didn't respond right away. She needed to process the statement for a moment. By this point, James "Whitey" Bulger had been on the run from the FBI for more than thirteen years. In that time, he'd

become something of a ghost story, a larger-than-life criminal who'd been written about in books and mythologized on the big screen, whose exploits had become crazier than fiction. His ability to evade capture had grown his legacy into infamy—instead of being a mob murderer and henchman, he'd become a folk hero.

Bamford's decree was nothing new. Every SAC of the Boston field office had made similar pledges before. His predecessor, Kenneth Kaiser, had pumped out his chest after taking the job in 2003 and promised that he'd do everything in his power to arrest the fugitive crime boss on his watch.

"I will do whatever it takes to get this guy," Kaiser told reporters then. "I don't care who catches him; I just want it over and done with. My goal is to have him caught and move on."

That didn't happen.

But Bamford was a quiet leader, and more methodical than the bombastic Kaiser. As a kid, Bamford watched the Efram Zimbalist Jr. television drama *The FBI*, and knew that's what he wanted to be when he grew up. A native of Lowell, Massachusetts, and a former US Marine, Bamford had served on the FBI's Hostage Rescue Team and was sent as a sniper to the deadly standoff at Ruby Ridge and the siege at David Koresh's Branch Davidian compound in Waco, Texas.

Tellingly, Bamford did not fire a single shot at either tragic event.

Bamford understood that cooperation between all the agencies—the FBI, state police, US Marshals, and US Attorney's office—was imperative in ending the now thirteen-year-old manhunt for America's most wanted mob boss. Bamford also needed someone who was smart and action oriented to lead the effort. He believed that he'd found the perfect candidate in Noreen Gleason.

"You were a state trooper in New Jersey and I think you'll have a good rapport with our counterparts. They'll respect you. We need everyone rowing in the same direction if we're going to pull this off."

"If catching Bulger is the priority of the office, that's what I'm gonna do," she told her boss.

Like Bamford, Gleason had always dreamed of a career in law enforcement. She entered the New Jersey State Police Academy in 1985 and served as a road trooper for the next seven years, eventually becoming an instructor teaching state police cadets defensive tactics, physical training, and water safety.

But Gleason wasn't satisfied with her career working for the New Jersey State Police.

"I felt it wasn't a truly professional organization and

it didn't respect women," Gleason says. "The FBI offered me more."

She entered the FBI Academy at Quantico in 1991 and was schooled in an advanced level of academics, firearms, and physical training. She took these skills to New York City, where she worked as a field agent investigating Dominican and Jamaican gangs. Gleason was driving into Manhattan to rendezvous with her squad for an undercover drug buy when the Twin Towers came down on 9/11. She was immediately dispatched into the toxic smoke and debris at Ground Zero to join the bucket brigade on top of the smoldering pile of twisted metal and ash.

Like everyone in New York that fateful day, the attacks affected Gleason personally. She immediately moved from monitoring drug dealers to counterterrorism, where she interviewed and vetted terror suspects for imprisonment and deportation.

After a year on that job, Gleason moved to FBI headquarters in Washington, DC, for leadership training. She has always felt that she had the organizational and interpersonal skills to be a good boss.

She eventually returned to Manhattan, where she supervised eleven agents and six New York City police officers on the Metro Gang Task Force, a unit

whose mission it was to penetrate murderous organizations like the Crips, Bloods, Latin Kings, and the ultraviolent MS-13, an international gang originating in El Salvador and known to dispatch death squads to eradicate perceived enemies.

Gleason was not only committed to putting street killers behind bars, she also felt the added responsibility of protecting innocent people from getting caught up in gang life.

"It's the underbelly of America. It's the most impoverished segment of society," she says. "I always felt very comfortable in that environment helping people live a better life there."

One person she could not protect was a valuable female informant who was executed in cold blood by a gang member in front of her two children.

"It bothers me to this day, the sheer brutality of it all. To murder a woman purposely with her two kids watching. I feel a responsibility for what happened to her to this day."

When she saw a posting for the Boston office, she jumped at the chance despite its sullied reputation following revelations that a former agent, John Connolly, had conspired to help Bulger.

"John Connolly had left a terrible black mark on the

entire Bureau," she says. "It bothered me personally about what he did with Whitey Bulger."

Indeed, Gleason was not alone in feeling this way—many others shared her disgust about the mark Connolly had left on the Bureau. The fallout at the Boston office after details of Connolly's corruption spread had been extreme—even now all these years later in 2008, the office still had not recovered its reputation.

What Connolly had done during his career as an FBI agent was to protect Whitey Bulger at all costs while working with the gangster to eliminate his rivals. After Bulger disappeared in late 1994, no one believed that the Bureau was serious in its effort to bring him to justice. When Gleason moved to the seaside town of Scituate, Massachusetts, and told new friends that she was an FBI agent, they immediately presumed she was corrupt.

"Are you like John Connolly?" one neighbor asked her.

"They were so mistrusting of the FBI," Gleason recalls today. "I'd never experienced that before in New York City or DC. People were respectful of the work we do, but not in Massachusetts."

Gleason wasn't alone. As she stared into the eyes of each agent now working on the Bulger case, she saw

men and women who were going through the motions and had all but given up the ghost.

"They were so ingrained in that Boston downtrodden, woe-is-me head space that I knew we had to shake things up," she said.

Gleason brought the team in for a huddle and gave them the cold reality.

"You guys simply aren't getting it done," she told them. "We're gonna bring in some fresh eyes and see what we can do."

In Gleason's mind, it was time to bring in the heavy hitters.

She was the newest agent working in the Boston FBI office and she was already the least popular. Agents who had been working the Bulger case for months and years were both stunned and offended by her decision to shake things up and bring in so-called ringers from the outside, but she forged ahead, undaunted.

"What have you guys been doing?" she asked the team.

Gleason already knew the case agents had aggressively investigated a potential sighting of Bulger and Catherine Greig in Sicily in the spring of 2007. The Bureau had secured a photo and video of an elderly couple fitting their description walking the cobblestoned streets of Taormina, a hilltop village near Mount Etna.

The man in question looked similar to Whitey, with snowflake-white hair and sunglasses, and the woman appeared to be roughly Greig's age. But the FBI's facial recognition analysis on both was inconclusive. The images were later used in an episode of Germany's equivalent of *America's Most Wanted*. A German couple immediately recognized themselves on TV from their vacation to Italy and called the hotline to report the bizarre case of mistaken identity.

It was typical of the way the probe had unfolded for years. To Gleason, the Bulger investigation seemed to be a never-ending series of missed calls and dead ends.

The case agents even told her they believed that Whitey was now traveling with someone else, that he'd killed Catherine Greig and had found another girlfriend.

Gleason didn't buy it. She believed deep down that the couple was still together and that was something she could work with. "The investigation had always been about Whitey," she recalls. "I hate to say it, but for most male criminals, their downfall is their women. That's often been the case for our male fugitives—their wives and girlfriends are their weak links."

She demanded that the agents shift their focus in a big way.

"Let's look at the women in his life," she told the team. "Let's look at Catherine and her twin sister."

By now, Gleason was spending much of her time dismantling and then rebuilding the investigative team—the so-called Bulger Task Force.

One agent she thought would be perfect for this case was a man she had worked with in New York City named Tommy MacDonald.

"Tommy Mac was one of the most tenacious agents I'd ever seen," she says. "He was especially good at old stale cases."

The hunt for Whitey Bulger had become just that—an old stale case.

MacDonald was a member of the FBI's Joint Bank Robbery Task Force with the NYPD. The unit was created in the late 1970s at the beginning of the crack epidemic, when violent addicts were starting to pull bank jobs. It was a great assignment for MacDonald, who'd always dreamed of a job in the FBI. The youngest of seven kids, Tommy was raised in Ridgefield, Connecticut. His father had a corporate job in New York while his mother worked part time as a secretary. A natural athlete and star basketball player, Tommy Mac earned an athletic scholarship to the University of New Hampshire, where he was selected captain during his senior year, in 1994. The six-foot-two guard averaged nearly ten points a game during his college career. He was good, but not good enough to play professionally, so he

doubled his efforts to gain acceptance into the Bureau. He worked days and went to law school at Fordham University at night. Once he'd earned his law degree, he was selected to go to Quantico.

Like Gleason, Tommy Mac was assigned to the New York office right out of the gate. It was a dizzying time for the FBI rookie, as he fought to keep up with the thousand other field agents working cases in Manhattan and beyond. One agent he particularly looked up to was Lenny Hatton Jr., a seasoned FBI specialist in evidence recovery and a father of four. Lenny was also a volunteer firefighter. On September 11, 2001, Hatton was on his way to work when he saw the black plume of smoke shoot out of the North Tower of the World Trade Center. He rushed to the scene to help and then witnessed the second plane crash into the South Tower. When Hatton reached Ground Zero, he hooked up with one of the rescue companies from the New York City Fire Department (FDNY) and entered the South Tower, where he and countless others disappeared forever.

"I went to the hospitals looking for Lenny," MacDonald remembers. "It was so eerie. The hospitals in Manhattan were virtually empty of patients. There were doctors and nurses just waiting to help but there was no one to treat."

Lenny Hatton's remains, like those of so many other Ground Zero victims, would never be found.

In the mid-2000s, Tommy Mac inherited a notorious and truly disturbing case from another agent who'd been reassigned elsewhere. MacDonald was asked to investigate the disappearance of five-year-old Etan Patz. The little boy vanished on his way to catch a school bus in SoHo in May 1979. The case generated headlines around the world, and Etan's smiling face was the first to appear on the back of a milk carton under the banner MISSING.

Investigators had a prime suspect in the case, a junk collector and convicted pedophile named José Ramos. The man dated a woman who was hired to walk Etan and other neighborhood children. He'd even admitted to being with Etan that morning. It all made perfect sense.

Or did it?

Tommy Mac was skeptical. Some pieces to the puzzle just didn't fit. So he pulled the puzzle apart and started again from the beginning. He went back and interviewed witnesses and worked diligently in his reexamination of the case. MacDonald revealed promising leads that he'd continue to pursue for years until he and other agents would later identify Etan's true killer Pedro Hernandez in 2012 and locked him up for twenty-five years to life in

prison. Etan Patz's body has never been found. The date of his disappearance, May 25, is designated as National Missing Children's Day.

The case of Etan Patz had been old and stale until it wasn't. For Noreen Gleason, MacDonald was the ideal agent for the Bulger case, which had cast a dark shadow over Boston—and the FBI—for nearly two decades.

Tommy Mac got the call from Gleason while he was sitting on the back porch of his Danbury, Connecticut, home enjoying a cold beer with his wife, Susie. After exchanging the usual pleasantries, the newly appointed ASAC got right to the point.

"I want you to come up here to Boston and find Whitey Bulger."

MacDonald knew the name. He'd played college basketball in New England and his brother was a schoolteacher in Boston. Tommy had also chased down Bulger leads in Manhattan that had gone nowhere.

Holy crap, he thought to himself.

The Whitey Bulger case was the proverbial white whale of the FBI. Gleason might as well have said that she wanted his help finding Bigfoot.

Gleason asked her old friend to sleep on it. Tommy had a lot of thinking to do. He'd been fighting in the FBI trenches for nine years and it was time for a change. But his young sons were now playing travel baseball.

How could he just leave his family? He wrestled with the question for a couple of days.

Finally, one day after one of his kids' baseball games, the entire family was grabbing chicken wings at a local restaurant. Tommy Mac was sitting at the table across from his father. The son revealed his dilemma. MacDonald's dad listened and then leaned across the restaurant table.

"It's Whitey Bulger, son, you gotta go to Boston. You gotta go."

2

After agreeing to join Gleason's team in Boston, Tommy Mac spent the next two months immersed in the Bulger case as his temporary duty assignment was getting finalized. While sitting on a beach along the Connecticut shoreline, MacDonald familiarized himself with the case file and read every news report and book about the near mythical mobster.

MacDonald could hardly believe there were still some people, especially in Southie, who glamorized and even idolized Whitey.

"This guy's committed nineteen murders," MacDonald told himself. "Why are there still people out there defending him and working against those of us who are trying to catch him?"

To find the answers, he had to go back to December 23, 1994—and everything that came after it.

It was just two days before Christmas, and the city of Boston was in full sparkle in anticipation of the holidays. A gigantic Norway spruce stood tall on Boston Common, its decorations illuminating the park, while in South Boston, less than two miles away, neighbors adorned their stoops, doors, and windows with strings of multicolored lights and festive yuletide wreaths.

Whitey Bulger, leader of the Winter Hill Gang, Boston's violent Irish mafia, was planning to take his longtime girlfriend Teresa Stanley downtown to Copley Plaza for some last-minute shopping at the fashionable clothing store Neiman Marcus. The city was a hive of holiday activity as folks were flowing in and out of shops, picking up their last-minute gifts. Forecasters were tracking a powerful winter nor'easter that was expected to slam New England and much of the east coast on Christmas Eve.

But Whitey was more concerned about another storm, one that was churning inside the US Attorney's office, where prosecutors were getting ready to pounce on Bulger and his longtime partner in crime, Stevie "The Rifleman" Flemmi.

Whitey had Stanley in the car when his beeper

buzzed with a message from Kevin Weeks, his thick-necked protégé and right-hand man. Bulger drove over to the Rotary Variety store and adjacent South Boston Liquor Mart, which served as the gang's headquarters. Weeks worked a day job there behind the cash register.

Weeks climbed in the backseat of Whitey's blue Ford LTD and the three of them drove north into downtown Boston. Weeks kept his mouth shut in the car. He was worried that the vehicle was bugged. Whitey had taught him well.

Born in Southie in 1956, Kevin Weeks was the fifth of six children of John and Margaret Weeks. John was a World War II vet and boxer who worked for the city of Boston's housing authority. The family lived in the same Old Colony housing project in Southie where Bulger and Connolly grew up. Weeks and his brothers learned to box from their dad and Kevin showed skills with his hands at a young age, accepting all challengers in the rough Southie projects.

He first met Whitey while working at a Commonwealth Avenue bar called Flicks. He later became a bouncer at Triple O's, where Whitey noticed his talent for handing out beat-downs and recruited him to be his personal bodyguard and driver. He worked for a time for Boston's public transit system, the MBTA, doing rail maintenance. He moonlighted collecting

from bookies with Whitey and soon ditched the day job. Weeks escalated to loan-sharking, strong-arming, and cracking heads for the Irish mob boss, and eventually, helping commit murders.

Now, shortly before Christmas 1994, Bulger and Weeks parked near Boylston Street, which was crowded with holiday shoppers passing by with gift bags bulging under their arms. There was a sense of merriment in the air even with a potentially killer blizzard on the horizon.

Whitey stuffed a wad of cash in Teresa's hand and sent her ahead. He then motioned Weeks to join him near the trunk of his car, which was illegally parked. The young, burly gangster told his boss that he'd just been visited by retired FBI agent John Connolly, Whitey's longtime man on the inside at the Bureau. Connolly had left the FBI in 1990 and now had a high-paying job as security chief for Boston Edison. Retired or not, Connolly still maintained relationships and shared secrets with many of his former colleagues.

During that earlier conversation in the walk-in beer cooler of the liquor mart, away from prying eyes and presumably prying ears, an anxious Connolly told Weeks that Whitey and Stevie Flemmi would soon be arrested on extortion and racketeering charges involving the shakedowns of two local bookies named Chico

Krantz and Jimmy Katz, and that the indictments were imminent.

In hushed tones, Weeks repeated the information to Whitey verbatim, just as Connolly had ordered him to. Bulger showed no emotion. He knew the feds would be coming sooner or later.

In fact, he had planned for it.

Whitey then whistled to Stanley and ordered her back in the car. The holiday shopping excursion was abruptly canceled. They would be going on a long trip instead.

Whitey then called Flemmi.

"The indictments are coming down," Bulger warned his partner. "There's a memo in Washington that the indictments are there and they'll be coming down in a week."

Bulger told Flemmi that he'd learned of the impending crackdown from another corrupt FBI agent named John Morris and not Connolly, perhaps in an attempt to shield his longtime friend from trouble. Whitey had lived his life stacking lies on top of lies, keeping the truth from even his closest friends and business partners.

Bulger dropped Weeks off back at the liquor store at 4:30 p.m. The sky was dark, cold, and windy and the waves were crashing to shore along nearby Carson

Beach. Whitey took one last look at the patch of land that he'd controlled for decades. He'd raped and murdered here in Southie. He'd created his own mythology as a gentleman gangster here, a Robin Hood–like figure who was respected and even revered, all the while preying on his neighbors, stealing their innocence and money, and destroying their dreams.

He turned the car around and headed south on Interstate 95 with Teresa Stanley by his side. There was a storm ahead, but Whitey Bulger was prepared.

The couple arrived in New York City sometime later and holed up in a hotel, where they spent Christmas Eve watching the snow pile up on the streets below. Stanley wished that she were spending Christmas back home with her children and grandkids, but this was the life she had chosen. She knew that her man might be forced one day to go on the run and completely detach himself from his past. Shortly before, Whitey had taken her on a trip to Europe, visiting romantic cities like Venice and Rome. They also flew to London and Dublin. Bulger had tried to convince Stanley that the sole purpose of the vacation was to strengthen their relationship after Teresa had caught him cheating with another woman. Once again, Whitey was stacking lies

upon lies. In truth, he was preparing for his life as a fugitive.

While the two were marveling at historic sites, Whitey was also scouting banks for a safe deposit box to hide some cash. In London, while treating Teresa to the elegant accommodations of Le Meridien Piccadilly in the city's West End, he stopped into a nearby Barclays bank, where he'd opened another safe deposit box two years prior under both his name and Stanley's. He accessed the deposit box and stuffed it with $50,000 in cash along with his Irish passport, should he be forced to go underground in the land of his ancestors. Bulger's Irish temper exploded on that trip while riding a packed train through London's Underground. He bumped into another rider and said sorry. The guy called Whitey a "bloody Yank" and Bulger unleashed on him, hitting him with several punches as fellow riders looked on in shock.

After their stay in New York City, Whitey and Teresa continued their journey down the east coast. Bulger listened to the car radio, trying to pick up intelligence about what the cops knew. He switched from news station to news station as they crossed state line after state line. As they drove from one motel to the next, Bulger was bleeding stress. They'd argue and he would lunge

at her with fists clenched. To escape another beating, a terrified Teresa would run and hide in the bathroom.

They arrived in New Orleans just in time for New Year's Eve. They stayed at Le Richelieu, a small yet stately hotel in the heart of the French Quarter. That night, another tourist from Boston named Amy Silberman was killed by a stray bullet fired while revelers stood on New Orleans' promenade watching holiday fireworks.

Local police and the FBI were called in to investigate the stray bullet death, which meant Bulger would have to be especially cautious. Making things even worse for him was that reporters from Boston also came to New Orleans to investigate the startling death of Silberman, a thirty-one-year-old executive assistant. Suddenly, the Crescent City was too risky for Whitey, so he and Teresa left and drove to Florida. Bulger owned a condominium in Clearwater, as he once planned to retire there like some aging insurance salesman. He didn't go near the place this time, though, because he'd purchased the condo a year before in his own name. Instead, he emptied another safe deposit box, grabbing cash and a fake ID.

He'd been on the run unofficially since December 23, but it was now almost two weeks later and there

was still no word on the indictments. Had Whitey received bad intelligence from his former FBI handlers?

Teresa Stanley was homesick and wanted to go back to Boston. She told Whitey that she wasn't cut out for life as a fugitive. He agreed and set course for the colder climate up north. What he didn't know was that the atmosphere had grown white hot back home.

On the night of January 5, 1995, DEA agents and detectives from the Massachusetts State Police swept in and arrested Stevie Flemmi outside Schooners, a restaurant owned by his son in Boston's Financial District. Flemmi was squiring around a new Chinese girlfriend and the pair was about to leave in her white Honda Accord when law enforcement closed in. State troopers driving an unmarked car thrust the vehicle forward, slammed on the brakes, and blocked the Honda, preventing any escape. Flemmi scrunched down in the passenger seat. He thought it was an assassination attempt by rival gangsters but made no effort to shield his girlfriend.

DEA agent Dan Doherty ripped open the car door and shoved his pistol against Flemmi's skull.

"Put your hands where I can see them, Stevie!"

The agent frisked Flemmi and found a hunting knife and mace in his pocket. They whisked the gang-

ster over to the FBI office close by at One Center Plaza, where he'd be held overnight until his first appearance in federal court the following day.

Whitey and Teresa were driving through Connecticut when they learned of Flemmi's arrest in a radio news flash. Authorities had made a run at Bulger too but had no luck. They showed up in force at Teresa's home on Silver Street in Southie and also at another home in nearby Quincy, where Whitey's longtime mistress lived.

Her name was Catherine Greig.

3

Whitey phoned Kevin Weeks and told him about the situation with Teresa. She had too many attachments, most importantly her family, which kept her tethered to her old life in Southie. There was no way that she could cut it as a fugitive because Bulger had no plans to return to Boston. Still, Whitey felt that he couldn't run alone. He was fifty-five years old now and had a bad heart. Similar to his criminal enterprises, Bulger didn't live in the moment, but instead had his head far into the future. He had enough money stashed away to live comfortably for the next thirty years. But he knew that his body would eventually turn on him as he got older and he would need someone to take care of him. Whitey was also acutely aware that it would be

easier to blend in and disappear with a woman by his side instead of going it alone.

"Nobody looks twice at an older couple," he told himself. "It's the single guy that stands out."

Bulger ordered Weeks to get in touch with Catherine Greig, have her pack a bag, and tell her to be ready to go at a moment's notice. Greig didn't need to know where they were going. She didn't care. What mattered to her was that he had finally chosen her over her romantic rival, Teresa Stanley. Life with Whitey on the run would force Catherine to remain in the shadows, but she no longer had to pretend that she didn't exist in Whitey's world.

Bulger was hers now and hers alone.

Teresa was kept in the dark about Whitey's plan to flee with Greig, although she probably suspected it. In the beginning, Teresa believed that she and Bulger would grow old together. Although she didn't have a wedding band on her finger, they had treated each other like husband and wife. Whitey and Teresa began living together in 1976 when Bulger purchased a two-story, eight-room colonial on Silver Street near South Boston High School and the monument at Dorchester Heights, a historic tourist spot where General George Washington's forces successfully repelled the British army without firing a shot in 1776.

HUNTING WHITEY • 33

Whitey moved Teresa, a divorcee, and her four children out of the Old Colony housing project and into his home. At first, Bulger lied and told Teresa that he worked in the construction trade, but she learned soon enough what he did and the nighttime hours he kept. Whitey, however, made sure that he was home just about every night for dinner with Teresa and the kids, Karen, Joan, Nancy, and Billy.

He was the father figure they'd never had. He took them on trips and even lectured them about the importance of homework. Teresa's children didn't call him "Dad"; instead they called him Charlie, a name he would become quite fond of in the years to come.

Whitey had strong paternal instincts and was still devastated by the death of his own child years before. Prior to dating Teresa, Bulger had spent twelve years with another woman named Lindsey Cyr, who gave birth to their son, Douglas Glen Cyr, in 1967. The child bore a striking resemblance to his father, with a head of blond hair that was almost white and piercing blue eyes. Photographs of the boy as a toddler give the appearance of a happy childhood, with the young lad grinning from ear to ear. Whitey was a doting dad in private. He kept the child's existence a secret from his friends and associates for fear they would target the boy

for kidnapping or worse if they knew he was the son of Whitey Bulger.

When Douglas was six years old, he was suddenly overcome by extreme nausea and a high fever as a result of a severe reaction to taking aspirin. The boy suffered from Reye's syndrome, a rare disease that causes swelling to the liver and brain.

His mother rushed him to Massachusetts General Hospital, where doctors fought desperately to save him. Bulger held vigil at the boy's bedside until he died.

"When he died, Jimmy [Whitey] was out of his mind," Lindsey Cyr later recalled. "Tears were streaming down Jimmy's face."

Bulger blamed himself for the boy's death and Lindsey proved to be a constant reminder of the tragic loss. Whitey ended the relationship, but continued to see her occasionally after he'd taken up with Teresa Stanley.

Although Whitey enjoyed playing Ozzie to Teresa's Harriet, the day-to-day demands of a domestic lifestyle ran counter to his true self. He was a criminal first and foremost and he prided himself on that. He got frustrated with her easily and beat her on occasion.

Once, in the early 1990s, Bulger assaulted Stanley in a summer cabana hangout in South Boston. The attack was sudden and vicious. Whitey curled his fist and punched her out like a thug he'd beat up on the street.

Whitey eventually moved out of the home but still supported Teresa and her kids and kept her believing that she was his one and only. She was dependable and Bulger liked that, but she was no longer exciting to him, so he looked elsewhere and soon found an attractive and seductive mistress who was much younger than Teresa.

Bulger was old enough to be Catherine Greig's father. Twenty-two years separated the pair, but they had much in common, especially a mutual love for animals.

Catherine, or Cathy as she was called, grew up in Southie in a three-family home on East Fourth Street. Her father worked for Raytheon as a machinist, while her mother worked part-time as an usher at the Colonial Theatre downtown. Greig had a younger sister, Jean, and brother, David, but she was closest to her sister Margaret—her identical twin.

"We ran with different crowds but we were close," Margaret (Greig) McCusker remembers. "[We] had a wonderful childhood despite the fact that our father was an alcoholic."

The twin sisters took ballet lessons together as youngsters and both later attended South Boston High School, where Catherine was voted prettiest girl in her senior class. Upon graduation, she enrolled in a two-

year program at the Forsyth School for Dental Hygienists and quickly married her first boyfriend when she was just twenty years old. His name was Bobby McGonagle, and he was a Boston firefighter whose brother Paulie happened to be the leader of a local gang.

Catherine was a homebody, while her new husband liked to go out and party. He had an affair and that ended the marriage in its infancy. As Catherine was going through the throes of her divorce, she met and fell in love with Whitey Bulger.

Some believe that it wasn't fate that brought them together. Instead, the thought is that Catherine had pursued Whitey at his local haunts like Triple O's lounge in a vendetta against her soon-to-be ex-husband.

Whitey had killed two of her husband's brothers in cold blood.

Margaret McCusker, who was no stranger to betrayal herself, blessed the relationship.

"He seemed very nice," McCusker recalls. "I didn't know exactly what he [Whitey] did but I knew who he was. Everybody knows who he is around here."

McCusker liked her sister's new boyfriend, whom she described as very charismatic and easy to get along with. Whitey had a reputation as a gangster, but that didn't raise any eyebrows in the Greig family.

This was Southie after all.

Whitey took care of Catherine much like he did Teresa and tried to keep both worlds from colliding. Stanley didn't know about Greig, but Catherine sure knew about her, and she seethed with jealousy.

In the autumn of 1994, things came to a head and one of Bulger's great lies was finally exposed.

Catherine called Teresa's home on Silver Street looking for Whitey. When Stanley told her that Bulger was out, Greig asked for a private talk.

"Something bad is going on," she said.

Catherine picked Teresa up at home in her green Ford Explorer and together they drove to Greig's house in nearby Quincy. The home, a four-bedroom split-level ranch, had been a gift from Whitey.

The two women in Bulger's life entered the living room and lit cigarettes. Catherine took a deep drag, exhaled, and then went into her story. She confessed to Teresa that she had been having an affair with Whitey for nearly two decades.

Her role as Bulger's mistress was no longer enough for Catherine. She wanted more. She wanted Whitey to make a choice between Teresa and her. This was quite a gamble for Greig, but she felt that it was time to place her chips on the table and go all in.

The revelation startled Teresa, who had been liv-

ing in a state of ignorant bliss with Bulger. Stanley had kept blinders on for decades. She didn't even know that Whitey had fathered a child who died.

Instead of getting hysterical, Teresa thanked Catherine for her honesty. There was a sense of calm in the room, but it lasted just a few short moments before a red-hot Whitey arrived and pounded on the front door. Catherine let him inside and Bulger pushed past her, followed by Kevin Weeks, and headed toward Stanley, ordering her to get up on her feet and go.

He grabbed Teresa forcefully by the arm while she informed him that his mistress had just revealed everything to her. Catherine interrupted and demanded that Whitey choose between them right then and there.

Bulger exploded, grabbing Greig by the neck, choking her. Catherine's eyes went wide with panic. Fearing that Whitey was going to kill her, Weeks pulled his boss away and tried to get him out the door.

Stanley left also and during a heated car ride back to Southie, Whitey withstood her barbs and pledged his love for her. He promised his girlfriend of thirty years that he'd never see Catherine's face again.

It was just another of Whitey Bulger's lies.

Months later, as Catherine prepared herself to join Whitey on the run, she and her sister Margaret walked

close together, huddled against the winter chill on the steep hill of Dorchester Heights.

"We're going on a trip," Catherine told her twin. "I'm leaving with Jimmy and I'll be in touch when I can."

Catherine didn't say where they were going, but Margaret wasn't overly concerned as Whitey, or "Jimmy," as he was called by friends, often took her sister on lavish getaways. Money was never an object for them. At her home in Quincy, Whitey had a globe in the middle of their dining room that opened up to store liquor. But Bulger used it to store cash—$20, $50, and $100 bills. When Catherine needed something, she'd just reach into the globe.

"Oh, my God, do you know how much you're spending?" Margaret would ask her twin. "Do you even know?"

Catherine would shrug and smile.

There was nothing lavish or romantic about Bulger's final moments with Teresa Stanley. They slipped back into Massachusetts and Whitey dropped her off in front of a Chili's restaurant in Hingham, a suburb just a few miles south of Boston. One of Stanley's daughters lived nearby and had offered to fetch her mother.

Whitey said, "See ya." Teresa replied the same.

He turned the car around and never looked back. Bulger was out of her life for good, but Teresa Stanley would have the last laugh one day soon.

Catherine waited alone near the bottom steps of the Dorchester Heights Monument. Margaret had helped her pack and had even handed over her driver's license to her twin in case the couple got pulled over and questioned by police. Margaret also promised to look after Catherine's two beloved dogs, French poodles named Nikki and Gigi.

Suddenly a pair of headlights flashed in Catherine's eyes as a black Pontiac Bonneville pulled slowly to the curb. She opened the passenger door and got in. She was dressed smartly and her platinum-blond hair was freshly done. The interior of the vehicle was soon filled with the aroma of Catherine's perfume. She'd chosen Whitey's favorite for the occasion. Kevin Weeks was behind the steering wheel, his eyes focused on the rearview mirror. He'd circled the location for more than an hour to make sure he wasn't being followed. It was part of the tradecraft for both spies and sinners like him. He lived in a world where one slip-up could get you captured or killed.

Weeks drove in a winding path through Southie, taking random turns down lonely streets while constantly searching for a tail. Once convinced they weren't under

the watch of the FBI or state police, Weeks drove Greig to a quiet spot in Dorchester called Malibu Beach. The place was popular with sunbathers in the summertime but was silent on a bitter winter night like this one.

Weeks pulled the car over and he and Catherine stepped out. At that moment, Whitey emerged from the darkness. He was dressed all in black and wearing a matching cowboy hat.

Catherine could no longer hide her excitement. She draped her arms around Whitey's neck and pulled him close for a long embrace. It reminded Weeks of a scene between Bogart and Bergman from *Casablanca*.

This was the moment she'd been dreaming of for years. They were finally together.

Whitey led her to his Mercury Grand Marquis and helped her inside. Weeks got into the backseat and they drove around Southie for about an hour. Bulger soaked in the atmosphere, taking mental pictures of the street corners and neighborhood taverns where he had consolidated his power. He also voiced his concern about Stevie Flemmi. Whitey didn't think he could last long behind bars and might commit suicide as a way out.

Bulger then drove his protégé back to his car and said good-bye. They shook hands and Weeks slipped him a new phone number where he could be reached.

Seconds later, Whitey and Catherine were gone.

4

S tevie Flemmi was now behind bars at the Plymouth House of Correction awaiting trial, but Kevin Weeks was still a free man. He would visit Flemmi often. At first, Flemmi had laughed off the charges against him, but now he doubted whether he'd ever see the outside of a prison again. With a glass partition between them and a phone to their ears, Weeks listened as Flemmi complained about the jailhouse conditions and especially the food. When the topic of conversation got around to Whitey, Flemmi just shrugged.

"It's better for my case that the other guy is out there," he told Weeks. "Tell him to stay free."

In May 1995, Bulger called Weeks and said, "Meet me at the Lions."

Kevin understood what this meant, so he hopped on an Amtrak train to New York City. He met his boss in front of the main branch of the New York City Public Library, where the statues of two marble lions named Lady Astor and Lord Lenox sat proudly guarding the entryway.

Bulger was with Catherine, who was her typical cheery self. Whitey wore sunglasses and a baseball cap. Surveillance photos of Whitey taken sometime before showed him in similar dress. These photos were now plastered inside every FBI office and police station in America. The aging crime boss had done nothing to alter his appearance while on the run.

Catherine stepped out of earshot so Whitey and Weeks could talk privately.

Surprisingly, Bulger was hopeful about the future. He'd heard there was bad blood between the FBI and Massachusetts State Police, and that the case against him was crumbling because one key witness was now dead of natural causes and another was ill and not expected to make it to trial.

Whitey and Catherine were now traveling under the names Thomas F. Baxter and Helen Marshall. They masqueraded as a married couple, which fulfilled Greig's long-held fantasy.

Bulger had been using the alias for years. He'd ob-

tained a Massachusetts driver's license with Baxter's name, Social Security number, and birth date and renewed it every four years as required by the state. The real Tom Baxter died in 1979. In 1990, Whitey got another license from the state of New York. Like the last one, it featured Baxter's information alongside Bulger's photograph. The address he gave on this one was from Selden, Long Island, where Kevin Weeks's cousin lived.

Other members of the gang had not planned their escape as meticulously as Whitey had and were not so lucky. Following the capture of Stevie Flemmi, more dominoes began to fall. In January 1995, Massachusetts State Police detective Steve Johnson learned that Bulger's attack dog John Martorano might be hiding out in Florida. Martorano was a prized catch, as he'd been the poisoned tip to Whitey's spear. Martorano was heavyset with curly black hair and looked like the late comedic actor John Belushi. But he was no funnyman. John Martorano was suspected to have committed several murders, including the brazen daytime slaying of a Tulsa, Oklahoma, businessman on Bulger's orders.

At the time, Johnson had been hunting a bookie turned fugitive who just happened to be close friends with Martorano. After tracing the bookie's phone, the

detective noticed a number that he suspected was Martorano's in Boca Raton, Florida. Johnson and a partner flew to Boca Raton and followed Martorano for three days, waiting for the perfect opportunity to strike. He'd been living with his girlfriend under the name Vincent Rancourt.

The detective knew that his prey was a stone-cold killer and that if he didn't handle the situation carefully, it was likely that someone would get killed, possibly even an innocent bystander.

He needed to take Martorano down when he was most vulnerable. Johnson seized the opportunity one early evening when the hit man visited a local ice cream shop with his nine-year-old son and the boy's friend.

Johnson approached Martorano and called him by his real name.

"You've got the wrong man," the mob killer protested quietly.

The detective ordered Martorano to roll up his shirtsleeves. The gangster did so, revealing two tattoos on each forearm. On the right was a drawing of a blue jay with the name *Nancy* written underneath. On the left was the inking of a cross accompanied by the initials *IHS* (*in hoc signo*), Latin for "In this sign thou shalt conquer." To Johnson, the tattoos represented the marks of the beast, and right there he knew he had

his man. The Winter Hill Gang's most notorious killer surrendered with less than a whimper.

In August 1995, investigators lured another infamous Boston gangster into their net. Francis "Cadillac Frank" Salemme was the reigning godfather of Boston's *La Cosa Nostra*. He wasn't part of the Winter Hill Gang, but he was especially close to Stevie Flemmi and had been named in the same sweeping thirty-five-count racketeering and extortion indictment handed down earlier that year. Like Martorano, Salemme had fled New England for the warmer climate of Florida.

He was living in West Palm Beach with his longtime girlfriend Donna Wolf, who'd recently traveled back to Massachusetts to attend the funeral for Salemme's son and namesake who had died of lymphoma. Investigators trailed Wolf back to the tiny $600-per-month condo she rented at Sandalwood Lake Village, which was a far cry from the nearby Mar-a-Lago club owned by Donald J. Trump.

Salemme had been featured on the Fox television program *America's Most Wanted*, which resulted in twenty-seven tips, including two from Florida.

The Boston Mafia boss had spent most of his time on the run sunbathing in his backyard, working out, and feeding ducks. His lack of elusiveness was surprising given that Salemme had gone on the run once before

in the late 1960s after blowing up the car owned by mob rat Joe "The Animal" Barboza. Salemme remained free for three years until he was arrested in New York City by a young FBI agent named John Connolly, Whitey's man on the inside of the Bureau. What Salemme didn't know until decades later was that Connolly had been tipped off to Salemme's whereabouts by the mobster's close friend Stevie Flemmi.

Like Martorano, Salemme was caught off guard by investigators. FBI agents and local police approached the condo in West Palm Beach just before midnight on Friday, August 13, 1995, and arrested Cadillac Frank while he was relaxing in his pajamas.

After leaving Kevin Weeks in New York City, Whitey and Catherine drove out to Long Island and stayed for eight days at a Best Western hotel in the town of Holtsville, just ten minutes from Selden. He booked room 335 under the alias Thomas Baxter and paid cash for the accommodations, $535.29 in total.

The purpose of Whitey's visit was most likely to dip into a steel safe held at the home of Kevin Weeks's relatives, where Bulger had stuffed wads of cash over time.

From there, Whitey drove west with Catherine by his side. A history buff, Bulger visited the site of Custer's last stand at the Battle of Little Big Horn and

also the Little Big Horn casino at the crossroads of Highways 212 and 90 on the Crow Native American reservation in Montana.

Bulger was there to gamble and wash his money, replacing old bills with new ones. The casino was drab and dysfunctional, and according to Whitey, not up to par with the Indian casinos back home in New England. The casino floor was virtually empty, which should have been a welcome sight for a fugitive on the run, but not for Bulger.

Instead of staying quiet and in the shadows, he demanded to speak to a manager.

"You can make some real money here if you add some things and change some other things around," Bulger told the casino boss. "This could be a really nice thing for you guys if you put some money in it."

The manager didn't want to take any advice and paid little attention to the white-haired stranger. This indifference frustrated the South Boston crime boss to no end.

Why would Bulger jeopardize his cover to help strangers at an Indian casino? In truth, Whitey had a genuine love for Native American culture dating back to the nearly three years he spent serving time for bank robbery at the world's most infamous prison—Alcatraz—from 1959 to 1962.

As prisoner number 1428 AZ, Whitey befriended and remained very close to a Native American inmate named Clarence "Joe" Carnes, aka "The Choctaw Kid."

Carnes was only eighteen years old when he arrived on the Rock in 1945, making him the youngest man ever incarcerated there. He was an Oklahoma native who was first sent to prison for killing a garage attendant during a holdup. In 1946, he was involved in what became known as "the Battle of Alcatraz" when he and five other inmates attempted a daring escape. Two prisoners were killed, along with two prison officers. Carnes didn't participate in the murders of the officers, so he wasn't sentenced to death. He remained on the Rock until it closed in 1963 and was paroled in 1973. He was sent back to prison for parole violations and corresponded regularly with Whitey from behind bars.

In a letter written by Bulger and obtained exclusively for this book, Whitey described one of their conversations.

He told me on the phone in 1988 how he wanted to be free . . . after a life time since 17 yrs of age behind bars so he took off with [some] money and had a period of wine women + song, thought it would never end but it did and back to prison—he

was due to be released Oct 15 1988. When I heard
where he was . . . [I] told him "Stay Strong" . . .
I'll be out in time to pick you up on Oct 15th and
you will be all set in life—told him to pick out car
he'd like will get it upon release Etc.

Jim Bulger

Carnes never made it out of prison. He died while incarcerated in Springfield, Missouri, in October 1988. "The Choctaw Kid" was buried unceremoniously nearby with no family members present to say goodbye. Whitey learned of this final, ultimate insult to his friend sometime later and paid $10,000 to have Carnes's body exhumed and reburied on sacred Choctaw soil in Carnes's hometown of Daisy, Oklahoma.

Despite not being able to help his friend, Bulger would look back fondly on his time locked up at Alcatraz, referring to the notorious island jail as his alma mater—a Harvard University for criminals.

While traveling with Catherine across the American West, Bulger wore a reminder of his past life and his friend "The Choctaw Kid" around his trim waist—a brass belt buckle decorated with an Alcatraz insignia. Whitey put 65,000 miles on his Mercury Grand Marquis during his first months on the run.

Eventually he made his way back to the southern

coast of the United States. In September 1995, a cop in Long Beach, Mississippi, spotted a green car with New York plates that was stopped at a red light. The driver looked in his rearview mirror and saw the cop. The officer ran the plate and it too came back to Thomas Baxter of Selden, New York. But Baxter's record was clean, so the officer let him go.

Bulger stayed clear of Clearwater, Florida, on this trip south and instead opted for a small barrier island off the coast of Louisiana called Grand Isle. But there was nothing grand about the island except for its name.

Although more than six thousand vacationers invaded the tiny island during the summertime, the place was virtually dead in early fall. Just over one thousand people lived there year round, most working in the shrimp business or on oil rigs in the Gulf of Mexico.

Bulger pulled his Grand Marquis off Louisiana Highway 1 and traveled across a drawbridge toward the seaside community known as the "Cajun Bahamas." He and Catherine had already cased out the town once before and found it to be the perfect hiding spot. They rented a seasonal camp that was built on stilts for a cheap price. No one there looked twice at the aging couple, and Whitey strongly considered staying in Grand Isle for good.

5

As Tommy Mac read through the files trying to understand facts of the Bulger case, the documentation wasn't just about Bulger's known travels since fleeing from Boston. By 2008, there had been a lot of ink spilled about the work of various agents. The paperwork told the stories of false leads and near misses the FBI had with the fugitive since he'd gone missing, while also detailing the hard work of a handful of agents who, contrary to popular belief, had labored tirelessly during the early years of Bulger's fugitive case to bring him to justice.

By the time Whitey went on the run, Boston FBI agent John Gamel had been on the Bulger beat for the first four years, slowly building a case against the mobster for extortion, gambling, and most importantly,

murder. In an office later smeared by corruption involving Bulger, Gamel was a straight arrow who'd been diligently trying to apprehend the mobster. Indeed, even before Gamel knew about John Connolly's role in Bulger's crimes, there was something about Connolly that didn't sit right with him.

"People would talk about him in a way that he was supposed to be famous, a larger-than-life character," Gamel says. "He had an ego the size of Alaska and he was impressed with himself and wanted to impress us. I really felt that I never wanted anything to do with him."

Gamel was in this to apprehend his suspect, so once Bulger disappeared, he was determined to pull him out of hiding and lock him up.

"I'm just a simple guy from Springfield, Massachusetts," he said years later.

Gamel's journey to the FBI was not a straight line and was anything but simple. Instead, he took many divergent paths before ultimately being tasked with bringing down Boston's most notorious gangster. He was the son of a high school principal who died when Gamel was just thirteen years old. Fearing that young John would lose focus in the wake of his father's death, his mother sent him off to prep school at nearby Northfield Mount Hermon, where Gamel eventually boosted

his grades and was accepted into Colgate University to study English. After college, he joined the US Navy in hopes of flying fighter missions in faraway Vietnam. With great vision and decision-making skills, Gamel aced his aptitude tests. But nothing went smoothly once he got into the cockpit. John and his instructors soon realized that he was a lousy pilot. Gamel was discharged early from the Navy and then enrolled at Boston University, where he earned a master's degree in journalism. He worked in local television and radio for several years, until his life changed forever in 1975 while covering the shocking murder of a rookie cop in Shrewsbury, Massachusetts.

Officer James Lonchiadis was shot through the heart after pleading for his life during a bungled car theft. His killer later used the officer's gun in a robbery to steal a getaway car. The crime shocked the relatively quiet town of Shrewsbury and it was a major story for Gamel to cover as a young journalist. The case took twenty months to crack and during that time, Gamel spent hours speaking with the FBI agents assigned to the case. Gamel was fascinated by their work and one of the agents told him, "Ya know, this FBI job is pretty good and you might want to think about it."

Gamel researched the idea and liked what he saw. He then told his wife, Beth, that he wanted to join the

Bureau and she went along with this new adventure. But there was one major problem. Gamel was thirty-four years old at the time and almost considered too old to apply. Most new agents were in their early twenties, and Gamel was a virtual dinosaur despite being one of the top-ranked recruits in the country.

He began new agents training at Quantico, Virginia, with more than thirty fellow recruits and spent eight hundred hours learning self-defense, defensive driving, how to manage and run criminal investigations, interview and interrogation tactics, and, of equal importance, how to shoot. A reporter's notepad and a reliable pen were once the tools of Gamel's trade, but now the journalist-turned-FBI recruit was spending his days firing off more than five thousand rounds of ammunition as he learned how to handle pistols, shotguns, and submachine guns.

After completing his training, Gamel was assigned to the Boston field office, where he worked on the fugitive squad and investigated the corruption of public officials including the case against Massachusetts congressman Nick Mavroules, who later spent more than a year in prison for bribery, extortion, and racketeering. He learned early in his FBI career that there was often a blurred line between politicians and gangsters in Massachusetts.

Gamel was then recruited to join the FBI's SWAT team and also worked on the counterterrorism squad, where he investigated a plot by the Red Army Faction to blow up a branch of Sun Myung Moon's Unification Church in Gloucester, Massachusetts. The would-be bomber, a Japanese terrorist named Yu Kikumura, had visited the rugged New England fishing town just before he was arrested following a police chase in New Jersey. A search of the vehicle uncovered canisters loaded with gunpowder and attached to wires, flashbulbs, and nine-volt batteries.

Gamel was also the Boston office's top tracker of skinheads and neo-Nazis.

"As a group, they were somewhat dangerous because they could feed off each other," Gamel recalls. "But individually, they were scared shitless and the first ones to run away if you attempted to confront them."

But the Whitey Bulger investigation was different. For four years, Gamel had dealt with a criminal who was bold and dangerous.

John Gamel had faced gangsters associated with Bulger as a member of the FBI SWAT team. During an ambush of armored car robbers outside a bank in Abington, Massachusetts, in 1991, Gamel had encountered an Irishman named Pat Nee, a former rival-turned-associate of Bulger and a man suspected

of helping Bulger pull off one of his most shockingly brazen crimes, the murders of Brian Halloran and his friend Michael Donahue in May 1982.

Brian Halloran was a thug who made his living collecting unpaid mob debts through threats or worse. He hated Bulger and the feeling was mutual. Halloran had information that could put Whitey away, so he took it to the FBI. John Connolly, Bulger's man on the inside, heard the news and told Whitey that Halloran had turned snitch.

Connolly had signed Brian Halloran's death warrant.

Bulger got a tip that Halloran was drinking at the Pier restaurant, a bar on the edge of Southie popular with fishermen and dockworkers. Whitey rendezvoused with Kevin Weeks, handed him a walkie-talkie, and ordered him to keep an eye on the tavern from a lookout point across the street. The front door to the bar had a large window, and that offered Weeks a near perfect view inside.

"When Balloonhead gets up, lemme know," Bulger told his protégé. Halloran was known as Balloonhead on the streets because he had a massive skull, which made him look like he was constantly suffering from some kind of allergic reaction.

The gangster had asked his buddy Michael Donahue

for a ride home to Dorchester. Donahue was about to open a bakery with his wife and had no ties to Whitey Bulger or organized crime, for that matter. His only crime, it seemed, was being friends with Brian Halloran.

Michael Donahue had no idea that Halloran was using him as a human shield, as one of the unwritten rules of the mob jungle was that noncombatants were strictly off-limits. Halloran knew that he was being targeted by Bulger and a host of other underworld figures that he'd double-crossed over the years.

Donahue left the bar first to pull around his car, a blue Datsun that he'd borrowed from his father for the day. Halloran finished his drink, paid the tab, and followed.

"The balloon is rising," Weeks told Bulger over the two-way radio.

As Halloran pushed open the front door and stepped outside, Weeks pressed the talk button once again.

"The balloon is in the air."

Whitey swung into action and drove his Chevy Malibu alongside Donahue's car.

"Hey Brian!" he yelled as he peered out the driver's-side window. Halloran and Donahue looked in Bulger's direction and saw the carbine rifle in his hand. They had zero time to react as Whitey opened fire while an-

other man, later identified in court by Stevie Flemmi as Pat Nee wearing a mask, began shooting from the backseat of Bulger's Malibu. Donahue was cut down instantly by a hail of bullets as the Datsun rolled slowly across the street. Halloran managed to stumble out of the car before falling to the pavement. Whitey pulled a quick U-turn and lowered the carbine toward Halloran's position. More bullets flew, each one striking Whitey's target with such force that Halloran's blood-soaked body bounced off the ground.

Brian Halloran was shot twenty-two times in all.

After making his getaway, Whitey sent a voice message to his partner Stevie Flemmi's pager: "The balloon has burst."

The story of the Halloran-Donahue murders was fresh in Gamel's mind when he left the FBI office at One Center Plaza one winter evening in the early 1990s and decided to check on Bulger's whereabouts in Southie. This was in the years before Bulger became a fugitive when the FBI was actively investigating him. Driving a rental car, a gray Ford Crown Victoria, Gamel made his way to Rotary Variety, the convenience store where Whitey and his gang ran much of their business, but the place was quiet except for a few folks buying their weekly lottery tickets. He then took a turn past Teresa

Stanley's home on Silver Street, but again there was no sign of the Irish crime boss.

"He must be at Catherine's place," Gamel surmised.

The agent weaved his way through South Boston and onto the expressway toward Quincy.

It was just past 8 p.m. when Gamel spotted Bulger driving with Greig along Quincy Shore Drive heading toward Squantum, another small barrier island, where Catherine lived at the time.

Gamel followed two to three car lengths behind, using the surveillance skills he'd learned and mastered during his years with the Bureau. Whitey had no clue that he was being followed.

As Bulger turned right toward Catherine's split-level ranch house on Hillcrest Drive, Gamel continued on over a large hill, passing several small, well-kept homes in the quiet bedroom community.

When the agent came back down the hill, he saw the headlights of Whitey's car approaching in the distance. Gamel's rental car was similar to a vehicle driven by one of Bulger's gang members, so Whitey waved as the two cars passed each other.

When Bulger got a closer look at Gamel, he made a quick U-turn in the middle of the street and began following the FBI man.

"Okay, this may not end well," Gamel told himself as Whitey continued his pursuit. "Let's see how far he'll follow me. He's crazy but he's not stupid."

But Gamel came dangerously close to losing that bet with himself. When the two men approached a stoplight, the agent was stunned to see Bulger getting out of his car. Gamel placed his hand on his .40-caliber Glock and waited.

He's well known for coming up with a knife, so let's see what he does, Gamel thought as he watched Whitey approach slowly.

Suddenly, the dead quiet was broken by the sound of laughter and Bulger looked to his right, where he saw five uniformed policemen standing outside a Dunkin' Donuts sharing stories and sipping their nightly coffees.

Bulger got back in his car, followed Gamel for a couple more miles, and soon disappeared into the night.

With run-ins like this, Gamel knew Bulger and the case as well as anyone, so once his criminal investigation of Bulger turned into a fugitive case, the agent devoted himself to shaking the trees. He believed it would only be a matter of time before Whitey and Catherine were captured and brought home to face charges.

One sensitive pressure point for the gangster had always been his family—most importantly his brother

Billy Bulger, the Senate president of Massachusetts and the most powerful politician in the state.

One day early on in the investigation, Gamel walked from his office up the hill to the golden-domed Massachusetts Statehouse and asked to talk to the lawmaker face-to-face.

"I'd like to speak with the Senate president," Gamel told Bulger's secretary as he handed her his card. "I need to see him now or make an appointment."

Billy Bulger's gatekeeper sized up the FBI agent and offered a fake smile.

"The Senate president is very busy," the secretary told him.

"Please ask him to give me a call so that we can discuss his brother's status," Gamel said before leaving.

Less than two hours later, as Gamel was working in his office cubicle, Bulger's secretary called his office line.

"Please hold for the Senate president," she advised.

Gamel rolled his eyes as he waited for the emperor-like Billy Bulger to come on the line. The agent spoke to Billy, explaining the purpose of his recent visit, and asked the lawmaker for a formal interview.

"I'm not interested at all in helping you," Billy Bulger said deliberately before slamming the phone in Gamel's ear.

Gamel's attempt would be repeated throughout the years of Whitey's run from the law, but Billy Bulger would remain elusive, beyond the FBI's grasp and protected by a powerful attorney along with his own reputation as one of the most influential men in the history of Massachusetts politics. While there were always suspicions about what Billy and other members of the Bulger family knew about their brother's whereabouts, he was never forced to address them directly. But in 2019, Billy Bulger sat down with the authors of this book to share for the first time his deep thoughts about his killer brother.

"He at different times of his life became wayward," Billy Bulger said, looking back. "But that's part of the mystery of why people do what they do, our own motivations and our own purposes. He was his own person and did his own thinking and he insisted on charting his own course."

That course was set early on in Whitey's life. His father, James Joseph Bulger, was born in Newfoundland and came to Boston in 1894 when he was eleven years old. Small in stature but powerful nonetheless, the elder Bulger rode freight trains looking for work as a teenager at the turn of the twentieth century and was almost killed when he attempted to jump a train but

fell beneath its wheels. His left arm was nearly severed in the accident and couldn't be saved, so doctors were forced to amputate the badly injured limb.

James Bulger was fitted with a crude wooden hand that he kept hidden in his pocket for the rest of his life. He had two wives. The first was a woman named Ruth Pearce, whom he was married to briefly beginning in 1916. A decade later, he married a Charlestown girl twenty-two years his junior named Jane "Jean" McCarthy—Whitey's mother.

"They were both faithful to their task—their family," Billy Bulger says. "My father had a job as a night watchman over at the docks because no one else wanted the job. He was a good provider and even worked holidays when no one else would do it."

Whitey, the couple's second child, was given the name James Joseph after his father. He was welcomed into the Bulger family on September 3, 1929, just as the world was plunging into the Great Depression.

The growing family moved from Everett, Massachusetts, just north of Boston, to the neighborhood of Dorchester on the city's southern shoulder. Younger brother Billy came along five years later, just before the Bulgers made their final move to a housing project in Southie with its neighborhood parish of St. Monica's, the patron saint of difficult children.

"He [Whitey] kept comic books under his mattress, not Batman & Robin and Superman and such," Billy Bulger recalls. "He had true crime comic books and I would always be seeking them out to read them. Maybe he thought that that was the way to go."

Billy spoke softly in his thick Boston accent, tinged with a hint of Irish brogue, while reminiscing about his brother. A true academic with a vast and impressive vocabulary, he's rarely spoken about Whitey and had not made any public comments about his brother for more than a decade when he broke his silence with the authors. He sat at the wooden kitchen table in the same modest home where he has lived for decades, right in the heart of the very neighborhood where his brother's actions made countless mothers, wives, and girlfriends cry. The townhouse-style home is located directly across the courtyard from the longtime home of Mary Flemmi—Stephen Flemmi's mother—where cops once found a cache of weapons Whitey and his gang used to commit all sorts of atrocities. During the conversation, Billy was guarded, but he opened up about their childhood. With his wife, Mary, sitting by his side, he recalled how as a child, Whitey was particularly fascinated by a pair of killers from Texas—Clyde Barrow and his lover, Bonnie Parker. This attraction eerily foreshadowed his future on the run with Catherine

Greig. In a letter written to a friend decades later in 2014, Bulger presented a photograph of the murderous bandits with this description.

> *2 of my favorite out laws*
> *"BONNIE + CLYDE"*
> *Died together, shot down*
> *from ambush by Frank*
> *Hamer Texas Ranger*
> *Tombstone for Clyde*
> *Barrow Read;*
> *"Gone But Not Forgotten"*
> *James Bulger 1428 AKA "Whitey"*

But South Boston wasn't a crime-ridden place back then and it isn't now. Southie residents went to work, attended Catholic church, and had pride in their neighborhood. Trouble existed, but one had to find it and Whitey found plenty of it, which caused great pain to his father, James Joseph.

The elder Bulger and his wife, Jean, had six children—three boys and three girls. When young Whitey got out of line, his father beat him severely. He once ran away with the Ringling Bros. and Barnum & Bailey Circus just to escape his father's wrath.

While the other Bulger children maintained good

grades in school and kept away from trouble, Whitey struggled in the classroom and felt inferior—weak. On the streets, he was strong. He lifted weights and marched through the neighborhood with a distinctive swagger that he would maintain his whole life.

At sixteen, Whitey began his life of crime when he stole merchandise off delivery trucks and fenced them for a good price. It was called "tailgating," and it had a long and rich history in Southie dating back before World War I. That's when the Gustin Gang, which took its name from a street just a block long in the heart of their own territory in South Boston, targeted delivery trucks at city intersections. By handing down a serious beating to the driver, or simply by the mere threat of one, the gang terrorized Southie and then spread fear to other city neighborhoods. Known originally to police as the Tailboard Thieves, the Gustin Gang grew and diversified during Prohibition to the point that they controlled much of the illegal booze coming into New England. What shipments they didn't control became theirs through other means. Armed with fake badges of the kind used by government agents, the Gustin Gang confiscated cases of liquor from rival bootleggers and then sold them through their distribution network in Southie.

The Gustin Gang also owned and operated more

rum-running boats than most of their rivals combined. Their vessels would steam out of Boston Harbor several times a week to rendezvous with liquor ships stationed three miles offshore in international waters. The bootleggers would stock up along "Rum Row" and head back to Boston, where eager patrons were happy to plunk down twenty-five cents for a watered-down beer that would have cost only a nickel before Prohibition.

Those early gangsters were legends to young Whitey, pulled right out of the true crime comics he kept stuffed under his bed. But what the comics failed to show was the price often paid for committing even the most minor crime. Once Whitey's name became known to police, they pulled him in at every opportunity and roughed him up for information.

"He talked often about police beatings and abusive police officers," Billy Bulger remembers. "I thought it was a bit of an exaggeration at first."

Whitey would later reveal that a cop had once stuffed a pistol in his mouth while another beat him so bad that he thought his arm was broken. In detailing Whitey's early life, Billy Bulger chooses his words carefully, and speaks pointedly and deliberately, as if to exonerate himself from responsibility while explaining his brother's life of crime.

"I'm not sure how one persuades or dissuades some-

one who's made up his own mind," he says. "At times he became impatient with me as I urged him into a different behavior . . . I wished it all could have been different."

When Whitey was eighteen years old, he was charged with assault with intent to rape. The victim was a young woman who claimed that she'd been mauled in a car by Bulger and two friends. Bulger wound up pleading guilty to a reduced charge—assault and battery—and paid a $50 fine. His family urged him to leave Southie, so he enlisted in the US Air Force.

While in the service, he earned his high school diploma and learned how to fix airplanes. He was arrested in Oklahoma City for going AWOL in 1950. He received an honorable discharge two years later despite more scrapes with the law, which included a charge of rape while stationed at a base in Montana.

Once back home in Southie, Whitey slipped right back into his previous life of crime, stealing, and eventually graduating to robbing banks.

His first big score came in 1955 when he and a small group of bandits robbed a bank in Pawtucket, Rhode Island. The heist took only four minutes and the robbers walked away with more than $42,000.

Two more bank robberies followed, including one in Hammond, Indiana. Waving a pistol at the terrified

tellers, Bulger said, "We're not here to hurt anyone, but we have to make a living. Dillinger did."

Later, one of his bank-robbing buddies snitched to police and a warrant was issued for Whitey's arrest. This prompted Bulger to go on the lam for the first time, driving to Chicago, Utah, Reno, and San Francisco. He returned to Boston once he felt the heat had cleared but walked around Southie in disguise, wearing horn-rimmed glasses and dyeing his fair hair jet black.

A tip came into the Boston FBI office that a wanted bank robber was in town, so a young, flamboyant federal agent named Paul Rico followed the lead to a bar in Revere, just north of Boston, and arrested Bulger without incident. Neither man knew it at the time, but their meeting proved to be prophetic, as Rico and Bulger would join forces decades later to commit murder and mayhem on a grand scale.

Whitey was sentenced to twenty years in prison and was taken off the streets just before a mob war exploded in Boston between two Irish gangs that would leave fifty-six men dead in a span of just three years. There's little doubt that Bulger would have gotten caught up in the neighborhood combat, but instead, he sat in a prison cell where he read Machiavelli and waited patiently for the time that he could return to Boston and take over the city.

During his interview with the authors, Billy Bulger painted a romantic picture of Whitey's early years while also trying to distance himself from his brother's emerging criminal behavior. But Billy was no innocent bystander. During his career in Massachusetts politics, he benefited from his brother's reputation, which struck fear into his opponents. In the 1970s, Billy battled Boston mayor Kevin White over forced busing in Southie, which Billy vigorously opposed. The mayor strongly believed that he'd be set up for assassination by Whitey.

"I was never more scared in my life," Kevin White later admitted in an interview. "Whitey would be crazy enough to do it. And if they shoot me, they win all the marbles."

Throughout his storied political career, Billy Bulger was simultaneously haunted and elevated by his brother's reign of terror. He was guilty by association in the court of public opinion and always wore the scarlet letter of corruption due to Whitey's infamy. Every action he took on Beacon Hill throughout his career was met by hallway whispers about him being Teflon because of his crime lord brother. Tucking line items into budgets to cut state police funding, horse-trading government jobs, or working back channels to strong-arm political rivals frequently raised eyebrows and fueled specu-

lation that he was in cahoots with Whitey, despite no hard evidence. Whitey was always an albatross around Billy's neck that he could never lift, and he certainly did nothing to remove it during the sit-down with the authors. In fact, he shrugged his shoulders and sighed when asked about his brother's life on the lam and what he knew about it. He was straightforward in his answers about why his brother chose the path he did, but was evasive about what he knew about his brother's fugitive escapades, just as he was throughout his entire career.

6

Much like Billy Bulger, Whitey's other siblings weren't talking about their fugitive brother's whereabouts in the months after he fled Boston. But just because they weren't talking didn't mean that they were immune from scrutiny.

Gamel figured that if he couldn't find Bulger, he could at least inflict pain on him from afar. Gamel huddled with then–US Attorney Donald K. Stern on an idea to seize Whitey's portion of a $14.3 million lottery jackpot he'd claimed back in 1991.

The lottery win had been another one of Bulger's brilliant schemes to launder his drug, extortion, and loan-sharking money. Back in the summer of 1991, a winning Mass Millions lottery ticket had been purchased at the South Boston Liquor Mart by Michael

Linskey, who was the brother of a Bulger underling named Patrick Linskey. The FBI had learned that once Whitey heard about the jackpot, he ordered the real winner to sign the ticket over, with Whitey and two associates paying $2.3 million cash for 50 percent of the winnings. Bulger himself paid Michael Linskey $700,000. Although Linskey lost money in the deal, he really had no choice. It came down to selling the ticket or risking his life. Kevin Weeks, whose name also appeared on the winning ticket, later claimed that Linskey had purchased a large batch of tickets to hand out as Christmas gifts and promised to split any winnings with Bulger and Weeks. But Weeks's story makes little sense; the so-called Christmas gifts were purchased during the dog days of summer.

The gang took the winning ticket over to the South Boston Savings Bank, where they received a lottery check split four ways among the Linskey brothers, Bulger, and Weeks. The scam set up a twenty-year legitimate income stream for Whitey, where he earned $119,000 each year.

When news first broke about Whitey's lottery winnings in 1991, many in South Boston rose to his defense.

"God bless him, his number came up," said one local resident.

"He had the same chance to lose, right?" said an-

other. "I think he ought to pay his taxes and keep the winnings."

Lottery officials took some heat, but they too called Whitey's lotto win legitimate.

"The only person that probably would have caused more trouble is if my mother had won," Massachusetts treasurer Joe Malone said at the time.

There was still $1.6 million left for Bulger to claim in 1995, so John Gamel won approval from the US attorney to serve the Massachusetts State Lottery with a federal seizure warrant to confiscate the remainder of his winnings. The forfeiture suit would require Whitey Bulger to appear in court in thirty days or give up any rights to his lottery prize, which was scheduled to be paid out until 2010.

There was a lot of money on the table, and Gamel relished the fact that he'd just scored one for the good guys and might possibly smoke Whitey out from hiding. The runaway mobster didn't show up to court the next month, but his older sister did. Jean Holland came forward and demanded that she be made receiver of her brother's estate in his absence.

When Gamel first heard that Whitey's sister wanted to lay claim to his lottery money, he drove to her house and tried to interview her on the front porch.

"I want you to understand what it means to harbor a

fugitive," he told her. "If you are knowingly harboring your brother in any way, we can lock you up for a full year."

Holland looked at the agent with utter contempt. She said nothing and disappeared through her front door. Soon after, her attorney called Gamel in his office and berated him for "intimidating" his client.

Gamel locked eyes with Whitey's sister once again when she arrived at the Norfolk Superior Courthouse in Dedham, Massachusetts. Cameras packed the courthouse as Holland filed her claim to Whitey's winnings, stating that her brother had disappeared and that she had no idea where he was. Holland was treating her brother as if he were a missing person instead of the fugitive from justice that he truly was.

The fight between Whitey Bulger's sister and the US government would be tied up in court for the next several years. Ultimately, the Bulger family wouldn't receive a penny from the lottery winnings.

7

Although Whitey was long gone, Teresa Stanley still lived in fear of her former mate. After all, he'd killed women before. She was never out of Bulger's reach, as Kevin Weeks kept close tabs on her during the months that his boss was crisscrossing the country with Catherine Greig. Teresa had a treasure trove of information about Whitey's meticulous planning for his possible life on the run, but she remained elusive to the FBI and had refused to sit down for an interview. Stanley was now dating another alleged hoodlum from South Boston named Alan Thistle. Word on the street was that Thistle was an FBI informant working directly for Gamel, earning $1,500 each month. How much information about Bulger Thistle may have learned through pillow talk with Stanley and shared

with Gamel is not known. But the Bureau's lack of results during this time spoke volumes.

To get to Stanley, John Gamel needed some solid backup. Enter FBI agent Charlie Gianturco.

Gianturco was a classic street cop, having worked for years chasing New York's most powerful Mafia bosses, including Gambino family godfather Paul "Big Paul" Castellano and the man who'd seized power from him through the barrel of a gun, John Gotti. On Gotti's orders, Castellano and his driver were assassinated in 1985, gunned down in spectacular fashion in front of Sparks Steak House in midtown Manhattan.

Gianturco, who had been schooled on mob life by none other than legendary FBI agent Joe Pistone, aka Donnie Brasco, maintained wiretaps on Castellano's home and then on Gotti's headquarters in New York's Little Italy. The wiretaps on the Ravenite Social Club provided federal agents with countless hours of tapes incriminating Gotti in five murders, along with loan-sharking and a slew of other mob-related crimes. The "Dapper Don" was convicted on all charges in 1992 and sentenced to life in prison, where he died of throat cancer a decade later.

"The difference between Gotti and Bulger is that John Gotti was a thug and a hijacker of trucks out of the airport in Queens, New York. That's where he made

his bones. He had a big fucking mouth and that's what got him into trouble," Gianturco says. "Whitey Bulger was a user of people. He used people and spit them out. But he was very smart."

The Bureau wanted a set of fresh eyes on the hunt for Whitey Bulger. John Gamel briefed Gianturco and two other agents on the case and set them loose.

Gianturco reviewed the file and tried to put the manhunt in its simplest terms.

"It's a guy from Southie versus a guy from Chelsea," he said, staring at a surveillance photo of Bulger. "Let's see how smart you are, Whitey."

For Gianturco, everything was about competition. Like Gamel, Gianturco came from Massachusetts, but Charlie was a Boston boy born and raised. He grew up playing football, basketball, and baseball in the predominantly Italian neighborhood of Chelsea, which had always been controlled by local wise guys. "In my neighborhood, you got two educations, one on the streets and one in school," he says. The son of a local doctor, Charlie went to private school at St. John's Prep in nearby Danvers, Massachusetts, and then the University of Dayton (Ohio).

His street smarts served him well out of the gate on the Bulger case. Gianturco understood that the key was Teresa Stanley, Whitey's longtime companion. But

how do you engage her? Browbeating her into talking wouldn't work. Instead, Stanley had to be wooed and comforted. She was an abused and now scorned woman. The financial support Whitey had offered her for decades had dried up. She had no job; she had no savings. Teresa was also angry about the fact that he'd taken up with Greig again so quickly and easily, which is why she started dating Alan Thistle. Stanley hoped it would drive Bulger crazy with jealousy.

These feelings of financial desperation and personal rejection were tools that Gianturco could use to the Bureau's advantage. He visited Teresa at her home and asked her to lunch. Scanning Teresa's living room, it appeared that all evidence of her previous life with Bulger, photographs and such, was now gone, save for a replica sports magazine cover with a picture of Teresa and Whitey dressed as hockey players from the Montreal Canadiens on it. It was most likely a gift from Stanley's son-in-law Chris Nilan, a former NHL player who'd earned the nickname "Knuckles" as a longtime enforcer for the storied Montreal hockey club and later the Boston Bruins.

Gianturco's lunch with Stanley proved successful. They continued to talk for several more days. On the second day of long talks, Teresa served up some major bombshells. First, Stanley told Gianturco and his FBI

partner Bob Walther about Whitey's safety deposit box in London.

"He's also using an alias," she confided. "He's going by the name Thomas Baxter."

Bingo, Gianturco thought.

Within an hour, the agents ran the Baxter alias through the Massachusetts Department of Motor Vehicles database and immediately got a hit. The name Thomas Baxter came up as a Massachusetts driver's license, but the identification card had Whitey Bulger's photo on it. The license was then transferred to New York.

"Baxter was a small-time guy from Woburn and Charlestown who died back in the '70s," Gianturco says. "Bulger found out that he died and got his hands on the license and brought it in to get his own photo on it."

The agents knew that Bulger must have had someone working for him on the inside at the Registry of Motor Vehicles, but they couldn't get anyone there to cooperate with the investigation.

"We couldn't puncture the registry," Gianturco recalls. "Everybody said, 'This is Billy Bulger's registry' and we got no support."

Gianturco believes that Whitey's all-powerful brother stymied this critical part of their investigation.

But the agents finally got the information they needed about the fake Massachusetts and New York licenses and then wondered, exactly how many licenses had Whitey made in how many states?

Gianturco then conducted an off-line search across the National Crime Information Center (NCIC) to see if Thomas Baxter's plates had been run by any member of law enforcement anywhere in the country. That's when he first learned about Bulger's visit to Mississippi, and another near miss in Sheridan, Wyoming, where a security guard at a veterans' hospital ran the out-of-state plates, and a third sighting of a Grand Marquis registered to Tom Baxter of Selden, New York, down in Louisiana.

"It looks like he's not crossing the borders into Canada or Mexico, or even fleeing to Europe," Gianturco said to himself. He thought the mad dash to Europe by investigators after the London safe deposit box was exposed by Stanley would be fruitless.

"It was all bullshit," the agent recalls. "Why put a safety deposit box in your own name like he did in London? He wasn't going back there. He'd changed his identity by then. He was someone else."

8

Whitey Bulger and Catherine Greig did their best to fit in with the slower-paced crowd in Grand Isle, Louisiana. Bulger was still using the Tom Baxter alias, while Greig kept the name Helen Marshall. They did most of their shopping at a massive Walmart in nearby Galliano, Louisiana, where Catherine also purchased a pair of prescription eyeglasses.

She told the clerk that she was from New York and was visiting friends on the island. The Walmart employee remembered her as being very talkative. Bulger didn't say much, but his accent suggested that he was from somewhere up north.

The couple befriended a local family, mostly because of their mutual love for dogs. Catherine was missing her poodles Nikki and Gigi terribly and struck up a

conversation with a town worker named Penny Gautreaux and her son Glenn Jr., known as "Bruiser," who owned two black Labrador retrievers.

"I was seventeen years old at the time I met him," Glenn Jr. said in a recent interview. "He was awesome. We called him Uncle Tom and her Aunt Helen."

The Gautreauxs invited the couple to their home for dinner, where they met Penny's husband, Glenn Sr., and the couple's other children. Penny served up fried fish and French fries, satisfying Whitey's appetite and also his love for family dinners.

Just as Catherine had missed her beloved dogs, Whitey longed for the good old days of sitting down with Teresa Stanley and her kids around the dinner table.

"He loved how tight our family was, the way we all took care of each other," Glenn Jr. recalls. "And we treated both of them as family also."

Whitey showed up at each meal with cartons of orange juice.

"You all need to drink your O.J.," he'd tell them. "You gotta stay healthy."

Like those family suppers with Teresa, Bulger insisted that the Gautreaux children sit at the table and not over on the couch, and even lectured them about

the importance of a solid education and staying out of trouble.

Glenn Jr. got the nickname "Bruiser" because he got into a lot of fights in school. One day, his uncle Tom aka Whitey pulled him aside and stressed to the teen that there was a better way.

"I used to get into fights all the time too," Whitey told him. "You gotta cut out all that bullshit. It'll only lead to problems."

When one of the teenager's dogs got pregnant, Whitey offered him money to build a proper pen for the puppies. When one of the puppies got sick, Bulger paid the veterinarian bill.

"The vet couldn't help her, so I had to put the puppy down," Glenn Jr. remembers. "I dug a ditch while [Whitey] held the dog in his arms. He was crying real hard. He made me put down a bowl of food and water by the hole so the puppy could have a last meal while I dug."

Glenn Jr. retrieved his rifle and Whitey reluctantly handed over the sick dog.

"Do what you gotta to, but don't shoot her until after I walk away," he told the teenager. "I just can't bear to see it."

Bulger turned his back and began to walk. After

about a hundred yards he heard the gunshot. Whitey didn't look back. Instead, he put his face in his hands and wept.

But it wasn't just household pets that had such an emotional effect on Whitey. When he'd take Glenn Jr. fishing, Bulger also had to look away as the boy retrieved his catch.

"It's just a fish," Glenn Jr. would tell him. "We eat 'em every night."

"Yeah, but they don't hurt anybody," Bulger replied. "I don't like seeing any kind of animal or even a fish in any kind of pain."

The comments were representative of Whitey's sociopathic behavior. The man had no fear or hesitation when it came to pumping bullets into the body of Brian Halloran. But he couldn't stomach any violence against a defenseless animal, or even a fish.

Whitey and Catherine became surrogate grandparents to the Gautreaux kids, and that meant bringing groceries to their house for home-cooked meals and taking the children out on spending sprees at the local Walmart.

"I'd walk in front of him and every time I'd pass and look at something like a new fishing rod or shotgun shells, he'd follow me and put it in the shopping cart

and buy it for me," Glenn Jr. says. "We had no money, so they really took good care of us."

They also took on the responsibility of paying for an eye exam and glasses for Glenn Jr. In all, Whitey would later claim that he'd spent about $40,000 on the family. When asked by the clerk about her relationship to the teenager, Greig told her that he was her nephew. While there, Catherine ordered four boxes of contact lenses, a year's supply, for herself. "We travel and I want to make sure I have enough contacts," she told the clerk.

The clerk found it a bit odd but did not ask Greig aka Helen Marshall where they planned to travel next. There was a good chance that Catherine did not know herself.

The Gautreauxs grew to love "Uncle Tom," but they were also exposed to his dark side and were disturbed by the way "Tom" treated "Helen." He'd clap his hands or snap his finger as a signal to her that he needed something and she would always come running. He treated her much like a servant—not a wife.

When she needed time to herself, Catherine would take quiet walks on the beach or strolls through town, no doubt grappling with her decision to embark on this new and secret life. But she loved him. There was no doubt about that. Whitey was set in his ways, and she'd

have to adapt to his lifestyle if she wanted to stay with him.

With all the miles that Whitey and Catherine were putting on the car, it was only a matter of time before Bulger swapped out the Grand Marquis for a new car. A reliable vehicle was critical to the aging gangster's freedom.

When Teresa Stanley gave up the Selden, New York, address of Kevin Weeks's cousin to Gianturco, the FBI sent an agent from its resident agency in Garden City by the home every day for four months, but there was no sign of the fugitive Bulger. Then, on a Friday night in 1996, an agent making his rounds by the Selden address spotted the Grand Marquis. The car Whitey Bulger had been driving for months had suddenly appeared in a Long Island driveway.

Gianturco was in Boston enjoying a retirement party for a friend when he got the call.

"I got an eye on the car. It's in the driveway," the agent told him.

Gianturco recalled what it felt like when he first learned the news. "You almost shit your pants when you hear something like that," he says.

He immediately reached out to his partner Bob Walther, and the two drove down to see for themselves.

The resident agency in Garden City had only six agents working in the office and they were pulling night shifts watching the Selden address. They didn't have the manpower to handle surveillance of the vehicle. The case could break at any time, so it was paramount that Gianturco take control quickly.

When he and Walther arrived in Selden, they noticed that the home was in a quiet neighborhood at the end of a cul-de-sac.

"That posed a major problem," Gianturco remembers. "We needed a good surveillance position, but there was no rental property on the street that we could slip into unnoticed. There wasn't any way to keep watch on the house."

Gianturco drove through the neighborhood and spotted a home on another street whose backyard faced the driveway. He watched the place for a few hours before approaching the homeowner.

"I believed he was an Italian guy, so I spoke to him as one Italian to another," he recalls.

It was less than a month after the tragedy of TWA Flight 800, which mysteriously crashed into the Atlantic Ocean off East Moriches, New York, killing all 230 people on board. Long Island was crawling with federal agents at the time, which gave Gianturco an idea.

He knocked on the neighbor's door and introduced himself.

"We're in a sensitive situation. This has to do with Flight 800," Gianturco lied. "We need to be in this area to get some information."

"My brother's NYPD, I'll give you whatever you guys need," the neighbor said. "What can I do to help?"

The neighbor allowed Gianturco to park a van in his wooded backyard, where he and three other agents conducted surveillance on the Grand Marquis working in eight-hour shifts over the next forty days.

The car did not move and there was no sign of Bulger.

Each day, the owner of the Selden home, a man married to Kevin Weeks's cousin, started the car and ran it for a few minutes before switching off the ignition and going back inside. The surveillance job was tedious work as the agents sat huddled in the tin can, watching and waiting.

Finally on the forty-first day, the homeowner got into the Grand Marquis and drove it to his work. Gianturco had previously run background checks on everyone inside the home. Although the wife was Weeks's cousin, there did not seem to be anything nefarious about the family. The husband was a straight guy who ran an

honest business, and they had a daughter attending the US Naval Academy.

"How do we approach this guy?" Gianturco asked Walther. They didn't want to embarrass him at his house or his business. They needed to wait until the man was on the move.

The agents watched the man's store until closing time, which was after dusk. That's when he locked up his business and walked across a parking lot toward the Grand Marquis. Gianturco stepped out of the shadows and made the approach.

"Excuse me, sir, can I talk to you a second?"

Gianturco pulled out his badge and a small wanted poster with Bulger's face plastered on it.

"This guy's no good," Gianturco said, pointing at the photo.

"Oh, Tom?" the man replied.

"No, take a good look. Look who it is. It's not Tom Baxter. His name is Whitey Bulger and he's a murderer and a drug dealer, and you don't want him around your children."

The man was stunned. To him, the aging gentleman was Tom Baxter, a longshoreman who just needed an address for his mail and paid the family money to store his car and a safe at their home.

"Bulger co-opted these people," Gianturco says. "They were naive, yes, but they weren't criminals."

The man handed over the car without argument and swore total secrecy to Gianturco and Walther.

Gianturco had the car brought to a bay at the Nassau County Police Department. He drove back to Boston to pick up a forensic analyst and a mechanic he trusted.

"This is on the QT, so just tell your wives that you'll see them tomorrow," Gianturco told them.

He drove them down to New York and watched as they went to work.

"Now, Whitey, let's see where you've been," Gianturco said aloud as the lab technician and mechanic disassembled the Grand Marquis piece by piece.

They removed the vehicle's tires and took samples of the soil stuck in the grooves, as that might tell them what part of the country Bulger was traveling in. They ripped open the cushions and pulled up the rugs inside the vehicle.

"He was very involved in keeping his car in good shape," Gianturco recalls. "He'd been driving about two hundred miles per day, so he had new tires, new oil filters and everything."

The interior rug was attached to rails and when they pulled it up, the forensic analyst spotted a crumpled-up

piece of paper underneath. Using a pair of gloves, he lifted the paper and handed it over to Gianturco.

"What's this?" the veteran agent said to himself as he eyeballed the evidence.

It was a receipt for coat hangers, milk, hair dye, and two other items from a Walmart Supercenter in Galliano, Louisiana.

Bingo.

Gianturco also found a Jiffy Lube in Galliano and learned that the Grand Marquis had been serviced there.

"You make your own luck," Gianturco says. "If you work hard enough, you're gonna catch a break."

He called an agent friend named Don Dixon, who worked for the FBI in Lake Charles, Louisiana.

"Don, what's down in the Bayou?" Gianturco asked. "I'm going down there on a case."

"Charlie, there's nothing fucking down there," Dixon told him. "The only place is Grand Isle. It's a summer resort with a hotel and a big marina, but that's it."

Gianturco and Walther caught a plane to New Orleans, grabbed a rental car, and headed for Galliano, driving along a four-mile-wide road with swamps on both sides dotted by run-down fishing huts and shrimp boats in the distance.

"This place is funky," Gianturco told Walther, who nodded in agreement.

When they arrived in Galliano, the agents canvassed the Walmart Supercenter and the local Jiffy Lube. There wasn't much else to see. The heat was stifling and the humidity caused Gianturco to sweat through his dress shirt. He and Walther walked around a bit, hearing the occasional conversation in Cajun French spoken by residents there.

"This doesn't make sense," Gianturco said. "There's no beaches to walk here. It's a pretty desperate place. Whitey's not here. He only shops here."

Then he recalled what his friend Don Dixon told him about nearby Grand Isle.

"Let's get back in the car," he told Walther.

They drove fifty-two minutes farther south and crossed the bridge onto the barrier island. Gianturco swung the rental car by the police station, where they asked to speak to the chief.

Gianturco offered the police chief the same photo of Bulger he'd shown Weeks's relative back in Selden. The chief recognized him immediately. He'd gotten to know "Tom Baxter" a little bit and would even wave hello each time they passed one another in town.

"Yeah, he walks the beach here every winter with

a woman. They're supposed to be coming back here pretty soon."

Bingo.

Neighbors who knew Bulger as Tom Baxter said that he'd feed stray dogs biscuits from the back of his Grand Marquis.

Gianturco spent the next several months living quietly in Grand Isle, waiting for Bulger and Catherine to reappear. He stayed at the Sand Dollar Motel, the only motel there. The Bureau allowed only one agent at a time to conduct surveillance on the island, and Gianturco swapped out with Walther every two weeks. He couldn't believe that the FBI wasn't committing more resources in covering this valuable lead. To Gianturco, this was a cheap way to conduct FBI business and it was also dangerous.

"The guy's probably got fourteen fucking guns on him," he said to himself. "And they [the FBI] assign only one agent to catch this guy?"

He was also concerned that Bulger would fight back if he was ever stopped by a patrolman while using the Tom Baxter identification. He pushed his superiors to include the words "armed and dangerous" to Baxter's (Bulger's) driver's license description in the National Crime Information Center (NCIC) database. In a sense,

this was perpetuating Bulger's fraud, as the FBI was reluctant to declare that it was Bulger who was using the phony Baxter ID. A major concern was that Bulger himself might have access to the NCIC database and could be checking to see if his cover had been blown.

"What if some local cop pulls him over?" Gianturco argued to his FBI bosses. "They'll have no idea the danger Tom Baxter truly poses. We gotta protect that patrol officer. We'll be responsible if they get killed."

Finally, the FBI granted the okay. It was a small but important victory as Gianturco watched and waited for Bulger to return, praying each day that the stakeout had not been compromised.

9

Teresa Stanley felt guilty. She'd betrayed Southie's code of silence in her attempt to hurt her longtime lover. Stanley could not keep this secret for long. When Kevin Weeks paid another visit to her Silver Street home, he realized immediately that she was hiding something. Teresa was nervous and fidgety, lighting up one cigarette after another. First, Weeks peppered her with questions about her new beau, Alan Thistle.

"He's with Cathy; I have to live my life," Teresa told Weeks.

"There's plenty of guys out there to go out with. Why him?"

Weeks told Teresa that Thistle was an informant who was only sleeping with her to get information about Whitey.

"Well it's too late," Stanley finally admitted. She told Weeks that she'd already spilled her guts to the FBI. "Where Jimmy [Whitey] and I were in New York, the name Tom Baxter he was using, everything," she said.

Stanley clenched her teeth and braced for a beating. She probably thought Weeks would kill her right there in her own kitchen. Instead, he told her that he'd get back to her and he walked out the door.

Weeks immediately drove to Plymouth, where Stevie Flemmi was still locked up awaiting trial. He wrote a note on a piece of paper and pressed it to the glass partition between them. Flemmi read what Stanley had done and wrote his own note back ordering Weeks to contact Whitey. Until now, that had not been part of their arrangement. Whitey would reach out to Weeks when he needed something, not the other way around.

Kevin finally called Bulger and told him about Teresa. Whitey remained calm.

"Thank God, at least I know," Bulger said. "I'll call you back."

Whitey had a plan. He always had a plan.

When he got back in touch with Weeks, Whitey told him to find his younger brother Jackie Bulger, who looked enough like him with a head of fair hair brushed back atop a broad forehead, and take some photos that he could use for new identification.

"I've grown a mustache now," Bulger told Weeks. "Make sure Jackie's wearing a mustache."

Weeks then suggested killing Teresa's new boy-friend Alan Thistle, but Whitey refused to sanction the hit. He felt that going out with a low-level creep like Thistle was enough punishment for his former mate.

Jackie Bulger worked as the clerk magistrate of Boston Juvenile Court, and that made him, like his brother Billy, a sworn officer of the court. But blood always trumped the law in Southie. Not only was Jackie game to help his fugitive brother, he'd been paying the rent on Whitey's safe deposit box in Clearwater, Florida. Weeks drove to Jackie Bulger's house in Southie and performed a makeshift photo shoot, complete with a blue cotton sheet used as a backdrop and a prop—a fake mustache. Jackie Bulger posed like his tough older brother and Weeks selected the best four photos to use as he compiled the fake documents needed to deliver his boss a new driver's license, birth certificate, and Social Security card.

Whitey and Catherine couldn't leave Grand Isle without saying good-bye to the Gautreauxs. "Bruiser" was in bed when he heard a knock on the front door late at night.

"We gotta go, there's been a family emergency," Bulger told them. "You probably won't see me again,

at least not in person. You may hear about me or read about me."

Oh shit, something must be really wrong, Glenn Jr. thought to himself.

Whitey and Catherine hugged each member of the Gautreaux family and left their home in tears.

Charlie Gianturco was still holed up in the Bayou in the midst of one of the longest stakeouts of his FBI career. While waiting for Whitey to reappear, he and a small team of agents interviewed everyone who'd come in contact with "Tom and Helen" on the sleepy barrier island and in nearby Galliano. Another team member, FBI agent Mike Carazza, hunted down the Gautreauxs, but they weren't saying much.

"Ain't no way that's him," Glenn Jr. said when he was shown an FBI wanted poster of Bulger. "You got the wrong guy."

Bruiser Gautreaux had no idea where the couple had fled, but even if he did know, he sure wasn't going to tell the FBI.

His mother, Penny, refused to talk also.

"She had to be compelled by a federal judge in Boston to testify before the Grand Jury," Carazza recalls. "It surprised us because here was a guy [Bulger] who

was wanted for murder and she was pleading the Fifth until a judge ordered her to cooperate."

There was no doubt now that Whitey had been living in Grand Isle. The only question now was, would he return?

During a trip back to Boston, Gianturco visited Teresa Stanley, who confessed that she'd tipped off Whitey through Kevin Weeks. Gianturco knew there was no way that the fugitive crime boss would return to the Bayou now, knowing that the FBI had infiltrated Grand Isle.

Teresa figured she was now in big trouble, but Gianturco understood the incredible strain she was under.

"I told Teresa not to worry about it," Gianturco recalls. "This woman had been used all her life. I wanted her to know that we weren't the same as the bad guys."

While in Boston, Gianturco interviewed Whitey's former FBI handler, John Connolly, in Connolly's executive office at Boston Edison inside the Prudential Center. At this point in 1996, the extent of Connolly's crimes remained hidden—in fact not only was Connolly's corruption still unknown, he'd landed the cushy job with Billy Bulger's help upon his retirement from the Bureau.

For his part, Gianturco knew Connolly well. He and Connolly had played handball together, but more importantly, Gianturco's brother Nick had been Connolly's longtime partner in the FBI. Still, Gianturco refused to allow old friendships to get in the way of his investigation. He knew Connolly well enough not to trust him.

"He was in it for himself, always. He [Connolly] never did any real work. You gotta question a guy like that."

When he was first assigned the case, he asked Dick Swensen, then special agent in charge of the Boston Bureau, if they'd ever interviewed Connolly about Bulger's possible whereabouts. Shockingly, Swensen said no.

"We're now two years into the hunt for Whitey and no one's ever talked to John Connolly?" Gianturco says. "You do that on Day One!"

During their interview, Connolly nonchalantly told Gianturco and another agent that Bulger and Stevie Flemmi had been offered protection against prosecution by the FBI because they'd been "such good informants." While Gianturco and his partner knew that Bulger and Flemmi had been informants, they were floored by the news that they'd been offered protection against prosecution.

"I've known Jimmy Bulger since I was a kid," Connolly told them. "He used to buy me ice cream at a soda fountain in Southie. It's a great story and I'm thinking about using it in a book I'm working on about our relationship." Connolly had dreams that a Hollywood superstar like Tom Cruise might even play him in an eventual movie.

Connolly then recounted a dinner with Bulger and Flemmi at the home of FBI supervisor John Morris in the historic town of Lexington, Massachusetts.

"He was in his cups," Connolly said of Morris, meaning he was drunk. "He told Bulger and Flemmi that they were so good as informants that he could get them off for anything short of murder."

Morris would later confess to taking $6,000 in bribes from Whitey Bulger, including $1,000 to bring his girlfriend to a 1982 Drug Enforcement Administration conference in Georgia as well as cases of French Bordeaux.

Connolly stressed that Morris promised Bulger and Flemmi they could continue to commit crimes like loan-sharking and illegal gambling as long as they fed the FBI information about Italian Mafia operations in Boston's North End. Connolly credits Bulger with providing him with knowledge used to obtain a wiretap of local Mafia boss Gennaro "Jerry" Angiulo's headquar-

ters on Prince Street in the North End back in 1981. Connolly and a team of agents then arrested Angiulo as he sat down for a plate of pork chops at his favorite restaurant.

"I'll be back before my pork chops get cold," Angiulo said defiantly as Connolly placed him in handcuffs. Jerry Angiulo would spend the next twenty-four years in prison before dying a free man at ninety years old.

In Gianturco's opinion, Bulger and Flemmi should have been closed as informants after the Angiulo case. Instead, once the Mafia was crippled by prosecutions, Whitey's gang quickly filled the underworld void.

"Everyone knew this but no one wanted to go up against Connolly," Gianturco says.

Connolly also told Gianturco and his partner that Bulger and Flemmi were indicted for things that they'd been told they wouldn't be indicted for.

"Bulger probably feels like he's been framed by the government," Connolly said incredulously. "I hope you guys never catch him."

For a long time, Connolly got his wish.

10

Kevin Weeks had money invested in a local orthopedic rehabilitation office and he often used the space for clandestine conversations with Whitey. Weeks would go to the office on Sunday nights and wait for further instructions from his boss. Sometimes, Bulger would order Kevin to drive from South Boston all the way to New Hampshire just to take a quick phone call at a secluded spot. During one of these calls, Bulger told him to meet up in Chicago. He and Catherine had ditched their car by then and were traveling by train from New York to the Midwest under the names Mark and Carol Shapeton.

Weeks met up with Whitey and Catherine at Water Tower Place, a huge shopping mall in downtown Chicago. Kevin had driven fifteen hours in a rented car

from Boston, stopping overnight in South Bend, Indiana. He had the photos of Jackie Bulger with him.

They dined for lunch alfresco and walked around the city. Weeks had brought along a girlfriend to keep Catherine company. Greig looked good, radiant even, with smooth tanned skin and a toned body. Bulger looked better than he had in years, fit and happy and free of the anxiety he'd felt earlier while hiding with Teresa Stanley. Kevin was a giant ball of stress, however. So far, he'd escaped the noose of federal prosecutors, but he was looking over his shoulder every minute of every day waiting for an indictment against him to drop.

"If anything ever comes down, put it on me," Bulger told him during their walk.

But when Weeks showed Whitey the photos he took of Jackie, the boss shook his head in disgust. The mustache was all wrong. The fake one was much bushier than the pencil-thin facial hair Whitey was now sporting. They bought another Polaroid camera and a set of blue bedsheets to use as a backdrop and then went to Bulger's hotel room to take more photographs. The fugitive crime boss came up with four new aliases complete with Social Security numbers.

Evening had fallen and Whitey was hungry. He suggested they all go to a Japanese restaurant close by.

The couples left the hotel and Catherine walked ahead with Weeks's girlfriend. Three young men catcalled the women as they walked by. Whitey exploded with rage.

"What're you looking at, you motherfuckers?" he shouted as he pulled a switchblade knife from a sheaf on his calf. Weeks whipped out his own knife, both blades now shining in the moonlight. They were ready for war, but the three young guys took off running down the street before any blood could be spilled.

When they entered the Japanese restaurant, Whitey pulled his protégé aside.

"Every day out there is another day I beat them, every good meal is a meal they can't take away from me."

They took a table in the back of the restaurant and devoured several dishes of chicken, beef, and vegetables while washing them down with some cold beer.

The next morning, Whitey and Catherine hopped on an Amtrak train and returned to Penn Station in New York while Kevin drove back to Southie to finish making Whitey's new IDs. Weeks was more paranoid than ever now. He swore that he heard the rotor blades of helicopters hovering over his house and he felt that he was being tailed everywhere he went. Instead of traveling himself, he asked a friend to deliver the phony identification cards to Whitey in New York. Bulger

later convinced Weeks to meet him for one last rendezvous back at "the Lions," outside the main branch
of the New York City Public Library. Whitey was feeling good, brazen even. While walking with Weeks and
Greig in Manhattan, he stopped to ask a police officer
for directions.

"The best place to get lost is a big city," Bulger said,
trying to comfort Kevin after the brief encounter with
the cop. "People are just walking around thinking
about their own problems. You don't stand out there."

When Bulger put Weeks on a train back to Boston,
the protégé had no idea that it would be the last time
they'd see each other during Whitey's time on the run.

"I'll be in touch," Bulger told him. Weeks never
heard from him again.

Charlie Gianturco had watched Bulger slip through
the FBI's net back in Grand Isle and he felt down,
but not defeated. He knew that Bulger would not be
careless enough to return to the Bayou, but his instincts told him that Whitey was still crisscrossing the
South.

"We only have to be lucky once," he told himself
over and over again. The feds were still monitoring the
phone lines of Whitey Bulger's family and friends, and
they got two hits for calls coming into the Southie ad-

dress of a Bulger family neighbor from a calling card. One call was made in Slidell, Louisiana, and the other in Mobile, Alabama. The calls were both placed at gas stations along busy Interstate 10. Gianturco and his partner drove the route from Texas to Jacksonville, Florida, stopping at every resident FBI agency along the way. The trip took two weeks. Gianturco showed up at each FBI branch office with a stack of Bulger wanted posters.

"This guy's very familiar with the territory," he told his fellow agents. "And you may see him."

In the fall of 1997, Gianturco picked up a ping on a phone call to Southie while tracking Whitey in Mississippi. He says the call was made to one of Whitey's relatives from a pay phone near Biloxi.

Gianturco believes he was close to nailing Whitey in Mississippi when suddenly he got a call from a superior at the Bureau.

"We'd like you to return to Boston ASAP to discuss an important matter," the superior said.

"Now? I'm about to collar Whitey *fucking* Bulger!" Gianturco responded incredulously.

"Yes, right now. It can't be helped. Another agent will take the lead on Bulger."

Gianturco was frustrated, but he followed his orders and returned to Boston. The lead died there. Looking

back now, it's hard for him not to have suspicions about the timing of that call back to Boston.

"I was about to arrest Whitey Bulger," he says today. "And someone inside the Bureau did not want that to happen."

In reality, Whitey Bulger was a ghost. Just as Gianturco and other agents were getting close to him in the Deep South, Bulger and Greig both vanished again, returning to Chicago, where Whitey met up with an old buddy from Alcatraz named Barney "Dirty Shirt" Grogan. A convicted bank robber, Grogan had earned his nickname by smuggling steaks under his shirt out of the prison kitchen. His real name wasn't Grogan at all, but John Joseph O'Brien. Whitey always found a way to connect with his prison pals, especially those who'd served with him at Alcatraz—his alma mater. Before he'd gone on the run, Whitey visited with another old inmate friend in Youngstown, Ohio. The former prisoner was down on his luck until Bulger appeared and lifted the trunk of his car. Inside were stacks upon stacks of dollar bills. Whitey took a few stacks out and placed them in the man's hands before going on his way.

After his brief reunion with "Dirty Shirt" Grogan, Whitey and Catherine boarded a train headed west. They rode the Southwest Chief through the Great

Plains and the Rocky Mountains until tall pine trees gave way to desert palms before arriving at Union Station in Los Angeles.

They booked a modest, quiet motel nearby and camped out there while Whitey plotted his next move. He considered heading north to Washington State, but the weather there was too damp for his aging bones; the same with San Francisco, which would have allowed him a sweeping view of his former home on Alcatraz. Bulger bought a map and unfolded it on the bed, studying it for several hours until Catherine urged him to get some sleep. Sleep would not come easy for him, though. It never did. Whitey had suffered from insomnia followed by frightening nightmares since his prison days in the 1960s, when he'd volunteered to take part in a covert CIA program called MK-Ultra in exchange for time shaved off his sentence. Bulger and the other prisoners were lied to and told that they were participating in a study to find a cure for schizophrenia. In reality, the CIA was working on a mind control weapon. Whitey was injected with LSD for weeks at a time, and he suffered terrifying hallucinations as he envisioned blood pouring from his cell walls while his prison bars transformed into slithering black snakes. He felt his head change shape and heard haunting voices. Years later he read that LSD also caused chro-

mosome damage, and he blamed the drug for the death of his only son.

On one of their first days in Los Angeles, Bulger awoke in the early morning to the sound of a helicopter hovering over their motel. It was no hallucination. It was real.

This is it, he thought to himself. *It all ends here.*

He rushed to the window for a peek outside and saw a caravan of television news trucks passing by without stopping. Bulger then flicked on the television set to see what the commotion was all about. Turns out, the media including the news chopper hovering overhead were all scrambling to cover the O. J. Simpson civil trial, which was now unfolding nearby at the Santa Monica Courthouse. Instead of breathing a sigh of relief, Bulger ordered Catherine to pack her stuff immediately. They were leaving the motel as soon as possible to find something quieter and far away from the O.J. media circus. Their next stop was Venice Beach.

Before he'd even accepted the job to join the Bulger task force in 2008, Tommy Mac knew the story of Kevin Weeks. Every FBI agent did. Weeks's decision to flip had been one of the most important moments in the hunt for Bulger, not only because it provided them with fresh intelligence on Whitey, but because it had finally laid bare the FBI's role in Whitey's criminal enterprises.

Reading through the FBI's paperwork on Weeks, it was hard not to be shocked all over again by what had transpired. The capture and confession of Weeks would have huge ramifications on the search for Bulger, ramifications that even in 2008, as Tommy Mac was joining the task force, continued to reverberate. Weeks's eventual testimony implicated high-level officials at the

Boston FBI office, but it also overshadowed all of the aggressive work that agents had been doing to catch him. All those near misses, all that good detective work, had been lost in the taint of scandal.

Suddenly, the whole hunt for Bulger became suspect. And somehow, in 2008 it still was.

By the mid-1990s, the capture of Weeks had been building for some time. After he and Bulger met for the last time in the spring of 1996, Kevin Weeks gravitated toward John Connolly. Having no contact with Bulger, Weeks and Connolly met more than three dozen times. If Weeks wanted a sit-down with the former federal agent turned private-sector security chief, he'd call Connolly's office and give the receptionist a fake name.

"Tell Mr. Connolly that Chico called."

Connolly would then call a relative of Weeks to set up the meeting.

Bulger's onetime man on the inside at the Bureau told Weeks about a turf war being waged between the FBI on one side and the Massachusetts State Police aligned with the DEA on the other. Connolly was right. Nobody trusted anybody when it came to the Bulger investigation.

"I called State Police Colonel Tom Foley early on in my investigation and asked that we share informa-

tion and resources," Charlie Gianturco recalls. "But he wanted no part of us."

Foley and others had long suspected that John Connolly, John Morris, and other federal agents were protecting Whitey Bulger and Stevie Flemmi and that this bad blood extended to every other agent in the Boston FBI office—corrupt or not. Foley had launched his own investigation and search for Bulger and Greig. He had a strong hunch that the pair was now living in Cuba, but the lack of diplomatic relations between the Clinton White House and Fidel Castro destroyed any chance of going there to find out.

"He had all the money in the world," Foley said in an interview later. "It was one of the areas we thought could be a real good spot for him."

What Foley didn't know at the time was that Bulger and Flemmi had also corrupted a member of the state police. A former lieutenant named Richard Schneiderhan had been feeding Flemmi information for years. It was Schneiderhan who had tipped off the gang to a state police bugging operation of their headquarters, a garage on Lancaster Street in Boston, back in 1980. He'd later tell Weeks that the FBI was tracking phone calls made from the homes of Billy and Jackie Bulger.

Schneiderhan had a warm spot for Billy Bulger. The dirty state cop was a member of a Catholic church that

was spared from the wrecking ball when Billy helped it gain designation as a national historic site.

Kevin Weeks was now managing the relationship with Schneiderhan, who enjoyed playing wise guy as it boosted his ego. The gang had penetrated the ranks of the FBI and the state police, and they were relationships that kept on giving. But Weeks never asked himself what the feds wanted in return.

He found out one night in the spring of 1997, when he learned through a TV news report that Flemmi had testified during an evidentiary hearing that he and Bulger were longtime FBI informants—*rats.*

Weeks was stunned. At first he didn't think he'd heard it right. He continued to flip through the channels, and every local station had topped its newscast with the blockbuster revelation.

"It made no sense. We *killed* guys because they were informants," Weeks would later write in his memoir. "And now I was learning that Jimmy [Whitey] and Stevie were informants themselves."

For more than two decades, Kevin Weeks, Whitey's loyal soldier and surrogate son, had believed that it was Bulger who was corrupting the FBI, paying them for information that allowed him to stay two steps ahead of the law. But instead it was the FBI that had struck a Faustian bargain with the Irish mob boss to supply

them with a steady stream of intelligence that would put his friends and criminal associates behind bars.

Whitey Bulger's life of crime had been fueled by one big lie. While rumors had swirled in the criminal underworld and among law enforcement for years that Bulger and Flemmi might be protected informants, the first time the duo was publicly accused surfaced in a 1988 report by the *Boston Globe*'s Spotlight Team. Although the documentation was a bit veiled in the story, the newspaper reported that the Southie crime lord had a "special relationship" with the FBI. James F. Ahearn, who was then special agent in charge of the FBI in Boston, denied any improper relationship between the Bureau and Bulger, telling the Spotlight Team, "That is absolutely untrue . . . We specifically deny that there has been special treatment of this individual."

Kevin Weeks had made his reputation as a tough guy who preyed on criminals and the innocent alike. But now he was the target. Weeks figured that rivals on the street would believe that he too was an informant for the FBI. He carried two pistols with him at all times under a long coat with the pockets cut out so he could keep his hands gripped tightly on two .45s that were sticking out of his large waistband.

He met with Flemmi behind bars and accused him

of putting a bull's-eye on his back. Flemmi tried to downplay the situation, but Weeks stormed out of the jailhouse visit. Later, John Connolly offered his own take on the double dealing. To him, it was a simple case of survival of the fittest.

"The Mafia was going against Jimmy [Whitey] and Stevie," Connolly explained to Weeks. "So Jimmy and Stevie went against them."

As Weeks was trying to put the pieces together in his own head, the Massachusetts State Police and DEA swooped in and plucked him off the streets. He was arrested in November 1999 with a concealed weapon—a knife in his pocket.

Weeks was charged with twenty-nine counts including extortion, money laundering, and racketeering and held without bail. He was forty-three years old, the father of two teenage boys, and he was facing hard time. He was sent to a federal holding facility in Rhode Island. Normally, he would have been placed in Plymouth, but that's where Flemmi was and authorities didn't want them communicating now that both were in jail.

Weeks's lawyer pulled the 661-page ruling from Mark Wolf, the federal judge assigned to the Bulger and Flemmi case, and gave it to his client to read. Weeks studied each page outlining their relationship

with the FBI. Flemmi had been ratting on his friends since the mid-1960s, while Whitey was brought into the Bureau's fold a decade later.

Bulger's surrogate son had a decision to make: either keep protecting his boss and his boss's lies, or protect himself and cut his own deal. It was a no-brainer. Kevin Weeks offered to cooperate with prosecutors. He knew where the bodies were buried—literally.

On the frigid morning of January 13, 2000, Weeks took investigators on a tour of the gang's greatest hits. He brought them to Hallet Street in Dorchester, across from Florian Hall, which is the Boston firefighters' union hall, as well as a banquet facility where Boston politicians hold rallies and many Irish wakes are celebrated.

Weeks pointed to the patch of snow where underneath lay the bodies of three Bulger victims—a safecracker named Bucky Barrett, a boat mechanic turned smuggler named John McIntyre, and a twenty-six-year-old woman named Deborah Hussey, the stepdaughter of Stevie Flemmi.

Weeks had reburied the bodies there more than a decade earlier. On Halloween 1985, Weeks served as an armed lookout while Flemmi and Bulger dug the ditches under the cover of darkness. While Whitey and Stevie were working their shovels, the area was illumi-

nated by headlights as a car pulled in and stopped a few yards away. Flemmi and Weeks hid as the driver got out, stumbled a bit, and unzipped his fly to take a piss. He got back in his car a few moments later and drove away. Weeks kept his eye and his trigger trained on the drunken motorist but didn't act.

"I told you that if anybody spots us, to shoot 'em," Flemmi told Weeks.

"Ah, c'mon Stevie, the guy's drunk. He just stopped to take a leak. He didn't see us and won't remember anything in the morning," Weeks replied.

"If anybody else comes here, you put 'em in the ground," Flemmi ordered. "Or one of these ditches will be for you."

As snow began to fall on the night of January 13, 2000, the sound of a large backhoe could be heard near Florian Hall, where state police and the DEA performed the grisly task of recovering the bodies, or what was left of them.

A short time later, investigators found bones. Deborah Hussey's tibia was still connected to her ankle and her foot was covered by a rotting shoe. Weeks told authorities that Hussey was choked to death by Whitey Bulger in early 1985. Kevin had witnessed the whole thing. It happened inside a home on East Third Street in Southie, which was owned by the brother of Bulger

associate Pat Nee. They called the place "The Haunty," because of the grim undertakings that took place in its basement. Whitey was on the floor strangling Hussey with his bare hands, his legs wrapped around her. The attack was violent and took several horrific minutes. Her body was carried to the basement. Flemmi feared that she wasn't quite dead, so he strangled her some more and then pulled her teeth out to prevent identification before he buried her in the dirt basement.

Hussey's murder was a violent end to a long and abusive relationship she had with Flemmi—her stepfather, the one she called Daddy and who had driven her to school as a child. The young woman had threatened to expose the incestuous relationship to her mother, Marion, Flemmi's common-law wife. Before luring the younger Hussey to her death, Flemmi brought her on a shopping spree, buying her clothes that he knew she'd never wear.

Deborah Hussey's bones were found buried near the remains of John McIntyre. He too met his fate in The Haunty, on November 30, 1984. Whitey was worried that McIntyre was snitching about Bulger's involvement in a 1984 shipment of seven tons of guns including 163 assault rifles from Gloucester, Massachusetts, to Ireland to support the Irish Republican Army's war of terror against Great Britain. McIntyre was a crew mem-

ber aboard the fishing boat *Valhalla*, which carried the weapons, all hidden in caskets, and transferred them to a boat off the coast of Ireland. The guns never made it to shore, as the second vessel was quickly seized by Irish authorities. After McIntyre returned home, he wanted to go clean and start living a normal life. He reached out to the DEA to make a deal and word got back to John Connolly, Whitey's man on the inside. Bulger brought McIntyre to The Haunty and interrogated him at gunpoint while Flemmi tied him up with handcuffs and leg shackles. McIntyre confessed to everything, including tipping the DEA off to a large boat shipment of marijuana that was supposed to earn Bulger and his gang $3 million.

"I'm sorry, I was weak," McIntyre cried.

After six hours of questioning, McIntyre was led to the basement in chains. Whitey pulled out a rope and wrapped it around the smuggler's neck. Bulger tightened it with his strong forearms, but the rope was too thick to do the job. McIntyre just gagged and vomited. Whitey then reached for his pistol and waved it at his victim.

"Would you like one in the head?" the executioner offered.

"Yes, please," McIntyre pleaded.

Bulger shot him once in the back of the head and then several more times in the face, turning McIntyre's flesh into hamburger. Flemmi later pulled the man's tongue out with a pair of pliers. When McIntyre first disappeared, his family believed that he'd been taken out by a hit squad sent by British Intelligence because of his support for the IRA. When McIntyre's father began demanding answers, he was approached by a mysterious man who offered a warning: "Remember, you have another son."

But the first man murdered inside The Haunty was Arthur "Bucky" Barrett, a safecracker who was involved in a daring burglary at the Depositors Trust Bank in Medford, just north of Boston, in 1980. The robbers had entered the bank by breaking through a four-inch concrete wall from an adjoining eye doctor's office. Then they had to drill through another eighteen inches of steel and concrete to gain access to the vault, where they stole $1.5 million worth of cash, gold, silver, and jewels. The gang included several cops. Barrett's role was to bypass the bank's security system. Whitey was due $100,000 from the heist as a tribute, but Bucky refused to pay. Bulger was patient, though. He waited three years before making his move. On July 26, 1983, Whitey had a friend invite Barrett to The Haunty to

inspect a cache of stolen diamonds. When he got there, Bulger met him with a nine-millimeter machine gun with a silencer.

"Bucky Barrett, freeze!" Whitey ordered, pointing the gun at the safecracker's heart.

Barrett was chained to a chair and grilled for information about a rival's drug business and then was ordered to pay Whitey the money he was owed.

Bulger and Flemmi stuffed Barrett in a car and drove to his home in Quincy, where Bucky retrieved $47,000 in cash and collected another $10,000 from a bar that he owned at Faneuil Hall Marketplace. They returned to The Haunty and Whitey announced that Barrett was going downstairs to "lay down."

Flemmi and Kevin Weeks knew what this meant.

As Barrett was led down the basement steps, Whitey stuck his gun to the back of his head and pulled the trigger, but the gun safety was on. Bulger fixed the problem and fired again, and this time the back of Barrett's head exploded and his body tumbled down the stairs.

Whitey went back upstairs and ordered Weeks to help Flemmi clean up the mess.

"I'm gonna lie down," Bulger said as he walked toward a bedroom and closed the door.

Barrett was buried in the dirt basement, where he

was later joined by McIntyre and Hussey. The macabre decision to unearth the bodies from The Haunty and move them to the Hallet Street site was made by Bulger because Nee's brother sold the house.

Now they were getting dug up again—this time by authorities.

Another Bulger death pit would be unearthed later that year. By this time, his brother Billy had retired from politics and was serving as president of the University of Massachusetts, earning more than $200,000 per year. Billy's crowning achievement as president was securing the first debate of the 2000 presidential election between Texas governor George W. Bush and Vice President Al Gore for the UMass Boston campus. Just so happens, while the candidates were taking the stage, excavation crews were digging for more Bulger victims nearby.

"The victims include strangers who happened to be in the wrong place, longtime criminal associates, friends and others," said US Attorney Donald Stern at the time.

12

Whitey's well-crafted persona as a gentleman gangster and the Robin Hood of South Boston was virtually shattered once the city's newspapers and television stations described his death pits in gruesome detail. As the facts came to light, investigators continued forensic work day and night on Hallet Street, utilizing sifting screens, spoons, and small tools under yellow-and-white-striped tents to keep the burial ground out of sight.

The unearthed bodies ended any doubt about Bulger's murderous ways and ran counter to the image of Whitey that many people, especially those in Southie, had fixed in their minds. Before he went on the run, Bulger was spotted handing out turkeys to needy families in the projects on Thanksgiving. He sent

money to the canteen accounts of jailed Southie prisoners. He donated to youth sports programs. He literally helped old ladies cross the street.

"You had a husband giving a wife a hard time, that's the stuff you went to him for," said then–City Councilor Peggy Davis-Mullen, a South Boston native who represented the district. "Even growing up, there was this dichotomy. You knew that he was a guy that was involved in organized crime, but you also had—I've got to be honest with you—regard for the man. I don't know what he did when he was doing his business, whatever his business was, but I know that he was a guy on the street and that he was good to people that were poor."

This myth was even perpetuated by the local media, especially longtime *Boston Globe* columnist Mike Barnicle, now a high-paid talking head on MSNBC's popular *Morning Joe* program. After Whitey had scammed his way to the lottery jackpot in 1991, Barnicle insisted that he had won it fair and square and told his readers so.

"So, lay off Jimmy Bulger. For the first time in his life, he got lucky, legitimately, and won the lottery," Barnicle wrote at the time. "Knowing him, he probably already handed out money to St. Augustine's, figuring that when he goes—and the odds on that are

better than winning Mass Millions—there will be some people left behind who will say, 'Not a bad guy.'"

While he still had friendly columnists in his back pocket, the burial ground's discovery finally provided incontrovertible evidence of what an evil, murderous man Whitey Bulger truly was.

One person who knew the real Whitey Bulger was John Connolly, and now the former FBI agent found himself in handcuffs. He was arrested just before Christmas 1999 at his home in Wakefield, Massachusetts. Connolly was recovering from the flu when agents yanked him out of his stately colonial home and escorted him across his well-manicured lawn and into an FBI vehicle. Connolly, who wore expensive suits and $100 haircuts, was sick and disheveled on this day. His hair was a mess and he was dressed in a jogging suit. He looked like any other mobbed-up thug.

Charlie Gianturco and others had been chasing Connolly for some time and they finally got the break they needed when Frank Salemme, the cagey head of the Boston Mafia, testified that it was Connolly who had tipped him and Whitey off to the impending indictments years earlier, allowing them to escape.

Connolly was soon out on bail and was called a scapegoat by his attorney. He also received a phone call from Billy Bulger, who later told a federal grand jury

that he was "just expressing interest in his situation and giving him a call to tell him that I still have confidence in him."

Gianturco was elated by Connolly's arrest, but he soon got pulled down and nearly drowned in the corrupt agent's wake.

Kevin Weeks, still wheeling and dealing, told a federal judge that Whitey had six FBI agents on his payroll including Connolly, John Morris, and an FBI supervisor named James Ring who received cash and gifts from the gang. He then pointed an accusing finger at Gianturco and his brother Nicky.

Nick Gianturco was Connolly's longtime FBI partner, and he'd been cozy with Bulger since Whitey allegedly warned him that he'd been marked for death by other gangsters. Nick dined with Whitey and even presented him with the Alcatraz belt he still wore proudly around his waist. In return Bulger gave him some expensive crystal stemware, an attaché case, and an Oriental figurine.

"At the time it did not dawn on me that it was something that I probably should not have done," Gianturco said later.

Nick Gianturco had long since retired and like Connolly, found a job in corporate security. But his younger

brother Charlie was still an active agent and presumed guilty by association.

"The Bureau didn't back me," Charlie Gianturco recalls. "They said go down to Washington, you need to get polygraphed."

Charlie passed the lie detector test, but he knew that he was dead in the water when it came to the Whitey Bulger investigation. He asked Barry Mawn, then special agent in charge of the Boston office, whom he had worked with on the FBI's bank robbery squad in New York City, to take his name off the case as case agent but to keep his team intact. Gianturco was ready to jump ship but offered to assist on the Bulger case behind the scenes.

"This was personal to me. My reputation was on the line. I understood Whitey Bulger better than anyone," Gianturco says. "I got deep into his head. He didn't follow the criminal code and would sacrifice anyone and anything to survive. He was a vicious killer of women and yet he depended on a woman to survive. But there were other forces working against me, including some of my so-called *friends* in the Bureau."

Charlie Gianturco went on to work several other cases, including helping nab infamous terrorist Richard Reid, the "Shoe Bomber," and breaking up a human

trafficking ring that included the kidnapping and exploitation of a thirteen-year-old girl.

"I took a beating from feds in Washington who whispered that I was dirty, when in fact they were the dirty ones," Gianturco says with disgust. "Collaring Richard Reid at Logan Airport in Boston was like redemption for me. I had arrested this notorious terrorist and gained information from him that put him behind bars for life."

More satisfying for Charlie Gianturco was saving the thirteen-year-old girl from the gang of sex-traffickers. "I celebrated each birthday with her and was there when she finally graduated high school. She had lost her innocence but we fought hard to get her life back."

While he remained on the outside looking in when it came to the Bulger case, Gianturco routinely called his FBI colleague Roberta Hastings in the Boston office with new information and fresh ideas.

"We all wanted that son of a bitch caught, but none more so than Charlie Gianturco," says Hastings.

13

While his dark secrets were getting dug up from the frozen ground in Boston, Whitey and Catherine were enjoying all the sunshine and warm weather that Southern California had to offer. He was now facing nineteen murder charges back home in addition to the extortion and bribery counts. Stevie Flemmi, his partner in crime, was charged with participating in ten of those slayings.

But Bulger was deep underground now, and the west coast provided him with the perfect place to hide. He'd vacationed there years before with Teresa Stanley, although he didn't mention that to Catherine. Whitey was playing the role of devoted husband now and Greig soaked up all the attention.

After leaving the motel near the O. J. Simpson media

circus, they stayed in Venice Beach, an eclectic artsy community that was plagued by an exploding homeless population with desperate forgotten people huddled in encampments living in tents under murals of rock icons like Jim Morrison and Jerry Garcia. The down-on-their-luck crowd were easy marks for the aging gangster on the run.

Bulger was always looking for new identification cards. Fake IDs were as good as gold to him. While in Venice Beach, he spotted a homeless woman lugging an old suitcase down the street. Whitey and Catherine approached her and offered to buy her a new suitcase at a store nearby. The woman had moved to California decades before in hopes of finding stardom, but now she was living on the streets and in and out of hostels. Bulger pulled out $40 cash to pay for the luggage and then offered the woman another $200. He told her that he and Catherine had moved to California from Canada and they needed some documentation to stay in the country. The homeless woman offered him her Social Security card and another ID in exchange for the money.

Catherine had grown tired of life on the road, bouncing from one motel room to the next. She yearned for somewhere to call home. They found a place to

settle down in nearby Santa Monica. The seaside community cultivated an interesting mix of people, from the Hollywood elite to college students, pensioners, and vacationers, who flocked to its famous pier with its towering Ferris wheel and other amusement rides that glimmered off the Pacific Ocean each night after sunset. The city's name also had a special meaning for Whitey. Living in Southie as a child, he'd attended St. Monica–St. Augustine Church. Now he was living once again under the protection of the patron saint of difficult children.

With the Tom and Helen Baxter names compromised, the couple was now going by Charlie and Carol Gasko. Bulger took the name from a mentally disabled homeless man he'd encountered during one of his walks through town. The homeless guy's name was actually Charles Gaska. Whitey paid him cash for his Social Security card and altered the name slightly to Gasko. Then, he and Catherine placed a $300 cash deposit on a two-bedroom apartment with a balcony overlooking the street at the Princess Eugenia. The rent there was $837 a month.

The twenty-seven-unit building was just a few blocks from the beach. It wasn't a slum, but it was plain-looking and worn. Princess Eugenia's best days

were behind her. The complex had originally housed art students from the J. Paul Getty Museum. There were still some students there now, along with retirees. The place was rent controlled when they first moved in, which was attractive to Whitey and Catherine. Plus, they didn't have to sign their names on a lease, provide any references, or undergo a credit check. The building's management had made it all too easy for the mob boss turned fugitive. After moving in, the couple kept mostly to themselves, which was the way Whitey wanted it.

When he got to Santa Monica, he tried to track down one of his former Alcatraz associates, a bank robber named Frank Hatfield, who'd served six years on the Rock. Hatfield was known for his ability to use printing presses to craft fake checks and identification cards. Bulger searched for Hatfield hoping he could create fake IDs for him and Catherine. He never connected with Hatfield, perhaps not knowing that the man had actually gone straight and become a US park ranger who gave guided tours of Alcatraz.

Whitey got lucky one day while walking through Palisades Park when he struck up a conversation about the weather with a man who appeared to be down on his luck.

"Do you have a driver's license?" Bulger asked.

The man said he had a license from the state of Nevada.

"Do you have any drunk driving charges or points against it?" Bulger pressed.

The man shook his head no.

"I'll give you $200 for it."

"I've got a Social Security card and a Sam's Club card," the man told him.

"I'll give you another $50." Bulger smiled.

He paid the man, stuck the IDs in his pocket, and walked away.

Their first few months living at Princess Eugenia were like a honeymoon. Whitey loved the old-time penny-crushing machines he found in the boardwalk arcade at the Santa Monica Pier. He enjoyed crushing the pennies and giving them to Catherine as little tokens of his affection, once handing her one engraved with the words "I love you."

Together, they would stroll to the Rose Garden at Palisades Park and shop at Barnes & Noble, where Bulger would browse the true crime section looking for books written about him or other mob figures. Once they returned to Third Street, Whitey would remind Catherine that the neighborhood had once been home to one of his favorite comedians, Hollywood legend Stan Laurel. Bulger explained that one of the few luxu-

ries he had enjoyed while behind bars at Alcatraz was watching Laurel & Hardy movies on a screen in the mess hall.

When Catherine would get her hair done at a local salon, a place appropriately called The Haircutters on Wilshire Boulevard, she'd chat with her hairdresser Wendy Farnetti about her husband "Charlie." For her, it was much-needed "girl time."

Greig appeared every two to three weeks wearing a visor to protect her face from the sun while pulling a cart filled with groceries from a nearby Whole Foods. She was no longer coloring her hair, which had turned white like Bulger's. Catherine kept it short in the front, long on the sides, and shaggy in the back. It was a bit punkish, and she resembled some aging 1980s rocker.

Catherine told Farnetti that her husband suffered from prostate problems and other ailments.

The hairdresser noticed that Catherine, or "Carol," spoke with a Boston accent and surprisingly, Greig told her that she was originally from Massachusetts. She also seemed to be always stressed out. Farnetti never saw her client's beau and began to jokingly refer to him as Carol's fictional husband.

Despite occasional forays out in the bright sunshine, Bulger became a virtual shut-in while his girlfriend hungered for contact with the outside world.

"Why don't you bring him in so I can cut his hair?" Farnetti asked.

"No, he doesn't go out for a haircut," she replied. "He's bald and just does a buzz on his hair."

Farnetti offered Carol her own tale of woe and confided to her that she was a "bum magnet" when it came to men.

The two had much in common.

"I like the bad boys," Catherine confided to the hair stylist. "I knew he was a bad boy when I married him, that's what attracted me to him. But he's older and has mellowed out now."

There was once a gap between visits to the beauty parlor that lasted over a month, and Farnetti was concerned until suddenly Catherine reappeared one day. Her hair was a mess and she acted distraught and nervous. Farnetti believed that her client had been pulling her own hair out because of some kind of stress.

"What's wrong?" the hairdresser asked.

"You don't know, you just don't even know," Greig replied.

Farnetti thought it was best to not pry further and just left it alone.

Catherine also struck up a friendship with their elderly neighbor Catalina Schlank after bumping into her

one day. Catalina had been living in the United States since emigrating from Argentina in 1963.

"When she saw that I was trying to get my newspaper from the front entranceway, she said, 'Don't do that, I will pick it up for you,'" Schlank remembers.

Whitey and Catherine didn't own a car, so she'd wake up every day at 6 a.m. and push a shopping cart eight blocks to the nearest market for food and other supplies. Greig would also walk to Pavilion's Place at the corner of Montana and Ninth Street or over to the farmer's market on Arizona and Third Street. Whitey never came downstairs to help her haul the groceries. Schlank thought it was unusual for the couple not to have a car, especially in California.

"I thought they just had a big accident and maybe had their driver's licenses taken away," she says.

When Greig picked up Catalina's newspaper each morning, she'd place a piece of fruit or another food item on top. The elderly neighbor wanted to return the favor, but Catherine would always smile and wave her off. Still, Schlank would place sweets and chocolates, perfumed soaps, and mango slices outside their front door.

"She felt that it was important to give something to me, and not to receive it," Schlank says. Catherine sent

their elderly neighbor cards for each major holiday and showered her with thank-you notes.

Good morning Catalina, thank you for the "yummy" surprise. We are saving it for dessert. I know you appreciate these "neighborly gestures," please no need for gifts. My gift—I love seeing your plants again on the balcony!!!

Whitey did show some kindness to Catalina when the woman received a visit from a relative from Argentina.

"My niece arrived and I went to pick her up at the airport. I drove her to my building and we were unloading in the carport," she recalls. "He [Bulger] came up and offered to take the suitcases to my apartment and he did."

Schlank says that Bulger had a nice, sweet face and that she never knew he was bald because he always wore a hat with the brim down.

Greig continued to shower Catalina with kind notes and greeting cards celebrating Passover and other religious holidays. Nearly every card ended with the words, *If we (Charlie and me) can ever lend a hand or do an errand—just give this neighbor a call. Thank you again, Carol and Charlie Gasko (303).*

Greig always included their home phone number.

If Whitey wanted to call his family back home, he certainly wouldn't use his landline. Instead, he and Catherine would buy a car with cash. They'd choose something dependable but not flashy and take off for a few weeks at a time, making their way from Santa Monica to Detroit, Michigan, some 2,297 miles away. Bulger and Catherine wouldn't drive straight there. Instead, he'd take a winding path through several states, staying at motels and buying food and gas with cash. Once he made it to Detroit, he'd leave his girlfriend and purchase a throwaway phone to call his brother Billy back in Boston.

Whitey later said that he strategically chose Michigan in an attempt to confuse any listening ears—especially the FBI if they were tracing the call. The crafty gangster said that he wanted the feds to believe that he and Catherine were living in Canada, not California, and coming down to Detroit to make phone calls to his family.

Catherine Greig wasn't as careful. Once back in Santa Monica, she'd sneak out to call her sister Margaret McCusker to check on life back home and the well-being of Nikki and Gigi, the French poodles she missed so much.

"She called me from California," McCusker says. "We probably talked once a month or every two

months. We'd also talk about everyday things like the weather and such. I knew they were in Santa Monica. We didn't talk about her coming home. That was her business but I wasn't concerned about her being on the run with him. He'd always been very kind."

Despite the regular conversations, McCusker never told anyone where her sister and her boyfriend—the nation's most wanted fugitive—were living.

14

Like most every other American, Whitey Bulger was glued to the television set watching in horror as the World Trade Center towers collapsed into themselves on September 11, 2001. Despite being a gangster and a cold-blooded killer, Bulger also considered himself a patriot and a proud veteran. Making the tragedy feel even more personal to him, one of the doomed flights, American Airlines Flight 11, had taken off from Boston's Logan Airport before crashing into the World Trade Center's North Tower.

The attacks on 9/11 also impacted his life as a fugitive in two important ways.

With the murders of nearly three thousand Americans in Lower Manhattan, the Pentagon, and a field in Shanksville, Pennsylvania, at the hands of Islamic ter-

rorists, the FBI would need to shift much of its focus to fighting the War on Terror. This meant that resources being used to track him and Catherine down would need to be shifted elsewhere.

Michael Sullivan, a Republican former district attorney in southeastern Massachusetts, was awaiting confirmation from the US Senate to become the next US attorney in Boston on the day the planes struck the towers. Sullivan grew up on the South Shore of Massachusetts and knew the toll that the Winter Hill Gang's crimes took on countless lives in Boston and neighboring communities. After being appointed by President George W. Bush, he read books on Whitey to get up to speed as he prepared to lead the global manhunt. After September 11, 2001, he was quickly confirmed and his mission, like that of all federal prosecutors, drastically changed, especially since two of the hijacked planes came out of Boston.

"Leading up to my appointment, not once did national security or terrorism come up as a priority interest for the US Attorney's office in Boston," Sullivan recalled. "After 9/11, that was the only priority of the Department of Justice. All your resources should be put against national security, anti-terrorism.

"Still, in the back of your mind, you're saying there

are other things that are important as well and one of them was the Bulger investigation," he added.

While the infamous terror attacks took much of the heat off Bulger, the ensuing security crackdown impacted him too. Now, he was stuck in the United States. Any dreams of taking off to Europe or South America were gone. Airport security was tightened to the highest levels in American history and there was no way that his phony IDs would pass inspection.

Following 9/11, terror mastermind Osama bin Laden, a man whose name had been unfamiliar to most people, had now catapulted to the top of the FBI's list of Most Wanted Fugitives, right above Whitey.

The FBI was offering a $250,000 reward for Bulger's capture. His case had been profiled several times on *America's Most Wanted*, the popular Fox television show hosted by John Walsh. After one broadcast, the FBI received a tip from Fountain Valley, California, a city in greater Los Angeles whose motto is simply "A Nice Place to Live." Actress Michelle Pfeiffer graduated from high school there before going on to play the girlfriend of fictional Miami mob kingpin Tony Montana in the Al Pacino flick *Scarface*.

Catherine Greig, the girlfriend of a real mob kingpin, had almost blown their cover while getting her hair

colored at a Vietnamese-owned salon called Fountain Hair & Nails, where the prices were cheap. Catherine showed up with her own blond hair dye and apologized to the owner that she was pressed for time, as her husband was waiting outside with their car idling. The owner later described Greig as pretty and petite, with lovely blue eyes.

Catherine paid $16 cash for a coloring plus a healthy tip. She thanked the owner with a smile and walked out the door toward Whitey's car. Catherine climbed in and they disappeared.

After seeing Bulger's story on television, a salon customer called the tip line saying that she recognized him as the man who was watching Catherine closely from his car parked right outside the store.

Years later, there was suspicion that Bulger could have been involved in a string of bank robberies in Orange County and as far south as San Diego. The robber, known as the "Geezer Bandit," sported a baseball cap and dark sunglasses, which had become a Bulger trademark. The thief hit fourteen banks in all and routinely handed a note to the tellers that read *Give me $50,000 or I will murder you.*

The "Geezer Bandit" was never caught, but it wasn't Whitey Bulger. He was shorter than the man identified as the bank robber. Catherine had done a marvelous job

keeping her man out of trouble while on the run, despite his natural instincts and urges to create mayhem.

When occasionally traveling by car, Whitey and Catherine hit the casinos in Las Vegas and Reno, Nevada, once again to wash their money. Bulger would use some of the cash to stockpile weapons from local gun shows. He browsed tables at the Big Reno Gun Show and at the Crossroads of the West Gun Show in Las Vegas under signs reading *Got Ammo?* and *Buy—Sell—Trade*, always looking to add to his growing arsenal. As one of America's most wanted fugitives, Bulger shopped with little fear of getting caught, thanks to a gaping loophole in federal law that allowed him to buy weapons and ammunition from private sellers without showing any identification or submitting to a background check. Unlike sellers at a gun store, private vendors at gun shows didn't even need to record the sale. Bulger paid cash, carried the weapons and ammo to his car, and drove away without peeking over his shoulder.

With FBI agent Charlie Gianturco off the case and John Gamel in retirement, coupled with the focus on terrorism, many people, including members of the media, thought that the FBI was spinning its wheels and had no real intention of catching Whitey Bulger.

They criticized the Bureau for, among other things, taking fifteen months to question Teresa Stanley after his escape and even longer to interview John Connolly.

"They were sniffing for footprints that were 15 months old with Teresa Stanley. That's a tangible example of a fugitive hunt that really wasn't real," argues Jonathan Wells, a former *60 Minutes* producer who also had headed the *Boston Herald*'s investigative team for years and led the paper's aggressive Bulger coverage. "John Connolly and by extension Whitey Bulger still had people in the Bureau, in the Boston office, who believed this was ridiculous, that they were hanging this longtime informant out to dry and indicting him. And now they're going to chase after him? Because they believed Whitey did his service and he was one of them. He was an Irish guy and the whole office back then was all Irish."

Conspiracy theorists were convinced the FBI was hiding Bulger, perhaps on a military base somewhere, to prevent him from revealing more of their dirty secrets. Others even suggested Whitey had been murdered— taken out by a team of government assassins.

The reality was far less nefarious: there just weren't the same resources being devoted to the hunt the longer it dragged on. For all that the FBI had gotten close over the years, the pursuit of Bulger had never

relented. Even after the Boston office became the epicenter of one of the largest corruption investigations in FBI history, there were still agents working hard to try to catch Whitey. But as bad as the stain on the Boston office was, perhaps nothing changed the search for Bulger more than 9/11.

By the mid-2000s, both the FBI and Massachusetts State Police had little to show for their efforts and had spent millions of dollars chasing down leads across the globe in places like Piccadilly Circus in London and later in Manchester, England. It was a cushy gig for agents working on the Bulger Task Force.

While the Bureau was focused on enforcing President George W. Bush's Patriot Act to combat terrorism after 9/11, the Bulger Task Force operated under the radar, jetting around the world to picture-postcard locales in Britain, Ireland, France, and Italy with little oversight. The notion that agents assigned to hunt down Whitey were out seeing the world on the Bureau's dime gnawed at many law enforcement officers who believed that more attention should have been paid to Bulger sightings around the United States.

15

I f the feds couldn't find Whitey and Catherine, they could still make life hard on their loved ones.

Margaret McCusker and her friend Kathleen McDonough were indicted for lying to a grand jury investigating the case about receiving calls from Catherine. Both pleaded guilty and were sentenced to six months' house arrest and fined $2,000.

According to court testimony, McCusker and McDonough would go to the home of McDonough's aunt to make or receive calls from Catherine. When the aunt asked why they needed to call from her home, the women replied, "You never know who's listening."

One topic that Margaret tried to stay away from during the calls was how Catherine's prized poodles were doing. McCusker, who was grieving the death of

her only son from suicide, had made a strange decision to euthanize her sister's beloved dogs Nikki and Gigi.

She never told Catherine. Greig heard the news from someone else and was devastated.

"Their relationship was always dysfunctional at best," says FBI agent Mike Carazza. "There was a love-hate thing going on between Catherine and Margaret and this is an example of that."

Jackie Bulger was also indicted for lying to the grand jury about his communications with his brother and about paying the rent for Whitey's safe deposit box in Clearwater, Florida. His lawyer said that Jackie had made a mistake, but that he only lied out of "brotherly concern."

The family loyalty excuse was dismissed and a federal judge sentenced Jackie to six months in federal prison, as his family members, including Billy Bulger, looked on.

Billy Bulger avoided charges like those faced by his relatives, but he was put on the hot seat before Congress when he was ordered to testify in a sweeping congressional probe of the FBI's use of informants, namely his brother.

On June 19, 2003, wearing a dark suit and powder-blue tie, he testified before the House Committee on

Government Reform on live TV. This was Billy's second appearance before the committee. The first time around, he pleaded the Fifth and refused to answer any questions.

Lawmakers were investigating the FBI's decades-long misuse of informants starting with another Boston-area gangster, Joe "The Animal" Barboza, who had served as a guinea pig for the Bureau's Top Echelon Informant program. The program began in the 1960s and was essentially created by infamous FBI director J. Edgar Hoover and his longtime nemesis, US Attorney General Bobby Kennedy, in a campaign to bring down the Italian Mafia.

Barboza was recruited to rat for the FBI by Boston agents Paul Rico, who had collared Whitey Bulger for a bank job back in the 1950s, and his partner Dennis Condon. The agents convinced Barboza, a notorious hit man who had collected as many as twenty-six mob pelts, to lie on the stand in three criminal trials against the most powerful gangsters in New England, including La Cosa Nostra boss Raymond Patriarca of Providence and Gennaro "Jerry" Anguilo of Boston's North End. Barboza was hidden by the FBI and the US Marshals Service on Thacher Island off the coast of picturesque Rockport, Massachusetts. There, "The Animal" practiced his testimony while the Mafia did

everything in its power to kill him, including sending a hit squad to the island by boat in hopes of blowing Barboza's head off with sniper rifles. Ultimately, Barboza's testimony put Patriarca and others behind bars, including four men framed for the murder of a gangster named Edward "Teddy" Deegan, which had actually been carried out by Barboza and Stevie Flemmi's brother Vincent "Jimmy the Bear" Flemmi, a true psychopath. J. Edgar Hoover had strong evidence that Barboza was lying at the time but still allowed him to send the men, many of whom were noted gangsters, to jail for life. Some of the men died in prison while two others, Joe Salvati and Peter Limone, were eventually freed after spending thirty years behind bars. The case would lead to the biggest settlement in the history of the United States Justice Department as a federal judge ordered the government to pay $101 million to the families of the wrongly accused.

The House committee heard from the innocent men and their families and also from Paul Rico, now retired from the FBI. Rico represented all that was wrong with the Boston office of the FBI, so perhaps it wasn't surprising that he and his partner Condon recruited Stevie Flemmi as an informant. It was Rico and Condon who groomed a young FBI agent from Southie named John Connolly to cozy up to Whitey Bulger. Rico would

later face murder and conspiracy charges for his role in one of Whitey's most brazen hits, the assassination of millionaire businessman Roger Wheeler in Tulsa, Oklahoma. Rico died in the hospital before he could be brought to trial.

After Rico's testimony it was Billy Bulger's turn. As Bulger, president of the University of Massachusetts, took his seat behind a microphone, committee chairman Tom Davis of Virginia called the hearing to order.

"We are here today to receive testimony from William Bulger," he announced. "James 'Whitey' Bulger was an informant for the FBI in Boston. Whitey Bulger was repeatedly able to avoid arrest due to information illegally leaked to him by his FBI handler John Connolly . . . This hearing will focus on whether the relationship between John Connolly and Whitey Bulger benefited Whitey Bulger's brother William Bulger while he was a high-ranking elected official in Massachusetts."

Being granted immunity by the committee, Billy Bulger was sworn in and then read from a prepared statement.

"Please allow me to speak plainly, I do not know where my brother is," Billy claimed. "I do not know where he has been over the past eight years. I have not

aided James Bulger in any way while he was a fugitive. Do I possess information that could lead to my brother's arrest? The honest answer is no!"

The hearing was carried live on C-SPAN and barrooms across Southie were packed as patrons sipped from pints of Guinness, glued to the television screens hung over the beer taps as if it were the fourth quarter of a close New England Patriots game.

Meanwhile, in apartment 303 at the Princess Eugenia, Whitey and Catherine watched intently as Billy, once the most powerful politician in Boston, squirmed on the national stage.

Under oath, Billy claimed to have had just one telephone conversation with Whitey back in 1995 and said that after that, he was "unable to penetrate the secretive life" of his older brother. He also criticized the FBI's leaking of information about Whitey's status as an informant to the *Boston Globe*.

"I believed that the FBI wanted James Bulger killed," Billy told the panel. ". . . I know my brother stands accused of many things, serious crimes, brutal crimes. I do still live in the hope that the worst charges against him will prove groundless."

When questioned by lawmakers, including Congressman Steve Lynch of South Boston and Massachusetts representative Marty Meehan, who would go on

to become president of UMass, Billy admitted that he had maintained a close friendship with Connolly but denied any real relationship with Kevin Weeks and others, including corrupt former state trooper Richard Schneiderhan.

Another Massachusetts congressman then asked Billy if he'd been interviewed by the FBI before being compelled by a grand jury investigating the case.

"If you have a memory, were you interviewed by the FBI prior to 2001 as to the whereabouts of your fugitive brother?" asked Representative William Delahunt.

"I don't believe I was," Billy replied.

"Were you not?" Delahunt stressed again.

"I don't think I was," Billy repeated.

He later claimed that the first direct effort by the FBI to question him about Whitey came eight years after his brother went on the lam.

Congressman Chris Shays of Connecticut later jumped in on the same topic.

"I'm asking you whether you gave a signal to the FBI that you did not want to answer their questions, and that they should not ask you and that they should leave," Shays pressed.

"I don't recall meeting the FBI. I really don't recall it."

"Did the FBI ever come to your offices?"

"No, I don't think so."

Right there, federal investigators suspected Billy Bulger was lying before Congress. Shortly after Billy's hours-long testimony, someone from the Bureau reached out to John Gamel, now retired, as he was about to go on a fishing trip.

"Did you ever contact Billy Bulger?" the investigator asked.

"Of course, I went to his office myself," Gamel replied. "He later called me and said he refused to help us find Whitey. He slammed the phone down on me. I wrote up a 302 about it right after. It's gotta be still there in the files."

An FD-302 form is used by FBI agents to summarize interviews they conduct while working a case. The Bureau went digging for the 302 regarding Gamel's conversation with Billy Bulger from early 1995 and found it. The FBI wanted to use this piece of evidence to bring formal perjury charges against the university president, but for some mysterious reason, those actions were not taken by the US Attorney's Office.

Billy's lawyer argued that his client didn't perjure himself before Congress. "He [Bulger] offered his memory. He reserved the notion that his memory might not be perfect," Attorney Tom Kiley insisted.

"The truth is, memories do change and memories do fail over eight years."

Still, Billy Bulger wasn't out of the woods yet. He'd been appointed president of UMass in 1996, nearly a year after Whitey had gone on the run, with support from then-Governor William Weld. Billy's annual salary was a whopping $357,000.

Mitt Romney now sat in the corner office of the Massachusetts Statehouse and Billy's testimony was nothing short of an embarrassment for Romney, who was eyeing a run for president of the United States. Romney, the future Republican presidential nominee, launched an immediate campaign to oust Billy from UMass.

"The shadow over the university is real and . . . the interests of the university are being harmed," Romney told the press.

Romney exerted pressure on the UMass Board of Trustees, who then applied their own pressure on Billy.

Less than two months later, Whitey's brother resigned from his prestigious post. On his way out the door, Billy blasted Mitt Romney for targeting him with "a calculated political assault."

The congressional hearing had resulted in a death blow to Billy's reputation and his career in public life.

After his resignation, he disappeared from view, only to be comforted by a pension that would pay him more than $200,000 each year for the rest of his life.

Meanwhile, the hunt for his fugitive brother continued.

16

San Diego sheriff's deputy Rich Eaton knew the Whitey Bulger story well. A native of Hyannis, Massachusetts, Eaton grew up on Cape Cod surrounded by news stories and neighborhood tales that mythologized the Irish mobster, who had vacationed in Provincetown at the tip of the Cape in years past.

Hollywood was first attracted to the dark world of Whitey Bulger in the early 2000s when acclaimed director Martin Scorsese decided to fictionalize the crime boss's exploits in the Oscar-winning film *The Departed,* starring Jack Nicholson, Leonardo DiCaprio, and Boston native Matt Damon, who'd put Southie on the Tinsel Town map with his own Oscar-winning effort *Good Will Hunting.* Like that movie, *The Departed* was filmed on location in Boston, on the same

neighborhood streets that Bulger had once controlled in his death grip.

Rich Eaton was living in San Diego at the time and working as a detective in the North County Regional Gang Task Force. His job brought him in close contact with killers from the Mexican cartels. In early October 2006, Eaton found himself testifying in a drug trial at the federal courthouse. The judge had called for an extended break, which gave the detective and his partner three hours of free time.

"Hey, *The Departed* just opened," Eaton's partner James Mancuso told him. "First showing is at eleven. We should go check it out."

"It'd be good to see if Scorsese gets the Boston mob story right," Eaton responded as the two walked across the street to a multiplex cinema adjacent to a galleria mall called Horton Plaza.

They purchased their movie tickets and entered the theater, which was surprisingly crowded for a weekday.

Eaton dug into a bucket of popcorn and briefly scanned the crowd before the lights dimmed. His eyes immediately focused on a man sitting alone four rows away. The man looked to be in his seventies. He was wearing a black floppy bucket hat and a neatly trimmed white beard covered his jawline.

Is that Whitey fucking Bulger? Nah, that's absurd,

he thought to himself. *Who would imagine that Whitey would be sitting in this theater with me watching Jack Nicholson act out his life story?*

Yet as the film ran, Eaton paid little attention to the screen and instead studied the man just a few rows away.

"I could see him reacting viscerally to Nicholson's portrayal," Eaton says, sharing his full story exclusively with the authors. "He was laughing at certain moments, shaking his head in disagreement at other times. My weird hunch suddenly became very real to me."

As the screening ended, Eaton slipped out of the theater ahead of his partner and waited for the mysterious older man to walk out. Several matinee-goers filed past him until the older man finally came into view. He was wearing cargo shorts, New Balance sneakers, and an oversized polo shirt that could not hide a peculiar bulge.

He's carrying, Eaton thought to himself.

As the older man walked by, Eaton caught his stare. The man looked at him menacingly with his pale blue eyes before quickly looking away, and the detective was convinced.

"I had just found Whitey Bulger," he recalls.

Eaton felt for his pistol, which was normally strapped to his ankle, and remembered it was not there. He'd

had to turn over his service weapon and his handcuffs earlier that morning as he entered the federal courthouse for trial. He forgot to retrieve them at the break.

Fuck. He's armed and very dangerous, the detective reminded himself. There was no way he could approach the fugitive without a gun to protect himself.

Eaton watched Bulger walk out the door and kept a safe distance as he monitored the mobster's next move. The detective saw Whitey walk toward an oncoming Blue Line trolley that was headed for San Ysidro, California, on the border with Mexico.

"That made sense to me," Eaton recalls. "We'd all heard that Bulger might be living in or close to Mexico, where he could get cheap heart medication. I watched him get on the train and then hightailed it back to the courthouse to grab my gun and cuffs."

Once armed, Eaton and his partner jumped into a police car and raced to San Ysidro in hopes of beating the train. With one hand on the steering wheel, Eaton fished for his cell phone and dialed the number for the San Diego office of the FBI.

"We have the fugitive James 'Whitey' Bulger on a southbound trolley headed for the Mexican border," Eaton told the FBI officer assigned to the fugitive squad. "We will meet the train and are in need of assistance for his apprehension."

The detective arrived at the station several minutes later and ahead of the train. Eaton was shocked to see that he and his partner were the only law enforcement agents on scene. The FBI was nowhere in sight.

"We saw the train pull in and braced ourselves for what was to come," Eaton recalls. "We didn't believe that Bulger would be taken without a fight and we feared that a shootout could lead to innocent people getting killed."

The detectives watched as all the passengers stepped off the train at what was the last stop on the line, but James "Whitey" Bulger never appeared.

"Fuck, he got off early and gave us the slip," Detective Mancuso told Eaton.

"Yup. He's a crafty bastard," Eaton replied. "But he couldn't have gone too far."

Eaton called the FBI once more and was connected with the agent in charge of all Whitey Bulger sightings in Southern California.

"That's when I realized the fix was in," Eaton says. "This agent didn't have a clue. She didn't know what Bulger looked like, didn't have any real understanding about the case, and this was one of the agents that the FBI had placed in charge of finding Whitey Bulger on the west coast. She couldn't solve a murder if it happened in front of her."

Detective Eaton recognized the problem immediately. He believes that the old guard of the FBI did not want Bulger captured, fearing that the fugitive mob boss had more secrets to reveal and more careers to ruin regarding his long-standing relationship with the Bureau, while the younger agents had no idea who Whitey was, even though he was now the Bureau's number-two-ranked fugitive behind Osama bin Laden.

"Corruption and sheer incompetence allowed this killer to remain on the run," Eaton contends.

Eaton continued to hunt for Bulger in San Diego, establishing patrols on the beaches of Coronado Island and anywhere else an elderly couple could blend in, but just like the elusive character Keyser Söze from the movie *The Usual Suspects*—poof . . . he was gone.

Eaton then pulled the surveillance video from Horton Plaza, which showed an elderly man fitting Bulger's description riding an escalator. He immediately called his friend Danny Simmons, a Boston native now working as a DEA agent in San Diego. Simmons forwarded the clip to fellow DEA agent Dan Doherty back in Boston. Doherty promised to run the tape by Kevin Weeks.

"Weeks tends to think not," Doherty told Simmons in a phone call. "He said that Whitey was a germophobe and he's touching the handrails of the escala-

tor in the video. Plus the guy has cargo shorts on and Whitey only wore long pants."

"Remember, Whitey's on the run," Simmons countered. "You're gonna mix it up a little bit when you're on the run. You'll wear a hat when you wouldn't have, wear shorts when you wouldn't have."

Simmons believes that Eaton had found his man. "Right time and right place for Richie, yeah. Unfortunately he couldn't get his hands on him. That was more than likely him [Bulger] despite what Kevin Weeks has to say."

An FBI agent who worked closely with Eaton in San Diego is also confident that he'd spotted the fugitive crime boss. The agent is still active with the Bureau and asked us not to use his name for this book.

"Over the years, there were allegations that Bulger was seen in San Diego years before and they were investigated very hard, but deemed not to be credible," the agent says. The FBI had interviewed Bulger look-alikes walking the beach or at their homes and met with dead end after dead end.

"But it was different here," the agent points out. "I had worked previously with Rich Eaton and he had identified a homicide fugitive that I had that I would not have been able to identify myself. We even knew where the guy was, but he looked completely different

and Rich identified him within a fraction of a second correctly. Rich is so sharp and such a good detective that if he's said he'd just seen Jesus, I would have believed it."

Eaton called the agent immediately and informed him of the sighting. The agent then contacted the FBI's organized crime squad and he said, "This is the real thing."

The agent provided the contact information for Eaton, but those assigned to the case never bothered to reach out to the detective directly about this highly promising lead.

"I can't justify that. The first thing that I would have done is call the detective," the agent says. "In any case, you need to interview the source and that wasn't done here. You don't interview a detective like Rich with his creds. Are you kidding me?"

The agent doesn't believe that the FBI purposely avoided following up on Eaton's tip in an attempt to keep Whitey out in the cold. Instead, the agent says that colleagues in the Bureau just weren't competent enough at that point to track him and Catherine down successfully.

"The other agents out here didn't understand the background of the case or the bigger picture here."

17

The game finally changed when Noreen Gleason took over the case in February 2008. There would be no more missed opportunities or lack of effort in following up credible leads. Indeed, this was a unit designed with one purpose in mind: catching Whitey Bulger. Gleason provided much-needed leadership to the task force and she had the full support of her boss Warren Bamford, who allowed her to bring in valuable resources from outside the Boston FBI office.

Gleason now had Agent Tommy MacDonald on the case, while she worked hard to deconstruct the Bulger mythology and paint for the public an accurate portrait of an insidious criminal.

When the FBI announced that it was increasing the reward for Whitey's capture from $1 million to $2 mil-

lion on the gangster's seventy-ninth birthday in 2008, Gleason used that opportunity to speak directly to those who still thought Whitey was a man of honor.

During a press conference, Gleason went off script and announced publicly for the first time that the FBI had uncovered evidence that Bulger was not just a killer, but a pedophile.

"He preyed on innocent girls, as young as twelve years old," Gleason told reporters. "These are sad, troubling, and disturbing stories that most people have not been privy to . . . [Bulger] is a truly deadly crime figure, not a folk-hero. The gravity of Mr. Bulger's crimes is egregious and has not been diminished over time."

The child molester rumors had been around for years, but had first gone public in 2001 when a low-level former Bulger associate named Eddie MacKenzie claimed that members of the Winter Hill Gang regularly preyed on underage girls—including some from a Southie parochial school. Girls were lured to MacKenzie's gym—nicknamed "The Dog Room"—where they were secretly watched and videotaped having sex through a two-way mirror. Whitey was a regular participant in the sex romps and was also known to have trysts with underage girls at Triple O's.

Gleason knew that she was potentially digging a hole

for herself, as her comments were not part of the official statement that had been approved by the US Attorney's Office.

"I got so emotional about this stuff because Southie thought he was a hero," she recalls. "This guy [Bulger] was the biggest piece of crap on so many levels."

US Attorney Michael J. Sullivan went wild. He'd been caught completely off guard by Gleason's comments and immediately called her boss Warren Bamford, screaming.

"We could press charges against her for saying that," Sullivan yelled. "He's not charged with being a pedophile."

Gleason's frustration with the US Attorney's Office had reached its peak. She'd long held the belief that federal prosecutors were working against the FBI and blamed them for the malaise that had nearly derailed the manhunt for Bulger.

"When case agents brought strong prosecutorial cases to the US Attorney's office, they were turned down," Gleason claims. "The office wasn't eager to work with the Bureau. That was really frustrating for a lot of people in the Boston office. I'd never experienced that before. You could see it was very deflating to the agents. And now they were threatening to come after me."

Gleason also blamed federal prosecutors for dropping the ball on pursuing charges against Billy Bulger for obstruction of justice. Under her leadership, the task force learned years later that Whitey had been communicating with Billy by telephone. According to Tommy Mac, he'd get word to a neighbor and order them to bump into Billy on the street in Southie and tell him to be at their house at a specific time, usually in the afternoon, because that was when Whitey would call that house.

"We had a strong case against Billy," Gleason says. "We knew he'd been in contact with his brother. It made me wild. The US Attorney was as complicit as anyone in not finding Whitey. How do you not hold Billy accountable and why are you making the Boston FBI office pay for our father's sins regarding John Connolly? It made me question where their loyalties lie."

Billy has always denied helping his brother while he was on the run, but he eventually confirmed that he did in fact take at least one call from him while he was a fugitive. It strains credulity, given how close the brothers were, their relationship with Connolly, and how their lives intertwined, that Billy Bulger did not stay in contact with Whitey during his years on the run. Gleason was surprised to see that her team was losing support from some within the FBI family, most notably retired

agent John Gamel. She'd seen him interviewed on television saying that he didn't think Bulger would ever be caught.

"I was livid, I got to the office and said, 'Gimme that guy's number. I gotta call him,'" Gleason remembers. "I called Gamel and laid him out. I said, 'Now you've become part of the problem we're facing. How dare you?'"

Gamel met with Gleason in her office and the two finally cleared the air.

"You gotta stay positive," she stressed. "You can't be focused on old history. This is a new day."

Gleason wasn't paying lip service to this problem. The new day meant a new stable of agents, including Tommy Mac and another manhunter Gleason had appointed to the team, Special Agent Phil Torsney.

Torsney was working out of the FBI office in Cleveland at the time. He'd been running the Fugitive Task Force there for nearly two decades.

"I've always been an adrenaline guy," he says. "I'm not an accountant; I'm not a foreign language guy. I'm just an FBI cop; I chased people for a living. Finding guys and bringing them in, I loved the work."

Before working the Bulger case, Torsney's most high-profile fugitive pursuit involved an Ohio doctor who'd killed his wife by feeding her calcium cap-

sules that he'd emptied and refilled with hand-crushed cyanide. The doctor's name was Yazeed Essa. He'd vanished in 2005 shortly after being questioned by police. He had a license to practice medicine, but Essa was a stupid criminal. When mourners gathered at his home immediately after his wife's death, the doctor tossed back shots of liquor and joked with his buddies that at least he wouldn't have to sneak other women into their house anymore. Using fake travel documents, Essa made his way to Lebanon, leaving the couple's young children behind. Working with INTERPOL, Phil Torsney created a flier with Essa's photo, his fingerprints, and details of the murder. That document was then translated into several languages and sent to law enforcement agencies across the globe. But since Lebanon had no extradition treaty with the United States, the accused killer was untouchable while living in Beirut. Torsney and his partners at INTERPOL kept track of the doctor's movements and waited for their break. Fortunately for the manhunters, Essa had wanderlust and decided to book a trip to the island of Cyprus. That's when Torsney and the team sprung into action, arresting the doctor the moment he stepped off the plane. Yazeed Essa would eventually be brought back to Ohio to face charges. He was tried for the murder of his wife and sentenced to life in prison.

When Torsney got the offer to join the Bulger Task Force, he felt that he'd already had a bit of a head start on the case.

"When Whitey was first indicted, I was following him right away," he recalls. "He'd been featured on *America's Most Wanted* and we were getting inundated with look-alike sightings. Any older guy with a baseball cap and sunglasses was fair game and we questioned a lot of them. Noreen Gleason brought me up to Boston because I knew how to work fugitives. I knew there was some bad shit happening there previously with Connolly. At one point, it felt like everybody in the Boston office was corrupt. But when I got there, I found out that wasn't the case at all."

Torsney reported to Boston on October 6, 2009. He checked into a hotel in Charlestown and went for a run. The crisp fall air felt refreshing, opening his lungs and clearing his head for the major task at hand. When he returned to the hotel sweaty but reenergized, he met his new partner, Tommy Mac, in the lobby. They'd spoken on the phone for a few months to familiarize themselves with one another, but they never mentioned where they'd be staying. Both were excited to know they'd be living under one roof, because this was the type of case that would be all consuming. The agents would have to work day and night.

"The Bulger case was like a bird flying around in my head," Tommy Mac recalls. "I'd wake up in the middle of the night and wonder, why am I thinking about this case? We're coming into this case fourteen years after he's been on the run. They'd already made a movie about him with Jack Nicholson, so what the hell are we gonna do?"

Phil Torsney felt the same way. But Noreen Gleason had placed her faith in the agents and together they devised a sound plan.

"We put an emphasis on facial recognition, as the technology had improved vastly and we felt that Whitey wouldn't be able to keep up with it," Torsney explains. "So we're looking to find any and all IDs for either of them. Another big thing was knocking on doors, even if witnesses had already been interviewed four or five times. We also wanted to recommit ourselves to tracking phone calls."

Phil and Tommy Mac were told that they'd be assigned to the Bulger case for three years of temporary duty unless they caught him first.

The clock was running.

They'd barely had time to unpack when the new partners requested a meeting with the US Attorney's Office. Despite a mutual mistrust, the FBI agents understood they'd need cooperation from federal pros-

ecutors, especially in the effort to place taps and trace orders, or pen registers, on the phones of the four people closest to Whitey and Catherine: Billy Bulger, Jackie Bulger, Jean Holland, and Margaret McCusker.

"If I wanted to find out about your life, I'd look at who you talked to on the phone," MacDonald explains. "Those conversations tell us all the little things that may lead to big things. We wanted to have that information on the key Bulger family members who may still be in touch with the fugitives."

Next, Torsney and Tommy Mac went exploring through Whitey's old neighborhood in Southie. The previous investigative team had long given up on knocking on the doors of Whitey's friends and family, but the partners wanted everyone to know that this was a new day and the heat was back on.

They first approached the home of Billy Bulger and asked to speak with the former lawmaker and college president. His wife, Mary, answered the door.

"We're from the FBI and would like to ask your husband a few questions," Phil asked kindly.

Mary Bulger nodded, smiled, and informed the agents that her husband wasn't home. Phil found it odd, as Billy's car was parked in the driveway. "By all accounts, I'd heard that Mary Bulger was a saintly woman," Phil says. "When she said that to us, I'm

thinking to myself, 'She's probably gonna have to go to confession because she just lied to me.'"

The visit to Billy's house prompted a call from his lawyer, Tom Kiley. The attorney left a voice mail for Tommy Mac saying that he represented Billy Bulger and all of his siblings along with their spouses and children. Kiley stressed once again that the Bulger family—the entire Bulger family—would not assist or support the hunt for Whitey.

Tommy Mac shook his head in frustration. "Who the fuck does this guy think he is?" he asked aloud. "Does he represent half of Boston? We're not gonna back down."

The Bulger family's posture was firm and clear. Collectively, they were saying, "Fuck you, FBI."

18

Joey Hipp moved to Santa Monica with his wife in 2007 when she was offered a position in a local law firm. Hipp's brother lived on Third Street and Joey wanted to be nearby, so the couple grabbed the first apartment they saw—which happened to be across the street from the Princess Eugenia.

They moved in with their tiny white dog, a West Highland terrier named Joplin, and as they walked Joplin one afternoon, they were approached by a nice older couple.

"Can we talk to your dog?" the woman asked.

She was with a man who dressed all in white and was impeccably groomed.

"The whole town is filled with rich film industry

people, so I thought he was a retired studio executive," Hipp recalls.

In fact, the young man had just come face-to-face with one of the most wanted men in America.

The older couple patted the dog and Joplin took a quick liking to them. The couple introduced themselves as Charlie and Carol Gasko.

"He shook my hand," Hipp says. "He's one of those guys who looks you right in the eye and tries to break your hand and sees if you break eye contact. I let it go."

"Where are you from?" the old man asked.

"Philly."

"You Irish?"

"Yeah," Hipp replied. That seemed to lighten Charlie's mood. Still, he kept up with the line of questioning. Bulger was making sure their story added up.

"Once he realized that we were just a couple across the street with a white dog, we were okay," Hipp says.

Catherine told him they were both dog lovers but couldn't have a dog of their own. Joe and his wife would see them from time to time on afternoon strolls, and Joplin would strain at his leash and wag his little tail when he knew they were close by.

"Carol and Charlie" always had chewy dog toys to present to Joplin. One day while the couple was playing

with the dog, Hipp reached for his phone and wanted to take a photo for social media.

"Yeah, take a picture of the dog with the toy," Charlie said. He and "Carol" then slipped behind Hipp to make sure they were out of the shot.

Hipp was fascinated by stories about organized crime. His hometown had no shortage of classic real-life mob tales, including the bloody reign of Mafia boss Nicky Scarfo, who ordered more than a dozen gangland hits in the late 1970s and early '80s. He'd devoured mob books like T. J. English's *The Westies*, and he'd even read a book about Whitey Bulger.

"I was aware of who he was," Hipp says. "But I had no idea that it was the guy living across the street from us. Carol was very nice to my wife. She took care of the stray cat up on the corner. There's a hotel across from their building, the cat belonged to the owner, someone that died or left. It was a stray that never left the property. She would feed it and go make sure it was alright."

Joey and his wife walked Joplin each afternoon and they'd normally run into Carol, but eventually there was no sign of her husband.

"I haven't seen Charlie in a while," Hipp asked her one day. "Is he alright?"

"He's got a bit of Alzheimer's and gets scared and doesn't like to come out," she told him.

The last time Hipp saw his sweet, elderly neighbor, he asked her once again about "Charlie."

"He's not well," she said. "But he wants to know how Joplin is doing. Do you have any pictures that I could show him?"

"That's a shame," Hipp replied. "Tell him that I wish him well. I'll print out a couple of pictures and bring them over."

Carol showed concern on her face. She didn't want Hipp anywhere near their apartment. "Just print a couple out and put them in an envelope and write 303 on them."

Whitey was no doubt watching the exchange with a pair of binoculars from his third-floor balcony. That was the perch where he could study every face that came and went by the building. He was always on alert for a stranger who didn't belong there.

Just as Osama bin Laden had lived in seclusion inside his compound in Pakistan before he was killed by US Special Forces, Bulger too was technically a free man, but his movements were now severely limited. He was a prisoner of sorts inside the apartment building, where he'd sleep in the rear bedroom with tinfoil-covered windows to block out the light. Yet, his room was also filled with flickering candles.

"I need them to sleep," he later told investigators.

"They help with all the nightmares." Nightmares caused by years of prison LSD experiments.

He'd spend his waking moments watching television, exercising, and keeping a lookout for the FBI or someone he'd double-crossed on the streets back home.

Whitey had a punching torso used by mixed martial artists standing inside the living room next to the sliding glass doors leading out to the balcony. He'd positioned it there with a fedora on its head to confuse any would-be assassin who might try to take a shot at him from the street or a nearby apartment.

"If you walked past at night, you'd see something in the window. He had a workout dummy torso that he would dress and put in the window, so it would look like someone looking out the window," Hipp remembers.

Bulger was also working on a manuscript about his life, one he hoped his family would get published for him. He didn't like what had been written about him by Kevin Weeks and others and wanted to set the record straight—at least his version of events.

When Hipp finally saw "Charlie" on the street again, his view of the man changed dramatically. The old man had already done the tough-guy routine by squeezing Joey's hand when they had first met, but this exchange was different. This was ugly.

"We were standing there and this young pregnant black woman walked down the other side of the street," Hipp recalls. "He let out a horrible racist rant just loud enough so she could hear it. According to him, every problem in Santa Monica was caused by minorities. He used the N word repeatedly."

"This is what's wrong with everything," the old man screamed. "Blacks and Mexicans!"

Hipp was appalled by the outburst. "I felt like just clocking the guy. But I thought, 'Ah he's an old man. He's not going to change his views.'"

After the racist rant, Joey took his dog Joplin and continued on his way. He promised to stay clear of "Charlie Gasko" from then on.

19

Whitey and Catherine stayed hunkered down in Santa Monica but occasionally traveled to Las Vegas to gamble. He had a VIP playing card at the Four Queens Casino, located two miles off the famous Strip, where you could book a room for as low as $42. Bulger was obsessed with washing his money and keeping his cash flow clean. He also went there to buy guns and knives.

Catherine kept up with the monthly bills paying with cash or money orders, getting to know the manager of the Princess Eugenia, Birgitta Farinelli, shortly after they moved in. A native of Göteborg, Sweden, Farinelli took the job after years working at LAX for New Zealand Air and Swiss Air. She was fluent in several languages, which made it easy to communicate with

foreign guests at the Princess Eugenia and its sister building, the Embassy Hotel apartments located across the street. Farinelli got to know "Carol Gasko" when she came into the office to drop off the rent. She always paid cash, and the two would often sit down and chat. Being from Sweden, the hotel manager couldn't place Carol's accent, so she inquired about it.

"I know that you don't have a New York accent," Farinelli told her. "But you have some kind of accent from the East Coast."

"Well, we're from Chicago," Catherine replied.

Despite Farinelli's inquisitive nature, Greig looked forward to their talks. If Farinelli was busy working in her office, Catherine would sit in the lobby and wait until she was free. Then she'd hand the property manager a white envelope stuffed with $1,165 in rent money. The bills, $100s, $50s, $20s, and $5s, always looked crisp and were neatly stacked.

"Well, did you rob a bank again, Carol?" Farinelli joked.

"Oh no," she replied nervously. "I just went to the bank and had to do some errands."

Greig asked Farinelli where she got her hair and nails done and would give her small gifts, like a silk scarf and a water bottle. One day, Farinelli knocked on the couple's apartment to notify them that the fire de-

partment had to cut the phone lines between the Princess Eugenia and Embassy Hotel apartments because of dangerous faulty wiring. When the manager entered the home, she could barely see. All the windows were covered by blackout shades.

"Oh, it's so dark in here," Farinelli observed to Carol.

Bulger was sitting in a fold-up chair, watching television.

"Charlie has a hard time sleeping," Greig said. "So he sleeps during the day." For once, Catherine wasn't lying, at least, not quite.

"We don't really need a phone," she told the manager. "Nobody ever calls us and we don't call anybody."

Farinelli was concerned about Charlie's health and would ask Carol about it.

"Well, he's always sick," Catherine explained. "He was smoking so much when he was younger that he has emphysema."

In truth, Bulger had never smoked and despised those who did.

Still, no one suspected a thing. Their cover stories worked well, and the fact that their case wasn't generating any media coverage in Southern California allowed Whitey and Catherine to conceal their true identities with ease.

Despite his being featured on the *America's Most Wanted* television show sixteen times, including a final appearance in October 2010, few people on the west coast knew who Whitey Bulger was and that's exactly how the elderly fugitive wanted it.

Whitey was spending less and less time outside their apartment at the Princess Eugenia. When he'd see Catherine chatting with neighbors in the hallway, he'd grumble for her to get back inside.

They'd occasionally visit a local dentist, signing in under the names "John R." and "Mary R."

After one agonizing trip, Bulger complained about his tooth pain to Farinelli.

"It's really hurting," he told her.

"You should get some Vicodin," she advised. "That makes you fly up to the sky. I have some. I can give it to you."

"No thanks," Whitey said, waving her off. "I'll tough it out."

Coupled with his tooth pain, Bulger was also suffering from severe arthritis. During a visit to an urgent care clinic in Los Angeles, the aging gangster was offered a cortisone shot for relief but said no. The shot cost $160, but it wasn't the money that Bulger was concerned about.

"I'm scared of needles," he told the doctor.

It was a childlike response that belied a mean temper. According to clinic physician Dr. Reza Ray Ehsan, Bulger shouted at the nurses and demeaned Catherine by introducing her as "his girl."

Greig smiled through the humiliation and did her best to stay healthy. She cut out new diet recipes and kept a thick binder in the apartment on the warning signs and treatment for osteoporosis, as their bones were starting to degenerate with age. She'd done everything she could to turn their tiny apartment into a home and made sure that Bulger realized how thankful she was, despite the circumstances. On Valentine's Day, Catherine expressed her love with a card that featured a drawing of a puppy on the cover with the whimsical wish for a day "that's tail waggin' fun." Under it she wrote: *"Happy Valentine's Day, 'Valentine'. Love always, Cxxxxoooo"*

There were photos of dogs and cats placed into frames on the walls, and pictures of her beloved poodles Nikki and Gigi were posted on a large piece of cardboard in the small kitchen. She bought everything in bulk, from Q-tips to Kleenex to bars of Dial soap, all stacked in orderly fashion in closets.

Catherine slept with a Claude Monet print above her bed, which stood opposite a pretty dresser with a makeup mirror and various blushes and perfumes

spread out neatly across a table covered by an embroidered cloth.

While her bedroom was decorated with a woman's delicate touch with accented lace and linen, his looked like a military barracks. A large map of the world was tacked up on the wall, no doubt fueling Whitey's imagination as to where they could flee to if they were ever spotted in Santa Monica. The map shared wall space with a poster of the US flag with the banner *God Bless America.*

Bulger collected dozens of books, which covered his desk and lined his small bookcase. His favorite subject was World War II, but he also read books on pirates and of course, tales about the mob. He even kept a copy of *Brutal,* the memoir penned by his protégé Kevin Weeks, on his shelf. He also owned a prized copy of *Escape from Alcatraz.* Whitey wasn't just reading for pleasure, though; he was also honing his skills as a fugitive.

He read *Soldier of Fortune* magazine religiously, along with a handbook on how to find missing persons and another that offered tips about how to survive worst-case scenarios including high-rise hotel fires and UFO abductions. One book that he studied cover to cover was *Secrets of a Back Alley ID Man: Fake ID Construction Techniques of the Underground.* The book promised to

reveal the most effective "new school" and "old school" techniques for fake IDs, including hologram reproduction, do-it-yourself templates for driver's licenses and official seals, and other evasive tricks for those on a tight budget, which most certainly appealed to Whitey.

He put this knowledge to work on another desperate man he'd met while strolling through Palisades Park named James William Lawlor.

Whitey did a double take when he first spotted Lawlor sitting on a bench. The man was bald, bearded, and Irish—just like Bulger. But Lawlor was also shorter than Whitey and paunchier, details that could possibly be overlooked on an ID card. Whitey sat with Lawlor and soon learned that he'd moved to California from New York after his wife died and that he had lost contact with his family. Lawlor also confided to Whitey that he had a drinking problem and was low on cash.

Bulger spotted a tattoo on Lawlor's right arm that read *US Army Irish*. Whitey offered him a few dollars but asked for nothing in return—at least not yet.

The two men would continue to talk in the park several more times and discovered they shared a mutual passion for history and reading. Finally, "Charlie" gave Lawlor his cover story—that he'd moved down from Canada illegally and he needed a valid California driver's license to get work.

Whitey forked over $1,000 for Lawlor's license, Social Security card, and birth certificate and morphed into Lawlor. He opened a bank account in the man's name and smartly convinced Lawlor to order a new senior citizen's identification card by mail. This time, Lawlor changed his description to say that he was five foot nine, 170 pounds, and had blue eyes. For this, Bulger gave him an additional $2,500 and even paid Lawlor's rent at a local hotel. Whitey also bought a car with cash and had Lawlor register it in his name so that he could drive around.

Bulger would continue to pay Lawlor's rent while urging him to seek help for his alcohol problem. In 2007, a couple of days after paying his rent with the money Whitey had given him, Lawlor died in his room. Bulger would never get over it. He couldn't claim the body as it would blow his cover, but Whitey was happy to learn later that Lawlor, an army veteran, was buried at a military cemetery some sixty miles away. Whitey drove the car back to Lawlor's neighborhood and parked it close by. He splashed some vodka around the front seat and left the keys in it. Bulger never drove again.

The years he'd spent prowling South Boston and preying on his neighbors were a distant memory for him now, but Whitey's criminal brain never stopped

working. Bulger had amassed great power in the underworld over several decades by using people on both sides of the law to serve his diabolical needs. Now, in the lion-in-winter phase of his life, Whitey exploited vulnerable men like James Lawlor to keep law enforcement at arm's length. His day-to-day life might have been more about toothaches and drawn shades, but his schemes were in constant view.

Whitey later befriended a young man named Josh Bond, who was hired to work with Birgitta Farinelli as a property manager for the Princess Eugenia in 2007. Bond was a musician and a recent graduate of Boston University, so he recognized Whitey's accent right away, although Bulger told him that he and his wife were from Chicago. He also lied and claimed he'd fought in the Korean War.

Bond lived in the apartment next to Whitey and Catherine and he played loud music at all hours. Surprisingly, Bulger didn't mind the noise. In fact, he liked the music.

"The first time I met Charlie, he brought me an old black Stetson hat and carrying case," Bond later recalled. "I thought that was strange."

The black cowboy hat was the same one he'd worn when he had first taken Catherine on the run years earlier. Now they were known in the neighborhood as the

couple that always wore white. She wore white blouses and slacks, and "Charlie Gasko" was never seen without his floppy hat and sunglasses.

The couple hung a sign on their front door asking people not to knock at certain times of the day. Like Farinelli, Josh Bond was one of the few people to ever get a look inside apartment 303. His eyes were immediately drawn to the torso dummy, which he thought was strange, but nothing else stood out to him.

It was clear that Charlie kept himself physically fit, and he gave Bond workout equipment including a curling bar and stomach crunch machine as gifts.

"If I didn't think the Gaskos were such a nice old couple, I would have thought that Charlie was trying to get me in shape because he was attracted to me," Bond says. "But since they didn't have any children of their own, they sort of treated me like a son."

Other presents included an Elvis Presley coffee-table book, a beard trimmer, and a bottle of Grand Marnier liqueur. As the apartment manager got closer to the couple, he learned that Whitey carried a knife at all times for protection after someone had creeped up on him from a flophouse down the street. Bond made the same mistake once and approached Bulger from behind. Whitey yelled at him for it.

He didn't like to be startled and tried to be observant

about his surroundings at all times. Bulger would leave copies of the local newspaper outside Bond's apartment door highlighting neighborhood crimes and other articles.

"He'd stay up all night," Bond remembers. "I could see him through a window sitting in his apartment with a pair of binoculars."

Josh Bond thought that Charlie Gasko was some kind of neighborhood watchman, an aging vigilante whose aim it was to protect his fellow residents. No one could have known that the man in apartment 303 was keeping a lookout for the FBI and was one of the most wanted killers alive.

20

Special Agent Phil Torsney had an idea. There was still much debate within the FBI about whether or not Whitey remained in communication with Billy Bulger or any of their siblings.

"What if we tell them that we think Whitey might be dead?" he told Tommy Mac. "What might their reaction be, shock? Or will they know we're lying because they're talking to him regularly? Let's get them out of their comfort zone."

The partners returned to Billy's house, knocked on the door, and were once again met by his wife.

"Mrs. Bulger, we have a DOA that may be James Bulger," Phil told her. "We'd like to make a determination on this, but we need your husband's cooperation by supplying his DNA for testing."

There was no reaction on Mary Bulger's face. She merely smiled and said that she'd pass along the request to her husband.

Torsney and MacDonald visited the other siblings, with only Whitey's younger sister Sheila consenting to an interview. Sheila McKeon was estranged from the family and lived with her husband in Hull, Massachusetts, twenty-five miles away from Southie. Out of all the Bulgers, Sheila looked to be the best bet.

"We need a sample of your DNA to compare it with this John Doe," the agents told her. "Because if it is Jim Bulger, we can put this thing to bed and stop bothering you folks and we can close the case."

Estranged or not, Sheila McKeon wouldn't assist them by giving up her DNA. Neither would any of the other Bulger family members.

When they returned to their office, the voice mail button on MacDonald's phone was flashing. He sat down at his cubicle and pressed play. Once again, the booming voice of Bulger family lawyer Tom Kiley could be heard loud and clear.

"You come to us with a body, and then maybe the family will talk," Tommy Mac recalled Kiley stating in the voice mail. "But we're not going to do anything to help you find James Bulger."

Tommy Mac was not dissuaded.

"Previous agents would have backed off, but Phil and I don't work that way," MacDonald says. "Whitey was wanted for killing nineteen people; this wasn't a tax case. We had a right to be there. I wondered how the Bulgers could sleep at night."

After interviewing Sheila McKeon, they waited and watched the pen registers on the phones of Billy and other family members. Would they immediately call each other? Would they call someone else?

FBI analyst Roberta "Bobby" Hastings was tasked with figuring it out. The only team member who'd been tracking Whitey since he went on the run back in the mid-1990s, Hastings had more skin in this game than anyone. For her, the hunt for Whitey was personal. Unlike the new members of the team, Hastings had enjoyed a friendship with disgraced agent John Connolly and felt burned by his betrayal.

A native of Clinton, Massachusetts, and a graduate of Western Kentucky University, Hastings joined the Bureau in 1980. As an FBI investigative analyst in the Boston office, Hastings had worked hand in hand with Charlie Gianturco before he was taken off the case. She analyzed and kept records on all tips, telephone calls, and meetings with those in Whitey Bulger's inner and outer circles. She cross-referenced every bit of information that was brought in and helped to put all the

puzzle pieces together, and then told the agents which pieces were still missing.

"We had a lot of good days, but a lot of bad days too. I'd wake up in the middle of the night with phone numbers running through my head. We'd get excited about a tip one minute and then learn it wasn't him. It was all-consuming," Hastings remembers. "Everybody, especially those in the media, also thought that we were all corrupt because of Connolly. We were all put into a category of liars and cheats. We were kicked down so low, but we had to pick ourselves up each morning and do the job. I knew John [Connolly] and I actually liked him. He was a flashy guy, but he treated me well. I had always thought of him as a nice guy, but then I reminded myself that nice guys don't murder people. We didn't know what he was doing behind closed doors. Connolly never brought me into that circle of his life."

By the time Gleason took over in 2008, Hastings was the unit's mother hen—the one who had been through it all and hadn't given up the fight. She was also a wizard when it came to researching data. And when it came to Billy Bulger's phone records, she analyzed all the phone numbers to narrow down common calls. One series of calls that stood out came from Billy's house to a location in Oxnard, California. The agents

figured that Billy was too smart to phone his brother directly, but it was still an unusual lead worth chasing.

Had Billy finally let his guard down? Tommy Mac traced the call to a woman living in Oxnard and flew out to interview her.

"She told us that she was an old classmate of Billy's," MacDonald says. "The woman said that the phone calls with Bulger concerned an upcoming class reunion and had nothing to do with Whitey."

MacDonald wasn't convinced.

After the interview, Tommy Mac drove south along the Pacific Coast Highway toward the FBI's Los Angeles office. After about an hour on the road, he stopped off in Santa Monica. The weather was gorgeous and MacDonald was hungry. He and a fellow agent on loan from the LA office parked their car and took a walk on the Santa Monica Pier, staring out at the Pacific Ocean and breathing in the salt air. While they grabbed lunch at the Bubba Gump Shrimp Company and discussed the case, MacDonald explained the unit's frustration, the mythology surrounding Whitey, and his determination to capture the mob killer, who unbeknownst to them was sitting in his apartment less than a mile away. After lunch, Tommy Mac and his fellow agent got back in their car and continued on to Los Angeles,

not knowing just how close they had come to solving this case once and for all.

Upon his return to Boston, MacDonald and Torsney took a new approach. If they couldn't unnerve the Bulger family, they'd do their best to embarrass them.

Tommy Mac printed up hundreds of fliers with photos of Whitey and Catherine on them. Under the pictures, the FBI wrote *Fugitives Wanted by the FBI* in the color blue for law enforcement, *19 Murder Victims* in the color red for blood, and *Reward $2 Million* in the color green for cash. MacDonald scribbled his cell phone number on the pieces of paper and then blanketed Billy Bulger's neighborhood, sticking the fliers in mailboxes and under windshield wipers. To the agents, this was psychological warfare and another attempt to get the family out of its comfort zone.

One of the fliers would later find its way to Whitey himself.

"We handed out business cards with New York printed on them for me and Cleveland for Phil," MacDonald says. "We also wanted to show them that the Bureau was investing its resources from outside the Boston office and we weren't going anywhere. We were getting the fire going. It had been years since a lot of the key people were approached. The answer we were getting from folks in Southie was that we weren't really

looking for Whitey. Or he's dead and we're wasting our time. We wanted people to know that we were committed to finding this guy. We didn't come to Boston to drink pints of Guinness at Faneuil Hall. This was no vacation."

Another investigator who was brought in to help supervise the Bulger probe was Rich Teahan, an agent who had spent a decade working in the FBI office in New Haven, Connecticut. Like Torsney, Teahan was a veteran manhunter, but he was also one with deep local roots. Teahan was Boston Irish. He grew up in Quincy, where his father worked as a trooper in the state police. When he landed in Connecticut, Teahan was handed one of the biggest fugitive cases in the country, the hunt for Alex Kelly, the "preppy rapist." Kelly was a former high school wrestling champion from Darien, Connecticut, who was accused of raping two teenage girls. Before his trial was set to begin, Kelly fled to Europe, where he stayed for seven years, bouncing around as a ski bum and living off money sent to him by his wealthy parents. The FBI long believed that Kelly's mother and father were supporting their son from afar. Finally, Rich Teahan and a team of agents swarmed the family home, executing a state police search warrant. Teahan discovered letters from the accused rapist and recent photos of the parents enjoying time with their

son overseas. The parents were charged with obstruction and Kelly finally surrendered in Switzerland. He was extradited back to the US to stand trial, where he was ultimately found guilty and sentenced to sixteen years in prison.

While on assignment in New Haven, Teahan also spent time chasing down Bulger leads and sightings, including one at a posh yacht club in Groton, Connecticut. The agent even had his own brush with a Bulger look-alike while touring World War II battlefields in Tunisia.

"I was sitting by the hotel pool having a beer when I look over and there's a guy who looks just like Whitey, and he's wearing a Boston Red Sox hat," Teahan recalls. "I listened to him speak and recognized a thick Boston accent."

Teahan observed the man for several more minutes. He'd heard Bulger's voice on surveillance tapes and remembered that his Southie dialect was more subtle. It turned out that the look-alike was a tourist from Somerville, Massachusetts.

"I thought you were someone else," the agent told the tourist. "I thought you were a top-ten FBI fugitive. I was gonna get a real nice reward for it."

Of course, federal agents were ineligible to cash in on the $2 million prize, but catching Whitey Bulger in

North Africa would have been the ultimate reward for any lawman.

In 2002, Teahan moved to Washington to work on the executive protection detail for then–FBI director Robert Mueller before jumping over to the national joint terrorism task force. Like Noreen Gleason, Teahan was known for his leadership and organizational skills. In 2006, he applied for Office of Preference, which was a wish list of where agents wanted to go. Rich Teahan wanted to go home for the first time in fifteen years. He had a wife and three kids and yearned to be close to his father, who was recently widowed. Teahan had a special bond with his father, who had retired as a lieutenant colonel in the state police and had inspired his son to join law enforcement. The father had been assigned to South Boston in the 1970s during a violent period of neighborhood unrest over a federal judge's decision to desegregate Boston schools. State troopers mobilized to protect African-American children as their school buses entered and left Southie while residents hurled bottles and racist insults in their direction. Whitey Bulger was among those who didn't want black students bused into his neighborhood. He tried to burn down an elementary school in the judge's hometown of Wellesley and then tossed a Molotov cocktail through the back door of President John F. Kennedy's

birthplace in nearby Brookline. The home, a historical landmark, was targeted by Whitey because Senator Edward Kennedy, JFK's younger brother, had been a vocal supporter of forced busing. Before fleeing the scene in a green Chevy Impala, Bulger spray-painted *Bus Teddy* on the sidewalk in front of the home.

When Rich Teahan agreed to supervise the Bulger Task Force, he too discovered the impenetrable wall that was put up around Whitey's siblings, especially Billy Bulger.

"What made me mad about that family was they wouldn't even talk to us without an attorney," Teahan recalls. "I had hunted enough people to know that the family was always the central thing. It's the central theme, and that's where you start and work your way out. It's like a dartboard and you focus on the family. That's what we did in the Alex Kelly case and just look at what that did for us. But the Bulgers were so insulated and so powerful. We were dealing with another level of power inside Massachusetts, like no other. Billy Bulger was titanium and we were not gonna break through."

21

Tommy Mac kept the heat on Whitey's family while Phil Torsney traveled across the country, chasing down Bulger's old pals from Alcatraz to see if there was any piece of information that had been missed over the past decade. Phil also flew up to Canada to check on Whitey sightings across the border. It made some sense that he and Catherine would be hiding there since Bulger had contacts in Canada through Teresa Stanley's son-in-law, former NHL player Chris Nilan, who had dragged money up there for Whitey in the past.

Back at the Boston FBI office, Rich Teahan also went on the offensive, giving media interviews to discuss the lack of cooperation offered by the Bulger family. It was Noreen Gleason's idea to lift the curtain and show the public what was being done to solve this case.

"You either feed the beast, or the beast feeds on you," Gleason says. "The FBI had been quiet for too long and that led to all the outrageous conspiracy theories about us hiding Whitey. It was so ridiculous to even think about."

Teahan was more than willing to engage with local reporters who had lost respect for the Boston office. It was his chance to turn them around. Still, most journalists working the Bulger beat remained skeptical about the Bureau's efforts.

"That was the single most frustrating thing about working this case," Teahan recalls. "We got the shit beat out of us every day. We were all very principled and ethical, but having the press beat you down every day and lump you in with John Connolly, Morris, and all the other dirty law enforcement that got into bed with this guy, it got to us. It gets down into your soul a little bit."

On a Sunday night in November 2009, Tommy Mac and Torsney decided to leave their hotel and drive to Quincy to pay a surprise visit to Kevin Weeks. It had been some time since anyone had spoken with Whitey's right-hand man, and the agents wanted to check his pulse and see if there was any nugget of information he had that previous agents could have overlooked.

"We didn't call the FBI first and ask permission to speak with Weeks," MacDonald says. "We knew we wouldn't have gotten the okay. The guy was part of the John Connolly conviction, so the US attorney had always told us to back off."

They found Weeks's apartment and knocked on the door. The former mob thug let the agents in and pointed them to a couch in the living room. Torsney looked around the well-kept apartment. The finely decorated digs were a far cry from the prison cell where Weeks had been locked up for five years before his parole in early 2005.

Weeks had a throw blanket wrapped around his large body and he was watching the fourth quarter of a tight New England Patriots game as his girlfriend hovered close by. Despite the interruption, Kevin patiently answered their questions for two straight hours.

"Do you think they're still together?" MacDonald asked him about Whitey and Catherine. "Could he have killed her by now?"

"I don't know about that," Weeks said. "They had a good relationship, they had a loving relationship, but there was one time where I witnessed violence between them that I had to pull Jimmy off Catherine because he was choking her to death."

Weeks was referring to the incident at Greig's house after she had confessed about their relationship to Teresa Stanley.

The agents scribbled in their notepads, thanked Weeks for his time, and then left.

The next morning, MacDonald and Torsney had breakfast together in the hotel restaurant. Tommy Mac had a plate stacked high with eggs, while his partner ate cereal with no milk. MacDonald had a hard time knowing that Phil was a vegetarian, as Tommy considered himself a proud carnivore and never met a steak he didn't like. Despite the differences in their diets, both got along well.

"Is Bulger a guy who's slick enough to kill or is he your typical old Irish guy who needs a good woman by his side to get through the day?" MacDonald asked.

"If he had killed her, she'd be a Jane Doe," Torsney replied. "Remember, she's never been arrested before so her fingerprints aren't on file. How can we search, dental records?"

"What about plastic surgery? What about breast implants?" MacDonald countered. "She was meticulous in her appearance and always tried to look young. If she's had a boob job, wouldn't the implants have serial numbers? If a medical examiner was performing an autopsy on a Jane Doe and she had breast implants,

you'd think they would take them out and record the serial numbers for identification."

Earlier in their investigation, police had found the torso of a female in the waters close to Grand Isle, Louisiana. It wasn't Catherine, but it got the agents thinking.

The agents posed the question to Bobby Hastings, who reminded them about a source close to Greig that was cultivated by agent Mike Carazza. That source had mentioned that Margaret McCusker had once dropped her twin sister off at a local hospital for a plastic surgery procedure.

On December 3, 2009, MacDonald and Torsney drove out to Newton-Wellesley Hospital with a subpoena. They quickly learned that Catherine had not only undergone breast enhancement surgery, but also had liposuction and other procedures performed at Plastic Surgical Associates in Newton, Massachusetts. Catherine was a woman who'd spent a lot of her time under the knife.

The medical practice now was run by Dr. Matthias Donelan and the FBI called his office requesting a meeting.

"Let's set up a time to talk by phone," the doctor told his secretary.

"No, the FBI wants to meet with you in person," she replied.

The Bureau didn't tell Donelan's assistant what the agents wanted to speak to him about, but the doctor knew all about Whitey Bulger and remembered that his longtime partner Dr. Eugene Curtiss had treated Catherine Greig as a patient before his retirement.

"She came into the office to have her eyelids done," Dr. Donelan recalls. "It was standard practice to take photographs for both face-lift patients and eyelid patients."

A few years later, Catherine had breast augmentation surgery performed by the same surgeon in the same office. When Donelan first met Tommy Mac, he told him that it was likely they had preserved her records. MacDonald was surprised at how willing the surgeon was to cooperate with the investigation.

"My father was an FBI agent," Donelan told him. The doctor's father, Charles Donelan, was a lawyer who worked for the Bureau for thirty-seven years and retired as assistant director and trainer at the FBI Academy at Quantico. He'd also served in the Bureau's New York office, just like Tommy Mac. For once, things were going right for MacDonald in the Bulger case.

"I'll check our files in storage; they're located in the bowels of our building," Dr. Donelan told him. "I'd be happy to help you catch Whitey Bulger."

A short time later, the plastic surgeon called Mac-Donald back. It was late in the day and the agent was pressed for time. Tommy Mac was just about to leave the office and head back to Connecticut to catch one of his son's baseball games.

"I've located the files you've been searching for," Dr. Donelan said. "I had to pull them out of storage."

"That's great," Tommy replied. "I'll swing by and pick them up in the morning."

"Do you want the photographs too?"

"You have photos?" MacDonald asked excitedly. "In that case, I'll be over in fifteen minutes."

Tommy Mac was dumbfounded. He didn't think that any photos of Greig existed outside the grainy surveillance pictures of her taken at a distance during a walk with Whitey several years before in Southie. In those images, Catherine wore a thick pair of sunglasses that took up half her face. To the investigators, they were useless.

When MacDonald arrived at the doctor's office, he was presented with a collection of high-resolution photographs of Catherine Greig. Unlike the surveillance pictures, these images were tight close-ups and side profiles of Bulger's longtime girlfriend. They were face, neck, and breast shots both before surgery and after.

"You could see every pore in her face," MacDonald remembers.

"We always had crappy pictures of her," adds Torsney. "Those pictures of Catherine became the backbone of the case."

But how could the FBI use them effectively? The agents huddled with Teahan and Noreen Gleason and came up with the strategy to target the medical and dental fields.

They took out advertisements showcasing the photos in industry news outlets like *Plastic Surgery News* and the American Dental Association's newsletter under the banner *Have You Treated This Woman?*

The advertisement listed all the plastic surgery procedures that she'd undergone and even listed the serial number of her breast implants, alerting doctors that Greig had the procedure done in 1982 and might be looking to replace them, along with information that she also suffered from a ragweed allergy and was sensitive to Valium.

Soon they were flooded with more tips, including a highly promising one from a dental office in Vancouver, British Columbia.

"She used to work here," the office manager told the FBI.

Was Whitey hiding in Canada after all?

MacDonald and Torsney flew out to Vancouver and rifled through the employment records. But like all the sightings of Whitey, this tip about his girlfriend proved to be another dead end.

Still, knowing they had the photos, the agents believed that it would be only a matter of time before someone came forward with the right information.

"We find her, and we'll find him," Noreen Gleason told her team.

But the Bulger Task Force unit needed support. Since both Tommy Mac and Phil Torsney were on temporary duty assignment in Boston, they would occasionally get pulled back to their home offices in New York and Cleveland.

"The powers that be thought, why are my agents in Boston chasing some old white guy when we have real fugitive cases in our own office?" MacDonald says.

Tommy was ordered back to Manhattan to investigate a rash of shootings in Yonkers, New York, while Phil was ordered home to Cleveland to handle a serial murder case. Anthony Sowell, the "Cleveland Strangler," had murdered eleven women inside his home. Sowell buried the bodies of his victims in the basement and in crawl spaces in the house.

"I was assigned the case, and when I got back there, I found that all the work had been done," Torsney recalls. "We'd recovered all the bodies and the killer had confessed to the murders. There was no need for me to be back in Cleveland as I had an active fugitive that I was chasing out of Boston."

22

Phil Torsney pleaded his case to the Bureau and was finally granted a permanent duty assignment in Boston with the sole purpose of catching Whitey Bulger. Torsney was fifty-five years old now and close to retirement. He hoped that he'd never have to look back on Whitey as the one that got away.

But with Tommy Mac still back in New York, Noreen Gleason needed additional assistance, so she looked outside the FBI to the US Marshals Service. It was a humbling experience, as there was still great animosity between law enforcement agencies and the FBI regarding Bulger, but Gleason wanted to be transparent about her efforts and the need for help.

"Look, there's not been a lot of collaboration and cooperation," she told David Taylor, the chief deputy

marshal of Boston. "I'm very sincere about this; let's try to get along. I know you don't trust us and I understand why. But it's a new day. Let's try to bury this hatchet and catch this guy. This affects all of us. This is a really bad dude who continues to have this terrible influence over this region."

In September 2010, the marshals assigned one of their own, a Massachusetts native named Neil Sullivan, to the case. When he reported to the Bulger Task Force, it consisted of two FBI agents (Teahan and Torsney) and an analyst (Hastings), along with a few state police detectives and correctional officers. The unit had once operated out of the Coast Guard building on Atlantic Avenue in the North End, but now, the Bulger team was back under the FBI's roof at its Boston headquarters at One Center Plaza, the so-called Land of Misfit Toys.

Sullivan grew up on Cape Cod and graduated from Barnstable High School, the same school that had produced another Bulger manhunter, San Diego sheriff's deputy Rich Eaton, although the two did not know each other.

Neil's father, William, worked a civilian job for the US Air Force on Cape Cod while his mother, Carrie, tended to their home. Neil joined the Air Force after graduating from high school and was assigned as a

security police officer, patrolling bases in the US and South Korea while undergoing heavy weapons training with Mark 19, 50-caliber, and M16 rifles and mortar teams.

"I wound up loving it and I knew that's exactly what I wanted to do in the civilian world," Sullivan says. "I enjoyed security police and saw some of the older guys get out of the service and into law enforcement jobs, so I followed their lead."

He enrolled at Salve Regina University in Newport, Rhode Island, where he studied criminal justice but left early to join the US Marshals. "When the Marshals offered me a job, I knew I had to take it as I didn't believe there would be any other good jobs out there when I graduated," he recalls.

Sullivan entered the US Marshals Academy in October 1995, eleven months after Whitey Bulger had gone on the run. As a young marshal, he worked court duty in Manhattan escorting gangsters like Gambino crime family honcho Vincent "Vinny the Chin" Gigante back and forth to trial.

"Gigante never gave me any trouble," Sullivan says. "He was the one feigning insanity. He was in character pretending that he was crazy at all times."

Two years later, he joined the warrant squad, earning the same salary, but this job was completely differ-

ent. Now Sullivan was on the streets breaking down doors and arresting accused killers, robbers, and rapists. It was a dangerous but rewarding job. Sullivan experienced a few close calls with fugitives, including one where a suspect rammed Neil's vehicle with a heavy-duty Ford Expedition. Sullivan jumped out of his car and opened fire on the Ford as it barreled toward him before crashing into a stop sign just a few feet away.

"If he'd been a foot or two to the right, I'd be dead," he says.

Sullivan admits that he was shaken by the incident and decided to take voluntary court duty for the next couple of months to heal himself psychologically.

"There had been a slew of marshals killed in the line of duty in recent years because we go after the most serious and desperate criminals," he explains. "When you're going after people like that, violent things are gonna happen."

After working a decade in New York, Sullivan joined the Boston office in 2010. At his going-away party in Albany, a colleague urged him to reach for the brass ring in Boston.

"When you get up there on day one, demand to work the Bulger case," the colleague said. "Say it immediately."

Sullivan packed his car and drove from upstate New

York to Boston with his wife, Eileen, a social worker who had counseled families of lost loved ones after 9/11.

After getting approached by Noreen Gleason, the marshals were searching for someone to join the FBI's team, and Neil Sullivan was the ideal candidate.

"My superiors recognized my work in New York and that I was good in the fugitive unit and a good investigator," he remembers. "The Marshal in Chief asked me if I'd be willing to go to the FBI and help them with the Bulger case. I said yes immediately."

There was no sophisticated layout at the Bulger Task Force headquarters. The unit didn't have its own office and instead had to share space across from the FBI gang squad (GS14), where agents worked violent street gang cases and other organized crime cases.

There were photos of Bulger and Greig tacked on bulletin boards, along with a world map covered in pins identifying all the places that the fugitives had been sighted since 1994, both real and imagined. Sullivan, Torsney, and Roberta Hastings were dropped into a pen surrounded by investigators who rolled their eyes and snickered, comparing the team to Mulder and Scully, the fictional agents in the hit show *The X-Files*, who chased after aliens and paranormal phenomena.

Were they hunting Whitey Bulger or the Abominable Snowman?

Roberta Hastings handed Sullivan a stack of case files and told him to start reading. The marshal could hardly believe the trail of blood left by Bulger and members of his gang through the streets of Southie, Dorchester, and other Boston neighborhoods.

"I had first heard about Whitey Bulger in the late 1990s. I had no idea who he was when he went on the run," Sullivan admits. "Growing up on Cape Cod, I was isolated from all the Boston crime news. My family only went to the city once a year for a Red Sox game and that was it."

It didn't take Sullivan long to hit a stone wall. He'd been handed the baton from Tommy Mac and he'd inherited the same resistance from those closest to Bulger. The marshal even flew down to Clearwater, Florida, and checked out Whitey's other old haunts to see if the fugitive had returned.

"I shared with my wife Eileen the frustrations I had about interviewing people who'd already been spoken to seven times," Sullivan recalls. "No one was giving us anything. There was a code of silence. In fact, they were offended that we were chasing after an old man."

The task force was beginning to lose ground on leads from the first campaign that utilized new photos of Catherine Greig to target plastic surgeons and dental offices. The investigators needed to rethink their strat-

egy once again. Sitting around the conference room at One Center Plaza, the agents spit-balled fresh ideas.

"What can we do to take control of our own message?" Rich Teahan asked the group. "We shouldn't be controlled by a media outlet like Fox's *America's Most Wanted* because Whitey's been aired on that show more than a dozen times and we have nothing to show for it."

Someone floated the idea of creating a commercial. The team brought in the FBI office's resident public relations professional to discuss whether it was feasible.

"We'll need a production company to build a public service announcement, and we'll need to target markets," the PR flack informed them. "We need to have a budget for those markets because one market may be more expensive than another market."

Teahan brought the idea to Noreen Gleason, who went to FBI headquarters to secure funding for the project. The FBI had never done something like this before and the approval process was painstakingly slow, but the team was confident that the strategy would net results.

Gleason managed to get only $50,000 allocated for the PSA's production and commercial costs.

"It wasn't a lot of money, but you can't look a gift horse in the mouth," Teahan says.

The FBI worked with a production company out of

Maine on the content for the spot and then chose fourteen markets to run it in.

"The common theme for us now was that Whitey had never left the country," Neil Sullivan remembers. "We created a chart of where we knew he was during the first two years and it was always in the US. If he was gonna go to Europe to hide, he would have done it in those first two years."

The team was also convinced that Bulger would be hiding someplace warm and near the ocean. That eliminated places like Oklahoma and Minnesota.

"We believed that he'd want to surround himself with fellow retirees someplace where he could walk and get around," Sullivan adds.

The investigators drew a map across the bottom of the United States from the Carolinas south to the Florida panhandle and over to the Gulf of Mexico and the west coast. Those were the regions they would spend money in.

But in California, the spot would only run in San Francisco because of Whitey's ties to Alcatraz, and not in the Los Angeles area, where the media market was too expensive to advertise.

While the FBI was plotting airtime, in Santa Monica, Catherine had been busy feeding and fretting over a stray cat they'd named Tiger. Tiger had helped her

make new friends, including a woman from Iceland named Anna Bjornsdottir, who struck up a conversation with her while Greig was feeding the cat outside. Anna was a former model who'd been crowned Miss Iceland in 1974. She'd moved to Southern California to kick-start her acting career and managed to get a few gigs, including a guest spot on the hit television show *Remington Steele.* She also appeared in Hollywood films including *More American Graffiti* and *The Sword and the Sorcerer.* Like Catherine, Anna was a cat lover, and they spent time together, especially at night, when Greig was feeding Tiger and Anna was returning home from one of her walks. Catherine, or "Carol," told Anna that she had a niece who'd once lived in Santa Monica and that's why they'd decided to move there.

It was as casual and innocent as every other stray conversation Catherine had since moving there—and it would be Whitey's undoing.

23

On Sunday night, May 1, 2011, Americans across the country and people around the world watched the breaking news coverage about the death of Osama bin Laden at the hands of US Special Forces in Abbottabad, Pakistan. President Barack Obama made the announcement from the East Room of the White House, interrupting a nationally televised baseball game between the New York Mets and the Philadelphia Phillies.

"Tonight I can report to the American people and to the world, the United States has conducted an operation that killed Osama bin Laden, the leader of al-Qaeda, and a terrorist who's responsible for the murder of thousands of innocent men, women and children," President Obama declared.

In Santa Monica, at Barney's Beanery on the Third Street Promenade, bar patrons broke into cheer; "USA, USA," they shouted. At an Italian restaurant nearby, diners waved American flags. At the popular Santa Monica pub Britannia, one grizzled barfly hoisted his mug in the air. "The bastard's dead. I'll drink to that!"

Inside apartment 303 at the Princess Eugenia, Whitey Bulger sat in his living room with Catherine, watching the announcement with a mixed feeling of pride and dread. The patriotic side of Bulger was elated to learn that members of SEAL Team 6 raided bin Laden's secret compound and sent the terror mastermind back to his maker with a bullet above his left eye. But with bin Laden's death also came an unnerving reality for the eighty-one-year-old former crime boss. James "Whitey" Bulger was now elevated to number one on the FBI's list of most wanted criminals, and that meant the pressure to find him would be intensified.

Would a Black Hawk helicopter soon land on the roof of their apartment building? Would armed men kick down his door and instigate a bloodbath?

He'd been planning for such a showdown for years as he built up his personal arsenal while purchasing weapons at Nevada gun shows. Whitey now owned more than thirty firearms, including a Ruger pistol and

several Smith & Wesson and Colt revolvers that he kept hidden inside cut-out walls and hollowed-out books, along with killing knives and $822,000 in cash. He also had two shotguns and two rifles stored under his bed and a pistol at his bedside.

All the weapons were loaded, and there was enough ammunition on hand to defend against a small army. Bulger was armed to the teeth and had vowed that he'd never be taken alive.

Back at One Center Plaza, Noreen Gleason and Rich Teahan were busy building a command post and call center to support the leads they had hoped to generate from the Catherine Greig PSA.

"We didn't really care how he was going to be found," Teahan says. "We didn't care if it was a local cop in Iowa or the DEA in Bogotá. All that mattered was catching the motherfucker."

The FBI bought 350 time slots during daytime TV shows that appealed to women, including *Live with Regis and Kelly*, *The View*, and *Ellen DeGeneres*. On June 21, 2011, the Bulger Task Force let the thirty-second commercial spot fly.

"This is an announcement by the FBI," a female narrator declared. "Have you seen this woman?" The high-resolution photos of Catherine Greig discov-

ered by Tommy Mac slid into the video frame next to the FBI shield, along with a reward in bold type of $100,000.

"Greig has had plastic surgeries," the narrator continued. "She's wanted for harboring James 'Whitey' Bulger, a fugitive on the FBI's Ten Most Wanted List."

Both Teahan and Gleason made sure that the commercial also evoked a sense of fear for Catherine's safety. They added a line about Bulger's violent temper, along with the fact that he was wanted for nineteen murders, in hopes of mobilizing a sisterhood of female viewers that might help rescue the girlfriend and pull her from harm's way.

What the investigators didn't realize was that the spot would generate major news because of the FBI's unique and innovative strategy to roll out a commercial on its own behalf. Rich Teahan's phone was inundated with interview requests from local, national, and international press, including CNN and the BBC. It didn't matter that the spot ran in only fourteen media markets, as Catherine Greig's photos were now plastered on TV screens and websites around the world.

Whitey Bulger was sitting in his apartment watching CNN when the news story flashed on the screen.

He realized its significance right away. He then turned to Catherine.

"That's it," he said somberly.

Neil Sullivan was manning the command post at One Center Plaza that day. The team got a series of tips including several from Biloxi, Mississippi. The young marshal was excited because the tips had come from such a small geographical area.

"I was the one sending all the information from the day shift to the cities, especially to Biloxi, and then just eliminating them one by one," Sullivan says.

Sullivan and Phil Torsney made a pact that if they got enthusiastic about a lead, they wouldn't just jump on the next plane, because that would have left all the other tips not being vetted by the right people.

"We knew more about the case now than anyone else and we didn't want any information to be dissected by other agents who didn't know what to look for," Sullivan adds.

By the end of the first day, they had run down all the Biloxi leads. Again, the sightings all wound up being look-alikes. Sullivan ended his day shift and handed over the duties to Torsney in the hope that he'd have better luck at night.

When the marshal returned to work the next day, he

was faced with a big pile of tips that had come in before dawn. Some of the leads had been written down by call center operators who'd answered them overnight, while others were e-mailed to Sullivan's computer. He and analyst Roberta Hastings began to sift through them all and recognized three different inquiries that had come from the same tipster—a woman named Anna Bjornsdottir from Reykjavik, Iceland. One tip was in the pile, another was buried in Sullivan's e-mail in-box, and a third was a voice-mail message. Anna Bjornsdottir had called frantically three times and it was clear that she wasn't getting the answer she wanted.

"The person that I think is him is living at Princess Eugenia Apartments in Santa Monica, California. Call me back immediately," Anna said in accented English. "They call themselves Charlie and Carol Gasko."

It was Anna Bjornsdottir who had once befriended Greig over their mutual love for the stray cat named Tiger. She had even provided an actual location and a name, which differentiated this tip from all the rest.

Sullivan and Hastings checked all the federal law enforcement databases available and found a Carol and Charles Gasko living at the Santa Monica address. The strange thing was that the couple had no birth dates listed, no Social Security numbers, no California driver's licenses or state identification cards. They were ghosts.

"Right away, red flags started going off in my head, so I called the tipster," Sullivan says.

She spoke with a trace of a Scandinavian accent and she was frustrated. Anna Bjornsdottir was adamant that she knew the couple Sullivan was looking for.

"Between the databases and what she was saying, I was quite convinced we had them."

Sullivan held his excitement in check. Although he was the newest member of the team, he'd heard enough stories from Torsney about dead ends and red herrings that he almost couldn't believe his own ears now. After sixteen long years and the near collapse of the Boston FBI office, had the team finally found its man?

Neil motioned Rich Teahan over and explained what was happening. Teahan then got in touch with Randy Jarvis from the FBI's Violent Crimes Task Force.

Scott Garriola is the best guy in L.A., Teahan wrote Jarvis in an e-mail. *We need him to chase down a promising lead on Whitey Bulger.*

Special Agent Scott Garriola had been working out of the Los Angeles office since 1991 and already had a colorful and celebrated career in the FBI, having hunted and captured dozens of dangerous fugitives, including many violent killers from the LA gang world and the murderous Mexican drug cartels. He'd also taken down a fugitive from the FBI's Top Ten List.

"Agent Garriola is a legend in the Bureau," Teahan says. "He's the only one I could fully trust for a job like this where we couldn't be boots on the ground ourselves. There's a small cadre of fugitive hunters in the FBI and he's on the top of the list with Phil Torsney."

But Garriola was on vacation and enjoying some well-deserved time off. He was with his kids at a local sporting goods store when Jarvis forwarded Teahan's e-mail. Garriola had worked Bulger leads in the Los Angeles area before. He also was very familiar with the east coast organized crime world, having grown up in the Bronx before attending college and law school in Southern California.

This is a 281, an organized crime case, Garriola typed back in a group e-mail to Teahan and Jarvis. *I'm off this week. Why don't you call in one of the O.C. guys?*

He stared at the message before sending and decided to delete it. This was Whitey Bulger after all.

Why don't you give me a call and show me what you got? Garriola responded instead.

Teahan phoned Garriola and brought him up to speed.

"I was still so pessimistic, having already covered so many Bulger leads over the years," Garriola says. "But something told me that I should go cover this one, so I

went and got a babysitter. My mother-in-law was home at the time, thank God, so I dropped my kids off and got to work."

Garriola summoned four members of his fugitive team from the LAPD to join him on the hunt in Santa Monica. He was very familiar with the area, having lived one block away from the Princess Eugenia while attending law school at Loyola Marymount.

We got a lead on Whitey Bulger and I'll see you there in about an hour, Garriola wrote in a group text.

A response came immediately: *Who's Whitey Bulger?*

You ever see the movie The Departed? *It's kinda based on him,* Garriola texted back.

Although Bulger's face and a list of his crimes, including nineteen murders, were plastered all over the FBI website and now on television, a generation of younger agents and law enforcement professionals had little or no institutional knowledge about America's most wanted fugitive.

Garriola had to get his team up to speed quickly while also devising a plan to capture Bulger properly and safely. Most importantly, he wanted to make damned sure they were looking for the right guy. He called Teahan back during the drive to Santa Monica.

"Who talked to the tipster?" Garriola asked.

"A US marshal," Teahan told him.

"Well, as you know, Rich, the FBI and the marshals don't really get along, so I need to speak to the tipster myself."

Once again, his pessimism set in. He recalled that an influx of Russian Jews had immigrated to Santa Monica during his time living there and figured that's what this was. The couple in question probably didn't have a big footprint in terms of identification cards because they didn't speak the language, didn't know the culture, and were unfamiliar with US document requirements.

Garriola's mind changed when he was put in touch with Anna Bjornsdottir.

"We called the Los Angeles office about this and didn't get a great response, so we called your headquarters in Washington and then Boston," Bjornsdottir told the agent on the phone. "He [Bulger] claimed he was from Chicago, but I have traveled around the country and I knew it wasn't a Chicago accent. It was a Boston accent. I got into several arguments with him. He's a racist and very anti-Obama. But the woman he is with was very pleasant."

"How sure are you that the couple you met are the fugitives we are looking for?" the agent asked her.

"I'm not 100 percent sure," the tipster replied. "I'm 200 percent sure it's them!"

That was good enough for Garriola. He started peppering Rich Teahan with requests. He needed a subpoena and was hyperfocused on the utilities of the apartment.

"Who controls the utilities?" Garriola asked him. "What were the names on the bill? Do they match the names that were called in on this tip?"

Teahan and Sullivan confirmed the information and then warned Garriola that they believed the aging crime boss was armed and would not give himself up without a fight.

"We had to get him away from the ability to shoot through walls and barricade himself inside with her [Catherine]. We feared that he'd use her as a hostage," Teahan recalls. "He wouldn't have come out of that apartment, not with the amount of firepower he had and everything he had to lose."

Scott Garriola went silent at that point. He was now operational.

Apartment manager Josh Bond was napping on the couch in his apartment when he was awakened by a coworker who told him that the FBI was in the office inquiring about a tenant. Bond then called Garriola's cell phone.

"Can we do this tomorrow?" Bond asked. "I'm off today."

"Well, I was off today too, pal. We need to take care of this now. It'll only take a few minutes of your time," Garriola said sternly.

Bond went down to his office across the street at the Embassy Hotel, where he was met by the FBI agent, who showed him photos of Whitey and Catherine.

"I'll make this real quick, I'm looking for a couple of fugitives," Garriola told him. "Are these the people living in apartment 303 at Princess Eugenia?"

Bond stared at the photos of his friends Charlie and Carol and put his head in his hands.

"That's my neighbor and his girlfriend," Bond said. "Yes, 100 percent it's them."

Garriola told the manager their real names and that they were wanted for serious crimes including murder. Bond was shocked.

"I know who Whitey Bulger is," Bond told him. "I went to school in Boston." The manager said that he'd lived in Boston for five years and had been working at the Princess Eugenia for five years too.

"You had ten years, and you never put two and two together that this was Whitey Bulger?" Garriola asked.

"I never saw a picture of him before."

"Well, it's him and I need some information from you."

Bond was unsure whether to cooperate.

"Umm, can we talk downstairs?"

Garriola didn't like that answer. He thought that maybe Bulger had set up a trip wire through the apartment manager to lure him somewhere long enough for Whitey to make his escape. The FBI agent called in his LAPD team members for backup.

"Okay, you should meet your team in the back of their building," Bond advised. "He's always on the balcony with a pair of binoculars looking up and down the street."

Garriola couldn't believe how clueless the manager was.

"And you didn't think that was odd as well?" he asked incredulously.

Bond was getting frustrated, as he didn't want to be late for a concert he was planning to attend that evening. He then inquired about a subpoena. Garriola quickly mentioned the big FBI reward for Whitey's capture and that certainly triggered the manager's interest.

"Somebody's already in line for the $2 million reward for leading us to Bulger's doorstep," the agent said. "But there's another $100 thousand reward for Catherine."

Garriola didn't know if the money was available or not. He was just throwing it out there to get the manager's cooperation.

"What can I do to help?" Bond asked.

Garriola asked for an apartment in the Embassy Hotel so that his team could run surveillance on Bulger's third-floor balcony. Bond complied.

"Where do you live?" he asked the manager.

"I live right next door to Charlie and Carol."

"Okay, I'd like to set up a ruse. We can shut the power off or tell him there's a plumbing leak going down from Bulger's apartment to the floor below. Or what if I get a UPS uniform and deliver a fake package?"

Josh Bond told Garriola that he didn't think any of the plans would work.

"No one's ever allowed in their apartment."

The agent told Bond to meet him in the back alley of the Princess Eugenia. The two men then went upstairs to the third floor and Garriola pressed his ear against the front door of apartment 303.

There was silence. He had to find another way inside.

Back in Boston, the Bulger Task Force waited patiently while Garriola and his team set the trap. Phil Torsney was now in, leading the command post as

night shift commander. Both Sullivan and Teahan had reluctantly gone home for the evening but were monitoring all developments through texts with Garriola.

The Boston team felt it didn't need to micromanage Garriola from three thousand miles away. They had ultimate faith that the renowned manhunter would get the job done.

But the question remained—would anyone be harmed or even killed in the process?

After about thirty minutes of radio silence, Torsney texted Garriola for an update.

Busy, Garriola texted back.

More waiting . . .

Scott Garriola sneaked down to the garage underneath the apartment building and walked toward a set of storage lockers that were assigned to each unit. He found the locker for apartment 303 with the name *Gaskos* written in crayon.

The fugitive hunter had an idea. He'd retrieve a set of bolt cutters and cut the lock off. He'd then take some stuff out of the locker and toss it on the ground to make it look like a burglary in hopes of luring Bulger downstairs.

The agent then called in for more backup. He needed three more officers to guard the exits of the Princess Eugenia while Garriola's team took position in the ga-

rage. It took another hour for the officers to arrive, as they'd been stuck in traffic. Garriola told them to fan out across one block and keep an eye out for an older couple with white hair.

Garriola then phoned Bond.

"Call the Gaskos and tell them to meet you at their storage locker," Garriola ordered.

Bond placed the call, but there was no answer.

"What do I do now?" the manager asked the agent.

"I want you to go knock on the door."

Bond smartly wasn't willing to put his life on the line for his job.

"I don't want to do that. What if he pulls a gun on me? I just Googled his name. He's killed nineteen people!"

A moment later, a call came in to Bond's phone. It was Catherine Greig, or "Carol Gasko," on the line.

"Hi, Josh, did you just call?"

"Yes, Carol. I have some bad news. Your storage unit was broken into. Do you want me to call police or meet me down in the garage?"

Greig turned to Bulger and relayed the information.

"Charlie wants to meet you in the garage," she replied.

"Okay, I'll be over in a minute," Bond told her. "I'm helping a guest right now."

Moments later, Catherine appeared on the balcony. She looked down at the street and saw nothing unusual, so she went back inside.

"What do you want me to do now?" Bond asked Garriola.

"Stay where you are. We'll handle it from here."

Garriola fired off another quick text to Boston:

Looking good, standby

After receiving the call from Bond, Whitey Bulger grabbed his white hat, stepped out of the apartment, and took the elevator down to the garage. Bulger described the scene in vivid detail in a letter to author Michael Esslinger, which was shared with the authors of this book:

> When I entered the elevator, I kind of hesitated. I stood there for a minute after the doors closed and stared at the button . . . looking intently at the worn buttons on the panel. I gathered my thoughts, but was thinking I didn't want the cops called or have this turn into anything big. When I got off the elevator and started to walk around a parked car, I could see my locker. I noticed that the door was hanging off. I knew something wasn't right. What first caught my eye was that I saw a few pieces of colored tape on the cement as if to mark posi-

tions like on a stage. There was a stillness that just seemed off . . . Hard to describe in words, but my instinct told me something was off.

As I started walking toward my locker, a light was shined on me and quite a few men in full combat gear and armed with M4 Carbines—fully automatic machine guns and a couple point Glock hand guns—took aim at me. I remember almost every word that was said in the garage that day. Some were omitted by the FBI on purpose. The agent in charge yelled: "Who are you?" He quoted me as responding back: "Who the fuck are you?" What I actually said was: "Who the fuck are you, Homeland Security?"

I felt I was the calmest person in the garage at that moment. Things were so tense I expected they may kill me.

The agents demanded that he get on his knees. But Bulger didn't want to kneel in the spot where they wanted him because there was a small pool of oil. Sixteen years on the run, millions in law enforcement spending, and years of unfathomable agony for his victims' loved ones, all had come to this moment: a deadly standoff over whether Whitey would get his pants dirty.

*They were screaming, "We will shoot," and I re-
sponded, "Go ahead . . . I'm not kneeling down in
the oil." I told them that there was a clean place to
my right and for him to take two steps to the right
to that area and then I'd comply.*

*He was screaming, "Don't try it or I'll shoot!" I
thought, "I'm going to die," and I knew it might be
my last step, but I told them, "Here is step number
one," and I took it. I debated with myself: do I dare
chance another step? The tension was rising, but I
said, "Fuck it, I'm not backing down" and I said,
"Here's step number two." They screamed, "Don't
or we'll shoot!!!" I had that feeling I had as a kid
waiting to feel the bullet in the back.*

But the agents didn't shoot.

Shit, is this guy gonna try to run on us? Scott Garriola thought.

But cornered with no chance to escape, Bulger put
his hands up. He'd feared this moment for the past sixteen years and now it was finally here.

"What's your name?" Garriola asked with his gun
trained on Whitey's chest.

"You know who I am," Bulger said defiantly.

"Okay, Whitey. We have a warrant for your arrest!"

Garriola then took out a pair of handcuffs and tied them to Bulger's wrists.

"Is Catherine upstairs?"

Whitey nodded.

"Do you have any guns up there?"

"Yeah," Bulger replied. "And they're all loaded."

"What do you mean? Do I need to call a SWAT team to get her outta there?"

"No, no," Whitey assured him. "All the guns are mine. Most of them are in my bedroom. She's never held a gun and she's not allowed in my bedroom."

Bulger offered to call Catherine to get her down to the garage.

"No, give me your key," Garriola said. "I'll go up and I'll treat her like a gentleman and I'll bring her down here."

Garriola sent another group text to Teahan, Sullivan, and Torsney:

One in custody and one to go. Bulger captured. Standby for Catherine.

The agent got a female detective to accompany him to apartment 303.

"Santa Monica PD," Garriola shouted. "Open the door."

Catherine walked to the door and turned the knob

slowly. She opened the door and then let out an exasperated sigh.

"I knew it!" she said tersely. "I knew the FBI was here."

Garriola sent another group text to his fellow agents in Boston:

Catherine in custody without incident. Scene secure.

Everyone stared at their cell phone screens in near disbelief.

"He's under arrest!" Torsney shouted to the young agents manning the phones at the FBI command center.

"They looked up at me as if to say, 'Holy shit!'" he recalls.

Agents started hugging one another.

"Tears came to my eyes. I've done a lot in my career and I'm not too proud to say that, but this was next level," Torsney says. "For the Boston office to finally put this to rest? I mean, are you shitting me?"

For Sullivan and Teahan, the moment was equally satisfying.

The marshal reached into the refrigerator of his rented condo on St. Botolph Street and grabbed a cold Stella Artois, popped the cap, and chugged. He then hugged his wife, Eileen.

"She couldn't believe it," Sullivan recalls, "that we'd actually completed the task that took sixteen long years to accomplish."

The celebrations were contagious.

"It was just unbelievable to me," Noreen Gleason says. "I almost cried when I heard. I sat down and thought, *oh my God, this is awesome!*"

The hunt for Bulger had been a team sport also involving the Massachusetts State Police, DEA, and US Marshals Service, but for the Bureau, it marked the beginning of a recovery. The stain of John Connolly and other corrupt agents had finally been lifted.

"I took my phone and threw it across the room and jumped in the air in celebration," Teahan remembers. "My wife had been dealing with my heartache and pressure. She was in the room when I got the text and she was just as thrilled. It was vindication. and the sweet thing was that it was the FBI that got him!"

Tommy Mac was attending a family celebration when he first learned of Bulger's capture. He threw his arms up like a boxer after a knockout win. He wasn't surprised that it had happened so quickly after the PSA was released. "If we never found those photos of Catherine Greig, Bulger would be sitting on the couch in Santa Monica right now scratching his balls and watching TV," MacDonald says. "Those images changed the case."

Roberta Hastings was also elated. She'd been working on the case longer than anyone. Her first phone call was to her former colleague, the now retired Charlie Gianturco.

"We got the son of a bitch!" she told him.

FBI director Robert Mueller called Rich Teahan, his former protector, at home.

"Rich, Director Mueller here. You did a great job. Your team did a great job."

The news had triggered a seismic reaction at FBI headquarters in Washington, DC.

"Oh my god, you gotta be kidding me. They just caught Bulger!" Andrew McCabe, the future director of the FBI, shouted when he heard.

McCabe had just been given an assignment to build the high-value detainee interrogation group and while the Bureau's focus remained on national security, the hunt for Whitey Bulger had always been a priority and a personal mission for every agent in every FBI office.

"The Bureau's Criminal Investigation Division [CID] had always bristled by the amount of attention that was generated by counterterrorism agents," McCabe explains. "That's why this was so special. It was a huge accomplishment for the FBI and one that echoes back to the core of who we are and what we do. FBI agents live their entire careers with the belief

that we never forget, that we never stop looking. The search for Bulger was the perfect example of that. It was a highly significant event."

For Noreen Gleason, the magnitude of putting this operation into play and having it be successful was overwhelming. "Arresting Whitey was a team sport with the marshals, state police, and finally the US Attorney's Office involved, but for the FBI, it was much more personal. This marked the beginning of a recovery for the people of Boston and for every good FBI agent that ever worked in the office. I felt so proud of what we had accomplished together. Bulger was no hero. He was a dangerous sociopath who committed heinous crimes and eluded capture for so many years until we got him."

24

As Scott Garriola was placing Bulger into custody in the carport at the Princess Eugenia, a neighbor entered the garage to do her laundry.

"I think I can help you," Janus Goodwin told the agent. "This man has dementia. So if he's acting oddly that could be why."

Goodwin lived on the same floor as Whitey and Catherine and had been told like so many others that "Charlie Gasko" suffered from mental illness.

Garriola got nervous for a moment. Had he just arrested a delusional elderly man with Alzheimer's disease?

He turned to Bulger. "This woman over here says you have a touch of Alzheimer's."

"Fuck her. Don't listen to her. She's fucking nuts. I'm James J. Bulger."

A few minutes later, Garriola asked the captured crime boss to grant the FBI permission to search apartment 303. He signed the consent form *James J. Bulger.*

"That's the first time I've signed that name in a long time," he sighed.

Garriola asked Bulger whether he was relieved that he didn't have to look over his shoulder anymore as the sixteen-year manhunt had come to an end.

"Are you fucking nuts?" Whitey answered.

Catherine was wearing a revealing halter top and asked to change into something more appropriate, so a female officer led her to the bathroom. Meanwhile, Whitey was busy walking Garriola through the apartment.

"He showed us where all his 'hides' were, where his stashes were," the agent recalls. "He had a Derringer in a hollowed-out book and of course all that money and weapons in the walls. Whitey was a tough son of a bitch. He looked pretty feisty when we got him. If we'd met up with Bulger a few years earlier, he would have given us a helluva fight."

Bulger and Greig were led out of the apartment building in handcuffs and placed into separate squad cars and driven off to Los Angeles, where they'd be

jailed separately overnight as they awaited their first court appearance the following day. It was after 8 p.m., so Garriola had to get special permission from the Bureau of Prisons to bring the fugitives in at such a late hour.

With Bulger safely in custody, Phil Torsney left his Boston office in the early morning hours and drove home in the driving rain. He didn't have time to sleep, as he was to meet Neil Sullivan and Rich Teahan at Logan Airport to catch the first flight out to Los Angeles.

When Neil Sullivan saw Whitey Bulger for the first time in person at the Federal Courthouse in LA, the aging gangster was wearing an orange prison jumpsuit and was doing push-ups in his cell.

"He looked very fit and was doing a lot of push-ups for an old man," Sullivan remembers. "I'd heard some reporters whispering that Bulger may be senile, but that wasn't true. He was totally with it and physically strong for an eighty-one-year-old."

The marshal also saw Catherine Greig in her cell. She was subdued and didn't say a word.

Sullivan escorted Bulger into court, where it was standing room only. This was the biggest criminal case to hit Los Angeles since O. J. Simpson, and everyone strained to get a look at the Irish mob boss from South

Boston and his aging moll. There were not enough seats available, so Neil had to stand with his gun on his hip. Both Whitey and Catherine remained quiet during the proceedings, which was a relief to the marshal.

"I wasn't worried about security in court," Sullivan says. "The place was airtight. I wasn't worried either about someone sneaking in firearms or that he'd make an outburst. That didn't seem to be his style."

While Bulger and Greig were in court, an FBI team continued to canvass their apartment at the Princess Eugenia.

Agents couldn't believe the amount of weapons Bulger had collected and hidden or the nearly $1 million he had squirreled away. They were also surprised to see how the couple had stockpiled everyday items like cleaning products and soaps. When agents entered Whitey's bedroom, they spotted seven 64-ounce bottles with white tube socks stretched over the top. It looked like Bulger was busy trying to build Molotov cocktails, but that wasn't the case. He told investigators that he'd purchased the socks at a discount store and that they were too tight on his calves, so he was merely stretching them out.

"Some of the other stuff we found in the apartment showed a different side of Bulger," Phil Torsney says. "We found letters showing that he had assisted some

people with their legal fees. If you were loyal to him, he was pretty damn loyal to you. He also reached out to people he didn't know in Alabama after seeing their story on TV. He sent some cash to someone who'd killed a family member for molesting a child."

Scott Garriola was exhausted and longing to return to his vacation. Instead, he was ordered to join a teleconference with FBI director Robert Mueller. That didn't sit well with the agent. He asked if his bosses could do it instead but was told no.

"The call with Mueller got a little testy," the agent recalls. "I was so tired at the time. I cracked a joke and the director didn't like it. I cracked another and he threatened to send me to Afghanistan and it went downhill from there."

Mueller had worked in Boston as the interim US attorney in 1986–87 and knew the Bulger case well. The FBI director was only interested in the facts and had no sympathy for the agent's fatigue. Mueller did recognize and express his appreciation to Garriola for his work on the case a few months later.

The FBI director then sent his own private Learjet for Sullivan, Teahan, and Torsney to escort America's most wanted man and his girlfriend back to Boston. Sullivan placed the belly chain and the leg restraints on Bulger and walked him carefully onto the plane.

Whitey and Catherine were separated when they got on board. She was led to the front of the plane and was watched closely by a deputy, while he was placed in the back in a rectangular seating area with two chairs facing backward and two chairs facing front. Bulger was joined by Sullivan and the two FBI agents. They had only six hours to interview Whitey and they weren't going to let one second go to waste.

"It's not often that you get to chase someone and hunt someone and then get the chance to interview them—and they're actually consenting," Teahan says.

Phil Torsney led the questioning. He called the captured fugitive James and not Whitey or Mr. Bulger.

"It was really hard not to be a crook anymore," Bulger told him. "I really lost focus. Years and dates kinda ran together."

"Like any other retiree?" Torsney said.

"Yeah." Bulger smiled. "But I went back to Boston a few times to handle unfinished business. The last time was five or six years ago and I was armed to the teeth."

The agents didn't believe him. They felt that it was just Whitey's attempt to remain relevant in a criminal world that has passed him by. Bulger wanted the investigators to believe that he was still menacing and that he still had clout.

"I'm done," Bulger told them. "I'll plead guilty tomorrow if you let Catherine go. She's the only reason I don't commit crimes. She doesn't deserve to be in jail. She deserves a fucking medal. There won't be a trial. I need to face the consequences but she's innocent and doesn't deserve any of this."

Whitey also tried to protect his old handler John Connolly. "I feel responsible for John Connolly. I never really dealt with him though. I was dealing with John Morris, not Connolly."

Bulger even claimed that Morris, the former FBI supervisor, had offered him money to kill his wife. He was rewriting history to benefit himself.

Whitey then took the agents down memory lane, or his version of it anyway, reminiscing about the old days in South Boston during the busing crisis.

"If blacks came across my territory in Southie, I'd beat the shit out of those niggers."

Teahan was surprised by how racist Whitey was. "He threw the N-word around like he was drinking a cup of water. He complained about blacks in South Boston and black people in Santa Monica."

But the agents had to work around Bulger's nasty disposition. He was a killer and a liar after all. They didn't want him to shut down. They needed him to keep talking.

"Do you have any money left in safety deposit boxes?" Rich Teahan asked.

"Why the hell would I tell you?"

Bulger then confided that he had a plan if he ever got real sick. He said he was going to go to Nevada and fall into a mine shaft, killing himself so that no one would ever find his body.

"I wanted to keep the mystery going," Whitey told them. "Fuck the FBI. I never wanted you guys to find me. I wanted you to all look like failures. I don't know why I'm telling you all this. I'm giving you the fugitive's playbook."

Rich Teahan watched Whitey Bulger in amazement as the elderly gangster's personality shifted. One minute he'd be normal and the next minute he'd snap.

"His eyes would turn steel blue," Teahan recalls. "You could see it. It was like a lion watching its prey, totally disarming one minute and devouring you the next."

As the Learjet flew over the Grand Canyon, Torsney took his attention off Bulger and looked out the window, as he'd never flown over the majestic site before. Whitey wasn't amused.

"He looked at me as if to say, 'You've finally got an opportunity to interview me and you're looking at the

fucking Grand Canyon?'" Torsney says. "'Don't you know who I am? I'm Whitey fucking Bulger.'"

"I couldn't believe his ego and his bragging," Sullivan remembers. "He'd describe crimes in vivid detail but he refused to admit his involvement."

Instead of placing himself at the scene of a mob murder, Whitey spoke as if he were a narrator reading a true crime book in the third person.

Bulger would play word games like "This guy did this thing or that thing and that's what got him killed." When one of the investigators asked Whitey if he'd ever spent time in San Diego, the mobster smiled. "They have nice theaters there," he said, corroborating the earlier sighting by Sheriff's Deputy Rich Eaton at a screening of *The Departed*.

Six hours later in late afternoon, the Learjet carved through the clouds above South Boston. Whitey Bulger was coming home.

On the approach to Logan Airport, Whitey looked out the window of the jet and down onto the rooftops of Southie.

"Where's that?" he asked. He didn't have a smile on his face. He wasn't joking. Whitey didn't recognize his old neighborhood. It had been that long since he'd fled.

PART II

The Trial

25

In late June 2011, Whitey Bulger made his first court appearance in Boston. Billy was seated in the second row of the John Joseph Moakley Courthouse, named after a former congressman and childhood friend of the Bulgers. Whitey's eyes lit up when he spotted his brother.

"Hi," he mouthed.

Billy smiled back.

It was the first time that the disgraced politician and former college president had seen his gangster brother in more than a decade. It was also the first time that many reporters had ever set their eyes on Whitey in person. To them, he was a specter known only through grainy surveillance images, court documents, and neighbor-

hood rumors. One spectator compared the hearing to something from the days of Al Capone in Chicago.

"If you could go back in time to be in that courtroom [for Capone] wouldn't you?" she asked.

Another gawker stood outside the courthouse amazed at the amount of television cameras present to cover the proceeding. "It's quite a bit of celebrity for a criminal," he remarked. "But around these parts, he's pretty famous so it doesn't surprise me."

But among the curious onlookers were those who had felt the pain of Bulger's brutality and reign of terror up close and personal. Tommy Donahue, whose father had been gunned down by Whitey during the hit on Brian Halloran in 1982, seethed when he saw Bulger for the first time in court. Donahue wanted the judge to inflict as much bodily harm on his father's killer as possible.

"He should get the electric chair," Donahue told reporters. "I'm an electrician, I know."

Security was beefed up around the courthouse for the hearings. The US Coast Guard sent two boats with mounted machine guns, along with a state police boat and a Boston police patrol boat, to guard against an attack on Bulger from the adjacent Boston Harbor.

Whitey looked fit and bronzed by the California sun, wearing a white hooded shirt and blue jeans as he was

led into court. America's most wanted, now caught, fugitive sat quietly while the judge read the laundry list of indictments against him, including nineteen counts of murder.

"Can I have a public defender represent me?" Bulger asked.

The request was shot down immediately as prosecutors reminded the judge of the more than $800,000 seized from the Santa Monica apartment. "He clearly didn't make that on a paper route on Santa Monica Boulevard," quipped prosecutor Brian Kelly.

He then stared out at the courtroom, spotting brother Billy and other family members. "We feel he has access to cash," Kelly argued.

During the second of back-to-back hearings that day, the magistrate judge asked Whitey if he could afford an attorney.

"I could if you give me my money," Whitey groused, inciting laughter in the courtroom.

Bulger didn't enter a plea that day, leaving all to wonder if he had any more cards to play.

Catherine appeared in the same courthouse later in the day with her twin sister, Margaret, watching from the front row. Unlike Bulger, she appeared gaunt and exhausted. All the stress of the past sixteen years on the run was now evident in the lines across her once

delicate face. As the judge recited the charges against her, including harboring a fugitive, Greig started shaking and her court-appointed lawyer had to place his hand on her frail shoulder to support her.

After the initial court hearing, Catherine was sent to the Wyatt Detention Center in Central Falls, Rhode Island, which had housed some notorious Mafia figures and also one of the prime suspects in the infamous art heist at Boston's Isabella Stewart Gardner Museum. Whitey was taken by motorcade to the Plymouth County Correctional Facility, the former home of Stevie Flemmi and the so-called Shoe Bomber, Richard Reid.

Whitey had not seen the inside of a prison cell since the early 1960s, when he spent time at Atlanta, Leavenworth, Lewisburg, and of course Alcatraz. The town of Plymouth had its own rock a short drive away where the Pilgrims had landed. No feast awaited Bulger when he arrived, though. It was back to bland prison food.

The elderly former mob boss was placed into the administrative segregation unit, where he had no contact with any other inmates and was never allowed to mix with anyone besides the guards and his visitors.

Both Billy and their brother Jackie made the hour drive south to Plymouth on a weekly basis. Since Jackie

was now an ex-convict himself, he needed special clearance to meet with Whitey.

Bulger was housed in Unit G of the prison, where he was in lockdown twenty-three hours per day with one hour for recreation. There were fourteen cells in the unit. On the top tier, inmates were doubled up. Bulger had a single cell on the bottom floor called Southwest 108, tucked away in the corner. The guards kept cell 107 empty to provide Whitey with a buffer.

As he'd done at the federal courthouse in Los Angeles, Bulger made the most of his confined space, doing hundreds of push-ups every day. When he was allowed to walk the floor, he'd chat up other inmates through their cell doors. One jailhouse snitch always tried to get Whitey to discuss mob murders that he'd either ordered or carried out on his own, but Bulger would never take the bait.

Ken Brady worked in the investigations unit at Plymouth. The biggest concern for authorities there was that Bulger would attempt suicide. Brady spoke with Whitey every day.

"He was frustrated that he wasn't the feared gangster that he used to be," Brady recalls.

Instead, Whitey felt that he was being humiliated on a regular basis. There was an incident on the floor of Bulger's unit that prompted a search of all the in-

mates' cells. Ken Brady had to conduct a strip search of Whitey. The old man stood up from his bunk and clenched his fists, preparing to fight.

"I'm not fucking doing it," Whitey growled. "I'm sick of this shit. I'm not doing it!"

Brady didn't want to pin down the geriatric prisoner and tear off his clothes, but he would if he had to. Bulger wasn't giving an inch of cell space.

"Listen, Whitey, I'm not playing games with you anymore," Brady commanded. "Knock it off and let's go. Strip or I'm ripping off your clothes anyway!"

Brady had always called him Mr. Bulger. It was the first time he'd called him Whitey and that got him even angrier. He wasn't the intimidating figure he'd once been or feared like he was decades ago in Southie. Whitey could show Brady that he was still tough, but attacking the prison guard would not help his situation, so he finally backed down.

"I'm sorry," Bulger apologized the next day. "I was frustrated."

To keep his brain alert, Whitey traded books with people, mostly history books. He also wrote letters and responded to anyone who wrote him. He talked about his time in Grand Isle, Louisiana, and his friendship with the Gautreaux family.

"These people were so poor and desolate, I'd buy

them new appliances for their house," Bulger bragged as he tried to resurrect the image he'd carefully crafted as a Robin Hood–style bandit. He wrote Glenn Gautreaux Jr. a letter, asking him about the family and describing his time on the run and also the circus in Boston:

> When they brought me back here, it looked like a parade. We traveled a lot over the years and even visited Tombstone, Arizona. But Grand Isle is the best place we ever visited.

Glenn Jr. wrote Whitey back, telling him how much the family loved and missed him and "Aunt Helen."

Bulger was also doing anything he could to gain leverage with the guards. He'd try to guess their lineage. "Are you Irish?" he'd ask. "Do you have a family? Where do you live?"

The prison guards wouldn't entertain the questions. To them, Bulger wasn't the crime lord he once was. He wasn't running the Winter Hill Gang anymore. In fact, the gang no longer existed. Whitey was just an old man who was about to be put away for the rest of his life, however long that lasted.

Ken Brady monitored all of Bulger's calls and visits from his family. Emotions got high during one jailhouse

meeting with his brother Billy. Separated by a partition of thick glass and speaking over the phone, Whitey complained about his unfair treatment in prison and had questions about his emerging defense. He was in full martyr mode, blaming everyone else including the FBI for his predicament. Finally, his younger brother had heard enough.

"Do you have any idea what this has put the family through for the past sixteen years?" Billy asked him.

Those words turned Whitey red with anger.

"What I've put the family through? Look at me. I'm locked up!" he shouted. "My girlfriend is in jail! If you could give me a poison pill right now, I'd take it!"

Ken Brady was listening in on the conversation and ran into the room to put an abrupt end to the visit. He then placed Whitey Bulger under suicide watch. If anything happened to Whitey while in Plymouth, the punishment for the guards would be severe. The US Attorney's Office was in charge now and they wanted Bulger treated with white gloves as he awaited trial.

While Whitey was adjusting to his life behind bars, Catherine was trying to avoid hers. A month after Catherine's initial court appearance in Boston, her new lawyer was fighting hard for her release. Attorney Kevin Reddington asked the judge to release Greig on

bail pending her trial and painted her not as Whitey's girlfriend, but as another one of his victims.

"This woman is not a violent person," Reddington argued during her bail hearing. "Her only crime is a crime of passion—falling in love with this gentleman [Bulger]."

FBI agent Mike Carazza, who had followed Bulger's trail down to the Bayou with Charlie Gianturco, testified at the hearing and described how domineering Whitey was toward Catherine and how subservient she was toward him. Prosecutors asked Carazza whether the Gautreaux family had ever said that Greig was being held against her will while living with Whitey in Grand Isle, Louisiana.

"They never indicated that," the agent replied.

Carazza looked over at Catherine sitting at the defense table. She was no longer the fragile prisoner that had first appeared in court a month before. She had regained her strength and projected a new attitude at the hearing.

"She was stoic, defiant, and loyal in court," Carazza recalls.

Attorney Reddington also claimed that Catherine was unaware of all the weapons and money stashed in the Santa Monica apartment.

Prosecutors argued that she was no unwitting ac-

complice and pointed to her efforts to help Bulger secure fake IDs and how she called her sister regularly while on the run.

"The defendant learned the tricks of the fugitive trade," said Assistant US Attorney James Hebert. "She was a willing, active participant in their joint effort to avoid arrest."

Tommy Donahue, son of victim Michael Donahue, then took the witness stand and called Greig "a creep." He said that allowing Catherine to be free would be unbearable to his family and the loved ones of Bulger's eighteen other murder victims.

"The sixteen years with her lover on the run are the sixteen years that we cried," he told the judge.

Reddington did his best to attempt to separate Bulger's crimes from his client, who was accused only of helping Whitey elude capture.

"She has nothing to do with any of those murders or acts of violence," the defense attorney said.

One year later, in 2012, Catherine Greig was sentenced to eight years in prison after pleading guilty to charges of conspiracy to harbor a fugitive, identity fraud, and conspiracy to commit identity fraud. As part of the plea deal, Catherine could not be compelled to testify against Whitey.

Attorney Reddington had appealed to the judge for

leniency and asked that she serve only twenty-seven months behind bars.

"Catherine Greig fell in love with Mr. Bulger, and that's why she was in the situation she was in," Reddington argued again. "Miss Greig did not believe that Mr. Bulger was capable of these homicides."

The lawyer's claim drew both heavy sighs and laughter in the courtroom.

Prosecutors pushed for a stiffer sentence, saying this was no "romantic saga."

Whitey and Catherine weren't Romeo and Juliet. Theirs was a modern-day version of Bonnie and Clyde.

"We are all responsible for what we do," US District Court judge Douglas Whitlock told Greig. "There is a price to be paid."

After Catherine was escorted out of the courtroom in shackles, her attorney was asked whether she felt any remorse for sticking by Whitey Bulger.

"He's the love of her life and she stands by him," Reddington noted. "Of course she has no regrets."

There was still a question about additional money, believed to be in the millions, that Whitey had stashed away in safe deposit boxes. The US Marshals had already taken control of everything that was found in the Santa Monica apartment. The asset forfeiture, including the $822,000, would go to the families of Bulger's

victims, but investigators believed that was just the tip of the iceberg.

"We wanted to bring Catherine in to the grand jury to talk about the money, but she wouldn't do it," says Rich Teahan. "So she was held in contempt of court."

For her unwillingness to cooperate, Greig, then sixty-one years old, would have an additional twenty-one months tacked on to her prison sentence.

Whitey Bulger meets with fellow Winter Hill mobster George Kaufman at the crew's headquarters at the Lancaster Street garage in Boston in 1980. *(United States Attorney evidence photo)*

Bulger *(center)* eventually learned that law enforcement was bugging and videotaping clandestine meetings at the Lancaster Street garage. *(United States Attorney evidence photo)*

Stephen "The Rifleman" Flemmi *(left)*, Whitey *(middle)*, and Kevin Weeks *(right)* stroll Castle Island on the South Boston waterfront. *(United States Attorney evidence photo)*

Whitey (*left*) and Weeks on Castle Island in Southie just before Whitey went on the run in 1995. This is one of the last known photos of Bulger in Boston. *(United States Attorney evidence photo)*

Whitey's de facto headquarters, Triple O's Lounge, was a blood-soaked barroom on West Broadway in South Boston. Today, it is home to an upscale gastropub and a luxury condo building. *(United States Attorney evidence photo)*

Whitey holds mob executioner John Martorano's son, John Jr., at the boy's christening in Boston in this undated photo. Martorano admitted killing twenty people as the Winter Hill Gang's top triggerman and implicated Whitey in more than a dozen killings. *(United States Attorney evidence photo)*

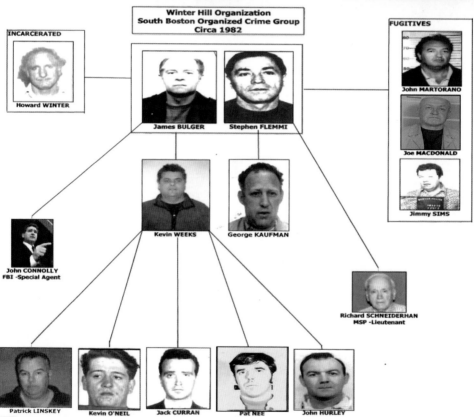

US Attorney's office organization chart for the Winter Hill Gang, including corrupt FBI agent John Connolly and corrupt Massachusetts state trooper Richard Schneiderhan as associates of the gang. *(United States Attorney evidence photo)*

Boston-born businessman Roger Wheeler, the fifty-five-year-old president of World Jai Alai, was executed in his car by John Martorano as he left a Tulsa, Oklahoma, country club in 1981. Wheeler was targeted for death after discovering Bulger and his crew were skimming from the Jai Alai operation. *(United States Attorney evidence photo)*

The bullet-riddled blue Datsun driven by Michael Donahue after an ambush by Whitey outside a bar on the South Boston waterfront in 1982. Whitey, wearing a wig, fake mustache, and floppy hat and brandishing a machine gun, executed Donahue, an innocent bystander, and Brian Halloran, who Bulger feared was cooperating with the FBI. *(United States Attorney evidence photo)*

FBI mugshots of Whitey and Flemmi taken in 1983 when they were suspects in the 1982 murder of former World Jai Alai president John B. Callahan in Miami. Callahan, forty-five, was from the Boston suburb of Medford and was killed because of what he knew about the Wheeler murder. *(United States Attorney evidence photo)*

Stephen Flemmi's mistress Debra Davis was strangled to death in the basement of The Haunty because Whitey feared she would talk to the FBI. While Flemmi testified Bulger killed the twenty-six-year-old beauty, the jury made no finding on Bulger's guilt in her slaying. The no-finding verdict on the Davis murder was labeled a victory for Whitey by his lawyers. *(United States Attorney evidence photo)*

Cops dig up bones at Tenean Beach in Dorchester. Three badly decomposed bodies were found at the site, including the remains of Paulie McGonagle, Debra Davis, and boxer Tommy King, who had the distinct honor of once having beaten up Whitey at Triple O's. *(United States Attorney evidence photo)*

Remains of one of three bodies unearthed from the burial site on Tenean Beach in 2000. *(United States Attorney evidence photo)*

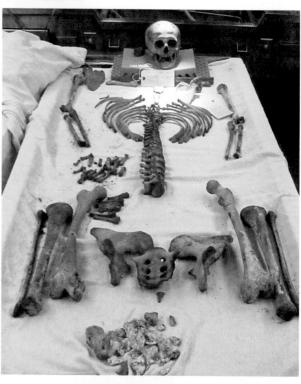

Below: Masks used by the Winter Hill Gang in armed robberies and shootings were unearthed, along with dozens of guns, in 1980 from the East Third Street home of Flemmi's mother, Mary, who lived across a courtyard from Whitey's powerful politician brother, Billy Bulger. *(United States Attorney evidence photo)*

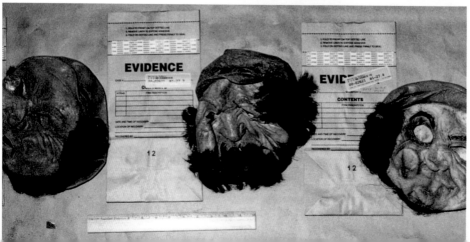

Whitey's brother, former Massachusetts State Senate president Billy Bulger, spoke to the authors for hours at this South Boston home on the left in the summer of 2019. The house on the right across the courtyard, 832 East Fourth St., was home to Flemmi's mother, Mary, for decades. It is now vacant. *(Photo by authors)*

Bulger and his crew killed at least three people and buried them in the basement of "The Haunty" murder house at 799 East Third St. in Southie. Built in 1890, the house was purchased for just $120,000 in the 1980s and sold for $3.5 million in 2019. At publication, it was slated for demolition for a new condo building in the heavily gentrified neighborhood. *(Photo by authors)*

Whitey's girlfriend Catherine Greig (*left*) and her twin sister, Margaret McCusker, in an undated photo. *(Photo courtesy of Margaret McCusker)*

A never-before-published fake ID used by Bulger in New York, immediately after he went on the run, under the name "Charles Gaska." He would later amend the name to Charles Gasko. *(United States Attorney evidence photo)*

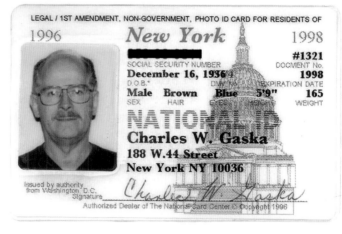

LEGAL / 1ST AMENDMENT, NON-GOVERNMENT, PHOTO ID CARD FOR RESIDENTS OF

1996 **New York** 1998

#1321

SOCIAL SECURITY NUMBER DOCUMENT No.

December 16, 1936 1998

D.O.B. DMV No. EXPIRATION DATE

Male Brown Blue 5'9" 165

SEX HAIR EYES HEIGHT WEIGHT

NATIONAL ID

Charles W. Gaska

188 W.44 Street

New York NY 10036

Issued by authority from Washington D.C. Signature

Authorized Dealer of The National Card Center © Copyright 1996

Whitey got this California driver's license by paying a US Army veteran named James Lawlor for his personal information. *(United States Attorney evidence photo)*

DMV **CALIFORNIA** DMV

DRIVER LICENSE

EXPIRES 11-09-07 S0620560 CLASS:C

JAMES WILLIAM LAWLOR
1538 SAWTELLE BLVD APT 29
W LOS ANGELES CA 90025

SEX:M HAIR:WHT EYES:BLU
HT:5-08 WT:170 DOB:11-09-36

RSTR: CORR LENS

09/23/2002 235 RB FD/07

Whitey stood watch on the third floor of the Princess Eugenia Apartments (*top right unit*) in Santa Monica, California, where he hid in plain sight for years as an unassuming retiree while the nation's number one fugitive. Bulger was arrested in 2011 by FBI agents in the underground garage in the bottom left of the photo. *(Photo by Authors)*

Whitey and Catherine lived in this unit, #303, at Princess Eugenia Apartments in Santa Monica for years until cops lured him out of the apartment and arrested him in the building's underground parking garage in 2011. *(Photo by Authors)*

Charlie and Carol Gasko—the aliases of Whitey Bulger and Catherine Greig—befriended their elderly neighbor Catalina Shlank. The Argentinian woman thought they were retirees and said Whitey regularly helped her with her groceries. *(Photo by Authors)*

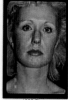

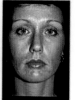

The FBI scored a major breakthrough in the case when agents found photographs of Catherine Greig that were taken when she underwent plastic surgery. *(Photo courtesy of the FBI)*

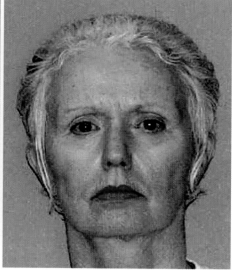

Booking photos for Whitey and Catherine following their arrests in 2011.
(Photo courtesy of US Marshals Service)

FBI Special Agent Scott Garriola handcuffs James J. "Whitey" Bulger in the underground parking garage at the Princess Eugenia Apartments in Santa Monica, on June 22, 2011.
(Photo courtesy of Scott Garriola and LAPD/ Miguel Mejia)

FBI Special Agent Scott Garriola escorts Whitey in cuffs while FBI agent James Ross escorts Catherine Greig to a federal prison detention center in Los Angeles in 2011.
(Photo courtesy of Scott Garriola and LAPD/Miguel Mejia)

Authorities retrieved more than $800,000 and dozens of guns and weapons stashed in wall hides such as this one inside unit #303 at the Princess Eugenia Apartments in Santa Monica. *(United States Attorney evidence photo)*

A cache of guns belonging to Bulger that were seized following his capture in Santa Monica. *(United States Attorney evidence photo)*

Whitey's living room in Santa Monica where he used a punching dummy wearing a fedora as a decoy for anyone who might want to shoot him through the window. *(United States Attorney evidence photo)*

Sgt. Richard Eaton of the San Diego County Sheriff's Department claims to have identified Whitey at a screening of the Oscar-winning film *The Departed* in 2006. *(Photo courtesy of Sgt. Richard Eaton, San Diego County Sheriff's Department)*

FBI Assistant Special Agent-in-Charge Noreen Gleason led the Bulger Task Force and put together the team that ultimately captured the fugitive crime boss. Gleason is credited with making the call to focus the investigation on tracking Catherine Greig, a pivotal move that ultimately led to the key break in the case. *(Photo courtesy of Noreen Gleason)*

US Marshal Neil Sullivan is the agent who got the tip that led authorities to Bulger's hideout in Santa Monica. *(Photo courtesy US Marshals Service)*

Assistant US Attorney Brian Kelly was part of the prosecution team that put Whitey away for good in 2013. Kelly received death threats that required security for him and his family because of his work on the Bulger case. *(US Attorney's office photo)*

Zach Hafer, a seasoned organized crime prosecutor, had a front seat to the courtroom theatrics as part of the team in the Boston US Attorney's office that brought Whitey to justice. *(US Attorney's office photo)*

Unit 303 in the Princess Eugenia Apartments where Whitey and Catherine hid out for years was renovated in 2019 and rented to a new tenant. *(Photo by authors)*

FBI manhunters Tommy MacDonald and Phil Torsney were brought in to spearhead the task force that captured Whitey. *(Photo courtesy of Federal Bureau of Investigation)*

A rare photo of Whitey Bulger in prison, seen here with his art teacher Clement "Chip" Janus at USP Tucson in 2014. *(Photo courtesy of Clement "Chip" Janus)*

Another rare photo of Whitey Bulger in USP Tucson in 2014 with his art teacher "Chip" Janus and others. *(Photo courtesy Clement "Chip" Janus)*

On Right Chip - "The Artist"   July 2014

A man who found himself in this place where so many waste away accomplishing very little.

Oscar Wilde said it over a hundred years ago:

"Vile Deeds Like Poison Weeds
    Bloom Well in Prison Air
It is only what is Good in Man
    That Wastes and Withers there."

So True. But Chip is the exception – fortunately for us who appreciate the fruits of his talent.

James Whitey Bulger 1428 AZ

A letter written by Whitey to his friend Clement "Chip" Janus in 2014.
(Courtesy of Clement "Chip" Janus)

Springfield mobster Fotios "Freddy" Geas, one of Bulger's accused killers, was a lieutenant in the powerful western Massachusetts Mafia faction run by Alfredo "Big Al" Bruno. The crew answered to John Gotti and the New York La Cosa Nostra and used this Springfield, Massachusetts, strip club as its headquarters. *(Photo by authors)*

Suspected Bulger killer Fotios "Freddy" Geas, who is serving life for murder and racketeering in the United States Penitentiary in Hazelton, West Virginia, where Whitey was killed, is shown with his daughter Taylor in this undated photo from the 1990s. *(Photo courtesy of Taylor Geas)*

Whitey is buried here with his parents, Mary and John, in a cemetery in the West Roxbury section of Boston. Whitey's name is not on the grave. *(Photo by authors)*

26

The Moakley Courthouse stood as an impenetrable fortress on the Boston waterfront. The city was still recovering from the deadly Boston Marathon bombings that tore through downtown in April, leaving three spectators dead, including an eight-year-old boy, and hundreds more critically wounded.

Terror suspect Dzhokhar Tsarnaev had been brought to the courthouse for his initial hearings, bringing with him throngs of media from around the world.

Now armies of reporters had returned as James "Whitey" Bulger, the city's proverbial white whale, was on deck. Network satellite trucks were fixtures on Seaport Boulevard, drawing gawking stares from tourists and locals alike. There were lines wrapped around

the courthouse for spectators seeking to witness history.

"I'm sick to my stomach," said Tommy Donahue.

"He's a cold-hearted murderer," Donahue told reporters. "Got a kick out of it like most of these people would . . . His demeanor is still the same. He could care less about what's going on, what feelings were hurt, who was killed."

Inside the courtroom, prosecutors were preparing for what they knew would be difficult weeks of proceedings. Of all those on the prosecution team, Zachary Hafer was the one true outsider. Raised in Philadelphia, Hafer graduated cum laude from Dartmouth College and got his law degree at the University of Virginia. He married a Boston girl and moved to Boston in 2007 after clerking in New York City for a federal judge and working for a private law firm.

In the US Attorney's Office, Hafer started on the drug task force. In 2009, he headed the prosecution of an international cocaine trafficking ring that resulted in the extradition of thirteen Colombian drug lords who were manufacturing drugs in Colombia and smuggling them into Boston. In 2011, Hafer won a conviction for money laundering against mob lawyer Robert George, who previously represented Frank Salemme and John Martorano. And in 2012, Hafer prosecuted

Trevor Watson, a gang member who served time for the 2000 stabbing of Boston Celtic great Paul Pierce, for attempting to kill an informant.

Tall and lean with light brown hair, Hafer was getting to know Boston, and more specifically, its criminal underworld, when he was thrust into the Bulger case. After Bulger was captured, Hafer was recruited to join the prosecution team and started doing much of the pretrial grunt work—reviewing old transcripts and case files, tracking down witnesses, and finding experts and cops who worked on the original murders. The young prosecutor's knowledge of the case came mostly from reading news clips and books and seeing the film *The Departed*, which was part of his curriculum at UVA law school. When he saw the first pictures of Bulger in custody, Hafer knew there would be an identification issue because the aged gangster looked so different than he did on the streets of Southie in the 1970s, '80s, and '90s. So it fell to Hafer to file for a court order mandating that Bulger shave off his gray beard.

"He looked completely different. Some of these witnesses hadn't seen him in thirty-five years," Hafer said. "As we were getting ready to file it, months into the litigation, eventually one day he just showed up and had shaved."

For Hafer, joining the Bulger team was "the opportunity of a lifetime," and he marveled at the rotating cast of characters paraded in and out of Judge Denise Casper's courtroom.

"You had the Italian bookmakers, the Jewish bookmakers, the loan sharks, the Irish bookmakers," Hafer said. "The huge Southie dopers, the victims' families, the victims' children. You'd go from laughing, to being angry, to hearing this really poignant emotional testimony. There was really never a dull moment. It was just incredibly colorful."

The case would be a history lesson of a bygone era when Cadillac-driving gangsters in fedoras and scally caps shook down business owners and bookies, took bets on pay phones, wrote them down on scraps of paper, and paid off cops with paper bags of cash.

"Historically, these kinds of people, you don't really have that as much anymore," Hafer says. "You don't have such a hierarchical criminal organization running a city. It's almost like a relic of a time gone by.

"So much of it had been suppressed for so long, with John Connolly, with the corruption, with Bulger being a fugitive," he added. "It was time to air it all out."

Leading Hafer through the maze of murder, death, and mayhem were veteran federal prosecutors Fred Wyshak and Brian Kelly. The team also included

DEA agent Dan Doherty, state trooper Steve Johnson, Department of Justice investigator Jim Marra, and IRS agent Sandy Lemanski. Conspicuously absent from the prosecution team was a member of the FBI. That was by design so as not to give even the slightest appearance of conflict or bias, given the history of corruption.

Wyshak, a veteran prosecutor who joined the Boston office in 1989, grew up in Boston's South End in the 1960s and '70s—the same neighborhood where Stevie Flemmi was raised. His family immigrated to Boston from the Middle East during the Depression. Flemmi, a jailhouse artist, was aware of Wyshak's Middle Eastern heritage and once sent him an oil painting he'd created behind bars of Lebanese poet Kahlil Gibran, author of *The Prophet*. Wyshak had to return the painting, however, due to ethics concerns. Other works by Flemmi are said to be on display at a Bureau of Prisons headquarters in Pennsylvania. It was all just part of the game within the game played by Flemmi and Bulger for decades, and they weren't going to stop now that they were in prison.

Wyshak attended New York University and got his law degree from St. John's University before taking a job in the Brooklyn district attorney's office in 1977. He stayed there until 1986, when he moved to New

Jersey and became an assistant United States attorney. He worked mob cases in Jersey and became an expert at prosecuting organized crime, which led him in 1989 to Boston to work on the ever-expanding Bulger case as head of the Organized Crime Strike Force.

"I just started working on a few cases that were directed at the Winter Hill associates, a lot of the bookies and loan sharks and drug dealers, and they sort of coalesced into the 1995 indictment of Bulger, Flemmi, Salemme," Wyshak recalled.

Like many who had pursued Bulger, Wyshak was eager to see Bulger in person in handcuffs. He was underwhelmed by what he saw in Courtroom 11 upon the start of the case.

"I had never seen him before except in pictures. He certainly didn't look anything like what I expected him to look like," Wyshak said. "He looked like an old man at that point, with a beard. Not the vicious individual that had been described to us by numerous individuals. I guess he had lost a lot of muscle tone. I would say it was a bit disappointing."

Hafer, Wyshak, and Kelly worked under Boston US Attorney Carmen Ortiz, who had been appointed to the post in 2009 by President Obama. She made her presence felt quickly in Boston in 2010 when she locked up crooked State Senator Diane Wilkerson and Boston

City Councilor Chuck Turner for taking bribes. It was a sensational sting in which Wilkerson was caught on video stuffing cash into her bra. A year later Ortiz's team convicted corrupt Massachusetts Speaker of the House Salvatore F. DiMasi—arguably the state's most powerful public official—for taking kickbacks from government contracts. Public corruption was her hallmark when the Bulger case landed in her lap.

The prosecutors' expertise in corruption would serve them well as they laid out the Bulger case and exposed in broad detail how cops and government officials crossed over to the dark side and enabled the gangster's bloody reign of terror.

27

On the eleventh floor of the gleaming waterfront courthouse, Judge Denise Casper, a middle-aged African-American jurist, presided. Casper grew up in New York, got her law degree at Harvard University, and worked for Boston powerhouse law firm Bingham McCutcheon before being appointed to the federal bench by President Obama in 2010. Bulger, an unabashed racist, sat just feet away as Casper oversaw the proceedings. It was karma that a liberal, black female judge now controlled the fate of the prejudiced Irish gangster, who fought integration and busing in Southie in the 1970s and would later support the right-wing politics of President Donald J. Trump.

Just weeks before the trial, Casper decimated Bulger's defense in a landmark ruling. Bulger's lawyers

wanted to argue that Whitey was under an immunity agreement with a former US attorney named Jeremiah O'Sullivan. According to the attorneys, the gangster was told by O'Sullivan that he could never be charged with any crime—short of murder—as long as he kept feeding the feds information, mainly on Boston's La Cosa Nostra. At the time of the supposed secret deal, O'Sullivan was chief of the New England Organized Crime Strike Force, a shadowy unit that operated under the US Attorney's Office. The defense team provided no details about the deal and no documentation. O'Sullivan wasn't talking either. He was long dead.

In the 1970s and '80s, O'Sullivan, along with the FBI, was under intense pressure to take down the Italian Mafia at any price. It had been the primary mission of the Bureau since the 1960s and the days of J. Edgar Hoover.

Under O'Sullivan, the heat was turned up high on Boston's Italian mob, which was led by Gennaro "Jerry" Angiulo and his North End crew. The local faction answered to Raymond Patriarca's crime syndicate, which was based in Providence, Rhode Island. It had always been an odd criminal arrangement in New England. Despite Boston being a much larger city than Providence, the Rhode Island capital had a far stronger and more influential Mafia presence that was linked

directly to New York. As a result, Boston's mob always answered to Patriarca.

As O'Sullivan built his case against the Boston Mafia, a federal wiretap picked up chatter of a potential hit on him, which left the young prosecutor and father of two spooked. Bulger claimed O'Sullivan cut the immunity deal with him in exchange for protection from mobsters who wanted him dead.

As proof of the deal, Bulger's attorneys filed an eleventh-hour appeal before the trial seeking to have the original jurist, Judge Richard Stearns, removed from the case. The attorneys argued that Stearns was conflicted because he worked in the US Attorney's Office at the time O'Sullivan chaired the Strike Force and knew or should have known about the supposed arrangement.

In the pleading, Bulger's attorneys pointed to a 1978 race-fixing case at Suffolk Downs racetrack in East Boston that led to the indictments of thirteen people—most connected to the Winter Hill Gang—and two unindicted coconspirators. Those two unindicted coconspirators were Bulger and Flemmi. The racket netted millions in winning bets made in Chicago, Philadelphia, New York, and other locales. The crooked gamblers were told who to bet on, in which race, and were instructed not to make bets at Suffolk

Downs, nearby Wonderland Greyhound Park, or any other Massachusetts racetrack.

In 2002, O'Sullivan testified before a congressional hearing probing FBI corruption in the Bulger case and acknowledged dropping Bulger and Flemmi from the race-fixing indictment, but claimed it was because evidence against the others was stronger. During that same hearing, O'Sullivan, who died in 2009 at age sixty-six, testified under oath that he never gave Bulger or Flemmi immunity.

But that didn't stop Bulger's legal team. J. W. Carney, the lead defense attorney, also wrote in the pleading that he planned to call as a witness former FBI director Robert Mueller, who worked in the US Attorney's Office with O'Sullivan and Stearns and was a close friend of the latter.

The strategy worked as Stearns was removed from the case, but no ruling was ever made on Bulger's immunity deal. After Whitey was caught in Santa Monica in 2011, one of the questions he asked FBI agents Phil Torsney and Rich Teahan on the flight back to Boston was whether O'Sullivan was still the US attorney.

After Stearns's removal, Casper was assigned the case and her first order of business was to rule on Bulger's immunity claim with O'Sullivan.

"Because O'Sullivan is deceased, there's obviously

no evidence of that agreement," Hafer explains. "We scoured all the files. There's no affirmative evidence of that agreement anywhere."

While Carney claimed it was a secret deal, the government fought it aggressively, arguing that even if Carney's unsubstantiated claims were true, it wouldn't have held up bureaucratically or legally.

"Under no circumstances would someone in Jerry O'Sullivan's position ever have been authorized to make such a deal," Hafer said. "No sentient human being would have made that agreement . . . There is no such thing as an agreement to allow someone to commit undefined future acts, including acts of violence . . . It was like grasping at smoke. There was no detail provided."

Judge Casper agreed and tossed out Carney's claim, delivering the first of many legal blows to Bulger. Carney was resolute, though, and vowed that his client would take the stand and blow the lid off the corruption in the FBI. It made for sensational headlines and exhilarating pretrial theatrics, but prosecutors were not impressed.

"He insinuated, he wrote in a pleading, unsworn, not under oath, not by a witness with personal knowledge," Hafer said. "But he never backed it up with anything."

The trial was slated to start on June 10, 2013, but Carney filed a last-minute motion to delay after it was revealed that a state trooper interfered with a probe into the criminal activity by Bulger hit man—and government star witness—John Martorano. Casper dismissed Carney's motion, the jury was seated, and the runway was cleared for Boston's trial of the century.

On June 12, 2013, Whitey arrived at the Moakley Courthouse with great fanfare. He walked slowly in shackles along the Boston waterfront, clad in an orange prison jumpsuit and wearing noise-canceling headphones, escorted from a helicopter by heavily armed US marshals to a waiting prison van. The image of the aged gangster's perp walk dominated the news cycle and was broadcast across the globe.

As the trial got underway, Boston Harbor was partially shut down. The US Coast Guard and Boston Police patrolled the waters surrounding the courthouse. Armed officers guarded a nearby marina. Bomb-sniffing dogs scoured the city blocks around the courthouse. Just down the street in Southie, where Bulger plied his trade for decades, the coffee shops and dark barrooms were abuzz.

In his opening statement, Kelly began the prosecution's case by painting a chilling portrait of Bulger as a bloodthirsty, Machiavellian killer. In methodical and

dramatic fashion, the prosecutor described how Bulger murdered at least nineteen people while running a criminal enterprise that destroyed families, corrupted law enforcement, and flooded Boston with drugs and despair for three-plus decades.

"It's a case about organized crime, public corruption, and all sorts of illegal activities ranging from extortion to drug dealing, to money laundering to possession of machine guns to murder, nineteen murders," Kelly told the hushed courtroom. "It's about a criminal enterprise, which is a group of criminals who ran amok in the City of Boston for almost thirty years . . . At the center of all this murder and mayhem is one man, the defendant in this case, James Bulger.

"He was no ordinary leader," Kelly continued. "He did the dirty work himself because he was a hands-on killer."

Wearing a green sweater tucked into jeans and white sneakers, Bulger, then eighty-three, sat at the defense table listening intently, sandwiched between his attorneys, J. W. Carney and Hank Brennan. His brother Jackie, a disgraced court clerk, sat behind him, but Billy, mysteriously, was not in the courtroom. Hard-nosed beat reporters and columnists who had covered the Bulger gang for decades sat attentive while dozens of reporters from across the country and the world

were herded into an overflow room with closed-circuit TVs to watch the trial unfold.

Kelly laid out the case, showing organizational charts of the Winter Hill Gang through the decades, illustrating Bulger's rise in the organization. And then he started laying out the murders. It was a shocking and macabre journey through Boston's darkest criminal era.

Kelly said Bulger made "a fortune" shaking down bookies and drug dealers, loan-sharking, and trafficking drugs in his hometown—a sharp jab at Bulger, who built his legend on the fabricated claim that he kept drugs out of Southie.

"Bulger liked to promote the myth that he had nothing to do with drugs," Kelly argued. "But you will hear from these drug dealers that in the 1980s, Bulger was deeply involved in the distribution of drugs in the South Boston area, especially cocaine. And he and his gang made millions at it."

The prosecutor laid out the charges: twenty-three counts of money laundering, two racketeering counts, five weapons charges, two extortion counts, and of course, nineteen murders.

He detailed how Bulger and his cohorts paid off cops "so they could get tipped off to investigations and stay one step ahead of the honest cops who were actually trying to make a case against them.

"It was part of a strategy they had, and it worked," Kelly said.

Kelly piled on the Southie crime lord and hit him where it hurt: he called him a *rat* in open court.

"Even though Bulger told people he didn't like rats, the evidence will be that Bulger was one of the biggest informants in Boston," Kelly said.

"Bulger routinely met with FBI agent John Connolly and gave him information, some true, some false, but all designed to protect himself and mislead other investigators, or get the competitive edge that he wanted," Kelly said.

Bulger's double dealing was one of the case's "grotesque ironies," because he regularly executed others suspected of being informants, the prosecutor added.

There was no better example of Bulger's informant executions than the case of Brian Halloran and Michael Donahue, the two men who were gunned down in 1982 as they left a waterfront bar. Halloran knew about Oklahoma businessman Roger Wheeler's murder and was giving information to the feds. His death warrant, and unfortunately the innocent Donahue's as well, were signed when Bulger found out Halloran was talking.

"Bulger learned from his own corrupt FBI connections that Halloran was trying to give information to

law enforcement," Kelly said. "This offended him . . . Bulger took action because he did not want the FBI to learn the truth about Roger Wheeler."

Wheeler, CEO of the lucrative Florida gambling business World Jai Alai, was shot right between the eyes in Oklahoma by John Martorano outside his country club in Tulsa after finishing a round of golf. Bulger and his crew had their sights set on taking over World Jai Alai with the help of the business's crooked accountant, John Callahan, who was skimming cash from the gaming operation and paying off Bulger's gang.

After Martorano gunned down Wheeler in Oklahoma, he killed Callahan in Florida.

"By the time this 1982 murder of Halloran and Donahue had occurred, Bulger and his coconspirators had already killed another thirteen people, because this little murder spree had been going on since the early '70s," Kelly told the court. "All of these murders were committed to promote or protect Bulger's criminal enterprise."

Kelly went into detail about the earliest murders, including the slayings of six men in the 1970s during the Southie gang wars. Bulger's role was often to drive the "crash car" behind the shooters, which required him to slam his car into another vehicle to cause chaos for arriving cops.

He told the tale of Eddie Connors, a Bulger hench-man whose fatal mistake was bragging about helping Bulger's gang. Flemmi and Bulger executed him in cold blood at a pay phone, spraying the booth with bullets. A stomach-churning picture of Connors slumped down, covered in blood and broken glass, was shown to jurors on a massive wide screen.

Kelly also prepared the jury for the parade of killers they would soon be hearing from, including Martorano and Flemmi. The gangsters had already cut controversial deals with prosecutors by pleading guilty to racketeering charges. Both, Kelly said, would implicate Bulger as a murderer and the mastermind behind the gang's reign of terror.

"You'll hear that Martorano ultimately got a sentence of fourteen years—not enough," Kelly conceded. "He did confess and he did cooperate and he did help solve crimes that had been unsolved for three decades."

He called Flemmi "a vicious killer" who was not only Bulger's partner in crime and murder, but also "in the informant business." The two mobsters fed John Connolly information about "criminal rivals" and together they "paid thousands" to corrupt agents and crooked cops.

He told the sordid stories of Flemmi's girlfriend, a beautiful blonde named Debbie Davis, and Flemmi's

stepdaughter Deborah Hussey, both of whom had been strangled to death. He then slowly read off the names of all nineteen murder victims.

"That, ladies and gentlemen, is what this case is about," he said. "A defendant, James Bulger, who was part of a criminal gang which extorted people, paid off cops, earned a fortune dealing drugs, laundered money, possessed all sorts of guns, and murdered people. Nineteen people."

Kelly let that number—nineteen—hang in the air inside the courtroom.

Carney countered with the only card he had to play: government corruption. He wove an elaborate tale about how the FBI used Bulger, and others, as part of a decades-long mission to topple La Cosa Nostra.

"What happened was, beginning with Robert Kennedy, when he was the Attorney General, and J. Edgar Hoover, when he was the head of the FBI, was that a commitment was made, a focus was made by federal prosecutors to smash the organization known as the Mafia," Carney said. "This became a nationwide crusade on the part of every prosecutor and the majority of the FBI agents working for the federal government."

Carney then claimed that Flemmi was a "top echelon" informant for Connolly, but declared that Bulger was "never an informant for John Connolly."

"There were two reasons for this. Number one, James Bulger is of Irish descent, and the worst thing that an Irish person could consider doing was becoming an informant because of the history of the troubles in Ireland," Carney said. "The second reason was . . . James Bulger was not deeply tied to the Italian Mafia."

He noted that although Bulger had Mafia associates, he never would have gotten inside information on the organization because he wasn't Italian. Instead, Carney claimed Flemmi was the one giving Connolly all the goods. The reports in Bulger's FBI file amounted to "junk tips" that were meaningless, or duplicates of information from other informants. The real FBI relationship with Bulger worked the opposite way, Carney claimed, saying Bulger paid for information to keep himself out of trouble.

Bulger handed Connolly lump sums of cash—$5,000, $10,000, and $50,000—which allowed the rogue agent to lead a "lavish lifestyle." Bulger also paid Connolly's boss, John Morris, $5,000, and greased up other cops and agents.

"He wanted information for when there would be a wiretap set up, a situation where a bug is placed in a room or in a car," Carney told jurors. "And in return for these payments, he was told where the bugs were placed.

"He wanted to know when searches were going to be executed so that he could make sure to clear his stuff out of those locations. And that when the police showed up to execute a search warrant and hopefully find drugs or evidence of illegal gambling or illegal loans, there was nothing there," Carney said. "And, finally, if he ever was going to be indicted, he wanted a heads-up so he could leave town. That's what he was paying for."

Carney also laid the groundwork for jurors to look with disgust upon the government's star witness, John Martorano, portraying him as an opportunist who cut an astonishing deal with prosecutors that allowed him to serve just twelve years in prison for twenty murders in exchange for testifying against Connolly and Bulger. The deal also meant Martorano would not be prosecuted on state charges for the murders of Roger Wheeler in Oklahoma and John Callahan in Florida, where he could have received the death penalty.

Martorano also negotiated immunity for his girlfriend, who harbored him for years, and assurances that he wouldn't have to testify against his brother, Jimmy Martorano, who Carney said "had also been committing murders." In addition, he wouldn't have to testify against fellow Bulger gang member Pat Nee, whom Carney also called "a murderer."

The cherry on top was the $26,500 Martorano received from the feds for his cooperation, as well as being allowed to keep the $250,000 he got for his book deal.

"The federal government was so desperate to have John Martorano testify in a manner that they wanted against John Connolly and James Bulger that they basically put their hands up in the air and said, 'Take anything you want,'" Carney said.

The defense attorney also blasted another key witness, Kevin Weeks, who admitted to his role in five murders but served just five years in prison. He too was allowed to keep money he received for his book and movie rights, the attorney added.

But Carney saved the best for last. Stevie Flemmi, he said, agreed to flip on Bulger to save his own life. The feds took the death penalty off the table for the Wheeler and Callahan murders, and in addition, Flemmi's brother, a crooked Boston cop named Michael Flemmi, was allowed to keep property Flemmi bought with "illegal" gains, Carney said.

He blamed the murders of Davis and Hussey on Flemmi. He said Davis had been cheating on Flemmi and making fun of him for being "old" behind his back. Hussey, meanwhile, was a drug addict and prostitute who was molested by Flemmi for years when she was

a teenager. When she revealed the molestation to her mother, who was Flemmi's common-law wife, Flemmi killed her because he feared she would go to the police, Carney claimed.

The crafty defense attorney didn't stop there.

He also incredulously claimed that Bulger had nothing to do with the Wheeler and Callahan murders. Instead, he alleged that Flemmi and Martorano hatched the plan with corrupt FBI agent Paul Rico, who had once busted Bulger and served as Flemmi's handler.

While acknowledging Bulger had "an unbelievably lucrative criminal enterprise in Boston," the Southie crime boss "had nothing, no interest, no motivation, no reason to go out of his comfort zone and ever get involved in anything in Florida, where he knew no one," Carney told the jury.

Carney's true strategy, as the trial unfolded, was to plant the seed with jurors that Bulger had been given immunity by the federal government, hoping that perhaps just one might believe such an outlandish claim and have "reasonable doubt" to deadlock the jury. It was a legal "Hail Mary."

28

On the morning of June 14, 2013, most Bostonians were exhausted from staying up until 1 a.m. to watch the heartbreaking first game of the Stanley Cup Finals, in which the Chicago Blackhawks came back to beat the Boston Bruins 4–3 in triple overtime. Reporters, lawyers, court officers, and trial spectators talked about the crushing defeat, and many looked haggard at the Moakley Courthouse.

That morning, Bobby Long, a grizzled former Massachusetts state trooper who had chased Bulger for years, woke up early in his Norwell home, showered, shaved, and slipped on his favorite court suit. The retired cop was like a kid on the first day of school. He'd thought this day would never come, but here he was, about to head into Boston federal court to take the

stand and testify against his longtime nemesis, Whitey Bulger.

Four months earlier, Long was at his retirement home on Marco Island, Florida, and fell off the roof of his garage as he was making some repairs. He suffered several compound fractures and was airlifted to a Level 1 trauma center. He nearly died.

He had been using crutches and occasionally a cane to walk ever since the accident, but on the day of the trial, he was determined to walk into that courtroom on his own. And he did exactly that when he took the stand as the first witness in the *United States v James J. Bulger* trial. Packed with media, relatives of the nineteen victims killed by Bulger and his crew, fellow cops, and lawyers, Long was ready to face the man who had terrorized his city for decades.

"Nobody ever thought he'd be brought to justice," Long recalls. "Our eyes connected once. I wasn't going to take mine off of his. He eventually looked away."

Long's history with the Winter Hill Gang and Bulger stretched back to the early 1970s. In 1977, Boston led the nation in truck hijackings as Winter Hill and other gangsters targeted trailers on a regular basis to swipe things like razor blades, Polaroid film, appliances, TVs, seafood, or anything else of value. The state was seeing an average of two hijackings a day. By

comparison, California had two a year. Drivers were being threatened, kidnapped, and beaten. Trucking companies were shutting down because they couldn't get insurance for their loads in Massachusetts.

Despite interagency mistrust, the state police through Bobby Long and the FBI through an agent named Dave Brady, who reported to FBI supervisor John Morris in the Boston office, joined forces to bust up the truck hijacking rings. As it happened, Nick Gianturco, Charlie's brother who would later be implicated in Bulger-related corruption, was looking to get back to the Boston FBI office at the time and called his friend John Connolly to help him get transferred home. Connolly recommended that Nick Gianturco join "Operation Lobster" with Dave Brady and Long. Long says Gianturco did a "great job" working undercover as they broke up several hijacking rings over three years.

"It was a tremendous success. From averaging two hijackings a day, there was only one in all of 1979," Long recalls.

The honeymoon between the state police and the FBI was short-lived, however. After Operation Lobster, which made national news, the agencies agreed they would work informants together and share information. But the day after the Operation Lobster arrests, two FBI agents went to Walpole State Prison to

try and flip one of the hijackers arrested in the sweep, without telling state police.

A few months later, the state police stumbled upon the infamous Lancaster Street garage in Boston's old West End, which served as a hideout and meeting spot for all of Boston's top gangsters, including Bulger, Flemmi, Boston mob capo Donato Angiulo, who was Jerry Angiulo's brother, and lieutenants from the Patriarca crime family.

"We knew we had a gold mine there," Long says. "Anybody who was anybody in organized crime was coming to that garage. I was saying to myself, 'How can they operate so openly and no one is doing anything about it. Boston police don't know anything about it? The FBI doesn't do anything about it?'"

Long, despite the interagency rift, went to US Attorney Jeremiah O'Sullivan for funding to pay for surveillance at the garage, telling the young federal prosecutor that he could work the case with Brady, so long as Brady wouldn't have to report back to the FBI.

"I can't do that," O'Sullivan told him.

Long had already suspected that John Connolly was feeding Bulger information and was a major weakness, at the very least, in the Bureau.

"I never liked him [Connolly] from the day I met him," Long says.

He told O'Sullivan that the operation couldn't involve the FBI, but that they'd work with any other federal agency: the Drug Enforcement Administration, US Customs, the Bureau of Alcohol, Tobacco and Firearms, but no FBI.

"I can't do that. It would be political suicide for me," O'Sullivan told him.

O'Sullivan funded the operation jointly anyway and ordered the FBI and state police to work the case, along with the Suffolk County district attorney. Long and Brady set up in a flophouse across the street from the garage, which sat in a then-run-down neighborhood filled with hookers, junkies, and grifters.

Now decades later in the summer of 2013, with Bulger sitting just feet away in the packed courtroom, Bobby Long identified grainy black-and-white photographs of Bulger, Flemmi, and Donato Angiulo at the garage. It was like a gangster history class. He pointed out mobsters and victims, like Bucky Barrett, from video surveillance footage shown to the jury.

He recounted how he and Dave Brady watched a parade of rogues come through the garage chitchatting brazenly about their crimes and both believed they were going to bust the city's underworld wide open. But the flow of gangsters at Lancaster Street came to a sudden stop and Bulger's loose lips on audio bugs

tightened. In fact, he stopped talking at all, except to make wisecracks faux-praising the job state police were doing on the Massachusetts Turnpike. The jig was up.

The operation was compromised—by both the state police and the FBI. Turns out, Long testified, corrupt state trooper Richard Schneiderhan met with Flemmi in Braintree and told him he believed the Lancaster Street garage had been bugged. Flemmi went to Connolly, who confirmed the bug with O'Sullivan. Connolly told Bulger and the operation was dead on arrival.

Long, who retired in 1990 and became a licensed private investigator, continued to track down tips on Bulger after he fled in 1995, including once being hired by a Boston TV station to track down a tip that Bulger was hiding in Cuba. The tip proved false.

Like many in the Massachusetts State Police from that era, Long has no love lost for the FBI. In fact, his hope was that the trial would serve two purposes: putting Bulger away for life and exposing corruption at the highest levels of the Bureau. It was, after all, Long's former boss, Colonel Jack O'Donovan, who was the first to sniff out that Bulger was getting tipped off by crooked FBI agents. Long wished the colonel were alive to witness the corruption being exposed once and for all.

29

As the trial unfolded, the prosecutors paraded a wide array of characters in and out of Judge Casper's courtroom, many right out of central casting. Their interactions with Bulger were daily theater. Their casual tones when talking about murder and violence and their colorful language incited everything from gasps to laughs to tears, depending on the day.

One day, Hafer called James Katz, a Dorchester bookie who initially refused to testify before a 1994 grand jury because he was afraid of Bulger and his henchmen. He later flipped after he was offered a reduced sentence and entry into the Witness Protection Program.

"If I were to testify, I felt my safety would . . . . It

would have been compromised probably," Katz testified.

Katz was in jail at the time of the grand jury and told the court he feared he could be killed in prison if he flipped on the Bulger gang.

"I knew that the people I would testify against . . . they could even reach me in jail," Katz told the court.

"And who were those people you were concerned about?" Hafer asked.

"The Bulger group. Stevie and Whitey," he said.

Katz told of an elaborate network of bookies in and around Boston and reported that you needed to pay "rent" to either the Mafia or Bulger's gang. He said Bulger and Flemmi hiked the "vig"—a fee for making a bet—to ensure the gang made more money from gamblers. He talked about "shylocks," which were described as loan sharks who charged exorbitant interest, clandestine meetings at the Lancaster Street garage, payoffs to Winter Hill mobsters at coffee shops and barrooms, and gangsters with memorable names like William "The Midget" McDonough and Joe "The Barber" Spaziani.

Katz, who was convicted of wire fraud, bookmaking, and money laundering in Massachusetts and South Carolina, went into the Witness Protection Program alone, leaving behind his wife and three daughters.

The family reunited in the late 1990s when he dropped out of the program and relocated to "start a new life," he testified.

Hafer asked him about the Bulger gang's reputation for violence.

"You could wind up in the hospital, let's put it that way," he said. "In those days, it was murder and a lot of beatings."

Another bookie who took the stand was Dickie O'Brien, an eighty-four-year-old Korean War veteran from Quincy. O'Brien was feeble and needed an oxygen tank to breathe.

O'Brien testified that, starting in the late 1950s, he took illegal bets on horse racing and sports and ran numbers. The numbers were a black-market lottery based on a number that ran in the newspaper daily, as there was no legal state lottery back then. He worked for Raymond Patriarca and recalled meeting with the mob boss in Providence the day Jimmy Hoffa was arrested.

Patriarca was distracted by the Hoffa arrest, so he directed O'Brien to go work under the Angiulos in Boston.

After the Angiulo mob was broken up by the feds and several top capos went to prison, O'Brien was "independent." He said Bulger summoned him to a

Quincy restaurant and strong-armed him into working for Winter Hill. He paid Bulger $2,000 a week, he testified.

"I said I was with the North End," O'Brien testified. "He said, 'Forget the North End. If you want to be in business, you're with us.' And that was put down as law."

Bulger showed his true colors a few times during the trial, including once as O'Brien was grilled by Hafer about the tale of a bookie who owed a large amount of money and was trying to break away from the organization. The bookie, George "Chickie" Labate of Brockton, was ordered to a meeting with O'Brien, Bulger, and Martorano at a hotel in Braintree, Massachusetts.

"Mr. Bulger came over to him and said, 'You're going to go your own way?'" O'Brien testified. "He said, 'You know, we have a business besides bookmaking.' Labate says, 'What's that?' Mr. Bulger said, 'Killing assholes like you.'"

Whitey erupted in laughter at the defense table. Judge Casper shot him a look. Hafer recoiled and looked at Wyshak in disbelief. Carney and Brennan glared at their client. When Bulger's chuckles subsided, he looked at Judge Casper and said, "Excuse me."

O'Brien, who was jailed for lying to a grand jury probing the Bulger gang in 1993, was friends with

Martorano and served time with him and Flemmi in the Plymouth House of Correction. The elderly ex-bookie told of a couple of brushes with death of his own, including once in Florida when Flemmi paid him an unexpected visit.

"If I'm not home in twelve hours or so, go to the FBI in Miami," he told his daughter before the meeting. "And don't go home."

It was exactly the type of fear that Hafer, Wyshak, and Kelly needed to get in front of the jury. These witnesses feared Bulger would end their lives for a buck.

As O'Brien left the stand, it was clear that he was one of the lucky ones who got away.

For all the gravity of the proceedings, the trial often had a circus-like atmosphere. Academy Award–winning actor Robert Duvall, who was in Boston shooting the legal thriller *The Judge*, dropped in to watch the spectacle one day. There was an endless conga line of rogues and plug-uglies brought to the stand that gave the trial a feeling of a *This Is Your Life* TV episode starring Whitey.

Grainy footage of gangsters in track suits, mobsters in Cadillacs, and gruesome autopsy photos were shown daily. Videos of a young and fit Bulger, his muscles

bulging from tight T-shirts, stood in stark contrast to the elderly gangster sitting at the defendant's table, although marshals and correctional officers in charge of watching Bulger before and after court said he regularly did push-ups in his cell, in defiance of his advanced age.

Wyshak, tall with short gray hair, carried himself with an air of calm but spoke quite powerfully and with stark authority when pressed. He and his fellow prosecutors had a front-row seat and regularly heard Bulger gruffly barking out orders to his attorneys, muttering under his breath, and chuckling inappropriately at various moments throughout the proceedings.

"The first time he opened his mouth, you could tell he was a vicious guy. Just that voice. He had a voice," Wyshak said. "He was complaining we took all his money from him. It was the way he spoke. You could see he had disdain for everyone and everything."

The only break during the two-month trial, besides weekends, came over the July 4th holiday. The Fourth of July was on a Thursday, so Judge Casper sent the jury home on Wednesday for a long weekend.

On Monday, when court resumed, the prosecutors were preparing at their table opposite Bulger's defense team, attorneys Carney and Brennan. Carney, bald and bespectacled and with a scholarly air about him, was

red-faced with an "Irish tan." He had obviously been in the sun all weekend.

Bulger was brought into court by the marshals and plopped into his chair between his lawyers. He had spent the long weekend in isolation in the Plymouth House of Correction and was not in a good mood.

"Morning, Jim. How was the weekend?" Carney said in an affable tone.

Bulger was incensed. He glared at Carney and said, "How the fuck do you think it was, Jay?"

Carney did attempt to keep Whitey's spirits up while he was behind bars, however. As he was awaiting trial, Bulger wrote love letters to Greig on Carney's legal pad. The attorney carried them on visits to Greig in prison, where he allowed her to read them. She wept, as did Bulger when he read her responses, again delivered by Carney. Ethical questions were raised by prosecutors and others about Carney delivering the missives, but the barrister dismissed them, saying, "There is no regulation or law that should prevent two people from expressing love."

Whitey was hands-on with his defense team, and at times seemed to direct them on who to cross-examine and who to leave alone. Drug trafficker Billy Shea, a longtime friend of Bulger, was greeted warmly by the gangster.

"Billy," Bulger said, nodding to Shea as he took the stand.

"Jim." Shea nodded back. It was like two old friends running into each other in a coffee shop. Except it was in a federal courtroom in the biggest criminal case Boston had seen perhaps in its entire history.

Shea testified for an hour and a half about the scope of drug dealing that he and Bulger did together. He told a story of how Bulger, Flemmi, and Weeks once walked him downstairs to an alley in Southie. It was a dramatic tale that had everyone in the courtroom on the edge of their seat. Shea thought his "number was up," but was let go without being harmed.

Bulger seemed as riveted by the story as anyone in the courtroom. As Shea continued his testimony, Bulger wrote a note and slipped it to Carney. Shea had never cooperated against Bulger in the past. His testimony was devastating on the drug charges and Hafer expected he would be torn apart on cross-examination. Instead, Carney read Bulger's note, stood up, and said, "I have no questions."

"We saw that scenario play out several times," Hafer said. "It seemed that if Bulger thought he was a stand-up guy or liked the person, he didn't want his lawyer cross-examining him."

There were many explosive moments throughout

the trial, but none as big as when news broke that Stephen "Stippo" Rakes, one of Bulger's extortion victims—and a potential witness in the case—was found murdered. Rakes, whose liquor store was stolen from him by Bulger and his crew, had attended the trial every day.

On July 16, 2013, he left the courthouse. His body was found the next day on a rural roadside in Lincoln, Massachusetts. A state trooper called prosecutor Brian Kelly with news of Rakes's death.

"Are you still planning to use Rakes?" the trooper asked Kelly.

"We're still trying to figure that out," he answered.

"Well you're not using him now. We just found him in Lincoln," the trooper said.

The story sent shock waves through the courthouse and sparked fears that Bulger had somehow reached out from behind the prison walls to kill a witness. Hafer says the news had some jurors "petrified."

"It was 2013, this kind of stuff doesn't happen anymore," he said. "We knew [Bulger] didn't like him."

Prosecutors were concerned about the impact Rakes's death could have on the jury, but were also worried he might have committed suicide because they took him off their witness list. The day he left the courthouse for the last time, Kelly told Rakes they wouldn't be calling

him. Rakes, who had a previous perjury conviction, had expressed a burning desire to take the stand to face Bulger in court.

"When he turned up dead and there were no visible signs—he wasn't stabbed or shot or beaten—we thought he had committed suicide," Wyshak said. "It was almost like this case had become his life. That we didn't want to call him as a witness, we thought he may have harmed himself. We didn't actually think someone killed him for Bulger."

Others, though, wondered if maybe, just maybe, Bulger still had the clout to reach out from prison and have a witness killed. The satirical website *The Onion* had a field day with the news, posting a fake story the next day with the headline "Everyone in Whitey Bulger Trial Found Dead in Woods Outside Dorchester."

Kelly laughed at the *Onion* story but, like Wyshak, was pretty sure there was no conspiracy.

"We doubted there were still Bulger loyalists out there killing witnesses, but we didn't know what was going on," Kelly said.

He and Wyshak had faced death threats in the past from Whitey's crew, including in the early 1990s when they were building the case that became the 1995 indictment. Back then, the US Marshals office was so concerned about the threats against the two prosecu-

tors that they sent agents to their homes to beef up security, including putting alarms on their cars to warn them if a bomb was installed.

Kelly's kids were toddlers at the time. He didn't tell his wife about the threats and assured her it was routine for marshals to protect prosecutors. But he knew otherwise.

"It was concerning," he admits. "It probably would have been more concerning if I had realized at the time how vicious and crazy the Bulger gang really was."

The Rakes mystery was solved quickly, as authorities revealed it was unrelated to the Bulger trial. It turned out he was poisoned by a disgruntled business associate named William Camuti, who laced Rakes's Dunkin' Donuts iced coffee with cyanide. Camuti was convicted of Rakes's murder in 2017 and sentenced to life without parole.

It was yet another stranger-than-fiction tale in the Bulger saga—and it wouldn't be the last.

30

For Wyshak, who had spent a career chasing the mob, getting in bed with a murderous killer like John Martorano was a necessary evil in order to finish off Whitey. A confessed killer of at least twenty people, Martorano was the star witness for Wyshak, Kelly, and Hafer. It was Wyshak who struck the devil's deal with Martorano in 1995 that gave him twelve years in prison in exchange for his testimony against Flemmi, Connolly, and Bulger. The deal was made all the easier for Martorano to cut after he learned that Flemmi and Bulger were lifelong rats.

Wyshak had already used Martorano to put Flemmi and Connolly away, including helping Florida prosecutors convict Connolly of murder for the Callahan slaying. As sweet as those cases were for Wyshak, the real

prize was always Bulger, and now it was time for Martorano to finish the job.

An imposing figure with salt-and-pepper receding
hair, beefy jowls, and deep lines on his face, the seventy-
two-year-old walked into the courtroom through a side
door and made a passing glance at Bulger, who sat at
the nearby witness table.

The two friends and former partners in murder
hadn't seen each other in person since 1982 and both
were a far cry from the muscular pair seen in surveillance photos throughout the previous days of the
trial. Born in the Winter Hill stronghold of Somerville,
Massachusetts, Martorano was the son of a gangster
bar owner who hailed from Sicily. His father owned
Luigi's, a restaurant on Washington Street in Boston's
South End that was a rowdy after-hours spot for mobsters.

The family moved when Martorano was young to
East Milton, where he attended private school and
was a football star playing on the same squad as future *60 Minutes* correspondent Ed Bradley. Martorano
turned down several athletic scholarships to college
and instead got into the family business: bookmaking
and strong-arming. He started hanging out in Boston's notorious—and now nonexistent—Combat Zone,
where he fell under the tutelage of Flemmi.

On the day of the trial, Martorano walked into court a free man, having served his time and fulfilled all obligations to the court. He drove a silver Mercedes-Benz and lived a quiet, suburban life with his girlfriend in Milford, a leafy suburb about thirty miles outside of Boston.

Wearing a mobster's black power suit, a light blue shirt, and matching pocket square, Martorano filled the witness box with his brawn. He wore glasses but swapped another pair on and off as he needed one to look at the courtroom—and Bulger—and another to read the documents provided by Wyshak that grimly detailed his three-decades-long killing spree.

A father of five, Martorano admitted taking part in twenty murders. His testimony started with Wyshak leading him through a string of slayings stemming from barroom and street-corner disputes between him, his brother, James, and a crew of gangsters from East Boston, Somerville, and Roxbury. He described casually gunning down a Southie boxer named Tony Veranis in a nightclub packed with thirty people. He was never charged.

He talked about stalking rivals to their homes and executing them in cold blood, with zero consequences. He talked about dumping bodies at North Station, near Boston Garden, and Blue Hills, a woodsy state reserva-

tion just south of Boston, as calmly as one might discuss the weather.

He regaled the courtroom with gangster tales of after-hours brawls in the Basin Street Club in Boston's South End, and traveling to Providence with Flemmi to meet New England Mafia boss Raymond Patriarca to get protection during the 1960s gang wars. He told stories of paying off jockeys to fix horse races.

He testified that he stabbed a rival named Jack Banno in an alley off Boylston Street while out on a date. He drove Banno to the hospital and planned to drop him off to get treated, but instead finished him off when Banno woke up and continued arguing. Banno was stabbed twenty times.

He recalled going to Montreal with Winter Hill Gang boss Howie Winter and Brian Halloran in the early 1970s to visit Flemmi while Flemmi was a fugitive. He said he gave money to Flemmi's common-law wife, Marion Hussey, to help him remain on the run.

He recalled meeting Bulger in 1972 when Bulger came into Martorano's restaurant, Chandler's, for an infamous meeting where Howie Winter ordered a truce between the feuding Mullins and Killeen gangs. Martorano brokered the meeting where Winter called for peace between Bulger, who was the lone survivor on the

Killeen side, and a trio from the Mullins gang: Tommy King, Pat Nee, and Jimmy "The Weasel" Mantville.

"They patched it up," Martorano testified. "Whitey seemed to surface as the leader."

The reconfigured crew, led by Bulger, started working with Martorano to run the gaming, loan-sharking, and strong-arming rackets in Southie. In 1973, the gang was called upon by Jerry Anguilo to kill a bookie named Al Notarangeli, who owed Anguilo and the Boston mob money. Martorano told a chilling tale of how gangsters scoped out neighborhoods in search of Notarangeli in a deadly game of cat-and-mouse.

There were several failed hits. In one, Bulger drove a "crash car" equipped with a police scanner, while Howie Winter and Martorano were in two separate vehicles. All of the vehicles were equipped with walkie-talkies so they could talk to each other. They followed a brown Mercedes leaving a bar called Mother's, believing they were tailing Notarangeli. The crew pulled up beside the sedan and Martorano and Winter peppered it with machine gun spray, killing one of the occupants.

Only it wasn't Notarangeli. It was a bartender named Michael Milano. Milano was killed while passengers Diane Sussman de Tennen and her boyfriend, Louis Lapiana, survived. Lapiana was paralyzed and spent

his life in a Veterans Administration hospital before dying in 2001. Sussman de Tennen, who was twenty-three the night of the shooting, recalled the horrific assault, telling teary-eyed jurors that Lapiana was the love of her life.

"All of a sudden there was this noise, this continuing stream of noise, gunfire," Sussman de Tennen testified. "Nonstop. Dozens and dozens of shots. It was a machine gun . . . When I heard the sound, I ducked. That's probably the only reason I am here today."

Eleven days after the March 8, 1973, botched hit, Bulger orchestrated another failed attempt to kill Notarangeli. The gang pulled off another drive-by and blasted another vehicle, killing Al Plummer, a father of six from Andover, Massachusetts, and wounding two organized crime figures, including bookie Frank Capizzi. Notarangeli was not with them.

"I had been hit in the head and felt warm blood running down my neck," Capizzi testified. He said one hundred bullets hit the vehicle and that he sustained more than thirty wounds from gunshots, glass, or shards of metal. After the attack, he fled Boston with his family.

"My wife and children were living in the throat of the dragon for forty years without any help from any-

one," Capizzi told the jury. "I never wanted to get killed."

A few days after the Plummer execution, Martorano gunned down Notarangeli's brother, Joe "Indian Joe" Notarangeli, at a pay phone inside a Medford restaurant. The hit man said he wore "a construction yellow hat, a pair of sunglasses, a full beard and a long meatcutter's coat" as a disguise.

Wyshak guided Martorano through the grim sequence of senseless hits that culminated when the crew finally caught up with Al Notarangeli on February 11, 1974, at a restaurant. Notarangeli had a Bible and $50,000 in cash he hoped to pay Martorano to give to Angiulo as a peace offering. Instead, Martorano shot him point blank in the head inside the car, killing him. He and Bulger put the body in the trunk of a stolen Buick and dumped it in Charlestown, where it was restolen by some unknowing teens—with the body in the trunk, Martorano told the jury.

He ran through killing after killing, answering Wyshak's questions methodically as the prosecutor went through a staggering body count and timeline that included fathers, sons, brothers, and husbands. Some were bookies, some were killers, some were informants, and some were innocent.

Martorano provided the first implication in the trial of Bulger's powerful politician brother Billy. The hit man said he met John Connolly in the mid-1970s and was told by Whitey that the G-man was an old friend from Southie. Whitey told him his brother helped Connolly get his FBI job and that Billy, in return, asked Connolly to watch out for Whitey.

"Bulger said that John Connolly is an FBI agent, that he grew up in Southie," Martorano said, recalling the conversation with Bulger. "He just got assigned to Boston, and he went to see his brother Billy and told Billy, 'I owe you for keeping me honest and making me finish this thing and become an FBI agent and stay out of trouble and if there's anything I can do for you, let me know.'"

Billy told him, "If you could keep my brother out of trouble, that would be helpful to me," Martorano testified.

In a 2019 interview with the authors, Billy Bulger drew a sharp line between his brother's criminal life and his own life of public service.

Asked if Whitey ever put pressure on him to help his criminal enterprises, Billy Bulger said, "No, I don't think so. He was very respectful of that. I think that he knew that I had a point of view that was as strong in my sense, as his was in his. So, I could even play back

his own words, and say 'Now you don't want me to go awry and I don't want you to.' That sort of thing."

Wyshak laid Martorano's deal out for the jury, pushing him to reveal why he flipped on his friends. The burly gangster said he felt betrayed. It was Flemmi and Bulger who tipped off the feds to his Florida hideout, where he was arrested in 1995 after sixteen years on the run. Martorano was one of the mobsters indicted in the 1978 race-fixing case, but Bulger and Flemmi gave him a heads-up that the bust was coming and he went on the run. Over the years as a fugitive, Martorano continued to work with Bulger and Flemmi, running rackets and executing rivals on command.

"They were my partners in crime, they were my best friends, they were my children's godfathers," Martorano testified. He said his youngest son was named James Steven in tribute to Bulger and Flemmi.

"After I heard that they were informants, it sort of broke my heart," he told the court. "They broke all trust that we had, all loyalties. I was just beside myself with it."

Bulger sat slumped in his chair and seemed disinterested in the proceedings. Martorano, who has a variety of nicknames, including "The Basin Street Butcher" and "The Executioner," had the courtroom riveted as the serial killer held nothing back.

Wyshak asked how he made a living currently and Martorano replied, "Social Security," eliciting snickers from the gallery. The prosecutor read from his lengthy plea agreement and slowly read the names of twenty people murdered by Martorano. The hit man confirmed killing each of them, including Wheeler and Callahan.

Martorano testified that the order came from Bulger and Flemmi to kill Callahan, a close friend and long-time associate of Martorano, because he was going to implicate the crew in Wheeler's May 27, 1981, murder. Callahan was a sharp-dressed accountant by day, but drank and caroused with gangsters by night.

"Did you ever hear the phrase 'Wannabe gangster'?" Wyshak asked.

"That's what he was," Martorano answered.

A millionaire industrialist, Wheeler had sniffed out a skimming operation at World Jai Alai in Florida in which the Winter Hill gang, with Callahan's help, was embezzling from the gambling business. Callahan originally suggested the gang force Wheeler to sell the business to them, but when Wheeler balked, the decision was made to kill him.

Crooked FBI agent H. Paul Rico, who was retired from the Bureau, was Callahan's head of security and set the wheels in motion for Wheeler's slaying.

"Callahan wanted to get Mr. Wheeler killed so he wouldn't get in trouble," Martorano testified. "He said that he discussed it with Paul Rico."

Flemmi and Martorano both pleaded guilty to Wheeler's murder and were going to testify against Rico, but he died before he went to trial on murder charges.

Martorano told the jury it was Rico who provided him Wheeler's golf schedule and description. Flemmi sent him a murder "kit"—a suitcase filled with machine guns, pistols, and masks—which Martorano picked up at a Tulsa bus station. He said he put on a fake beard and sunglasses, approached Wheeler in the parking lot of Southern Hills Country Club in Tulsa, and shot the businessman in the face.

"I saw a guy coming over the hill carrying a brief-case," Martorano said. "It looked like him. He was heading toward that car. So I head toward that car. He opened the door and got in. So I opened the door and shot him. Between the eyes."

The jury was shown a graphic autopsy photo of Wheeler's face with a bullet hole in the middle of his forehead. He said Callahan paid him $50,000 for the slaying, which he split with Flemmi, Bulger, and Joe McDonald, a Winter Hill associate who went with him to Tulsa.

Wyshak walked Martorano through the maze of death, illuminating for the jury how the brazen Wheeler killing touched off a string of murders as the gang desperately scrambled to contain the situation and gain control of World Jai Alai.

Callahan got drunk one night back in Boston and told his pal Brian Halloran about the Wheeler murder and who was behind it. Halloran was facing charges in an unrelated case and sought to trade info about the Wheeler killing and the Winter Hill Gang's role in hopes of getting a lighter sentence.

Bulger ended Halloran's negotiations on a South Boston street when he gunned him down, along with Michael Donahue. Martorano said Connolly—whom he referred to by his nickname "Zip"—signed Halloran's death warrant by telling Bulger that Halloran was talking to the feds.

"He said that Halloran had went to the FBI and told them that I had killed Wheeler," Martorano testified. "Bulger said he learned this from his friend Zip."

Callahan was the next victim in the World Jai Alai bloodbath because Bulger feared he would rat out the gang. The decision to kill Callahan was made in a 1982 meeting he attended in New York with Bulger and Flemmi.

"[Bulger] said that Zip told him that Callahan is

going to get so much pressure on him that he is going to fold and we are all going to go to jail for the rest of our life," Martorano testified. "Bulger did all the talking. Stevie just listened. They thought that he wouldn't hold up. They wanted to take him out."

Martorano considered Callahan a "friend" and said he "objected" to the execution but was overruled.

"I didn't want to kill Callahan," he said. "Eventually, they convinced me. It was two against one and it was three of us. And I finally agreed, 'It has got to be done. It has to be done.' "

Martorano was such close pals with Callahan that Callahan gave him money while he was on the run and let him use his condo and car in Plantation, Florida. Still, on August 1, 1982, Martorano picked him up in a van at Fort Lauderdale International Airport, shot him in the head, and dumped his body in the trunk of his own car.

When he and a cohort moved the body from the van to Callahan's car, they heard him "moan," so Martorano shot him again. Then they drove around the Little Havana neighborhood of Miami and tossed his belongings out of the car "to make it appear drug-related." The car was dumped at Miami International Airport, where it was found days later. After the slaying, Martorano and Flemmi met in Florida with Rico,

the retired FBI agent, to discuss the future of World Jai Alai. Martorano remained on the run for another thirteen years until he was arrested in 1995 in Delray Beach.

While Martorano coldly detailed the murders he committed, it was all about tying Whitey to each body, which Wyshak did one after the other. The wily prosecutor steered Martorano to the 1975 killing of Tommy King, a Mullins gang member, bank robber, and rugged Southie boxer who famously beat up Bulger at Triple O's in 1975.

"Him and Tommy couldn't get along. They were always butting heads together," Martorano told jurors. "He wanted to get rid of Tommy."

Martorano said Bulger came up with a "ruse" to set up King's murder that involved lying to King about helping them kill a deadbeat bookie named "Suitcase" Fidler. Martorano, Bulger, Howie Winter, and King all met at Carson Beach in Southie, where Flemmi handed out guns, supposedly to use to kill Fidler. King, who was wearing a bulletproof vest, was given a gun with blanks in it.

With Bulger driving, Winter and Martorano got in the backseat and Martorano executed King with a gunshot to the back of the head. The crew drove toward a pre-dug grave at Tenean Beach in Dorches-

ter, a marshy area along the Neponset River, just off Interstate 93 under an MBTA Red Line bridge. Martorano and Winter got out of the vehicle and went back to Somerville to check on a horse race, while Bulger drove on and buried King in a chest-deep hole along the river.

King's wife, Margaret, testified that she went to Triple O's when her husband didn't come home and confronted Bulger.

"Where is my husband?" she asked the mob boss.

"He's probably in Canada robbing banks," Bulger responded.

Over the ensuing years, Bulger was infamously caught on a DEA bug saying to pals as they drove on I-93 past the river, "Tip your hat to Tommy." The comment was a mystery until October 2000, when Weeks led cops to the burial ground. King's body was unearthed on the beach, along with the decaying corpses of Debbie Davis and Paul McGonagle, Catherine's former brother-in-law. Bulger lived for many years in a condominium that overlooked the burial ground.

Martorano's testimony was exhaustive as the jury heard three days of him confessing to murder after murder, including eleven he says he committed with Bulger, as well as a day and a half of Brennan and Car-

ney lambasting him as a liar, a "serial killer," and an opportunist.

"You even lied to your best friend, John Callahan, before you murdered him," Brennan said.

"Correct," Martorano answered. "To me that was a necessity. I couldn't tell him I wanted to shoot him."

Brennan asked him if he was a "serial killer."

"Serial killers kill until they get caught or stopped," Martorano answered. "I didn't. I wasn't a serial killer.

"A serial murderer kills for fun, they like it," he added. "I don't like it. I never did like it."

He was also asked if he was remorseful.

"Yes," he responded flatly.

As Martorano left the court, he smiled at Bulger.

It was a devil's grin.

31

After three days of Martorano's ghoulish testimony, the prosecutors needed the jury to hear from the loved ones of those left behind by the gang's bloody reign. So Wyshak, Hafer, and Kelly brought in a string of tearful relatives of Bulger's murder victims who helped shed light on the wreckage, as well as the depths of the corruption.

Sandra Castucci, wife of murder victim Richard Castucci, took the stand and laid the foundation for prosecutors to start painting a vivid picture of the deadly coordination that went on between Whitey and the FBI. Richard Castucci was a mobbed-up strip club owner and bookie. He was golfing buddies with Sammy Davis Jr. and palled around with the Rat Pack. A photo

was shown to the jury of Castucci with Frank Sinatra at Sammy Davis's wedding.

Castucci was in deep to loan sharks and was executed in Somerville in December 1976 by Martorano, with Flemmi and Bulger standing by. The mobsters tossed his body in the trunk of Castucci's Cadillac and dumped it in Revere, a city known for its mob boneyards, where it was discovered during a snowstorm.

Sandra Castucci testified after her husband's murder that she was strong-armed out of his nightclubs by New England mob boss Raymond Patriarca, who told her he was taking them because her husband owed the Mafia money. The real reason Castucci was killed, though, was that word leaked to Whitey and Flemmi that he was an FBI informant. Whitey was an FBI rat at the time of the killing. This marked the first known occasion that he participated in a murder while under the Bureau's watch. In 2009, the Castucci family won a $6 million wrongful death suit against the federal government.

The seventy-six-year-old widow's testimony set the stage for James Marra, a special agent with the Justice Department's Office of the Inspector General, who provided the most damning evidence of Whitey's status as an FBI mole. Marra read from Bulger's seven-hundred-page informant file over four long days, mak-

ing him one of the longest witnesses of the trial. He
revealed that Whitey was known officially to the Bureau as "BS 1544," a secret code number used to protect his status as an informant.

Marra's testimony was visibly uncomfortable for
Whitey and his defense team, who made clear from
the outset of the trial that they would seek to dismantle
claims that he was a protected FBI informant. It meant
nothing legally to the charges in the case but was obviously a priority for Bulger, who at that point had nothing left but his street reputation and legacy.

Marra, who spent thirty-five years in the DOJ, was
an expert in internal affairs matters in the FBI. He had
investigated dozens of federal agents for wrongdoing
over the years. He was part of the US attorney's prosecution team in 1994 that won a landmark $58 mil-
lion settlement against the Teamsters labor union for
embezzlement, kickbacks, and bribery. And he was a
key witness in Connolly's 2008 murder trial in Florida,
which ended with the disgraced G-man being found
guilty of second-degree murder and getting forty years
in prison.

For Wyshak, Kelly, and Hafer, Marra was a key
witness, as Bulger's informant file did much more than
shed light on his decades-long relationship with the
FBI. It also corroborated many of the killings Whitey

was charged with—including several that were chillingly outlined to the jury by Martorano.

As Marra sat in the witness booth, just fifteen feet from Whitey, he read from report after report drafted by several different FBI agents and their supervisors detailing Bulger's status as an informant. The eighty-five-year-old gangster's blood boiled.

"The glares he gave to me on the stand, you could feel and sense the evil in him," Marra told the authors of this book in 2019. "If looks could kill."

As lawyers talked at sidebar with Judge Casper about Bulger's voluminous FBI informant file and how it should be presented to the jury, the disgraced mob boss slouched in his chair, angrily muttering.

"I'm not a fucking informant," he seethed.

It was one of the more intense moments of the trial up to that point and exposed Bulger's nasty side as his lawyers desperately sought to spin the facts and rewrite history.

Wyshak at one point had enough of the defense team's charade, telling Judge Casper, "I understand that for whatever reasons, whether it's the ego of the defendant or attempting to preserve his reputation, he does not want to be called an informant, but I am not going to tailor my questions in a manner that preserves that ridiculous contention."

Marra's testimony was crippling. He said Bulger began working as an FBI informant in 1971, but was shut down because he wasn't providing useful information. He was put back into the program in 1975 and became a "Top Echelon—Organized Crime" informant for the next fifteen years, until Connolly retired. His primary handler was his Southie pal Zip Connolly, but he also provided information to other agents through the years, including Dennis Condon, John Morris, and James Ring, Marra testified.

"He'd be considered to be a very valuable source of information," Marra said, referring to the official FBI status Bulger had for decades.

The reports Marra detailed showed that Bulger met with several FBI agents, not just Connolly, further blunting the defense claim that the informant file was filled with false information crafted by Connolly to hoodwink his superiors. The records showed Dennis Condon wrote multiple reports about contacts with Bulger in 1971. FBI agent James Scanlon was his supervisor at the time.

Bulger was released as an informant in 1971, but in 1975, he was back on the books under Connolly's purview. Scanlon was also Connolly's supervisor for two years, until 1978 when Morris took over. In November 1980, then–special-agent-in-charge of the Boston

office Lawrence Sarhatt wrote a memo saying that he met with Morris, Connolly, and Bulger for "four hours" at an East Boston hotel. Flemmi was conspicuously absent from the meeting, lending more credence to prosecutors' assertions that Bulger himself was feeding information to the FBI and wasn't just along for the ride with Flemmi.

Whitey told Sarhatt at that meeting that the Massachusetts State Police were "aware of his informant role with the FBI."

"However, he is not concerned with his personal safety because no one would dare believe that he is an informant," Sarhatt wrote. "It would be too incredible. Notwithstanding this notoriety, he indicated to me that he wants to continue the relationship with the FBI."

From February 1983 through May 1990, James Ring was Connolly's supervisor and wrote several reports about Bulger and Flemmi. He too noted that he met personally with them, including multiple meetings in 1984.

"I have met with these informants on approximately four occasions," Ring wrote in an October 17, 1984, report.

Marra read through a slew of Connolly's informant reports on Bulger, all littered with information about murders, gun running, drug deals, and bank robber-

ies. Bulger spun elaborate lies to his handlers to deflect the investigative spotlight away from himself.

After the 1982 Brian Halloran/Michael Donahue murders, he was particularly vocal with Connolly as he planted fabricated stories designed to throw agents off his trail. Two days after the murders, Bulger told Connolly that Halloran might have been killed by the Mafia because he was talking to the feds.

Then he claimed the Mafia put a "hit" on Halloran because Halloran gunned down a rival in a restaurant and was planning to pin the killing on mobster "Cadillac" Frank Salemme's brother Jackie. The mob, Bulger told the agent, wanted Halloran dead because Halloran was a "weak person" who "might make a deal" to implicate Jackie Salemme.

He also claimed Halloran's mind was "blown out on coke" and that he was shaking down drug dealers all over Southie, suggesting his unpredictable street antics could have led to his murder. He suggested Halloran could have been targeted by Jimmy Flynn and Jimmy "The Weasel" Mantville, two Charlestown associates who knew Halloran's brother was a state trooper and suspected he was a rat.

Finally, he gave yet another scenario: that Halloran was killed by Jimmy Flynn because several Irish mobsters were afraid he would tell the feds about a murder

in Canada. Bulger told Connolly the crew held a fund-raiser at an Irish civic club in Malden, Massachusetts, to raise money to send Flynn on the run. Halloran knew all about it and was going to squeal to the feds, which is why he was targeted for death, Bulger said, according to Connolly's reports.

Based on the bogus info, Flynn was arrested and charged in the slaying but was acquitted at trial in 1986. He went on to run the Teamsters movie crews in Boston, and appeared in several made-in-Boston films, including playing a judge in a scene with Matt Damon in *Good Will Hunting*. In an ironic twist, Flynn was the Teamsters' transportation supervisor during filming in Boston for *The Departed*.

Marra also outlined a series of damning FBI reports and memos detailing the murders of Wheeler and Callahan, many of which exposed Connolly as being complicit.

The informant files remained sealed for years and were first acknowledged following Bulger's 1995 indictment. But they remained redacted until a landmark 2003 decision by Congress that gave the DOJ's Office of the Inspector General full oversight to investigate all federal agencies, including the FBI, Bureau of Prisons, Bureau of Alcohol, Tobacco and Firearms, DEA, and even the US Attorney's Office. The FBI had fought

tooth-and-nail to keep them sealed during the 1995 case and the ruling opened up the floodgates.

"The FBI was happy policing itself," one source said.

The detail Marra outlined in court was stark. Had the legislation not been changed in 2003, the reports never would have seen the light of day. The way they were written made it clear that Connolly and his fellow agents assumed they never would have been made public.

Whitey's lawyers challenged the veracity of the reports, saying there was "missing information" to verify their authenticity. And they pointed the finger at the DOJ for allowing Bulger's reign of terror to go on for decades.

"Certainly the DOJ needs to protect the fact that they let somebody they believe is a killer run loose, kill people throughout the Boston area, and never charge him," Brennan told the court.

Marra was subjected to one of the longest and nastiest cross-examinations of the trial as Brennan pointed out lies in Connolly's reports, challenged Marra's knowledge of the truth behind the reports, and questioned whether the information led to any prosecutions.

"Hank Brennan was ruthless on him, trying to prove Bulger wasn't an informant," Hafer recalled.

"I'm sure that was driven by Bulger because it really didn't mean much legally."

The defense was relentless in pushing their narrative of Connolly as a rogue agent who made up information from Bulger, or attributed information to Whitey that actually came from Flemmi.

Wyshak called their claim "fiction" and pointed to volumes of reports not only from Connolly, but from Condon, Ring, Morris, Scanlon, and others.

"Unless it is Mr. Bulger's contention that all of these agents got together to fabricate this file for some reason, his contention that he was not an FBI informant is simply absurd," Wyshak said.

Former FBI supervisor John Morris, who was retired and living in Florida, was called by prosecutors and took the stand for two days. He told a sordid tale of corruption in the Boston FBI office, including fudging reports with Connolly to protect Bulger and Flemmi. The disgraced agent, who was granted immunity and flipped on Connolly, met with Bulger scores of times, took at least $7,000 in bribes, and hosted dinners with the gangsters at his home while in charge of the Boston FBI.

"I knew I was completely trapped," Morris said. "I was in so far I could never get out of it. I didn't know what to do. I felt awful."

Morris admitted he was the agent who anonymously first leaked Bulger's relationship with the FBI to the media in 1988. As he did with Marra, Bulger expressed hostility toward Morris in court, at one point muttering under his breath, "You're a fucking liar."

Brian Kelly was furious at the comment and asked Judge Casper to order the gangster to watch his tongue.

"I know he spent his whole life intimidating people, including fifteen-year-old boys in Southie, but he shouldn't be allowed to do it here," Kelly said.

Judge Casper said she didn't hear the comment but advised him to let his lawyers do the talking.

"Do you understand?" she asked.

"Yes," Bulger responded.

When it came time for Bulger's team to lay out their case, they didn't call any of the agents Marra mentioned who were still alive, including Sarhatt, who did testify at Flemmi's 1998 trial and was still alive in 2013. He died in July 2018.

In fact, there was only one agent who claimed Bulger wasn't an informant—Robert Fitzpatrick, who was the special agent in charge of the Boston office from 1981 to 1986. Fitzpatrick was the only witness at all called by the defense team, but rather than bolster Whitey's claims that he wasn't an informant, he told a series of

whopping lies that ultimately landed him a perjury conviction after the Bulger trial.

Fitzpatrick, who wrote a book about the case, testified that Whitey told him he wasn't an informant and claimed he was brought in to clean up the Boston office in 1980. Both turned out to be lies, but they weren't the most fantastical fabrications Fitzpatrick told on the stand.

He told the jury it was he who put the handcuffs on Boston mob boss Jerry Anguilo. He also said he personally recovered the rifle that James Earl Ray used to assassinate Dr. Martin Luther King at the Lorraine Motel in Memphis, Tennessee, in 1968. Both proved to be total fabrications.

Kelly grilled Fitzpatrick on the stand, which visibly angered Bulger. As the prosecutor started tearing into Fitzpatrick, Bulger shot him an angry look that sent chills down Kelly's spine.

"He turned around really quickly and glared at me," Kelly said. "I really went at Fitzpatrick hard. He clearly didn't like it. He turned around really fast and I thought, 'This guy is just a maniac.'

"For an old guy, he was threatening looking," he added. "He had this aura of evil, even as an old man, sitting in the courtroom when he looked at you. I was glad the marshals were there."

Three years after Bulger's trial, Fitzpatrick was convicted of six counts of perjury and six counts of obstruction of justice because of his lies on the stand. He was sentenced to twenty-four months' probation and fined $12,500.

"Fitzpatrick admitted that he lied when he testified at Bulger's trial that he tried to end Bulger's relationship with the FBI and target Bulger for prosecution but was overruled by higher authorities in the FBI," US Attorney Carmen Ortiz said.

The testimony was a disaster for Bulger's defense, but it would only get worse.

32

Whitey's politically connected family was largely spared throughout the trial, as Billy Bulger had already been publicly pilloried during his circus-like 2003 congressional testimony, after which he was forced to resign his lofty perch as president of the University of Massachusetts.

But a handful of other relatives were dragged into the case in July 2013 when the jury was played recordings of a series of jailhouse conversations between Whitey and his family. Ken Brady, the investigator and guard at Plymouth, burned all the calls to a disk and handed them over to prosecutors.

In one recording, the mobster was heard telling Billy Bulger's son, William Bulger Jr., and his sister

about the 1975 murder of Edward Connors, a Dorchester tavern owner gunned down in a Dorchester phone booth.

"Pa-pa-pa-pa-pow," Bulger whispered in the October 13, 2012, call, mimicking machine gun fire.

Connors was one of the nineteen victims Bulger was charged with killing.

"Somebody threw my name in the mix," Whitey told his nephew and niece, who could be heard laughing on the tape.

"As usual," William Bulger Jr. says.

In another taped conversation with his brother Jackie, a disgraced ex–clerk magistrate for the Boston Juvenile Court, Whitey talked about pointing a shotgun at kids casing out his Southie liquor store.

"They're getting ready to stick the joint up, so I picked up a shotgun and I'm aimin' it at them. And the guy looked up and, 'Oh,'" Whitey says in the December 11, 2012, recording, while breaking into laughter.

"See you later," Jackie chimed in.

"And I put one in the chamber," Whitey said. "One went this way, one went that way. . . . We were lucky they didn't try to do nothing."

While the tape was played, Whitey was smirking at the defendant's table.

Bulger had nothing to laugh about when his protégé Kevin Weeks strolled into court to testify against his former boss and mentor.

Weeks's name was sprinkled throughout the trial and it was already well established that he'd turned on Whitey. Now it was time for the jury to learn about the six decomposed corpses that he'd led investigators to at two separate makeshift burial grounds in Boston's Dorchester neighborhood.

Like Martorano, Weeks was a free man, despite his admitted role in five murders. He too had cut a sweetheart immunity deal with the government in exchange for his testimony against Bulger and Flemmi, and he was living just down the street from the courthouse in his old Southie neighborhood.

A former bouncer at Whitey's haunt, Triple O's, Weeks earned the nickname "Two Weeks" in 2000 because he flipped on Bulger and Flemmi after just a few weeks in federal prison in Rhode Island.

Whitey didn't show much interest in most witnesses, but when Weeks came in—his surrogate son, whom he hadn't seen in seventeen years—he sat up in his chair and craned his neck to watch the beefy thug take the stand.

"I was with him over twenty years," Weeks told the jury. "Sometimes I'd beat somebody up."

They shook down landlords, businessmen, bookies, and drug dealers. They moved kilos of cocaine across Boston, sometimes up to twenty-six kilos—fifty-seven pounds—at a time. He recalled shaking down a drug dealer named "Red" Shea for $15,000 plus $1,500 monthly payments, using a fake Uzi machine gun given to Whitey by Connolly as a gag gift.

One bookie who wanted out had to pay the gang $500,000. Whitey called it "severance." He recalled shaking down a bookie named Kevin Hayes—the father of National Hockey League players Kevin and Jimmy Hayes—for $25,000 cash plus $1,000 a month in rent during football season. Hayes later testified that he was brought to the basement of The Haunty, where Weeks threatened to shoot him in the head if he didn't pay. There was a plastic tarp on the floor.

Weeks said the gang had gun "hides" all over Southie, including one that had a sliding electronic wall where they stashed machine guns, silencers, masks, and ammo. He said the gang regularly oiled and wiped down firearms to remove fingerprints. After shooting people, they would destroy the guns. He recalled moving stashes of weapons after the indictments came

down in 1995. They had handcuffs to restrain people during shakedowns and murders and knives to use for "intimidation."

He testified about paying off Connolly, Morris, Schneiderhan, and other cops and FBI agents. He described Whitey as his "mentor." And he verified infamous surveillance photos showing him, Whitey, and Flemmi having clandestine criminal meetings while casually walking around Southie's Castle Island. He said he made as much as $2 million in the roughly fifteen years he was partnered with Bulger.

For the prosecutors, Weeks, like Martorano, was another key to checking off murders as Weeks was involved in the planning, execution, and cleanup of several of the killings in the indictment. Weeks had the courtroom on edge as he described the May 1982 killings of Halloran and Donahue on South Boston's waterfront. Halloran was targeted because, he said, "we got word that he was cooperating with the FBI on a couple of murders." The crew didn't even know who Donahue was.

After the drive-by double murder, Whitey had dinner at Teresa Stanley's house. Then they drove back to the murder scene, which by then was surrounded by police tape and mobbed with cops, and they grabbed a

hubcap that flew off Whitey's "hit car" after the shooting. Whitey bragged about the shooting later that night to Flemmi and another gangster.

A couple of days after the murders, Whitey, Flemmi, and Weeks brazenly went and marveled at the bullet-riddled Datsun in a South Boston tow lot where the car was being stored by police.

"Let's get out of here before someone spots us," Whitey told the crew after examining his handiwork for a few minutes.

Days later, Weeks got the guns out of the backseat of the Chevy Malibu and removed the stock from a carbine because Bulger "liked that stock." He kept the stock but tossed the guns into the ocean at Marina Bay, an ocean pier in nearby Quincy.

Asked how he felt after the slayings, Weeks told the jury, "I just was involved in a double homicide, so there was no getting out. I knew I was in."

His second day of testimony got more gruesome as Weeks recalled the string of murders at The Haunty. He talked about watching Bulger execute Bucky Barrett and watching Flemmi pull out the victim's teeth. He, Flemmi, and associate Pat Nee buried the body.

He recalled Whitey telling him about the Tommy King and Paulie McGonagle murders and the strangulation of Debbie Davis. He said Bulger told him that

Flemmi wrapped the twenty-six-year-old beauty's face in duct tape and told her "you're going to a better place" before she was strangled. Whitey was unclear about who strangled her—him or Flemmi, he testified.

Weeks later led cops to those three bodies at another makeshift burial ground on Tenean Beach, along the shores of the Neponset River in Dorchester.

He admitted making fake IDs for Whitey and delivering them to him in Chicago in 1996 while Bulger was on the lam. He talked with him regularly on pay phones and met with him several times at the New York Public Library.

Defense attorney Jay Carney dragged Weeks through an agonizing and intense cross-examination that went on for hours and exploded when the topic of Whitey being an informant came up. Referencing Weeks's light sentence for his convictions and participation in five murders, the attorney said, "You won against the system."

"What did I win? What did I win? Five people are dead!" Weeks shouted. "We killed people that were rats, and I had the two biggest rats right next to me."

With that, Whitey's anger spilled over once again.

"You suck," Bulger said.

"Fuck you, okay," Weeks shot back.

"Fuck you too," Whitey snarled.

"What do you want to do?" Weeks bellowed. He was ready to fight his former boss in the middle of the courtroom.

Judge Casper was livid.

"Hey, Mr. Bulger," the judge said, her voice rising. "Mr. Bulger, let your attorneys speak in this court for you."

After Weeks's turn wrapped up, he left the stand, glaring at Whitey. The judge called the attorneys to sidebar and admonished Carney and his partner Hank Brennan.

"Is it fair to say that you're going to speak to your client after today's session about this outburst?" Judge Casper said.

"Yes, your honor," Carney replied.

But there was still one final courtroom confrontation to come.

33

Hearing Kevin Weeks call him a rat rattled Whitey enough to scream "fuck you" in Judge Casper's courtroom, but what came next from Bulger's lifelong criminal partner Flemmi brought out perhaps the darkest moments of the two-month trial.

Bulger was dressed sharply in a pressed blue button-down suit the day his former right-hand man took the stand to publicly turn against him. It was a long time coming and the tension was high as Flemmi walked into the courtroom, marking the first time the two gangsters had seen each other in eighteen years. Both men had aged, but Flemmi's longer stretch behind bars made him look more withered than his former friend.

The prosecutors knew Flemmi was key to corroborating most of the murders, the drug dealing, gambling,

and racketeering, but the biggest question was whether he would be able to help them nail Whitey for the murders of Debbie Davis and Deborah Hussey. Would the jury believe this lifelong criminal and admitted killer who turned informant to save his own life?

Wearing a green prison jumpsuit and matching green windbreaker, Flemmi took the stand and immediately set the tone by saying emphatically they were both informants since the early 1970s and that Whitey was the boss when it came to their FBI snitching. The pair met with agents "hundreds of times," but it was Bulger who called the shots and "did all the talking" with their notorious handler, John "Zip" Connolly.

"He was the one that was really friendly with Connolly," Flemmi, slumped in the witness chair, testified.

It was another blow to the defense. The two gangsters, once inseparable and united in ruling Boston's underworld, squared off in the courtroom at one point with Flemmi standing defiantly with his hands on his hips, staring at Whitey.

"Fuck him," Bulger grumbled under his breath.

"Really?" Flemmi shot back.

Flemmi, who is serving life but was spared the death penalty in the Oklahoma and Florida murders for agreeing to turn on Whitey, casually ran through

the roster of murders as though discussing his breakfast. He repeatedly implicated Bulger, including in the grim strangulations of Flemmi's stepdaughter, Hussey, and his mistress, Debbie Davis.

According to Flemmi, Hussey was killed because Whitey determined she was a junkie who might talk to cops, while Davis was considered to be a "vulnerability" because she knew they were FBI informants.

Recalling Davis's murder, Flemmi said, "She walked in the entrance there, and he [Bulger] grabbed her by the neck. I couldn't do it. He knew it. He told me, 'I'll take care of it.'" Davis's family sobbed in the gallery, as did one juror.

Asked by Wyshak how it made him feel to stand and watch helplessly as Whitey choked the life out of the twenty-six-year-old beauty, he said, "It affected me. It's going to affect me until the day I die."

He added, coldly, "I loved her, but I wasn't in love with her."

Whitey dragged her to the basement, where she was stripped naked and her teeth were yanked out, per the usual routine. Flemmi said Bulger then went upstairs to lie down. Flemmi, Pat Nee, and another associate buried the woman's mutilated body at Tenean Beach.

He told a similar tale about Hussey's killing, but things turned ugly when Bulger's attorney, Hank Bren-

nan, grilled Flemmi about having sex with Hussey, his stepdaughter. The attorney needled Flemmi that the girl, who was seventeen years old when he admitted having oral sex with her, called him "Daddy."

"That was a consensual relationship," Flemmi said, fuming. "On just two occasions. Moments of weakness. And I regretted it all my life."

As Brennan pressed him about discrepancies in his stories about Hussey's murder over the years, the defense attorney suggested that it was Flemmi who killed her because she told her mother—Flemmi's common-law wife, Marion—that he molested her. Enraged, Flemmi blurted out an oft-repeated rumor about Whitey having a penchant for underage girls in his heyday.

"You want to talk about pedophilia, right over there at that table," Flemmi said, pointing to Bulger sitting at the defense table. "He had a young girlfriend, sixteen years old, he took to Mexico."

While Whitey had erupted at far less scandalous accusations during the two-month trial, Flemmi's bombshell barely elicited a sigh from Bulger, who didn't have the energy or strength to defend his own lies anymore.

The final witness to testify for the prosecution was a foe from Bulger's more recent past.

FBI manhunter Scott Garriola flew in from Los Angeles to walk jurors through Whitey's final hours as America's most wanted criminal.

There would be no outbursts from Bulger this time. The Irish mob boss and accused killer respectfully observed Garriola as he took the witness stand and described how he managed to lure Bulger out of the apartment at the Princess Eugenia and also the cache of weapons they found inside apartment 303.

Prosecutor Zach Hafer asked the FBI agent if Whitey had stocked up on all those weapons for an eventual shootout with those coming to arrest him.

"I asked him that question," Garriola told the jury. "He paused. And then he told me, 'No, because a stray bullet may hit someone.'"

As the exhaustive eight-week trial wrapped up, there was one key figure whose name came up repeatedly in the Moakley Courthouse and who hadn't been heard from: Pat Nee.

The notorious bank robber, gunrunner, and triggerman was supposed to be a star witness for Bulger. Jay Carney was prepared to call him, but Nee told Judge Casper he would refuse to testify by invoking his Fifth Amendment right against self-incrimination. Nee's attorney, a seasoned Southie criminal defense

lawyer named Steven Boozang, felt Bulger was using his client for no other reason than courtroom theatrics—and he and Nee weren't going along for the ride.

"It's become readily apparent that this is not a legal defense, but a client-run defense," Boozang said.

An Irish national and loyal gunrunner for the IRA, Nee was a violent bank robber and enforcer who had a long, storied history with Bulger. There were some who believed he too was a protected FBI informant.

Born in Rus Muc, a Gaelic-speaking village in Galway, Ireland, Nee was the oldest of six children. His dad was a laborer and his mom cleaned office buildings. The family immigrated to Boston on an English cruise ship and settled on East Sixth Street in Southie, right around the corner from the Bulger clan.

Young Pat seamlessly fell into a life of crime, stealing Hummel ceramic figures and jewelry during home break-ins.

"I learned how to steal and I liked the adrenaline rushes and the excitement," Nee told the authors of this book.

He joined the Mullen gang at age fourteen and immersed himself in the bloody gang wars that rocked Boston in the 1950s and '60s. He briefly abandoned his criminal career when he joined the Marines and went to Vietnam, where he became a US citizen while fight-

ing the war. He returned to Southie in 1966 and re-joined the Mullen gang.

Whitey and Nee played a dangerous game of cat-and-mouse during the 1970s as they took turns stalking each other as rival members of the feuding Mullen and Killeen gangs. One night in Charlestown, Nee and Bulger chased each other through a housing project, firing bullets at one another. Bulger carried a German-made submachine gun while Nee brandished a .30-06—"30 odd six"—military rifle outfitted with a scope. At one point, Nee spotted Bulger across a court-yard. He dropped to one knee and tried to get Bulger in his crosshairs, but the Southie gangster escaped.

Their final violent clash came when Whitey am-bushed him at the corner of N and Fifth Streets in Southie one night. Nee and another thug were in Nee's brother's car when Whitey and two henchmen pulled up, got out, and opened fire, riddling the sedan with bullets. Nee hid on the floor and was shredded by shat-tering glass, receiving cuts all over his face and body.

"I saw the flashes of the guns," Nee said. "I have no idea how they missed me."

Nee and Whitey reluctantly joined forces when Bulger took control of the Winter Hill Gang. The former rivals put aside their differences for the good of their criminal careers, but Nee says he "never trusted" Bulger.

The jury heard from Weeks and others how Nee was the one who orchestrated the Valhalla gun-running scheme and helped Weeks lure John McIntyre to the basement of The Haunty. Nee was implicated in several slayings, including the killings of Bucky Barrett, Brian Halloran, and Michael Donahue, but was never prosecuted.

"Pat Nee is a stone-cold killer," Donahue's son, Tommy, told reporters after closing statements in the case. "He has been his whole life. He was involved in my father's murder . . . No charges were brought upon him. He's involved in countless violent crimes."

According to Weeks, Nee helped him and Flemmi exhume the remains of McIntyre, Hussey, and Barrett from the basement of The Haunty when the death house was sold. Flemmi, Weeks, and Bulger reburied the bodies across from Florian Hall, where they were later found, thanks to Weeks. Nee wasn't allowed to help with the second burial because Whitey didn't trust him, Weeks testified.

Nee told the authors of this book that Whitey confessed to him that he was an FBI informant. He said it was him who helped the FBI wire the Mafia's North End hideout.

"He told me at one point, before I took off on the

Valhalla case," Nee said. "We were out at Castle Island with Weeks and O'Neil. He pulled me aside and said 'I helped Zip with the bug at Prince Street.'"

Nee went on the run for several years after being charged in the Valhalla case until he was arrested in 1987. He served just two years in federal prison for the gun-running case, which could have landed him a life sentence. Upon his release, he started a crew that robbed armored trucks. He served ten years of a thirty-seven-year sentence for a 1991 armored truck heist in Abington, Massachusetts, that was foiled by authorities, including FBI agent John Gamel.

Nee said that after serving his sentence for Valhalla, he avoided Whitey and hid his criminal endeavors from the Southie crime boss.

"He was an informant. I didn't talk to him at all," Nee said. "He kept us all either in prison or on the run. We were never able to piece it all together."

During the trial, like Martorano and Weeks, Nee was a free man. He still lived in Southie and walked the streets freely. In fact, it was announced during the trial that he'd be starring in a Discovery Channel reality show about bookies called *Saint Hoods*. None of it sat well with jurors and some were scared.

"People looked sick in the beginning," juror Scott

Hotyckey said. "I think they were terrified. People asked me, 'What if Pat Nee comes to your house?'"

With Nee bowing out of the courthouse drama, all that was left was for Whitey to take the stand. The crime lord's pretrial pledge to expose government corruption at the highest level had the courthouse buzzing, but ultimately fell flat, as he decided not to testify.

It was disappointing to prosecutors, who were eager to grill the mob boss.

"Carney touted from day one, 'Wait until he takes the witness stand. Wait until he testifies. Wait til you hear what he has to say,'" Fred Wyshak said. "He was essentially threatening the government that he was going to expose all their wrongdoing, saying, 'When everybody hears his side of the story, we're going to have a very different picture.' At the last minute, as usual, he didn't testify."

Zach Hafer added, "There was a real disappointment that Bulger didn't testify. And that was calculated.

"If he had testified, he could have been asked about all this stuff. He knew that. It sort of enabled just this little bit of doubt to be out there. Was he really an informant? Did he meet with Jeremiah O'Sullivan? If he had taken the stand and been confronted with the absurdity of some of the claims, and the lack of any kind of backup, that little bit of residual doubt would

be gone . . . We wanted the jury to hear that. That was part of the story."

After the demise of Whitey's much-anticipated final stand, the jury got the case and delivered its verdict after five long days of deliberation. They pored over piles of sickening crime scene photos and mountains of evidence.

On the day of the verdict—August 12, 2013—Bulger was picked up before dawn at the sally port of the Plymouth County Correctional Facility by state police and US marshals with guns drawn. He was transported by motorcade forty miles north to Boston, where along the way he passed the death pits that had hidden his secrets for so long, and his old neighborhood where his notorious legend was constructed over decades. Traffic along the busy highway into the city came to a standstill as motorists craned their necks to catch a glimpse of the former crime boss as he sped by.

The jury of eight men and four women convicted Whitey on thirty-one of thirty-two counts in the racketeering case, with the only not guilty delivered on the extortion of bookie Kevin Hayes.

They also found Bulger guilty of eleven of the nineteen murders, including the strangulation of Deborah Hussey, as well as the killings of Wheeler,

Callahan, Halloran, Donahue, Tommy King, Edward Connors, Richard Castucci, Bucky Barrett, and John McIntyre. The jurors deadlocked on the killing of Debra Davis.

Her younger brother Steven Davis, who had been a fixture at the trial, holding court outside the courthouse and always willing to give a colorful quote to reporters, was stunned by the ruling.

"It's hard to digest," he said moments after the verdict came down. "With all the years since '81, I've been looking for answers, searching for answers, and I come out with an NF [No Finding]. It's not good enough . . . I believe I deserve more than an NF. I'm disappointed."

Wyshak, Hafer, and Kelly were also disappointed at the "no finding" on the Davis killing. It was the one small victory for Whitey and a tough loss for the prosecutors, as they hoped to deliver justice to the Davis family while also proving undeniably that Bulger was a heartless killer of women.

Still, the verdict, after four decades, finally held Bulger accountable for his evil reign.

"This day of reckoning for Bulger has been a long time coming," US Attorney Carmen Ortiz told reporters. "So many people's lives were so terribly harmed by the criminal acts of Bulger and his crew . . . We hope they find some degree of comfort in the fact . . .

that Bulger is being held accountable for his horrific crimes."

Hafer, who previously worked in public corruption in the US Attorney's Office, said that despite Whitey's refusal to testify, the case did hold several corrupt public officials accountable.

"It's important for the public to have confidence that when assistant US attorneys who prosecute corruption cases are confronted by corruption by police officers or law enforcement, that we're just as offended by it as members of the public and we're going to expose it," he said. "That level of corruption by someone as high in the FBI as John Connolly was, for people who do this job for all the right reasons, is repugnant."

Fred Wyshak, who had worked on Bulger-related cases most of his career, said the verdict affirmed the hard work of a small group of dedicated investigators who refused to cave to political, bureaucratic, or institutional pressure and corruption.

"The group of people who did this case . . . had to fight the department," Wyshak said. "Elements in the FBI didn't like this case from the beginning, didn't want this case to happen, and tried to pull a lot of strings to derail it over the years . . . So what you had was a small group of prosecutors and investigators who basically fought the system to make this case happen."

Jay Carney, for his part, wasn't impressed and said he was "very pleased" with the verdict because he thought it vindicated Whitey on the Davis killing and also exposed deep corruption in the FBI and beyond.

"Mr. Bulger knew as soon as he was arrested that he was going to die behind the walls of a prison . . . or be injected with a chemical that would kill him," Carney said. "This trial was never about Jim Bulger being set free."

Some of the victims' families were relieved with the results but felt bad for the families of the eight victims that did not get a guilty finding.

Donahue's son, Tommy, said of the verdict: "It's a good feeling. But my heart also goes out to those families who were searching for that closure."

For Kelly, the case marked the end of a twenty-plus-year chapter in his life. When he started chasing Bulger's gang, his kids were toddlers. When the verdict was handed down, he had one son in college and two other children in high school.

"It was a case well worth doing," he reflected. "It exposed corruption that had to be exposed. It held accountable murderers and drug dealers who had to be held accountable. As much of a time drain as it was, it was well worth it. I'd gladly do it again."

As Whitey left the courtroom in shackles, he smiled

and gave a thumbs-up to his brother Jackie and nieces and nephews. It was a sickening moment for the victims, but they'd soon take solace in knowing that Whitey's reign of terror was truly over and his life in prison would be anything but peaceful.

PART III
The Murder

34

It's never news when an aging retiree leaves the cold confines of Boston for the dry, warm climate of Arizona, but Whitey Bulger was no ordinary retiree and he was going to no ordinary place.

After the guilty verdict, the now convicted mob killer was shipped from Plymouth to the Metropolitan Detention Center in Brooklyn. Following a quick stay there, he was shipped to the federal transfer center in Oklahoma City before finally being sent to the United States Penitentiary in Tucson, Arizona. He'd never see his beloved Boston or Massachusetts again.

Whitey loved the Southwest and had traveled there extensively while he was on the run. But this time he wouldn't get to visit Tombstone or the Painted Desert.

With any luck, he'd never get to see the outside of a prison wall for the rest of his life.

The US Penitentiary in Tucson housed 1,552 inmates in its high-security facility. There were few inmates that were deemed more high security or high profile than Whitey.

But he was eighty-four years old now, and the years he'd spent in jail before and during his sensational trial had taken their toll. The regimen of daily push-ups helped; however, his body and mind were slowing down. Not even the notorious Whitey Bulger could defeat Father Time.

During his first few days as a federal prison inmate, Bulger befriended a young convict named Clement "Chip" Janus.

Janus, a member of the Rosebud Sioux tribe, grew up on the Crow reservation in Pryor, Montana. His mother died from a drug overdose and his father wasn't around, so Chip was raised on the reservation by his grandfather, a US Marine veteran. The grandfather was also an artist and he saw promise in Chip, so instead of giving him toys for Christmas, he put art supplies under the tree. But life on the reservation was particularly bleak, so Chip created his own excitement, drinking, carousing with friends, and boosting cars. He did a short stint in prison but was later sent back on federal gun charges.

"I was mad at the world and ran around with a huge chip on my shoulder thinking somebody owes me," he recalls.

He was incarcerated in Tucson for two years before Whitey Bulger walked into his life. By then, Chip had committed himself to doing his time and pursuing a career as an artist when he got out. The warden was so impressed by his talent that he put Chip in charge of the prison art room, where he taught oil painting and charcoal sketching to other inmates.

One day, while he was putting the finishing brush-strokes on several uncompleted projects, Whitey strolled into the art room with his customary gray sweatpants, white shirt, and a white baseball cap to inspect his work. Chip specialized in Native American art, so there were a number of paintings of tribe members in their traditional dress. Bulger was a huge fan of Native American art also, and he took his time studying each piece quietly without disrupting the artist's concentration.

The next morning, as Chip Janus made his way across the prison yard under the constant surveillance of rifle-toting guards perched atop gun towers, he bumped into a friend who said, "Whitey wants to shake your hand."

Chip didn't break stride, as he had only ten min-

utes to get from his cell to the art room, where he was scheduled to teach that day.

"It's a very controlled movement inside the yard," he explains. "The guards warn you that they'll shoot you if there are any problems."

He walked swiftly over to Bulger and extended his hand.

"Nice to meet you, but I gotta go."

"Can I come and talk to you?" Whitey asked.

"Alright, yeah," Chip answered. "I'll be in the art room."

Bulger made his way to the art room the next day.

"Wow," he sighed as he took his eyeglasses off and browsed Janus's artwork up close. "You did this?"

The prison art instructor nodded. "Yeah, I did that."

"You have great talent," Whitey told him. "I've been around the world. I saw the *Mona Lisa* in Paris. Do you know who I am? Did you know I was in Alcatraz?"

"Nah, I didn't know any of that stuff," Chip said. "How was it in Alcatraz?"

In truth, Chip Janus was vaguely aware of who Whitey was by now. When Bulger first got to Tucson, prisoners from the east coast marked his arrival with whispers and surrounded him like hungry sharks.

"Oh my God, is that him?" some inmates would ask.

But to convicts from the western United States, the

geriatric former crime boss wasn't the most infamous inmate in the yard. Also housed in Tucson was Brian Mitchell, the man who kidnapped and raped Elizabeth Smart; former US Army private Steven Green, who was one of five American soldiers that gang-raped a fourteen-year-old Iraqi girl and then murdered her family; and Colombian cartel boss Diego Montoya Sánchez.

"Some old guy is trying to make friends with me, says he was in Alcatraz," Janus told a guard.

"Yeah, that's Whitey Bulger," the guard replied. "He was the mobster that was on the run."

It didn't appear that Whitey had made any friends in Tucson, so he began hanging around the art room with Chip, and soon their conversations would spill over to the yard.

"There was a big art heist back in Boston at a place called the Isabella Stewart Gardner Museum. Everybody thinks I have the paintings but I never laid my hands on 'em." Whitey laughed.

In 1990, at the height of Whitey's power, two robbers disguised as police officers entered the museum after hours, tied up the security guard, and stole thirteen pieces of priceless art including Vermeer's *The Concert* and Rembrandt's dramatic work *Christ in the Storm on the Sea of Galilee*. It was the richest art theft

in the world. As his former protégé Kevin Weeks once said, "When we learned about it, we pulled in every crook we knew and gave them a good beat down for information but we never found them." The FBI maintains a $10 million reward for the safe return of the stolen art.

Whitey also told Chip about the letters and phone calls that his lawyer received from filmmakers that were developing *Black Mass,* a Hollywood biopic eventually released in 2015 about Bulger's life of crime starring Johnny Depp in the lead role.

"He's a good person [Depp]. But I don't understand why he took the role," Bulger said. "Even Johnny doesn't believe I was an informant. My lawyer is talking to Depp's agent. I'm gonna decline because I can't stand the *Boston Globe* guys that wrote it. If I was out, they wouldn't be writing that shit about me."

Whitey bragged to Janus that he'd once shot up a *Boston Globe* printing press with a machine gun. He told the prison art teacher that if he were to ever sit down for an interview, he'd speak only to Barbara Walters. The legendary television journalist had interviewed world leaders like Fidel Castro and countless Hollywood stars. Bulger felt that he was deserving of the same celebrity treatment.

He also schooled Chip about his life at Alcatraz and

Joe "The Animal" Barboza, another notorious Boston mobster turned government rat.

"Barboza was killed for being an informant," Bulger said in mock disgust. "They reached out and touched him in San Francisco for being a rat. He was a big player in the game and lots of stuff happened with him. He was a hit man who turned informant and was blown off his feet because of it."

"How'd you manage to stay on the run all those years?" Chip asked him.

"They thought I was outta the country when I left." Whitey shook his head and laughed. "There were sightings of me overseas but that never happened. I was right there in front of 'em the whole fucking time."

He also explained that it was his and Catherine's love of pets that led to their capture.

"We'd go outside our apartments for walks in Santa Monica and every morning we'd feed this cat. That cat was gonna be the death of me. Some days I didn't want to go out there but Catherine would wanna feed the cat. I told her to just leave the fucking thing alone, but she had this thing for this stray animal. If she didn't feed that cat, we wouldn't have gotten to know all those people. I didn't wanna build any relationships. I never wanted to spend any money either because I didn't want to attract any attention."

Their conversations also centered on Bulger's friendship with Joe Carnes. Whitey commissioned Janus to paint some portraits of Carnes wearing a traditional Choctaw headdress that he could send as a gift to his brother Billy back home in Southie.

"I can't pay you any money, but I can write you some stories and send you some signed photos. Trust me, they're worth something."

As the two men sat on a bench in the prison yard, Bulger's menacing stare constantly shifted, watching every prisoner who passed by. He'd count how many times they'd walk by and then get up to confront them.

"Hey, what're you doing?" the eighty-four-year-old gangster would ask in a stern voice. "I'm trying to have a conversation here, you walked by a few times. What're you doin'? You wanna ask me something?"

Bulger understood that he was a high-level target for any prisoners looking to make a name for themselves and expected that someone would take a run at him sooner or later.

"When they give it to me, I hope they give it to me quick, because I gave it quick," he told Janus.

One prisoner that Bulger kept a close eye on was Louis Eppolito, a former New York City police detec-

tive turned hired Mafia killer for the Lucchese and Gambino crime families. Eppolito was serving life in prison for several gangland slayings and also had been contracted for failed hits on John "Junior" Gotti and notorious mob rat Sammy "The Bull" Gravano. Like most people with deep knowledge of the underworld, Eppolito didn't buy Bulger's story that he was never an informant for the FBI.

During one controlled movement in the prison yard, Eppolito stood directly behind Whitey and shouted, "Fucking rat!"

Bulger pretended not to hear the insult, as he didn't want to draw the attention of some trigger-happy prison guard standing in the gun towers above. But Eppolito never tried to exact mob justice on Whitey. Instead, Bulger was nearly killed in an attack he didn't see coming.

Four months after he had arrived in Tucson, Whitey's luck almost ran out when he was jumped by another prisoner who went by the nickname "Retro."

Whitey was bringing photos of Joe Carnes to Janus's art room when Retro, a well-known heroin addict, rushed him and stabbed him in the skull and neck with a homemade knife. The wounds were nearly fatal. Bulger was rushed to the prison infirmary, where doctors worked desperately to stop the bleeding. Some-

how, even at the advanced age of eighty-four, Whitey was strong enough to survive the assault.

He stayed in the prison infirmary for more than a month while Retro was tossed into solitary confinement, which had been his goal. The attacker owed drug money to some prisoners in the yard and had no way to pay them. By trying to kill Bulger, he saved himself from a similar fate at the hands of the inmates he'd welched on.

"It's called a check-in move," Janus explained. "Retro attacked Bulger to get taken out of the yard, thrown into solitary, and out of his debt. He also knew that if he killed Whitey, he'd go down in history."

While Bulger was recovering from his stab wounds, he sent photos of Carnes to Chip Janus for reproduction.

"Somebody put them in my art teacher's locker," Janus recalls. "He also sent me a note telling me that he would be fine and for me to say hello to everyone. I laughed because he didn't have any friends—just me. But he was showing that he had the prison wired and that he could get things to me."

While in the infirmary, Bulger sought counseling from a female prison psychologist. He was falling into a deep depression as he longed for his girlfriend, who was still in prison thousands of miles away. Follow-

ing her guilty plea, Catherine was sent to the Waseca Federal Correctional Institution, a low-security facility with 660 female inmates in Minnesota.

The young psychologist became intrigued by the aging, lovelorn gangster. The two spent hours together, according to Janus.

"I get to write to Catherine," Bulger told his friend after he was released from the prison hospital. "The psychologist came up with some brilliant story so I'd get to write to Catherine. I know the woman's grandmother. She was from South Boston."

Soon, someone at the Tucson prison complained about the relationship between Bulger and the staff member. Officials began investigating whether the psychologist slipped Whitey a cell phone that he used in prison and if she sold autographed photos that Bulger had given her.

"He was the master at charming people," Chip Janus recalled.

Prosecutor Brian Kelly agreed. "It's no surprise that he's been breaking the rules and trying to manipulate the system," Kelly said. "He's been doing that his whole life."

In Southie, Bulger was revered like some kind of god. He maintained that cult of personality while incarcerated in Arizona, where he regaled younger inmates

like Chip with stories about Alcatraz and sweet-talked staffers into giving him special treatment. But Whitey could not rely on his fearsome reputation any longer. He needed to allow his advancing age to work in his favor. For prisoners and prison workers alike, any attention bestowed on them by a celebrated, old-school gangster such as Bulger was considered an honor.

He carried himself with an air of invincibility and his reputation preceded him, but he was also old and frail. The combination of his gangster cred, jailhouse celebrity, and frailty gave him some protection in Tucson, but what really kept him safe was that he was in a prison specifically designated by the Bureau of Prisons as a safe haven for high-profile informants. At Tucson he was far away from hard-core mobsters who would want to kill a rat like him. But before he could really grow his power behind the Arizona prison walls, officials shipped him off again, this time to a federal lockup in central Florida.

35

Bulger's health steadily deteriorated shortly after he was placed into the humid confines of the Coleman Federal Correctional Complex, a massive 555,000-square-foot facility about fifty miles northwest of Disney World in central Florida. The prison sits about ten miles outside the town of Coleman, which is known as the "Cabbage Capital of the World."

As in Tucson, Whitey was just one of several high-profile prisoners that now called Coleman home including Leonard Peltier, the Native American activist serving life in prison for murdering two FBI agents during a shootout in 1975, and Amine El Khalifi, an Al Qaeda supporter convicted of plotting to attack the US Capitol building by suicide bombing in 2012.

Bulger was housed in an adjacent complex known as

Coleman II, which, like USP Tucson, was deemed safe for informants and gang members. Alone and isolated, he began to write his friend Chip Janus right away. The night terrors induced by LSD experiments he'd been subjected to in the 1960s were creeping back, making it impossible for him to get a good night's rest. At 12:18 a.m. on December 2, 2014, he picked up a pencil and crafted a letter to the prison art teacher in Tucson:

I prefer Tucson because of the yard time I enjoyed there and because it had the best art department of any place I've been. I have to give credit to the Native American artists. Marilyn Monroe seems to be their favorite American icon. If I was an artist, I'd be doing pictures of American gangster[s] like N.Y Mobster + Bank Robber "Legs Diamond."

Whitey then got more serious about his physical condition and his legal battle, as he appeared confident that he'd one day get back in front of a jury to plead his case:

My health is going down hill—I'm now in a wheel chair and in intense pain—finally got x ray, [and was]told "you have arthritis." Fell down using

walker, knocked out and cut head—took anti-biotics to knock out infection but pain is back . . . headaches . . . Hope to get to hospital sooner or later.

I'll receive new trial, my 2 [second] lawyer fighting for me via appeal—did not receive fair trial and not allowed to bring facts to jury plus witnesses against me who were facing the electric chair and death by lethal injection in O.K and Florida received big deal by Gov. [presumably Flemmi and Martorano before they agreed to testify against Bulger]. All witnesses against me [except for Flemmi] are free + wealthy. Gov. let them keep their assets.

Bulger promised to keep Janus up to date on his case.

At 85 years now, don't have too much more time—especially as every time I turn around something else is wrong with my health. Come what may, I consider I had a good life—a great family—and many adventures along the way.

I remain your friend always,

James Bulger (1428 AZ my lucky number those were the Good Old Days) Keep Smiling!

Now wheelchair bound, Whitey could do nothing but reflect on his life of crime. His mind remained sharp, but his brittle body had robbed him of vitality and strength. While continuing to deny that he was a killer of women and an FBI informant, he never apologized for the path he chose. He was at peace with the idea that he could not outrun impending death, but was saddened with knowing that his version of events would never be fully told.

Bulger had been working on a manuscript about his life when he was captured in Santa Monica. The unfinished book was taken into evidence and its whereabouts are still unknown.

Instead, he continued to share his sordid tales with prisoners he paid to push him around the prison yard and fetch his breakfast and lunch.

"When I first saw Whitey, I didn't realize he was Whitey," former Coleman inmate Nate Lindell recalled. "He looked like a pale, white-haired geezer in a wheelchair. Probably a chomo [child molester], I thought. [I] Couldn't see him robbing a bank, killing people, or any other respectable crime."

According to Lindell, Bulger looked frail but always wore a scowl on his face as a repellent against those who might do him harm. The attack he survived in Tucson was still fresh in his mind, and his increasing head-

aches were most likely the result of the knife wound to his skull.

While his prison bodyguards managed successfully to shield Bulger, there were times that the crippled gangster was left alone.

One day while Whitey was napping in the prison yard, an inmate known for selling used shoes tried to steal his sneakers while they were still on his feet.

"Hey stop that," Nate Lindell shouted. "He ain't dead yet!"

The prisoners all laughed and Bulger went back to sleep.

Whitey was an easy mark at Coleman, and although he wasn't beaten up by the sneaker thief, the incident hurt his pride. Had the prisoner tried that even ten years earlier, he'd surely be dead. But Bulger was defenseless now. Even worse, he was a joke.

Bulger daydreamed about his former life as the most feared gangster in Boston and as a young inmate at Alcatraz, a place where real criminals were treated with respect. He began corresponding with a writer named Michael Esslinger, who was working on a book chronicling the history of the Rock. Whitey was all too eager to chat about his "alma mater." But he also wrote Esslinger about his affection for Catherine.

"He deeply loved her. He wrote about her every time," said Esslinger. "He always communicated to me that he loved his life there [in Santa Monica] with Catherine . . . He looked back at it as the best days of his life."

Whitey also shared his feelings about Catherine in other letters to his friend Chip Janus, where he even stated that he was willing to die for her:

My woman—wife of 40 years met her when she was 23, I was 45—poor girl she has had a rough go of it. She's in prison in Waseca (MN)—she is an instructor for the "Paws Program" training dogs to be service dogs for the Handicapped and Autistic Children—one of the more worthwhile projects in prison—great utilization of prison man hours (womans—woman hours) She has moved up in the program—we write daily so she fills me in on how they train the dogs . . . Took 2 years and 11 months before we could write each other—tried to be considered common law husband + wife— Rejected in a country that recognizes "Same Sex Marriages!" . . . Don't know when ordeal ends for her . . . Will do the best I can to settle down. [I] want to live to see Catherine free when I am ready for the next and final stage.

Catherine had $100,000 for her reward and capture. Catherine + I on the run for 16 years that flew by too fast. We were together night + day and never had an argument or cross word. But years of our lives were taken from us after capture and both put in isolation. Her, no bail and had no police record . . . I offered if they would free her that I'd plead guilty to all charges and will accept execution and no appeal. I will opt for fast track for execution in one year (to save them $$$ + time). She has never hurt anyone—her only crime was loving me. They (prosecutors) refused.

By this time, Hollywood was gearing up for the anticipated release of the feature film *Black Mass*, a project that the real Whitey Bulger wanted nothing to do with. The Warner Bros. movie about the gangster's rise to power was filmed in the Boston area in 2014. Director Scott Cooper chose to shoot in neighborhoods like Dorchester and Cambridge, but never Southie out of respect for victims' families. It wasn't that Whitey was completely against the idea of a movie about his life, he just wanted it told his way: his well-crafted story of a gentleman gangster who became a Robin Hood–type figure for needy families in his beloved South Boston. This image had been shattered at his trial as all of his

dark truths were revealed in court. Bulger had even invited Mark Wahlberg, who'd costarred in *The Departed*, to visit him while he was behind bars in Plymouth in the hope that the Dorchester-bred actor might share his biased vision.

"He wants me to come down and visit him," Wahlberg said during an interview with a Boston radio station at the time. "Maybe he'll give me the exclusive rights to tell his story, 'cause ya know, we do it better than anybody else."

But Wahlberg never pursued it, and another home-grown project led by Ben Affleck and Matt Damon failed to get off the ground. Bulger did allow recorded conversations with his lawyer Jay Carney to be used in a documentary that was heavily slanted in his favor, as it continued to float the balloon that he was never an FBI informant.

After *Black Mass* was released in theaters and then on DVD, Bulger wrote Chip Janus once again to express his feelings about the movie and its star:

> *(Depp) played John Dillinger in "Public Enemies," saw it and enjoyed it—never saw "Black Mass"—have no desire—not at all accurate—wish I had accepted (Depp's) offer to meet, felt I couldn't or I'd look like I endorsed the picture—Hollywood and*

John Morris. Will explain some day—too weary to
begin. A Long Healthy Life and Lots of Happiness.
Your friend—Jim Bulger 1428 AZ

Inside Coleman, far from the glitz and glamour of
Hollywood, Whitey was subjected to humiliation after
humiliation. First, an inmate had tried to steal his
sneakers; next, he was placed in solitary confinement
for allegedly masturbating in his cell. He was caught by
a guard making his rounds at 3 a.m. Sexual activity of
any kind was forbidden at the prison. Bulger claimed
that he was innocent of the lewd offense. He told prison
officials that he was applying medicated powder to his
genitals to soothe an itch he was too embarrassed to
report to the medical staff.

"I never had any charges like that in my whole life,"
Bulger stated in his disciplinary report. "I'm 85 years
old. My sex life is over. I volunteer to take a polygraph
test to prove my answer to this charge." As he wrote to
Janus:

Frustrating to think I'm in a place where anyone
can make an accusation against you and it sticks.
Never had this feeling before in any prison—can't
shake feeling that I'm somebody's target. Kind of a
mystery to me—Why? Revenge?

Prison officials didn't buy Whitey's excuse and placed him in solitary for thirty days, revoked his commissary privileges, and confiscated his personal property from his jail cell.

By early 2018, Bulger's health was getting worse. He was sitting each day in his cell trapped in a cage within a cage, slumped in a wheelchair, experiencing blackouts and dependent on nitroglycerin pills to keep his weak, damaged heart from exploding in his chest. Back in Tucson, Whitey had told his friend Chip Janus that he'd never allow himself to be in such condition and that he'd attack a guard and get himself shot instead of just fading slowly away.

The beginning of the end of Whitey's time in Coleman actually was in late February 2018. He had been living in a special housing unit there since April 19, 2017.

On February 23, 2018, he was living in a first-floor cell in special housing and paid regular visits to the prison's assistant health services administrator, Shanna Mezyk. At 8:45 a.m. that day, he was taken to the medical office complaining of chest pains. Mezyk checked his vital signs and performed a cardiac test. It was clear to her that Whitey was experiencing severe cardiac complications.

"We need to bring you to the prison emergency room," the nurse told him.

But for some unknown reason, Bulger refused to go.

"You're treating me like a dog," he complained. "You'll have your day of reckoning and you will pay for this. I know people and my word is good!"

Mezyk reported the threat to Coleman warden Charles Lockett, who was not only her boss, but also a close friend.

Whitey was charged with a "299"—making an implied threat to an employee. It was a less severe charge than a "203," which is when an inmate makes a direct threat to harm or kill a staffer.

Bulger claimed that Mezyk was lying. He told Coleman officials that he asked the nurse to supply him with a long-sleeved shirt for the visit to the ER and that Mezyk started harassing him over it. He argued that the "day of reckoning" comment meant that she was inducing him to have a massive heart attack because she was yelling at him so much.

"It was all blown out of proportion," Whitey argued. "I didn't threaten her."

Bulger was found guilty of the violation on March 16, 2018, and sentenced to thirty days in "DS"—disciplinary segregation. The punishment was

pretty standard, but what wasn't standard was what happened next.

After the thirty days were up, Lockett kept Bulger in the disciplinary segregation unit for the rest of his stay at Coleman. On April 10, 2018, the warden tried to have Whitey transferred out of Coleman, but the request was denied by the Bureau of Prisons central office in Washington, DC.

At the time, Bulger was classified as a "high-risk" inmate—the highest possible classification—while his medical classification was "Care Level 3," which is the second highest. According to the Bureau of Prisons, Care Level 3 inmates are "fragile outpatients who require frequent clinical contacts, and/or who may require some assistance with activities of daily living . . . (and) may require periodic hospitalization." Bulger, then eighty-eight, had suffered several heart attacks, was in a wheelchair, used a respirator to breathe, and required almost daily visits from medical staff.

Still, on October 8, 2018, a month after his eighty-ninth birthday, Whitey was mysteriously switched to the lower "Medical Care Level 2." The BOP defines this class as "those who are stable outpatients, requiring at least quarterly clinician evaluation. Examples

of such conditions are medication-controlled diabetes, epilepsy, and emphysema."

Warden Lockett claimed that Bulger's health had "dramatically improved" despite his suffering from aortic stenosis, prostate bladder issues, and high blood pressure. After his medical care level was lowered, his transfer to US Penitentiary Hazelton, located 911 miles away in Bruceton Mills, West Virginia, was approved. Joe Rojas, president of the union that represents USP Coleman correctional officers, said there was no valid reason for the transfer since Coleman has all the medical facilities Bulger required.

Furthermore, if Whitey was going to be transferred, he should have gone to the United States Medical Center for Federal Prisoners in Springfield, Missouri, or USP Terre Haute in Indiana—not Hazelton.

In the federal prison system, child predators and rats are generally restricted to three prisons known in the BOP as "The Triangle": USP Coleman, USP Tucson, and USP Terre Haute. Whitey had already been to two of those.

Inmates who have problems at one of the prisons in "The Triangle" are normally moved to one of the other two. For example, convicted child molester Larry Nassar, who systematically molested Olympic and college

gymnasts for decades, was the target of threats and assaults at Tucson, so he was moved to Coleman.

"Those inmates can only go in certain institutions," says Rojas, president of the American Federation of Government Employees Local 506 at Coleman. "Hazelton is one of the most violent prisons in our agency. And at Hazelton, you have a lot of mob guys there."

Regardless, on October 23, 2018, Whitey was moved to the Oklahoma City Federal Transfer Center, where he was held for six days in the special segregation unit. Six days later, on October 29, 2018, he was transferred to Hazelton, a prison so riddled with violence that it earned the name "Misery Mountain."

36

While Whitey was preparing for the transfer to West Virginia, notorious Springfield, Massachusetts, Mafia enforcer Fotios "Freddy" Geas was spending his days at Hazelton, calling shots in the prison yard as one of the most feared gangsters in a penitentiary filled with killers.

Freddy never really operated in Whitey's world of Southie, Charlestown, and Boston's North End because there are clear jurisdictional lines in the organized crime underworld between Boston and Springfield. In the Mafia hierarchy, Springfield falls under the jurisdiction of the Genovese crime family out of New York City, unlike Boston, which answers to the Patriarca mob or what's left of it in Providence, Rhode Island.

It's an odd setup, as Springfield is a much smaller and more rural city, but it has historically had far more Mafia clout than Boston.

With 150,000 residents, Springfield is the fourth largest city in New England behind Boston, Worcester, and Providence. It has a rich history, as it was the birthplace of basketball, the American dictionary, the motorcycle, and the gun. The first American musket and rifle were manufactured in Springfield, and today the city is home to the headquarters of global firearms maker Smith & Wesson.

Like so many troubled cities in the Northeast, economic downturns and the defection of industry overseas hit post–World War II Springfield particularly hard. Massive manufacturing buildings were abandoned, leaving behind blocks and blocks of vacant buildings and urban blight. In the shadows of these crumbling edifices, a ruthless black market run by the Mafia thrived in the 1970s, '80s, and '90s. Bookmaking, prostitution, drug dealing, strong-arming, loan-sharking, political corruption, violence, and murder became big business, all controlled by the New York mob.

Freddy Geas and his younger brother Ty seized upon this opportunity. Despite their Greek heritage, the brothers became feared hit men for the Italian mob. The brothers could never be made men as they

weren't Sicilian, but the Genovese capos needed muscle in Springfield to enforce their rackets and no one was better suited for the job than the feared Geas brothers.

Born in Springfield, Freddy was the oldest of three brothers. He moved to Huntington Beach, California, with his father when he was in seventh grade. A couple of months later, they were joined by Freddy's mother and his two brothers, Ty and Tom. Freddy had long, blond hair as a kid and fit right in with the surfing culture in Huntington Beach. He skateboarded and surfed, wore Vans slip-ons, loved fishing, and raved about the burgers on the boardwalk. Later, the family moved back to Springfield and Freddy's parents split up. Their mother abandoned the family and they never heard from her again.

Freddy's father ran a family diamond importing business, which Freddy helped run. Once back in Springfield and with their mom gone, Freddy and Ty immersed themselves in the seedy underbelly of the Mafia-infested western Massachusetts city. Their brother, Tom, joined the Marines.

"My uncle and aunt had a jewelry store," Freddy told the authors in an October 2019 letter. "We had a few wiseguys that shopped at the store and were also friends with my family so I got into moving football parlay cards and knock off merchandise at school.

"The money was easy," he continued. "The guys were serious and I liked the lifestyle . . . Life was pretty easy. On the one hand you're dealing with lowlifes and [on the other] all the other normal people. [It was] very easy to separate the two."

Freddy and Ty built rap sheets that were impressive from a young age. Ty was sentenced to a year in jail after shooting a weapon into the air during a brawl at a high school hockey game. He was just seventeen. Freddy too picked up a felony conviction for that brawl, for threatening to kill a witness to the mayhem. He was twenty-two years old at the time.

That same year, Freddy picked up another assault conviction for destroying an antique car during a melee at a Springfield nightclub called Sh-Booms. Freddy was charged with beating a cop in 1990, was nabbed in a 1996 truck heist, and went to jail for a pair of brutal baseball bat beatings. Ty got a year in jail in 2006 for bludgeoning a man at Mardi Gras, a sketchy strip club in a run-down section of downtown Springfield that served as the crew's headquarters.

Between the two brothers, they racked up more than seventy-five criminal arraignments and had been in and out of jail most of their adult lives.

Much like Whitey Bulger's stranglehold on Southie, the Geas brothers lorded over the Springfield under-

world of pimps, drug dealers, triggermen, and thieves. You crossed the brothers at your own peril and with the knowledge that they were feared enforcers for the Genovese crime family, serving at the pleasure of Springfield capo Anthony Arillotta and New York mob boss Artie "The Little Guy" Nigro.

Freddy's ranking with the Genovese family was well-known among thugs and cops and his toughness went unchallenged. One night at Mardi Gras, he was holding court with a room filled with members of the Latin Kings gang. It was well past closing time—around 3 a.m.—yet the drinks continued to flow and the nude women continued to dance. A bouncer named Leo discreetly approached Freddy, and whispered to him, "Hey Freddy, man, I hate to break this up, but I have a baseball game with my son at 8 a.m. tomorrow. Think we could wrap it up so I can get home?"

Freddy looked at the bouncer and nodded.

"Not a problem, Leo," he said.

Freddy stood up from his seat, put his hands up, and announced to the group of gangbangers that the party was over.

"Time to go, guys. I gotta get Leo out of here. He's got an early Little League game with his son. Let's go. Out," Freddy said.

And just like that, the gangbangers dispersed. The

room was cleared. That was the kind of respect that Freddy had in Springfield. He had the reputation of being a gentleman's gangster. He was a criminal to the core, but he respected civilians—like Leo—and honored those who were outside of their world trying to provide for their families.

To the outside world, Freddy is a bloodthirsty mob killer and career criminal doing life for two slayings, including the November 23, 2003, execution of Springfield mob boss Alfredo "Big Al" Bruno. Bruno was gunned down outside a Springfield social club on the orders of Nigro, which were carried out by Freddy, Ty, Arillotta, and Springfield mob capo Felix Tranghese. With the New York mob's blessing, the brothers hired the gunman, a low-level mobster named Frankie Roche, to execute Bruno so Arillotta and the Geas brothers could take over the Springfield mob.

In between all the brutality and murders, Freddy fought for a semblance of life balance.

He met his wife, Tracy, on a blind date. They married and had a son, Alex, and daughter, Taylor, but, as his criminal record grew and he was behind bars more and more, the relationship fell apart. They divorced in 2003, when Taylor was ten.

"My parents had the funniest divorce of all di-

vorces," Taylor Geas tells the authors in an exclusive interview. "They drove to the courthouse together, and then went to grab breakfast afterward."

The couple remained friendly and continued to have breakfast together regularly to catch up on the kids, in between Freddy's jail stretches.

"They loved us, and so nothing else really mattered," Taylor says. "We were their common ground. They put their differences aside because they both agreed that Al and I were the best things to ever happen to them."

Taylor and Alex grew up in Connecticut with their mother, who remarried in 2006. Both graduated from college and Taylor credits their dad—despite his dark side—with keeping them on the right path.

"The reason Al and I are the way we are is because although many people don't believe my dad is a good man, there's no denying that he's always been a good father," she said. "And that's why, plain and simple, my brother and I turned out the way we did."

She has fond memories of him taking them to the North End in Boston as kids to get pastries and to her first Red Sox game, where he transformed Taylor— then a Connecticut-raised Yankees fan—into a Red Sox fan. He even got her to partake in an obligatory

"Yankees Suck" Fenway Park chant. They sat near Boston's famed "Pesky Pole," named for Red Sox Hall-of-Famer Johnny Pesky, and caught a foul ball.

"It was always about the little things with my dad. It never took much to make him happy," she recalls. "We had our routines together, but even the ordinary and everyday things were better with him."

Taylor didn't know about her father's mob connections, though. To her, he was just a doting dad who was at every one of her softball games and loved taking them out for impromptu junk-food sprees at Burger King. While he was in and out of jail for most of her life, she was always told as a kid that he wasn't around because he was in the army. There were, though, occasional hints of her dad's violent streak.

At one of her softball games when she was in her early teens, there was a loudmouthed third-base coach for the opposing team. Taylor was pitching and the coach kept taunting her. Freddy was in the stands and had had enough. Stocky and in tip-top physical condition, Freddy stormed across the field to the third-base box and stood right behind the coach. The coach had no idea who Freddy was but knew he was in a pickle.

Freddy leaned toward him and said, loudly, "I'm gonna put you in a fucking coma if you don't shut the fuck up."

The game stopped. The opposing team had no idea what was going on. The stands were silent. The coach stood still, having no clue how close he had come to hospitalization or worse. Freddy walked back to the stands, sat down, and play resumed. No one said a word.

In 2008, the Geas brothers along with Arillotta were charged with extortion for shaking down mobbed-up nightclub owners' lucrative illegal poker machines. The case was an appetizer to squeeze witnesses as prosecutors built a murder indictment for the hit on Big Al Bruno.

In 2009, the Bruno murder and a laundry list of other violent crimes were bundled into a sweeping federal RICO racketeering indictment by the US attorney in the Southern District of New York. In all, nine Springfield mobsters and members of the Genovese family, including Freddy and Ty, were charged in a spectacular case that blew open Mafia secrets.

In addition to Bruno's killing, the brothers were charged with executing Arillotta's drug pusher brother-in-law, Gary D. Westerman, because they believed he was talking to the feds. It was Freddy who pumped two bullets into Westerman's head in November 2003 and the gang buried him in an eight-foot grave in the woods. Arillotta, who flipped on the Geas brothers

during the 2011 federal trial in New York, testified that Freddy dug the grave weeks earlier in preparation for the inevitable burial of an unspecified rival, but no one knew who it was going to be until Westerman's corpse was tossed in.

The night after the killing, Freddy, Ty, and Arillotta went to Morton's Steakhouse in Hartford to celebrate. After dinner, they drove back by the burial site and Freddy laughed, joked, and sang mockingly about the murder.

"Freddy started singing 'On top of Old Smokey . . . all covered in blood,'" Arillotta testified.

Westerman's remains were not recovered for seven years until Arillotta led law enforcement to the rural burial site.

Taylor Geas recalls learning about the federal RICO indictment and her father's arrest in Florida the night she was set to emcee her high school senior variety show. She was now wise to the fact that her father wasn't in the army, but instead was a soldier for the mob.

"I thought it was going to be totally fine," she said. "He'd been in and out all the time when I was a kid."

But it wasn't fine. Freddy, Ty, and Nigro were convicted in 2011 on the RICO case, including both murders and the attempted murder of a mobbed-up union boss, largely based on the testimony of Arillotta.

All three were sentenced to life without parole. Arillotta cut a deal and served just eight years, while Tranghese, who also flipped on the Geas brothers, served just four. Roche, the gunman who executed Bruno, also testified against the brothers, and Nigro and was sentenced to fourteen years.

Prosecutors said Arillotta wrestled with flipping on the brothers and tried to tell them to turn informant to spare themselves from life in prison.

"Arillotta appeared to take no pleasure from cooperating against people he claimed as some of his closest friends," prosecutors wrote in court filings. "Arillotta thereafter repeatedly expressed disappointment at the fact that his former friends—the Geases in particular—were not pleading guilty because he did not want to see them spend the rest of their lives in jail."

The Geas brothers' New York attorney, Frederick Cohn, recalled some "tense" fighting between Freddy and Ty during the trial.

"Freddy was very pleasant to me. His brother was very difficult," Cohn said. "And he was difficult for Freddy to control. I think Freddy tried to keep him under control in Springfield but was not totally successful.

"Freddy never expected much from the trial. We knew it was severely uphill," Cohn, who retired shortly

after the case, continued. "Really, once [prosecutors] decided they weren't going to go for the death penalty for him, it was pretty much written in the sky that he was going to go away forever. I can't say he was alright with it, but it was part of the game. That whole old school mafia thing . . . These guys expected to die in the street or in jail."

Freddy shook Cohn's hand at the end of the trial that sealed his fate. He still occasionally sends Cohn Christmas cards.

"He was always respectful," Cohn said. "I don't recall that we ever had a disagreement. I had generally a good feeling about him. I wouldn't want to stand between him and a big profit, though, if he had a weapon."

Just like Kevin Weeks, Pat Nee, and John Martorano, Arillotta is a free man after being released from prison in 2017. He was offered the Witness Protection Program but declined and moved back to Springfield, where he hasn't exactly kept a low profile. In July 2019, while still on federal probation, Arillotta was charged with making threats and assault and battery with a dangerous weapon for allegedly throwing a carton of lemonade at a female relative, striking her in the leg, during a dispute over a dog.

For Taylor Geas, the conviction was devastating. She

was just twenty-three years old and her dad was going away forever. A few days after her dad's conviction was splashed across the front page of the Springfield newspaper, she wrote an emotional piece portraying a different side of him.

"When I'm sitting across the table from him during our visits I don't see a monster, I see a flawed man that's paying for the choices he made," she wrote. "The person I know is the father that would tuck me in at night, and tell me funny stories until I fell asleep. He was the person that taught me how to throw a baseball, and got me my first pair of soccer cleats."

Taylor believes her father refused to flip on his codefendants to protect her and her brother Alex from possible retribution from mobsters.

"When the government offered him the option to become an informant, he didn't because of us," she says. "The hardest thing he's ever had to do was make the decision to not be in our lives anymore. And people think he did this because he's a thug who swears by the code, but his loyalty lies with us before anybody else. And so he made the decision to spend the rest of his life in federal prison so that Al and I could lead normal lives. Because of him, we don't have to live looking over our shoulders."

The brothers headed off to the catacombs inside the

federal prison system. But Freddy Geas's greatest mob
hit was still to come.

Freddy and Ty Geas were originally sent to a federal
prison together in Kentucky, but their shared incarcer-
ation didn't last long. In 2012, they were split up after
they brutally attacked and bludgeoned a child molester.
Taylor recalls that she didn't hear from her dad for six
months after the incident because he was in solitary.
While Ty stayed in Kentucky, Freddy was moved to
Hazelton.

Because of his Mafia status and brutal reputation,
Freddy became a shot-caller at Hazelton, meaning he
was a top gang leader in a unit filled with killers and
gangsters. While the Springfield and Boston mobsters
worked separately on the outside, inside the walls of
Hazelton, mobsters from both territories stuck together.
And there were plenty of Massachusetts gangsters on
Freddy's unit for him to join forces with, including several who had been betrayed by Bulger.

One was New England Mafia boss "Cadillac Frank"
Salemme, who was sent to Hazelton briefly following
his 2018 conviction in the unsolved 1993 murder of Steven DiSarro, owner of The Channel rock club in South
Boston.

Salemme and his son, Francis P. Salemme Jr., were

silent partners in the club and DiSarro was killed because Salemme believed he was talking to the FBI. Flemmi had also testified at Salemme's 2018 trial that he walked into Salemme's home in Sharon, Massachusetts, and saw the younger Salemme and another Boston mobster, Paul Weadick, strangling DiSarro. DiSarro's body was buried behind a Providence mill, where it was unearthed in 2016 thanks to an FBI tip.

Weadick was also convicted of the slaying and served time in Hazelton with Freddy. The younger Salemme died in 1995. Weadick has said he and Freddy were friends at Hazelton.

Another mobster Freddy befriended was Frederick Weichel, a South Boston man who was framed by Bulger for the murder of Robert LaMonica, who was gunned down in a parking lot outside his apartment in Braintree, Massachusetts, in 1980. Weichel believed that Whitey had set him up for a fall by giving his name to authorities.

Freddy Geas and Weichel became close in prison in Massachusetts and the Springfield mobster couldn't stomach the idea that his friend had spent thirty-six years locked up for a crime he didn't commit.

"We were at (Massachusetts Correctional Institution) Shirley together, talked every day," Freddy told

the authors of this book in a January 26, 2020, letter from USP Hazelton. "Nice guy."

Freddy said Weichel would have him "grab friends" in the Massachusetts prison to stand watch while Weichel worked out in the prison yard in the "sub-arctic" weather.

He said he has lost touch with Weichel but was glad to hear he was exonerated.

"The last time I was with him he was in court so I hope he has made it home," Freddy wrote.

Freddy's longtime attorney and friend, Daniel Kelly, said Freddy spoke to him of the injustice of Weichel's conviction.

"He referenced that [Weichel] was framed," Kelly said. "Freddy was a stand-up guy, the last of the Mohicans."

A friend of Weichel's even wrote Whitey a letter in prison, begging him to do the right thing and provide an affidavit or sworn testimony that Weichel was innocent. Bulger flat-out refused and denied that he was the one who fingered Weichel for the 1980 murder:

I have never testified against any man, have never caused any man to be put in prison. I too have been falsely accused.

Whitey did reveal that he knew the identity of the real killer but wouldn't give up any other information:

I won't name him—or force him, just as I choose not to tell the truth in my own trial about certain incidents even though the guilty lied—Strange perhaps but that's what I felt the thing to do— Keep Silent in a Corrupt Trial. No Regets, JB (James Bulger).

Despite a lack of cooperation from Whitey, a judge later overturned Frederick Weichel's conviction and granted his freedom in April 2017.

Despite his friend's freedom, Freddy Geas wanted Bulger to pay for his betrayal, but he never thought he'd get the opportunity to exact his own brand of justice on the notorious gangster turned FBI informant.

Instead, Geas had to manage the tribal politics inside "Misery Mountain," where inmates are classified by race and gang affiliation. Top-echelon gangsters like Freddy helped to organize crime within the prison walls and negotiate disputes between bloodthirsty gangs such as MS-13, the Bloods, the Crips, and the Latin Kings.

The daily routine and dangers of Hazelton wore

heavily on Freddy, but somehow he always remained upbeat when talking with his daughter, Taylor. He called and wrote his kids often and they visited him a few times a year.

The regular contact would soon be disrupted as Freddy Geas, the relatively unknown enforcer from western Massachusetts, would soon become a key figure in the history of organized crime in America.

37

When Whitey Bulger was transferred to Hazelton, he was wheeled into a powder keg of bureaucratic dysfunction and violence.

The notorious penitentiary already had two murders in 2018 and was in the midst of a staffing crisis that pitted the correctional officers' union in a nasty battle against Warden Joseph Coakley. The prison's problems were national news as the dispute made its way all the way to the White House.

Opened in 2004 in Bruceton Mills, West Virginia, a tiny rural town of just eighty-five residents in the northeast corner of the state, Hazelton came with a $129 million price tag and is the second largest federal prison in the country. With 1,300 hardened criminals

prowling its six buildings and sprawling yards, it's got a long history of violence that led to its nickname, "Misery Mountain."

Within the federal prison system, Hazelton is well-known as a place not safe for two types of inmates: pedophiles and informants. Violent attacks are a daily occurrence, and murders don't raise many eyebrows.

In October 2007, an inmate named Jesse Harris was stabbed to death by two inmates serving life sentences. In December 2009, Jimmy Lee Wilson, a twenty-five-year-old serving eleven years for armed robbery, was killed during a race-fueled brawl involving at least five other inmates. In 2017, the year before Whitey arrived, there were 275 reported violent incidents, which was up 15 percent from the previous year.

Besides the hiring freeze, the Trump administration ordered the federal Bureau of Prisons to eliminate six thousand unfilled positions. The cuts slashed more than 1,800 correctional officers' positions nationwide, including 127 at Hazelton.

The result at Hazelton was that Warden Coakley started shifting regular prison employees from their normal duties to work behind the walls in units. The practice, known as "augmentation," only added more stress to an already stressful and dangerous environ-

ment. The situation was at a breaking point in early 2018 as the officers' union took their complaints to Washington.

"With less corrections officers in the prisons, BOP has turned to augmentation . . . which means that cooks, foremen, secretaries, electricians, teachers, accountants, or counselors are augmented to replace officers inside the prison," David Cox, president of the American Federation of Government Employees, which represents federal correctional officers, said in February 2018. "Augmentation can result in one correctional worker supervising hundreds of dangerous prisoners, including terrorists, gangs, and murderers inside each facility with no backup."

As the staffing and overtime crisis took root, Coakley began putting only one officer on duty in units, in defiance of congressional mandates, angering the officers' union. Besides endangering the officers, single-staffed units meant fewer inmate shakedowns and searches and more opportunity for prisoners to hide weapons and cause chaos.

There was incentive for Warden Coakley to keep overtime costs down: he and other federal wardens and BOP administrators were raking in hefty bonuses for controlling costs. The Bureau of Prisons shelled out

$1.6 million in bonuses to executives and wardens in 2017 and 2018, and Coakley himself raked in more than $50,000 in bonuses from 2015 through 2018.

On February 25, 2018, Representative David McKinley, a West Virginia Republican whose district includes Hazelton, led a bipartisan effort that sought to force the Trump administration to hire more correctional officers. McKinley and fifty other members of Congress fired off a letter to Trump's then–attorney general Jeff Sessions to reinstate the six thousand positions that were on the chopping block.

"We must address the staffing crisis our corrections officers face before the safety in our prisons deteriorates further. Inadequate staffing creates dangerous conditions for our officers and our communities," McKinley wrote. "Our prison guards have never failed us when we've called them to duty. They risk their lives every day they enter these dangerous prisons to protect our communities from hardened criminals."

Regardless, the troubled prison's officer ranks were severely depleted as the hiring freeze wasn't lifted. Down more than ninety officers, COs at Hazelton were being forced to work overtime shifts, sometimes as many as three in a row. It wasn't uncommon for correctional officers to work double shifts with no sleep.

The troubles would only worsen. The prison was

locked down nine times in 2018 for violence and weapons incidents. Five officers were attacked. Already overburdened officers were reaching their breaking point when a pair of inmate killings escalated tensions. On April 2, 2018, Ian Thorne, a forty-eight-year-old Washington, DC, heroin dealer serving twenty years for orchestrating a prison murder, was killed by two shank-wielding inmates. A few months later, on September 17, 2018, Demario Porter, a twenty-seven-year-old who was serving a two-year sentence for probation violations, was killed by another inmate. Porter, who was charged at age sixteen in the 2007 slaying of an elderly barber in Washington, DC, had been at Hazelton for only two weeks.

In a letter to Congress sent on October 10, 2018—just two weeks before Whitey was sent to Misery Mountain—the Hazelton correctional officers' union pleaded for more resources and expressed fears that cuts were going to lead to bloodshed. Justin Tarovisky, a former college football player who headed the Hazelton correctional officers' union, warned Congress that Coakley's cost-cutting moves posed "significant danger," especially the decision to single-staff units. The move, the union argued, directly violated Congress's 2016 funding bill, which stated: "All BOP high security institutions would have at least two correc-

tional officers on duty in each housing unit for all three shifts."

"The staff at FCC Hazelton can no longer afford to stand by and let this particular administration place them in perilous situations," Tarovisky wrote. "The administration at FCC Hazelton has cultivated an atmosphere amongst all supervisors that places miniscule [sic] savings (what they believe to be cost-saving measures) over the safety and well-being of all staff working at this complex."

Just five days before Whitey arrived, five lawmakers responded swiftly to the union's call. US Senators Pat Toomey and Robert P. Casey Jr. of Pennsylvania and Joe Manchin III and Shelley Moore Capito of West Virginia, along with US Representative Bill Shuster, a Republican from Pennsylvania, wrote a letter to Sessions urging him to address "dangerous staffing issues" at federal prisons in both states.

The letter referenced the Thorne and Porter murders, as well as the brutal 2013 murder of Correctional Officer Eric Williams at USP Canaan in Pennsylvania. Williams, thirty-four, was just two hours away from the end of his shift and was working a unit at Canaan alone when he was ruthlessly set upon by a Mexican Mafia member named Jessie Con-ui. Williams was savagely shoved down a set of stairs by Con-ui, who pulled out

two homemade shanks and stabbed the officer more than two hundred times. Dozens of inmates did nothing as they watched the sickening eleven-minute attack, which was caught on video.

Congress boosted the BOP's $7 billion federal prison budget by $106 million in 2018 to address "dangerous continual understaffing," but the agency was still not increasing full-time hires, the lawmakers said.

"We are writing to express our deep concerns about the Bureau of Prisons' (BOP) staffing practices . . . and the failure to follow clear congressional directives to hire more full-time correctional officers," the October 25, 2018, letter states.

In September 2018, Taylor Geas, her mother, and brother traveled to Hazelton to visit Freddy. He normally didn't talk much about his case or his appeals, but on this visit, he was upbeat and chatty about the potential of his appeal because another inmate he knew had just beat a case for which he was serving 140 years.

They talked about Taylor's new job, and Freddy talked about the model airplane-building class he was teaching at Hazelton.

"He looked really good, looked like he was in good shape," Taylor remembers. "He had looked old and tired and stressed in the past. Every time we go, we

talk like he's coming home, for his own sanity. He was telling us not to lose hope."

In June 2018, just a few months before Bulger was transferred to Hazelton from Coleman, he told author Michael Esslinger that he missed being at the Tucson prison and preferred it to Coleman.

"He seemed to be at odds with the conditions there [at Coleman]," Esslinger recalled.

It was one of the last known missives from Whitey, and the frail ex–crime lord said he hoped that he'd one day be reunited with Catherine.

"He talked about Catherine and his hopes that when she got out, that he'd be able to see her again, that she could come visit him," Esslinger said. "He said she was the love of his life for sure."

Whitey wouldn't get his wish, as his fate would soon be sealed at Misery Mountain.

38

When Whitey Bulger entered Hazelton, he was a far cry from the muscled and menacing gangster who controlled Southie for decades. He wasn't even the fit-for-his-age old man who groused and was combative during his trial. He was now an invalid, and the Bureau of Prisons higher-ups, including Warden Coakley, threw him to the lions.

At 9:17 a.m. on October 29, 2018, Bulger was transported from the Oklahoma City federal prison transfer center. Even though he was there for only a short period of time, he was kept in a segregated unit during his stay.

At 6:45 p.m., he arrived at Hazelton. He was wheeled off a prison bus and brought into "intake," where his case file was reviewed and he was assigned a

cell in general population, despite the fact that the unit was filled with Italian Mafia members and associates, including several from Massachusetts.

"They sent him to the worst open yard," said Joe Rojas, head of the USP Coleman correctional officers' union. "This is an open yard with a lot of mobsters walking around, from Boston, Philly, and New York. Of course, Whitey Bulger walks in, they must have been drooling."

After dusk, at 8:35 p.m., Whitey was assigned to unit 229L—on the second tier of the unit—in a cell with Paul J. "Little Paulie" DeCologero, a Boston mobster serving twenty-five years for racketeering and conspiring to kill a nineteen-year-old woman named Aislin Silva. The DeCologero crew made its money selling drugs and kidnapping and robbing dealers, among other rackets. They were based in Burlington, Massachusetts, a toney suburb north of Boston, and the crew was run by DeCologero's uncle, Paul A. "Big Paulie" DeCologero, who ran drugs briefly for Whitey and Flemmi in the 1980s.

The gang answered to Providence's Patriarca mob and was involved in a beef in the 1990s between Whitey's rival, "Cadillac Frank" Salemme, and another Italian crew trying to muscle in on Salemme's Boston rackets. The elder DeCologero stopped running drugs

for the Winter Hill Gang after he got out of prison in 1992, which "irked the mob leaders." The dispute led Whitey to put out a contract on "Big Paulie."

"Little Paulie" was among several members of the crew rounded up in 2001 in a racketeering case that included the infamous—and gruesome—Silva killing. It was "Big Paulie" who made the call to kill the attractive blonde in November 1996 because they feared she'd rat out the gang after a cache of guns was found in the apartment she shared with one of the mobsters. First, they planned to give her a fatal "hotshot" of heroin by telling her it was "good cocaine." When that failed, she was taken to an apartment by three gang members who broke her neck, chopped her up with hacksaws, and dumped her remains behind an elementary school. Her remains weren't found for ten years.

"Little Paulie" had a cell at Hazelton just a few doors down from Freddy Geas, who was in number 219L. But because Bulger was in a wheelchair, he couldn't be housed on the second tier, so "Little Paulie" and Freddy wouldn't have their chance to meet the notorious crime lord that night. At 9:53 p.m., Whitey was sent to cell 132L on the first level of the 120-man unit.

Normally, inmates are segregated by race, but Bulger, an avowed racist, was assigned to bunk with a black inmate named Felix Wilson. A mentally ill,

thirty-five-year-old Buffalo man, Wilson was serving a thirty-month sentence for a gun rap. He had a history of violence and was stabbed in the neck in Buffalo in May 2011. That same month, he was convicted of attempted robbery, which prohibited him from carrying a firearm. On August 22, 2013, he was riding his bike on a Buffalo street when he was stopped by police and arrested for being a felon illegally carrying a .22-caliber handgun.

As Whitey was wheeled into the unit, the tiers were abuzz with news of the latest celebrity inmate. Word spread fast among the criminals and convicted killers.

"The minute they saw Bulger, I'm sure they couldn't believe it. He's known as a snitch," Rojas said.

"Hazelton is a yard where they don't accept that," added Justin Tarovisky, head of the Hazelton correctional officers' union. "There's a code. If they think you're a child predator or you've cooperated with law enforcement, they'll put a hit on you.

"They're gonna get you. That's the code of the yard. It's a city of criminals. It's hard to prevent that," he said.

Whitey entered the cell and would never leave again. He and Wilson went to sleep for the night. The cell doors opened automatically at 5 a.m. for the start of the prison day, as they do every day. Shortly thereafter,

Wilson left the cell. Sometime around 6 a.m., Freddy Geas and "Little Paulie" were seen on video going into Bulger's cell.

At some point before Wilson returned to his cell, Whitey was beaten to death with padlocks stuffed into tube socks. The "lock in a sock" was a common Hazelton killing tool.

The killers swung their makeshift weapons against Bulger's head as he lay in his bunk.

Whitey Bulger must have sensed trouble. He must have shown fear. As he gazed up at his attackers, the look in his pale blue eyes must have been similar to the startled gazes of his many victims when they realized they were staring into the face of the reaper.

The killers continued their attack as they beat Bulger without mercy across his body and head. Whitey's face was bashed in and his eyes were swollen shut. The weighted socks were smeared with his blood.

The tough-guy gangster who executed at will, strangled women, ordered hits like he was ordering lunch, strong-armed bookies, and pumped his beloved South Boston full of drugs that ended lives and destroyed families died helplessly and without putting up any fight. He wanted it quick—and he got it quick.

Bulger's killers slipped out of his cell as quietly as they had come.

There were reports that the killers tried to gouge out his eyes and cut out his tongue—a ruthless tactic used to send a message to rats. But according to a prison source who viewed the corpse, Whitey's body was not mutilated in any way, though Bulger's eyes were so swollen shut that it looked as if he had no eyes at all.

Felix Wilson returned to his cell after the murder and found Whitey covered with a blanket in his bed. He cleaned up the cell and threw several items into the garbage, which was put out with the morning trash. The trash from the cell was taken away and thrown into the prison's incinerator, destroying any potential physical evidence of the killing.

Wilson didn't alert the guards to his cellmate's violent demise and Whitey lay dead in his prison bed until around 8:21 a.m., when an officer walking around the unit called in to the cell and got no response. He went in and discovered the mobster's brutally beaten and lifeless body in the bed. Medical staff was called to the cell and Whitey Bulger was pronounced dead at 9:04 a.m.

He was wheeled out and taken to a triage unit while the coroner was called. The prison's internal special investigations unit was called in. The former public enemy number one, who made global headlines when his sixteen-year flight from justice ended at Princess Eugenia Apartments in Santa Monica seven years ear-

lier, lay deceased on a slab, clad only in his prison-issued boxers.

He had welts from the beating on his chest and his face was unrecognizable. There was a little blood trickling from his left eye, but no other blood. The medical staff tried to open his eyes to check his pupils but were unable due to the swelling.

A year before the murder, Whitey had written a letter to his old Alcatraz pal Charlie Hopkins and said he was tired of hospitals. He said he hoped he would die peacefully at Coleman.

"I prefer to stay here and hope to get a peaceful death," he wrote. "One of those he Died in his Sleep kind."

His death certificate listed his cause of death as "blunt force injuries of the head" as a result of "assault by other(s)."

News of Bulger's murder broke quickly, and the media began scrambling to report the details of how Boston's most infamous crime figure was killed. It didn't take long before Freddy Geas and "Little Paulie" DeCologero were named as suspects.

Both were dyed-in-the-wool mobsters convicted of crimes connected to La Cosa Nostra. Both lived by the gangster's code. Freddy Geas hated rats more than anything. This was personal for him. He knew

436 • CASEY SHERMAN AND DAVE WEDGE

that Whitey was the cold-blooded liar who put an innocent man—Fred Weichel—in prison for most of his life. Both Geas and DeCologero hailed from the brutal criminal underworld of Massachusetts and were lifers at Hazelton. What both understood more than anything else was that if they killed Whitey Bulger, they would be heroes to the Mafia and gangster legends inside and outside prison walls. When their names were mentioned anywhere, they would be known as the ones who killed Whitey Bulger.

In the end, it wasn't the FBI or Flemmi or Weeks or Martorano or Pat Nee or anyone else who was responsible for Whitey's death. He was responsible for his death. It was gangster karma, payback for a lifetime of deception and lying that cost countless people their lives. There has perhaps never been a starker example in the annals of American criminal history of the mantra "live by the sword, die by the sword."

Whitey Bulger got what was coming to him, and Geas and DeCologero were moved into disciplinary segregation at Hazelton immediately after the killing. So was Felix Wilson. The prison went into lockdown for the tenth time in 2018. Also moved into solitary with them was Geas's cellmate, Sean McKinnon, a thirty-two-year-old thief and drug dealer from Montpelier, Vermont. McKinnon was doing eight years for

stealing a cache of weapons from a gun store in Barre, Vermont, in March 2016. He traded five handguns for bags of heroin in Hartford, Connecticut, and was nabbed with forty-five bags of dope, pry bars, a shotgun, and ammo.

As Whitey Bulger's battered corpse was shuttled off to the coroner's office, the Bureau of Prisons began investigating the killing along with the FBI, the US Attorney's Office in West Virginia, and the BOP's Office of the Inspector General.

"Regarding the recent incidence of violence at FCC Hazelton, the BOP has sent a team of subject-matter experts to the complex to assess operational activities and correctional security practices and measures to determine any relevant facts that may have contributed to the incident," Bureau of Prisons officials said in a statement. "The team will make recommendations to the BOP's senior leadership to assist in mitigating any identified risks."

The questions over the circumstances surrounding Whitey's transfer to Hazelton were only just beginning. Bulger's attorneys, Jay Carney and Hank Brennan, would be leading the charge to find out what happened.

"[Bulger] was sentenced to prison," Carney said, "but as a result of decisions by the Federal Bureau of

Prisons, that sentence has been changed to the death penalty."

Even Freddy Geas's attorney, Fred Cohn, questioned the decision to put Whitey in the mob-infested prison with his former client and echoed Carney's sentiments.

"I would wonder about the decision to put Whitey Bulger particularly there, and in general population, which I think was tantamount to a death sentence," Cohn said.

The violence of Whitey's death was the latest illustration of jailhouse justice for a high-profile inmate. It echoed the violent demises of Jeffrey Dahmer, who was beaten to death with a mop wringer by a fellow inmate in a Wisconsin prison in 1994, and the 2003 murder of pedophile Boston priest Father John Geoghan, who was stomped to death in his cell at a Massachusetts maximum security prison by Joseph Druce. The Geoghan murder, like Bulger's, raised questions about jailhouse security as well as accusations of incompetence and corruption by prison officials.

But for the families of Whitey's victims, the killing was the ultimate justice.

"I was happy as hell when that happened," said Tommy Donahue, who was raised without a father after Bulger killed his dad, Michael, in 1982. "I chugged a beer."

For members of law enforcement who had chased Bulger for sixteen years, feelings were mixed.

"I was shocked when he was killed," Neil Sullivan said. "I thought he was going to Springfield, Missouri, the biggest federal medical facility in the country. A lot of old-time mob guys went there to die of old age. But Bulger wasn't allowed to go quietly."

Rich Teahan didn't like the smell of it either. "I'd put a lot of people in WITSEC [Witness Protection]. When you have a high threat prisoner, you have to do a threat assessment on the facility to ensure it is safe. Somebody fucked up. I don't wish that on anyone—not even Whitey Bulger."

Charlie Gianturco strongly disagreed with his fellow FBI agents' assessment. He relished Bulger's bloody end.

"You live by the sword, you die by the sword," he told the authors of this book before quickly correcting himself. "No, scratch that. It makes Whitey sound valiant, like a fucking knight. He was a slug. He was a killer of women. There's nothing valiant or romantic about that. He got the death he deserved, brutal and painful."

39

Fallout from Whitey's killing at Hazelton happened immediately, with ripple effects in Washington, DC, and Boston. The startling news had a karmic element, and raised simmering questions about whether Bulger was set up to be murdered, which ratcheted up the media frenzy to levels not seen since his 2011 capture made global headlines.

Zach Hafer got a call the morning of Bulger's slaying from a Bureau of Prisons official in West Virginia.

"I just want to let you know Bulger is dead," the official said.

"Thank you for letting me know," Hafer responded. The young prosecutor figured that Whitey had finally succumbed to one of the litany of health issues plaguing the elderly gangster.

"Sir, he was murdered," the voice added.

Hafer was stunned.

"It was shocking. I cannot believe that happened," Hafer reflected. "I cannot believe someone got access to him. But it's also amazing that it didn't happen to him sooner, with the number of dangerous people he crossed over the years."

Margaret McCusker said she spoke to her twin sister, Catherine Greig, by phone from prison shortly after news of the murder broke.

"She was very upset, understandably. It was a very difficult conversation," McCusker said. "I couldn't console her really . . . I felt really bad. I felt bad for my sister and for him. He was a good guy . . . I've read about [his crimes] but he wasn't like that with us."

The sensational jailhouse killing thrust Hazelton into the national spotlight and the crime was immediately used by the officers' union as proof that the BOP's policies were failing.

"Am I surprised there's been another murder? No," Hazelton correctional officers' union president Richard Heldreth said the day after the killing. "It wouldn't surprise me if there was another one tomorrow. We are severely understaffed."

As the investigation unfolded, Freddy Geas and

"Little Paulie" DeCologero remained in solitary confinement for months without being charged. While Geas has admitted he attacked Bulger, he claims he acted alone; officials have not commented on whether DeCologero admits or denies his alleged role in the murder. Whitey's cellmate Felix Wilson was released from prison on April 5, 2019, while Sean McKinnon, whose alleged role is unclear, remained at Hazelton.

In June 2019, Freddy Geas wrote the authors a letter from solitary at Hazelton, which was scrawled with a rubber pencil:

> *I'm in solitary as of now as the BOP . . . likes to play games with guys in my situation. [They] have us sit back here for years while they decide if they are going to charge us or handle it in the prison.*

In July 2019, Geas wrote another letter to the authors, saying, "I'm in the process of being transferred along with Paulie [DeCologero]." That transfer hasn't happened as of the publication of this book.

Geas expressed sympathy in the letter toward Francis "Cadillac Frank" Salemme, who was convicted in 2018 of the 1993 murder of Boston nightclub owner Steven DiSarro, based largely on testimony from Stephen Flemmi.

"Shame about Salemme," Geas wrote. "All the stuff the guy went through and then to go bad at the end."

Salemme was put in jail for eight years in 1995 for racketeering, thanks primarily to information provided to the FBI by Bulger and Flemmi. The North End mob boss was released early from prison in 2003 in exchange for testifying against John Connolly in the disgraced federal agent's 2002 racketeering trial. During that trial, and a subsequent congressional hearing, Salemme said Connolly gave him, Flemmi, and Bulger a heads-up that they were about to be arrested on the 1995 RICO case, allowing him and Bulger to go on the run.

While Freddy never met Salemme, the fact that he expressed sympathy toward Salemme's ultimate fate is a clear statement on just which side Freddy was on in the war between Whitey and the mob.

For Taylor Geas, news that her father was a suspect in the gangster's prison murder was another devastating blow. She didn't speak to her father for months after the killing as he sat in solitary. In January 2018, he wrote her a letter asking her to set up a GoFundMe page for him. Taylor was angry, as her dad had never asked her for money. He didn't need money for an appeal because there wasn't even a case, so Taylor couldn't figure out why he wanted a crowdsourcing page.

She wrote back to him and told him she was furious with the request and wouldn't do it. When he wrote back to her, he still didn't tell her why he wanted the page put up, but said only: *Just start the page kid.*

Taylor didn't do it, but believes he wanted it because he was afraid he would be sent into the catacombs of another facility—likely the federal "Supermax" penitentiary in Florence, Colorado—and disappear forever.

"He doesn't want to be forgotten," she said.

Geas's restrictions on both phone calls and visitors were lifted in summer 2019 but he still remained in solitary, virtually isolated from the outside world. He could make one phone call per month and get one visitor. During a September 2019 call to Taylor, he again said he thought he was getting transferred.

"He was looking forward to [leaving Hazelton]," she said. "He sounded OK, but he definitely sounded beaten down."

Taylor walks a fine line between love for her father and embracing the man she knows, while also staring the cold reality of his criminal career in the face.

"He's not a monster," she contends. "I'd like to believe that there was a much bigger thing going on . . . that there was a lot going on behind the scenes. Like, my dad was given a job and he had to do it."

She added, "If he did do this, then I really don't know anybody. Because I've never seen him like that."

Bulger's killing further exposed problems at Hazelton and the federal prison system and forced change. In the months after the murder, a wave of new officers was hired at Hazelton. The irony was not lost on prison officials.

"There's a saying among the guards now: Whitey Bulger is still helping out law enforcement from the grave," Justin Tarovisky, senior officer specialist at Hazelton, told the authors. "It took Whitey Bulger getting killed to bring light to the BOP and everything they were doing to us. It's really ironic that he was the straw that broke the camel's back here. It was a perfect storm of events that had to happen."

The union, as well as lawmakers and Bulger's family, have questioned the decisions that led to his demise. Tarovisky says Bulger should have been sent to "SHU"—a special housing unit—and that Warden Coakley should have made that call.

"We've had high-profile inmates here before and we've had more competent wardens who've sent them to SHU," he said. "This warden was not an officer. He obviously didn't understand the gravity of the situation. You're getting paid $180,000 to make these decisions. If you don't, look what happens."

In December 2019, Coleman's warden, Charles Lockett, retired in Florida. Three months later, in March 2019, Warden Coakley retired from Misery Mountain.

"It has been my great honor to serve as your warden," Coakley wrote in a letter to staffers. "I have had a full and rewarding career and I cannot think of a better duty station for which to close it out. I want to thank each and every one of you for the hard work and dedication you display every day! Stay safe!"

In April 2019, Charles Lockett went on national television and defended the decisions to move Bulger, claiming he believed the gangster "wanted to die."

"It's a tragedy, but I don't think anyone was deficient in their duty," he said.

Fred Wyshak, the man who chased Whitey for years and led his prosecution in Boston, was also among those looking for some answers.

"Whatever possessed the BOP to transfer him to a facility and put him in general population where there were Boston mobsters also in general population, is just astounding," he said. "The fact that this occurred within 24 hours of his arrival there is also something that is just mind-boggling."

Whitey's family had its own questions and once again demanded money. Members of the Bulger family, represented by Hank Brennan, the lawyer who cochaired

Whitey's defense, filed a $200 million wrongful death lawsuit against the federal government for his prison murder. The announcement was made just days after the death of Whitey's sister Jean Holland, who had unsuccessfully fought for his lottery winnings decades before.

"You almost have to go back to the people who made that fateful decision to place him in this place where he was killed," his brother Billy Bulger told the authors. "It's in the bureaucracy, isn't it? Of the system. It's very hard to find where the responsibility lies. But people frequently bring it up to me. It raised a big question in the minds of many people."

Sitting in the kitchen of their modest East Third Street home in South Boston, Billy Bulger and his wife, Mary, were somber as they reflected on Whitey's death. He was a serial killer, an extortionist, a drug dealer, and a crime boss to the world, but to them, he was family. And much like Taylor Geas, they say they didn't know that side of him.

"He got life, but they gave him death," Mary Bulger said.

"It seems in retrospect to have been a clear case of putting him into harm's way," Billy added softly. "I'm sorry that it happened. I'm sorry that it happened . . . I think in that case they were definitely wrong and it was

a foreseeable event. But after that I don't know what to say."

A valuable source in Washington, DC, told the authors that members of Congress were pursuing justice not only for the killers, but also those whose decisions put Whitey into the belly of the Hazelton beast.

"Certainly, the fact that there's something bad that happened at Hazelton was not a surprise," the source said. "The combination—short staff and the mismanagement under the previous warden—probably contributed to this. Clearly the fact he was transferred there is problematic. Some of this is attributed to BOP overall and the decisions being made . . . and some of it to local management per the local warden. It all kind of came to a head."

Catherine Greig was transferred from the federal women's prison in Waseca, Minnesota, to a halfway house on bucolic Cape Cod in spring 2019, where she was forced to wear an electronic monitoring bracelet. The decision to trim Greig's sentence was part of the government's First Step act, which is designed to give deserving prisoners an opportunity for shortened sentences and job training.

The sixty-eight-year-old former fugitive was released in September 2019 and moved in with Whitey

Bulger's niece—Billy's daughter Mary—in Hingham, Massachusetts. Her probation ends in July 2020.

"I am pleased to see that Catherine is moving on with her life," her attorney, Kevin Reddington, told the authors. "She is an incredibly strong woman whose only 'crime' was falling in love with Jim Bulger. She had sixteen happy years and those memories give her the strength to live day to day, realizing that she was fortunate to have such a relationship. I wish her the best."

Whitey Bulger's body was flown to Massachusetts and a private Catholic funeral mass was held for him on November 8, 2018, at St. Monica's Parish, in the heart of the Southie neighborhood he had controlled and terrorized for decades. Whitey's brothers, Billy and Jackie, attended, along with some of the gangster's nieces and nephews, his attorney Hank Brennan, and Margaret McCusker.

The Reverend James Flavin, a well-known Southie priest, presided.

"Out of respect for the family and those who were hurt, it was a private service just for the immediate family," he said. "The Church is certainly aware of the deep pain that innocent victims of crime and violence live with every day."

After a traditional service, he told the small congregation:

"It is finished."

Whitey was laid to rest at a private burial in sprawling St. Joseph Cemetery in the West Roxbury neighborhood of Boston. The atmosphere was serene and a far cry from the makeshift death pits that were dug under the cover of night for his many victims.

He is buried with his parents, James and Jean Bulger.

Whitey's name is not on the family grave.

Epilogue

April 2019

We had no plan. We had set up no interviews. But we just knew that we had to see the place for ourselves. Escaping the biting cold of Boston, where winter refused to submit to an early spring, we landed in Los Angeles, California, grabbed a rental car, and drove eleven miles from LAX to Santa Monica.

The weather was sunny and breezy, so we rolled down the car windows to let in the warm California air. We couldn't taste the smog as we'd feared, but traffic along Santa Monica Boulevard was heavy and we hit every red light along the way.

It gave us time to talk.

"Whitey and Catherine probably took this same stretch of road," my coauthor, Dave Wedge, said to me.

I nodded from behind the steering wheel.

"They didn't have a car during most of their time, so they probably took a bus or grabbed a cab," I theorized. "Of course they paid in cash."

We continued the drive to Santa Monica and we eventually found our way to Third Street. I parked our rented silver Nissan and we stepped out across the street toward a white three-story apartment building with the Victorian name—Princess Eugenia. There was no sign out front. It had been taken down long ago to discourage gawkers from taking selfies at the notorious address. We walked up the front steps and entered the vestibule, where Dave pressed the button for the building manager.

"I'm Dave Wedge and I'm here with my coauthor, Casey Sherman," he said. "We're writers from Boston and we're working on a new project about Whitey Bulger. Can you talk?"

"No, I don't wanna talk," said the voice on the intercom. "I'm all done talking."

"Well, can you at least let us in the building?" I asked.

There was no reply and the front door remained locked.

Seconds later, a young resident fresh from his morning run entered the vestibule. He asked us if we needed to get inside. We nodded. He then put his key in the door lock, pushed it open, and we followed him inside.

The interior hallway smelled of fresh paint, with yellow candy stripes covering each wall from floor to ceiling. A small portrait of Queen Elizabeth I hung in the lobby in an attempt to project a regal flair to the building. The queen's eyes followed us as we began knocking on door after door with no answer. We then stepped into the small elevator to the third floor and made our way to apartment 303. I rapped my knuckles on the front door, but again—silence.

We continued to gumshoe and spoke with a couple of residents who had heard about the story we were chasing, but weren't living in the building at the time.

"It's crazy that it happened here," one man said as he bounced a toddler on his shoulder.

We returned to the first floor and knocked on the apartment closest to the front entrance. An elderly woman named Catalina Schlank opened her door and welcomed us inside her home.

We stepped through a narrow hallway that was cluttered with a lifetime of memories and we both sat down on the couch.

"I was more friendly with her because she was help-

ful to me," Schlank offered with a smile. Her accent sounded European, but the old woman told us that she had emigrated from Argentina decades before. "I have lived here for forty-six years. They were very good neighbors."

Schlank then stood up and walked gingerly across her living room and pulled out a bag.

"Would you like to see the letters?" she asked before fanning a dozen or so cards out on her couch.

We examined the first one. It was a holiday card with an illustration of a red covered bridge in a field of snow. It was a beautiful New England scene. We opened the card and read the inscription.

Dear Catalina,
      May the special gifts of health, peace, joy and happiness be yours throughout the year.
                                    Merry Christmas,
                                    Carol & Charlie Gasko

I handed the card to Catalina and she stared at it for a moment and then sighed.

"You would never believe they were Mafiosi. He had a nice face, a sweet face."

After spending twenty minutes interviewing the elderly neighbor, we left the complex and were headed

toward our car when suddenly we were confronted by the building's maintenance man, who was waving his thick arms in our direction.

"Don't worry, we're leaving," I said, trying to quell his concerns.

"You're here to write a story about Bulger, right?" he asked.

"Yup," Dave replied. "We think we got everything we need. We don't mean to bother you."

"Would you like to see where they caught him?" the maintenance man asked excitedly.

We said yes, and he led us into the basement garage to the exact grease-stained spot where Whitey Bulger's more-than-half-century-long criminal odyssey had come to an abrupt and dramatic end in 2011. Dave took some photos with his phone as I chatted with the worker.

"We knocked on apartment 303, which was Bulger's apartment, but got no answer. Does anyone live there?"

The worker explained that the place was being renovated and that it would be available for rent in another month or so.

"Do you have the key?" I asked. "Can you take us inside?"

The maintenance man smiled and showed us to the elevator, where the three of us squeezed inside. Sec-

onds later, we found ourselves back on the third floor and headed toward apartment 303.

Dave and I took deep breaths. To our knowledge, no reporter had ever been inside the apartment where Whitey Bulger and his girlfriend Catherine Greig had lived as America's most wanted fugitive couple for more than a decade under the names Charles and Carol Gasko.

We stepped into the apartment, which had the rugs ripped up and had just been painted bleach white. There was a brick fireplace in the center of the living room and a screened balcony off to the side. The kitchen was quite small and led to two bedrooms in the back, where the couple had slept separately since the day they moved in.

Bulger was long gone, but you could still feel his ominous presence here. We toured the small apartment, going from room to room, trying to imagine what it had been like for both Whitey and Catherine while living in this space. While they must have felt some sense of relief that they were free, unlike Bulger's closest criminal partner and the crooked FBI agent who covered up many of their crimes, there was also likely a sense of dread that accompanied them each day.

It was the fear of getting caught.

We wonder if Whitey Bulger expressed fear mo-

ments before his murder in 2018. As he gazed up at the killers, the look in his pale blue eyes must have been similar to that of his victims, including two innocent women, before he snuffed out their lives. Whitey had survived for decades on the streets and years as a fugitive, but in the end, he could not outrun his own fate. In the words of William Shakespeare: "Time is the old justice that examines all offenders."

Acknowledgments

Our goal in writing this book was to deconstruct the mythology surrounding James "Whitey" Bulger and to apply greater focus on the men and women who banded together over a span of decades to bring this monster to justice.

The memories of his innocent victims such as Roger Wheeler, Michael Donahue, Debbie Davis, and Deborah Hussey clung to us during the course of this project.

I'd like to thank my soon-to-be wife, Kristin York, for her unwavering love and support.

This book could not have been written if not for the guidance of our editor, Matt Harper, and our super agent, Peter Steinberg. Thank you for trusting us to tell this story the right way.

I am indebted to former and current agents of the FBI for your honesty, transparency, and valuable insight. A special thanks to Kristen Setera, John Gamel, Charlie Gianturco, Roberta Hastings, Noreen Gleason, Scott Garriola, Phil Torsney, Tommy MacDonald, Rich Teahan, Mike Carazza, and former director Andrew McCabe for your countless hours answering my questions.

Thanks also to my fellow Barnstable High alums, Neil Sullivan and Rich Eaton, for taking us deep inside your pursuit of Bulger. You both make our Cape Cod community proud.

I also appreciated the openness and support of Chip Janus and his wife, Dorcas, who provided us with a treasure trove of Bulger's letters and photos that allowed us to re-create Whitey's life in prison.

A special thanks also to Glenn Gautreaux Jr., Catalina Schlank, Dr. Matthias Donelan, and Ken Brady for your time and kindness. I'd like to give a big shoutout as well to Mike McDonough for providing us some writing space at Work.local in Marshfield and story connections, and to Brian Rogers and John DiPietro for assisting with key interviews.

I'd also like to thank our television partners Jenette Kahn and Adam Richman at Double Nickel Entertainment as well as our Hollywood reps Ellen Goldsmith-

Vein and Tony Gil at Gotham Group, and our Fort Point Media partners Andrew Braverman and Parker Knight.

On the home front, of course I am always thankful for my incredible daughters, Bella and Mia Sherman. I'm also grateful to my mum, Diane Dodd, my hero in many ways, as well as my brother Todd Forrest Sherman and our uncle Jim Sherman.

I'd also like to thank the Goldsmith-York family, especially Martha Goldsmith for dissecting the Bulger letters for us.

A final thanks to my writing partner, Dave Wedge, for another incredible journey. Until we ride again.

—*Casey Sherman*

As a young reporter in my second year at the *Boston Herald* in 2000, I was in awe of the cloak-and-dagger exploits of the tabloid's I-Team, especially their work on the Bulger case. When I got the call to go cover the unearthing of Bulger's victims at Florian Hall and Tenean Beach in Dorchester, I was more than happy to take on the grim task. It was a baptism by fire, as I was thrust into the biggest crime story in Boston, and I was proud to take part. I'll always remember standing there in the snow, gazing at the lighted tents erected

around the macabre burial ground, as cops worked shovels and sifted through dirt to unearth the remains that ultimately held Bulger accountable once and for all. The pain and suffering he brought into Boston, and especially South Boston, is unfathomable. I've always felt sorry for the many families whose loved ones were killed or otherwise destroyed by Whitey's crimes.

There are so many people who helped us immensely to tell this story, and I'd like to thank, in no particular order: Taylor Geas, Christina Sterling and Elizabeth McCarthy in the US Attorney's Office, Fred Wyshak, Brian Kelly, Zachary Hafer, James Marra, Steve Boozang, retired Massachusetts state troopers Bobby Long and Thomas Murphy, *Springfield Republican* mob reporter Stephanie Barry, Attorney Dan Kelly, author Michael Esslinger, Justin Tarovisky and Joe Rojas of the correctional officers' unions at Hazelton and Coleman, journalist and friend Jonathan Wells, and Rebecca Mesple.

I would also like to thank our editor Matt Harper and the team at HarperCollins, our agent at Foundry Literary & Media Peter Steinberg, our team at Gotham Group, especially Tony Gill and Ellen Goldsmith-Vein, and our TV partners at Double Nickel. Also, thank you to my wife, Jessica, for supporting me and helping me manage my chaotic life while writing this book; my

kids, Danielle and Jackson, for making me smile every day; my good friend Kris Meyer for all the inspiring conversation and hikes in the woods to clear my head, my friend and counsel Attorney Keith Davidson, and of course, my dad, Roger, who may have taught me a few things about bookies over the years, but more importantly, instilled in me the importance of reading the news and understanding the world around us.

—*Dave Wedge*

Notes

Chapter 2

21 *"trying to catch him?"*: Ibid.

25 *"coming down in a week"*: Steven Flemmi Testimony, *United States v James J. Bulger*, 3rd superseding indictment, 1999

27 *looked on in shock*: Authors interview with Phil Torsney, 2019

Chapter 3

32 *"guy that stands out"*: Authors interview with Clement Janus, 2019

34 *"streaming down Jimmy's face"*: "Whitey Bulger Was His Dad: The Never Told Story of the Gangster and His Little Son," Stephen Kurkjian and Shelley Murphy, *Boston Globe*, April 3, 2012

34 *beat up on the street*: Authors interview with Jonathan Wells per his interview with Teresa Stanley, 2019

35 *"our father was an alcoholic"*: Authors interview with Margaret McCusker, 2019

36 *soon-to-be ex-husband: Whitey Bulger*, Kevin Cullen and Shelley Murphy, page 159, W.W. Norton & Company, 2013

36 *"Everybody knows who he is around here"*: Authors interview with Margaret McCusker, 2019

37 *"Something bad is going on"*: *Whitey Bulger*, Kevin Cullen and Shelley Murphy, page 307, W.W. Norton & Company, 2013

38 *out the door*: Authors interview with Phil Torsney, 2019

39 *"in touch when I can"*: Authors interview with Margaret McCusker, 2019

39 *"Do you even know?"*: Margaret McCusker Federal Grand Jury Interview, February 9, 2012

39 *Whitey said, "See ya."*: *Whitey Bulger*, Kevin Cullen and Shelley Murphy, page 321, W.W. Norton & Company, 2013

41 *from* Casablanca: *Brutal*, Kevin Weeks and Phyllis Karas, page 244, William Morrow, 2007

Chapter 4

43 *"Tell him to stay free."*: *Brutal*, Kevin Weeks and Phyllis Karas, page 247, William Morrow, 2007

46 *"You've got the wrong man"*: *Hitman: The Untold Story of John Martorano*, John Martorano and Howie Carr, page 394, Forge Books, 2012

48 *$535.29 in total*: *United States v James J. Bulger*, Exhibit 14

49 *"put some money in it"*: Authors interview with Clement Janus, 2019

51 *get it upon release. Etc.*: Letter from James "Whitey" Bulger to Clement Janus, 2014

51 *Daisy, Oklahoma*: Authors interview with Mike Carazza, 2019

51 *first months on the run*: Authors interview with Charles Gianturco, 2019

Chapter 5

54 *"never wanted anything to do with him"*: Authors interview with John Gamel, 2019

55 *"think about it"*: Ibid.

60 *wearing a mask*: Patick Nee's lawyer denies slayings, Laurel J. Sweet, *Boston Herald*, July 31, 2013

60 *bounced off the ground*: Kevin Weeks Testimony in James Bulger Murder Trial, July 7, 2013

62 *"but he's not stupid"*: Authors interview with John Gamel, 2019

63 *in Gamel's ear*: Ibid.

64 *"charting his own course"*: Authors interview with William Bulger, 2019

65 *"no one else would do it"*: Ibid.

66 *"the way to go"*: Ibid.

67 *AKA "Whitey"*: Letter from James "Whitey" Bulger to Clement Janus, 2014

71 *"Dillinger did"*: *Hammond Times*, November 24, 1955

72 *"all the marbles"*: "Kevin White: A Reporter Remembers," David Boeri, WBUR.org, January 12, 2012

Chapter 6

77 *"keep the winnings"*: "Hitting Pay Dirt in Southie: A Tale of the $14 Million Split," Christopher B. Daly, *Washington Post*, August 7, 1991

77 *Malone said at the time*: "Reputed Mobster Wins Lottery: State Treasurer Says No Way Was It Fixed," Eve Epstein, Associated Press, July 31, 1991

Chapter 7

81 *"he was very smart"*: Authors interview with Charles Gianturco, 2019
84 *"He was someone else"*: Ibid.

Chapter 8

85 *prescription eyeglasses*: *United States v James J. Bulger*, Exhibit 15
86 *"Aunt Helen"*: Authors interview with Glenn Gautreaux Jr., 2019
87 *"can't bear to see it"*: Ibid.
89 *$40,000 on the family*: *Brutal*, Kevin Weeks and Phyllis Karas, page 254, William Morrow, 2007
89 *he was her nephew*: *United States v James J. Bulger*, Exhibit 15
89 *"sure I have enough contacts"*: Ibid.
89 *not a wife*: Authors interview with Michael Carazza, 2019

Chapter 9

100 *"the name Tom Baxter"*: *Brutal*, Kevin Weeks and Phyllis Karas, page 250, William Morrow, 2007

100 *"I'll call you back"*: *Brutal*, Kevin Weeks and Phyllis Karas, page 253, William Morrow, 2007

102 *thought to himself*: Authors interview with Glenn Gautreaux Jr., 2019

103 *"ordered her to cooperate"*: Authors interview with Mike Carazza

104 *"on Day One!"*: Authors interview with Charles Gianturco, 2019

105 *"anything short of murder"*: "Testimony Cites Soft Spot for Bulger," Patricia Nealon, *Boston Globe*, August 11, 1998

Chapter 10

107 *Mark and Carol Shapeton*: *United States v James Bulger*, Exhibit 16

108 *"put it on me"*: *Brutal*, Kevin Weeks and Phyllis Karas, page 254, William Morrow, 2007

109 *blood could be spilled*: *Whitey Bulger*, Kevin Cullen and Shelley Murphy, page 331, W.W. Norton & Company, 2013

109 *"can't take away from me"*: *Brutal*, Kevin Weeks and Phyllis Karas, page 255, William Morrow, 2007

110 *"don't stand out there"*: *Brutal*, Kevin Weeks and Phyllis Karas, page 257, William Morrow, 2007

112 *John Joseph O'Brien*: *The Brothers Bulger*, Howie Carr, page 35, Grand Central Publishing, 2006

112 *before going on his way*: Authors interview with Phil Torsney, 2019

114 *next stop was Venice Beach*: Ibid.

Chapter 11

117 *"a real good spot for him"*: "Ex-Mass State Police Chief Rips FBI Over Bulger," Scott Croteau, *Worcester Telegram & Gazette*, May 5, 2012

118 *national historic site*: "Records: Ex-officer Admitted to Tipping Mobster to Probe," Shelley Murphy, *Boston Globe*, April 20, 2001

118 *"were informants themselves"*: *Brutal*, Kevin Weeks and Phyllis Karas, page 267, William Morrow, 2007

120 *"went against them"*: *Brutal*, Kevin Weeks and Phyllis Karas, page 269, William Morrow, 2007

122 *"ditches will be for you"*: Author Casey Sherman interview with Kevin Weeks at Curry College, 2008

126 *the safecracker's heart*: Kevin Weeks Testimony in James "Whitey" Bulger Trial, 2013

127 *"criminal associates, friends and others"*: "Two Boston Brothers, One Did Good, the Other Didn't," Elizabeth Mehren, *Los Angeles Times*, September 30, 2000

Chapter 12

130 *"people that were poor"*: "Most Wanted Listing Adds to Lore of South Boston Mob Boss," Elizabeth Mehren, *Los Angeles Times*, September 21, 1999

131 *"Not a bad guy"*: "Mike Barnicle: The Best Friend a Gangster Could Have," Steve Kornacki, Salon.com, June 23, 2011

132 *"confidence in him"*: William Bulger, testimony before federal grand jury in Boston, April 5, 2001

132 *Oriental figurine*: "Gangsters as FBI Partners," Edmund H. Mahoney, *Hartford Courant*, October 22, 2008

132 *"should not have done"*: "Gangsters as FBI Partners," Edmund H. Mahoney, *Hartford Courant*, October 22, 2008

133 *"friends in the Bureau"*: Authors interview with Charles Gianturco, 2019

Chapter 13

136 *in exchange for the money*: Authors interview with Phil Torsney, 2019

138 *guided tours of Alcatraz*: Authors interview with Michael Esslinger, 2019

139 *"another $50"*: FBI Witness Interview, February 18, 2011

141 *"mellowed out now"*: Massachusetts State Police Interview with Wendy Farnetti, July 18, 2011

142 *"pick it up for you"*: Authors interview with Catalina Schlank, 2019

143 on the balcony!!!: Card from Catherine Greig to Catalina Schlank, obtained by Authors 2019

144 *calls to his family*: Authors interview with Clement Janus, 2019

145 *"always been very kind"*: Authors interview with Margaret McCusker, 2019

Chapter 14

149 *"the Bulger investigation"*: Author interview with former US Attorney Michael Sullivan, May 10, 2019

150 *with their car idling*: "Mob Suspect May Have Been Spotted in O.C.," Meg James, *Los Angeles Times*, April 5, 2000

150 I will murder you: "Was James 'Whitey' Bulger an Active Senior in Orange County Before His Capture?", Matt Coker, *OC Weekly*, June 23, 2011

152 *"was all Irish"*: Authors interview with John Wells, 2019

Chapter 15

155 *"never know who's listening"*: FBI Agent Mike Carazza Testimony in Catherine Greig Hearing, July 11, 2011

156 *"an example of that"*: Authors interview with Mike Carazza, 2019

156 *"brotherly concern"*: "Mobster's Brother Sentenced to Six Months in Federal Prison," Matt Pratt, Associated Press, September 4, 2003

159 *"official in Massachusetts"*: Hearing before the Committee on Government Reform, 108th Congress, June 19, 2003

160 *"honest answer is no!"*: Ibid.

162 *"in the files"*: Authors interview with John Gamel, 2019

163 *"over eight years"*: "Ex-FBI Agent Contradicts UMass President," Fox Butterfield, *New York Times*, June 30, 2003

163 *Romney told the press*: "Romney Turns Up Pressure to Oust Bulger," Jennifer Peter, Associated Press, June 21, 2003

Chapter 16

166 *"go check it out"*: Authors interview with Richard Eaton, 2019

167 *"very real to me"*: Ibid.

171 *"when you wouldn't have"*: Authors interview with Danny Simmons, 2019

172 *"would have believed it"*: Authors interview with unnamed FBI agent, 2019

Chapter 17

174 *"diminished over time"*: "Whitey Bounty Hits $2M," Laurel Sweet, *Boston Herald*, September 4, 2008

174 *trysts with underage girls*: "Eyewitness to Evil; Gang videotaped sex acts in secret room at gym," *Boston Herald*, April 9, 2001

175 *"so many levels"*: Authors interview with Noreen Gleason, 2019

175 *"being a pedophile"*: Ibid.

175 *"come after me"*: Ibid.

177 *"I loved the work"*: Authors interview with Phil Torsney, 2019

179 *"wasn't the case at all"*: Ibid.

180 *"tracking phone calls"*: Ibid.

182 *"lied to me"*: Ibid.

Chapter 18

184 *"retired studio executive"*: Authors interview with Joe Hipp, 2019

185 *"it was alright"*: Ibid.

187 *"all the nightmares"*: Authors interview with Phil Torsney, 2019

Chapter 19

190 *"from the East Coast"*: Birgitta Farinelli Grand Jury Testimony, August 4, 2011

191 *"he has emphysema"*: Ibid.

192 *get back inside*: Federal Grand Jury Interview with Birgitta Farinelli, August 4, 2011

192 *"John R." and "Mary R.":* Catherine E. Greig's Statement of Facts, March 5, 2012

192 *"I'll tough it out":* Birgitta Farinelli Grand Jury Testimony, August 4, 2011

192 *"I'm scared of needles":* FBI interview of Dr. Reza Ray Ehsan, July 19, 2011

193 "Love always, Cxxxxoooo": Catherine E. Greig Government Exhibit, 2011

195 *to get work:* Ibid.

196 *never drove again:* Authors interview with Phil Torsney, 2019

197 *"thought that was strange":* FBI interview with Joshua Bond, July 12, 2011

198 *"treated me like a son":* Ibid.

199 *"pair of binoculars":* FBI interview with Joshua Bond, July 12, 2011

Chapter 20

202 *"close the case":* Authors interview with Tommy MacDonald, 2019

202 *"find James Bulger":* Ibid.

204 *"circle of his life":* Authors interview with Roberta Hastings, 2019

210 *in front of the home:* "Bulger Linked to '70's Antibusing Attacks," Shelley Murphy, *Boston Globe*, April 22, 2001

210 *"not gonna break through":* Authors interview with Rich Teahan, 2019

Chapter 21

212 *"ridiculous to even think about"*: Authors interview with Noreen Gleason, 2019

212 *"soul a little bit"*: Authors interview with Rich Teahan, 2019

213 *"choking her to death"*: Authors interview with Tommy MacDonald, 2019

215 *"meet with you in person"*: Authors interview with Dr. Matthias Donelan, 2019

216 *"eyelid patients"*: Ibid.

217 *"in fifteen minutes"*: Authors interview with Tommy MacDonald, 2019

220 *"chasing out of Boston"*: Authors interview with Phil Torsney, 2019

Chapter 22

222 *"influence over this region"*: Authors interview with Noreen Gleason, 2019

223 *"followed their lead"*: Authors interview with Neil Sullivan, 2019

225 *"said yes immediately"*: Ibid.

227 *"nothing to show for it"*: Authors interview with Richard Teahan, 2019

Chapter 23

232 *"I'll drink to that!"*: "Santa Monica Reacts to bin Laden's Death," Jason Islas, *The Lookout News*, May 3, 2011

233 *pistol at his bedside*: Inventory of Evidence in Bulger-Greig case, FBI, November 21, 2011

237 *"convinced we had them"*: Authors interview with Neil Sullivan, 2019

239 *"got to work"*: Authors interview with Scott Garriola, 2019

240 *"200 percent sure it's them!"*: Ibid.

242 *"100 percent it's them"*: Joshua Bond Federal Grand Jury Interview, July 28, 2011

249 bullet in the back: Letter from James J. Bulger to author Michael Esslinger, March 22, 2012

254 *"highly significant event"*: Authors interview with Andrew McCabe, 2019

Chapter 24

256 *"I'm James J. Bulger"*: Authors interview with Scott Garriola, 2019

256 *"in a long time"*: Authors interview with Phil Torsney, 2019

256 *"a helluva fight"*: Authors interview with Scott Garriola, 2019

258 *"be his style"*: Authors interview with Neil Sullivan, 2019

259 *"for molesting a child"*: Authors interview with Phil Torsney, 2019

260 *"they're actually consenting"*: Ibid.

261 *"doesn't deserve any of this"*: Ibid.

262 *"would I tell you?"*: Authors interview with Rich Teahan, 2019

263 *"admit his involvement"*: Authors interview with Neil Sullivan, 2019

Chapter 25

268 *"[for Capone] wouldn't you?"*: "Bulger and Girlfriend Appear in Boston Federal Court," WBUR Radio, June 24, 2011

268 *"it doesn't surprise me"*: "Crime Lord Returns to Boston to Face Raft of Charges," Abby Goodnough, *New York Times*, June 24, 2011

269 *"on Santa Monica Boulevard"*: Ibid.

272 *"your clothes anyway!"*: Authors interview with Ken Brady, 2019

273 *"best place we ever visited"*: Authors interview with Glenn Gautreux Jr., 2019

275 *"this gentleman [Bulger]"*: "Whitey Bulger's Girlfriend Offers Glimpse of Her Defense," Associated Press, July 14, 2011

275 *"defiant, and loyal in court"*: Authors interview with Mike Carazza, 2019

277 *"she has no regrets"*: "Catherine Greig Gets Eight Years

for Helping Whitey Bulger," Denise Lavoie, Associated Press, June 12, 2012

Chapter 26

280 *"sick to my stomach"*: "Boston mob boss trial underway," ABC News, June 13, 2013

280 *"who was killed"*: "LOL doesn't surprise Donahue," John Zaremba, *Boston Herald*, June 15, 2013

282 *Judge Denise Casper's courtroom*: Authors interview with Zachary Hafer, August 5, 2019

284 *"Bulger, Flemmi, Salemme"*: Authors interview with Fred Wyshak, June 12, 2019

Chapter 27

291 *"that agreement anywhere"*: Authors interview with Zach Hafer, 2019

291 *"backed it up with anything"*: Ibid.

293 *"a hands-on killer"*: USA v. James J. Bulger, trial transcripts, June 12, 2013

301 *"Take anything you want"*: Ibid.

Chapter 28

304 *"eventually looked away"*: Authors interview with Robert Long, June 18, 2019

308 *dead on arrival*: Ibid.

Chapter 29

310 *"would have been compromised probably"*: USA v. James J. Bulger, trial transcripts, June 14, 2013

311 *"a lot of beatings"*: Ibid.

312 *"put down as law"*: Ibid.

315 *"think it was, Jay?"*: Ibid.

315 *"from expressing love"*: "With sobs, Bulger and Greig Traded Jailhouse Love Letters," J.M. Lawrence, *Boston Globe*, January 10, 2014

319 *"Bulger gang really was"*: Author interview with Brian Kelly, October 3, 2019

Chapter 30

325 *"surface as the leader"*: USA v. Bulger trial transcripts, June 17, 2013

326 *"reason I am here today"*: USA v. Bulger trial transcripts, June 19, 2013

327 *"wanted to get killed"*: USA v. Bulger trial transcripts, June 20, 2013

328 *"helpful to me"*: USA v. Bulger trial transcripts, June 17, 2013

329 *"That sort of thing"*: Authors interview with Billy Bulger, June 24, 2019

329 *"beside myself with it"*: Ibid.

330 *"That's what he was"*: Ibid.

333 *"wanted to take him out"*: Ibid.

333 *"It has to be done"*: Ibid.

335 *"in Canada robbing banks"*: *USA v. Bulger* trial transcripts, June 24, 2013

336 *"I wanted to shoot him"*: *USA v. Bulger* trial transcripts, June 19, 2013

Chapter 31

340 *"If looks could kill"*: Authors interview with James Marra, September 5, 2019

340 *"I'm not a fucking informant"*: "'Whitey' Bulger says he's not a snitch, but FBI file tells a different story," CNN, June 25, 2013

340 *"that ridiculous contention"*: *USA v. Bulger* trial transcripts, June 21, 2013

341 *Bulger had for decades*: Ibid.

342 *"relationship with the FBI"*: *USA v. Bulger* trial transcripts, June 24, 2013

342 *October 17, 1984, report*: *USA v. Bulger* trial transcripts, June 21, 2013

343 *to implicate Jackie Salemme*: Ibid.

345 *"and never charge him"*: Ibid.

346 *"didn't mean much legally"*: Author interview with Zach Hafer, August 5, 2019

346 *"is simply absurd"*: *USA v. Bulger* trial transcripts, June 21, 2013

346 *"I felt awful"*: "'You're a F—cking Liar': Whitey Bulger and the FBI's Sordid History," The Daily Beast, July 1, 2013

347 *"Yes," Bulger responded*: Ibid.

348 *"glad the marshals were there"*: Author interview with Brian Kelly, October 3, 2019

349 *"higher authorities in the FBI"*: Department of Justice, US Attorney's Office, District of Boston press release, August 5, 2016

Chapter 32

352 *"didn't try to do nothing"*: US v. Bulger trial transcript, July 2, 2013

354 *"beat somebody up"*: US v. Bulger trial transcripts, July 8, 2013

358 *"this court for you"*: Ibid.

Chapter 33

360 *"really friendly with Connolly"*: US v. Bulger trial transcript, July 18, 2013

360 *Flemmi shot back*: "'Rifleman' gets a rise out of former partner in crime," Boston Herald, July 19, 2013

361 *"wasn't in love with her"*: US v. Bulger trial transcript July 19, 2013

362 *"regretted it all my life"*: US v. Bulger trial transcript, July 21, 2013

362 *"he took to Mexico"*: "Henchman accuses Boston mob boss 'Whitey' Bulger of pedophilia," Reuters, July 23, 2013

363 *"may hit someone"*: US v. Bulger trial transcript, July 26, 2013

364 *"a client-run defense"*: "Bulger team tries to build its defense in trial's final days," *Boston Globe*, August 1, 2013

364 *"and the excitement"*: Authors interview with Pat Nee, July 15, 2019

365 *Southie gangster escaped*: Ibid.

365 *"they missed me"*: Ibid.

366 *"countless violent crimes"*: "Pat Nee Testimony a Point of Contention in Bulger Trial," WGBH, July 25, 2013

368 *"comes to your house?"*: "Crime-steeped witnesses raised jurors' ire, suspicions," *Boston Globe*, August 14, 2013

368 *"he didn't testify"*: Authors interview with Fred Wyshak, June 12, 2019

369 *"part of the story"*: Authors interview with Zach Hafer, August 5, 2019

370 *"I'm disappointed"*: "High Life Brought Low: Jury Finds Whitey Bulger Guilty in Killings, Racketeering," Deborah Feherick, CNN, July 13, 2013

371 *"his horrific crimes"*: " 'Whitey' Bulger found guilty of racketeering, murders," *Boston Globe*, August 13, 2013

371 *"is repugnant"*: Authors interview with Zach Hafer, June 12, 2019

371 *"make this case happen"*: Authors interview with Fred Wyshak, June 12, 2009

372 *"being set free"*: " 'Whitey' Bulger found guilty of racketeering, murders," *Boston Globe*, August 13, 2013

372 *"searching for that closure"*: "Range of emotions among victims' families," *Boston Globe*, August 13, 2013

372 *"gladly do it again"*: Author interview with Brian Kelly, October 3, 2019

Chapter 34

381 *"There was a big art heist"*: Authors interview with Chip Janus, 2019
382 *"We pulled in every crook"*: Author Casey Sherman interview with Kevin Weeks at Curry College, 2008
382 *"He's a good person"*: Authors interview with Clement Janus, 2019
387 *"It's no surprise"*: "Even in Prison, Whitey Bulger Is Pushing Boundaries," Shelley Murphy, *Boston Globe*, February 7, 2015

Chapter 35

391 "sooner or later": Letter obtained by authors from Bulger to Janus, December 2, 2014
392 *"other respectable crime"*: "My Memories of Being in Prison with Whitey Bulger," Nate A. Lindell, The Marshall Project, March 17, 2016
393 *"went back to sleep"*: Ibid.
394 *"best days of his life"*: Authors interview with Michael Essinger, 2019
394 next and final stage: Letter obtained by authors from Bulger to Janus, July 25, 2015
395 They (prosecutors) refused: Letter obtained by authors from Bulger to Janus (undated)

396 *"better than anybody else"*: "Mark Wahlberg: Whitey Wants Me to Visit," WAAF FM Radio, January 2012

397 Jim Bulger 1428 AZ: Letter obtained by authors from Bulger to Janus, January 12, 2017

397 *"answer to this charge"*: Internal Disciplinary Data, James J. Bulger, Coleman II, October 31, 2018

397 "Why? Revenge?": Letter obtained by authors from Bulger to Janus (undated)

399 *"my word is good!"*: "After Whitey Bulger Killing, Warden of 'Misery Mountain' Faces Removal," Danielle Ivory, *New York Times*, November 30, 2018

400 *office in Washington, DC*: Internal Disciplinary Data, James J. Bulger, Coleman II, October 31, 2018

401 *"facilities Bulger required"*: Authors interview with Joe Rojas, 2019

402 *"lot of mob guys there"*: Ibid.

Chapter 36

405 *never heard from her again*: Letter to authors from Taylor Geas, June 7, 2019

406 *most of their adult lives*: "Murder plots, truck heists and brawls: The backstory of Freddy Geas, suspect in 'Whitey' Bulger death," Masslive.com, November 3, 2018

409 *"to ever happen to them"*: Ibid.

412 *"all covered in blood"*: Ibid.

412 *"when I was a kid"*: Author interview with Taylor Geas, September 10, 2019

413 *"their lives in jail"*: "Audacious homecoming," *The Republican* (Springfield, Mass.), May 8, 2017

414 *"in the street or in jail"*: Author interview with Frederick Cohn, June 12, 2019

415 *"first pair of soccer cleats"*: "Freddy Geas case viewed with a daughter's eye: Reader viewpoint," *The Republican* (Springfield, Mass.), Jan. 21, 2016

416 *club in South Boston*: "This man may have waited 38 years for his revenge on Whitey Bulger," *New York Post*, November 1, 2018

417 *friends at Hazelton*: "The mystery deepens: Why was Bulger left in harm's way?", *Boston Globe*, November 1, 2018

418 *"last of the Mohicans"*: Ibid.

419 JB (James Bulger): "Whitey Bulger Won't Help Man Claiming Wrongful Conviction," Shelley Murphy, *Boston Globe*, October 16, 2016

Chapter 37

422 *from the previous year*: " 'Misery Mountain': The jail where 'Whitey' Bulger was slain has history of murder and violence," *Washington Examiner*, October 30, 2018

423 *"with no backup"*: "Exclusive: As federal prisons run low on guards, nurses and cooks are filling in," *USA Today*, February 13, 2018

424 *from 2015 through 2018*: "Federal prison officials get bonuses as staffing shortages, management problems persist," *USA Today*, July 16, 2019

424 *"from hardened criminals"*: McKinley Fights for Corrections Employees; Bipartisan Effort to Stop Bureau of Prisons Staffing Cuts, Rep. David McKinley (R-WV) News Release, February 22, 2018

425 *two shank-wielding inmates*: "Lorton Slaying Catches Up With Inmate," *Washington Post,* October 21, 2000; "James 'Whitey' Bulger's killing is just the latest in a string of troubling violence for W.Va. prison," *Boston Globe,* October 30, 2018

425 *for only two weeks*: "Officials: Inmate killed in fight at federal prison," Associated Press, September 19, 2018; "Barber Slain in Apparent Robbery," *Washington Post,* June 16, 2007

426 *"working at this complex"*: Letter from AFGE Local 420 executive vice-president Justin Tarovisky to members of Congress, October 10, 2018

427 *"more full-time correctional officers"*: Congressional letter to Attorney General Jeff Sessions, October 25, 2018

428 *"not to lose hope"*: Author interview with Taylor Geas, September 10, 2019

428 *"love of his life for sure"*: Author interview with Michael Esslinger, May 20, 2019

Chapter 38

430 *"must have been drooling"*: Author interview with Joe Rojas, executive vice-president of the American Federation of Government Employees Local 506 at USP Coleman, September 25, 2019

430 *Whitey and Flemmi in the 1980s*: US v. Paul A. DeCologero, John P. DeCologero, Jr., Paul J. DeCologero and Joseph F. Pavone; United States Court of Appeals, First Circuit decision, June 23, 2008

431 *"irked the mob leaders"*: Ibid.

431 *a contract on "Big Paulie"*: "Bulger suspect's brother says families had bad blood," *Boston Globe*, November 3, 2018

431 *weren't found for ten years*: US v. Paul A. DeCologero, John P. DeCologero, Jr., Paul J. DeCologero and Joseph F. Pavone; United States Court of Appeals, First Circuit decision, June 23, 2008

432 *a .22-caliber handgun*: New Hampshire Man Pleads Guilty to Gun Charge, Department of Justice press release, November 28, 2016

432 *"hard to prevent that"*: Author interview with Justin Tarovisky, executive vice-president of the American Federation of Government Employees Local 420 at USP Hazelton, August 25, 2019

435 *"Died in his Sleep kind"*: "In letters from prison, Bulger wished for 'peaceful death,'" *Boston Globe*, November 29, 2018

435 *"assault by other(s)"*: James J. Bulger death certificate

437 *a shotgun, and ammo*: "Montpelier man among prisoners isolated over Whitey Bulger killing," *VT Digger*, November 20, 2018

438 *"changed to the death penalty"*: "'Whitey' Bulger, One of the Most Feared Men in Boston's History, Has Been Killed in Prison," WBUR, October 30, 2018

438 *"tantamount to a death sentence"*: Author interview with Attorney Fred Cohn, 2019

438 *"I chugged a beer"*: Authors interview with Tommy Donahue, 2019

439 *"to go quietly"*: Authors interview with Neil Sullivan, 2019

439 *"not even Whitey Bulger"*: Authors interview with Rich Teahan, 2019

439 *"brutal and painful"*: Authors interview with Charlie Gianturco, 2019

Chapter 39

442 *"crossed over the years"*: Authors interview with Zachary Hafer, 2019

442 *"wasn't like that with us"*: Authors interview with Margaret McCusker, 2019

442 *"severely understaffed"*: "Mafia hit man is suspected in former mob boss 'Whitey' Bulger's beating death in prison," *Los Angeles Times*, October 31, 2018

443 *remained at Hazelton*: Federal Bureau of Prisons inmate locator

443 handle it in the prison: Letter to authors from Freddy Geas, 2019

445 *"doesn't want to be forgotten"*: Authors interview with Taylor Geas, 2019

445 *"sounded beaten down"*: Ibid.

446 *"had to happen"*: Author interview with Justin Tarovisky, executive vice-president of the American Federation of Government Employees Local 420 at USP Hazelton, August 25, 2019

447 *"Stay safe!"*: "Hazelton federal prison warden to retire March 31," *MetroNews of West Virginia*, February 6, 2019

447 *"deficient in their duty"*: "Whitey Bulger's prison warden: 'I think he wanted to die,'" NBC News, April 29, 2019

447 *"just mind-boggling"*: Authors interview with Fred Wyshak, 2019

448 *"minds of many people"*: Authors interview with Billy Bulger, 2019

448 *"they gave him death"*: Authors interview with Mary Bulger, 2019

450 *"wish her the best"*: Author interview with Kevin Reddington, October 2019

451 *"It is finished"*: "At Whitey Bulger's funeral, a coda: 'it's finished,'" *Boston Globe*, November 8, 2018

Epilogue

456 Carol & Charlie Gasko: New Year Card from Catherine Greig to Catalina Schlank obtained by Authors 2019

References

Author Interviews

William Bulger, former Massachusetts Senate president

Andrew McCabe, former FBI director

Noreen Gleason, former FBI ASAC, Boston Office

Charlie Gianturco, former FBI agent, Boston Office

John Gamel, former FBI supervisor, Boston Office

Rich Teahan, former FBI supervisor, Boston Office

Roberta Hastings, former FBI analyst, Boston Office

Tommy MacDonald, FBI agent, Boston & New York Office

Phil Torsney, FBI agent, Boston & Cleveland Office

Mike Carazza, FBI agent, Boston Office

Scott Garriola, FBI agent, Los Angeles Office

Neil Sullivan, US Marshals Service

Richard Eaton, former detective, San Diego Sheriff's Office

Danny Simmons, DEA Agent

Robert Long, former Massachusetts State Police detective

Brian Kelly, United States Attorneys Office

Zach Hafer, United States Attorneys Office

Fred Wyshak, United States Attorneys Office

James Marra, United States Department of Justice investigator

Mary Bulger, wife of William Bulger

Catalina Schlank, Bulger neighbor

Joe Hipp, Bulger neighbor

Glenn Gautreaux Jr., Bulger neighbor

Margaret McCusker, Grieg's sister

Taylor Geas, Freddy Geas's daughter

Frederick Cohn, Freddy Geas's attorney

Ken Brady, Plymouth County correctional officer

Pat Nee, Bulger associate

Kevin Weeks, Bulger associate

Clement "Chip" Janus, Bulger friend

Michael Esslinger, Bulger friend and author

John Wells, journalist

Dr. Matthias Donelan, plastic surgeon

Joe Rojas, president, USP Coleman Correctional Officers Union

Justin Tarovisky, Senior Officer Special at USP Hazelton

Tommy Donahue, Bulger victim's son

Michael Sullivan, former United States attorney

Thomas Murphy, retired Massachusetts State Police detective

Correspondence

Fotios "Freddy" Geas

Documents and Books

Whitey Bulger Letters to Clement "Chip" Janus (2014–2018)

New Year Card from Catherine Greig to Catalina Schlank

Steven Flemmi Testimony, *United States v James J. Bulger*, 3rd superseding indictment, 1999

United States v James J. Bulger, Exhibit 14

United States v James J. Bulger, Exhibit 15

United States v James J. Bulger, Exhibit 16

United States v James J. Bulger, trial transcripts, 2013

Catherine E. Greig's Statement of Facts, March 5, 2012

Catherine E. Greig Government Exhibit, 2011

Hearing before the Committee on Government Reform, 108th Congress, June 19, 2003

Massachusetts State Police interview with Wendy Farnetti, July 18, 2011

Inventory of Evidence in Bulger-Greig case, FBI, November 21, 2011

FBI interview with Joshua Bond, July 12, 2011

William Bulger, testimony before federal grand jury in Boston, April 5, 2001

Internal Disciplinary Data, James J. Bulger, Coleman II USP, October 2018

Letter from AFGE Local 420 executive vice president Justin Tarovisky to members of Congress, October 10, 2018

Congressional letter to Attorney General Jeff Sessions, October 25, 2018

Whitey Bulger, Kevin Cullen and Shelley Murphy, W.W. Norton & Company, 2013

Brutal, Kevin Weeks and Phyllis Karas, William Morrow, 2007

Hitman: The Untold Story of John Martorano, John Martorano and Howie Carr, Forge Books, 2012

About the Authors

CASEY SHERMAN is a multiple *New York Times* bestselling author of *The Finest Hours* (now a major motion picture), *12: The Inside Story of Tom Brady's Fight for Redemption*, and eight other books including *Above & Beyond, Boston Strong*, cowritten by Dave Wedge and the inspiration for the feature film *Patriots Day; The Ice Bucket Challenge*, also coauthored by Wedge and now in development for a major motion picture; and *Animal: The Rise and Fall of the Mob's Most Feared Assassin* (now in development for a major motion picture).

Sherman is also an award-winning journalist and recipient of the Edward R. Murrow award for Journalistic Excellence, the prestigious Truth & Justice Award given by the Cold Case Research Institute, and has been

nominated for an EMMY award. He is also a contributing writer for *Time*, *The Washington Post*, *Esquire*, *Huffington Post*, and *Boston* magazine. Sherman is a featured weekly columnist for the *Boston Herald* and has appeared on more than one hundred television programs including *The Today Show*, *Unsolved Mysteries*, *ABC World News Tonight*, *The CBS Evening News*, and *The View*, and on the networks CNN, FOX News, C-SPAN, The History Channel, The Travel Channel, and Discovery. He is the founding partner of Fort Point Media.

He is also a sought-after public speaker and is represented by APB Speakers Bureau. Sherman can be reached on Facebook and on Twitter at *caseysherman123*.

He is a proud graduate of Barnstable High School, Fryeburg Academy, and Boston University. He lives in Massachusetts.

DAVE WEDGE is a *New York Times* bestselling author and writer based in Boston. He has cowritten three books with acclaimed author Casey Sherman, including *Boston Strong: A City's Triumph Over Tragedy*, a nonfiction drama about the 2013 Boston Marathon Bombings adapted for the 2017 movie *Patriots Day*; *The Ice Bucket Challenge: Pete Frates*

and the Fight Against ALS, which was released in October 2017 and is in development as a feature film; and *12: The Inside Story of Tom Brady's Fight for Redemption*, which was released in 2018 and was on the *New York Times* bestseller list for eight weeks. He cofounded Fort Point Media, a content development and production company, with Sherman.

Dave has also written for *VICE*, *Esquire*, *Newsweek*, and *Boston* magazine and was an award-winning investigative journalist for the *Boston Herald* for fourteen years. He has also been a radio host on WRKO in Boston and has appeared on CNN, MSNBC, FOX News Channel, *Good Morning America*, CBC (Canada), CNBC, E! Entertainment Network, CBS, and many other local and national networks.

Follow him on Twitter @DaveWedge and Instagram @davidmwedge

HARPER
LARGE PRINT

We hope you enjoyed reading
our new, comfortable print size and found it
an experience you would like to repeat.

Well – you're in luck!

Harper Large Print offers the finest in
fiction and nonfiction books in this same larger
print size and paperback format. Light and easy to read,
Harper Large Print paperbacks are for the book lovers
who want to see what they are reading without strain.

For a full listing of titles and
new releases to come, please visit our website:

www.hc.com

HARPER LARGE PRINT

SEEING IS BELIEVING!